"The conspectus of patristic exposition that this series offers has been badly needed for several centuries, and the whole Christian world should unite to thank those who are undertaking to fill the gap. For the ongoing ecumenical conversation, and the accurate appreciation of early Christian thought, and the current hermeneutical debate as well, the Ancient Christian Commentary on Scripture will prove itself to be a really indispensable resource."

J. I. PACKER
Board of Governors Professor of Theology
Regent College

"In the desert of biblical scholarship that tries to deconstruct or get behind the texts, the patristic commentators let the pure, clear waters of Christian faith flow from its scriptural source. Preachers, teachers and Bible students of every sort will want to drink deeply from the Ancient Christian Commentary on Scripture."

RICHARD JOHN NEUHAUS
President, Religion and Public Life
Editor-in-Chief, **First Things**

"The fathers of the ancient church were enabled, by the grace of God, to interpret the divine Scriptures in a way that integrates spirituality and erudition, liturgy and dogma, and generally all aspects of our faith which embrace the totality of our life. To allow the fathers to speak to us again, in our contemporary situation, in the way that you have proposed in your project, provides a corrective to the fragmentation of the faith which results from the particularization and overspecialization that exists today in the study of the Holy Bible and of sacred theology."

FR. GEORGE DRAGAS
Holy Cross Seminary

"This new but old Ancient Christian Commentary on Scripture takes us out of the small, closed-minded world in which much modern biblical scholarship is done into an earlier time marked by a Christian seriousness, by robust inquiry and by believing faith. This Commentary is a fresh breeze blowing in our empty, postmodern world."

DAVID F. WELLS
Andrew Mutch Distinguished Professor of Historical and
Systematic Theology, Gordon-Conwell Theological Seminary

"Composed in the style of the great medieval *catenae*, this new anthology of patristic commentary on Holy Scripture, conveniently arranged by chapter and verse, will be a valuable resource for prayer, study and proclamation. By calling attention to the rich Christian heritage preceding the separations between East and West and between Protestant and Catholic, this series will perform a major service to the cause of ecumenism."

AVERY DULLES, S.J.
Laurence J. McGinley Professor of Religion and Society
Fordham University

"The initial cry of the Reformation was *ad fontes*—back to the sources! The Ancient Christian Commentary on Scripture is a marvelous tool for the recovery of biblical wisdom in today's church. Not just another scholarly project, the ACCS is a major resource for the renewal of preaching, theology and Christian devotion."

TIMOTHY GEORGE
Dean, Beeson Divinity School, Samford University

"Modern church members often do not realize that they are participants in the vast company of the communion of saints that reaches far back into the past and that will continue into the future, until the kingdom comes. This Commentary should help them begin to see themselves as participants in that redeemed community."

ELIZABETH ACHTEMEIER
Union Professor Emerita of Bible and Homiletics
Union Theological Seminary in Virginia

"Contemporary pastors do not stand alone. We are not the first generation of preachers to wrestle with the challenges of communicating the gospel. The Ancient Christian Commentary on Scripture puts us in conversation with our colleagues from the past, that great cloud of witnesses who preceded us in this vocation. This Commentary enables us to receive their deep spiritual insights, their encouragement and guidance for present-day interpretation and preaching of the Word. What a wonderful addition to any pastor's library!"

WILLIAM H. WILLIMON
Dean of the Chapel and Professor of Christian Ministry
Duke University

"Here is a nonpareil series which reclaims the Bible as the book of the church by making accessible to earnest readers of the twenty-first century the classrooms of Clement of Alexandria and Didymus the Blind, the study and lecture hall of Origen, the cathedrae of Chrysostom and Augustine, the scriptorium of Jerome in his Bethlehem monastery."

GEORGE LAWLESS
Patristic Institute and Augustianum, Rome

"We are pleased to witness publication of the
Ancient Christian Commentary on Scripture. It is most beneficial for us to learn
how the ancient Christians, especially the saints of the church
who proved through their lives their devotion to God and his Word, interpreted
Scripture. Let us heed the witness of those who have gone before us in the faith."

METROPOLITAN THEODOSIUS
Primate, Orthodox Church in America

"As we approach the advent of a new millennium there has emerged across Christendom a
widespread interest in early Christianity, both at the popular and scholarly level. . . .
Christians of all traditions stand to benefit from this project, especially clergy
and those who study the Bible. Moreover, it will allow us to see how our traditions are
both rooted in the scriptural interpretations of the church fathers while at
the same time seeing how we have developed new perspectives."

ALBERTO FERREIRO
Professor of History, Seattle Pacific University

"The Ancient Christian Commentary on Scripture fills a long overdue need for scholars and
students of the church fathers. . . . Such information will be of immeasurable
worth to those of us who have felt inundated by contemporary interpreters and novel theories
of the biblical text. We welcome some 'new' insight from the
ancient authors in the early centuries of the church."

H. WAYNE HOUSE
*Professor of Theology and Law
Trinity University School of Law*

Chronological snobbery—the assumption that our ancestors working without benefit of
computers have nothing to teach us—is exposed as nonsense by this magnificent
new series. Surfeited with knowledge but starved of wisdom, many of us are
more than ready to sit at table with our ancestors and listen to their holy
conversations on Scripture. I know I am.

EUGENE H. PETERSON
*James Houston Professor of Spiritual Theology
Regent College*

"Few publishing projects have encouraged me as much as the recently announced Ancient Christian Commentary on Scripture with Dr. Thomas Oden serving as general editor. . . . How is it that so many of us who are dedicated to serve the Lord received seminary educations which omitted familiarity with such incredible students of the Scriptures as St. John Chrysostom, St. Athanasius the Great and St. John of Damascus? I am greatly anticipating the publication of this Commentary."

FR. PETER E. GILLQUIST
Director, Department of Missions and Evangelism
Antiochian Orthodox Christian Archdiocese of North America

"The Scriptures have been read with love and attention for nearly two thousand years, and listening to the voice of believers from previous centuries opens us to unexpected insight and deepened faith. Those who studied Scripture in the centuries closest to its writing, the centuries during and following persecution and martyrdom, speak with particular authority. The Ancient Christian Commentary on Scripture will bring to life the truth that we are invisibly surrounded by a 'great cloud of witnesses.' "

FREDERICA MATHEWES-GREEN
Commentator, National Public Radio

"For those who think that church history began around 1941 when their pastor was born, this Commentary will be a great surprise. Christians throughout the centuries have read the biblical text, nursed their spirits with it and then applied it to their lives. These commentaries reflect that the witness of the Holy Spirit was present in his church throughout the centuries. As a result, we can profit by allowing the ancient Christians to speak to us today."

HADDON ROBINSON
Harold John Ockenga Distinguished Professor of Preaching
Gordon-Conwell Theological Seminary

"All who are interested in the interpretation of the Bible will welcome the forthcoming multivolume series Ancient Christian Commentary on Scripture. Here the insights of scores of early church fathers will be assembled and made readily available for significant passages throughout the Bible and the Apocrypha. It is hard to think of a more worthy ecumenical project to be undertaken by the publisher."

BRUCE M. METZGER
Professor of New Testament, Emeritus
Princeton Theological Seminary

ANCIENT CHRISTIAN COMMENTARY ON SCRIPTURE

NEW TESTAMENT
VII

1-2 CORINTHIANS

EDITED BY

GERALD BRAY

GENERAL EDITOR
THOMAS C. ODEN

InterVarsity Press
Downers Grove, Illinois

InterVarsity Press
P.O. Box 1400, Downers Grove, IL 60515
World Wide Web: www.ivpress.com
E-mail: mail@ivpress.com

InterVarsity Press® is the book-publishing division of InterVarsity Christian Fellowship/USA®, a student movement active on campus at hundreds of universities, colleges and schools of nursing in the United States of America, and a member movement of the International Fellowship of Evangelical Students. For information about local and regional activities, write Public Relations Dept., InterVarsity Christian Fellowship/USA, 6400 Schroeder Rd., P.O. Box 7895, Madison, WI 53707-7895.

Cover photograph: Scala / Art Resource, New York. View of the apse. S. Vitale, Ravenna, Italy.

Spine photograph: Byzantine Collection, Dumbarton Oaks, Washington D.C. Pendant cross (gold and enamel). Constantinople, late sixth century.

ISBN 0-8308-1492-2

Printed in the United States of America ∞

Library of Congress Cataloging-in-Publication Data

1-2 Corinthians/ edited by Gerald Bray.
     p.   cm.—(Ancient Christian commentary on Scripture. New
  Testament; 7)
   Includes bibliographical references.
   ISBN 0-8308-1492-2 (cloth: alk. paper)
   1. Bible. N.T. Corinthians Commentaries.   2. Fathers of the
  church.   3. Bible. N.T. Corinthians—Criticism and interpretation,
  etc.—History—Early church, ca. 30-600 Sources.   I. Bray, Gerald
  Lewis.   II. Title: First-second Corinthians.   III. Series.
  BS2675.3.A179   1999
  227'.2077—dc21
                                          99-23125
                                            CIP

| 26 | 25 | 24 | 23 | 22 | 21 | 20 | 19 | 18 | 17 | 16 | 15 | 14 | 13 | 12 | 11 | 10 | 9 | 8 | 7 | 6 | 5 | 4 | 3 |
| 22 | 21 | 20 | 19 | 18 | 17 | 16 | 15 | 14 | 13 | 12 | 11 | 10 | 09 | 08 | 07 | 06 | 05 | 04 | 03 | 02 | 01 | 00 | |

ANCIENT CHRISTIAN COMMENTARY
PROJECT RESEARCH TEAM

GENERAL EDITOR
Thomas C. Oden

ASSOCIATE EDITOR
Christopher A. Hall

TRANSLATIONS PROJECTS DIRECTOR
Joel Scandrett

RESEARCH DIRECTOR
Michael Glerup

EDITORIAL SERVICES DIRECTOR
Susan Kipper

TRANSLATION EDITOR
Dennis McManus

GRADUATE RESEARCH ASSISTANTS

Vincent Bacote	*David Fox*
Brian Brewer	*Konstantin Gavrilkin*
Thomas Buchan	*J. Sergius Halvorsen*
Jill Burnett	*Alexei Khamine*
Hunn Choi	*Sergey Kozin*
Meesaeng Lee Choi	*Michael Nausner*
Joel Elowsky	*Wesley Tink*
Jeffrey Finch	*Bernie Van De Walle*

COMPUTER & TECHNICAL SUPPORT
Michael Kipper

ADMINISTRATIVE ASSISTANT
Colleen Van De Walle

Contents

General Introduction

The Ancient Christian Commentary on Scripture has as its goal the revitalization of Christian teaching based on classical Christian exegesis, the intensified study of Scripture by lay persons who wish to think with the early church about the canonical text, and the stimulation of Christian historical, biblical, theological and pastoral scholars toward further inquiry into scriptural interpretation by ancient Christian writers.

The time frame of these documents spans seven centuries of exegesis, from Clement of Rome to John of Damascus, from the end of the New Testament era to A.D. 750, including the Venerable Bede.

Lay readers are asking how they might study sacred texts under the instruction of the great minds of the ancient church. This commentary has been intentionally prepared for a general lay audience of nonprofessionals who study the Bible regularly and who earnestly wish to have classic Christian observation on the text readily available to them. The series is targeted to anyone who wants to reflect and meditate with the early church about the plain sense, theological wisdom and moral meaning of particular Scripture texts.

A commentary dedicated to allowing ancient Christian exegetes to speak for themselves will refrain from the temptation to fixate endlessly upon contemporary criticism. Rather, it will stand ready to provide textual resources from a distinguished history of exegesis that has remained massively inaccessible and shockingly disregarded during the last century. We seek to make available to our present-day audiences the multicultural, multilingual, transgenerational resources of the early ecumenical Christian tradition.

Preaching at the end of the first millennium focused primarily on the text of Scripture as understood by the earlier esteemed tradition of comment, largely converging on those writers that best reflected classic Christian consensual thinking. Preaching at the end of the second millennium has reversed that pattern. It has so forgotten most of these classic comments that they are vexing to find anywhere, and even when located they are often available only in archaic editions and inadequate translations. The preached word in our time has remained largely bereft of previously influential patristic inspiration. Recent scholarship has so focused attention upon post-Enlightenment historical and literary methods that it has left this longing largely unattended and unserviced.

This series provides the pastor, exegete, student and lay reader with convenient means to see what Athanasius or John Chrysostom or the desert fathers and mothers had to say about a particular text for preaching, for study and for meditation. There is an emerging awareness among Catholic, Protestant and Orthodox laity that vital biblical preaching and spiritual formation need deeper grounding beyond the scope of the historical-critical orientations that have governed biblical studies in our day.

Hence this work is directed toward a much broader audience than the highly technical and specialized scholarly field of patristic studies. The audience is not limited to the university scholar concentrating on the study of the history of the transmission of the text or to those with highly focused philological interests in textual morphology or historical-critical issues. Though these are crucial concerns for specialists, they are not the paramount interest of this series.

This work is a Christian Talmud. The Talmud is a Jewish collection of rabbinic arguments and comments on the Mishnah, which epitomized the laws of the Torah. The Talmud originated in approximately the same period that the patristic writers were commenting on texts of the Christian tradition. Christians from the late patristic age through the medieval period had documents analogous to the Jewish Talmud and Midrash (Jewish commentaries) available to them in the *glossa ordinaria* and catena traditions, two forms of compiling extracts of patristic exegesis. In Talmudic fashion the sacred text of Christian Scripture was thus clarified and interpreted by the classic commentators.

The Ancient Christian Commentary on Scripture has venerable antecedents in medieval exegesis of both eastern and western traditions, as well as in the Reformation tradition. It offers for the first time in this century the earliest Christian comments and reflections on the Old and New Testaments to a modern audience. Intrinsically an ecumenical project, this series is designed to serve Protestant, Catholic and Orthodox lay, pastoral and scholarly audiences.

In cases where Greek, Latin, Syriac and Coptic texts have remained untranslated into English, we provide new translations. Wherever current English translations are already well rendered, they will be utilized, but if necessary their language will be brought up to date. We seek to present fresh dynamic equivalency translations of long-neglected texts which historically have been regarded as authoritative models of biblical interpretation.

These foundational sources are finding their way into many public libraries and into the core book collections of many pastors and lay persons. It is our intent and the publisher's commitment to keep the whole series in print for many years to come.

Thomas C. Oden
General Editor

A Guide to Using This Commentary

Several features have been incorporated into the design of this commentary. The following comments are intended to assist readers in making full use of this volume.

Pericopes of Scripture

The scriptural text has been divided into pericopes, or passages, usually several verses in length. Each of these pericopes is given a heading, which appears at the beginning of the pericope. For example, the first pericope in the commentary on 1 Corinthians is "1:1-3, An Apostle Called by God." This heading is followed by the Scripture passage quoted in the Revised Standard Version (RSV) across the full width of the page. The Scripture passage is provided for the convenience of readers, but it is also in keeping with medieval patristic commentaries, in which the citations of the Fathers were arranged around the text of Scripture.

Overviews

Following each pericope of text from 1 and 2 Corinthians is an overview of the patristic comments on that pericope. The format of this overview varies within the volumes of this series, depending on the requirements of the specific book of Scripture. The function of the overview is to provide a brief summary of all the comments to follow. It tracks a reasonably cohesive thread of argument among patristic comments, even though they are derived from diverse sources and generations. Thus the summaries do not proceed chronologically or by verse sequence. Rather they seek to rehearse the overall course of the patristic comment on that pericope.

We do not assume that the commentators themselves anticipated or expressed a formally received cohesive argument but rather that the various arguments tend to flow in a plausible, recognizable pattern. Modern readers can thus glimpse aspects of continuity in the flow of diverse exegetical traditions representing various generations and geographical locations.

Topical Headings

An abundance of varied patristic comment is available for each pericope of these letters. For this reason we have broken the pericopes into two levels. First is the verse with its topical heading. The patristic comments are then focused on aspects of each verse, with topical headings summarizing the essence of the patristic comment by evoking a key phrase, metaphor or idea. This feature provides a bridge by which modern readers can enter into the heart of the patristic comment.

Identifying the Patristic Texts

Following the topical heading of each section of comment, the name of the patristic commentator is given. An English translation of the patristic comment is then provided. This is immediately followed by the title of the patristic work and the textual reference—either by book, section and subsection or by book-and-verse references.

The Footnotes

Readers who wish to pursue a deeper investigation of the patristic works cited in this commentary will find the footnotes especially valuable. A footnote number directs the reader to the notes at the bottom of the right-hand column, where in addition to other notations (clarifications or biblical crossreferences) one will find information on English translations (where available) and standard original-language editions of the work cited. An abbreviated citation (normally citing the book, volume and page number) of the work in a modern edition is provided. A key to the abbreviations is provided on page xv. Where there is any serious ambiguity or textual problem in the selection, we have tried to reflect the best available textual tradition.

For the convenience of computer database users the digital database references are provided to either the Thesaurus Lingua Graecae (Greek texts) or to the Cetedoc (Latin texts) in the appendix found on pages 317-22.

Abbreviations

ACW   Ancient Christian Writers: The Works of the Fathers in Translation. Mahwah, N.J.: Paulist, 1946-.

AF   J. B. Lightfoot and J. R. Harmer, trans. *The Apostolic Fathers*. Edited by M. W. Holmes. 2nd ed. Grand Rapids, Mich.: Baker, 1989.

AHSIS   Dana Miller, ed. *The Ascetical Homilies of Saint Isaac the Syrian*. Boston, Mass.: Holy Transfiguration Monastery, 1984.

CSEL   Corpus Scriptorum Ecclesiasticorum Latinorum. Vienna, 1866-.

CWS   Classics of Western Spirituality: A Library of the Great Spiritual Masters. Mahwah, N.J.: Paulist Press, 1978-.

FC   Fathers of the Church: A New Translation. Washington, D.C.: Catholic University of America Press, 1947-.

FGFR   *F. W. Norris. Faith Gives Fullness to Reasoning: The Five Theological Orations of Gregory Nazianzen*. Leiden and New York: E. J. Brill, 1990.

HOP   Ephrem the Syrian. *Hymns on Paradise*. Edited by S. Brock. New York: St. Vladimir's Seminary Press, 1990.

JTS   *Journal of Theological Studies*. (Citations in this volume are from Origen, "Fragments on the Pauline Epistles," JTS 3 [1902]; JTS 9-10 [1908-1909]; JTS 13-14 [1912-1913].)

LCC   J. Baillie et al., eds. The Library of Christian Classics. 26 vols. Philadelphia: Westminster Press, 1953-1966.

MOT   *Ronald E. Heine, ed. The Montanist Oracles and Testimonia*. North American Patristic Monograph Series 14. Macon, Ga.: Mercer University Press, 1989.

NPNF   P. Schaff et al., eds. A Select Library of the Nicene and Post-Nicene Fathers of the Christian Church. 2 series (14 vols. each). New York: Christian Literature, 1887-1894. Reprint, Grand Rapids, Mich.: Eerdmans, 1952-1956. Reprint, Peabody, Mass.: Hendrickson, 1994.

NTA 15   K. Staab, ed. *Pauluskommentare aus der griechischen Kirche: Aus Katenenhandschriften gesammelt und herausgegeben* (Pauline Commentary from the Greek Church: Collected and Edited Catena Writings). NT Abhandlungen 15. Münster in Westfalen: Aschendorff, 1933. (Commentators: Didymus the Blind of Alexandria, pp. 6-44; Severian of Gabala, pp. 225-98; Theodore of Mopsuestia, pp. 172-200; Theodoret of Cyr, pp. 226-460; Gennadius of Constantinople, pp. 118-19; Oecumenius, pp. 432-46.)

OFP   Origen. *On First Principles*. Translated by G. W. Butterworth. London: SPCK, 1936. Reprint, Gloucester, Mass.: Peter Smith, 1973.

PG   J.-P. Migne, ed. Patrologia Graeca. 166 vols. Paris: Petit-Montrouge: apud. J.-P. Migne, 1857-1886.

PL   J.-P. Migne, ed. Patrologia Latina. 221 vols. Paris: Migne, 1844-1864.

SFPSL   S. Brock, trans. *The Syriac Fathers on Prayer and the Spiritual Life*. Kalamazoo, Mich.: Cistercian Publications, 1987.

Introduction to 1-2 Corinthians

How is it possible to smooth the way for a modern reader to explore 1 and 2 Corinthians through the eyes of the ancient Christian writers? To help in this task, we must first consider four different questions:

1. Who wrote the epistles to the Corinthians?
2. Why are the epistles to the Corinthians important?
3. How were the patristic quotations used here selected?
4. How has the process of reading them been made easier for you?

Who Wrote the Epistles to the Corinthians?

On the question of the authorship of 1 and 2 Corinthians, virtually all commentators, both ancient and modern, agree that the author of the epistles was the apostle Paul, though there are doubts about whether the current form of 2 Corinthians in particular is original to him. Even in ancient times, there was a suspicion that Paul wrote other letters to the Corinthians, and it was not clear even then whether or to what extent their content had found its way into the canonical texts as we have them. Dating the epistles is therefore a complicated procedure, especially if we have to take a later redaction into account. In any case, we know that they cannot have been written before A.D. 49-51, when Paul was in Corinth, and it seems most likely that they should be dated at some point between A.D. 52 and A.D. 56, with the second epistle coming a year or so after the first.

Why Are the Epistles to the Corinthians Important?

The all but unanimous agreement about the authorship of the epistles is matched by an equally widespread consensus concerning their importance. First Corinthians is the longest of Paul's epistles, and furthermore, it was written to the church in the largest and most important city of Greece at that time. Second Corinthians follows up the themes of the first epistle, bringing out certain fundamental themes that were touched on though not fully dealt with in the earlier letter. The epistles are important because of what they tell us about the difficulties encountered by one of the most important churches planted by Paul. Many of these difficulties focused around the vexing questions of authority and leadership. The Fathers do not explicitly state that monarchical episcopacy was the solution to the Corinthians' problems, though that message must have been clear enough to their readers, since Paul is portrayed as insisting that only he or those specially delegated by him would be able to resolve the difficulties of the church.

The nature of the problem becomes clear in the second epistle, where the apostle feels obliged to defend his record and his qualifications. The awkwardness of this comes across in every line, and the Fathers were not slow to pick up Paul's mood. They were accustomed, thanks to their familiarity with classical rhetoric, to the uses of irony, and they responded to Paul's defense with instinctive sympathy. Furthermore, they were acutely aware that unhappiness with the apostle meant unhappiness with his teaching, which in turn meant heresy. This was a living issue in the fourth century, when there were false prophets like Arius and Eunomius, who appeared to be doing the same thing to the church of their day that the false prophets at Corinth did in theirs. The close link in the patristic mind between doctrinal heresy and immorality comes across clearly. None of the Fathers seems to have doubted that the man who slept with his stepmother (1 Cor 5) was also the church's leading heresiarch.

Uncertainties about leadership at Corinth had produced a situation in which the church was in danger of dissolving into competing factions based on personalities, some of whom were teaching false doctrine as well. From the experiences of their time, the Fathers were aware that unity and truth went together, and they constantly emphasized this link in their commentaries on these epistles. At the same time, however, it is interesting and important to note that they knew little more, and perhaps even less, than we do about the people Paul mentions. Particularly revealing in this respect is the confusion over the expression "Chloe's people" in 1 Corinthians 1:11. Some of the Fathers apparently thought that Chloe was a place, not the name of a person, which demonstrates that by the fourth century there were conflicting traditions about the earliest days of the Corinthian church.

The epistles do not deal directly with the problem of relations between Jews and Gentiles in the way that Galatians and Romans do, but the question is never far from the surface. The epistles are important because they reveal the nature of the problem of sanctification in a Gentile milieu. Jews solved this problem by segregation. They refused to eat meat that had been sacrificed to idols, and often they maintained few if any social relations outside their own communities. Gentiles did not have this option, even though some Jewish Christians tried to impose it on them. Gentiles had to live in their own milieu without being contaminated by it and without giving offense to those who did not or who could not understand the subtleties of their position. Paul's basic response, here as elsewhere, was that they should defend the principles of Christian freedom against both the law of Moses and paganism, but when this caused personal difficulties they should graciously sacrifice their private opinions for the sake of peace. This meant not eating food sacrificed to idols, which might offend Jews, but it also meant being willing to socialize with pagans and even to maintain marriages already contracted with them.

At another level Gentile Christians were also forced to reconcile the competing claims of philosophy and religion. In the Greek world these things were separate and often mutually hostile. Many philosophers followed Plato in regarding religion as an irrational superstition that should be put aside. Much pagan religious practice, by contrast, had little to do with morality and occasionally involved practices like ritual fornication. These were still living issues in the fourth and fifth centuries, and here the Fathers are genuinely closer to the mindset of the first Christians than we are.

Neither philosophy nor religion had much to say about practical considerations of charity, which take up a major slice of 2 Corinthians. Generosity toward fellow believers in distress was a hallmark of ancient Christians because it was unheard of in the pagan world. Once again the Fathers were more conscious of this than we are, if only because we have inherited centuries of tradition in which charity has become associated with almsgiving.

The Fathers sensed that the epistles were important because of what they say about basic Christian doctrines. Many of the early commentators knew that the Corinthian epistles are less doctrinal than is the epistle to the Romans, but this did not mean that 1 and 2 Corinthians are not full of fundamental Christian teaching. The resurrection of the body was the most obvious example of this, but that immediately raised the question of Christ's incarnation and divinity. Spiritual gifts were another matter, and this issue forced the Fathers to consider both the divinity of the Holy Spirit and the nature of the Christian life. What did it mean to be born again in baptism and receive divine grace? Why did Christians in the fourth century not speak in tongues or prophesy in the way that the first Christians had apparently done? The witness of these epistles forced the Fathers to define their understanding of the Christian life both in this world and in the resurrection. These definitions were intimately connected with the Christian understanding of God, and the Fathers lost no opportunity to demonstrate that the apostle Paul taught the doctrine of the Trinity, the basic and most distinctive Christian belief.

How Were the Patristic Quotations Used Here Selected?
The epistles to the Corinthians have always been among the best known and most frequently quoted New Testament texts. From the patristic period there are thousands of quotations and allusions, all of which can be recovered without difficulty, thanks to the possibilities that have been opened up by computer research. The combined resources of the Thesaurus Linguae Graecae (TLG) and of the Centre de Textes et Documents (Cetedoc), as well as the digital version of the Patrologia Latina, have made it possible to obtain a virtually complete collection of patristic references to Corinthians that, if they were all reproduced, would take up several volumes. For our purposes, many of these references can be ignored. Some are merely passing allusions to the text that shed little or no light on its meaning. Others are quotations that are intended to reinforce a point made on the strength of some other part of Scripture, and more often than we would like, they are there taken out of context.

Allusions to the text of 1 and 2 Corinthians are almost all that we have to go on for the earliest period (before A.D. 200), and so a few quotations from authors like Irenaeus and Tertullian have been given in order to give readers a flavor of how the Corinthian epistles were used before commentary writing became common. These allusions must be used with a certain degree of caution, since in many cases the writer was making some other point and using Corinthians in order to bolster his argument. For the purposes of this collection, an effort has been made to ensure that such references do have a genuine link with Paul's epistles, but even so, readers will be well advised to treat this material with discretion.

We do possess a few commentaries on the epistles, though the material available in this form is much less than for the epistle to the Romans. The first full-length commentary that has survived is also the greatest produced in the ancient church. It was the work of an unknown scholar, writing in Rome sometime between 366 and 384. He wrote in Latin, and throughout the Middle Ages his identity was merged with that of Ambrose of Milan (d. 397). It was not until Erasmus (1466-1536) examined the text that it became clear that this attribution was a mistake. The commentary on this and on the other Pauline epistles was the work of a much greater scholar than Ambrose, whom Erasmus somewhat punningly chose to call Ambrosiaster, the name by which he has been known ever since.

Ambrosiaster wrote a literal commentary, and he was fully aware of many of the problems posed by historical and textual criticism. His work can easily stand comparison with modern writings on the subject, so close were his methods to those generally employed today. Who Ambrosiaster was is a matter of speculation, the most intriguing suggestion being that he may have been a monk known as Isaac the Syrian, who was a converted Jew in Rome. If that is true, it would certainly explain Ambrosiaster's deep and sympathetic knowledge of Judaism, though we are constrained by lack of evidence from making any definite decision on the question. Whoever he was, he was soon being widely read and imitated, though never altogether successfully. It is a pity that his work is not available in English translation, and so it is unknown to most readers. For that reason, this edition contains rather more of Ambrosiaster than might otherwise be the case, since in effect it is introducing him to a wider reading public for the first time. We are indebted to Dr. Janet Fairweather of Cambridge for much of the translation of Ambrosiaster in this volume.

Contemporary with Ambrosiaster are a number of Greek commentators whose work survives only in fragments. They are Didymus the Blind of Alexandria (313-398) and Severian of Gabala (fl. c. 400). Their work may be found in the Staab edition of *Pauluskommentare aus der Griechischen Kirche* (NTA). Severian represents the Antiochene school of biblical exegesis, which concentrated heavily on the literal interpretation of the texts and which is full of historical details, textual criticism, and so on. The fragmentary nature of the surviving material means that it is impossible to do justice to these commentators, but the selection presented here will give some idea of how they went about their task. Didymus wrote from Alexandria, which was the great rival of Antioch and where an allegorical interpretation of Scripture was more favored. Nevertheless Didymus himself resisted this tendency to a large extent, and the style of his commentary is not noticeably different from that of the others.

The next full-length work to appear in Greek was the sermon series of John Chrysostom (347-407), the famous preacher who became patriarch of Constantinople but was exiled by the court because of his boldness in criticizing its corruption. Chrysostom has left us forty-four homilies on the first epistle and thirty on the second, all of which are verse-by-verse expositions of Corinthians. Each homily concludes with a long section relating to practical application, most of which has had to be omitted from the present edition. It is, however, readily available in English translation. As is to be expected from homilies, Chrysostom's style is more rhetorical than that of the others, and he often tends toward ad hominem arguments. At the same time, he was a good historian and critic, and his conclusions about the authorship and dating of Corinthians are what most commentators today would still propose. For a book like this one, which aims to reach pastors and ordinary Christians rather than professional scholars, he is often the most user-friendly commentator of them all.

Contemporary with or slightly later than Chrysostom is Theodore of Mopsuestia (350-428), another Antiochene whose work survives only in fragments. Theodore was a truly great commentator, and if his work survived in toto he would rank with Ambrosiaster or even higher. His feeling for Paul's language and meaning was deep, and his critical sense was acute. His judgments were almost always apposite, and it is our good fortune that so many of them have survived in the Catenae[1] even though the complete text has disappeared.

After Theodore's time, there were further commentaries in Greek, of which the most notable was written by Theodoret of Cyr (Cyrrhus) (393-466). This survives, almost uniquely among the Antiochene commentaries, although it is not available in English translation. Theodoret was dependent on Theodore of Mopsuestia, and from him we can catch a glimpse of the greatness of the Antiochene tradition. He eschews allegory, concentrates on historical and grammatical details and stays close to the apostle's original intention. His comments are usually helpful and retain their freshness even after the passage of time. He is particularly inclined to draw the reader's attention to other parts of Scripture that support what the apostle is saying to the Corinthians. Because of all this, we have chosen to offer a fairly extensive selection of his work, so that both he and the tradition he represents may be made more familiar to modern readers.

After Theodoret's time there was a commentary by Gennadius of Constantinople (d. 471), of which only a few fragments survive, and another by Oecumenius (sixth century), which is likewise fragmentary though more extensive. These texts also may be found in Staab (NTA). On the whole the text of Gennadius is prone to speculation when it does not follow earlier sources, and it is of relatively little value.

---

[1] Chains of quotations selected and anthologized, rather like the present volume.

In addition to the commentaries that are available, there is a wide choice of other patristic works in which particular passages or verses of Corinthians are mentioned and commented on. In making a selection of them for this volume, two considerations have guided our choice. The first of these is the prominence and representativeness of the writer or source being used. There is little point in quoting an obscure author or writing in order to demonstrate a knowledge of his or its existence. But this is often the only way that gives us access to Syriac and Coptic sources, and an exception to this rule has been made for them. Otherwise we have preferred to rely on mainstream writers whose works have entered the spiritual tradition of the church and who may therefore be taken as more fully representative of patristic thought as a whole.

A special word of explanation is needed regarding the inclusion of the archheretic Pelagius (c. 354-c. 420) in this commentary. Pelagius's original text was presumably explicitly heretical in more ways than the present redacted version displays. What we have now is largely unexceptional, even if it is possible to detect points of disagreement with Augustine. Some earlier version of the text, predating this one, was undoubtedly written by Pelagius and survived for many centuries because it was thought to have been the work of Jerome. The text as we now have it was probably reworked and brought closer to orthodoxy in the sixth century either by Cassiodorus or Primasius or both.

The textual problems associated with the commentary of Pelagius remain highly controverted.[2] The original commentary, written before 412 by Pelagius, was probably revised before 432 by a Pelagian redactor (possibly Caelestius), eliminating certain phrases of the commentary in light of the condemnation of Pelagius and Caelestius. These revisions are preserved in the Pseudo-Jerome tradition of Pelagius's commentary. Over a century later the commentary was revised by Cassiodorus and his students at the Vivarium, who were unaware that Pelagius was the author of the commentary.[3] Seeing that the commentary was still marred by Pelagian errors, Cassiodorus and his students revised, "improved" and softened the commentary so as to make it more acceptable within Western orthodoxy. This version was attributed to Primasius, and its redaction by the school of Cassiodorus was not recognized until the twentieth century.

There remain crucial variants in key passages of the various manuscript traditions—chiefly the Karlsruhe, Balliol, Paris and St. Gall versions—which can be read in either a more Pelagian or Augustinian tone, chastened perhaps by the Council of Orange in 529. What this means for readers is that text here attributed to Pelagius is not an uncorrupted text by Pelagius himself; it has probably been decontaminated from many more overtly objectionable "Pelagian" ideas. The aim of this commentary is to present so far as it is discernible the more consensual traditions of early Christian

---

[2]For a discussion of the probable redaction and transmission of the text, see studies by H. J. Frede, Georges de Plinval, Alexander Souter, R. F. Evans and Theodore de Bruyn.
[3]Cassiodorus thought it had been written by Pope Gelasius.

exegesis. While Pelagius himself does not qualify as an exemplar of consensuality on those points that were clearly rejected, this redacted version of his earlier manuscript has been considered much less objectionable from the point of view of consensuality. Hence it is included in this collection.

How Has Reading the Commentaries Been Made Easier for You?

Access to writings that were produced long ago in ancient languages is never an easy matter, and translations into English do not always help us. A number of such translations were made in the nineteenth century, which was a great age of patristic scholarship, but the style of the English is often dated almost as much as that of the original text. Modern readers do not want to plow through long sentences full of subordinate clauses and polysyllabic words whose meaning is clear only to those with a classical education. It is also the case that the Fathers wrote to be read aloud, not silently, and they are therefore much more rhetorical in their style than we would be. Sometimes this is attractive, but more often than not the modern reader finds it high-blown and irritating. It can also become unnecessarily repetitive and even disjointed in places, as speech often is.

In this edition all that has been smoothed out. Contemporary style has been preferred, even when this has meant interpreting the literal wording of the original text. Because we are presenting extracts and not complete quotations, it has sometimes been necessary to supply bridging material that is not in the original text but that is either implied by it or contained there at much greater length. It did not seem worthwhile to quote an entire page merely to retain the odd sentence. Rather than do that, we have at times used ellipses to condense such paragraphs into a sentence or two, so as not to detract from the essence of what the Father in question was trying to say. Existing English translations have been consulted and used to some extent, but we have felt free to alter them to fit the style and needs of the present edition, so that only occasionally their wording has been preserved intact. In particular we have tried to establish some consistency in the rendering of theological terms, and whenever possible we have opted for the variants that are normally used by theologians today. All this may cause a certain amount of irritation to the professional scholar, but it should be remembered that the purpose of this commentary is to allow the Fathers to speak to the present generation, not to give people the impression that it is necessary to have a Ph.D. in order to understand them.

When selections are taken from complete commentaries such as Ambrosiaster's, minimal references are given. It is assumed that anyone wishing to consult the original will have only to look up the relevant chapter and verse of the commentary in question. Fragments and quotations from other works are referenced according to source. Where possible, reference is also made to the best available English translation, though what is found in this book is at most an adaptation of that and probably not a direct quotation.

Furthermore, each group of verses is accompanied by an overview that gives the reader some idea of what the discussion is about. Where there are notable differences of opinion among the Fathers or where one of them has presented a particularly significant argument, this is also noted, so that readers may be alerted to the importance of the selections that follow.

It only remains to be said that the main purpose of this volume is to edify the communion of saints, so that Christians today may be encouraged to examine and appropriate what the writers of an earlier time, many of whom have been canonized by the tradition of the church and all of whom are worth reading, had to say about two of the greatest books ever written—the apostle Paul's epistles to the Corinthians. May God by his grace open the hearts and minds of all who read these texts, and may we, together with them, come to that perfect peace and joy that is the inheritance of the saints in light.

Gerald Bray
Feast of St. Augustine of Canterbury

THE FIRST EPISTLE
TO THE CORINTHIANS

OVERVIEW OF THE FIRST EPISTLE: It was Paul who first brought the gospel to Corinth, and he therefore took special interest in the nurture of this community of faith. Corinth was a place where all the evils of the pagan world were on display. New Christians were tempted either to return to the practices of the law or to revert to the pagan environment. Ambrosiaster had no difficulty sketching at least ten motivations that led Paul to write this letter to Corinth. Most of these had to do with problems faced by the church that Paul knew about. So he provides doctrinal correction, moral admonition and pleas for unity and charity. Paul himself had suffered deeply in Corinth, where wealth and wisdom were prone to make the inhabitants proud. Among the problems and questions in Corinth were perfectionism, pride in spiritual gifts, marriage, fornication (CHRYSOSTOM), divisiveness, pseudo-philosophy and the pretense of eloquence (THEODORET OF CYR). Paul demonstrated their intrinsic interconnection and how they could all be remedied by the right reception of the gospel. These remain problems faced by churches of other times and places.

TEN REASONS PAUL WROTE TO CORINTH. AM-BROSIASTER: Prompted by the Lord's command, Paul stayed with the Corinthians for eighteen months and taught the Word of God among them. It is because of this that he treats them with great confidence and loving affection, sometimes warning and sometimes censuring them, and sometimes treating them fondly as if they were his own children. There are quite varied reasons why he was writing to them:

The first is that some godly people were disagreeing with one another in partisanship, wanting to be called followers of Paul, of Peter or of Apollos rather than of Christ. Paul strongly disapproved of this. Others disagreed with all of the above and declared themselves partisans of Christ alone.

The second reason is that the Corinthians were beginning to find pleasure in eloquence and worldly philosophy, with the result that although they were nominally Christian, they were imbued with philosophical notions which were contrary to the faith.

The third reason is that they were puffed up with anger, frustrated because Paul had not been to visit them.

The fourth reason concerned someone who was guilty of fornication, whom they had allowed to remain in their midst.

The fifth reason was Paul's need to remind the Corinthians of a previous letter which he had written before the one which we call the "first."[1]

The sixth reason is that the Corinthians were behaving unlawfully and fraudulently toward one another and preferred to seek redress in the pagan courts.

The seventh reason is that, although Paul was allowed to accept financial support, he refused to do so, so as not to set a precedent for wild or false apostles.

The eighth reason was that they were beginning to be thrown into confusion by heretics on the subject of marriage.

The ninth reason was his assertion that everyone should remain steadfast in what he had taught them to believe.

The tenth reason concerned virgins, about whom Paul had given no instructions.

And there are other reasons as well, which will soon become apparent in the body of the text. COMMENTARY ON PAUL'S EPISTLES, PROEM.[2]

THE CORINTHIAN SETTING AND ITS PROBLEMS. CHRYSOSTOM: Corinth is still the first city of Greece. In ancient times it prided itself on many temporal advantages, above all on its great wealth. The city was full of orators and philosophers, one of whom [Periander] was considered one of the seven wise men of his time. These things are not just ornamental details. They help us in understanding Paul's epistles.

Paul also suffered many things in this city, where Christ appeared to him and told him to speak [Acts 18:9-10]. In the time of Gallio, Paul was beaten here in front of the judgment seat. The devil, seeing that a great city had accepted the truth and received the Word of God with great eagerness, set about dividing it. He knew that even the strongest kingdom, if divided against itself, would not stand. He had a choice weapon for doing this in the wealth and wisdom of the inhabitants, which made them exceedingly proud.

In addition to this, there was another sin

committed there, namely, a person who had slept with his stepmother not only escaped rebuke but even became a leader of the people and gave them occasion to be conceited. There were also some people who regarded themselves as more perfect than the rest. Out of gluttony some flaunted their freedom by eating meat which had been sacrificed to idols. They would even do this in the temples, bringing the whole church to conflict. Other people, fighting over money, took their cases to the secular courts. Some of the men wore long hair, and others ate by themselves in church, refusing to share their food with the needy. Others were puffed up with spiritual gifts, which was also the main reason why the church was split. The doctrine of the resurrection was also disputed among them, because some people refused to believe in the resurrection of the body. All these things were the result of the influence of heathen philosophy. The divisions in the church reflected those among the philosophers themselves.

The Corinthians had written to Paul by the hand of Fortunatus, Stephanas and Achaicus, not about all these matters but more particularly about marriage and virginity. Paul gave them instructions both about the things they had asked about and about these other matters as well. He sent Timothy with the letters, knowing that their force would be backed up by the recollection of his own emissary.

Those who had divided the church tried to hide their wickedness by claiming that they were teaching more perfect doctrines and that they were wiser than the others. Paul attacks the root of the problem first, before going on to deal with the issue of division. He is not afraid to be bold in what he says, because these were

---

[1]The "previous letter" referred to in 1 Cor 5:9-11. It contained instructions "not to associate with immoral persons" (1 Cor 5:9). No text is available. [2]CSEL 81.3-4. Among the motivations for writing were doctrinal correction, moral admonition, apologetic persuasion, Christian unity and benevolence to the saints.

his own converts, and some of them, at least, were weaker than Christians elsewhere. But it is most unlikely that the entire church was corrupted. Rather it appears that there were some among them who were very holy. Paul said as much in the epistle [1 Cor 4:3, 6]. The evils in the church sprang from the pride of some of its members, and it was that which the apostle attacked first of all. HOMILIES ON THE EPISTLES OF PAUL TO THE CORINTHIANS, PROEM.[3]

To WHOM ADDRESSED. THEODORET OF CYR: St. Paul was the first to bring the message of salvation to the Corinthians. He had already spent a considerable amount of time there. After eighteen months he left and went on to preach the Gospel in other cities. But the Corinthian church was in a place where it could easily develop a taste for philosophical arguments and academic affectations. The church became divided into many factions, each with powerful speakers as its leader. Each of them promoted its own beliefs, and they argued with one another over them. One of these eloquent leaders even dared to take his stepmother as his mistress. Those who belonged to his faction paid no attention. They were merely drawn to his eloquence, which they admired. For this reason St. Paul, at the beginning of his letter, condemns their idea of wisdom and demonstrates that there is something missing in their preaching, in spite of its vigor. He also criticizes them for feuding among themselves and taking their differences to the secular magistrate. He also forbids eating meat which has been sacrificed to idols, insinuating thereby that some of them were doing just that. In passing, he also gives good advice concerning virginity and widowhood and discourses at some length on spiritual gifts, explaining how they differ from one another. He argues that speaking in tongues is given not for self-promotion but for the edification of others. He especially expounds to them the doctrine of the resurrection. It appears that some people were trying to persuade them that there was no physical resurrection of the body. In addition there are a few other things which he inserts into his letter and which are generally useful for everyone. He says relatively little about Christian doctrine, because having spent such a long time with them he had already taught them exactly what they should believe, and Apollos, who came immediately after him, had confirmed it all. Paul imitated the best of physicians and applied the right medicines to their feelings and sicknesses. The bearers of the letter were Stephanas, Fortunatus and Achaicus, who had been sent to him by the Corinthians, as he tells us at the end of the letter. He also sent St. Timothy to them, but independently of the letter. COMMENTARY ON THE FIRST EPISTLE TO THE CORINTHIANS 163-64.[4]

---

[3]NPNF 1 12:1-2. [4]Migne PG 82:226-27.

1:1-3 AN APOSTLE CALLED BY GOD

[1]*Paul, called by the will of God to be an apostle of Christ Jesus, and our brother Sosthenes,* [2]*To the church of God which is at Corinth, to those sanctified in Christ Jesus, called to be saints together with all those who in every place call on the name of our Lord Jesus Christ, both their Lord and ours:*

³Grace to you and peace from God our Father and the Lord Jesus Christ.

Overview: The letter is addressed not only to those who are already cleansed from their sins (Ambrosiaster) but also to those still looking toward the fuller reception of sanctifying grace (Origen). Its instruction is not limited to the Corinthians but is applicable to all Christians everywhere (Chrysostom). Grace comes from the Father through the Son (Ambrosiaster, Theodoret of Cyr). Paul first establishes his apostolic authority (Ambrosiaster), as distinguished from those whose presumed calling is explained by human motives (Theodoret of Cyr). To be called as an apostle by the will of God is to have all pride disarmed, since it comes wholly on God's initiative (Chrysostom). Paul identifies his companion Sosthenes as a brother who had suffered persecution in Corinth along with Paul (Theodoret of Cyr, Pelagius).

1:1 Called by God

An Apostle. Ambrosiaster: Paul begins this epistle differently, because his subject matter is different. He writes that he is an apostle by the will of God, alluding to those false apostles who had not been sent by Christ and whose teaching was not true. There were many sects which had emerged and which preached Christ according to their own whims. They broke up churches, and some of their dried-up branches are still with us today. For this reason, Paul sets out everything which is opposed to the heresies and asserts that he is a true preacher because he has been sent by Christ, according to God's will. Commentary on Paul's Epistles.[1]

Called by God's Will. Chrysostom: From the very beginning Paul casts down the Corinthians' pride, in that he speaks of himself as "called." "For what I have learned," says Paul, "I did not discover myself, but it was while I was persecuting the church that I was called. It was

God who willed that you too should be saved in this way." We have done nothing good by ourselves, but by God's will we have been saved. We were called because it seemed good to him, not because we were worthy. Homilies on the Epistles of Paul to the Corinthians 1.1.[2]

Our Brother. Pelagius: By calling Sosthenes his brother, Paul is both demonstrating his own humility and pointing out that Sosthenes is a fellow worker in the gospel. Commentary on the First Epistle to the Corinthians 1.[3]

Not Called by Man. Theodoret of Cyr: Paul is saying in effect: "You Corinthians have been called by men, but I have been called by God." I think that Sosthenes was a Corinthian. He is mentioned in Acts [18:17], where Luke says that in the time of Gallio the Greeks arrested him and beat him. Commentary on the First Epistle to the Corinthians 165.[4]

1:2a To the Church at Corinth

Sanctified in Christ. Origen: Why did Paul write "to those called to be saints" as well as to those who are already "sanctified" and in the church? Surely this means that the letter is addressed not only to those who are already cleansed from their sins but also to those who still await cleansing, though they are among those whom God has called. Commentary on 1 Corinthians 1.1.7.[5]

1:2b Those Called to Be Saints

---

[1]CSEL 81.4. For an explanation of the omission here of book, section and subsection numbering in line-by-line commentaries, see the introduction (p. xxiii). [2]NPNF 1 12:3. [3]Migne PL 30:717B. For an explanation of the inclusion here of comments attributed to the archheretic Pelagius, see the introduction (p. xxii). [4]Migne PG 82:227-30. [5]JTS 9:232.

THE CHURCH AS A WHOLE. AMBROSIASTER: Paul writes to the church as a whole, because at that time leaders had not yet been appointed for individual churches. He censures them for many things, but in spite of that he still says that they have been sanctified. However, they later began to behave badly, so that although the whole church was sanctified in Christ, some members of it had been deflected from the truth by the wicked teaching of the false apostles.

The Corinthians were called to be saints, which means that they could not deviate from the narrow path of sanctification. Paul linked them, as Gentiles, with the true Jews, because salvation is of the Jews, so that wherever there are Gentiles who call on the name of the Lord Jesus Christ and wherever there are true Jews, both are united in him. But the false apostles, who preached the name of Christ in accordance with the wisdom of this world, criticized the law and the prophets. Like Marcion and Mani, they maintained that Christ was not really crucified but that it merely appeared that he had been. Neither did they believe in the resurrection of the body. COMMENTARY ON PAUL'S EPISTLES.[6]

THE LETTER WRITTEN TO THE SAINTS. PELAGIUS: Paul is writing to those who have preserved their sanctity, not to those who have lost it. The former he honors with his letter; the latter he admonishes with his authority. COMMENTARY ON THE FIRST EPISTLE TO THE CORINTHIANS 1.[7]

1:2c All Who Call on the Lord Jesus Christ

THE ONE ASSEMBLY ALL OVER THE WORLD. CHRYSOSTOM: The church ought to be united because it belongs to God. It does not exist only in Corinth, but all over the world, and it is one, for the church's name (*ekklēsia*) means "assembly." It is not a name of separation, but a name of unity and concord. HOMILIES ON THE EPISTLES OF PAUL TO THE CORINTHIANS 1.1.[8]

TO HEAL DIVISIONS. THEODORET OF CYR: Everything Paul mentions here is meant to be a remedy for the disease of schism. They are meant to heal division and display the church's unity. COMMENTARY ON THE FIRST EPISTLE TO THE CORINTHIANS 165.[9]

1:3 Grace and Peace from God and Jesus Christ

GRACE FROM THE FATHER. AMBROSIASTER: Paul teaches that Christ should be invoked in prayer but all grace comes from the Father. The two are one in their divinity, but primacy belongs to the authority of the Father. COMMENTARY ON PAUL'S EPISTLES.[10]

GRACE AND PEACE. CHRYSOSTOM: If our peace comes from God's grace, why are you so proud, since you are saved by grace? How can anyone find grace with God, except through humility? HOMILIES ON THE EPISTLES OF PAUL TO THE CORINTHIANS 1.3.[11]

FATHER AND SON ARE ONE. THEODORET OF CYR: Paul says that Christ is their benefactor as well as the Father, demonstrating that the two are one. COMMENTARY ON THE FIRST EPISTLE TO THE CORINTHIANS 166.[12]

---

[6]CSEL 81.5-6. [7]Migne PL 30:717B-C. [8]NPNF 1 12:3. [9]Migne PG 82:230. [10]CSEL 81.6. [11]NPNF 1 12:4. [12]Migne PG 82:230.

1:4-9 THANKSGIVING

⁴*I give thanks to God*^a *always for you because of the grace of God which was given you in Christ Jesus,* ⁵*that in every way you were enriched in him with all speech and all knowledge—* ⁶*even as the testimony to Christ was confirmed among you—* ⁷*so that you are not lacking in any spiritual gift, as you wait for the revealing of our Lord Jesus Christ;* ⁸*who will sustain you to the end, guiltless in the day of our Lord Jesus Christ.* ⁹*God is faithful, by whom you were called into the fellowship of his Son, Jesus Christ our Lord.*

a *Other ancient authorities read* my God

OVERVIEW: Paul puts himself in the position of a father; he gives thanks for his children, the Corinthians, all the time, regardless of what they have done (ORIGEN). They are called to be one with all believers in Christ (ORIGEN). Paul begins with praise in order to prepare the Corinthians (CHRYSOSTOM) for the admonition that is to come (THEODORET OF CYR). Some of the Corinthians were no longer living according to their faith, so as to appear to make void the grace they had once received (AMBROSIASTER, PELAGIUS). On the day of the Lord (JEROME), unbelievers will know the truth of what they disbelieved. Christians will find that what they believed is wonderful beyond what they had imagined (AMBROSIASTER).

1:4a Thanking God for Them

ALL THE TIME. ORIGEN: Paul does not just give thanks for the Corinthians some of the time, nor only when they do good. He puts himself in the position of a father, who is thankful for his children all the time, whatever they may have done. COMMENTARY ON 1 CORINTHIANS 1.2.1-15.[1]

1:4b The Grace of God Given in Christ Jesus

BY FAITH ALONE. AMBROSIASTER: God has decreed that a person who believes in Christ can be saved without works. By faith alone he re-

ceives the forgiveness of his sins. COMMENTARY ON PAUL'S EPISTLES.[2]

NOT BY WORKS. CHRYSOSTOM: You were saved by grace, not by works. And who gave you this grace? It was not Paul, or another apostle, but Jesus Christ himself. HOMILIES ON THE EPISTLES OF PAUL TO THE CORINTHIANS 2.3.[3]

A SWEET BEGINNING. THEODORET OF CYR: Paul takes care to sweeten their ears before starting to admonish them. What he says is true, however: He gives thanks to God because of the gifts which have been given to them. COMMENTARY ON THE FIRST EPISTLE TO THE CORINTHIANS 166.[4]

1:5 Enriched with Speech and Knowledge

SPEECH GOES FURTHER. ORIGEN: Knowledge shows what there is to know. Speech goes further and explains it. COMMENTARY ON 1 CORINTHIANS 1.2.29-30.[5]

STEADFAST IN GRACE TO ACQUIRE KNOWLEDGE. AMBROSIASTER: This means that the Corinthians have remained steadfast in the grace which they have received and in the preaching

---

[1]JTS 9:232-33. [2]CSEL 81.6-7. [3]NPNF 1 12:6. [4]Migne PG 82:230. [5]JTS 9:233.

of the doctrine of truth, because they have acquired spiritual knowledge. Paul therefore gives thanks to God for these things. COMMENTARY ON PAUL'S EPISTLES.[6]

ONCE BLESSED WITH GRACE. PELAGIUS: When the Corinthians came to faith in Christ they were blessed with all grace. But now that they were no longer living according to their faith, they had made void the grace which they had received. COMMENTARY ON THE FIRST EPISTLE TO THE CORINTHIANS 1.[7]

TO UNDERSTAND AND TO SPEAK. CHRYSOSTOM: There is knowledge which goes beyond speech. Many have knowledge which they cannot express—for example, those who are uneducated and unable to express themselves clearly. But the Corinthians were not like them. They were able both to understand and to speak. HOMILIES ON THE EPISTLES OF PAUL TO THE CORINTHIANS 2.3.[8]

1:6 The Testimony to Christ

CONFIRMED IN US. ORIGEN: The testimony of Christ is confirmed in us if we can say, like the apostle Paul, "I am persuaded that neither life nor death etc. can separate us from the love of God in Christ Jesus our Lord" [Rom 8:38-39]. But if we are upset by every little thing that happens, then Christ's testimony has not been confirmed in us at all. COMMENTARY ON 1 CORINTHIANS 1.2.35-40.[9]

THE TESTIMONY STRENGTHENED BY FAITH. AMBROSIASTER: The testimony of Christ has been confirmed in them because they have been strengthened by their faith. They had come to put no trust in human things. Rather, all their hope was in Christ, for they were ensnared neither by pleasure nor by the enticements of pleasure. COMMENTARY ON PAUL'S EPISTLES.[10]

1:7a Lacking No Spiritual Gift

PRAISE BEFORE CRITICISM. CHRYSOSTOM: These praises are not uncritical, as the rest of the epistle makes clear. But they are inserted in order to prepare the Corinthians for the criticism which is to come. For whoever starts out with unpleasant words antagonizes his hearers. Paul starts by praising them in order to avoid this. HOMILIES ON THE EPISTLES OF PAUL TO THE CORINTHIANS 2.5.[11]

UNIMPEACHABLE IN THE PRESENT. JEROME: Although we lack no gift, nevertheless we await the appearance of our Lord Jesus Christ. He will then keep us secure in all things and present us unimpeachable when the day of our Lord Jesus Christ comes. The end of the world shall arrive, when no flesh may glory in his sight. AGAINST THE PELAGIANS 2.8.[12]

1:7b The Revealing of Our Lord Jesus Christ

WAITING FOR THE REVEALING. ORIGEN: In this life the righteous person does not yet enjoy what he hopes for but rather endures suffering and danger. He is waiting for the revelation of Christ to come. COMMENTARY ON 1 CORINTHIANS 1.2.48-51.[13]

BELIEVERS AND UNBELIEVERS AWAIT THAT DAY. AMBROSIASTER: It is clear that Paul was a circumspect man who was full of concern as he awaited the day of judgment. On that day the Lord Jesus Christ will be revealed both to believers and to unbelievers. Then unbelievers will realize that what they did not want to believe is in fact true. Believers will rejoice, finding that what they believed in is more wonderful than they had imagined. COMMENTARY ON PAUL'S EPISTLES.[14]

THE REVELATION IS NOW HIDDEN. PELAGIUS:

---

[6]CSEL 81.7.　[7]Migne PL 30:718B.　[8]NPNF 1 12:6.　[9]JTS 9:233.　[10]CSEL 81.7.　[11]NPNF 1 12:7.　[12]FC 53:307.　[13]JTS 9:233.　[14]CSEL 81.7-8.

Christ's second coming is described as a revelation, because now it is hidden from us. Commentary on the First Epistle to the Corinthians 1.[15]

1:8 Sustained by Christ

Sustained Forever. Origen: Who sustains us? Christ Jesus, the Word and Wisdom of God. Moreover, he sustains us not merely for a day or two, but forever. Commentary on 1 Corinthians 1.2.52-54.[16]

Guiltless in the Day of Our Lord. Ambrosiaster: Paul is confident that the Corinthians will persevere in righteousness until the day of judgment. People who could not be shaken in spite of so many turmoils and disagreements proved that they would remain faithful to the end. In praising them, Paul is also challenging those who had been corrupted by the errors of the false apostles, for in proclaiming the faith of the former, he is calling the latter to repentance. Commentary on Paul's Epistles.[17]

Hidden Reproof. Chrysostom: This is not praise but backhanded reproof, since the Corinthians were far from "guiltless," as the rest of the epistle makes clear. Homilies on the Epistles of Paul to the Corinthians 2.7.[18]

If Now Guilty, Then Guiltless. Theodoret of Cyr: By saying that he hopes that they will be guiltless in the day of Christ Jesus, Paul is indicating that right now they are guilty. Commentary on the First Epistle to the Corinthians 167.[19]

1:9a God Is Faithful

The God Who Is Faithful. Clement of Alexandria: That God is faithful means that we can trust his self-revelation. His Word reveals him. He is the God who is faithful. Stromata 2.27.3.[20]

The Problem Is Not with God. Chrysostom: Paul says this so that the Corinthians will not fall into despair when he criticizes them. He reminds them that God is not the problem. We are, because of our sin and unbelief. Homilies on the Epistles of Paul to the Corinthians 2.7.[21]

1:9b Called into Fellowship by God

Called to Be One with Christ. Origen: Believe in Christ always, because you were called for no other purpose than to be one with us in him. Commentary on 1 Corinthians 1.3.[22]

Be Faithful to Your Adoption. Ambrosiaster: Fellowship is brotherhood. Just as Paul declares God's unfailing faithfulness toward us in this regard, so we ourselves must not be found to be faithless or dishonorable with respect to our adoption. Rather we must remain faithful in it. Commentary on Paul's Epistles.[23]

---

[15]Migne PL 30:718C. [16]JTS 9:234. [17]CSEL 81.8. [18]NPNF 1 12:7. [19]Migne PG 82:231. [20]FC 85:176. [21]NPNF 1 12:7. [22]JTS 9:234. [23]CSEL 81.8.

1:10-16 THE SCANDAL OF DIVISION

[10]*I appeal to you, brethren, by the name of our Lord Jesus Christ, that all of you agree and that there be no dissensions among you, but that you be united in the same mind and*

the same judgment. [11]*For it has been reported to me by Chloe's people that there is quarreling among you, my brethren.* [12]*What I mean is that each one of you says, "I belong to Paul," or "I belong to Apollos," or "I belong to Cephas," or "I belong to Christ."* [13]*Is Christ divided? Was Paul crucified for you? Or were you baptized in the name of Paul?* [14]*I am thankful* [b] *that I baptized none of you except Crispus and Gaius;* [15]*lest any one should say that you were baptized in my name.* [16]*(I did baptize also the household of Stephanas. Beyond that, I do not know whether I baptized any one else.)*

b *Other ancient authorities read* I thank God

OVERVIEW: The Corinthian church was divided into factions (ORIGEN). Paul wanted them to be united in the teaching he had given them (AMBROSIASTER). Some were making Christ the head of a faction (CHRYSOSTOM), and thereby in their disunity rejecting Christ himself (THEODORET OF CYR). Baptism, the sacrament of unity, had become the point of division. The efficacy of baptism lies in the one whose name is invoked in the baptism (CHRYSOSTOM). In addition to addressing these great issues of truth and unity, the Fathers speculated about details, such as whether Chloe was a family (THEODORET OF CYR), a person or a place, or had some symbolic reference (AMBROSIASTER).

1:10a *An Appeal for Unity*

LET THERE BE NO DISSENSIONS. ORIGEN: The visible church is a mixed body, consisting of both righteous and unrighteous people. This is why Paul praises some of its members and criticizes others. The person who agrees with the right doctrine and the church's teaching concerning the Father, Son and Holy Spirit, as well as with the dispensation concerning us, with resurrection and judgment, and who follows the rules of the church is not in schism. COMMENTARY ON 1 CORINTHIANS 1.4.[1]

APPEAL IN CHRIST'S NAME. THEODORET OF CYR: Paul was right to add the name of Christ here, because that is what the Corinthians were re-ally rejecting. COMMENTARY ON THE FIRST EPISTLE TO THE CORINTHIANS 167.[2]

1:10b *United in Mind and Judgment*

UNITED IN THINKING. AMBROSIASTER: Paul prays that the Corinthians will all think one thing, namely, that those who have been born again are children of God. He wants them to be perfectly united in the teaching which he had given to them. He challenges them to think this way and to defend his teaching. COMMENTARY ON PAUL'S EPISTLES.[3]

UNITED IN JUDGMENT. CHRYSOSTOM: It is possible to agree on a form of words but still harbor dissent, which is why Paul speaks the way he does here. It is also possible to share the same opinion with someone but not the same feelings. For example, it is possible to be united in faith without being united in love. This is why Paul says that we must be united both in mind and in judgment. HOMILIES ON THE EPISTLES OF PAUL TO THE CORINTHIANS 3.2.[4]

1:11 *A Report from Chloe*

WHETHER CHLOE IS A PLACE. AMBROSIASTER: Some people think that "Chloe's people" are those who remain faithful and bear fruit in

---

[1]JTS 9:234. [2]Migne PG 82:231. [3]CSEL 81.9. [4]NPNF 1 12:11.

the faith of Christ. Others think that Chloe is a place, as if one were to say "Antioch's people," for example. But others think that she was a woman devoted to God, in whose company there were many faithful worshipers. Commentary on Paul's Epistles.[5]

Paul's Source Not Personally Identified. Chrysostom: Paul is careful to mention who his informers are without singling out one particular person. This gives his criticisms plausibility without allowing the Corinthians to direct their feelings toward any one person. Homilies on the Epistles of Paul to the Corinthians 3.3.[6]

Whether Chloe Is a Family. Theodoret of Cyr: Perhaps there was a family at Corinth called Chloe, but Paul does not give any details so as not to reveal their identity and start more quarreling. Commentary on the First Epistle to the Corinthians 168.[7]

1:12 Factions Within the Church

Corinth Had a History of Partisanship. Clement of Rome: Inspired by God, Paul wrote to you concerning himself and Cephas and Apollos, because even then you were given to faction. But that factiousness involved you in less guilt, because then you were partisans of highly reputed apostles and of those commended by them. Epistle to the Corinthians 47.3-4.[8]

All Good Teachers. Ambrosiaster: Paul exposes their error without mentioning the names of the people responsible. The men whom he names here were all good teachers, but by alluding to them in this way he is really getting at the false apostles. For if the Corinthians were not to boast of their devotion to any of these men, how much more would this be true in the case of false teachers, whose corrupt doctrine he refers to next? Commentary on Paul's Epistles.[9]

Is Christ the Head of a Faction? Chrysostom: The quarreling at Corinth was not over trivial matters but over something fundamental. Even those who said they were of Christ were at fault, because they were implicitly denying this to others and making Christ the head of a faction rather than the head of the whole church. Homilies on the Epistles of Paul to the Corinthians 3.5.[10]

A Ridiculous Conflict. Theodoret of Cyr: In reality the Corinthians called themselves after other teachers, but Paul uses his own name and that of Apollos and Peter in order to make his point. By adding the name of Christ to the rest, he showed them how ridiculous the whole conflict was. Commentary on the First Epistle to the Corinthians 168.[11]

1:13 Is Christ Divided?

How Christ Becomes Divided. Ambrosiaster: By believing different things about Christ, the people have divided him. One person thought that Christ was a mere man, another that he was only God. One says that he was foretold by the prophets, while another denies it.

Paul starts with himself, so that nobody will think that he is disparaging the status of others. If Christ died for us, how can we attribute his grace and blessing to men, thereby doing him a grave injustice? Commentary on Paul's Epistles.[12]

The Question Rhetorical. Chrysostom: Whenever Paul uses rhetorical questions, as he does here, he implies that the whole argument is absurd. Homilies on the Epistles of Paul to the Corinthians 3.5.[13]

---

[5]CSEL 81.9. [6]NPNF 1 12:11. [7]Migne PG 82:231. [8]FC 1:46. Clement of Rome was writing in the A.D. 90s to the church at Corinth, recalling the tendency to partisanship "even then," in the times of Paul. [9]CSEL 81.10. [10]NPNF 1 12:11-12. [11]Migne PG 82:234. [12]CSEL 81.10-11. [13]NPNF 1 12:12.

1:14 *Paul Baptized Only Crispus and Gaius*

Claiming Baptism in the Wrong Names. Ambrosiaster: These Corinthians were like the Novatianists and the Donatists of today, who claim baptism for themselves and do not recognize anybody else's. Those who are so baptized glory in the names of Novatian and Donatus, having been deprived of the name of Christ. Crispus and Gaius are called as witnesses, because although they were baptized by Paul, they never suggested that he should be given any glory because of it. Commentary on Paul's Epistles.[14]

The Name Evoked in Baptism. Chrysostom: The greatness of baptism does not lie in the baptizer but in the one whose name is invoked in the baptism. Furthermore, although baptism is important and even necessary in order to obtain the kingdom, still it is much less than preaching the gospel. A person of no singular excellence can baptize, but only the truly gifted can preach the gospel. Homilies on the Epistles of Paul to the Corinthians 3.6.[15]

1:15-16 *Baptized in Paul's Name?*

Paul Not Seeking Glory. Chrysostom: Paul downplays his own role in order to show that he was not seeking honor or glory for himself. Homilies on the Epistles of Paul to the Corinthians 3.6.[16]

---

[14]CSEL 81.11-12. [15]NPNF 1 12:12. [16]NPNF 1 12:13.

1:17-19 PREACHING THE GOSPEL

[17]*For Christ did not send me to baptize but to preach the gospel, and not with eloquent wisdom, lest the cross of Christ be emptied of its power.*
[18]*For the word of the cross is folly to those who are perishing, but to us who are being saved it is the power of God.* [19]*For it is written,*
"I will destroy the wisdom of the wise,
and the cleverness of the clever I will thwart."

Overview: Not everyone who baptizes is competent to preach the gospel (Ambrosiaster). Preaching is a gift given to few, and it must not be confused with eloquence, which is superficial (Theodoret of Cyr). The truth of the message does not depend on the cleverness of the messenger; otherwise fishers would not be chosen to preach (Ambrosiaster). The power of the cross is not recognized by those who are perishing (Chrysostom).

1:17 *Sent to Preach the Gospel*

Why Fishers Were Chosen to Preach. Ambrosiaster: Because it is a greater thing to preach the gospel than to baptize, Paul says that he was sent to do the former, not the latter. Not everyone who baptizes is competent to preach the gospel, for the words used at baptism are an established formula. When Cornelius became a believer, the apostle Peter gave orders that he should be baptized along with his household, but he did not bother to do it himself when he had his assistants standing by.[1] It was because Christian preaching does not need elaborate refinement of verbal expression that fishers, who were uneducated, were chosen to preach the gospel.[2] In that way the truth of the message would be its own recommendation, and it would not depend on the cleverness or ingenuity of human wisdom. The false apostles were doing just that, and moreover they were omitting the things which the world does not believe, like the virgin birth of Christ and his resurrection from the dead. COMMENTARY ON PAUL'S EPISTLES.[3]

PAUL'S APOSTOLIC OFFICE TOOK PRECEDENCE. PELAGIUS: Paul did not usurp the functions of the lower offices when he was able to exercise the higher ones. It would be as if nowadays a bishop or even a priest were to do the work of a deacon. COMMENTARY ON THE FIRST EPISTLE TO THE CORINTHIANS 1.[4]

1:17b Not with Eloquent Wisdom

THE CROSS STANDS CONTRARY TO HUMAN WISDOM. CHRYSOSTOM: If human wisdom is at war with the cross and fights against the gospel, it is not right to boast about it. Rather, we should recoil in shame. HOMILIES ON THE EPISTLES OF PAUL TO THE CORINTHIANS 3.7.[5]

PREACHING IS A GIFT. THEODORET OF CYR: Anyone can baptize if he is a priest, but preaching is a gift given to few, and it must not be confused with mere eloquence, which is purely superficial. COMMENTARY ON THE FIRST EPISTLE TO THE CORINTHIANS 169.[6]

1:18 Folly to Those Who Are Perishing

A DIVINE DEFENSE AGAINST THE DEVIL. ORIGEN: Who was capable of destroying the plague of ignorance, darkness and destruction? Not a prophet, nor an apostle, nor any other righteous man. Rather there had to be a divine power coming down from heaven, capable of dying on behalf of us all, so that by his death there might be a defense against the devil. COMMENTARY ON 1 CORINTHIANS 1.6.8-12.[7]

THE MADNESS OF REJECTING GOOD MEDICINE. CHRYSOSTOM: The power of the cross is not recognized by those who are perishing, because they are out of their minds and act like madmen, complaining and rejecting the medicines which bring salvation. HOMILIES ON THE EPISTLES OF PAUL TO THE CORINTHIANS 4.1.[8]

1:19 Destroying the Wisdom of the Wise

THWARTING THE CLEVERNESS OF THE CLEVER.[9] AMBROSIASTER: By doing this, God shows that actions speak louder than words. COMMENTARY ON PAUL'S EPISTLES.[10]

FOOD FOR DECEPTION. THEODORET OF CYR: Paul speaks about the wisdom of this world and not merely the eloquence, for God has given it also. It was God who divided the languages and gave each one its own character. It was he who gave the Greek language its splendor. But those who abuse these gifts have prepared food for deception and have preached false tales. What Paul objects to is not their eloquence as such but the false teaching which lies behind it. COMMENTARY ON THE FIRST EPISTLE TO THE CORINTHIANS 170-71.[11]

---

[1]Acts 10:46-48. [2]See Mt 4:18-19. [3]CSEL 81.12-13. [4]Migne PL 30:719D. [5]NPNF 1 12:13. [6]Migne PG 82:234. [7]JTS 9:235. [8]NPNF 1 12:16. [9]Is 29:14. [10]CSEL 81.14. [11]Migne PG 82:235.

1:20-25 TRUE WISDOM

²⁰*Where is the wise man? Where is the scribe? Where is the debater of this age? Has not God made foolish the wisdom of the world?* ²¹*For since, in the wisdom of God, the world did not know God through wisdom, it pleased God through the folly of what we preach to save those who believe.* ²²*For Jews demand signs and Greeks seek wisdom,* ²³*but we preach Christ crucified, a stumbling block to Jews and folly to Gentiles,* ²⁴*but to those who are called, both Jews and Greeks, Christ the power of God and the wisdom of God.* ²⁵*For the foolishness of God is wiser than men, and the weakness of God is stronger than men.*

OVERVIEW: Since God's way of reasoning is in accord with things of the spirit, it confounds the reasoning of this world (AMBROSIASTER). The cross is a stumbling block to those who are unbelievers, but to believers it is salvation and eternal life (IGNATIUS OF ANTIOCH). Both Greek wisdom and Jewish law are humbled before it (AMBROSIASTER, SEVERIAN OF GABALA, PELAGIUS). Both the wise and the prudent are foolish insofar as they reject the wisdom of God (HILARY OF POITIERS). The simplicity of God's wisdom makes those who have it appear foolish in the eyes of the world (ORIGEN). The philosophers could not achieve what a few unlearned men accomplished, namely, the conversion of the whole world (CHRYSOSTOM, AUGUSTINE). True philosophy is conveyed through the Son (CLEMENT OF ALEXANDRIA). The apostles won their case, not without a sign but by something that appeared to go against all the known signs—the cross (CHRYSOSTOM). God's power is intricately interwoven with God's wisdom (GREGORY OF NYSSA).

1:20a The Wise Man, the Scribe and the Debater

THE CROSS A STUMBLING BLOCK. IGNATIUS OF ANTIOCH: My spirit has become an offscouring of the cross, which is a stumbling block to those who are unbelievers, but to us it is salvation and life eternal. Where is the wise man? Where is the debater? Where is the boasting of those who are called prudent? EPISTLE TO THE EPHESIANS 18.[1]

THE HUMBLING OF GREEK WISDOM AND JEWISH LAW. AMBROSIASTER: Here Paul attacks the Jews as much as the Gentiles, because their scribes and doctors of the law think that it is foolish to believe that God has a Son. Gentiles also laugh at this, but the Jews' unbelief is based on the fact that the matter is not openly stated in the law, whereas the Gentiles think it is silly because the reasoning of the world does not accept it, claiming that nothing can be made without sexual union. The debater of this age is a man who thinks that the world is governed by the conjunction of the stars and that births and deaths are brought about by the twelve signs of the zodiac. Is there anything more foolish than the belief that the Creator does not care about the world he has made? What would be the point of making it in that case? It is because they see some people enjoying life and others not, because they see the righteous suffering while the wicked boast, that they have come to believe that God does not care. But to say this is to say that God is malevolent and unjust.

---

[1] AF 67.

COMMENTARY ON PAUL'S EPISTLES.[2]

THE WISE AND THE PRUDENT. HILARY OF POITIERS: In this matter the wise and the prudent are silent, for they have rejected the wisdom of God. THE TRINITY 2.12.[3]

SEVERIAN OF GABALA: The wise man is the Greek, the scribe is the Jew. PAULINE COMMENTARY FROM THE GREEK CHURCH.[4]

1:20b Making the World's Wisdom Foolish

THE TRUE WISDOM. ORIGEN: The wisdom of this world and the wisdom of God are not the same thing. God's wisdom is the true one, without any additives to corrupt it. The world's wisdom is foolish, even though the simplicity of God's wisdom makes those who have it appear foolish in the eyes of the world. Believers have received this divine wisdom and thus in this world appear to be fools. COMMENTARY ON 1 CORINTHIANS 1.7.1-7.[5]

1:21a The World Did Not Know God Through Wisdom

GOD'S WISDOM CONVEYED THROUGH HIS SON. CLEMENT OF ALEXANDRIA: Paul says that the wisdom of God is teaching in conformity with the Lord, which will show that true philosophy is conveyed through the Son. STROMATA 1.90.1.[6]

GOD'S WISDOM HAS BECOME INCARNATE. ATHANASIUS: Given that men had rejected the contemplation of God and were looking for him in nature and in the material world, making gods for themselves out of mortal men and demons, the loving and general Savior of all, the Word of God, took to himself a body and walked about like a man, in order to meet the senses halfway, so that those who think that God is corporeal might perceive the truth by observing what the Lord accomplishes in his body, and through him recognize the Father.

ON THE INCARNATION 15.[7]

1:21b Saving Those Who Believe

PREACHING THAT SEEMS FOOLISH. AMBROSIASTER: The world has not recognized God but has attributed divine majesty to his creatures and to the elemental powers of the universe, thinking that visible things ought to be worshiped.[8] God has therefore chosen a form of preaching which will seem foolish to such people. Those who reject what the apostles preach will be condemned, while believers are being saved. COMMENTARY ON PAUL'S EPISTLES.[9]

HUMAN WISDOM DOES NOT CONVERT. CHRYSOSTOM: To believe in the one who was crucified and buried and to be fully convinced that he rose again does not need more reasoning but faith alone. The apostles themselves were converted not by wisdom but by faith. Once they had that, they surpassed the heathen wise men in both wisdom and intellectual depth. . . . Plato was cast out not by another philosopher of more skill but by unlearned fishers. HOMILIES ON THE EPISTLES OF PAUL TO THE CORINTHIANS 4.4.[10]

THE FOLLY OF THE CROSS DISTINGUISHED FROM TWO OTHER KINDS OF WISDOM. THEODORET OF CYR: Paul enumerates two or even three different kinds of wisdom here. First there is what the world calls folly, wisdom greater than the others. Then there is the wisdom given to human beings by which we reason and act, by which we develop and invent things and by which we can know God. Finally, there is a third kind of wisdom, which is found in the contemplation of the creation. The wisdom which is folly to the world is given to us by the Savior, so that people who know God by natural wis-

---

[2]CSEL 81.14-15. [3]FC 25:46. [4]NTA 15:228. [5]JTS 9:236. [6]FC 85:91. [7]LCC 3:69. [8]See Rom 1:22. [9]CSEL 81.16. [10]NPNF 1 12:17, 18.

dom and who are led to him by contemplating the created order may attain the salvation which neither of these kinds of wisdom can provide and be delivered from error. COMMENTARY ON THE FIRST EPISTLE TO THE CORINTHIANS 171.[11]

1:22 Demanding Signs, Seeking Wisdom

JEWS DEMAND SIGNS, GREEKS SEEK ARGUMENTS. AMBROSIASTER: The Jews seek signs because they do not reject the possibility that things like this can happen. What they want to know is whether it has actually occurred, like Aaron's rod, which sprouted and bore fruit,[12] and Jonah who spent three days and nights in the belly of the whale before being spewed out alive.[13] But the Greeks seek wisdom, refusing to believe anything which does not accord with human reason. COMMENTARY ON PAUL'S EPISTLES.[14]

BOTH EVIDENCE DISBELIEF. PELAGIUS: The Jews want signs, because that is what the prophets gave them, but even then they do not believe. The Greeks, on the other hand, want clever academic arguments. COMMENTARY ON THE FIRST EPISTLE TO THE CORINTHIANS 1.[15]

1:23 Preaching Christ Crucified

EMPOWERMENT THROUGH THE CRUCIFIED. ORIGEN: What has empowered us is belief in Christ crucified. To the extent that we are lacking something in our faith, then we are missing out on what the power of God has to offer us. COMMENTARY ON 1 CORINTHIANS 1.8.1-4.[16]

A STUMBLING BLOCK AND FOLLY. AMBROSIASTER: It is a stumbling block to the Jews when they hear Christ calling himself the Son of God yet not observing the sabbath. It is foolishness to the Gentiles because they hear things like the virgin birth and the resurrection being preached but regard them as irrational. COMMENTARY ON PAUL'S EPISTLES.[17]

1:24a Jews and Greeks Are Called

THE WISDOM OF THE FATHER KNOWN THROUGH THE SON. AMBROSIASTER: When Jews believe in Christ, they understand that he is the power of God. When Greeks believe in him, they understand that he is the wisdom of God. He is God's power because the Father does everything through him. He is God's wisdom because God is known through him. It would not be possible for God to be known through anyone who was not from him in the first place. No one has seen the Father except the Son and whomever the Son has chosen to reveal him to. COMMENTARY ON PAUL'S EPISTLES.[18]

THE OFFENSE AND THE CALL. CHRYSOSTOM: The gospel produces the exact opposite of what people want and expect, but it is that very fact which persuades them to accept it in the end. The apostles won their case, not simply without a sign, but by something which appeared to go against all the known signs. The cross seems to be a cause of offense, but far from simply offending, it attracts and calls believers to itself. HOMILIES ON THE EPISTLES OF PAUL TO THE CORINTHIANS 4.5.[19]

1:24b Christ the Power and Wisdom of God

GOD'S POWER IS SUFFICIENT. CLEMENT OF ALEXANDRIA: The Savior's teaching is sufficient without additional help, for it is the power and wisdom of God. STROMATA 1.100.1.[20]

GOD'S WISDOM IS INTERWOVEN WITH GOD'S POWER. GREGORY OF NYSSA: Through this description of Christ we derive notions of the divine which make the name an object of reverence for us. Since all creation, both perceptible

---

[11]Migne PG 82:235. [12]See Num 17:8. [13]Jon 1:17—2:10. [14]CSEL 81.16. [15]Migne PL 30:720D. [16]JTS 9:236. [17]CSEL 81.16-17. [18]CSEL 81.17. [19]NPNF 1 12:18. [20]FC 85:98.

and imperceptible, came into being through him and is united with him, wisdom is necessarily interwoven with power in connection with the very definition of Christ, the maker of all things. On Perfection.[21]

The Cross as Pattern. Pelagius: Note that Paul does not say that the divinity of Christ is God's power and wisdom, but rather the pattern of the cross. Commentary on the First Epistle to the Corinthians 1.[22]

Preaching the Cross. Theodore of Mopsuestia: The power and wisdom of God is not the divinity of Christ as such but the preaching of the cross. Pauline Commentary from the Greek Church.[23]

1:25 The Seeming Foolishness of God

God's Wisdom Confounds Human Reasoning. Ambrosiaster: When Paul speaks of the "foolishness of God," he is not implying that God is foolish. Rather he is saying that since God's way of reasoning is in accord with things of the spirit, it confounds the reasoning of this world. It is wiser than human reasoning, because spiritual things are wiser than carnal ones. Spiritual things do not exist through carnal ones, but the other way around. Therefore carnal things are understandable in relation to spiritual ones.

Similarly, what belongs to heaven is stronger than what belongs to earth. So what seems like the weakness of God is not really weak at all. Christ appeared to be defeated when he was killed, but he emerged as the victor and turned the reproof back on his persecutors. Commentary on Paul's Epistles.[24]

Christ's World Mission Carried Out by the Unlearned to Evidence God's Power. Chrysostom: The folly and the wisdom spoken of here are more apparent than real. For the philosophers could not achieve what a few unlearned men accomplished, namely, the conversion of the whole world. The philosophers spoke about trivialities and convinced only a few. The apostles spoke about God, righteousness and judgment and converted a great many. Homilies on the Epistles of Paul to the Corinthians 4.6.[25]

The Gospel Truth. Augustine: There is no way that this gospel truth could have been made acceptable to some philosophers and debaters. They follow a way of life that does not stand in the truth but is only an imitation of it. They deceived themselves and others. Letter to Consentius 120.[26]

---

[21]FC 58:101. [22]Migne PL 30:721A. [23]NTA 15:174. [24]CSEL 81.17. [25]NPNF 1 12:19. [26]FC 18:304.

1:26-31 THE UPSIDE-DOWN CHURCH

[26]*For consider your call, brethren; not many of you were wise according to worldly standards, not many were powerful, not many were of noble birth;* [27]*but God chose what is foolish in the world to shame the wise, God chose what is weak in the world to shame the strong,* [28]*God chose what is low and despised in the world, even things that are not, to bring to nothing things that are,* [29]*so that no human being might boast in the presence of God.* [30]*He is the source of*

your life in Christ Jesus, whom God made our wisdom, our righteousness and sanctification and redemption; [31]*therefore, as it is written, "Let him who boasts, boast of the Lord."*

Overview: A little learning is a dangerous thing, for it makes people unwilling to learn more (Chrysostom). The world does not understand that the Savior's sufferings have become the source of power, for through these sufferings Christ vanquished death (Ambrosiaster). Christ gave himself as an atonement on our behalf, ransoming us from death with his own life (Gregory of Nyssa). No one should glory in human works (Augustine, Theodore of Mopsuestia). If only the most eloquent people had been chosen as preachers, they would have gloried in their own abilities and been damned for it (Theodoret of Cyr).

1:26 Considering Their Call

Worldly Standards. Chrysostom: The man who is wise according to the standards of this world is really very foolish, because he will not cast away his corrupt teaching. A little learning is a dangerous thing, because it makes those who have it unwilling to learn more. The unlearned are more open to conviction, because they are not so foolish as to think that they are wise. Homilies on the Epistles of Paul to the Corinthians 5.2.[1]

Not Many Were Powerful. Theodoret of Cyr: Paul did not say that there was nobody like this in the church, only that there were not many. Commentary on the First Epistle to the Corinthians 173.[2]

1:27 Shaming the Wise by What Is Foolish

Weak Things a Source of Power. Ambrosiaster: The two most "foolish things of the world" are in particular the virgin birth of Christ and his resurrection from the dead. The wise are confounded because they see that what a few of them deny, the many profess to be true.

There is no doubt that the opinions of the many faithful take precedence over those of a small number. Likewise, those who are mighty in this world can easily see the so-called weak things of Christ overturning demons and performing miracles. To the world the injuries and sufferings of the Savior are weak things, because the world does not understand that they have become the source of power through Christ who submitted to suffering in order to overcome death. Commentary on Paul's Epistles.[3]

Getting the Better of the Philosophers. Chrysostom: In human terms, it was not possible for fishers to get the better of philosophers, but that is what happened by the power of God's grace. Homilies on the Epistles of Paul to the Corinthians 5.5.[4]

1:28 Bringing to Nothing Things That Are

God Chose What Is Low. Ambrosiaster: God chose ignoble and contemptible things to exalt. It is not that they are really ignoble and contemptible; this is how the world sees them. By believing in Christ they have overturned worldly reasoning. God did this in order to destroy things which are really ignoble and contemptible, because those who judged were more deserving of judgment and condemnation. Their teaching was asserted in words but not demonstrated in power, and so it was destroyed. Our teaching is proved true not only by words but by power as well. Commentary on Paul's Epistles.[5]

Things That Are Not. Theodore of Mopsuestia: Paul uses the expression "things that are

---

[1]NPNF 1 12:23. [2]Migne PG 82:238. [3]CSEL 81.18-19.
[4]NPNF 1 12:25. [5]CSEL 81.19.

not" differently here from the way he uses it in his epistle to the Romans. Here it means simply that which is vile and contemptible, as opposed to "things that are," which are beautiful, powerful and respected. Pauline Commentary from the Greek Church.[6]

1:29 No Human Boasting in God's Presence

Under the Judgment of God. Ambrosiaster: Under the judgment of God the wisdom of the flesh can only blush at its miscalculations. Commentary on Paul's Epistles.[7]

Humbling Those in High Places. Chrysostom: God did not just choose the unlearned, but also the needy, the contemptible and the obscure, in order to humble those in high places. Homilies on the Epistles of Paul to the Corinthians 5.3.[8]

The Harm of Boasting. Theodore of Mopsuestia: Boasting, even if it is of good works, harms the soul of the boaster. Anyone who boasts of worldly achievements is highly worldly himself. Pauline Commentary from the Greek Church.[9]

Attacking Pride. Augustine: Paul's intention is perfectly clear—to accost the pride of man, that no one should take glory in human works and that no one should glory in himself. Predestination of the Saints 5.9.[10]

The Temptation of the Eloquent. Theodoret of Cyr: If Paul had chosen only the most eloquent and gifted people as preachers they would have gloried in their own abilities and been damned for it, whether they preached the truth or not. Commentary on the First Epistle to the Corinthians 173.[11]

1:30 The Source of Life in Christ Jesus

God Made Christ Our Sanctification. Ambrose: Christ was made our sanctification, not

so that he might change what he was but that he might sanctify us in the flesh. The Holy Spirit 3.4.26.[12]

Our Redemption. Ambrosiaster: Christ did what he did in order to strengthen believers, for no one can redeem something which did not originally belong to him. Therefore, whether it is because we have been redeemed, or because we have been sanctified (i.e., purged from the works of the flesh and the filthiness of idols), or because we have been justified (for it is just to worship only the Creator and spurn everything else) or because we are wise, having learned that worldly people are unwise—all this is a gift of God through Christ. But this is our redemption—when the devil desires it, Christ offers himself to the devil so that he may cancel sin and rescue the devil's captives. Commentary on Paul's Epistles.[13]

Our Ransom. Gregory of Nyssa: We are taught by the knowledge that Christ is redemption, because he gave himself as an atonement on our behalf, that when he bestowed immortality on us as our own possession, he ransomed us from death with his own life. On Perfection.[14]

Our Salvation. Chrysostom: God did not just make us wise, righteous and holy in Christ. He gave us Christ so that we should never need anything else for our salvation. Homilies on the Epistles of Paul to the Corinthians 5.4.[15]

1:31 Boasting of the Lord

Boast of the Lord. Ambrosiaster: What Jeremiah [as quoted here] says is commendable, because the person who glories in the Lord will not be confounded. Commentary on Paul's Epistles.[16]

---

[6]NTA 15:174. [7]CSEL 81.19-20. [8]NPNF 1 12:24. [9]NTA 15:174. [10]FC 86:228. [11]Migne PG 82:239. [12]FC 44:163. [13]CSEL 81.20. [14]FC 58:103. [15]NPNF 1 12:24. [16]CSEL 81.20-21.

2:1-5 PAUL'S PREACHING POWER

[1]When I came to you, brethren, I did not come proclaiming to you the testimony[c] of God in lofty words or wisdom. [2]For I decided to know nothing among you except Jesus Christ and him crucified. [3]And I was with you in weakness and in much fear and trembling; [4]and my speech and my message were not in plausible words of wisdom, but in demonstration of the Spirit and of power, [5]that your faith might not rest in the wisdom of men but in the power of God.

c Other ancient authorities read mystery (or secret)

OVERVIEW: Paul was not without natural fear when he was beaten and persecuted (CHRYSOSTOM) as a direct result of his preaching (AMBROSIASTER). When demonstration is made by the wisdom of human words, the worse argument often overcomes the better one, so as to encourage the arguer to boast of his own achievement (CHRYSOSTOM). The false teachers were embarrassed by the Word incarnate (AMBROSIASTER) and dull to sublime teachings (AUGUSTINE) of the one through whom God accomplished our salvation on the cross and in the resurrection (MARIUS VICTORINUS). Faith is elicited not by philosophical rhetoric but by the power of God demonstrated (ORIGEN).

2:1 No Lofty Words or Wisdom

FALSE TEACHERS EMBARRASSED BY THE WORD INCARNATE. AMBROSIASTER: What Paul calls the testimony here is God the Word incarnate, hidden from all ages with God. Heretics played fast and loose with these things. They preached their wicked doctrine with great eloquence, following the wisdom of the world. They emptied Christ's cross of its power. They were embarrassed to be ridiculed by the world. COMMENTARY ON PAUL'S EPISTLES.[1]

2:2 Knowing Only Christ Crucified

JESUS CHRIST FREED US. MARIUS VICTORINUS: It was the incarnate Word who accomplished the mystery of our salvation. It was he who freed us and redeemed us. We believe in him who is our Savior through the cross and through his resurrection from the dead. AGAINST ARIUS IA.[2]

DULL TO SUBLIME TEACHINGS. AUGUSTINE: Paul said this because he was speaking to those who were unable to grasp the more sublime teachings of the divinity of Christ. TRINITY 1.12.[3]

2:3 In Weakness, Fear and Trembling

PROVOKING PERSECUTION. AMBROSIASTER: By preaching Christ in what appeared to be folly to human wisdom, Paul provoked hatred and persecution against himself. COMMENTARY ON PAUL'S EPISTLES.[4]

IN MUCH FEAR. CHRYSOSTOM: Was Paul really afraid of danger? Yes, he was, for even though he was Paul, he was still a man. This is not to say anything against him but rather about the infirmity of human nature. Indeed it is to the credit of his sense of determination that even when he was afraid of death and beatings, he did nothing wrong because of this fear. Therefore those who claim that Paul was not afraid of being beaten not only do not honor him, they

---

[1]CSEL 81.21-22. [2]FC 69:165. [3]FC 45:35. [4]CSEL 81.22.

diminish his greatness. For if he was without fear, what endurance or self-control was there in bearing dangers? Homilies on the Epistles of Paul to the Corinthians 6.2.[5]

2:4 Not Words of Wisdom

Not in Plausible Words of Wisdom. Origen: If our Scriptures had persuaded people to believe because they had been written with rhetorical art or philosophical skill, there is no doubt that our faith would be said to depend on the art of words and on human wisdom rather than on the power of God. On First Principles 4.1.7.[6]

Demonstration of Power. Chrysostom: It does not belittle the gospel to say that it was preached without wisdom. On the contrary, this is the gospel's great glory, the clearest sign that it is divine and that it comes from heaven. When demonstration is made by the wisdom of human words, the worse argument often overcomes the better one, because the one who argues for it has greater rhetorical skills. But in this case it is not so, because the Spirit does not enter an unclean soul, nor can he ever be overcome, however much clever speech is used to attack him. The demonstration by works and signs is more powerful than mere words. Homilies on the Epistles of Paul to the Corinthians 6.3.[7]

2:5 Faith Rests in the Power of God

God's Power Is Eternal. Pelagius: Human wisdom is temporal. The power of God is eternal. Commentary on the First Epistle to the Corinthians 2.[8]

Wisdom's Boast. Chrysostom: Human wisdom denied the cross, but faith proclaimed the power of God. Wisdom not only failed to reveal the things which people sought after, but also it encouraged them to boast of their own achievements. But faith not only gave them the truth, it also encouraged them to glorify God. Homilies on the Epistles of Paul to the Corinthians 6.3.[9]

---

[5]NPNF 1 12:30. [6]CWS 177. [7]NPNF 1 12:30. [8]Migne PL 30:722C. [9]NPNF 1 12:30.

2:6-12 GOD'S SECRET WISDOM

[6]*Yet among the mature we do impart wisdom, although it is not a wisdom of this age or of the rulers of this age, who are doomed to pass away.* [7]*But we impart a secret and hidden wisdom of God, which God decreed before the ages for our glorification.* [8]*None of the rulers of this age understood this; for if they had, they would not have crucified the Lord of glory.* [9]*But, as it is written,*

"What no eye has seen, nor ear heard,

nor the heart of man conceived,

what God has prepared for those who love him,"

[10]*God has revealed to us through the Spirit. For the Spirit searches everything, even the*

depths of God. ¹¹For what person knows a man's thoughts except the spirit of the man which is in him? So also no one comprehends the thoughts of God except the Spirit of God. ¹²Now we have received not the spirit of the world, but the Spirit which is from God, that we might understand the gifts bestowed on us by God.

OVERVIEW: Even those who crucified the Lord (OECUMENIUS) were not beyond the range of forgiveness (CHRYSOSTOM), unless they refuse to repent and persist in their unbelief (THEODORET OF CYR). The depths of God (CLEMENT OF ALEXANDRIA) cannot be understood without the Spirit of God (AMBROSIASTER, THEODORET OF CYR), who is one with the Father and the Son (SEVERIAN OF GABALA). Human searching alone (AMBROSIASTER, OECUMENIUS) cannot penetrate these depths (ORIGEN, CHRYSOSTOM). Faith is not grasped by the deceptive spirit of the world (AMBROSIASTER). Worldly wisdom is of this age (ORIGEN), but the gospel sets forth wisdom of the age to come, when the truth of God will be manifested to those who now deny it (AMBROSIASTER, THEODORE OF MOPSUESTIA). God's wisdom is so great that it makes human wisdom appear foolish (CHRYSOSTOM). The gospel is not merely a riddle (THEODORET OF CYR). It is hidden not in words but in power (AMBROSIASTER). It has been stored up for us before we were born (CHRYSOSTOM). Both those who deny that Christ was fully human (APOLLINARIANS) and those who claim that God suffers in his essential nature as Word (ARIANS) misunderstand the phrase "they crucified the Lord of glory" (PELAGIUS). Although the Fathers debated the source of Paul's quotation in 2:9 (AMBROSIASTER, CHRYSOSTOM), they agreed on the central importance of Christ's death (AUGUSTINE). Wherever the quotation came from, it shows how bright a spiritual body can be (ORIGEN) and how God foresees and foreknows our human choices (SEVERIAN). The rulers are every spiritual or demonic power that deliberately sets itself up against God (AMBROSIASTER).

2:6 Imparting Wisdom to the Mature

WORLDLY WISDOM. ORIGEN: When Paul talks about the wisdom of the rulers of this world he seems to be talking not about one wisdom common to them all but about different kinds of wisdom which are peculiar to each. ON FIRST PRINCIPLES 3.3.1.[1]

THE MATURE. AMBROSIASTER: The mature are those who preach the cross as wisdom because of the witness of Christ's power at work. They know that actions speak louder than words. Their wisdom is not of this age but of the age to come, when the truth of God will be manifested to those who now deny it. COMMENTARY ON PAUL'S EPISTLES.[2]

TRUE WISDOM FOUND IN THE CROSS. CHRYSOSTOM: Paul is saying that when he, a man thought to be foolish and a preacher of folly, gets the better of the wise, he overcomes their wisdom, not by foolishness but by a more perfect wisdom. This wisdom is so broad and so great that the other kind appears to be foolishness. True wisdom is the gospel, the means of salvation through the cross of Christ. The perfect are those who believe. They are indeed "perfect," because they know that all human things are utterly helpless, and therefore they ignore them, being convinced that they have nothing to gain from them. This is what true believers are like. HOMILIES ON THE EPISTLES OF PAUL TO THE CORINTHIANS 7.1.[3]

2:7 The Hidden Wisdom of God

[1]OFP 223. [2]CSEL 81.23. [3]NPNF 1 12:34.

Impossible in Human Terms. Ambrosiaster: Paul testifies that he has been sent to reveal a secret wisdom which the princes of this world do not know and which they therefore label stupid. The wisdom of God is hidden because it is not in words but in power. It is impossible in human terms, but it can be believed by the power of the Spirit. God foresaw the future sins of the world and therefore decreed this in order to confound those who would turn his wisdom into their own stupidity, and also to glorify us, who would believe it. Commentary on Paul's Epistles.[4]

From the Beginning. Chrysostom: Paul is keen to point out that God always loved us, even from the very beginning, when we did not yet exist. For if he had not loved us, he would not have foreordained our riches. Look beyond the broken relationship which has come in between, and you will see that God's love for us is more ancient still. Homilies on the Epistles of Paul to the Corinthians 7.4.[5]

The Whole Dispensation. Theodore of Mopsuestia: By *wisdom* Paul means the cross and the whole dispensation of salvation. Pauline Commentary from the Greek Church.[6]

Not a Riddle. Theodoret of Cyr: Paul does not mean that he is now communicating in secrets and riddles but that the message he preaches was once hidden. Commentary on the First Epistle to the Corinthians 175.[7]

2:8a Rulers of This Age Do Not Understand

Every Demonic Power Against God. Ambrosiaster: The rulers of this age are not only those who were great among the Jews and the Romans but also every spiritual power which sets itself up against God. The Jewish rulers cannot be called rulers of this age, because they were subject to the Romans. Nor did the Romans

crucify Jesus, because Pilate himself said that he found no fault in him. The rulers who crucified him were the demons. They knew that Jesus was the Messiah but not that he was the Son of God, and so it can be said that they crucified him in ignorance. Commentary on Paul's Epistles.[8]

2:8b Crucifying the Lord of Glory

Condemned by Ignorance. Pelagius: Pilate, Caiaphas and the rest were condemned by their ignorance, because they should have known the truth. There are two kinds of heretics who misinterpret this passage. The first are the Apollinarians, and the second are the Arians. The Apollinarians are wrong because they do not accept that Christ's human nature was perfect. The Arians err because they claim that the Word of God can suffer. Arius did not believe that it was the Lord of glory who took on a human nature, and therefore he thought that the Word, being only human, could suffer. Commentary on the First Epistle to the Corinthians 2.[9]

Even the Crucifiers Are Not Beyond Forgiveness. Chrysostom: Could Herod and the priests who wanted to crucify Jesus have been forgiven? Yes. If they repented, they were forgiven. Even Paul, who persecuted the church, was forgiven when he repented, and so they could have been as well. The ignorance of the rulers was not concerning Christ's person but rather concerning the significance of the event which was taking place on the cross. Jesus prayed that they might be forgiven, not because they did not know him but because they did not understand what they were doing. Homilies on the Epistles of Paul to the Corinthians 7.5.[10]

---

[4]CSEL 81.24. [5]NPNF 1 12:35. [6]NTA 15:174. [7]Migne PG 82:242. [8]CSEL 81.24-25. [9]Migne PL 30:722D—723A. [10]NPNF 1 12:35-36.

What If Christ Had Not Died? Augustine: But if Christ had not been put to death, death would not have died. The devil was overcome by his own trophy, for the devil rejoiced when, by seducing the first man, he cast him into death. By seducing the first man, he killed him.[11] By killing the last man, he lost the first from his snare. The Ascension 263.[12]

Those Who Persist in Unbelief. Theodoret of Cyr: God forgave Pilate, Herod, Annas, Caiaphas and the rest for their ignorance at the time of the crucifixion, but after Christ had risen and ascended into heaven, and the Holy Spirit had come, and the apostles had performed many miracles, he handed them over for punishment, because they persisted in their unbelief. Commentary on the First Epistle to the Corinthians 176.[13]

Who Killed the Lord of Glory? Oecumenius: This applies to Herod and Pilate. It does not apply in the same way to the high priests and scribes, because they knew that Jesus was the Christ. They were more like the workers in the vineyard who said: "This is the heir. Let us kill him, and the vineyard will be ours."[14] Pauline Commentary from the Greek Church.[15]

2:9 What God Has Prepared

Good Things to Come. Isaac of Nineveh: When it says "which eye hath not seen, nor ear hath heard" and the rest, Scripture has declared to us that the good things to come are incomprehensible and have no similarity to any thing here. Ascetical Homilies 2.[16]

A Spiritual Body. Origen: From this we may gain an idea of how great the splendor, the beauty and the brightness of a spiritual body is. On First Principles 3.6.4.[17]

Paul's Source? Ambrosiaster: These words

were expressed somewhat differently by Isaiah,[18] and they are also found in the apocryphal Apocalypse of Elijah.[19] Paul uses them to refer to the incarnation of Christ, which not only goes against human perception but is beyond the understanding of heavenly powers as well. Commentary on Paul's Epistles.[20]

A Paraphrase? Chrysostom: Where are these words written? Either they are a paraphrase of some passage [such as Isaiah 52:15], or they were written in some book which has now disappeared. In fact, many books were destroyed, and very few survived the first[21] captivity intact, as we know from the documents which have survived. Not all the words of the prophets are extant, but Paul, who was learned in the law and was also speaking by the Spirit, would have known them all accurately. Homilies on the Epistles of Paul to the Corinthians 7.6.[22]

God Foresees Human Choices. Severian of Gabala: One should not think that God has indiscriminately revealed the mystery to some and allowed the rest to perish in ignorance. Rather one should know and be persuaded that by the foreknowledge of his power God prepared the right thing for each person according to his deserts, for he foresees what each one will choose even before it happens. Pauline Commentary from the Greek Church.[23]

2:10 The Spirit Searches Everything

The Deep Things of God. Clement of Alexandria: Those who possess the Spirit seek out the deep things of God, that is, the hidden secrets that surround prophecy. Stromata 2.7.3.[24]

---

[11]Gen 3:1-19. [12]FC 38:392. [13]Migne PG 82:242. [14]Mt 21:38. [15]NTA 15:432. [16]AHSIS 11. [17]OFP 250. [18]Is 64:4. [19]See K. Berger, "Zur Discussion über die Herkunft von 1 Kor 2:9," *New Testament Studies* 24 (1977-1978): 271-83. [20]CSEL 81.26. [21]Babylonian. [22]NPNF 1 12:36. [23]NTA 15:232. [24]FC 85:161.

The Limits of Human Searching. Origen: Only the Spirit can search everything. The human soul cannot do this, which is why it needs to be strengthened by the Spirit if it is ever going to penetrate the depths of God. Commentary on 1 Corinthians 1.10.6-10.[25]

Only God Can Reveal God. Ambrosiaster: God revealed these things through his Spirit to believers, because the things of God cannot be understood without the Spirit of God, who is of God and therefore knows everything about him. Commentary on Paul's Epistles.[26]

Accurate Knowledge of God Is Beyond Our Searching. Chrysostom: If the Spirit, who knows the secret things of God, had not revealed them to us, there is no way that we could ever have known them. The word *search* does not imply that the Spirit was ignorant but refers rather to accurate, detailed knowledge. It is the same usage as when Paul speaks of God, saying that he searches the human heart.[27] Homilies on the Epistles of Paul to the Corinthians 7.7.[28]

The Spirit's Understanding. Theodoret of Cyr: Whoever has received the revelation of the Spirit has also received the Spirit's understanding. Commentary on the First Epistle to the Corinthians 177.[29]

2:11 Only the Spirit Comprehends God's Thoughts

Spirit of Man—Spirit of God. Ambrosiaster: The Spirit of God has taught us what he knows by nature, not what he has been taught himself. Furthermore, he has taught us about the mys-

tery of Christ, because he is not just the Spirit of God but the Spirit of Christ as well. Commentary on Paul's Epistles.[30]

Unity of Father and Spirit. Severian of Gabala: God and the Holy Spirit are two persons, whereas a man and the spirit in him are not two persons but one man. What Paul means is that just as in the man there is a cohesion in knowing, so the knowledge of the Father and the Spirit is one. What the Spirit searches is therefore already known to him. Pauline Commentary from the Greek Church.[31]

2:12 Receiving the Spirit from God

Not Possessed by the Deceptive Spirit of the World. Ambrosiaster: The "spirit of the world" is the one by which different people are possessed. It does not know the truth but can only guess at it, and therefore it both deceives others and is itself deceived by appearances. Commentary on Paul's Epistles.[32]

Human Wisdom. Oecumenius: I think that by "spirit of the world" Paul means human wisdom and learning. Pauline Commentary from the Greek Church.[33]

Not the Spirit from God. Theodoret of Cyr: Paul shows by saying this that the Holy Spirit is not a creature but has his own divine nature. Commentary on the First Epistle to the Corinthians 178.[34]

---

[25]JTS 9:239. [26]CSEL 81.27. [27]Rom 8:27. [28]NPNF 1 12:37. [29]Migne PG 82:243. [30]CSEL 81.27-28. [31]NTA 15:233. [32]CSEL 81.28. [33]NTA 15:432. [34]Migne PG 82:243.

2:13-16 SPIRITUAL PEOPLE

[13]*And we impart this in words not taught by human wisdom but taught by the Spirit, interpreting spiritual truths to those who possess the Spirit.*[d] [14]*The unspiritual*[e] *man does not receive the gifts of the Spirit of God, for they are folly to him, and he is not able to understand them because they are spiritually discerned.* [15]*The spiritual man judges all things, but is himself to be judged by no one.* [16]*"For who has known the mind of the Lord so as to instruct him?" But we have the mind of Christ.*

d *Or interpreting spiritual truths in spiritual language; or comparing spiritual things with spiritual* e *Or natural*

OVERVIEW: A spiritual truth must be viewed not in isolation but in comparison to other spiritual truths, such as Jonah's deliverance, Christ's resurrection and Sarah's birthing (CHRYSOSTOM). The soul that pretends to see without the Spirit may become a danger to itself, as if eyes were trying to see without light (CHRYSOSTOM). Such a person is prone to become contented with blindness (THEODORET OF CYR, CHRYSOSTOM). One whose mind is formed by God's revelation is better able to assess philosophical arguments than the philosopher is able to assess revelation (ORIGEN). The enemies of faith view falsehood as true (AMBROSIASTER). Everything we know about our salvation comes from the mind of Christ (CHRYSOSTOM, AMBROSIASTER) through the Holy Spirit (PELAGIUS), revealing the mind of the Father (OECUMENIUS). It is not that faith knows everything (CHRYSOSTOM) but that everything sufficient for our salvation is adequately revealed (THEODORET OF CYR). Only one who lives in the Spirit is prepared to teach Christianity (THEODORET OF CYR).

2:13 Taught by the Spirit

INTERPRETING SPIRITUAL TRUTHS. CHRYSOSTOM: Some spiritual truths are unclear and need to be interpreted, but this can be done only by comparing them with other spiritual things. For example, when I say that Christ rose again, I compare this to the deliverance of Jonah from the belly of the whale.[1] And when I say that he was born of a virgin, I compare this to the miraculous childbearing of barren women like Sarah, Rebekah and so on.[2] HOMILIES ON THE EPISTLES OF PAUL TO THE CORINTHIANS 7.8.[3]

NOT A TOTAL DISAVOWAL OF HUMAN WISDOM. THEODORET OF CYR: This does not mean that Paul did not have any human wisdom but that he preached in the wisdom of the Spirit. COMMENTARY ON THE FIRST EPISTLE TO THE CORINTHIANS 178.[4]

2:14a A Folly to Unspiritual Persons

THE UNSPIRITUAL TRY TO SEE WITHOUT LIGHT. CHRYSOSTOM: God gave us a mind in order that we might learn and receive help from him, not in order that the mind should be self-sufficient. Eyes are beautiful and useful, but if they choose to see without light, their beauty is useless and may even be harmful. Likewise, if my soul chooses to see without the Spirit, it becomes a danger to itself. HOMILIES ON THE EPISTLES OF PAUL TO THE CORINTHIANS 7.9.[5]

[1]Jon 2:10. [2]Gen 21:1-7; 25:21. [3]NPNF 1 12:37. [4]Migne PG 82:243. [5]NPNF 1 12:38.

2:14b Spiritual Gifts Are Spiritually Discerned

THE UNSPIRITUAL ARE UNABLE TO UNDERSTAND. CHRYSOSTOM: The man who can see sees everything which belongs to the blind man, but no blind person can tell what he is doing. Likewise, we who believe can understand both our own affairs and those of unbelievers, but they are helpless when it comes to trying to understand us. HOMILIES ON THE EPISTLES OF PAUL TO THE CORINTHIANS 7.11.[6]

CONTENTED WITH BLINDNESS. THEODORET OF CYR: The unspiritual man is one who is happy enough with his own ideas and who neither accepts nor understands the teaching of the Spirit. COMMENTARY ON THE FIRST EPISTLE TO THE CORINTHIANS 178.[7]

2:15 The Spiritual Person Judges All Things

THE SPIRITUAL MAN. ORIGEN: The spiritual man is able to judge everything, whether it is Greek or barbarian, wise or foolish. He cannot be judged by anyone because of the depth of his understanding and his responses. COMMENTARY ON 1 CORINTHIANS 1.11.44-45.[8]

THE ENEMIES OF FAITH REGARD FALSEHOOD AS TRUE. AMBROSIASTER: Who can condemn a man who tells the truth? When such a person states that all the enemies of the faith regard falsehoods as true, their accusations are reduced to nothing because they are condemned by the judgment of the truth. COMMENTARY ON PAUL'S EPISTLES.[9]

THE GIFT OF TEACHING. THEODORET OF CYR: The person who has received the Spirit's gift is equipped to teach others. Otherwise what he says is of no value at all. COMMENTARY ON THE FIRST EPISTLE TO THE CORINTHIANS 179.[10]

2:16 Who Knows the Mind of the Lord?

PARTAKERS OF THE MIND OF CHRIST. AMBROSIASTER: Paul says this because believers are partakers of the divine wisdom.[11] COMMENTARY ON PAUL'S EPISTLES.[12]

THE ILLUMINATION OF THE HOLY SPIRIT. PELAGIUS: We have the mind of Christ because we have the Holy Spirit. COMMENTARY ON THE FIRST EPISTLE TO THE CORINTHIANS 2.[13]

DO WE KNOW ALL THAT CHRIST KNOWS? CHRYSOSTOM: We know the things which are in the mind of Christ, which he has willed and revealed to us. This does not mean that we know everything which Christ knows but rather that everything which we know comes from him and is spiritual. HOMILIES ON THE EPISTLES OF PAUL TO THE CORINTHIANS 7.12.[14]

NOTHING LACKING. THEODORET OF CYR: Paul demonstrates with sufficient clarity that there is nothing lacking in God's teaching. It is not simply that it contains the sum of all knowledge, but God also imparts wisdom so that we may understand it properly. COMMENTARY ON THE FIRST EPISTLE TO THE CORINTHIANS 179.[15]

THE FATHER IN US. OECUMENIUS: The "mind of Christ" refers to the Father. Paul is saying that we have the Father of Christ in us. PAULINE COMMENTARY FROM THE GREEK CHURCH.[16]

---

[6]NPNF 1 12:39. [7]Migne PG 82:246. [8]JTS 9:241. [9]CSEL 81.30-31. [10]Migne PG 82:246. [11]Is 40:13. [12]CSEL 81.31. [13]Migne PL 30:724B. [14]CSEL 81.39. [15]Migne PG 82:246. [16]NTA 15:432-33.

3:1-4 UNSPIRITUAL PEOPLE

[1]*But I, brethren, could not address you as spiritual men, but as men of the flesh, as babes in Christ.* [2]*I fed you with milk, not solid food; for you were not ready for it; and even yet you are not ready,* [3]*for you are still of the flesh. For while there is jealousy and strife among you, are you not of the flesh, and behaving like ordinary men?* [4]*For when one says, "I belong to Paul," and another, "I belong to Apollos," are you not merely men?*

OVERVIEW: The Holy Spirit dwells and remains in believers who stay firm in the conviction of their new birth (AMBROSIASTER). Solid food is found in the teaching of the Father and the Son in the New Testament, prefigured in the manna of Moses in the Old Testament (ORIGEN, CAESARIUS OF ARLES). To be ready only for milk is to be fixated on miracles (SEVERIAN OF GABALA). For these hearers the level of teaching must be downwardly adjusted (THEODORET OF CYR). Recall that the Lord displayed his glory on the mountain to only three disciples, who were told to say nothing about what had happened until his resurrection (AMBROSIASTER). Factionalism produces jealousy, deepens carnality and takes away the freedom to hear the gospel (CHRYSOSTOM). Paul's emphasis on the spiritual person is not to be understood as a Manichaean rejection of the body (AUGUSTINE).

3:1 Babes in Christ

ADDRESSED AS CARNAL PEOPLE. AMBROSIASTER: These people were carnal because they were still slaves to the desires of the present age. Although they had been baptized and had received the Holy Spirit, they were carnal because after their baptism they had returned to their old lives, which they had renounced. The Holy Spirit dwells in a person into whom he has poured himself if that person stays firm in the conviction of his new birth. Otherwise he departs, but only provisionally. If that person repents, the Spirit will return, for he is always ready for what is good, being a lover of repentance. COMMENTARY ON PAUL'S EPISTLES.[1]

NOT A MANICHAEAN REJECTION OF THE BODY. AUGUSTINE: Paul was not speaking of their bodies but of their carnal spirits. CITY OF GOD 22.21.[2]

3:2a Fed with Milk, Not Solid Food

SOLID FOOD. ORIGEN: In spiritual matters, "solid food" means the teaching about the Father and the Son. In the Old Testament, solid food appears under the guise of typology, as, for example, when we read about the serpent which Moses lifted up in the wilderness.[3] This serpent was a picture, or type, of Christ, which explains why it was that the people were saved when they looked at it. COMMENTARY ON 1 CORINTHIANS 1.12.17-23.[4]

CHRISTIAN TEACHERS, LIKE COWS, FEED BY TWO UDDERS. CAESARIUS OF ARLES: Not unfittingly, dearly beloved, do elders seem to bear a likeness to cows. Just as a cow has two udders to nurse her calf, so also elders ought to feed the Christian people with two udders: both the Old and the New Testaments. SERMONS 4.4.[5]

ONLY MILK. SEVERIAN OF GABALA: By "milk" Paul means moral teaching and miracles. Solid food, by contrast, is the proclamation of the

---

[1]CSEL 81.31-32. [2]FC 24:473. [3]Num 21:8-9. [4]JTS 9:242. [5]FC 31:31.

doctrines of God. PAULINE COMMENTARY FROM THE GREEK CHURCH.[6]

3:2b Not Yet Ready

NOT READY. AMBROSIASTER: Although they had been born again in Christ, they were not yet fit to receive spiritual things. Although they had received the faith which is the seed of the Spirit, they had produced no fruit worthy of God, but like babies, they were eager for the sensations of imperfection. But Paul, who was a man of God and a spiritual physician, gave to each of them according to his strength, so that no one should suffer scandal where spiritual matters were concerned because of imperfection or inexperience. Paul is also arguing strongly against those who were complaining that they had not heard anything spiritual for a long time, when in fact they were not worthy to hear it. The false apostles conveyed their message indiscriminately to anyone who would listen, but it is generally agreed that our Lord and Master spoke one way in public and another way to his disciples in private, and that even among the latter a distinction was made, for he displayed his glory on the mountain to only three disciples and told them to say nothing about what had happened until he should rise again from the dead. COMMENTARY ON PAUL'S EPISTLES.[7]

WITHOUT EXCUSE. CHRYSOSTOM: The Corinthians' inability to receive solid food was not by nature but by choice, so they were without excuse. HOMILIES ON THE EPISTLES OF PAUL TO THE CORINTHIANS 7.3.[8]

ADJUSTING THE LEVEL OF TEACHING. THEODORET OF CYR: Paul is saying that he adjusted the level of his teaching to their lack of understanding. COMMENTARY ON THE FIRST EPISTLE TO THE CORINTHIANS 179.[9]

3:3 Jealousy and Strife

STILL OF THE FLESH. CHRYSOSTOM: Here Paul talks about the particular problem which made the Corinthians carnal. There were other matters, like fornication and uncleanness, which he would deal with later, but first he wants to tackle something which he has clearly been trying to put right for some time. If jealousy makes people carnal, every one of us ought to be crying out because of our sin and covering ourselves in sackcloth and ashes. Who is not tainted with this? I say this of others only because I know how true it is of me. HOMILIES ON THE EPISTLES OF PAUL TO THE CORINTHIANS 8.3.[10]

3:4 Behaving as Mere Humans

FACTIONALISM. CHRYSOSTOM: It was the factionalism of the Corinthians that produced jealousy, and that in turn made them carnal. Once they were carnal, they were no longer free to hear truths of a more spiritual kind. HOMILIES ON THE EPISTLES OF PAUL TO THE CORINTHIANS 8.5.[11]

---

[6]NTA 15:236. [7]CSEL 81.32-33. [8]NPNF 1 12:44. [9]Migne PG 82:246. [10]NPNF 1 12:44-45. [11]NPNF 1 12:45.

3:5-10 SERVANTS OF GOD

[5]*What then is Apollos? What is Paul? Servants through whom you believed, as the Lord assigned to each.* [6]*I planted, Apollos watered, but God gave the growth.* [7]*So neither he who plants nor he who waters is anything, but only God who gives the growth.* [8]*He who plants and he who waters are equal, and each shall receive his wages according to his labor.* [9]*For we are God's fellow workers; you are God's field, God's building.*

[10]*According to the grace of God given to me, like a skilled master builder I laid a foundation, and another man is building upon it. Let each man take care how he builds upon it.*

OVERVIEW: Only one who is planted in the Lord's house, the doctrines of the church, will bring forth flower and fruit (JEROME). In this process only God gives growth (AUGUSTINE, AMBROSIASTER, THEODORET OF CYR). God the Spirit gives life even where there is not yet a visible baptism, as in the case of martyrs (AMBROSIASTER). Differing gifts and tasks may be inspired by the one Spirit (CHRYSOSTOM). The unity of God's building is protected against splitting by the boundaries of ecumenical consent (CHRYSOSTOM). What we build now must cohere with the foundation (AMBROSIASTER). Christ is the only foundation (CHRYSOSTOM), which must be preserved, not overthrown (THEODORET OF CYR). We are not slaves but God's fellow workers in our preaching (THEODORE OF MOPSUESTIA). The poison of pride is resisted with the medicine of true humility (CAESARIUS OF ARLES). It is a great thing to be a servant so as to be used by God to bring others to faith, but compared with the root of all good, this is nothing (CHRYSOSTOM, PELAGIUS). Paul wants to avoid the temptation to idleness that results when everybody is treated as though equal in virtue (CHRYSOSTOM, AMBROSIASTER, PELAGIUS).

3:5 Servants Through Whom They Believed

APOLLOS AND PAUL AS SERVANTS. PELAGIUS: If Paul and Apollos counted for nothing, what can we say about those who glory in the flesh? COMMENTARY ON THE FIRST EPISTLE TO THE CORINTHIANS 3.[1]

PREACHING AND SERVING. CHRYSOSTOM: Paul denigrates himself in order to show the Corinthians that he is not mistreating them. It is a great thing to be a servant, used by God to bring others to faith, but compared with the source and the root of all good, it is nothing. Note also that Paul called Apollos and himself servants, not evangelists. This is because they had not merely preached the gospel, but had also ministered to the people at Corinth. The first was a matter of word only, whereas the second includes deeds as well. HOMILIES ON THE EPISTLES OF PAUL TO THE CORINTHIANS 8.5.[2]

3:6 God Gave the Growth

GOD THE SPIRIT GIVES GROWTH. AMBROSIASTER: To plant is to evangelize and to bring to faith, to water is to baptize with the approved form of words. To forgive sins, however, and to give the Spirit belongs to God alone. We know that

---

[1]Migne PL 30:724D. [2]NPNF 1 12:45.

the Holy Spirit is given by God without the laying on of hands, and it has happened that an unbaptized person has received the forgiveness of his sins. Was such a person invisibly baptized, considering that he received the gift which belongs to baptism? Commentary on Paul's Epistles.[3]

Putting Down Roots in the House of the Lord. Jerome: I have been planted in the house of the Lord, I mean in the church; not in the walls but in its doctrines. Everyone who has been planted in the house of the Lord, who has put down roots there, brings forth flowers. Homily 21.[4]

Differing Gifts. Chrysostom: Paul and Apollos had different functions, but everything they did was of God. Homilies on the Epistles of Paul to the Corinthians 8.5.[5]

3:7 Only God Is Anything

Planters and Waterers Are Nothing. Ambrosiaster: In relation to God's honor, human honor is nothing. As far as the ministry is concerned, a man may be honored in the way that a servant is honored. Commentary on Paul's Epistles.[6]

Only God Gives Increase. Augustine: Since the apostles would not have accomplished anything if God had not given the increase, how much more true is this of you or me, or anyone else of our time, who fancies himself as a teacher. Letters 193.[7]

Labor in Vain. Theodoret of Cyr: Our labor is in vain without the help of God. Commentary on the First Epistle to the Corinthians 180.[8]

3:8 Receiving Wages According to Labor

A Greater Reward. Ambrosiaster: Even though they are equal, the one who preaches the gospel is still greater than the one who baptizes and will receive a greater reward. Commentary on Paul's Epistles.[9]

Hired Hands. Pelagius: Paul points out that he and Apollos are merely hired hands on someone else's farm. They have nothing apart from the payment they get for their labor. Commentary on the First Epistle to the Corinthians 3.[10]

Avoiding the Temptation to Idleness. Chrysostom: Paul says this in order to show that the Corinthians have no reason to think that some of them are superior to others. He did not allow those who worked hard to regard themselves as superior to those who did less, nor did he permit the latter to be jealous of the former. But in order to avoid the temptation to idleness which naturally results when everybody is treated equally, whether they have worked hard or not, Paul adds that the rewards will be distributed to each one according to the work accomplished. Homilies on the Epistles of Paul to the Corinthians 8.6.[11]

3:9 Fellow Workers

The Unity of God's Building. Chrysostom: The building does not belong to the workman but to the master. If you are a building, you must not be split in two, since then the building will collapse. If you are a farm, you must not be divided but rather surrounded with a single fence, the fence of unanimity. Homilies on the Epistles of Paul to the Corinthians 8.6.[12]

Workers Are Not Slaves. Theodore of Mopsuestia: Paul calls us God's fellow workers, not his servants or slaves. Pauline Commentary from the Greek Church.[13]

---

[3]CSEL 81.34. [4]FC 48:173. [5]CSEL 81.46. [6]CSEL 81.34. [7]FC 30:301. [8]Migne PG 82:247. [9]CSEL 81.35. [10]Migne PL 30:725A. [11]NPNF 1 12:46. [12]NPNF 1 12:46. [13]NTA 15:175.

The Medicine of Humility. Caesarius of Arles: Coworkers of God are those who, when once they see the poison of pride creeping into the heart of a brother, with all haste try to destroy it with the medicine of true humility. Sermons 233.6.[14]

3:10 Laying a Foundation

Build Properly on the Foundation. Origen: This warning applies to you and me as well. If I do not build properly on the foundation already laid for me, then the fire will consume my work on the day of judgment. Commentary on 1 Corinthians 1.15.18-20.[15]

What We Build Coheres with the Foundation. Ambrosiaster: The wise master builder is one who preaches the same gospel as that which was preached by the Savior. Afterward other people build on the foundation, sometimes well and sometimes badly. We need to pay attention to make sure that what we build coheres with the foundation, because if it is crooked or lightweight it will collapse, though the foundation itself will remain intact. Even when people have taught badly, the name of Christ endures, because it is the foundation, although the bad teaching collapses. Commentary on Paul's Epistles.[16]

Christ Is the Foundation. Chrysostom: Paul is not exalting himself by taking the example of a skilled master builder, because whatever skill he possesses comes entirely from the grace of God that has been given to him. Furthermore, because it is grace, it is not divided but rests securely on the one foundation, which is Christ. Homilies on the Epistles of Paul to the Corinthians 8.6.[17]

Preserving the Foundation. Theodoret of Cyr: We need to build on the foundation, not overthrow it. Commentary on the First Epistle to the Corinthians 181.[18]

---

[14]FC 66:196. [15]JTS 9:244. [16]CSEL 81.35. [17]NPNF 1 12:46. [18]Migne PG 82:247.

3:11-15 THE PRINCIPLES OF DIVINE ARCHITECTURE

[11]*For no other foundation can any one lay than that which is laid, which is Jesus Christ.* [12]*Now if any one builds on the foundation with gold, silver, precious stones, wood, hay, straw—* [13]*each man's work will become manifest; for the Day will disclose it, because it will be revealed with fire, and the fire will test what sort of work each one has done.* [14]*If the work which any man has built on the foundation survives, he will receive a reward.* [15]*If any man's work is burned up, he will suffer loss, though he himself will be saved, but only as through fire.*

Overview: Paul uses the metaphor of architecture to describe the Christian life: There is no other foundation (Ambrosiaster) than Jesus Christ (Origen) to which the faithful are firmly cemented (CHRYSOSTOM). This same foundation was laid for the Gentiles in Paul's ministry (ORIGEN). Though the foundation is the same for all the faithful, they may choose to build with different moral materials (CHRYSOSTOM, THEODORET OF CYR). To sin after repentance and faith is to build once again on hay and straw (ORIGEN). On a scale from the highest-grade materials (jewels) to the lowest (straw), the builder chooses materials for good or ill (PELAGIUS). Each one's quality of work will be tested in final judgment (AUGUSTINE) and will become clear (AMBROSIASTER). Wood, hay and straw will not survive the fire of judgment (PELAGIUS). One who is saved by faith may yet have to be tested by fire (AMBROSIASTER). When one who has faith continues to pursue a wicked life, his faith will not protect him from punishment, because his work will be burned like hay in the fire, as distinguished from gold (CHRYSOSTOM). The good works offered up by faith must be offered in this life, for when the gate of death once closes there is no future opportunity in the world to come for human freedom to repair sins (GREGORY THE GREAT). Though heretics may want to be called Christian, the substantial proclamation underlying the name *Christian* is not honored (AUGUSTINE). The eternal destiny of the teacher does not finally depend exclusively on the irresponsible choices of his pupils (THEODORET OF CYR).

3:11 *Jesus Christ the Foundation*

THE FOUNDATION LAID FOR THE GENTILES. ORIGEN: The other apostles laid this foundation among the Jews, while Paul and Barnabas laid it among the Gentiles. COMMENTARY ON 1 CORINTHIANS 1.15.41-42.[1]

NO OTHER FOUNDATION. AMBROSIASTER: Nobody can lay another foundation, because even if some people are heretics, they do not teach except in the name of Christ. They cannot commend the inventions of their error in any other way. So through the dignity of his name they try to make contradictory and absurd ideas acceptable. COMMENTARY ON PAUL'S EPISTLES.[2]

CEMENTED TO THE FOUNDATION. CHRYSOSTOM: The foundation is already in place, and no one can change it. Let us therefore build on it and cling to it in the way that branches cling to the vine, so that there is no gap between us and Christ. For the minute a gap opens up between the vine and its branches, the branches wither and perish. Similarly, if a building is not cemented to its foundation, it will collapse. Therefore, let us not merely cling to Christ, but let us be cemented to him, for if we stand apart we shall perish. HOMILIES ON THE EPISTLES OF PAUL TO THE CORINTHIANS 8.7.[3]

THE PRETENSE OF THE HERETICS. AUGUSTINE: It should not be denied that this is the distinctive basis of the orthodox faith, just because it is shared between us and certain heretics as well. For if we think carefully about the meaning of Christ we shall see that among some of the heretics who want to be called Christians, the name of Christ is held in honor, but the reality to which the name points is not. ENCHIRIDION 2.5.[4]

3:12 *Precious or Common Building Materials*

BUILDING ON WOOD, HAY AND STRAW. ORIGEN: If we think what is right and good, then we are building on a foundation of gold. If we repeat every holy word that has been spoken without corrupting it, then we are building on a foundation of silver. If all our works are good, then we are building on precious stones. But if I sin after laying the foundation, then I am building on wood; if I continue, I am building on hay, and

---

[1]JTS 9:244-45. [2]CSEL 81.36. [3]NPNF 1 12:47. [4]LCC 7:339.

finally, if I still go on, I am building on straw. COMMENTARY ON 1 CORINTHIANS 1.15.46-55.[5]

TYPES OF BUILDING MATERIALS. PELAGIUS: The house does not build itself; somebody has to put the walls up. This is the role of teachers in the church. The gold, silver, etc., represent six different types of hearers. Gold stands for good respondents, silver for better ones (because silver is stronger than gold) and precious stones for the best of all. Similarly, wood stands for bad people, hay for those who are worse and straw for the worst of all. COMMENTARY ON THE FIRST EPISTLE TO THE CORINTHIANS 3.[6]

THE FOUNDATION IS THE SAME FOR ALL THE FAITHFUL. CHRYSOSTOM: Our faith is the foundation, and it is the same for everyone. But in life, not everyone is the same. Some are diligent, others lazy. Some are high achievers, others more average. Some do well in greater things, others shine in lesser matters. Some people's mistakes are more serious than others'. This is why we find the variety here. Furthermore, the judgment applies to the effort, not to the results. A teacher cannot be faulted merely because his pupils refuse to listen. HOMILIES ON THE EPISTLES OF PAUL TO THE CORINTHIANS 9.5.[7]

MORAL MATERIALS. THEODORET OF CYR: Some people think that this refers to the development of Christian doctrine, but a glance at the context will show that Paul is talking about morals and behavior here. COMMENTARY ON THE FIRST EPISTLE TO THE CORINTHIANS 182.[8]

3:13 Fire Will Test One's Work

TESTED BY FIRE. AMBROSIASTER: In the fire, bad teaching will become clear to everyone, though for the moment it is deceiving some. COMMENTARY ON PAUL'S EPISTLES.[9]

FINAL TESTING. AUGUSTINE: The fire will try the quality of everyone's work. If his work remains,

he will receive his reward. If his work burns, he will lose his reward, but he himself will be saved. In this fire neither man will be lost forever, though the fire will profit the one and harm the other, being a test for both. CITY OF GOD 21.[10]

SURVIVING THE FIRE OF JUDGMENT. PELAGIUS: Gold, silver and precious stones will survive the fire of judgment, but wood, hay and straw will be burned up. COMMENTARY ON THE FIRST EPISTLE TO THE CORINTHIANS 3.[11]

3:14 Receiving a Reward

GLORIOUS WORK BUILT ON THE FOUNDATION. AMBROSIASTER: If anyone's work proves lasting, he will receive his wage. He will be just like the three brothers in the fiery furnace,[12] destined to receive as his wage heavenly life with glory. COMMENTARY ON PAUL'S EPISTLES.[13]

3:15 Saved Only As Through Fire

THE FIRE WILL TEST THE WORK. AMBROSIASTER: To suffer loss is to endure reproof. For what person, when subjected to punishment, does not lose something thereby? Yet the person himself may be saved. His living soul will not perish in the same way that his erroneous ideas will. Even so, however, he may suffer punishments of fire. He will be saved only by being purified through fire. COMMENTARY ON PAUL'S EPISTLES.[14]

GOLD SURVIVES FIRE, HAY BURNS. CHRYSOSTOM: If someone has the right faith but leads a wicked life, his faith will not protect him from punishment, because his work will be burned up. A man in gold armor will pass through a river of fire and come out shining all the more brightly, but a man who passes through it with

---

[5]JTS 9:245. [6]Migne PL 30:725C—726A. [7]NPNF 1 12:51. [8]Migne PG 82:250. [9]CSEL 81.37. [10]FC 24:400-401. [11]Migne PL 30:726B. [12]Dan 3:1-10. [13]CSEL 81.37. [14]CSEL 81.37-38.

hay will lose it all and destroy himself besides. HOMILIES ON THE EPISTLES OF PAUL TO THE CORINTHIANS 9.5.[15]

THE FAITHFUL TEACHER WILL RECEIVE HIS REWARD. THEODORET OF CYR: The teacher teaches what is right. Some follow him; others do not. Those who follow will be like gold and silver—purified by the fire and shining when they emerge from it. The others will be burned up. But the teacher will not lose anything by this. If he has been faithful, he will receive his reward regardless. COMMENTARY ON THE FIRST EPISTLE TO THE CORINTHIANS 183.[16]

AVOIDING FALSE ASSURANCE. CAESARIUS OF ARLES: There are many people who understand this text incorrectly, deceiving themselves with a false assurance. They believe that if they build serious sins upon the foundation of Christ, those very offenses can be purified by transitory flames, and they themselves can later reach eternal life. This kind of understanding must be cor-

rected. People deceive themselves when they flatter themselves in this way. For in that fire it is slight sins which are purged, not serious ones. Even worse, it is not only the greater sins but the smaller ones as well which can ruin a person. SERMONS 179.1.[17]

OPPORTUNITY FOR PURGING OF SIN IN THIS LIFE AND THE NEXT. GREGORY THE GREAT: We should remember that in the world to come no one will be purged of even his slightest faults unless he has deserved such a cleansing through good works performed in this life. DIALOGUE 4.41.[18]

---

[15]NPNF 1 12:51. [16]Migne PG 82:250. [17]FC 47:450. [18]FC 39:249. Gregory is often considered to be a chief contributor to the early medieval doctrine of purgation. This hypothesis does not negate what he says elsewhere about the priority of grace to faith active in love. A balanced reading of Gregory's intent must link his speculation about the purgation required for the celestial life to his (largely Augustinian) teaching of grace. Any good works to be offered up in the life of faith must be offered freely before the time of death, for once closed there is no future opportunity for human freedom to engage in temporally willed acts in the world to come.

3:16-17 CHRISTIAN IDENTITY

[16]Do you not know that you are God's temple and that God's Spirit dwells in you? [17]If any one destroys God's temple, God will destroy him. For God's temple is holy, and that temple you are.

OVERVIEW: God the Spirit lives in his own temple: we ourselves (AMBROSIASTER). Those who have become spiritual according to their confession of faith may nevertheless still live as though they were carnal, thus becoming an insult to the Holy Spirit who dwells in them

(THEODORE OF MOPSUESTIA). Paul pricks the conscience of those who would treat God's holy temple as a profane place (AMBROSIASTER), as in the case of fornication (CHRYSOSTOM).

3:16 The Spirit Dwells in God's Temple

The Spirit Lives in Us. Ambrosiaster: It is necessarily the case that God lives in his own temple. Note that because he says that the Spirit of God lives in us, the word *God* must be taken to refer to the Holy Spirit [in this verse]. Commentary on Paul's Epistles.[1]

Insulting the Spirit. Theodore of Mopsuestia: The one who believes in Christ receives the Holy Spirit, who dwells in him by the washing of rebirth, and thus he is spiritual. But if such people then turn around and serve worldly passions, in that respect they are carnal. Paul says that those who have become spiritual according to their confession of faith may nevertheless still live as though they were carnal so as to become an insult to the Holy Spirit who dwells in them. Pauline

Commentary from the Greek Church.2

3:17 You Are God's Temple

God's Temple Is Holy. Ambrosiaster: Paul says this in order to prick the consciences of those who have corrupted their bodies through evil living, especially the man who was having an affair with his father's wife.[3] Commentary on Paul's Epistles.[4]

Profaning God's Temple. Chrysostom: God's temple is holy, but anyone who has committed fornication is profane. Homilies on the Epistles of Paul to the Corinthians 9.7.[5]

---

[1]CSEL 81.38. [2]NTA 15:176. [3]1 Cor 5:1-5. [4]CSEL 81.38. [5]NPNF 1 12:52.

3:18-23 THE UPSIDE-DOWN PERSON

[18]Let no one deceive himself. If any one among you thinks that he is wise in this age, let him become a fool that he may become wise. [19]For the wisdom of this world is folly with God. For it is written, "He catches the wise in their craftiness," [20]and again, "The Lord knows that the thoughts of the wise are futile." [21]So let no one boast of men. For all things are yours, [22]whether Paul or Apollos or Cephas or the world or life or death or the present or the future, all are yours; [23]and you are Christ's; and Christ is God's.

Overview: Whatever human beings think apart from God is foolishness (Ambrosiaster). The faithful may look like fools to this world when they despise earthly wisdom, while the wise are caught in their craftiness when they imagine they can do without God (Chrysostom, Theodoret of Cyr). What the wise thought true has turned out to be false (Ambrosiaster) and unable to save (Pelagius). Whatever the worldly wise may have, it may be stolen (Origen). In this way Paul returns to his

original theme (Chrysostom, Ambrosiaster).

3:18 Becoming a Fool to Become Wise

Recapitulation. Ambrosiaster: Here Paul is returning to what he said [in the first chapter]. Commentary on Paul's Epistles.[1]

---

[1]CSEL 81.39.

A Wisdom Not Learned Through Study.
Isaac of Nineveh: Those who are tiny of body[2] and those who, being wise in the world, abandon their knowledge and . . . become like babes of their own free will, will learn a wisdom which is not learned through study's labors. Ascetical Homilies 72.[3]

Dead to the World. Chrysostom: Paul asks us to become dead to the world, and this deadness is of benefit to us, because it is the beginning of new life. So also he bids us become foolish toward the world, thereby introducing us to true wisdom. You become a fool to this world when you despise earthly wisdom and are persuaded that it contributes nothing to your understanding of the faith. For Christians, everything is just the opposite of what it seems. Homilies on the Epistles of Paul to the Corinthians 10.2.[4]

3:19 Worldly Wisdom Is Folly with God

Catching the Wise in Their Craftiness.
Chrysostom: How does God catch the wise in their own craftiness?[5] By showing them that while they imagined they can do without God, just then they would have all the more need of him. They are reduced to such a strait as to appear inferior to fishers and illiterates, whose wisdom they cannot now do without. Homilies on the Epistles of Paul to the Corinthians 10.3.[6]

Lacking Grace. Theodoret of Cyr: The wisdom of this world is that which lacks the grace of God. It is purely human in character. Commentary on the First Epistle to the Corinthians 184.[7]

3:20 The Futility of Worldly Wisdom

What They Thought False Was True. Ambrosiaster: Knowing that their thoughts are vain, God rebukes their wisdom in order to prove that they are foolish, showing that what

they thought was false is true and vice versa. Commentary on Paul's Epistles.[8]

The Thoughts of the Wise. Pelagius: The thoughts of the wise[9] contribute nothing to a person's salvation. Commentary on the First Epistle to the Corinthians 3.[10]

3:21 No Boasting of Human Reason

All Things Are Yours. Origen: The believer owns everything there is, but the unbeliever is effectively penniless. Anything he may have has been stolen. Commentary on 1 Corinthians 2.17.12-14.[11]

Trying to Think Apart from God. Ambrosiaster: Human reasoning is unwise and weak, so one should not glory in man but in God, whose word cannot be altered. Whatever human beings think apart from God is foolishness. Commentary on Paul's Epistles.[12]

3:22 All Things Are Yours

A Word of Encouragement. Chrysostom: Having criticized the Corinthians, Paul now turns to encourage them once more. He even puts down the pride of the teachers by implying that they ought to be grateful to the others, for whose sake they were made what they are. Homilies on the Epistles of Paul to the Corinthians 10.4.[13]

3:23 Belonging to Christ

You Are Christ's. Ambrosiaster: We are Christ's because we were made by him, both physically and spiritually. Commentary on Paul's Epistles.[14]

---

[2]Cf. Ps 114:6. [3]AHSIS 352. [4]NPNF 1 12:54. [5]Job 5:13. [6]NPNF 1 12:55. [7]Migne PG 82:251. [8]CSEL 81.40. [9]Ps 94:11. [10]Migne PL 30:727A. [11]JTS 9:353. [12]CSEL 81.40. [13]NPNF 1 12:55. [14]CSEL 81.41.

We Are Christ's by Grace. Chrysostom: We are Christ's because we have been made by him [by grace]. But Christ is God's, not as a creature but as his own Son. Homilies on the Epis- tles of Paul to the Corinthians 10.4.[15]

[15]NPNF 1 12:55.

4:1-5 PAUL'S IDENTITY

[1]*This is how one should regard us, as servants of Christ and stewards of the mysteries of God. [2]Moreover it is required of stewards that they be found trustworthy. [3]But with me it is a very small thing that I should be judged by you or by any human court. I do not even judge myself. [4]I am not aware of anything against myself, but I am not thereby acquitted. It is the Lord who judges me. [5]Therefore do not pronounce judgment before the time, before the Lord comes, who will bring to light the things now hidden in darkness and will disclose the purposes of the heart. Then every man will receive his commendation from God.*

Overview: Paul defended himself against the unreasonable blame of others without pretending to be utterly blameless (Ignatius of Antioch, Origen, Chrysostom). He knew that he was unable to judge himself rightly but that God knew his heart (Chrysostom, Theodoret of Cyr). The timing of the verdict on our moral failures is for the final judge to say, not for us to preempt (Ambrosiaster, Theodoret of Cyr). God who sees into our secret depths (Chrysostom) does not focus upon incidentals (Origen). The servant of Christ will read the Scriptures carefully, but the steward of the mysteries of God will plumb their depths (Origen). The mysteries of God are not to be offered indiscriminately, but only to those prepared for them and to whom they are due (Chrysostom). We are called to be trustworthy stewards like the apostles (Origen, Ambrosiaster), ministering faithfully what has been entrusted to us (Chrysostom, Ambrose).

4:1 Servants of Christ

Steward of the Mysteries. Origen: There is a big difference between being a servant of Christ and a steward of the mysteries of God. Anyone who has read the Bible can be a servant of Christ, but to be a steward of the mysteries one must plumb their depths. Paul was acting as a steward of the mysteries when he commissioned Luke, for example, to write his Gospel, and when he sent Timothy[1] to sort out the Ephesian church. I would even dare to say that in Corinth Paul acted like a servant of Christ, whereas in Ephesus he became a steward of the mysteries of God.[2] Commentary on 1 Corinthians 2.18.10-16.[3]

In Accord with the Apostles. Ambrosiaster: Paul says this because some of the Corinthians

[1]1 Tim 1:1-4. [2]Eph 3:1-13. [3]JTS 9:354.

were denigrating him. He did not preach anything different from the apostles. By calling himself a servant of Christ and a steward of the mysteries of God, Paul implicitly points out who the false apostles are. He denies that what they preach is of Christ, because it is not in accord with apostolic tradition. COMMENTARY ON PAUL'S EPISTLES.[4]

MYSTERIES NOT GIVEN INDISCRIMINATELY. CHRYSOSTOM: Paul honors the Corinthians by calling them servants and makes this even more precise when he adds the term *stewards*. For we should not give the mysteries of God indiscriminately to everyone, but only to those to whom they are due and to whom it is right that we should minister. HOMILIES ON THE EPISTLES OF PAUL TO THE CORINTHIANS 10.5.[5]

4:2 Stewards Must Be Trustworthy

TRUSTWORTHY STEWARDS. ORIGEN: If Paul can say this of people like himself, Peter and Apollos, how much more will it be true of us? We ought to be on our guard to make sure that we are found to be trustworthy stewards. COMMENTARY ON 1 CORINTHIANS 2.18.25-27.[6]

ENTRUSTED BY THE MASTER. CHRYSOSTOM: A steward's duty is to administer well the things that have been entrusted to him. The things of the master's are not the stewards but the reverse—what is his really belongs to his master. HOMILIES ON THE EPISTLES OF PAUL TO THE CORINTHIANS 10.5.[7]

WHAT YOU HAVE IS FROM GOD. AMBROSE: As you receive everything, call upon God for everything. What you have is from God. Always acknowledge that you are his debtor. ON THEODOSIUS 22.[8]

SAFEKEEPING THE DEPOSIT. THEODORET OF CYR: No banker plays fast and loose with other peo-

ple's deposits. Rather he looks after them in order to keep them safe for the one who has entrusted them to him. COMMENTARY ON THE FIRST EPISTLE TO THE CORINTHIANS 188.[9]

4:3 Human Judgment a Small Thing

HIS CLEAR CONSCIENCE. AMBROSIASTER: It is obvious that Paul was not worried about himself because he had a clear conscience. COMMENTARY ON PAUL'S EPISTLES.[10]

HIS RELUCTANCE TO JUDGE HIMSELF. CHRYSOSTOM: Paul says this not to exalt himself but to humble others who were getting too full of themselves. Paul says that he would not even presume to judge himself, because he is not capable of making an adequate assessment. HOMILIES ON THE EPISTLES OF PAUL TO THE CORINTHIANS 9.2.[11]

EXAGGERATION AND CONDEMNATION. THEODORET OF CYR: Paul accuses the Corinthians of two things. First, they exaggerate their praise, and second, they condemn others when they have no right to judge. COMMENTARY ON THE FIRST EPISTLE TO THE CORINTHIANS 186.[12]

4:4 The Lord Judges

NOT ACQUITTED. IGNATIUS OF ANTIOCH: Through the wrongdoings of others I become a better disciple, but I am not thereby acquitted. EPISTLE TO THE ROMANS 5.[13]

UNAWARE OF ANYTHING AGAINST HIMSELF. ORIGEN: Paul knew that even if his heart was still prone to sin, his deeds were upright. COMMENTARY ON 1 CORINTHIANS 2.18.49-51.[14]

BLAMING UNREASONABLY. CHRYSOSTOM: Paul may

---

[4]CSEL 81.41. [5]NPNF 1 12:55. [6]JTS 9:354. [7]NPNF 1 12:56. [8]FC 22:317. [9]Migne PG 82:255. [10]CSEL 81.42. [11]NPNF 1 12:59. [12]Migne PG 82:254. [13]AF 77. [14]JTS 9:355.

have committed certain sins without knowing that they are sins. His purpose here is not to say that he is blameless but to stop the mouths of those who were blaming him unreasonably. God is our judge, because only he knows for sure what is going on in our hearts. HOMILIES ON THE EPISTLES OF PAUL TO THE CORINTHIANS 9.3.[15]

UNABLE TO JUDGE MYSELF. THEODORET OF CYR: If I am unable to judge myself, how shall I presume to judge others? COMMENTARY ON THE FIRST EPISTLE TO THE CORINTHIANS 187.[16]

4:5 Commendation from God

WHAT REACHES GOD'S EARS. ORIGEN: Why does Paul mention only commendation from God and say nothing about condemnation? The reason seems to be that only that which is commendable will reach God's ears; the rest will be passed over in silence. I would even go so far as to say that it is God who receives the commendable things we have done, whereas the rest goes straight to the devil. COMMENTARY ON 1 CORINTHIANS 2.18.106-12.[17]

DO NOT PRONOUNCE JUDGMENT BEFORE THE TIME. AMBROSIASTER: God will judge in his own good time. A judge is insulted if a servant presumes to pronounce a verdict before the judge makes the decision known. COMMENTARY ON PAUL'S EPISTLES.[18]

GOD KNOWS OUR HEARTS. CHRYSOSTOM: Paul is not talking here about those sins that we all recognize and confess as such. Rather he is speaking about preferring one person before another and making invidious comparisons of moral behaviors. Only God, who knows all our secret doings, can judge that sort of thing with accuracy. Only he knows what is more and what is less worthy of punishment. HOMILIES ON THE EPISTLES OF PAUL TO THE CORINTHIANS 9.3.[19]

---

[15]NPNF 1 12:59. [16]Migne PG 82:255. [17]JTS 9:356-57. [18]CSEL 81.43. [19]NPNF 1 12:60.

4:6-13 THE IDENTITY OF THE CORINTHIANS

[6]*I have applied all this to myself and Apollos for your benefit, brethren, that you may learn by us not to go beyond what is written, that none of you may be puffed up in favor of one against another.* [7]*For who sees anything different in you? What have you that you did not receive? If then you received it, why do you boast as if it were not a gift?*

[8]*Already you are filled! Already you have become rich! Without us you have become kings! And would that you did reign, so that we might share the rule with you!* [9]*For I think that God has exhibited us apostles as last of all, like men sentenced to death; because we have become a spectacle to the world, to angels and to men.* [10]*We are fools for Christ's sake, but you are wise in Christ. We are weak, but you are strong. You are held in honor, but we in disrepute.* [11]*To the present hour we hunger and thirst, we are ill-clad and buffeted and homeless,* [12]*and we labor, working with our own hands. When reviled, we bless; when*

persecuted, we endure; [13]*when slandered, we try to conciliate; we have become, and are now, as the refuse of the world, the offscouring of all things.*

Overview: Paul was gentle when the situation called for gentleness but firm when firmness was required (Chrysostom). The pettiness of the Corinthian quarrelers is contrasted with Paul, who in wrestling with spiritual wickedness became a spectacle to the world (Ambrose), to angels (Theodoret of Cyr) and to humans (Chrysostom). The faithful everywhere are ready to suffer without despair or anger, returning good for evil, bearing insults meekly that they might grow in patience (Chrysostom). All that the Corinthians had, they had received as a gift (Ambrosiaster, Chrysostom), and so they should not boast (Augustine).

4:6 Applied for Their Benefit

Applying Tact. Chrysostom: As long as there was a need for expressions as harsh as these, Paul refrained from drawing up the curtain and went on arguing as if he himself were the person to whom they were addressed. But when the time came to be gentler, he tore the curtain away and revealed who the people were whom he had concealed under the names of Paul and Apollos. This was not hypocrisy but gentleness and tact. For if he had said openly that the men whom the Corinthians were attacking were saints, they might have taken it badly. But by first humbling himself he gained their attention and respect. Homilies on the Epistles of Paul to the Corinthians 9.1.[1]

4:7 Receiving a Gift

Everything Is a Gift. Ambrosiaster: Paul wrote this to people who thought that it was better to be baptized by some people rather than by others, who had been led astray by their eloquence and who by some trick believed that perverse teachings were right. In fact, every-

thing these people had they had received from the apostle. Commentary on Paul's Epistles.[2]

You Have Received. Chrysostom: By showing that they have received all that they have from someone else, Paul points out the deficiencies of the Corinthians, which were not few in number. Homilies on the Epistles of Paul to the Corinthians 9.3-4.[3]

Boasting as If It Were Not a Gift. Augustine: The people who boast imagine that they are justified by their own efforts, and therefore they glory in themselves, not in the Lord. Letter to Valentine.[4]

4:8 Would That You Did Reign!

The Reprimand. Chrysostom: Arguments like these, which appeal to our sense of shame, have two advantages. On the one hand, they cut deeper than open invective would ever do. On the other hand, they cause the person reprimanded to bear that deeper wound with greater patience. Homilies on the Epistles of Paul to the Corinthians 12.4.[5]

4:9 The Apostles Have Become a Spectacle

A Spectacle. Ambrose: Paul was worthy to be watched by angels as he strove to win the prize of Christ, as he struggled to establish the life of angels on earth and confound the wickedness of angels in heaven. For he wrestled with spiritual wickedness. Rightly did the world watch him, to follow his example. Episcopal Election at Vercellae 63.71.[6]

---

[1]NPNF 1 12:64. [2]CSEL 81.44. [3]NPNF 1 12:65. [4]FC 32:59. [5]NPNF 1 12:66. [6]LCC 5:278.

The Contrast with Pettiness. Chrysostom: From the things by which he vilifies himself, Paul shows us how great he is. From the things that make the Corinthians proud he displays their littleness. Homilies on the Epistles of Paul to the Corinthians 12.6.[7]

Why the Angels Marvel. Theodoret of Cyr: The angels marvel at the apostles' fortitude. As for human beings, some rejoice in the apostles' afflictions, while others are moved to pity but have no help to offer. Commentary on the First Epistle to the Corinthians 189.[8]

4:10 Fools for Christ's Sake

Fools for Christ. Ambrosiaster: Those who love Christ are fools as far as the world is concerned. Commentary on Paul's Epistles.[9]

Held in Disrepute. Chrysostom: Paul said these things in order to provoke the Corinthians to consider that they should zealously seek to emulate the apostles in their dangers and their indignities, not in their honors and glories. For it is the former, not the latter, that the gospel requires. Homilies on the Epistles of Paul to the Corinthians 13.1.[10]

4:11 Physical Deprivations

The Constant Risk of the Athlete. Chrysostom: Paul is talking about the present as much as about the past, because the Christian must always be living in this way, and not just occasionally. The wrestler may be crowned after a single victory, but if he then goes on to lose, he will not be crowned a second time. Homilies on the Epistles of Paul to the Corinthians 13.2.[11]

4:12 Suffering and Endurance

Suffering Without Anger. Chrysostom: Paul is saying that the main point is not that he and his fellow apostles are suffering, for that is common to all. What is unique about them is that they are suffering without despair or anger. On the contrary, they are full of rejoicing, and they prove it by returning good for the evil they receive. Homilies on the Epistles of Paul to the Corinthians 13.2.[12]

4:13 Returning Good for Evil

Silence, Not Reproach. Chrysostom: Christ commanded us to bear insults meekly, both so that we might grow in virtue ourselves and that we might put our adversaries to shame.[13] That effect is best produced not by reproach but by silence. Homilies on the Epistles of Paul to the Corinthians 13.2.[14]

---

[7]NPNF 1 12:66. [8]Migne PG 82:258. [9]CSEL 81.47. [10]NPNF 1 12:72. [11]NPNF 1 12:73. [12]NPNF 1 12:73. [13]E.g., Mt 5:10-12. [14]NPNF 1 12:73.

4:14-21 PAUL'S FAMILY

[14]I do not write this to make you ashamed, but to admonish you as my beloved children. [15]For though you have countless guides in Christ, you do not have many fathers. For I became your father in Christ Jesus through the gospel. [16]I urge you, then, be imitators of

me. [17]*Therefore I sent*[g] *to you Timothy, my beloved and faithful child in the Lord, to remind you of my ways in Christ, as I teach them everywhere in every church.* [18]*Some are arrogant, as though I were not coming to you.* [19]*But I will come to you soon, if the Lord wills, and I will find out not the talk of these arrogant people but their power.* [20]*For the kingdom of God does not consist in talk but in power.* [21]*What do you wish? Shall I come to you with a rod, or with love in a spirit of gentleness?*

g *Or am sending*

OVERVIEW: Paul knew that he was the father of the Corinthians in faith (AMBROSIASTER), as distinguished from all their subsequent guides and mentors (ORIGEN). In this fatherly way he has showed his love for them (CHRYSOSTOM). Out of this relationship, Paul urged them to be humble and to be prepared to suffer (ORIGEN) as he has suffered (THEODORET OF CYR). The surgeon does not cure by leaving the disease alone but by treating its cause, even with the knife (AMBROSIASTER, CHRYSOSTOM). Only insofar as Paul imitates Christ does he exhort the people to imitate him (CHRYSOSTOM, AMBROSIASTER). Paul sent Timothy to correct them and keep them on course (CHRYSOSTOM) and remind them how consistent was their teaching with their way of life in Christ (ORIGEN, PELAGIUS). Some were accusing Paul of weakness (SEVERIAN OF GABALA) or pride (AMBROSIASTER). Paul couched his hope of coming to them within the framework of the will of God (AMBROSIASTER). But he warned that when he does come they should be prepared for correction (SEVERIAN). They must have no false expectations (CAESARIUS OF ARLES). Their behavior will speak louder than their words (ORIGEN, CHRYSOSTOM, THEODORET OF CYR). In what mood he will come will be up to the Corinthians to decide (CHRYSOSTOM). Love is hidden in the rod (ORIGEN) of the Spirit (SEVERIAN) in order to lead to comfort (AMBROSE).

4:14 Admonishing Them as Beloved Children

THE PHYSICIAN'S WORK. AMBROSIASTER: Paul is acting here like a good physician who alleviates the pain caused by his operation to remove the disease, so that the sick person will let himself be cured. COMMENTARY ON PAUL'S EPISTLES.[1]

THE KNIFE AND THE PAIN. CHRYSOSTOM: Not to speak against sins would have been impossible, since they would have remained uncorrected. To have left the wound untended after having spoken would have been harsh. Therefore Paul apologizes for being severe, because so far from destroying the effect of the knife it makes it sink in even deeper, while at the same time it looks toward soothing the pain of the wound. When a person is told that these things are being said in love and not in reproach, he will be more open to receiving correction. HOMILIES ON THE EPISTLES OF PAUL TO THE CORINTHIANS 13.3.[2]

4:15 Countless Guides, Only One Father

DISTINGUISHING THE TRUE FATHER FROM SUBSEQUENT GUIDES. ORIGEN: The father is the one who has sown the seed of the gospel in their souls. The guides are those who have taken the child later on and helped him develop. COMMENTARY ON 1 CORINTHIANS 2.21.9-11.[3]

I BECAME YOUR FATHER. AMBROSIASTER: Paul is telling the Corinthians that nobody else will

---

[1]CSEL 81.49. [2]NPNF 1 12:73. [3]JTS 9:361-62.

ever love them the way he does. Commentary on Paul's Epistles.[4]

The Love of a Father. Chrysostom: Paul is not claiming any dignity here, but rather he is showing the depth of his love. Dignity belongs to the teacher, but love is the mark of the father. Homilies on the Epistles of Paul to the Corinthians 13.4.[5]

4:16 Urgings to Imitate Paul

Be Humble. Origen: Paul is saying to the Corinthians: "Be humble as I am humble, suffer as I suffer. It is by your sufferings, not by your gifts, that you will be rated." Commentary on 1 Corinthians 2.21.12-14.[6]

Imitate Paul. Ambrosiaster: Paul wants them to be imitators of him in these things, so that just as he has endured many hardships from unbelievers for their salvation and is still doing so as long as he preaches the free gift of God's grace day and night, so they too ought to remain in his faith and doctrine and not accept the evil teachings of false apostles. Commentary on Paul's Epistles.[7]

Imitate Christ. Chrysostom: Paul's real aim was that the Corinthians should imitate Christ. But because of their weakness, he presents himself as an intermediate model to follow. It is only because he imitates Christ that he exhorts the people to imitate him. Homilies on the Epistles of Paul to the Corinthians 13.5.[8]

Be Prepared to Suffer. Theodoret of Cyr: By this Paul meant that if he was humble, they should also be humble. What he was prepared to suffer, they should be prepared to suffer. They were to glory in their hardships, not in their blessings. Commentary on the First Epistle to the Corinthians 190.[9]

4:17a Timothy an Emissary

Sending Timothy to Them. Chrysostom: Paul shows how much he loves the Corinthians by sending his dearly beloved child, Timothy, to them, choosing thereby to be separated from him for the Corinthians' sake. Homilies on the Epistles of Paul to the Corinthians 14.1.[10]

4:17b Reminders of Paul's Teachings

My Ways in Christ. Origen: By "ways in Christ" Paul means his embodied good deeds. He tells the Corinthians to remember them, because they are self-evident and do not need to be taught. Commentary on 1 Corinthians 2.21.20-22.[11]

Teaching and Life. Pelagius: Paul's behavior was completely consistent with his teaching. Commentary on the First Epistle to the Corinthians 4.[12]

4:18 Some Are Arrogant

The Corinthians' Pride. Ambrosiaster: Some of the Corinthians were angry that Paul had not come to them, not because they wanted him to but because they were proud and imagined that Paul thought they were unworthy of a visit. In fact, Paul wanted to go but had more important things to do. Commentary on Paul's Epistles.[13]

Some Thought Him Weak. Severian of Gabala: It is clear from this that what was being said was that Paul and his companions were weak, while the Corinthians were strong. Pauline Commentary from the Greek Church.[14]

4:19 Paul Will Visit Corinth

Paul Promises to Come. Ambrosiaster: Paul couches his promise to come in the will of God,

---

[4]CSEL 81.49. [5]NPNF 1 12:74. [6]JTS 9:362. [7]CSEL 81.49-50. [8]NPNF 1 12:74. [9]Migne PG 82:259. [10]NPNF 1 12:78. [11]JTS 9:362. [12]Migne PL 30:729B. [13]CSEL 81.50-51. [14]NTA 15:241.

because God knows more than man. If there was some advantage in Paul's going to Corinth, God would make it known, and if he did not turn up, the Corinthians would know that the Lord had not wanted him to. COMMENTARY ON PAUL'S EPISTLES.[15]

FOR CORRECTION. SEVERIAN OF GABALA: Paul promises to come, so that the Corinthians can prepare themselves for correction. On the one hand he was forced by his irritation to say "I shall come," but on the other hand he added "if the Lord wills," because of his sense of dependence on God. PAULINE COMMENTARY FROM THE GREEK CHURCH.[16]

4:20 Not Talk but Power

THE KINGDOM OF GOD AND POWER. ORIGEN: It is not smooth talk that reveals the presence of the kingdom of God, but power. When there is power in the words, then the kingdom is present in them. COMMENTARY ON 1 CORINTHIANS 2.22.6-8.[17]

NO HIDING BEHIND A WALL OF WORDS. CHRYsostom: "Actions speak louder than words," says Paul. "If those Corinthians who are now arrogant want to prove something, let them show me when I come whether they can do the same miracles I can do. I do not want to find them hiding behind a wall of words, for that sort of thing means nothing to me." HOMILIES ON THE EPISTLES OF PAUL TO THE CORINTHIANS 14.2.[18]

NOT PREACHING BUT BEHAVIOR. THEODORET OF CYR: It is not enough to preach the kingdom of God in order to be saved; one must also behave in a way which is worthy of the kingdom. COMMENTARY ON THE FIRST EPISTLE TO THE CORINTHIANS 191.[19]

NO FALSE SECURITY. CAESARIUS OF ARLES: Let us not deceive ourselves with a false security, believing that a nonresponsive faith lacking good works can deliver us against the day of judgment. SERMONS 209.3.[20]

4:21a What the Corinthians Wish

THE CHOICE. CHRYSOSTOM: Paul leaves it up to the Corinthians to decide how he should come to them. We too have a choice. Either we can fall into hell, or we can obtain the kingdom. But if you say that you are willing to do the right thing but not able, you are mistaken. All that means is that you are not willing strongly enough. HOMILIES ON THE EPISTLES OF PAUL TO THE CORINTHIANS 14.5.[21]

4:21b Severity or a Spirit of Gentleness?

LOVE HIDDEN IN THE ROD. ORIGEN: The rod does not mean that there is no love, but love is hidden behind its blows and is not perceived by the one who is on the receiving end. COMMENTARY ON 1 CORINTHIANS 2.23.6-8.[22]

FIRST THE ROD, THEN GENTLENESS. AMBROSE: Paul mentioned a rod first, that he might afterward comfort them with the spirit of meekness. SYNAGOGUE AT CALLINICUM 41.4.[23]

THE POWER OF THE SPIRIT. SEVERIAN OF GABALA: By "rod" Paul meant the compelling power of the Spirit, which he had used against Elymas and which God had used against him.[24] PAULINE COMMENTARY FROM THE GREEK CHURCH.[25]

---

[15]CSEL 81.51. [16]NTA 15:242. [17]JTS 9:362. [18]NPNF 1 12:79. [19]Migne PG 82:259. [20]FC 66:91. [21]NPNF 1 12:79. [22]JTS 9:363. [23]LCC 5:241. [24]Acts 13:4-12. [25]NTA 15:242.

5:1-8 CHURCH DISCIPLINE

¹*It is actually reported that there is immorality among you, and of a kind that is not found even among pagans; for a man is living with his father's wife.* ²*And you are arrogant! Ought you not rather to mourn? Let him who has done this be removed from among you.*

³*For though absent in body I am present in spirit, and as if present, I have already pronounced judgment* ⁴*in the name of the Lord Jesus on the man who has done such a thing. When you are assembled, and my spirit is present, with the power of our Lord Jesus,* ⁵*you are to deliver this man to Satan for the destruction of the flesh, that his spirit may be saved in the day of the Lord Jesus.*ʰ

⁶*Your boasting is not good. Do you not know that a little leaven leavens the whole lump?* ⁷*Cleanse out the old leaven that you may be a new lump, as you really are unleavened. For Christ, our paschal lamb, has been sacrificed.* ⁸*Let us, therefore, celebrate the festival, not with the old leaven, the leaven of malice and evil, but with the unleavened bread of sincerity and truth.*

h *Other ancient authorities omit* Jesus

OVERVIEW: Some forms of immorality are far more degrading than others (ORIGEN). The particular form of immorality reported at Corinth, a man living with his father's wife, was so intolerable that it was hard even to speak of openly (CHRYSOSTOM). Yet those who look the other way will not be innocent. Deputized in the power of Christ (AMBROSIASTER), Paul urged the man's immediate removal (CHRYSOSTOM). This person should be put out of the church and forced to live in the world, which is ruled by Satan (THEODORE OF MOPSUESTIA, SEVERIAN OF GABALA). The offender, who had already blasphemed of his own free will (JEROME), had better hope thereby for ultimate reconciliation by being cast out promptly than by being treated permissively (THEODORET OF CYR, THEODORE). Yet this should occur without undermining the spirit of cooperation (AMBROSIASTER). They could easily have predicted his judgment in advance (THEODORET OF CYR). Just as a little leaven leavens the whole lump, an evil life corrupts the whole person (AMBROSIASTER, CHRYSOSTOM). Sin will contaminate the whole body if it is uncorrected (AMBROSIASTER). Others have hindered the man from repenting by leaving his sin uncorrected (CHRYSOSTOM). The true teaching of the atonement (against false misrepresentations, the old lump) must come before moral reformation in the Christian community (AMBROSIASTER).

5:1 Immorality Beyond That of Pagans

SOME FORMS OF IMMORALITY ARE MORE DEMEANING. ORIGEN: We learn from this that there are different kinds of immorality, some of which are more serious than others. When God judges it, he will take extenuating factors into account and vary the punishment accordingly. In this case, Paul is teaching us that even when there has been a legal marriage ceremony, if it goes against the law of God, it is immoral and will be condemned accordingly. COMMENTARY ON 1 CORINTHIANS 2.23.15-20.[1]

---

[1]JTS 9:263.

Those Who Look the Other Way Are Not Innocent. Ambrosiaster: This person was clearly deserving of death for his crime,[2] but those who supported him were not innocent either. Commentary on Paul's Epistles.[3]

Too Intolerable to Discuss Publicly. Chrysostom: The extreme foulness of the deed causes Paul to shrink. He hurries over it with a sense of embarrassment, aggravating the charge by implying that even to speak about it was intolerable. Homilies on the Epistles of Paul to the Corinthians 15.2.[4]

5:2 Removing the Offender

Humbling Their Pride. Ambrosiaster: Paul humbles their pride, but in such a way that instead of making them angry he makes them willing to cooperate with him. Commentary on Paul's Epistles.[5]

5:3 Pronouncing Judgment

Paul Pronounces Judgment. Theodoret of Cyr: None would expect anything else, implies Paul, once again showing how important the matter was. Commentary on the First Epistle to the Corinthians 192.[6]

5:4 Judgment in the Lord's Name

Deputized in the Power of Christ. Ambrosiaster: The Corinthians were to eject this man not only by common consent among themselves but also in the power of Christ, whose deputy Paul was. Commentary on Paul's Epistles.[7]

Act Immediately. Chrysostom: Paul does not allow the Corinthians to wait for him to come but passes sentence from afar. He did this so as not to give the Corinthians any leeway for making excuses. They were to act immediately and in the very precise manner described. Homilies on the Epistles of Paul to the Corinthians 15.3.[8]

5:5 Acting to Save the Man's Spirit

The Contamination Infected Others. Ambrosiaster: If this man were not thrown out, the spirit of the church would not be saved on the day of judgment, because the source of the contamination was infecting them all. Commentary on Paul's Epistles.[9]

Deliver the Sinner to Satan. Jerome: Paul has delivered over to Satan those who had already blasphemed of their own free will. Against Rufinus 7.[10]

The Reconciling Intent. Theodore of Mopsuestia: This is not to be taken literally. What Paul means is that the person concerned should be put out of the church and forced to live in the world, which is ruled by Satan. That way he will learn to fear God and escape the greater punishment that is to come. Pauline Commentary from the Greek Church.[11]

Exposure to Life's Hardships. Severian of Gabala: When Paul says that this man must be delivered to Satan, he does not mean that he should be handed over to the power of the evil one. Rather, all the evils of this life, for example, diseases, sorrows, sufferings, and other circumstances, were attributed to Satan, and it is in this sense that Paul uses the term here. What he means is that this man should be exposed to the hardships of life. Pauline Commentary from the Greek Church.[12]

Separation from the Body of Christ. Theodoret of Cyr: We are taught by this that the devil invades those who are separated from the body of the church because he finds them de-

---

[2]According to Mosaic law. [3]CSEL 81.52. [4]NPNF 1 12:83. [5]CSEL 81.52. [6]Migne PG 82:262. [7]CSEL 81.53. [8]NPNF 1 12:84. [9]CSEL 81.54. [10]FC 53:112. [11]NTA 15:178. [12]NTA 15:243.

prived of grace. COMMENTARY ON THE FIRST EPISTLE TO THE CORINTHIANS 193.[13]

5:6 A Little Leaven

UNCORRECTED SIN CONTAMINATES. AMBROSIASTER: Just as the sin of one person contaminates many, if it is not dealt with once it is known, so also does the sin of the many who know what is happening and either do not turn away from it or pretend that they have not noticed it. Sin does not look like sin if it is not corrected or avoided by anybody. COMMENTARY ON PAUL'S EPISTLES.[14]

A PROBLEM FOR THE WHOLE CHURCH. CHRYSOSTOM: Paul says that the Corinthians are to blame, because by taking pride in this man they have hindered him from repenting. Here he indicates that the problem is one for the whole church, not just for an individual. This is why he uses the symbol of the leaven, which, although a small thing in itself, transforms the whole lump into its own nature. This man will do the same thing if he is allowed to go unpunished. HOMILIES ON THE EPISTLES OF PAUL TO THE CORINTHIANS 15.5.[15]

5:7a Cleansing Out the Old Leaven

SIN OF EVERY KIND. CHRYSOSTOM: Paul is not referring to this man only but to others as well. The old leaven is not just fornication but sin of every kind, which must be rooted out if the lump is to be pure. HOMILIES ON THE EPISTLES OF PAUL TO THE CORINTHIANS 15.5.[16]

5:7b Christ, Our Paschal Lamb

THE CROSS OUR PASSOVER PRECEDES MORAL

REFORMATION. AMBROSIASTER: The old leaven has a double meaning here. On the one hand, it refers to false teaching, just as Jesus warned his disciples to beware the leaven of the Pharisees.[17] On the other hand, it also refers to the sin of fornication being dealt with here. Paul teaches that the passover is the sacrifice, and not the exodus, as some people think. The sacrifice comes first, and then it is possible to make the transition from the old life to the new. For this reason it is the cross that is the saving reality signified by the passover in the Old Testament. COMMENTARY ON PAUL'S EPISTLES.[18]

5:8a Celebrating the Festival

THE OLD LEAVEN. CHRYSOSTOM: The old leaven refers among other things to the priests who allow an enormous amount of the old leaven to remain within the church, namely, the covetous, the extortioners and those guilty of doing anything that would keep them out of the kingdom of heaven. HOMILIES ON THE EPISTLES OF PAUL TO THE CORINTHIANS 15.11.[19]

5:8b In Sincerity and Truth

THE UNLEAVENED BREAD OF SINCERITY. AMBROSIASTER: Just as a little leaven leavens the whole lump, an evil life corrupts the whole man. Therefore Paul wants us to avoid not only evil acts but all interest in sin, so that sincerity may cleanse our lives and truth may exclude all deception. COMMENTARY ON PAUL'S EPISTLES.[20]

---

[13]Migne PG 82:262. [14]CSEL 81.55. [15]NPNF 1 12:85. [16]NPNF 1 12:85. [17]Mt 16:6-12; Mk 8:15; Lk 12:1. [18]CSEL 81.55. [19]NPNF 1 12:87. [20]CSEL 81.56-57.

5:9-13 DIFFERENT STANDARDS

[9]*I wrote to you in my letter not to associate with immoral men;* [10]*not at all meaning the immoral of this world, or the greedy and robbers, or idolaters, since then you would need to go out of the world.* [11]*But rather I wrote*[i] *to you not to associate with any one who bears the name of brother if he is guilty of immorality or greed, or is an idolater, reviler, drunkard, or robber—not even to eat with such a one.* [12]*For what have I to do with judging outsiders? Is it not those inside the church whom you are to judge?* [13]*God judges those outside. "Drive out the wicked person from among you."*

i *Or now I write*

OVERVIEW: Since immoral believers corrupt the church more than do unbelievers (ORIGEN), do not mix with them (AMBROSIASTER). They are to be withdrawn from table fellowship (THEODORET OF CYR). Only those who voluntarily decide to enter into the church fellowship are due the discipline that is fitting within the church (CHRYSOSTOM). The most extreme discipline consists in withholding the sacred mysteries of bread and wine from the recalcitrant believer (AMBROSIASTER). The whole people of God gain by being freed from such plagues as fornication, as has been true since the days of Moses (CHRYSOSTOM). Only with this cleansing does Christ again come to dwell in you (ORIGEN). Some argue that "my letter" refers to a previous letter (AMBROSIASTER), while others see it as a reference to this letter (THEODORET OF CYR).

5:9 Paul's Letter

A SECOND LETTER. AMBROSIASTER: Paul tells us here that he has already written to the Corinthians once. Because they failed to take action then, he is now writing a second time. COMMENTARY ON PAUL'S EPISTLES.[1]

WHICH LETTER? THEODORET OF CYR: Paul is not referring to another letter but to this one, for he has just said that a little leaven leavens the whole lump. COMMENTARY ON THE FIRST EPISTLE TO THE CORINTHIANS 193.[2]

5:10 Immoral Believers

IMMORAL BELIEVERS HARM THE CHURCH MORE THAN DO UNBELIEVERS. ORIGEN: Immoral unbelievers cannot harm the church, but immoral believers corrupt it from within, which is why they must be avoided and expelled. COMMENTARY ON 1 CORINTHIANS 2.26.23-26.[3]

DO NOT MIX. AMBROSIASTER: Paul means that it would be better to die than to mix with fellow believers who sin like the fornicator in question, because death would put an end to it sooner rather than later. COMMENTARY ON PAUL'S EPISTLES.[4]

5:11 Not Associating with Immoral Believers

WITHDRAWAL OF FELLOWSHIP NOT APPLICABLE TO UNBELIEVERS. AMBROSIASTER: Note that none of this applies to relations with unbelievers. COMMENTARY ON PAUL'S EPISTLES.[5]

---

[1]CSEL 81.57. [2]Migne PG 82:263. [3]JTS 9:366. [4]CSEL 81.57. [5]CSEL 81.58. Rather we speak of discipline *within* the community of faith.

No Table Fellowship. THEODORET OF CYR: Obviously if we are not to eat ordinary food with such people, we are not to admit them to the Lord's table either. COMMENTARY ON THE FIRST EPISTLE TO THE CORINTHIANS 194.[6]

5:12 Judging Fellow Believers

Barring from Sacraments. AMBROSIASTER: A bishop cannot do anything about unbelievers. But a brother who is caught doing such things he can bar not only from the sacraments but also from common intercourse with his fellows, so that when he is avoided he may feel ashamed and repent. COMMENTARY ON PAUL'S EPISTLES.[7]

Discipline Applicable Inside the Church. CHRYSOSTOM: Did Paul not care about those who were outside the church? Of course he did! But it was not until after they had received the gospel and he had made them subject to the teaching of Christ that he laid down requirements for them. As long as they despised Christ, it was pointless to speak to them about his commandments. HOMILIES ON THE EPISTLES OF PAUL TO THE CORINTHIANS 16.2.[8]

5:13 God Judges Unbelievers

Expel the Impenitent. ORIGEN: Do all you can to expel the wicked person, for once he is gone, Christ will dwell in you. COMMENTARY ON 1 CORINTHIANS 2.26.57-59.[9]

The Law Speaks with Severity. CHRYSOSTOM: Paul uses an expression taken from the Old Testament,[10] partly because he is hinting that the Corinthians will be great gainers in being freed from a kind of plague and partly to show that this kind of thing is no novelty but goes right back to the beginning. Even Moses the lawgiver thought that people like this should be cut off, but he did it with greater severity than is shown here. Moses would have had the man stoned, but Paul thinks only of trying to lead him to repentance. HOMILIES ON THE EPISTLES OF PAUL TO THE CORINTHIANS 16.3.[11]

---

[6]Migne PG 82:263. [7]CSEL 81.58. [8]NPNF 1 12:90. [9]JTS 9:367. [10]Deut 17:7; 19:19; 22:21; 24:7. [11]NPNF 1 12:90.

6:1-8 RESOLVING DIFFERENCES INSIDE THE CHURCH

[1]*When one of you has a grievance against a brother, does he dare go to law before the unrighteous instead of the saints?* [2]*Do you not know that the saints will judge the world? And if the world is to be judged by you, are you incompetent to try trivial cases?* [3]*Do you not know that we are to judge angels? How much more, matters pertaining to this life!* [4]*If then you have such cases, why do you lay them before those who are least esteemed by the church?* [5]*I say this to your shame. Can it be that there is no man among you wise enough to decide between members of the brotherhood,* [6]*but brother goes to law against brother, and that before unbelievers?*

[7]*To have lawsuits at all with one another is defeat for you. Why not rather suffer wrong?*

Why not rather be defrauded? [8]*But you yourselves wrong and defraud, and that even your own brethren.*

Overview: It is doubly wrong to take believers to court to be judged by unbelievers (Origen, Ambrosiaster, Chrysostom, Pelagius). Bringing suit may cause scandal to those outside the church (Theodore of Mopsuestia) and multiply guilt (Ambrosiaster, Chrysostom). Submit rather to arbitration (Chrysostom) within the community of faith (Ambrosiaster). It is a disgrace for Christians to be judged by outsiders over trivial matters (Chrysostom). Yet this was a common practice among the Corinthians (Theodoret of Cyr). The saints are destined finally to judge the world (Ambrosiaster), as the twelve apostles will judge the twelve tribes of Israel (Severian of Gabala). It remains in dispute as to whether the angels to be judged are false teachers (Severian), demons (Chrysostom, Theodoret of Cyr) or angels (Ambrosiaster). Few are wise enough to judge (Origen), but believers will be given such wisdom (Ambrosiaster). Even those least esteemed in the church will turn out to judge better than those who lack understanding and discernment in the Christian sense (Chrysostom, Severian). This passage is not opposed to the obedience to authorities commended in Romans 13 (Theodoret of Cyr).

6:1 Bringing Lawsuits Before the Unrighteous

Going to Law. Ambrosiaster: The Corinthians were wrong in two ways. First, they were unfaithful, and second, they were expounding God's laws with a show of respect but in reality attributing their authority to idols. Commentary on Paul's Epistles.[1]

Submitting to Unbelievers. Chrysostom: Paul says that Christians should not submit their disputes to outside arbitration. For how can it be anything other than absurd for a man who disagrees with his friend to choose their mutual enemy as their reconciler? How can you avoid feeling shame when a pagan sits in judgment on a Christian? And if it is not right to go to law before pagans about private matters, how can we submit other things of greater importance to them for a decision? Note too how Paul speaks. He calls the pagans not "unbelievers" but "unrighteous," and the Christians he calls "saints," using the appropriate description in order to deter them from getting involved with the secular courts. Homilies on the Epistles of Paul to the Corinthians 16.4.[2]

No Christian Judges at the Time. Pelagius: This proves that there were no Christian judges at that time, because Paul refers to them all as "unrighteous." Commentary on the First Epistle to the Corinthians 6.[3]

Avoid Scandal. Theodore of Mopsuestia: Paul did not want them to be judged by outsiders because he did not want the shortcomings of those who had been taught propriety and righteousness to become a scandal to those outside the church. Pauline Commentary from the Greek Church.[4]

6:2 Judging the World

Unbelief Will Be Finally Judged. Ambrosiaster: The saints will judge this world because the unbelief of the world will be condemned by the example of their faith. Commentary on Paul's Epistles.[5]

---

[1]CSEL 81.59. [2]NPNF 1 12:91. [3]Migne PL 30:731C. [4]NTA 15:179. [5]CSEL 81.59.

View Trivial Matters in the Perspective of the Last Day. Chrysostom: It is a disgrace for Christians to be judged by outsiders over trivial matters, when we shall judge them in far more important things. Homilies on the Epistles of Paul to the Corinthians 16.5.[6]

Who Will Judge? Severian of Gabala: The twelve apostles will judge the twelve tribes of Israel, if they have not believed and for that reason rejected Christ. The other saints, that is to say, the Gentiles, will judge those who have not abandoned idols and believed in the true God. Pauline Commentary from the Greek Church.[7]

6:3 Judging Angels

Believers Are to Judge Angels. Ambrosiaster: Angels are to be judged by us in the same way as the world is to be judged. Commentary on Paul's Epistles.[8]

Whether Demons Will Be Judged. Chrysostom: Some people say that Paul was thinking of corrupt priests when he said this, but that cannot be right. He is really talking about the demons. Homilies on the Epistles of Paul to the Corinthians 16.5.[9]

False Teachers to Be Judged. Severian of Gabala: Paul is not talking here about real angels but about the priests and teachers of the people who will be judged by the saints because of their false teaching about Christ. Pauline Commentary from the Greek Church.[10]

Are These Demons Who Were Once Angels? Theodoret of Cyr: By "angels" here, Paul means demons who once were angels. Commentary on the First Epistle to the Corinthians 195.[11]

Participating with Christ in Judgment. Cassiodorus: Who can conceive of such a miracle?

Who can mentally grasp such great glory? . . . All participate with Christ in judgment who do not oppose his commands, for with the devoted they too will share in his decisions. Explanation of the Psalms.[12]

6:4 Judging Trivial Cases

Even the Lowliest Believer. Severian of Gabala: The lowest person in the church is preferable in judgment to an unbeliever. Pauline Commentary from the Greek Church.[13]

Those Least Esteemed. Augustine: Therefore the apostle wished wise, holy, and faithful persons who were well established in the various places to be judges of such matters, and not persons who, in preaching, traveled about here and there. . . . If wise judges were lacking, he wished even the lowly and contemptible to be appointed so that the affairs of Christians might not be brought to the public eye. The Work of Monks 29.[14]

6:5 Judging Among Believers

Shame That There Are So Few Wise. Origen: Paul attacks the Corinthians because, although they are right in the middle of Greece, they have no truly wise people in their midst, even though many had gone to preach wisdom to them. Commentary on 1 Corinthians 2.27.20-22.[15]

Some Believers Are Wise Enough. Ambrosiaster: Paul meant that they were so unmanageable and thoughtless that they might choose inexperienced brothers as judges. There must, he said, be some people in the church wise enough to judge such cases, and they should be allowed

---

[6]NPNF 1 12:91. [7]NTA 15:245. [8]CSEL 81.60. [9]NPNF 1 12:91. [10]NTA 15:246. [11]Migne PG 82:266. [12]ACW 53:460-61. [13]NTA 15:246. [14]FC 16:386. [15]JTS 9:368.

to do so. He said this, incidentally, because at that time there was no official leader in their church. Commentary on Paul's Epistles.[16]

6:6 Going to Law Before Unbelievers

Settling Disputes Among Christians. Origen: We have rulers of the church to whom we should take our disputes, so that we will not be summoned before the law courts of unbelievers. Commentary on 1 Corinthians 2.27.27-28.[17]

Taking Believers to the Courts of Unbelievers Doubly Wrong. Pelagius: There is a double sin here. First, they were taking each other to court, and secondly, they were going to court before unbelievers. Commentary on the First Epistle to the Corinthians 6.[18]

The Need for Understanding and Discernment. Chrysostom: When brothers go to law against each other, there is no need for a mediator to show understanding and discernment. Brotherly feeling and relationship contribute greatly toward the settlement of such quarrels. To take such a quarrel before unbelievers merely makes everything that much worse and prevents a happy resolution of the problem. Homilies on the Epistles of Paul to the Corinthians 16.6.[19]

Implies No Disrespect for Civil Authorities. Theodoret of Cyr: This in no way contradicts Romans [13], where Paul tells people to respect the magistrates. He is not telling us to resist secular authorities, but rather we should not appeal to them. Commentary on the First Epistle to the Corinthians 195.[20]

6:7 Suffering Wrong

Bring the Case to the Church. Ambrosiaster: A Christian ought not to engage in litigation at all, but if the matter is too serious to be disregarded he should bring the case to the

church, so as not to incur an immediate penalty and personal downfall. Commentary on Paul's Epistles.[21]

Preventing Evil Consequences. Basil: In this manner we shall save our adversary also, even against his will, from evil consequences, and we ourselves will not violate the commandment of God, being as his ministers neither contentious nor avaricious, steadily intent upon the manifestation of truth and never overstepping the appointed limits of zeal. The Long Rules 9.[22]

Handling Conflict with Restraint. Chrysostom: The just man handles everything with restraint, demonstrating the remarkable degree of his own good sense and teaching not only those present at the time but also everyone in the future never to settle our differences with our relatives by feuding. Homily 33.8.[23]

What Were They Doing? Theodoret of Cyr: By saying all this Paul is showing that the Corinthians were doing the exact opposite. Commentary on the First Epistle to the Corinthians 196.[24]

6:8 Wronging Each Other

Defrauding Brothers. Ambrosiaster: Paul is rebuking the people whose wrongful behavior has started the quarrels. Not only are they liable to be charged for the fraud which they have committed; they also share in the fault of those who, compelled by their injurious or fraudulent actions, call upon unbelievers to pass judgment. Commentary on Paul's Epistles.[25]

Multiplying Guilt. Chrysostom: Here there may be as many as four crimes involved. The first is not knowing how to bear being wronged.

---

[16]CSEL 81.61. [17]JTS 9:368. [18]Migne PL 30:732A. [19]NPNF 1 12:92. [20]Migne PG 82:266. [21]CSEL 81.62. [22]FC 9:259. [23]FC 82:281. [24]Migne PG 82:266. [25]CSEL 81.62.

The second is to do wrong. The third is to reserve settlement of the matter to the unrighteous. And the fourth is that this kind of thing is being done to a fellow believer.

Homilies on the Epistles of Paul to the Corinthians 16.7.[26]

[26]NPNF 1 12:92.

6:9-11 WHAT MAKES CHRISTIANS DIFFERENT

[9]Do you not know that the unrighteous will not inherit the kingdom of God? Do not be deceived; neither the immoral, nor idolaters, nor adulterers, nor sexual perverts, [10]nor thieves, nor the greedy, nor drunkards, nor revilers, nor robbers will inherit the kingdom of God. [11]And such were some of you. But you were washed, you were sanctified, you were justified in the name of the Lord Jesus Christ and in the Spirit of our God.

Overview: Paul was not teaching the Corinthians something they did not already know (Ambrosiaster). Rather he was readying them for the righteousness that pervades the kingdom of God (Ignatius of Antioch, Ambrosiaster). Sex belongs within marriage (Origen). Adultery corrupts whole families (Ignatius). These sins are committed voluntarily, and hence they are harder to excuse (Ambrosiaster). Paul is not here giving a short list of particular sins but calling all to repentance (Chrysostom). One who is found unworthy to reign with Christ will perish with the devil (Caesarius of Arles). In faithful baptism the believer is washed clean from all sins, made righteous in the name of the Lord, and through the Spirit adopted as God's child (Ambrosiaster). After baptism one must avoid continuing sin (Pelagius). After baptism there is not a loss of concupiscence but a new reception of grace that does not obey its desires (Augustine), out of which come countless blessings (Chrysostom).

6:9 The Unrighteous Will Not Inherit the Kingdom

Adultery Corrupts Whole Families. Ignatius of Antioch: Do not be deceived, my brothers. Corrupters of houses will not inherit the kingdom of God. Epistle to the Ephesians 16.[1]

Sex Belongs Within Marriage. Origen: Let no one say: "I was young. Before I got married, I slept with prostitutes." Why did you not get married instead? Commentary on 1 Corinthians 2.27.48-49.[2]

Harder to Excuse Knowing Sin. Ambrosiaster: Paul indicates that they are not sinning unknowingly, and so it is that much harder to excuse them. Commentary on Paul's Epistles.[3]

6:10 Immorality Has No Part in the Kingdom

No Home for Immorality in the Kingdom. Origen: The kingdom of God must be purified of all sin and immorality, so that God may reign

[1]AF 67. [2]JTS 9:369. [3]CSEL 81.63.

in it. Commentary on 1 Corinthians 2.27.67-69.[4]

Readiness for the Kingdom. Ambrosiaster: Paul did not say this because the Corinthians did not know it already. He was rather reawakening their reverence for the divine commandment and bringing them closer to readiness for the kingdom of heaven. Commentary on Paul's Epistles.[5]

Convicting All. Chrysostom: Paul does not confine his accusations to a short list of types of sin but condemns all equally. He is not so much getting at particular sins as making a general admonition that will secretly convict anyone who may have such things on his conscience. Homilies on the Epistles of Paul to the Corinthians 16.8.[6]

Only Two Places to Go Eternally. Caesarius of Arles: If someone says that he does not want the kingdom of God, only eternal rest, he should not deceive himself. For there are only two places, and not a third. If a person does not deserve to reign with Christ, then he will most assuredly perish with the devil. Sermons 47.5.[7]

6:11 Washed, Sanctified, Justified

Washed from All Sin. Ambrosiaster: The Corinthians had received all the benefits of purity in their baptism, which is the foundation of the truth of the gospel. In baptism the believer is washed clean from all sins and is made righteous in the name of the Lord, and through the Spirit of God he is adopted as God's child. With these words, Paul is reminding them how great and how special is the grace which they

have received in the true tradition. But afterward, by thinking which is contrary to this baptismal rule of faith, they had stripped themselves of these benefits. For this reason he is trying to bring them back to their original way of thinking, so that they can recover what they had once received. Commentary on Paul's Epistles.[8]

Avoid Sin After Baptism. Pelagius: The Corinthians were not to bother about the sins they committed before baptism. All that should concern them now was that they should not sin again in the future. Commentary on the First Epistle to the Corinthians 6.[9]

Countless Blessings. Chrysostom: Paul says this to make the Corinthians feel ashamed of themselves. He asks them to think about the great evils from which God had delivered them. But God did not limit his salvation to mere deliverance. He greatly extended the benefit by making them clean, by going on to make them holy and finally by making them righteous in his sight. Even bare deliverance from our sins would have been a great gift, but God has gone on from that to fill us with countless blessings. Homilies on the Epistles of Paul to the Corinthians 16.9.[10]

Changed for the Better. Augustine: Paul says that they have been changed for the better, not so as to lose concupiscence altogether, a condition never realized in this life, but so as to not obey the desire to sin. Against Julian 16.49.[11]

---

[4]JTS 9:369. [5]CSEL 81.63. [6]NPNF 1 12:93. [7]FC 31:242. [8]CSEL 81.63-64. [9]Migne PL 30:732C. [10]NPNF 1 12:93. [11]FC 35:357.

6:12-20 RIGHT AND WRONG

[12]"All things are lawful for me," but not all things are helpful. "All things are lawful for me," but I will not be enslaved by anything. [13]"Food is meant for the stomach and the stomach for food"—and God will destroy both one and the other. The body is not meant for immorality, but for the Lord, and the Lord for the body. [14]And God raised the Lord and will also raise us up by his power. [15]Do you not know that your bodies are members of Christ? Shall I therefore take the members of Christ and make them members of a prostitute? Never! [16]Do you not know that he who joins himself to a prostitute becomes one body with her? For, as it is written, "The two shall become one flesh." [17]But he who is united to the Lord becomes one spirit with him. [18]Shun immorality. Every other sin which a man commits is outside the body; but the immoral man sins against his own body. [19]Do you not know that your body is a temple of the Holy Spirit within you, which you have from God? You are not your own; [20]you were bought with a price. So glorify God in your body.

Overview: "All things are lawful" does not imply a new slavery to desires (Chrysostom), lack of self-discipline (Clement of Alexandria) or pretending that no choices are wrong (Theodoret of Cyr). Nor does it mean anything that might go against natural law (Ambrosiaster). The rational soul is given to rule the body and draw it toward its true spiritual ends (Ambrosiaster). Having become members of the body that has Christ as its head, we must not defile the body or use it for purposes for which it was not created (Chrysostom). God finally brings to nothing what is intended primarily for the stomach (Clement of Alexandria). To worship food is to substitute one's belly for God (Novatian). If one belongs to Christ, one ought to know better than to indulge in sexual sins (Chrysostom). Treat the body as if it is risen with Christ's body (Chrysostom, Oecumenius). In joining oneself to a prostitute, one becomes one body with her (Ambrosiaster). One thereby sins both against his own body and against his wife, because the two are one flesh (Oecumenius).

As the soul of Jesus clung to God and became one spirit with him, so does the soul of faith cling to light and truth (Origen). To be united to the Lord is to become one spirit with him (Ambrosiaster). Christians understand that the body is a temple, not a prison (Tertullian). Bring nothing defiled into this temple (Novatian, Severian of Gabala). Keep your body uncontaminated (Ambrosiaster). The fornicator not only defiles his entire body, sinning against his own body and against his soul (Ambrosiaster), but also compounds the sins of others (Pelagius). We who have been bought with so great a price (Ambrosiaster, Chrysostom) must be aware of the deviousness of temptation (Theodoret of Cyr).

6:12 Not Enslaved by Anything

Premised on Self-Discipline. Clement of Alexandria: All things are lawful, but that is obviously premised upon self-discipline. Stromata 3.40.5.[1]

Qualifying "All Things." Ambrosiaster: By

---

[1]FC 85:280.

"all things" Paul presumably means those things which are contained in the natural law and which were also lawful for his fellow apostles. It would not refer to the law of Moses, because Moses forbade many things owing to the hardness of heart of an unbelieving and stiff-necked people. Commentary on Paul's Epistles.[2]

Avoid Slavery to Desires. Chrysostom: Paul means that if we are free to choose, then we should remain free and not become a slave to any particular desire. Anyone who orders his desires properly remains the master of them, but once he goes beyond this limit he loses control and becomes their slave. Homilies on the Epistles of Paul to the Corinthians 16.1.1.[3]

Some Choices Are Flatly Wrong. Theodoret of Cyr: Now that we are no longer under the law, we have the freedom to make choices, but we need to realize that some choices are right and others wrong. Commentary on the First Epistle to the Corinthians 19.7.[4]

6:13 The Body Is Meant for the Lord

Foods Will Come to Nothing. Clement of Alexandria: We must restrain the belly and keep it under the control of heaven. God will finally bring to nothing all that is made for the belly, as the apostle says. Christ the Educator 2.5.[5]

Pretending the Belly Is God. Novatian: One who worships God through food is almost like one who has God for his belly. Jewish Foods 5.9.[6]

Ruling the Body. Ambrosiaster: The body, being dedicated to God, will be rewarded with a spiritual reward for the merit of its ruler, which is the rational soul. Commentary on Paul's Epistles.[7]

Not an Attack on the Body. Chrysostom: Paul is not attacking the nature of the body but the unbridled license of the mind, which abuses the body. The body was not made for the purpose of fornication, nor was it created for gluttony. It was meant to have Christ as its head, so that it might follow him. We should be overcome with shame and horror-struck if we defile ourselves with such great evils, once we have been accounted worthy of the great honor of being members of him who sits on high. Homilies on the Epistles of Paul to the Corinthians 17.1.[8]

6:14 Raised by God's Power

Christ's Risen Body and Our Bodies. Chrysostom: If our body is a member of Christ and Christ has risen from the dead, our body will surely follow his lead. Homilies on the Epistles of Paul to the Corinthians 16.2.[9]

He Will Also Raise Us. Oecumenius: Paul did not write this because of Christ's resurrection, which had already taken place, but because of ours, so that we might believe and silence our opponents. Pauline Commentary from the Greek Church.[10]

6:15 Members of Christ

Do Not Demean Your Body. Chrysostom: Paul seeks to shame the fornicator by saying that if he really belongs to Christ he ought to know better than to indulge in such demeaning behavior. He speaks in graphic terms about the prostitute in order to startle his hearers and fill them with alarm. Nothing could be better suited to strike them with horror than this expression. Homilies on the Epistles of Paul to the Corinthians 17.1.[11]

Rise with Him. Theodore of Mopsuestia: You

---

[2]CSEL 81.64. [3]NPNF 1 12:96. [4]Migne PG 82:267. [5]FC 23:96*. [6]FC 67:152*. [7]CSEL 81.65. [8]NPNF 1 12:97. [9]NPNF 1 12:97. [10]NTA 15:434. [11]NPNF 1 12:100-101.

are all members of Christ because you have been united to him by being born again of the Spirit. You have the hope that you will rise again, just as he rose. PAULINE COMMENTARY FROM THE GREEK CHURCH.[12]

FORNICATION ROOTED IN THE FLESH. OECUMENIUS: Other sins like anger and greed come from the soul, but fornication has its roots in the flesh. Paul makes special mention of it here because it was the problem which he had to deal with at the time. Fornication is not self-evidently the worst sin of all. PAULINE COMMENTARY FROM THE GREEK CHURCH.[13]

6:16 Becoming One Flesh

UNITED WITH A PROSTITUTE. AMBROSIASTER: Paul says this because the person who involves himself in contamination is united with the person with whom he involves himself. Sexual immorality makes them both one,[14] in nature as well as in sin. COMMENTARY ON PAUL'S EPISTLES.[15]

THE TWO ARE ONE FLESH. OECUMENIUS: A man guilty of fornication and the impurity which comes from it insults his marriage and his wife. He sins against his own body and consequently against his wife, because the two are one flesh. PAULINE COMMENTARY FROM THE GREEK CHURCH.[16]

6:17 United to the Lord

ONE SPIRIT WITH HIM. ORIGEN: The soul of Jesus clung to God from the beginning of the creation in a union inseparable and indissoluble, as the soul of the wisdom and word of God, and of the truth and the true light. Receiving him wholly and itself entering into his light and splendor, it was made one spirit with him in a preeminent degree. This is what the apostle promises to those who imitate Jesus. ON FIRST PRINCIPLES 2.9.3.[17]

THE SPIRIT SHARED. AMBROSIASTER: The Spirit of God is shared between God and human beings when we are united to the Lord. COMMENTARY ON PAUL'S EPISTLES.[18]

6:18 Shun Immorality

SHUN VILE SERVITUDE. AMBROSE: Only by a swift flight can we shun the savagery of such a rabid mistress and escape from such vile servitude. CAIN AND ABEL 1.20.[19]

SINNING AGAINST BODY AND SOUL. AMBROSIASTER: If someone hangs himself or kills himself with a dagger, he does not sin against his body but against his soul, on which he inflicts violence. But to fornicate is a sin of the body which touches both the body and the soul. COMMENTARY ON PAUL'S EPISTLES.[20]

COMPOUNDING OTHERS' SINS. PELAGIUS: Fornication multiplies sins because two people are involved, and both perish together. COMMENTARY ON THE FIRST EPISTLE TO THE CORINTHIANS 6.[21]

THE ENTIRE BODY DEFILED. CHRYSOSTOM: What Paul says here obviously applies to the murderer, the covetous person and the extortioner equally well. But as it was not possible to mention anything worse than fornication, Paul magnifies the crime by saying that in the fornicator the entire body is defiled. It is a sin against one's own self in a way that the others are not. HOMILIES ON THE EPISTLES OF PAUL TO THE CORINTHIANS 18.2.[22]

BE AWARE OF THE PERNICIOUSNESS OF EVIL. THEODORET OF CYR: Note that Paul did not say that we should hate immorality, but that we should shun it as people who are aware of the perniciousness of evil. COMMENTARY ON THE

---

[12]NTA 15:181. [13]NTA 15:434. [14]Gen 2:24. [15]CSEL 81.67. [16]NTA 15:234-35. [17]OFP 110. [18]CSEL 81.67. [19]FC 42:379*. [20]CSEL 81.67-68. [21]Migne PL 30:733D. [22]NPNF 1 12:101.

First Epistle to the Corinthians 198.[23]

6:19 A Temple of the Holy Spirit

A Temple and an Altar. Anonymous Syriac Author: The body and heart in which our Lord dwells—also because the Spirit resides there—is in truth a temple and an altar, seeing that our Lord resides there. Book of Steps 12.2.[24]

The Body Not a Prison but a Temple. Tertullian: In the Platonic view, the body is a prison; in that of Paul, it is the temple of God because it is in Christ. On the Soul 54.5.[25]

You Are Not Your Own. Ambrosiaster: Paul said this with the intention that we should keep our bodies uncontaminated, so that the Holy Spirit may dwell in them. Commentary on Paul's Epistles.[26]

Corrupting the Temple. Severian of Gabala: The fornicator is also guilty of impiety, for by doing harm to his body he has corrupted the temple of the Holy Spirit. Pauline Commentary from the Greek Church.[27]

6:20 Glorify God in the Body

Bring Nothing Defiled into the Temple. Cyprian: Let us glorify God and bear him in a pure and spotless body and with more perfect observance. Let those who have been redeemed by the blood of Christ submit to the rule of our redeemer with the absolute obedience of servants. Let us take care not to bring anything unclean or defiled into the temple of God, lest he be offended and leave the abode where he dwells. The Dress of Virgins 2.[28]

Bought with a Price. Ambrosiaster: Someone who has been bought does not have the power to make decisions, but the person who bought him does. And because we were bought for a very high price, we ought to serve our master all the more, so that the offense from which he has bought our release may not turn us back over to death. Commentary on Paul's Epistles.[29]

We Are Not Our Own. Chrysostom: What is Paul trying to prove when he says that we are not our own? He wants to secure us against sin and against following the improper desires of the mind. We have many improper desires, but we must constrain them, and we can do so. If we could not, there would be no point in exhorting us like this. Paul does not say that we are under compulsion but that we have been bought—and bought with a great price, reminding us of the way in which our salvation was obtained. Homilies on the Epistles of Paul to the Corinthians 18.3.[30]

---

[23]Migne PG 82:270. [24]SFPSL 48. [25]FC 10:296*. [26]CSEL 81.69. [27]NTA 15:248. [28]FC 36:32-33. [29]CSEL 81.69-70. [30]NPNF 1 12:101.

7:1-7 MAN AND WOMAN

[1]Now concerning the matters about which you wrote. It is well for a man not to touch a woman. [2]But because of the temptation to immorality, each man should have his own wife and each woman her own husband. [3]The husband should give to his wife her conjugal

rights, and likewise the wife to her husband. [4]For the wife does not rule over her own body, but the husband does; likewise the husband does not rule over his own body, but the wife does. [5]Do not refuse one another except perhaps by agreement for a season, that you may devote yourselves to prayer; but then come together again, lest Satan tempt you through lack of self-control. [6]I say this by way of concession, not of command. [7]I wish that all were as I myself am. But each has his own special gift from God, one of one kind and one of another.

OVERVIEW: Marriage partners are called to submit to one another sexually (AMBROSIASTER). The wife rules over the husband's body, as the husband rules over the wife's body (ORIGEN). When a spouse denies the partner the marriage bed, anger, adulteries, fornications and the destruction of families are more likely to follow (CHRYSOSTOM, THEODORET OF CYR). Although devotion of marriage partners may be rekindled by occasional abstinence (AUGUSTINE), withholding sexual gratification for too long may tend toward the hazards of adultery (THEODORET OF CYR, AUGUSTINE). Marriage is a mystery to be approached with holiness (ORIGEN). The marriage of believers is a special spiritual gift (ORIGEN, THEODORET OF CYR). Paul allowed marriage (AMBROSIASTER), forbade fornication and praised chastity (THEODORET OF CYR, SEVERIAN OF GABALA). Paul's advice on marriage leaves room for personal choice (AMBROSIASTER), yet with a strong interest in avoiding fornication (AMBROSIASTER). Virginity is encouraged (CHRYSOSTOM), but in the desire for purity, one must not destroy one's spouse's happiness (ORIGEN). The command to have sex is not absolute (PELAGIUS). Do not imagine that the law of chastity applies less to men than women (THEODORET OF CYR, CHRYSOSTOM).

7:1 Questions About Marriage

WHETHER MARRIAGE SHOULD BE REJECTED. AMBROSIASTER: Stirred up by the depraved minds of the false apostles, who in their hypocrisy were teaching that marriage ought to be rejected in order that they might appear to be holier than others, the Corinthians wrote to Paul to ask him about these things. Because they were unhappy about this teaching, they ignored everything else and concentrated exclusively on this. COMMENTARY ON PAUL'S EPISTLES.[1]

PAUL'S REPLY. SEVERIAN OF GABALA: This is Paul's reply to those who had written to him about this subject. He forbade fornication because it was against the law, but he allowed marriage as being holy and an antidote to fornication. However, he praised chastity as more perfect still. PAULINE COMMENTARY FROM THE GREEK CHURCH.[2]

THEODORET OF CYR: The Corinthians were asking Paul whether it was right for lawfully married Christians, once they were baptized, to enjoy sexual relations with each other. Paul answered by praising chastity, condemning fornication and allowing conjugal relations. COMMENTARY ON THE FIRST EPISTLE TO THE CORINTHIANS 200.[3]

7:2 Honoring One's Spouse

DO NOT DESTROY YOUR SPOUSE'S HAPPINESS IN YOUR QUEST FOR HOLINESS. ORIGEN: You have given up your wife, to whom you are bound. This is a big step you have taken. You are not

---

[1]CSEL 81.70. [2]NTA 15:249. [3]Migne PG 82:271.

abusing her, you say, but claiming that you can be chaste and live more purely. But look how your poor wife is being destroyed as a result, because she is unable to endure your purity! You should sleep with your wife, not for your sake but for hers. Commentary on 1 Corinthians 3.33.23-25.[4]

The Command to Have Sex Is Not Absolute. Pelagius: People who want to be promiscuous argue that God commanded us to have sexual relations, so that the earth would be filled with human beings. But God is quite capable of making humans out of the earth, as he did at the beginning, so this is no excuse. Commentary on the First Epistle to the Corinthians 7.[5]

Encouraging Virginity. Chrysostom: Some people think that this was written primarily for priests, but judging from what follows, this cannot be right. If he had meant it only for priests, he would have said so, but throughout this [chapter] he speaks of persons in general. Paul permits marriage as a concession, but the very fact that it is designed to avoid fornication shows that he is really trying to encourage virginity. Homilies on the Epistles of Paul to the Corinthians 19.1[6]

7:3 Mutual Conjugal Rights

Husbands and Wives Submit to One Another Sexually. Ambrosiaster: Husband and wife must submit to one another in this matter, since the two of them are one flesh and one will, according to the law of nature. Commentary on Paul's Epistles.[7]

Husbands and Wives Called Equally to Sexual Accountability. Theodoret of Cyr: Human laws demand that women be chaste and if they are not they are punished for it, but they do not demand the same from men. Since it was men who made the laws, they did not make themselves equal with woman but allowed

themselves extra indulgence. The holy apostle, however, inspired by divine grace, was the first one who made the law of chastity apply to men as well. Commentary on the First Epistle to the Corinthians 201.[8]

7:4 Ruling Over Each Other's Body

The Wife Does Not Rule Over Her Own Body, Nor the Husband His. Origen: If this is so, a man should be able to refrain from exercising his authority [to receive his spouse's body]. And isn't a woman capable of doing likewise? Commentary on 1 Corinthians 3.33.41-46.[9]

Equality in Chastity. Chrysostom: The wife does not have power over her own body but is both the servant and the mistress of the husband. If you reject this, you have offended God. But if you want to withdraw yourself sexually, it should only be with your husband's permission, and then only for a short time. In other parts of Scripture the husband is given certain prerogatives in marriage, but not here. Where chastity is concerned, husband and wife have equal rights. Homilies on the Epistles of Paul to the Corinthians 19.1.[10]

7:5 Not Refusing One Another

The Holy Mystery of Marriage. Origen: The mysteries of marriage ought to be performed with holiness, deliberately and without disorderly passions. On Prayer 2.2.[11]

The Hazard of Refusing the Marriage Bed. Chrysostom: Great evils spring from this sort of continence, if it is overdone. Adulteries, fornications and the destruction of families have

---

[4]JTS 9:500-501. [5]Migne PL 30:734C-D. [6]NPNF 1 12:105. [7]CSEL 81.71. [8]Migne PG 82:271. This selection shows that among the ancient Christian writers there existed an awareness of the social location of men effecting legislative bias, which Christian ethics seeks to correct. [9]JTS 9:501. [10]NPNF 1 12:105. [11]CWS 83.

often resulted from this. If a married man commits fornication, how much more will he do so if his wife denies herself to him? Unless there is mutual consent, continence in this case is really a form of theft. HOMILIES ON THE EPISTLES OF PAUL TO THE CORINTHIANS 19.3.[12]

DO NOT REFUSE ONE ANOTHER. AUGUSTINE: According to this, if he had wished to practice continence but you had not, he would have been obliged to give in to you, and God would have given him credit for continence for not refusing intercourse out of consideration for your weakness, not his own, in order to prevent you from committing adultery. How much better would it have been for you, for whom subjection was more appropriate, to yield to his will in rendering him the debt, since God would have taken account of your intention to observe continence, which you gave up in order to save your husband from destruction. LETTER 262 TO EUDICIA.[13]

DEVOTION REKINDLED BY OCCASIONAL ABSTINENCE. AUGUSTINE: It is not arduous and difficult for faithful married people to do for a few days what holy widows have undertaken and which holy virgins do throughout their lives. So let devotion be kindled and self-gratification be checked. LENT 209.3.[14]

WITHHOLDING MAY ELICIT ANGER. THEODORET OF CYR: If a woman stays away from her husband, she will make him angry, and vice versa. That is why Paul insists that it must be by mutual consent. COMMENTARY ON THE FIRST EPISTLE TO THE CORINTHIANS 201.[15]

7:6 Concession, Not Command

A PERSONAL CHOICE. AMBROSIASTER: No one should be forced to do something unlawful on the ground that he is forbidden to do what is lawful. It is up to each person to discern which path to follow. COMMENTARY ON PAUL'S EPISTLES.[16]

7:7 Each Has a Special Gift from God

MARRIAGE AMONG BELIEVERS. ORIGEN: Marriage is a spiritual gift, but not if it is contracted with unbelievers. The Spirit of God is not given to dwell in those who are not believers. COMMENTARY ON 1 CORINTHIANS 3.34.42-45.[17]

PAUL AS EXAMPLE. CHRYSOSTOM: Paul often puts himself forward as an example when he is talking about difficult subjects. Here is another case in point. HOMILIES ON THE EPISTLES OF PAUL TO THE CORINTHIANS 19.3.[18]

AVOID FORNICATION. AMBROSIASTER: Paul's intention is to avoid fornication, not to put hindrances in the way of those seeking a higher way of life. COMMENTARY ON PAUL'S EPISTLES.[19]

MARRIAGE A GIFT OF GOD. THEODORET OF CYR: Paul comforts those who are married by saying that marriage is a gift of God. COMMENTARY ON THE FIRST EPISTLE TO THE CORINTHIANS 202.[20]

---

[12]NPNF 1 12:106. [13]FC 32:263. [14]FC 38:97. [15]Migne PG 82:274. [16]CSEL 81.72-73. [17]JTS 9:503. [18]NPNF 1 12:106. [19]CSEL 81.72. [20]Migne PG 82:274.

7:8-9 THE SINGLE LIFE

8To the unmarried and the widows I say that it is well for them to remain single as I do. 9But if they cannot exercise self-control, they should marry. For it is better to marry than to be aflame with passion.

OVERVIEW: The single life is commended to both the unmarried and to widows (AUGUSTINE). Marriage is an available remedy for lust (CHRYSOSTOM), yet lust remains a moral disease (AUGUSTINE). One who marries is not sinning against the covenant, but neither is he fulfilling the highest purpose of the gospel ethic (CLEMENT OF ALEXANDRIA).

7:8 Remaining Single

THE STRONG PULL OF CONCUPISCENCE. CHRYSOSTOM: Paul states that continence is better, but he does not attempt to pressure those who cannot attain to it. He recognizes how strong the pull of concupiscence is and says that if it leads to a lot of violence and burning desire, then it is better to put an end to that, rather than be corrupted by immorality. HOMILIES ON THE EPISTLES OF PAUL TO THE CORINTHIANS 19.3.[1]

WHETHER WIDOWS ARE SAID TO BE UNMARRIED. AUGUSTINE: We must not understand these words to mean that widows are not un-married because they once embraced the married state. Widows are unmarried, but not all unmarried are widows. That is why Paul makes a distinction here. THE EXCELLENCE OF WIDOWHOOD 2.[2]

7:9 Marriage Better Than Lust

AFLAME WITH PASSION. CLEMENT OF ALEXANDRIA: Such a person [who cannot exercise self-control] is not sinning against the covenant [by marrying], but neither is he fulfilling the highest purpose of the gospel ethic. STROMATA 3.82.4.[3]

THE REMEDY FOR LUST. AUGUSTINE: Why do you acknowledge that there is a necessary remedy for lust yet contradict me when I say that lust is a disease? If you recognize the remedy, then recognize the disease as well. AGAINST JULIAN 15.[4]

---

[1]NPNF 1 12:106. [2]FC 16:281. [3]FC 85:307. [4]FC 35:133.

7:10-16 MIXED MARRIAGES

10To the married I give charge, not I but the Lord, that the wife should not separate from her husband 11(but if she does, let her remain single or else be reconciled to her husband)— and that the husband should not divorce his wife.

 ¹²To the rest I say, not the Lord, that if any brother has a wife who is an unbeliever, and she consents to live with him, he should not divorce her. ¹³If any woman has a husband who is an unbeliever, and he consents to live with her, she should not divorce him. ¹⁴For the unbelieving husband is consecrated through his wife, and the unbelieving wife is consecrated through her husband. Otherwise, your children would be unclean, but as it is they are holy. ¹⁵But if the unbelieving partner desires to separate, let it be so; in such a case the brother or sister is not bound. For God has called us¹ to peace. ¹⁶Wife, how do you know whether you will save your husband? Husband, how do you know whether you will save your wife?

1 *Other ancient authorities read you*

OVERVIEW: The believer must take care not to be the cause of divorce (THEODORET OF CYR). Neither spouse may divorce the other if both are believers (AUGUSTINE). A Christian is not to marry an unbeliever but is to stay with the unbeliever once married (SEVERIAN OF GABALA). The sanctification of a believing spouse may overcome the uncleanness of the unbelieving spouse (CHRYSOSTOM). The unbelieving spouse, by the continuing good will of the believing spouse, may become inoculated from detesting Christ (AMBROSIASTER). As water and wine mixing, the believing spouse may sanctify the unbelieving, or the unbelieving spouse may corrupt the believing spouse (ORIGEN). The children are uncorrupted by unbelief when the faith of one parent wins out over unbelief (TERTULLIAN, SEVERIAN). It is not merely the opinion of Paul that urges against the separation of married people (CHRYSOSTOM) but the word of the Lord (THEODORET OF CYR). When the apostle says "I say, not the Lord" he means that this counsel cannot be found in the Old Testament (THEODORET OF CYR). If the husband turns away from the faith or desires to have extramarital sexual relations, the wife should neither marry another nor return to him (AMBROSIASTER). Annulment is better than idolatry (CHRYSOSTOM, PELAGIUS). One may enter celibacy after having been married (SEVERIAN). When one refuses to remain married because one's spouse is a Christian, the partners may sepa-rate without blame (AUGUSTINE). If an unbelieving partner wants to separate, the believing partner may separate innocently (THEODORET OF CYR). It is always possible that the unbelieving partner may come to believe (AMBROSIASTER).

7:10 Instructions to the Married

INSTRUCTIONS FROM THE LORD. CHRYSOSTOM: Paul's views on this subject do not come from himself but from God, who is speaking through him. HOMILIES ON THE EPISTLES OF PAUL TO THE CORINTHIANS 19.4.[1]

WHETHER ONE CAN LEAVE ONE'S SPOUSE. SEVERIAN OF GABALA: Paul did not intend this to apply to those who abandon their spouses for the service of Christ. PAULINE COMMENTARY FROM THE GREEK CHURCH.[2]

THE WORDS OF THE LORD. THEODORET OF CYR: Here Paul recalls the words of the Lord [in Matthew 5:32]: "Whoever puts away his wife, except for fornication, makes her an adulteress." COMMENTARY ON THE FIRST EPISTLE OF PAUL TO THE CORINTHIANS 204.[3]

7:11 Separating

THE HUSBAND SHOULD NOT DIVORCE HIS WIFE.

---

[1]NPNF 1 12:106. [2]NTA 15:250. [3]Migne PG 82:275.

AMBROSIASTER: A woman may not marry if she has left her husband because of fornication or apostasy, if he wishes to have sexual relations with her. But if the husband turns away from the faith or desires to have extramarital sexual relations, the wife may neither marry another nor return to him. The husband should not divorce his wife, but one should add the clause "except for fornication." COMMENTARY ON PAUL'S EPISTLES.[4]

AVOID SEPARATIONS. CHRYSOSTOM: Separations are best avoided if at all possible, but if not, the wife should not take another husband. HOMILIES ON THE EPISTLES OF PAUL TO THE CORINTHIANS 19.4.[5]

7:12 Do Not Divorce

NEITHER SPOUSE MAY DIVORCE. AUGUSTINE: We are here given to understand that neither spouse may divorce the other if both are believers. QUESTIONS 83.[6]

7:13 Unbelieving Spouses

WHEN A HUSBAND IS AN UNBELIEVER. AMBROSIASTER: Paul says this in the case of two Gentiles, one of whom has become a believer. Normally, a pagan detests Christianity, and a Christian does not want to be contaminated by paganism, which is why Paul says that if they are happy to stay together, they should continue to do so. COMMENTARY ON PAUL'S EPISTLES.[7]

STAYING WITH AN UNBELIEVER. SEVERIAN OF GABALA: Paul did not mean that a woman should marry an unbeliever, only that she should stay with him if she is already married. PAULINE COMMENTARY FROM THE GREEK CHURCH.[8]

7:14a The Unbeliever Consecrated

THE BELIEVING SPOUSE SANCTIFIES THE UNBELIEVING SPOUSE. ORIGEN: Husband and wife are one in the same way that wine and water are one when they are mixed together. Just as the believing partner sanctifies the unbelieving one, so the unbelieving partner corrupts the believing one. This is why a man who is not yet married should consider very carefully and either not marry at all or marry only in the Lord. COMMENTARY ON 1 CORINTHIANS 3.36.2-5.[9]

PROTECTION FROM DETESTING CHRIST. AMBROSIASTER: These unbelievers have the benefit of good will, which protects them from detesting the name of Christ. COMMENTARY ON PAUL'S EPISTLES.[10]

THE DISTINCTION BETWEEN A HARLOT AND A SPOUSE. CHRYSOSTOM: If a man joined to a harlot is one body with her, then it is clear that a woman joined to an idolater is one body with him. That is true, but in this case she does not become unclean as a result. On the contrary, her cleanness overcomes the uncleanness of her husband, just as the cleanness of a believing husband overcomes the uncleanness of his unbelieving wife. How can this be, if a husband is not condemned for casting out a wife who has played the harlot? The reason is that in this case there is hope that the lost member may be saved through the marriage, whereas in the other case, the marriage has already been dissolved through harlotry. An unbelieving man may be reclaimed by his believing wife if she is faithful to him. But for a harlot things are not so easy, because how can she reclaim someone whom she has wronged? The same is true for a believing husband who has an unbelieving wife. HOMILIES ON THE EPISTLES OF PAUL TO THE CORINTHIANS 19.4.[11]

7:14b Children Made Holy

---

[4]CSEL 81.74-75. [5]NPNF 1 12:106-7. [6]FC 70:220. [7]CSEL 81.75-76. [8]NTA 15:250. [9]JTS 9:505. [10]CSEL 81.76. [11]NPNF 1 12:107.

YOUR CHILDREN DESTINED FOR HOLINESS. TERTULLIAN: The children of believers were in some sense destined for holiness and salvation, and in the pledge of this hope Paul supported those marriages which he wished to continue. ON THE SOUL 39.4.[12]

THE FAITH OF THE PARENT OVERCOMES UNBELIEF. SEVERIAN OF GABALA: When the children are clean and holy, uncorrupted by unbelief, the faith of the parent has won. PAULINE COMMENTARY FROM THE GREEK CHURCH.[13]

7:15 Separating from an Unbeliever

IF THE UNBELIEVING PARTNER DESIRES TO SEPARATE. AMBROSIASTER: A marriage contracted without devotion to God is not binding, and for that reason it is not a sin if it is abandoned because of God. But the unbelieving partner sins both against God and against the marriage, because he or she is unwilling to live in a marriage relationship dedicated to God. It is not right to go to court over this because the one who leaves the marriage is doing so out of hatred for God, and for this reason he or she is not to be considered worthy of such attention. COMMENTARY ON PAUL'S EPISTLES.[14]

ANNULMENT IS BETTER THAN SACRIFICING TO IDOLS. CHRYSOSTOM: If an unbeliever wants his partner to join him in sacrificing to idols, it is better for the marriage to be annulled, so that there may be no breach in godliness. HOMILIES ON THE EPISTLES OF PAUL TO THE CORINTHIANS 19.4.[15]

REFUSAL TO REMAIN MARRIED. AUGUSTINE: A Christian husband may leave his wife without any blame, even if they are lawfully married, if she refuses to live with him because he is a Christian. EIGHT QUESTIONS OF DULCITIUS 1.[16]

LOYALTY TO GOD FIRST. PELAGIUS: The Lord must come before a husband or a wife. COMMENTARY ON THE FIRST EPISTLE TO THE CORINTHIANS 7.[17]

THE BELIEVER NOT TO BE THE CAUSE OF DIVORCE. THEODORET OF CYR: The believing partner is not to be the cause of the divorce. But if the unbelieving partner wants to separate, the believing partner is innocent and free from any accusation. COMMENTARY ON THE FIRST EPISTLE TO THE CORINTHIANS 205.[18]

7:16 Coming to Faith

THE UNBELIEVER MAY BELIEVE. AMBROSIASTER: Paul says this because it is always possible that the unbelieving partner will come to believe if he or she does not detest the name of Christ. COMMENTARY ON PAUL'S EPISTLES.[19]

---

[12]FC 10:271. [13]NTA 15:250. [14]CSEL 81.76-77. [15]NPNF 1 12:108. [16]FC 16:436. [17]Migne PL 30:737A. [18]Migne PG 82:278. [19]CSEL 81.78.

7:17-24 THE CONTENTED LIFE

[17]*Only, let every one lead the life which the Lord has assigned to him, and in which God has called him. This is my rule in all the churches.* [18]*Was any one at the time of his call*

already circumcised? Let him not seek to remove the marks of circumcision. Was any one at the time of his call uncircumcised? Let him not seek circumcision. [19]*For neither circumcision counts for anything nor uncircumcision, but keeping the commandments of God.* [20]*Every one should remain in the state in which he was called.* [21]*Were you a slave when called? Never mind. But if you can gain your freedom, avail yourself of the opportunity.*[x] [22]*For he who was called in the Lord as a slave is a freedman of the Lord. Likewise he who was free when called is a slave of Christ.* [23]*You were bought with a price; do not become slaves of men.* [24]*So, brethren, in whatever state each was called, there let him remain with God.*

x *Or make use of your present condition instead*

OVERVIEW: Outward circumstances do not stand in the way of one's becoming holy (THEODORE OF MOPSUESTIA). Paul's rule is that believers are to follow the life the Lord has assigned to them (AMBROSIASTER). Paul works this out in terms not only of marriage but also of circumcision and economic circumstance. Whether persons are married or single (ORIGEN) or of high or lowly status (PELAGIUS), they are to remain in the state in which they were called. God does not judge us by our external status (SEVERIAN OF GABALA), such as slave or free (AMBROSIASTER, THEODORET OF CYR). Similarly there is no reward for either circumcision or uncircumcision (SEVERIAN). Neither remove the marks of circumcision nor try to convert the uncircumcised to circumcision (PELAGIUS). Once it is cut away, flesh cannot be replaced (THEODORE). One enslaved by gluttony or passion can hardly be said to be free (CHRYSOSTOM). Having been bought by God, we must not become slaves of our fellow beings (AMBROSIASTER). Believers are free from real slavery (AMBROSIASTER, CHRYSOSTOM), being slaves of Christ and thus incomparably free in Christ (OECUMENIUS).

7:17 Lead the Life Assigned

KEEPING TO GOD'S ASSIGNMENT. AMBROSIASTER: God has assigned to each person the time of his salvation, that is, the time when he might believe, and he will keep that person until then.

Paul tells the Corinthians that this is his general rule, so that when they hear that others are expected to follow it, they will be more willing to do so themselves. It is always easier to do something when you see others doing the same. COMMENTARY ON PAUL'S EPISTLES.[1]

CIRCUMSTANCES DO NOT IMPEDE HOLINESS. THEODORE OF MOPSUESTIA: It is wrong to suppose that the circumstances which prevailed when a person was converted stand in the way of his becoming holy. PAULINE COMMENTARY FROM THE GREEK CHURCH.[2]

7:18 Circumcised or Uncircumcised

DO NOT REMOVE THE MARKS OF CIRCUMCISION. PELAGIUS: Someone who has been circumcised should not think that this is going too far, or regret it, because in its own day it was necessary. But neither should he seek to convert the uncircumcised to that practice. COMMENTARY ON THE FIRST EPISTLE TO THE CORINTHIANS 7.[3]

LET HIM NOT SEEK CIRCUMCISION. THEODORE OF MOPSUESTIA: It is not possible to replace flesh which has been cut off in this way, although the blessed Epiphanius of Cyprus says that it is.[4] Those who want to know more about the sub-

---

[1]CSEL 81.78. [2]NTA 15:182. [3]Migne PL 30:737C. [4]In *De Mensuris et Ponderibus (On Weights and Measures)* 16.

ject can consult what he has to say about it. PAULINE COMMENTARY FROM THE GREEK CHURCH.[5]

7:19 Keeping the Commandments

NO REWARD FOR CIRCUMCISION OR UNCIRCUMCISION. SEVERIAN OF GABALA: Circumcision means nothing by itself, but it was a command of God. On the other hand, uncircumcised is the way God made us, so there is no reward for that either. PAULINE COMMENTARY FROM THE GREEK CHURCH.[6]

7:20 The State in Which One Was Called

MARRIED OR SINGLE. ORIGEN: In itself, the state in which we are called is a matter of indifference. An unmarried man, for example, can live a life of purity, but he may also be deeply involved in sin. The same is true for a married man as well. If it were only Christians who practiced celibacy, then it would be possible to say that it was a pure and divine state. But the Marcionites also practice it, though not in the same way as Christians. Christians do it in order to please God, but the Marcionites do it in order not to succumb to the Creator. Celibacy is honorable only when it is clothed with the life and behavior of the church, with pure knowledge and truth. COMMENTARY ON 1 CORINTHIANS 3.37.35-43.[7]

STATUS HIGH OR LOW. PELAGIUS: God does not care about our social status but about our will and mind. COMMENTARY ON THE FIRST EPISTLE TO THE CORINTHIANS 7.[8]

SEVERIAN OF GABALA: Paul says this because it makes no difference to God either way. PAULINE COMMENTARY FROM THE GREEK CHURCH.[9]

7:21 Slave or Free

OUR SLAVERY AND OUR FREEDOM. ORIGEN: I am

a slave of that affair and care to which I am bound. For I know that it is written that whatever one is conquered by, to that he is delivered as a slave. . . . Who will free me from this most unseemly slavery except him who said, "If the Son shall make you free, you shall be free indeed"?[10] HOMILIES 13.[11]

A SLAVE WHEN CALLED. AMBROSIASTER: Paul encourages slaves to serve their earthy masters well, so that they may appear to them to deserve their freedom. A slave who did not do his work properly would blaspheme the name of Christ and do nothing to further God's cause. COMMENTARY ON PAUL'S EPISTLES.[12]

DO NOT USE RELIGION AS AN EXCUSE. THEODORET OF CYR: Paul is saying that no slave should run away, using religion as his excuse. COMMENTARY ON THE FIRST EPISTLE TO THE CORINTHIANS 207.[13]

7:22 A Freedman or a Slave of Christ

CALLED IN THE LORD. AMBROSIASTER: Whoever has been delivered from sin is truly free. The ancients used to say that anyone who acts unwisely is a slave. They called all wise men free, and all the unwise were slaves as far as they were concerned. In any case, even a free believer is a slave of Christ, for to be free from God is the greatest sin of all. COMMENTARY ON PAUL'S EPISTLES.[14]

FREEDOM FROM REAL SLAVERY. CHRYSOSTOM: A slave is free because he has been set free from the passions and diseases of the mind. Legal freedom is unimportant by comparison. HOMILIES ON THE EPISTLES OF PAUL TO THE CORINTHIANS 19.5.[15]

---

[5]NTA 15:182. [6]NTA 15:251. [7]JTS 9:507. [8]Migne PL 30:737D. [9]NTA 15:251. [10]Jn 8:36. [11]FC 71:374*. [12]CSEL 81.79. [13]Migne PG 82:279. [14]CSEL 81.80. [15]NPNF 1 12:108.

Slaves of Christ and Free in Christ. Oecu-menius: Paul wants to show that slave and master are equal. We are all freedmen of Christ because he has set us free from the tyranny of Satan, and we are voluntary slaves of Christ because, having set us free, he led us into his own kingdom. Pauline Commentary from the Greek Church.[16]

7:23 Not Slaves of Men

Bought Back. Origen: Christ came and "bought us back" when we were serving that lord to whom we sold ourselves by sinning. So he appears to have recovered as his own those whom he created. He has redeemed a people who chose to belong to another, who sought another lord for themselves by sinning. Homilies on Exodus 6.[17]

The Demonic Plot to Reverse Redemption. Basil: The price of man is the blood of Christ. "You have been bought," it is said, "with a price; do not become the slaves of men." The powers of the evil one are trying to render this price useless to us. They try to lead us back into slavery even after we are free. Homilies 21.[18]

So High a Price. Ambrosiaster: We have been bought at so high a price that only Christ, who owns everything, is able to pay it. Therefore whoever is bought with a price ought to serve all the more, in an effort to pay back the buyer. Having been bought by God, we must not once again become slaves of men. Slaves of men are those who accept human superstitions. Commentary on Paul's Epistles.[19]

Do Not Become Slaves of Men. Chrysostom: Free men can enslave themselves by agreeing to serve others out of gluttony, greed or a desire for power. Such a person may be technically free, but in reality he is more of a slave than anyone else. Homilies on the Epistles of Paul to the Corinthians 19.5.[20]

No Greater Price. Jerome: What greater price is there than that the Creator shed his blood for the creature? Homily 29.[21]

7:24 Remain with God

In Whatever State Called. Basil: The apostle himself practiced very meticulously what he preached to others. Concerning Baptism 12.[22]

The Command Repeated. Ambrosiaster: Paul repeats what he said above in order to underline its importance. Commentary on Paul's Epistles.[23]

---

[16]NTA 15:436. [17]FC 71:295*. [18]FC 46:344-45*. [19]CSEL 81.80-81. [20]NPNF 1 12:109. [21]FC 48:220. [22]FC 9:427. [23]CSEL 81.81.

7:25-31 MARRIAGE

[25]*Now concerning the unmarried,*[y] *I have no command of the Lord, but I give my opinion as one who by the Lord's mercy is trustworthy.* [26]*I think that in view of the present*[m] *distress it is well for a person to remain as he is.* [27]*Are you bound to a wife? Do not seek to be free. Are you free from a wife? Do not seek marriage.* [28]*But if you marry, you do not sin, and if*

a girl[z] marries she does not sin. Yet those who marry will have worldly troubles, and I would spare you that. [29]*I mean, brethren, the appointed time has grown very short; from now on, let those who have wives live as though they had none,* [30]*and those who mourn as though they were not mourning, and those who rejoice as though they were not rejoicing, and those who buy as though they had no goods,* [31]*and those who deal with the world as though they had no dealings with it. For the form of this world is passing away.*

y *Greek virgins* m *Or impending* z *Greek virgin*

OVERVIEW: Paul turns his attention to young people who are thinking about getting married. Without denying the validity of marriage, Paul commends the single state (AMBROSIASTER), partly to avoid worldly entanglements (ORIGEN) during this hazardous end time (AMBROSIASTER). His instruction is set in terms of a view of history in which the end is imminently expected. Every day the world gets older (AMBROSIASTER). In this context virginity has great advantages (SEVERIAN OF GABALA), and caring for children is especially put in doubt. The focus should be upon begetting spiritual children, not earthly ones (CAESARIUS OF ARLES). Those distinctly called to virginity should not marry (CHRYSOSTOM). There is no need for the unmarried actively to seek to be married (AMBROSIASTER). Those who know that the end of the world is near will soon be consoled (AMBROSIASTER). Paul commends his opinion on the unmarried state without imposing it as a command of the Lord (ORIGEN, SEVERIAN OF GABALA).

7:25 Concerning the Unmarried

THE OPTIONAL DISTINGUISHED FROM THE OBLIGATORY. ORIGEN: Some rules are given as commandments of God, while others are more flexible and left by God to the decision of the individual. The first kind are those commandments which pertain to salvation. The others are better, because even if we do not keep them, we shall still be saved. There is no merit in doing what is obligatory, but there is in doing that which is optional. COMMENTARY ON 1 CORINTHIANS 3.39.2-6.[1]

RECOMMENDING WITHOUT IMPOSING. SEVERIAN OF GABALA: It is clear that Paul says this not because he has no command to teach about virginity but because God has not told him that these people should practice chastity themselves. That is why he writes to them giving his opinion and recommending chastity, without imposing it on them. PAULINE COMMENTARY FROM THE GREEK CHURCH.[2]

AN OPINION, NOT A COMMAND. OECUMENIUS: Paul is coming here to a higher wisdom, but he is hesitant to impose it directly because that might show up the inadequacy of his hearers. Therefore he sets it out as an opinion rather than as a command. PAULINE COMMENTARY FROM THE GREEK CHURCH.[3]

7:26 Remaining as One Is

VIRGINITY BETTER. AMBROSIASTER: Here Paul teaches that virginity is better, not just because it is more pleasing to God but also because it is the more sensible course to follow in the present [end-time] circumstances. COMMENTARY ON PAUL'S EPISTLES.[4]

7:27 Married or Free

[1]JTS 9:508. [2]NTA 15:251-52. [3]NTA 15:436. [4]CSEL 81.82.

Do Not Seek Marriage if You Are Free. Ambrosiaster: Paul says that no one should be divorced from his wife except in a case of fornication. As for the unmarried, what advantage is there in giving in to the lusts of the flesh? Commentary on Paul's Epistles.[5]

7:28 No Sin in Marrying

Sparing Them Worldly Troubles. Origen: The virgin is spared earthly troubles and set free by her purity, as she awaits the blessed Bridegroom. Commentary on 1 Corinthians 3.39.51-52.[6]

If You Marry, You Do Not Sin. Ambrosiaster: The man who marries does not sin because he is doing something which is permitted. But if he refuses to do it, he earns merit and a crown in heaven, for it takes great self-control to avoid doing something which is not expressly forbidden. Commentary on Paul's Epistles.[7]

Those Called to Virginity Should Not Marry. Chrysostom: Paul is not speaking about the woman who has chosen virginity, for if such a woman decides to marry, she has indeed sinned. If widows are condemned for entering into second marriages,[8] how much more is this true of those called to remain virgins. Homilies on the Epistles of Paul to the Corinthians 19.7.[9]

7:29 The Appointed Time Is Short

The Time Has Grown Short. Ambrosiaster: Paul means by this that the end of the world is coming soon. Given this fact, believers should not worry about having children and instead should dedicate themselves to the service of God. For there will be many unprecedented pressures on them, and many will fall into the

devil's trap. No one among us who has a proper fear of the pressures which the Savior predicted will want to be caught like that. Commentary on Paul's Epistles.[10]

Marriage in the End Time. Severian of Gabala: If married people are supposed to live as if they were single, how is it possible not to prefer virginity? Pauline Commentary from the Greek Church.[11]

Beget Spiritual Children. Caesarius of Arles: Those who practice physical sterility should observe fruitfulness in souls, and those who cannot have earthly children should try to beget spiritual ones. All our deeds are children. If we perform good works every day, we shall not lack spiritual offspring. Sermon 51.3.[12]

7:30 Mourning, Rejoicing

Those Who Mourn Live as Though Not Mourning. Ambrosiaster: Those who know that the end of the world is near realize that they will soon be consoled, and they comfort each other with this hope. Commentary on Paul's Epistles.[13]

7:31 Dealings with the World

The Form of This World Is Passing Away. Ambrosiaster: Note that Paul says that the form of this world is passing away, not the substance of it. Therefore if the form of the world is going to perish, there is no doubt that everything in the world will vanish. It will all pass away. Every day the world gets older. Commentary on Paul's Epistles.[14]

---

[5]CSEL 81.82-83. [6]JTS 9:510. [7]CSEL 81.83. [8]Cf. 1 Tim 5:11-12. [9]NPNF 1 12:110. [10]CSEL 81.83-84. [11]NTA 15:252. [12]FC 31:258. [13]CSEL 81.85. [14]CSEL 81.85.

7:32-38 FREEDOM

³²*I want you to be free from anxieties. The unmarried man is anxious about the affairs of the Lord, how to please the Lord;* ³³*but the married man is anxious about worldly affairs, how to please his wife,* ³⁴*and his interests are divided. And the unmarried woman or girl* ᶻ *is anxious about the affairs of the Lord, how to be holy in body and spirit; but the married woman is anxious about worldly affairs, how to please her husband.* ³⁵*I say this for your own benefit, not to lay any restraint upon you, but to promote good order and to secure your undivided devotion to the Lord.*

³⁶*If any one thinks that he is not behaving properly toward his betrothed,* ᶻ *if his passions are strong, and it has to be, let him do as he wishes: let them marry—it is no sin.* ³⁷*But whoever is firmly established in his heart, being under no necessity but having his desire under control, and has determined this in his heart, to keep her as his betrothed,* ᶻ *he will do well.* ³⁸*So that he who marries his betrothed* ᶻ *does well; and he who refrains from marriage will do better.*

z *Greek* virgin

OVERVIEW: The married and unmarried are called to the same holiness of body and soul (AUGUSTINE). Marriage is up to the choice of the individuals and is not a matter of compulsion one way or the other (CHRYSOSTOM, AMBROSIASTER). One who marries without being firmly established in the Lord risks impropriety (OECUMENIUS). It is better to marry publicly than to behave badly in private (AMBROSIASTER). Caring for wife and family tends to elicit anxieties from which the single are spared (BASIL, AMBROSIASTER). If marriage is good, virginity is better (AMBROSE, AMBROSIASTER). Virginity is commended not because of the wrongness of sex but in order to concentrate the mind on the worship of God (SEVERIAN OF GABALA) and to reduce worldly concerns (OECUMENIUS). The wall of virginity protects the unmarried from distraction (AMBROSE). Anyone who tries to have a pure body but a corrupt soul will soon have to choose between them (AMBROSIASTER).

7:32 Free from Anxieties

READINESS FOR WORSHIP. SEVERIAN OF GABALA: Here Paul explains why virginity is preferable to marriage. It has nothing to do with the rightness or wrongness of sex. Rather it is a question of anxieties which prevent the mind from concentrating on the worship of God. PAULINE COMMENTARY FROM THE GREEK CHURCH.[1]

FREEDOM FROM ANXIETY. OECUMENIUS: To be concerned about the things of the Lord is not anxiety but salvation. Paul has just told them that he wants them to be free of anxiety. PAULINE COMMENTARY FROM THE GREEK CHURCH.[2]

7:33 The Concerns of Married Men

THE CONCERNS OF GOD AND MARRIAGE. BASIL: Paul allows marriage and considers it worthy of blessing, but he contrasts it with his own preoccupation with the concerns of God and hints

[1]NTA 15:253. [2]NTA 15:437.

that the two things are incompatible. THE LONG RULES 5.[3]

MARRIAGE AND TEMPTATION. AMBROSIASTER: Looking after a wife and family is a worldly thing. Sometimes, just to keep them happy, it even leads to doing things which ought to be punished. COMMENTARY ON PAUL'S EPISTLES.[4]

7:34a *Holy in Body and Spirit*

THE WALL OF VIRGINITY. AMBROSE: The unmarried woman has her wall of virginity, protecting her against the storms of this world. Thus fortified by the enclosure of God's protection, she is disquieted by no winds of this world. LETTERS TO PRIESTS 59.[5]

THE HUMAN SPIRIT TENDS TO SANCTIFY OR CORRUPT THE BODY. AMBROSIASTER: It is the human spirit which either sanctifies or corrupts the body. If anyone tries to have a pure body but a corrupt soul, he will soon have to choose between them. Either the soul must be honored, or the body will be drawn toward corruption. COMMENTARY ON PAUL'S EPISTLES.[6]

7:34b *The Concerns of Married Women*

THE SAME CALL TO HOLINESS IN A MARRIED WOMAN. AUGUSTINE: This should not be interpreted to mean that a married woman is not meant to be holy in body as well as in soul. THE EXCELLENCE OF WIDOWHOOD 6.[7]

7:35 *Undivided Devotion to the Lord*

TO PROMOTE GOOD ORDER, NOT TO RESTRAIN. AMBROSIASTER: What Paul has just said may seem harsh to some people, which is why he adds this here. COMMENTARY ON PAUL'S EPISTLES.[8]

FREE CHOICE OF INDIVIDUALS. CHRYSOSTOM: Paul makes his case for celibacy, but in the end

he leaves it up to the free choice of the individual. If after all this he were to resort to compulsion, it would look as if he did not really believe his own statements. HOMILIES ON THE EPISTLES OF PAUL TO THE CORINTHIANS 19.7.[9]

7:36 *Marriage Not a Sin*

BETTER TO MARRY PUBLICLY THAN BEHAVE BADLY IN PRIVATE. AMBROSIASTER: Paul always wants the best out of Christians. If someone really wants to get married, then it is better to marry publicly according to the permission given than to behave badly and be ashamed in private. COMMENTARY ON PAUL'S EPISTLES.[10]

7:37 *Having Desire Under Control*

BEING UNDER NO NECESSITY. CHRYSOSTOM: The evil is not in the cohabitation but in the impediment to purity in the life. HOMILIES ON THE EPISTLES OF PAUL TO THE CORINTHIANS 19.7.[11]

BE FIRMLY ESTABLISHED IN THE HEART. OECUMENIUS: It is clear from this that someone who has been overcome by apparent impropriety, even if married, is not yet firmly established in the work of the Lord. PAULINE COMMENTARY FROM THE GREEK CHURCH.[12]

7:38 *Refraining from Marriage*

DOING WELL, DOING BETTER. AMBROSE: The one is bound by marriage bonds, the other is free. One is under the law, the other under grace. Marriage is good because through it the means of human continuity are found. But virginity is better, because through it are attained the inheritance of a heavenly kingdom and a continuity of heavenly rewards. SYNODAL LETTERS 44.[13]

---

[3]FC 9:242. [4]CSEL 81.86. [5]FC 26:334. [6]CSEL 81.87. [7]FC 16:286. [8]CSEL 81.87-88. [9]NPNF 1 12:110-11. [10]CSEL 81.89. [11]NPNF 1 12:111. [12]NTA 15:438. [13]FC 26:226.

Delivered from Worldly Cares. Ambrosiaster: The one who refrains from marriage does better because he earns merit for her with God and delivers her from the cares of this world.

Commentary on Paul's Epistles.[14]

[14]CSEL 81.89-90.

7:39-40 WIDOWHOOD

[39]*A wife is bound to her husband as long as he lives. If the husband dies, she is free to be married to whom she wishes, only in the Lord. [40]But in my judgment she is happier if she remains as she is. And I think that I have the Spirit of God.*

Overview: If the husband of a divorced woman dies, she may remarry but only in the Lord (Ambrosiaster). Reconciliation is better than divorce (Augustine). Happy is the married woman, but still happier is the chaste widow. Happiest is the virgin who attains the highest prize without struggling (Pelagius, Hermas, Theodoret of Cyr, Severian of Gabala). It is the Spirit of God who enables good counsel (Ambrosiaster).

7:39 Guidelines for Wives

A Wife Is Bound to Her Husband. Ambrosiaster: Paul writes this in order to make it clear that a woman who has been rejected by her husband is not free to marry again. If he should die, then she may remarry, but only in the Lord, which means without any suspicion of wrongdoing and within the bounds of the church. Commentary on Paul's Epistles.[1]

Seek Reconciliation. Augustine: The death referred to here is clearly the death of the body, not of the soul. Forgiveness and attempts at reconciliation of the offending person are offered

as better solutions than divorce. Adulterous Marriages.[2]

7:40a Happier If She Remains Single

Remarriage Not a Sin. Hermas: If a wife or a husband falls asleep and the one left marries again, is that a sin? No, but if he remains single he covers himself with greater honor and glory in the sight of the Lord. Shepherd 4.4.[3]

Happy, Happier and Happiest. Pelagius: Happy is the woman who has a husband. Happier still is the widow who can remain chaste with little effort on her part. But happiest of all is the virgin, who can attain to the highest prize without struggling. Commentary on the First Epistle to the Corinthians 7.[4]

Entire Devotion to God Is Happier. Severian of Gabala: What Paul means is that she is blessed if she marries and has a husband to protect her, but she is more blessed if, for the sake of piety, she refuses marriage and devotes her-

[1]CSEL 81.90. [2]FC 27:57. [3]AF 185-86. [4]Migne PL 30:740D.

self entirely to God. Pauline Commentary from the Greek Church.[5]

Degrees of Happiness. Theodoret of Cyr: Note that Paul does not say that a woman who contracts a second marriage will be unhappy. Rather he says that she will be happier if she remains single. It is all a matter of degree. Commentary on the First Epistle to the Corinthians 212.[6]

7:40b *Having the Spirit of God*

The Spirit Enables Good Counsel. Ambrosiaster: Paul adds that he has the Spirit of God in order to show that his advice is reliable. Commentary on Paul's Epistles.[7]

---

[5]NTA 15:253. [6]Migne PG 82:286. [7]CSEL 81.91.

8:1-8 FOOD OFFERED TO IDOLS

[1]*Now concerning food offered to idols: we know that "all of us possess knowledge." "Knowledge" puffs up, but love builds up.* [2]*If any one imagines that he knows something, he does not yet know as he ought to know.* [3]*But if one loves God, one is known by him.*
[4]*Hence, as to the eating of food offered to idols, we know that "an idol has no real existence," and that "there is no God but one."* [5]*For although there may be so-called gods in heaven or on earth—as indeed there are many "gods" and many "lords"—* [6]*yet for us there is one God, the Father, from whom are all things and for whom we exist, and one Lord, Jesus Christ, through whom are all things and through whom we exist.*
[7]*However, not all possess this knowledge. But some, through being hitherto accustomed to idols, eat food as really offered to an idol; and their conscience, being weak, is defiled.* [8]*Food will not commend us to God. We are no worse off if we do not eat, and no better off if we do.*

Overview: Love builds up (Clement of Alexandria). Knowledge on its own puffs up and does not necessarily produce love (Augustine, Theodoret of Cyr). It may prevent the unwary from discovering love (Ambrosiaster) by making them proud (Chrysostom). To be known by God is the death of pride. We cannot even say how wrong our perceptions of God are (Chrysostom). The so-called gods that the idolatrous worship have no existence (Theodore of Mopsuestia). Though what we call

idols have no existence, it is necessary to avoid them so as not to give cause for scandal to those who are weak in the faith (Chrysostom) in the one God in whom Father and Son are one (Ambrosiaster, Severian of Gabala, Theodoret of Cyr).

8:1 *Food Offered to Idols*

Love Builds Up. Clement of Alexandria: Love builds up. It moves in the realm of truth, not of opinion. STROMATA 1.54.4.[1]

KNOWLEDGE WITH LOVE. AMBROSIASTER: Paul means that knowledge is a great thing and very useful to the person who has it, as long as it is tempered by love. COMMENTARY ON PAUL'S EPISTLES.[2]

KNOWLEDGE WITHOUT LOVE. CHRYSOSTOM: Paul rebukes those who think they are wiser than the rest by saying that everybody possesses knowledge—the self-appointed wise people are nothing special in this respect. If anyone has knowledge but lacks love, not only will he gain nothing more, but also he will be cast down from what he already has. Knowledge is not productive of love, but rather it prevents the unwary from acquiring it by puffing him up and elating him. Arrogance causes divisions, but love draws people together and leads to true knowledge. HOMILIES ON THE EPISTLES OF PAUL TO THE CORINTHIANS 20.2.[3]

KNOWLEDGE PUFFS UP. AUGUSTINE: Paul means that knowledge only does good in company with love. Otherwise it merely puffs a man into pride. CITY OF GOD 9.20.[4]

8:2 Not Knowing as One Ought

HE DOES NOT YET KNOW. AMBROSIASTER: Only when a person has love can he be said to know as he ought to know. COMMENTARY ON PAUL'S EPISTLES.[5]

OUR IMPERFECT KNOWLEDGE OF GOD. CHRYSOSTOM: Whatever knowledge we may have, it is still imperfect. How is it then that some people claim to have a full and precise knowledge of God? Where God is concerned, we cannot even say just how wrong our perception of him is. HOMILIES ON THE EPISTLES OF PAUL TO THE CORINTHIANS 20.3.[6]

LACKING LOVE, LACKING KNOWLEDGE. THEO-

DORET OF CYR: Paul shows not only that they have no love but that they have no knowledge either. COMMENTARY ON THE FIRST EPISTLE TO THE CORINTHIANS 215.[7]

8:3 Known by God

THROUGH LOVE GOD KNOWS US. CHRYSOSTOM: We do not know God, but he knows us. This is why Christ said: "You have not chosen me, but I have chosen you" (Jn 15:16). This is the fruit of love and the death of pride. HOMILIES ON THE EPISTLES OF PAUL TO THE CORINTHIANS 20.3.[8]

TO BE KNOWN BY GOD. AUGUSTINE: Paul says: "If one loves God, one is known by him." He certainly did not say "one knows God," a dangerous presumption, but "he is known by God." Elsewhere he remarks, "But now you know God," and then immediately corrects himself: "or rather you are known by God." TRINITY 9.1.[9]

8:4 No God but One

AN IDOL IS NOTHING. ORIGEN: "An idol is nothing," says the apostle. One who makes an idol makes what is not. But what is that which is not? A form which the eye does not see but which the mind imagines for itself. HOMILIES ON EXODUS 8.3.[10]

KNOWLEDGE WITHOUT LOVE. AMBROSIASTER: Paul now develops his argument in detail in order to show that knowledge without love is both useless and harmful. COMMENTARY ON PAUL'S EPISTLES.[11]

AN IDOL HAS NO REAL EXISTENCE. AUGUSTINE: Although man has made his own gods, he nevertheless became their captive once he was handed over to their fellowship by his act of

---

[1]FC 85:63. [2]CSEL 81.91. [3]NPNF 1 12:112. [4]FC 14:108. [5]CSEL 81.92. [6]NPNF 1 12:112. [7]Migne PG 82:290. [8]NPNF 1 1:113. [9]FC 45:269*. [10]FC 71:321*. [11]CSEL 81.93.

worshiping them. . . . For what are idols but things, as the Scripture says, which "have eyes and see not"?[12] City of God 8.[13]

8:5 So-Called Gods

Idols Do Not Exist. Theodore of Mopsuestia: Paul says "so-called" here because he is showing that they do not really exist. Pauline Commentary from the Greek Church.[14]

8:6a One God, the Father

There Is One God. Cyril of Jerusalem: We say "one" to stop anyone dreaming that there could be another. We say "one" lest you should hear of his work under manifold names. Catechetical Lectures 10.3.[15]

With, Through and in Him. Ambrose: When he says "through him," did he deny that all things were made in him, through whom he says that all things are? These words, "in him" and "with him," have this force, that by these is understood one and the same reality, not something contrary. . . . Scripture bears witness that these three phrases—"with him," and "through him," and "in him"—are one in Christ. The Holy Spirit 83.[16]

From Whom Are All Things. Augustine: You have made not only what is created and formed but also whatever can be created and formed. Everything which is formed from the formless must first be formless before it can be a formed thing. Confessions 12.19.[17]

Triune Language Embedded. Augustine: "From him" means from the Father. "Through him" means through the Son. "In him" means in the Holy Spirit. It is self-evident that the Father, the Son and the Holy Spirit are one God. Trinity 1.13.[18]

One God, One Lord.: Cyril of Alexandria: Just as there is one God the Father from whom are all things, so there is one Lord Jesus Christ through whom are all things. Letter 50.26.[19]

All Things Ascribed to God. Pseudo-Dionysius: So all things are rightly ascribed to God since it is by him and in him and for him that all things exist, are co-ordered, remain, hold together, are completed and are returned. The Divine Names 980.[20]

8:6b One Lord, Jesus Christ

One Name. Ambrose: It is written: "Go baptize the nations in the name of the Father, and of the Son, and of the Holy Spirit." "In the name," he said, not "in the names." So there is not one name for the Father, another name for the Son, and another name for the Holy Spirit, because there is one God, not several names, because there are not two gods, not three gods. The Holy Spirit 13.132.[21]

One God. Ambrosiaster: Everything which exists has been created by the Father through the Son. It is impossible for God not to be Lord as well, and since the Lord is God, it is clear that Father and Son are one. Commentary on Paul's Epistles.[22]

The Son Is No Less God Than the Father. Severian of Gabala: The Father is one, just as the Son is one. If the Son is called Lord, that does not make the Father any less Lord, just as when it is said that God the Father is one, the Son is no less God. Pauline Commentary from the Greek Church.[23]

One Lord and One God. Theodoret of Cyr: Note once more the apostle's wisdom. For having first demonstrated that the words *Lord* and *God* are synonymous, he then splits them up,

---

[12]Ps 113:5. [13]FC 14:68*. [14]NTA 15:183-84. [15]LCC 4:131. [16]FC 44:183*. [17]FC 21:389*. [18]FC 45:16*. [19]FC 76:225. [20]CWS 129. [21]FC 44:83*. [22]CSEL 81.93. [23]NTA 15:254-55.

calling the Father one and the Son the other. COMMENTARY ON THE FIRST EPISTLE TO THE CORINTHIANS 215.[24]

8:7 The Weak Conscience

THE WEAK CONSCIENCE FEELS DEFILED. Chrysostom: When people were forbidden to touch idols they would suspect that it was because they had power to do them harm. Paul therefore makes his position clear. He says categorically that there is no such thing as an idol but that it is necessary to avoid them so as not to give cause for scandal to those who are weak in the faith. HOMILIES ON THE EPISTLES OF PAUL TO THE CORINTHIANS 20.8.[25]

8:8 Eating or Not Eating

FOOD WILL NOT COMMEND US TO GOD. Chrysostom: Food by itself is neither here nor there. But as he goes on, Paul reveals all the harm which might arise from eating meat which had been sacrificed to idols. HOMILIES ON THE EPISTLES OF PAUL TO THE CORINTHIANS 20.9-10.[26]

NEITHER ABUNDANCE NOR LOSS. Augustine: "Neither shall we have any abundance if we do eat, nor shall we suffer any loss if we do not eat." That is to say: neither will the former make me rich, nor will the latter make me poor. CONFESSIONS 10.45.[27]

---

[24]Migne PG 82:290. [25]NPNF 1 12:114-15. [26]NPNF 1 12:115. [27]FC 21:303.

8:9-13 FREEDOM AND FAILURE

[9]Only take care lest this liberty of yours somehow become a stumbling block to the weak. [10]For if any one sees you, a man of knowledge, at table in an idol's temple, might he not be encouraged, if his conscience is weak, to eat food offered to idols? [11]And so by your knowledge this weak man is destroyed, the brother for whom Christ died. [12]Thus, sinning against your brethren and wounding their conscience when it is weak, you sin against Christ. [13]Therefore, if food is a cause of my brother's falling, I will never eat meat, lest I cause my brother to fall.

OVERVIEW: If we exercise our freedom at the wrong time (CHRYSOSTOM) or in the wrong way, the weak brother or sister may be undermined (THEODORET OF CYR, CHRYSOSTOM). It is the believer's responsibility not to trip up weaker persons (CHRYSOSTOM) who might think that there is some spiritual power in food offered to idols, a power they might acquire if they eat (AMBROSIASTER). Offer nothing to idols (TERTULLIAN). Do not do anything that causes another Christian to stumble (AMBROSIASTER, BASIL, CHRYSOSTOM). Christ died for the weak. the strong must protect the weak (AUGUSTINE).

8:9 Not a Stumbling Block

DO NOT TRIP UP THE WEAK. Chrysostom: Paul is saying that if we are not prepared to correct our weaker brethren, then at least we should not trip them up. HOMILIES ON THE EPISTLES OF PAUL TO THE CORINTHIANS 20.10.[1]

8:10 *In an Idol's Temple*

GIVE NOTHING TO AN IDOL. TERTULLIAN: Give nothing and take nothing from an idol! If it be against the faith to recline at table in the temple of an idol, what would you call it if one wore the garb of an idol? THE CHAPLET 10.[2]

AT TABLE IN AN IDOL'S TEMPLE. AMBROSIASTER: Paul is afraid that the weaker brother may be tempted to eat meat sacrificed to idols, not because he also possesses the knowledge that there is no such thing as an idol but because he might think that there is some spiritual power in such food, which he will acquire if he eats it. COMMENTARY ON PAUL'S EPISTLES.[3]

ILL-TIMED BEHAVIOR. CHRYSOSTOM: It is not only his weakness but also your ill-timed behavior which plots against him and makes him weaker. HOMILIES ON THE EPISTLES OF PAUL TO THE CORINTHIANS 20.10.[4]

HARMFUL ASSOCIATIONS. CHRYSOSTOM: Let us expand this thought so as to say: "If someone sees you who have knowledge of piety passing the whole day in those senseless and harmful associations, will not the conscience of the weak man be emboldened to pursue such actions more earnestly?" That blessed apostle said this to keep in check those who were heedless, even after having knowledge of piety, who were exposing themselves to places of idolatry and causing scandal to the rest. BAPTISMAL INSTRUCTIONS 6.16.[5]

SLAVES OF FOOD. CLEMENT OF ALEXANDRIA: There are two sorts of food, one ministering to salvation, and the other which is fitting to those who perish. . . . We ought not to misuse the gifts of the Father, then, acting the part of spendthrifts like the rich son in the Gospel.[6] Let us, rather, make use of them with detachment,

keeping them under control. Surely we have been commanded to be the master and lord, not the slave, of food. CHRIST THE EDUCATOR 2.9.[7]

8:11 *Destroying One for Whom Christ Died*

RESPONSIBILITY FOR THE WEAK. CHRYSOSTOM: There are two things which deprive you of any excuse in this mischief. The first is that he is weak, the second is that he is your brother. I should add a third excuse also, one which is even worse than the others. What is this? That whereas Christ died for him, you cannot even lift a finger to help him in the slightest. HOMILIES ON THE EPISTLES OF PAUL TO THE CORINTHIANS 20.10.[8]

CONSIDER WHO DIED FOR HIM. AUGUSTINE: If you love the weak person less because of the moral failing that makes him weak, consider the One who died on his behalf. QUESTIONS 71.[9]

THE WEAK PERSON IS DESTROYED. THEODORET OF CYR: Paul magnifies the accusation in order to prevent people from committing the crime. COMMENTARY ON THE FIRST EPISTLE TO THE CORINTHIANS 217.[10]

8:12 *Sinning Against Christ*

THE WOUNDING OF CONSCIENCE. BASIL: Consequently, either when something is done which is intrinsically evil and scandal results, or if the performance of a licit act and one within our sphere of competence causes scandal to one who is weak in faith or knowledge, then the penalty is clear and unescapable. . . . "It were better for him that a millstone were hanged

---

[1]NPNF 1 12:115-16. [2]FC 40:254. The issue Tertullian was discussing was the wearing of ceremonial garb for idolatrous events. [3]CSEL 81:95. [4]NPNF 1 12:116. [5]FC 31:99*. [6]Lk 15:11-14. [7]FC 23:101. [8]NPNF 1 12:116. [9]FC 70:185. [10]Migne PG 82:217.

about his neck."[11] CONCERNING BAPTISM 10.[12]

DESTROYING CHRIST'S WORK. CHRYSOSTOM: Those who wound a weak conscience sin against Christ. He considers the concerns of his servants to be his own. Those who are wounded make up his own body. These people are destroying the work which Christ built up by his own blood. HOMILIES ON THE EPISTLES OF PAUL TO THE CORINTHIANS 20.10.[13]

LOVING CHRIST IN THE MEETING WITH THE OTHER. AUGUSTINE: It is the very law of Christ that we bear one another's burdens. Moreover, by loving Christ we easily bear the weakness of another, even him whom we do not yet love for the sake of his own good qualities, for we realize that the one whom we love is someone for whom the Lord has died. QUESTIONS 71.[14]

8:13 Not Causing Others to Fall

ANALOGY WITH ADULTERY. AMBROSIASTER: It is all right to have a wife, but if she commits adultery she is to be rejected. Likewise, it is all right to eat meat, but if it has been sacrificed to idols it is to be refused. COMMENTARY ON PAUL'S EPISTLES.[15]

DO NOT CAUSE A BROTHER TO FALL. CHRYSOSTOM: This is like the best of teachers, to apply to himself the things he is speaking about. Paul is not concerned about the rights and wrongs of the issue in any objective sense. His only concern is that his brother should not stumble. HOMILIES ON THE EPISTLES OF PAUL TO THE CORINTHIANS 20.11.[16]

THE STRONG AND THE WEAK. AUGUSTINE: Those who are stronger and are not troubled by scruples are nevertheless commanded to abstain so as not to offend those who, on account of their weakness, still find abstinence necessary. THE WAY OF LIFE OF THE CATHOLIC CHURCH 71.[17]

---

[11]Lk 17:2. [12]FC 9:424. [13]NPNF 1 12:116. [14]FC 30:184-85. [15]CSEL 81.96. [16]NPNF 1 12:116. [17]FC 56:55.

9:1-6 PAUL'S SELF-DEFENSE

[1]*Am I not free? Am I not an apostle? Have I not seen Jesus our Lord? Are not you my workmanship in the Lord?* [2]*If to others I am not an apostle, at least I am to you; for you are the seal of my apostleship in the Lord.*

[3]*This is my defense to those who would examine me.* [4]*Do we not have the right to our food and drink?* [5]*Do we not have the right to be accompanied by a wife,*[n] *as the other apostles and the brothers of the Lord and Cephas?* [6]*Or is it only Barnabas and I who have no right to refrain from working for a living?*

n *Greek a sister as wife*

OVERVIEW: If any want to examine Paul's apostleship (THEODORET OF CYR), let them look at the Corinthians as a sufficient witness to his workmanship in the Lord (CHRYSOSTOM).

Paul's authorization as apostle withstood close questioning (Ambrosiaster). The whole world had him as its apostle (Chrysostom). His special role in the church is based on his calling as an apostle (Clement of Alexandria, Ambrosiaster). Faithful women possessing worldly goods ministered significantly to the apostles in the necessities of life (Augustine).

9:1 The Apostle's Workmanship

My Workmanship in the Lord. Chrysostom: The really great thing was that the Corinthian Christians were Paul's workmanship in the Lord. Even Judas was an apostle and saw Christ, but because he did not have the work of an apostle, these things were of no benefit to him. Homilies on the Epistles of Paul to the Corinthians 21.2.[1]

9:2 The Seal of Paul's Apostleship

An Apostle to the Corinthians. Ambrosiaster: Those Jewish believers who nevertheless continued to observe the law of Moses denied that Paul was an apostle because he taught that it was no longer necessary to be circumcised or to observe the sabbath. Even the other apostles thought that he was teaching something different because of this, and they denied that he was an apostle. But to the Corinthians Paul was an apostle, because they had seen the signs of God's power in him. Commentary on Paul's Epistles.[2]

He Became Everyone's Apostle. Chrysostom: Once again, Paul makes his point by concession, for the whole world had him as its apostle. Homilies on the Epistles of Paul to the Corinthians 21.2.[3]

9:3 A Defense

Paul's Defense. Ambrosiaster: Here Paul begins to develop the argument which he set out above, namely: "All things are lawful for me, but I will not be enslaved by anything" (6:12). Commentary on Paul's Epistles.[4]

To Those Who Would Examine Him. Theodoret of Cyr: Paul says that if anyone wants to examine his works, let him look at the Corinthians, for they are a sufficient witness to his labors. Commentary on the First Epistle to the Corinthians 219.[5]

9:4 The Apostle's Rights

Food and Drink. Ambrosiaster: This is what Paul meant when he said that all things were lawful to him. Commentary on Paul's Epistles.[6]

9:5 The Other Apostles' Practice

Accompanied by a Wife. Clement of Alexandria: The apostles concentrated on undistracted preaching and took their wives around as Christian sisters rather than as spouses, to be their fellow ministers to the women of the household, so that the gospel would reach them without causing scandal. Stromata 3.53.3.[7]

The Ministry of Sister Women. Augustine: When his identity has been established, he shows that the privileges granted to the other apostles are his also, namely, exemption from manual labor and livelihood in recompense for his preaching as the Lord appointed. This is stated most clearly according to the verses where St. Paul argues explicitly that faithful women, possessing the goods of this world, went along with the apostles and ministered to them from their own supplies that the servants of God might lack none of those commodities which constitute the necessities of life. . . . Certain persons, not understanding this passage, have interpreted it as "wife." The obscurity of the Greek word deceived them, since, in Greek,

---

[1]NPNF 1 12:119. [2]CSEL 81.97. [3]NPNF 1 12:119. [4]CSEL 81.97. [5]Migne PG 82:294. [6]CSEL 81.98. [7]FC 85:289.

the same word is used for wife and woman. Yet the apostle has placed the words in such a way that people should not be deceived, since he says not merely "a woman" but "a sister woman," and not "to take in marriage" but "to take about." The Work of Monks 2.[8]

The Right to Be Accompanied. Augustine: To what right does he refer unless it be to the one which the Lord gave to those whom he sent to preach the kingdom of heaven when he said: "Eat what they have; for the laborer deserves his wages"?[9] He offered himself as an exponent of this privilege. Very faithful women attended to the necessities of his life at their own expense. The Work of Monks 7.[10]

9:6 Paul's Livelihood

The Right to Refrain from Working. Ambrosiaster: Paul means by this that he and Barnabas do have this right, but they do not want to exercise it. Commentary on Paul's Epistles.[11]

Live by the Gospel. Augustine: The Lord directed those who preach the gospel to live by the gospel, that is, to maintain at the expense of the faithful that life for which food and clothing are essential. The Work of Monks 9.[12]

---

[8]FC 16:338*. [9]Lk 10:7. [10]FC 16:341*. [11]CSEL 81.98. [12]FC 16:346.

9:7-14 THE RIGHT TO COMPENSATION

[7]*Who serves as a soldier at his own expense? Who plants a vineyard without eating any of its fruit? Who tends a flock without getting some of the milk?*

[8]*Do I say this on human authority? Does not the law say the same?* [9]*For it is written in the law of Moses, "You shall not muzzle an ox when it is treading out the grain." Is it for oxen that God is concerned?* [10]*Does he not speak entirely for our sake? It was written for our sake, because the plowman should plow in hope and the thresher thresh in hope of a share in the crop.* [11]*If we have sown spiritual good among you, is it too much if we reap your material benefits?* [12]*If others share this rightful claim upon you, do not we still more?*

Nevertheless, we have not made use of this right, but we endure anything rather than put an obstacle in the way of the gospel of Christ. [13]*Do you not know that those who are employed in the temple service get their food from the temple, and those who serve at the altar share in the sacrificial offerings?* [14]*In the same way, the Lord commanded that those who proclaim the gospel should get their living by the gospel.*

Overview: The apostles are like soldiers standing firmly against the demonic powers, and at the same time they are like shepherds guiding rational souls (Chrysostom). They do not proceed by any human authority (Ambrosiaster).

They are exposed to dangers, slaughters and violent deaths (Chrysostom, Ambrosiaster). If God cares about oxen treading grain (Fulgentius), he will care much more for the labor of apostles (Origen, Chrysostom). Those who serve the gospel have the right to receive support from the churches and bodily nourishment for the spiritual nourishment they provide (Augustine). Those who contribute to the apostles receive in spiritual good far more than they give in material benefits (Chrysostom, Ambrosiaster, Augustine).

9:7 Serving as a Soldier

A Soldier Against the Demonic. Chrysostom: The apostleship was much more dangerous than being a soldier. For their warfare was not just with men but with demons as well. The apostles were both soldiers and husbandmen and shepherds, not of the earth, nor of irrational animals, nor in such wars as are perceived by the senses, but of rational souls and in battle array with the demons. Homilies on the Epistles of Paul to the Corinthians 21.4.[1]

The Propriety of Receiving Support. Augustine: The church has its own soldiers and its own provincial officers . . . its vineyard and its planters, its flock and its shepherds. . . . Thus some are rightly fed and clothed at the expense of the charitable rich. They accept nothing for their own necessities except from those who sell their goods. They are not to be judged and condemned by the more perfect members of Christ who furnish their own needs with their own hands—a higher virtue which the apostle strongly commends.[2] They in turn ought not to condemn as Christians of lower grade those from whose resources they are supplied. . . . The servants of God who live by selling the honest works of their own hands could, with much less impropriety, condemn those from whom they receive nothing than could those others who are unable to work with their hands because of some bodily weakness yet who condemn the very ones at whose expense they live. Letter to Hilarius 157.[3]

9:8 Scripture's Teaching

Written in the Law. Ambrosiaster: Paul indicates here that his position corresponds to the teaching of Scripture and that his refusal to accept any payment from the Corinthians was with good reason. Commentary on Paul's Epistles.[4]

9:9 Not Muzzling an Ox

God's Care for the Apostles. Origen: God's care was not only for the oxen[5] but moreso for the apostles, for whose sake he uttered these words. On First Principles 2.4.2.[6]

An Ox Treading Grain. Chrysostom: Why does Paul mention this, when he could have used the example of the priests?[7] The reason is that he wanted to prove his case beyond any shadow of doubt. If God cares about oxen, how much more will he care about the labor of teachers? Homilies on the Epistles of Paul to the Corinthians 21.5.[8]

Oxen and Men. Fulgentius: These animals accomplish their life and purpose in this world according to the incomprehensible will of the Creator. They render no account of their deeds because they are not rational. "Is God concerned about oxen?" Human beings, however, because they have been made rational, will render an account to God for themselves and for all the things which they have received for use in this present life. To Peter on the Faith 42.[9]

9:10 Speaking for the Apostles' Sake

Reasoning by Analogy. Ambrosiaster: The whole of Scripture applies to us by way of analogy. Commentary on Paul's Epistles.[10]

9:11 Sowing Spiritual Good

---

[1]NPNF 1 12:120. [2]Acts 20:36; 1 Thess 4:11. [3]FC 20:351*. [4]CSEL 81.98-99. [5]Deut 25:4. [6]OFP 98. [7]E.g., Lev 2:3, 10; 7:28-36; 10:12-15. [8]NPNF 1 12:121. [9]FC 95:87*. [10]CSEL 81.99.

SPIRITUAL GOOD AND MATERIAL BENEFIT. CHRYSOSTOM: Paul points out that those who contribute to their teachers receive more than they give. HOMILIES ON THE EPISTLES OF PAUL TO THE CORINTHIANS 21.6.[11]

MANUAL LABOR JUSTLY SUBSTITUTED. AUGUSTINE: Paul emphasizes the fact that his fellow apostles were not transgressing in any way when they did not engage in manual labor to provide the necessities of life, but, as the Lord directed, living on the gospel, they accepted, without offering payment, bodily nourishment from those to whom they in turn furnished spiritual nourishment without demanding payment. THE WORK OF MONKS 7.[12]

9:12 Giving Up One's Right

WE ENDURE ANYTHING. AMBROSIASTER: Paul does not exercise his rights because they might be an obstacle to the gospel. That left him free to argue that he was not one of the false apostles. COMMENTARY ON PAUL'S EPISTLES.[13]

9:13 Sharing in the Offerings

FOOD FROM THE TEMPLE. CHRYSOSTOM: The case of the apostles was much stronger than that of the priests. The priesthood was an honor, but the apostles were exposed to dangers, slaughters and violent deaths. In saying "We have seen spiritual good among you" he points to the storms, the dangers, the snares, the unspeakable evils endured in preaching. But Paul was unwilling to despise the things of the old law or to exalt what belonged to him. He even provided his own possessions. He reckoned their value not from the dangers but from the greatness of God's gift. He did not say "if we have exposed ourselves to danger" but "if we have sown spiritual things among you." HOMILIES ON THE EPISTLES OF PAUL TO THE CORINTHIANS 22.1.[14]

9:14 Their Living by the Gospel

LIVING FROM ONE'S LABOR. AMBROSIASTER: It was not by the law of Moses that God followed the practice of the Gentiles, but natural reason itself decrees that a person should live from his labor. COMMENTARY ON PAUL'S EPISTLES.[15]

THE RIGHT OF SUPPORT. AUGUSTINE: The apostle says this [here and in 2 Timothy 2:3-6] so that Timothy might understand that what he took from those for whom he was, as it were, fighting, and whom he was cultivating as a vine, or feeding as a flock, was not a sign of begging but an acknowledgment of a right. THE WORK OF MONKS 15.[16]

---

[11]NPNF 1 12:121. [12]FC 16:343. [13]CSEL 81.100. [14]NPNF 1 12:126. [15]CSEL 81.101. [16]FC 16:357*.

9:15-18 PAUL'S COMMISSION TO PREACH THE GOSPEL

[15]*But I have made no use of any of these rights, nor am I writing this to secure any such provision. For I would rather die than have any one deprive me of my ground for boasting.* [16]*For if I preach the gospel, that gives me no ground for boasting. For necessity is laid upon me. Woe to me if I do not preach the gospel!* [17]*For if I do this of my own will, I have a*

reward; but if not of my own will, I am entrusted with a commission. ¹⁸What then is my reward? Just this: that in my preaching I may make the gospel free of charge, not making full use of my right in the gospel.

OVERVIEW: Paul served freely as an apostle (AMBROSE). His reward was preaching itself (CHRYSOSTOM). He did not overreach his claim in being an apostle but expressed it fully (AMBROSIASTER). The servant sent by the Lord does what he has to do even under difficult circumstances, putting everything in end-time perspective (AMBROSIASTER). It is a serious offense to lead others astray (ORIGEN). That the laborer deserves his hire is permitted but not commanded in the case of support for ministry. Although Paul defended the right of pastoral leaders to receive support, he himself did not accept it (AUGUSTINE).

9:15a Not Using Rights

THE CLARITY OF THE TEXT EXCEEDS ITS EXPLANATIONS. AUGUSTINE: "The Lord directed that those who preach the gospel should have their living from the gospel. But I for my part have appealed to none of these rights." . . . What is clearer than this? What is more definite? My only fear is that, when I discuss the passage in an attempt to explain it, I may obscure that which is of itself patent and forceful. For, they who do not understand these words, or pretend that they do not understand them, understand mine much less. THE WORK OF MONKS 9.[1]

LOOK TO THE SAINTS FOR APPLICATIONS. AUGUSTINE: "For the laborer deserves his hire."[2] He showed that this practice[3] was permitted, though not commanded, lest perhaps a disciple who took some compensation for his personal needs from those to whom he was preaching might think he was doing wrong. That it was more commendable to omit this practice is shown clearly in the life of the apostle . . . [who] declared: "Nevertheless I have not used this right." . . . He possessed the right, but he did

not bind his followers by a command. Since we are, then, unable to comprehend many passages, we gather from the deeds of the saints how to understand those passages which may easily be misinterpreted if reference is not made to the example set by the saints. ON LYING 15.30.[4]

9:15b Willing to Die

WILLINGNESS TO DIE. ORIGEN: "It is better that I die" than that they ravish and plunder some of my brothers and by sly verbal deception lead captive the "little children" and sucklings in Christ. HOMILY ON GENESIS 4.6.[5]

I WOULD RATHER DIE. AMBROSIASTER: Paul says he would rather die because he knew it would be better from the standpoint of his future salvation. COMMENTARY ON PAUL'S EPISTLES.[6]

9:16 Necessity of Preaching the Gospel

PREACHING THE GOSPEL. AMBROSIASTER: The servant sent by the Lord does what he has to do even if he is not willing, because if he does not do it he will suffer for it. Moses preached to Pharaoh even though he did not want to,[7] and Jonah was forced to preach to the Ninevites.[8] COMMENTARY ON PAUL'S EPISTLES.[9]

9:17 Entrusted with a Commission

THE DISPENSATION OF THE WORD. ORIGEN: What then shall I do, to whom the dispensation of the Word is committed? Although I am an "unprofitable servant,"[10] I have, nevertheless, re-

---

[1]FC 16:345. [2]Mt 10:10. [3]The securing of provision. [4]FC 16:92. [5]FC 71:109*. [6]CSEL 81.101. [7]Ex 4:10; 5:1. [8]Jon 1:1—3:4. [9]CSEL 81.102. [10]Lk 17:40.

ceived from the Lord the commission "to distribute the measure of wheat to the master's servants."[11] Genesis Homily 10.[12]

In Charity of Spirit. Ambrose: Surely it is better to merit a reward than to serve as a steward. Let us not be bound by the yoke of slavery, but let us serve in charity of spirit. Letters to Priests 47.[13]

Dispensing and Partaking of Salvation. Augustine: Up to now I am so far restored in that glory that I confess I am ignorant not only how near I come to it but even whether I shall come to it at all. It is true I am a dispenser of eternal salvation along with my other innumer-able fellow servants. "For if I do this thing willingly, I have a reward." To be a dispenser of that salvation by word and sacrament is not at all the same as to be a partaker of it. Letter 261 to Audax.[14]

9:18 The Reward of Preaching

Reward. Chrysostom: What can equal preaching? For it makes men vie even with the angels themselves. Homilies on the Epistles of Paul to the Corinthians 22.3.[15]

---

[11]Lk 12:42. [12]FC 71:157*. [13]FC 26:248. [14]FC 32:259. [15]NPNF 1 12:127.

9:19-23 FLEXIBLE SERVICE

[19]For though I am free from all men, I have made myself a slave to all, that I might win the more. [20]To the Jews I became as a Jew, in order to win Jews; to those under the law I became as one under the law—though not being myself under the law—that I might win those under the law. [21]To those outside the law I became as one outside the law—not being without law toward God but under the law of Christ—that I might win those outside the law. [22]To the weak I became weak, that I might win the weak. I have become all things to all men, that I might by all means save some. [23]I do it all for the sake of the gospel, that I may share in its blessings.

Overview: Paul's empathy for all was not a cheap pretense (Ambrosiaster, Chrysostom, Augustine) but a sincere expression of his hope to save some (Chrysostom, Cyril of Alexandria). Paul found in Christ the pattern of empathy (Ambrose, Cyril of Jerusalem). Each one becomes like those he helps when he mercifully grants them what he would desire in that situation (Augustine). The apostle who was free from all became vol-untarily a slave to all (Origen) for their salvation (Ambrosiaster). Paul was content in time to share with the others the crowns laid up for them in eternity (Chrysostom). To be under the law of Christ (Theodore of Mopsuestia) is to be under the law of God, because everything that is of Christ is of God (Ambrosiaster).

9:19 That I Might Win the More

Free from All, Slave to All. Origen: The fact that he is completely free makes Paul the exemplary apostle. For it is possible to be free of immorality but a slave to anger, to be free of greed but a slave to boasting, to be free of one sin but a slave to another. Commentary on 1 Corinthians 3.43.1-5.[1]

Wanting Only Their Salvation. Ambrosiaster: Paul is free from all human claims because he preached the gospel without getting any praise for it and never wanted anything from anyone, except their salvation. Commentary on Paul's Epistles.[2]

Losing a Part to Gain All. Cyril of Alexandria: So also the blessed Paul "became all things to all men," not in order that he might gain some sort of advantage but that, with the loss of a part, he might gain all. Letter 76.[3]

9:20 As One Under the Law

Not a Pretense. Ambrosiaster: Did Paul merely pretend to be all things to all men, in the way that flatterers do? No. He was a man of God and a doctor of the spirit who could diagnose every pain, and with great diligence he tended them and sympathized with them all. We all have something or other in common with everyone. This empathy is what Paul embodied in dealing with each particular person. Commentary on Paul's Epistles.[4]

Not Being Under the Law. Chrysostom: Paul did not become a Jew in reality but only in appearance. How could it have been otherwise, since he was so determined to convert them and deliver them from their predicament? Homilies on the Epistles of Paul to the Corinthians 22.5.[5]

Not a Deception. Augustine: Paul was not pretending to be what he is not but showing compassion. Letter 82 to Jerome.[6]

Thinking Sympathetically. Augustine: A person who nurses a sick man becomes, in a sense, sick himself, not by pretending to have a fever but by thinking sympathetically how he would like to be treated if he were sick himself. Letter to Jerome 75.[7]

9:21 As One Outside the Law

Under the Law of Christ. Ambrosiaster: To be under the law of Christ is to be under the law of God, because everything which is of Christ is of God. Commentary on Paul's Epistles.[8]

Theodore of Mopsuestia: Paul states, somewhat surprisingly, that he is under the law of Christ, lest anyone think that he is under the law of Moses. Pauline Commentary from the Greek Church.[9]

Putting Oneself in the Other's Place. Augustine: He did this by compassion, not by lying. For each one becomes like him whom he wants to help when such great mercy prevails as that each one would wish for himself if he were in the same misery. And so he becomes like the other—not by deceiving him but by putting himself in the other's place. Against Lying 12.[10]

9:22a Winning the Weak

Not a Lie. Augustine: This is correctly interpreted to mean that he, not by lying but by sympathy, brought it about that he enabled their conversion by his own great love which made it seem as though he himself were afflicted with that evil of which he wished to heal them. On Lying 21.[11]

9:22b Becoming All to All

Christ as Pattern of Empathy. Cyril of Jerusalem: Everywhere the Savior becomes "all

---

[1]JTS 9:512-13. [2]CSEL 81.103. [3]FC 77:87. [4]CSEL 81.103. [5]NPNF 1 12:128. [6]FC 12:415. [7]FC 12:355. [8]CSEL 81.104. [9]NTA 15:185. [10]FC 16:159*. [11]FC 16:107*.

things to all men." To the hungry, bread; to the thirsty, water; to the dead, resurrection; to the sick, a physician; to sinners, redemption. SERMON ON THE PARALYTIC 10.[12]

PAUL THE IMITATOR OF CHRIST. AMBROSE: He who did not think it robbery to be equal with God took the nature of a slave. He became all things to all men to bring salvation to all. Paul, an imitator of him, lived as if outside the law while remaining accountable to the law. He spent his life for the advantage of those he wished to win. He willingly became weak for the weak in order to strengthen them. He ran the race to overtake them. LETTERS TO PRIESTS 54.[13]

ALL THINGS TO ALL PEOPLE. AMBROSIASTER: Paul became weak by abstaining from things which would scandalize the weak. COMMENTARY ON PAUL'S EPISTLES.[14]

9:22c Saving Some

TO SAVE SOME. CHRYSOSTOM: Paul became all things to all men, not in the expectation that he would win everybody but that he might save at least some. It was not possible for all the seed

to be saved, but neither could it be that all of it should perish. Someone as ardently zealous as Paul was sure to have some success at least. HOMILIES ON THE EPISTLES OF PAUL TO THE CORINTHIANS 22.5.[15]

9:23 Sharing in the Gospel's Blessings

FOR THE SAKE OF THE GOSPEL. ORIGEN: Only someone as mature in faith as the apostle Paul could say this. A sinner could never talk in this way. COMMENTARY ON 1 CORINTHIANS 3.43.49-50.[16]

CONTENT TO SHARE. CHRYSOSTOM: Do you perceive Paul's humility, how in the recompense of rewards he places himself as one of the many, even though he had exceeded all the others in his labors? It is obvious that his reward would be greater also, but he does not attempt to claim the first prize. On the contrary, he is content simply to share with the others the crowns which are laid up for them. HOMILIES ON THE EPISTLES OF PAUL TO THE CORINTHIANS 22.5.[17]

---

[12]FC 64:215. [13]FC 26:295*. [14]CSEL 81.105. [15]NPNF 1 12:128-29. [16]JTS 9:514. [17]NPNF 1 12:129.

9:24-27 THE RACE

[24]*Do you not know that in a race all the runners compete, but only one receives the prize? So run that you may obtain it.* [25]*Every athlete exercises self-control in all things. They do it to receive a perishable wreath, but we an imperishable.* [26]*Well, I do not run aimlessly, I do not box as one beating the air;* [27]*but I pommel my body and subdue it, lest after preaching to others I myself should be disqualified.*

OVERVIEW: The Christian life resembles a race. Lacking effort, there is no crown for the athlete (CLEMENT OF ALEXANDRIA, TERTULLIAN, CYPRIAN, SECOND CLEMENT, AMBROSE). It is

not enough to pretend to believe and then sit back passively (CHRYSOSTOM). Enabled by grace, the active fight against the powers of evil occurs with deeds, not words (AMBROSIASTER). Let the soul command the body (Jerome) through fasting (Ambrosiaster), so the lusts of the belly may be put in subjection (Chrysostom). We pray for grace in this difficult contest (Cassiodorus).

9:24 Obtaining the Prize

Not All Are Crowned. The So-Called Second Letter of Clement: So then, my brothers, let us strive, knowing that the contest is close at hand and that many make voyages for corruptible contests, but not all are crowned—only those who have labored much and striven well. The So-Called Second Letter of Clement 7.[1]

The Harsh Regimen of the Athlete. Tertullian: Your master, Jesus Christ, has anointed you with his Spirit and has brought you to this training ground. He determined long before the day of the contest to take you from a softer way of life to a harsher regimen, that your strength may increase. Athletes are set apart for more rigid training to apply themselves to the building up of their physical strength. They are kept from lavish living, from more tempting dishes, from more pleasurable drinks. They are urged on, they are subjected to tortuous toils, they are worn out. The more strenuously they have exerted themselves, the greater is their hope of victory. To the Martyrs 3.3.[2]

Greatness of Soul. Gregory of Nyssa: As far as you extend your efforts in behalf of piety, so far will the greatness of your soul extend through efforts and toils toward what the Lord urges us. On the Christian Mode of Life.[3]

The Diligence Required to Win. Chrysostom: Paul says this not because he thinks that only one person will be saved but because he wants to point out how much diligence is required in order to succeed. It is not enough merely to believe and then contend in any which way. Unless we have

run our race in such a way as to be blameless and to come near to the prize, it will not benefit us. Even if you think you are perfect in your knowledge you have still not obtained everything, so you must continue to run in order to obtain the prize. Homilies on the Epistles of Paul to the Corinthians 23.1.[4]

The Sacred Contest. Pseudo-Dionysius: The initiate is summoned to the sacred contests, which, with Christ as his trainer, he must undertake. For it is Christ who, as God, arranges the match, as sage lays down the rules, as beauty is a worthy prize for the victors, and more divinely as goodness is present with the athletes, defending their freedom and guaranteeing their victory over the forces of death and destruction. And so the initiate will quite gladly hurl himself into what he knows to be divine contests, and he will follow and scrupulously observe the wise rules of the game. . . . He will follow the divine tracks established by the goodness of the first of athletes. The Ecclesiastical Hierarchy 3.6.[5]

Willing and Running by Grace. Augustine: It is not from the one who wills nor from the one that runs but from God who has mercy that we obtain what we hope for and reach what we desire. Esau was unwilling and did not run. Had he been willing and had he run, he would have obtained the help of God who by calling him would have given him the power both to will and to run. To Simplician 10.[6]

9:25 An Imperishable Wreath

Athletes of Self-Control. Clement of Alexandria: No effort, no crown! Today there are people who place the widow above the virgin in terms of self-control, because the widow has rejected a pleasure which she once enjoyed. Stromata 3.101.4-5.[7]

---

[1]FC 1:69. [2]FC 40:23*. [3]FC 58:131. [4]NPNF 1 12:131-32. [5]CWS 207. [6]LCC 6:393*. [7]FC 85:320.

THE COMBAT. CYPRIAN: This combat was foretold by the prophets, engaged in by the Lord and carried on by the apostles. LETTERS 10.4.[8]

THE ATHLETE. AMBROSE: You are an athlete. Come to grips with your opponent, not with your head but with your arms. SIX DAYS OF CREATION 6.[9]

THE RULES. BASIL: No one is crowned except he strive lawfully. GIVE HEED TO THYSELF.[10]

REFRESHED BY HOPE. AUGUSTINE: When we enter upon the way of the Lord, let us fast from the vanity of this present life and refresh ourselves with the hope of the future life, not focusing our heart on things here but feasting it on things above. SERMON 263.[11]

9:26 Not Beating the Air

FIGHTING EFFECTIVELY. AMBROSIASTER: Paul means that he fights not merely with his words but with his deeds. COMMENTARY ON PAUL'S EPISTLES.[12]

INTO THE ARENA. AMBROSE: Like an athlete he comes last into the arena. He lifts his eyes to heaven. . . . He sees that his whole task awaits him. . . . He chastises his body so that it will not defeat him in the contest. He anoints it with the oil of mercy. He practices daily exhibitions of virtue. He smears himself with dust. He runs with assurance to the goal of the course. He aims his blows, he darts his arms, but not at empty spaces. . . . Earth is man's training ground, heaven his crown. LETTERS TO PRIESTS 49.[13]

PARRYING BLOWS. AMBROSE: Like a good athlete, Paul knew how to parry the blows of the opposing powers and even to strike them as they advanced to the attack. PARADISE 12.56.[14]

THIS WORLD AND THE NEXT. JEROME: So run in this world as to obtain in the next. AGAINST THE PELAGIANS 1.[15]

THE POWERS OF THE AIR. THEODORE OF MOPSUESTIA: The "air" here refers to the powers of evil. PAULINE COMMENTARY FROM THE GREEK CHURCH.[16]

9:27 Not Being Disqualified

LET THE SOUL COMMAND THE BODY. JEROME: Let our soul be in command and our body in subjection. Then Christ will come immediately and make his dwelling with us. HOMILY 9.[17]

POMMEL THE BODY. AMBROSIASTER: To pommel the body is to fast and to avoid any kind of luxury. Paul shows that he disciplines his own body so that he will not miss out on the reward about which he preaches to others. COMMENTARY ON PAUL'S EPISTLES.[18]

BEHAVIORAL CHANGE REQUIRED. CHRYSOSTOM: Here Paul is implying that the Corinthians are subject to the lusts of the belly and abandon themselves to it, fulfilling their own greediness under a pretense of perfection. If Paul, who had taught so many, was afraid of being rejected at the end, what can we say? Mere belief is not enough; we must behave in a way which is blameless if we hope to inherit salvation. HOMILIES ON THE EPISTLES OF PAUL TO THE CORINTHIANS 23.2.[19]

PAUL'S NEED FOR SELF-DISCIPLINE. CHRYSOSTOM: If Paul—a man of such caliber and stature, who traversed the whole world like a winged creation, who proved superior to bodily necessities and was privileged to hear those secret words that no one else to this day has heard—if he wrote these words, "I punish my body and

---

[8]FC 51:27*. [9]FC 42:264*. [10]FC 9:438*. [11]FC 38:396. [12]CSEL 81.106. [13]FC 26:256. [14]FC 42:335. [15]FC 53:348*. [16]NTA 15:106. [17]FC 48:67. [18]CSEL 81.106-7. [19]NPNF 1 12:132-33.

bring it into subjection lest while preaching to others I myself become disqualified," if then that man, the object of so great favor, despite such conspicuous prowess felt the need to pommel his body, bring it into subjection, submit it to the authority of the soul and place its impulses under the virtue of the soul . . . what then would we say, deprived as we are of these virtues and with nothing to show in addition to this beyond deep indifference? After all, this war admits of no truce, does it? It has no set time for the assault, does it? HOMILIES ON GENESIS, HOMILY 22.22.[20]

DISTINGUISHING THE JUSTIFIED SELF FROM THE EVIL CONSEQUENCES OF FREE ACTS. AUGUSTINE: Paul chastises what is of him and not what is himself. For what is of him is one thing, what is himself is another. He chastises what is of him

so that he, being just, may bring about the death of bodily wantonness. AGAINST JULIAN 24.[21]

THE UNEVEN CONTEST. CASSIODORUS: Free us, Lover of men, from the danger which Paul mentions, that while preaching to others I may myself be found false. You truly know how weak we are. You recognize the nature of the foe who oppresses us. In our uneven contest and our mortal weakness we seek you, for the glory redounds to your majesty if the roaring lion is overcome by the feeble sheep. EXPLANATION OF THE PSALMS, PRAYER.[22]

---

[20]FC 82:86*. [21]FC 35:85. He does not chastise the new man made just in faith but what is of or from the old man of sin. [22]ACW 53:468-69.

10:1-5 THE OLD AND THE NEW

[1]I want you to know, brethren, that our fathers were all under the cloud, and all passed through the sea, [2]and all were baptized into Moses in the cloud and in the sea, [3]and all ate the same supernatural° food [4]and all drank the same supernatural° drink. For they drank from the supernatural° Rock which followed them, and the Rock was Christ. [5]Nevertheless with most of them God was not pleased; for they were overthrown in the wilderness.

o *Greek* spiritual

OVERVIEW: All believers journey through a sea of baptism and under a cloud of grace (THEODORET OF CYR). Everything that happened to the wandering Hebrews is understood as a picture of the truth that has been revealed in Christ (AMBROSIASTER). As the crossing of the sea protected them from their enemies and gave them real freedom, so baptism protects us from our demonic enemies (GENNADIUS OF CONSTAN-

TINOPLE). The sea prefigures baptism with water; the cloud prefigures the grace of baptism in the Spirit (THEODORE, CYPRIAN, MAXIMUS OF TURIN). The supernatural food (THEODORE) and the water that flowed from the rock were figures (AMBROSE, PELAGIUS) of what we now eat and drink in remembrance of Christ (AMBROSIASTER). Those who ate manna died in the desert, but the food you receive is living bread for eternal life (Ambrose). From the rock of his humanity flows the endless stream of his redeeming blood (Ambrose, Caesarius of Arles). Moses and the children of Israel passed from the old life of slavery in Egypt to the new life of faith. Christians make the same spiritual journey when they are converted (Ambrosiaster). The children of Israel proved to be unworthy recipients of God's free gift (Origen).

10:1 The Cloud and the Sea

The Mission of the Lamb. Cyril of Jerusalem: There Moses was sent by God into Egypt; here Christ was sent from the Father into the world. Moses' mission was to lead out of Egypt a persecuted people; Christ's was to rescue all the people of the world who were under the tyranny of sin. There the blood of a lamb was the charm against the destroyer; here, the blood of the unspotted Lamb, Jesus Christ, is appointed your inviolable sanctuary against demons. Mystagogical Lecture 1 1.3.[1]

Grace and Baptism. Theodoret of Cyr: The cloud is the grace of the Holy Spirit, while the sea represents baptism. Commentary on the First Epistle to the Corinthians 226.[2]

Through the Sea. Maximus of Turin: What took place, as the apostle says, was the mystery of baptism. Clearly this was a kind of baptism, where the cloud covered the people and water carried them. But the same Christ the Lord who did all these things now goes through baptism before the Christian people in the pillar of his body—he who at that time went through the sea before the children of Israel in the pillar of fire. . . . Through this faith—as was the case with the children of Israel—the one who walks calmly will not fear Egypt in pursuit. Sermons 100.3.[3]

10:2 Baptized into Moses

The Baptism of the Law. Cyprian: The Jews

had already obtained that most ancient baptism of the law and of Moses. Letter 73, The Baptismal Controversy 17.[4]

Delivered from Death. Ambrosiaster: Paul says the Jews were under the cloud in order to point out that everything that happened to them is meant to be understood as a picture of the truth which has been revealed to us. Under the cloud they were protected from their enemies until they were delivered from death, analogous to baptism. For when they passed through the Red Sea they were delivered from the Egyptians who died in it,[5] and their death prefigured our baptism, which puts our adversaries to death as well. Commentary on Paul's Epistles.[6]

The Meaning of the Exodus. Augustine: The history of the exodus was an allegory of the Christian people that was yet to be. The Usefulness of Belief 8.[7]

Water and Spirit. Theodore of Mopsuestia: The sea is a figure of baptism with water; the cloud of the grace of baptism in the Spirit. Pauline Commentary from the Greek Church.[8]

The Sea of Protection. Gennadius of Constantinople: The cloud was a figure standing for the grace of the Spirit. For just as the cloud covered the Israelites and protected them from the Egyptians,[9] so the Spirit's grace shields us from the wiles of the devil. Likewise, just as the crossing of the sea protected them from their enemies and gave them real freedom, so baptism protects us from our enemies. That was how the Israelites came to live under the law of Moses. This is how we, in baptism, are clothed with the Spirit of adoption and inherit the cove-

---

[1]FC 64:154. [2]Migne PG 82:302. [3]ACW 50:227. [4]LCC 5:166. [5]Ex 14:28-29. [6]CSEL 81.107. [7]LCC 6:297. Cf. 1 Cor 10:1-11. [8]NTA 15:185. [9]Ex 14:19.

nants and confessions made in accordance with the commands of Christ. Pauline Commentary from the Greek Church.[10]

10:3 Supernatural Food

Food for the Soul. Gregory of Nyssa: The divine apostle also, in calling the Lord "spiritual food and drink," suggests that he knows that human nature is not simple, but that there is an intelligible part mixed with a sensual part and that a particular type of nurture is needed for each of the elements in us—sensible food to strengthen our bodies and spiritual food for the well-being of our souls. On Perfection.[11]

The Manna and the Bread of Life. Ambrose: All those who ate that bread [manna] died in the desert, but this food which you receive, this "living bread which came down from heaven," furnishes the energy for eternal life. Whoever eats this bread "will not die forever," for it is the body of Christ.[12] . . . That manna was subject to corruption if kept for a second day. This is foreign to every corruption. Whoever tastes it in a holy manner shall not be able to feel corruption. For them water flowed from the rock. For you blood flows from Christ. Water satisfied them for the hour. Blood satisfies you for eternity. The Mysteries 8.48.[13]

Taste and See. Ambrose: What we eat, what we drink, the Holy Spirit expresses to you elsewhere, saying; "Taste and see that the Lord is sweet. Blessed is the one who trusts in him."[14] Christ is in that sacrament, because the body is Christ's. So the food is not corporeal but spiritual. The Mysteries 56.[15]

Power of the Spirit. Theodore of Mopsuestia: Paul calls the food supernatural because it gave those who ate it the power of the Holy Spirit.[16] However, it did not of itself make them spiritual people. Pauline Commentary from the Greek Church.[17]

10:4 Supernatural Drink

The Rock Was Christ. Ambrose: This surely referred not to his divinity but to his flesh, which flowed over the hearts of the thirsting people with the perpetual stream of his blood. The Holy Spirit 1.2.[18]

The Word of the Creator. Ephrem the Syrian: I considered the Word of the Creator and likened it to the rock that marched with the people in Israel in the wilderness; it was not from the reservoir of water contained within it that it poured forth for them glorious streams. There was no water in the rock, yet oceans sprang forth from it. Just so did the Word fashion created things out of nothing. Hymns on Paradise 5.1.[19]

Figures of What We Now Eat and Drink. Ambrosiaster: The manna and the water which flowed from the rock are called spiritual because they were formed not according to the law of nature but by the power of God working independently of the natural elements.[20] They were created for a time as figures of what we now eat and drink in remembrance of Christ the Lord. Commentary on Paul's Epistles.[21]

Imitating the Rock. Gregory of Nyssa: We also will be a rock, imitating, as far as possible in our changing nature, the unchanging and permanent nature of the Master. On Perfection.[22]

The Rock a Symbol. Augustine: All symbols seem in some way to personify the realities of which they are symbols. So, St. Paul says, "The rock was Christ," because the rock in question

---

[10]NTA 15:418. [11]FC 58:107*. [12]Jn 6:49-58. [13]FC 44:22-23*. [14]Ps 33:9. [15]FC 44:27. [16]Ex 16:11-36. [17]NTA 15:185. [18]FC 44:36. [19]HOP 102. [20]Ex 16:11-36; 17:1-7. [21]CSEL 81.108. [22]FC 58:108.

symbolized Christ. City of God 18.46.[23]

Manifest a Life Worthy of Grace. Chrysostom: Why does Paul say these things? He was pointing out that just as the Israelites got no benefit from the great gift which they enjoyed, so the Corinthian Christians would get nothing out of baptism or holy communion unless they went on and manifested a life worthy of that grace. Homilies on the Epistles of Paul to the Corinthians 23.3.[24]

The Stream of His Blood. Caesarius of Arles: Surely this refers more to his physical body than to his divinity, for the hearts of the thirsty people were satisfied by the endless stream of his blood. Sermons 117.2.[25]

10:5 God's Displeasure

Unworthy Recipients of the Free Gift.

Origen: Paul wants to remind us that we are not saved merely because we happen to have been the recipients of God's free grace. We have to demonstrate that we are willing recipients of that free gift. The children of Israel received it, but they proved to be unworthy of it, and so they were not saved. Commentary on 1 Corinthians 4.45.2-5.[26]

Overthrown in the Wilderness. Chrysostom: The Israelites were not in the land of promise when God did these things to them. Thus it was that he visited them with a double vengeance, because he did not allow them to see the land which had been promised to them, and he punished them severely as well. Homilies on the Epistles of Paul to the Corinthians 23.4.[27]

---

[23]FC 24:168. [24]NPNF 1 12:133. [25]FC 47:178. [26]JTS 9:29. [27]NPNF 1 12:134.

10:6-13 LEARNING FROM EXPERIENCE

[6]*Now these things are warnings for us, not to desire evil as they did.* [7]*Do not be idolaters as some of them were; as it is written, "The people sat down to eat and drink and rose up to dance."* [8]*We must not indulge in immorality as some of them did, and twenty-three thousand fell in a single day.* [9]*We must not put the Lord* [p] *to the test, as some of them did and were destroyed by serpents;* [10]*nor grumble, as some of them did and were destroyed by the Destroyer.* [11]*Now these things happened to them as a warning, but they were written down for our instruction, upon whom the end of the ages has come.* [12]*Therefore let any one who thinks that he stands take heed lest he fall.* [13]*No temptation has overtaken you that is not common to man. God is faithful, and he will not let you be tempted beyond your strength, but with the temptation will also provide the way of escape, that you may be able to endure it.*

p *Other ancient authorities read* Christ

OVERVIEW: Baptism and holy Communion were prefigured in ancient prophecy (CHRYSOSTOM). Christians can learn from Israel's experience in the desert. We are being warned and chastised (ORIGEN, AMBROSIASTER) through our gluttony, idolatry, fornication (CHRYSOSTOM) and immorality (PELAGIUS). We are called to endure the suffering that leads to the crown (CHRYSOSTOM), not to grumble over receiving lesser gifts (THEODORET OF CYR) as did Judas (AMBROSIASTER). Beware. The penalties that come in the last day will not have a time limit but will be eternal (CHRYSOSTOM). Do not be proud of your standing, but pay attention so that you will not fall (CHRYSOSTOM, AMBROSIASTER). Providence permits temptations to strengthen the will (SEVERIAN OF GABALA). The ability to bear temptations comes by grace (CHRYSOSTOM, AUGUSTINE). In temptation God gives us not the certainty that we shall bear it but the gift that we shall be made able to bear it (ORIGEN).

10:6 Not Desiring Evil

WARNINGS FOR US. ORIGEN: These things were written as examples for us, so that when we read about their sins we shall know to avoid them. COMMENTARY ON 1 CORINTHIANS 4.46.[1]

PREFIGURED IN PROPHECY. CHRYSOSTOM: Just as the gifts are symbolic, so are the punishments symbolic. Baptism and holy Communion were prefigured in prophecy. In the same way the certainty of punishment for those who are unworthy of this gift was proclaimed beforehand for our sake, so that we might learn from these examples how we must watch our step. HOMILIES ON THE EPISTLES OF PAUL TO THE CORINTHIANS 23.4.[2]

10:7 Warnings Against Idolatry

GLUTTONOUS IDOLATERS. CHRYSOSTOM: Do you see how Paul even calls the Israelites idolaters?

He says it first, and then gives examples to support his contention.[3] He also gives us the reason for their idolatry, which is gluttony. HOMILIES ON THE EPISTLES OF PAUL TO THE CORINTHIANS 23.4.[4]

IDOLATRY AS PLAY. AUGUSTINE: What is as similar to the play of children as the worshiping of idols? QUESTIONS 61.[5]

10:8 Not Indulging in Immorality

THE ISRAELITES' IMMORALITY. PELAGIUS: Note that it was not just idolatry which led to death [but their immorality as well]. COMMENTARY ON THE FIRST EPISTLE TO THE CORINTHIANS 10.[6]

ANOTHER WARNING ABOUT FORNICATION. CHRYSOSTOM: Why does Paul mention fornication again, when he has said so much about it already? It is always Paul's custom, when he admonishes people of many sins, to put them down in order before proceeding to deal with them individually, and then to refer to earlier topics as he goes down the list. God himself does this in the Old Testament when, in mentioning each particular transgression he keeps going back to the golden calf, reminding the Jews of that sin.[7] Paul is doing this here, reminding them of the sin of fornication and pointing out that the cause of that evil was sloth and gluttony. HOMILIES ON THE EPISTLES OF PAUL TO THE CORINTHIANS 23.4.[8]

10:9 Not Testing the Lord

TESTING CHRIST. AMBROSIASTER: The Jews were putting Christ to the test, because it was he who spoke to Moses. Paul is warning us here

---

[1]JTS 9:29. [2]NPNF 1 12:134. [3]See Ex 32:6. [4]NPNF 1 12:134. [5]FC 70:121. [6]Migne PL 30:746D. [7]Deut 9:13-21. [8]NPNF 1 12:134.

not to do the same as they did. Commentary on Paul's Epistles.[9]

10:10 Destroyed by the Destroyer

Prefiguring Judas. Ambrosiaster: Those who were destroyed prefigured Judas, who betrayed Christ and was eliminated from the number of the apostles by the judgment of God.[10] Commentary on Paul's Epistles.[11]

Endure Suffering That Leads to the Crown. Chrysostom: What is required is not only to suffer for Christ, but to endure what we suffer nobly and with all gladness, since this is the nature of every athlete's crown. If we do not do so, punishment will come upon us who take disaster with bad grace. This is why the apostles rejoiced when they were beaten, and Paul gloried in his sufferings. Homilies on the Epistles of Paul to the Corinthians 23.4.[12]

Do Not Grumble. Theodoret of Cyr: Some of the Corinthians were grumbling that they had only received the lesser spiritual gifts, when they wanted them all. Commentary on the First Epistle to the Corinthians 227.[13]

10:11 Warning and Instruction

A Warning with Eternal Consequences. Chrysostom: Paul mentions the end of the ages in order to startle the Corinthians. For the penalties which come then will not have a time limit but will be eternal. Although the punishments in this world end with our present life, those in the next world remain forever. Homilies on the Epistles of Paul to the Corinthians 23.5.[14]

10:12 Taking Care Not to Fall

Take Heed. Ambrosiaster: Paul says this to those who, relying on their knowledge that it was lawful to eat anything, were a cause of scandal to their weaker brethren. Thinking that they had risen to a higher level, they in fact declined because of the teaching of the false apostles and condemned Paul when they were the guilty ones. Commentary on Paul's Epistles.[15]

Our Standing in This World. Chrysostom: Once again, Paul casts down the pride of those who think they know it all. For if the Israelites, who had such great privileges, suffered these things, and if some were punished merely because they were heard to complain, how much more shall we suffer if we are not careful. Anyone who relies on himself will soon fall. For the way in which we stand in this world is not secure and will not be until we are delivered out of the waves of this present life into the peaceful haven of eternal rest. Therefore, do not be proud of your standing, but pay attention so that you will not stumble. If Paul was afraid that it might happen to him, how much more ought we to be afraid also. Homilies on the Epistles of Paul to the Corinthians 23.5.[16]

10:13a Temptation Common to Humanity

The Purpose of Temptation. Severian of Gabala: Paul did not pray that we should not be tempted, for a man who has not been tempted is untried, but that we should be able to bear our temptations as we ought. Pauline Commentary from the Greek Church.[17]

10:13b Ability to Endure Temptation

God Enables Us to Bear Temptation. Origen: Many do not bear it but are conquered by temptation. What God gives us is not the certainty that we shall bear it but the possibility that we

---

[9]CSEL 81.110. [10]Mt 27:3-5; Acts 1:24-26. [11]CSEL 81.110.
[12]NPNF 1 12:135. [13]Migne PG 82:303. [14]NPNF 1 12:135.
[15]CSEL 81.111. [16]NPNF 1 12:135. [17]NTA 15:258.

may be made able to bear it. ON FIRST PRINCI-PLES 3.2.3.[18]

ABILITY TO BEAR TEMPTATION COMES FROM GRACE.

CHRYSOSTOM: Paul implies that there must be temptations which we cannot bear. What are these? Well, all of them in effect. For the ability to bear them comes from God's grace, which we obtain by asking for it. God gives us patience and brings us speedy deliverance. In this way the temptation becomes bear-

able. HOMILIES ON THE EPISTLES OF PAUL TO THE CORINTHIANS 24.1.[19]

NOT BY STRENGTH OF FREE WILL.

AUGUSTINE: Why is this written if we are now so endowed that by the strength of our free will we are able to overcome all temptations merely by bearing them? LETTER 179 TO BISHOP JOHN.[20]

---

[18]OFP 216. [19]NPNF 1 12:139. [20]FC 30:113.

10:14-22 THE BODY AND BLOOD OF CHRIST

[14]*Therefore, my beloved, shun the worship of idols.* [15]*I speak as to sensible men; judge for yourselves what I say.* [16]*The cup of blessing which we bless, is it not a participation[q] in the blood of Christ? The bread which we break, is it not a participation[q] in the body of Christ?* [17]*Because there is one bread, we who are many are one body, for we all partake of the one bread.* [18]*Consider the people of Israel;[a] are not those who eat the sacrifices partners in the altar?* [19]*What do I imply then? That food offered to idols is anything, or that an idol is anything?* [20]*No, I imply that what pagans sacrifice they offer to demons and not to God. I do not want you to be partners with demons.* [21]*You cannot drink the cup of the Lord and the cup of demons. You cannot partake of the table of the Lord and the table of demons.* [22]*Shall we provoke the Lord to jealousy? Are we stronger than he?*

q *Or* communion   a *Greek* Israel according to the flesh

OVERVIEW: Paul's argument now comes to a crucial turn (CHRYSOSTOM, SEVERIAN OF GABALA): We are to avoid any connection with idolatry (TERTULLIAN). People who are drawn to idolatry will expect something from it, and to trust in an idol is to turn away from God (AMBROSIASTER). Paul appealed to the Corinthians to judge for themselves, which indicates Paul is sure of his own case (CHRYSOSTOM). In this passage we find one of the few places in Scripture where holy Communion is described. As we hold the cup of blessing in our hands we sing a

hymn to God for having poured out this draft that we might be saved. We thereby do what lovers do—turn our eyes away from all others (CHRYSOSTOM). One who properly eats the body of Christ is incorporated in the unity of his body (AUGUSTINE), as partners of the living Christ (CHRYSOSTOM). Every soul is a house of bread (AMBROSE)—gathered, crushed, moistened and fired (AUGUSTINE). Many grains are made into one bread (CHRYSOSTOM). Anyone who eats at the table of demons revolts against the table of Christ (AMBROSIASTER). Though the demonic forces may work in pagan sacrifices (Ambrosiaster), the food offered to idols has no power in itself to corrupt (Theodoret of Cyr). The uncleanness lies not in the food but in the distorted intentions of the sacrificers (Chrysostom). Good food is profaned when offered to idols (Cyril of Jerusalem).

10:14 Shun Worship of Idols

Flee the Worship of Idols. Tertullian: When the apostle says: "Flee from the worship of idols," he means idolatry whole and entire. Look closely at a thicket and see how many thorns lie hidden beneath the leaves! The Chaplet 10.[1]

Undercut Temptation. Ambrosiaster: Paul is exhorting the Corinthians to avoid any connection with idolatry, so that not only their bodies but their minds as well might be separated from it in order to destroy any form of temptation. For anyone involved in idolatry will expect something out of it. To trust in an idol is to turn away from God. Commentary on Paul's Epistles.[2]

The Climax of the Argument. Severian of Gabala: You see that everything Paul has been saying up to now is to reinforce this single point. Pauline Commentary from the Greek Church.[3]

10:15 Judging for Themselves

The Accused Judge. Chrysostom: It is a sign that a man is very sure of the rightness of his case when he is prepared to let the accused be their own judges. Homilies on the Epistles of Paul to the Corinthians 24.2.[4]

10:16 The Cup of Blessing

We Do What Lovers Do. Chrysostom: Paul called it a cup of blessing, because as we hold it in our hands we exalt him in our hymns, wondering and marveling at his unspeakable gift, blessing him for having poured out this draft so that we might not abide in error, and not only for having poured it out but also for having imparted it to us all. This is what lovers do. When they see those whom they love desiring what belongs to strangers and despising their own, they give what belongs to themselves and so persuade them to turn away from the gifts of those others. Homilies on the Epistles of Paul to the Corinthians 24.3.[5]

You Are What You Have Received. Augustine: That chalice, or rather, what the chalice holds, consecrated by the word of God, is the blood of Christ. Through those elements the Lord wished to entrust to us his body and the blood which he poured out for the remission of sins. If you have received worthily, you are what you have received. Easter Sunday, Homily 227.[6]

10:17 All Partake of the One Bread

One Bread. Chrysostom: The body of Christ is not many bodies but one body. For just as the bread, which consists of many grains, is made one to the point that the separate grains are no longer visible, even though they are still there, so we are joined to each other and to Christ. But if we are all nourished by the same source and become one with him, why do we not also show forth the same love and become one in this respect too? This was what it was like in ancient times, as we see in Acts [4:32]: "For the multitude of those who believed were of one heart and one soul." Homilies on the Epistles of Paul to the Corinthians 24.4.[7]

Every Soul a House of Bread. Ambrose: Thus every soul which receives the bread which comes down from heaven is a house of bread,

---

[1]FC 40:254*. [2]CSEL 81.113. [3]NTA 15:259. [4]NPNF 1 12:139. [5]NPNF 1 12:139. [6]FC 38:196. [7]NPNF 1 12:140.

the bread of Christ, being nourished and having its heart strengthened by the support of the heavenly bread which dwells within it. Hence Paul says: "We are all one bread." Every faithful soul is Bethlehem, just as that is called Jerusalem which has the peace and tranquility of the Jerusalem on high which is in heaven. That is the true bread which, after it was broken into bits, has fed all humanity. LETTERS TO PRIESTS 45.[8]

THE BREAD GATHERED, CRUSHED, MOISTENED AND FIRED. AUGUSTINE: So by bread you are instructed as to how you ought to cherish unity. Was that bread made of one grain of wheat? Were there not, rather, many grains? However, before they became bread, these grains were separate. They were joined together in water after a certain amount of crushing. For unless the grain is ground and moistened with water, it cannot arrive at that form which is called bread. So, too, you were previously ground, as it were, by the humiliation of your fasting and by the sacrament of exorcism. Then came the baptism of water. You were moistened, as it were, so as to arrive at the form of bread. But without fire, bread does not yet exist. EASTER SUNDAY 227.[9]

ONE BODY. AUGUSTINE: The one who is properly said to eat the body of Christ and to drink his blood is the one who is incorporated into the unity of his body. Heretics and schismatics can receive the sacrament but to no avail—in fact, to their harm—since the result is to increase their pain rather than to curtail the length of their punishment. CITY OF GOD 21.25.[10]

10:18 *An Analogy from Israel*

PARTNERS IN THE LIVING CHRIST. CHRYSOSTOM: The Jews were partners in the altar, but this is different from Christian communion. The Jews shared in something which was burned, but we share in the living Christ. It is with him that we have communion. HOMILIES ON THE EPISTLES OF PAUL TO THE CORINTHIANS 24.5.[11]

10:19 *An Idol Is Nothing*

FOOD OFFERED TO IDOLS. THEODORET OF CYR: Paul does not want anyone to think that sacrifices as such have any power or that they can corrupt the one who eats them afterward. COMMENTARY ON THE FIRST EPISTLE TO THE CORINTHIANS 229.[12]

10:20 *Not Partners with Demons*

THEY OFFER TO DEMONS, NOT TO GOD. CYRIL OF JERUSALEM: For as the bread and wine of the Eucharist before the holy invocation of the adorable Trinity were ordinary bread and wine, while after the invocation the bread becomes the body of Christ and the wine becomes his blood, so these foods of the pomp of Satan, though of their own nature ordinary food, become profane through the invocation of evil spirits. MYSTAGOGICAL LECTURE 1.7.[13]

WHAT PAGANS SACRIFICE. AMBROSIASTER: Paul is saying that beneath the surface of the idol there is a demonic power which is out to corrupt faith in the one God. COMMENTARY ON PAUL'S EPISTLES.[14]

UNCLEANNESS NOT IN THE FOOD AS SUCH. CHRYSOSTOM: This is the reason why we should not eat food which has been sacrificed to idols. The uncleanness is not in the food but in the intentions of the sacrificers and the attitude of the receivers. HOMILIES ON THE EPISTLES OF PAUL TO THE CORINTHIANS 24.5.[15]

10:21 *Partaking of the Table of Demons*

---

[8]FC 26:236. [9]FC 38:197. [10]FC 24:396. [11]NPNF 1 12:140. [12]Migne PG 82:306. [13]FC 64:157. [14]CSEL 81.114. [15]NPNF 1 12:141.

CRUCIFYING CHRIST AGAIN. AMBROSIASTER: Anyone who drinks the cup of demons insults the cup of Christ, and anyone who eats at the table of demons revolts against the table of Christ, that is to say, the altar of the Lord, and crucifies his body again. COMMENTARY ON PAUL'S EPISTLES.[16]

10:22 Provoking the Lord's Jealousy

FROM THE LESSER TO THE GREATER. CHRYSOSTOM: Do you see how terribly Paul rebukes the Corinthians, shaking their very nerves and reducing them to an absurdity? Why, you may ask, did he not say this at the beginning? Because it is Paul's custom to prove his point by many details, placing the strongest last and prevailing in the argument by proving more than is strictly necessary. Thus he began here with the smaller matters and made his way up toward the greatest of evils, so that the minds of the Corinthians had been prepared by the things already said. In this way the last point is more easily absorbed. HOMILIES ON THE EPISTLES OF PAUL TO THE CORINTHIANS 24.6.[17]

---

[16]CSEL 81.115. [17]NPNF 1 12:141.

10:23-29 GOING TOO FAR

[23]*"All things are lawful," but not all things are helpful. "All things are lawful," but not all things build up.* [24]*Let no one seek his own good, but the good of his neighbor.* [25]*Eat whatever is sold in the meat market without raising any question on the ground of conscience.* [26]*For "the earth is the Lord's, and everything in it."* [27]*If one of the unbelievers invites you to dinner and you are disposed to go, eat whatever is set before you without raising any question on the ground of conscience.* [28]*(But if some one says to you, "This has been offered in sacrifice," then out of consideration for the man who informed you, and for conscience' sake—* [29]*I mean his conscience, not yours—do not eat it.) For why should my liberty be determined by another man's scruples?*

OVERVIEW: We come to the altar of sacrifice with fear and trembling (TERTULLIAN). Paul is concerned for the conscience of one who sees somebody else buying food that has been sacrificed to idols and thinks that it is wrong (SEVERIAN OF GABALA). Suppose someone finds out that the food has been sacrificed to idols and then decides to abstain. If one does so out of aversion toward the idolatry and not out of fear, that is acceptable in God's sight (CHRYSOSTOM). Believers are asked to consider whether what they do will benefit their brothers and sisters or cause them to stumble (AMBROSIASTER, OECUMENIUS). Nothing is unclean except by our unworthy intentions (CHRYSOSTOM, NOVATIAN, AUGUSTINE). We may eat what is set before us but must not take advantage of the statement "all things are lawful" (Clement of Alexandria).

10:23 What Is Helpful

What Is Permitted. Tertullian: It is much easier for one to dread what is forbidden if he has a reverential fear of what is permitted. The Apparel of Women 10.6.[1]

Taking Advantage. Clement of Alexandria: Those who take advantage of everything that is lawful rapidly deteriorate into doing what is not lawful. Christ the Educator 2.1.14.[2]

10:24 Seeking Another's Good

Not Doing What We Want to Do. Ambrosiaster: It is true that anyone who is an idolater will seek what pleases him alone. He will place scandals in the way of the weaker brother's conscience. This is why we ought to be quick to resist doing just what we want to do, for the love of Christ and for the salvation of our neighbors. Commentary on Paul's Epistles.[3]

Have a Conscience That Benefits Others. Oecumenius: The question is not merely whether you are eating with a clear conscience. It is whether what you are doing is of benefit to your brother. Pauline Commentary from the Greek Church.[4]

10:25 The Ground of Conscience

The Blessing of Creation. Novatian: Accordingly, it is evident that all these foods enjoy again the blessings they received at their creation, now that the law has ended. Jewish Foods 5.6.[5]

Eat with a Good Conscience. Chrysostom: Ignorance is bliss. The food is not unclean in itself; only human intentions might make it unclean. Those who do not know what those intentions are can therefore eat it with a good

conscience. Homilies on the Epistles of Paul to the Corinthians 25.1.[6]

Eat Without Scruple of Conscience. Severian of Gabala: The conscience referred to here is not the conscience of the one who knows that idols do not exist but the conscience of the one who sees somebody else buying food which has been sacrificed to idols and thinks that it is wrong for that reason. Pauline Commentary from the Greek Church.[7]

10:26 All Is the Lord's

The Earth Is the Lord's.[8] Chrysostom: Nothing is unclean, unless we make it so by our intentions and our disobedience. Homilies on the Epistles of Paul to the Corinthians 25.1.[9]

God's Fruit. Augustine: One does not sin who afterward unwittingly eats food which he had previously refused as belonging to idols. Vegetables and any kind of fruit grown in any field are God's who created them. Letters 47.[10]

10:27 Raising No Questions

Eat What Is Set Before You. Clement of Alexandria: We must shun gluttony and eat only what is necessary. But if some unbeliever invites us to a banquet and we decide to accept, the apostle tells us to eat what is set before us. We do not need to abstain from rich foods completely, but we should not hanker for them either. Christ the Educator 2.10.[11]

10:28 Considering Others

Abstaining Out of Aversion to Idolatry. Chrysostom: Notice Paul's balanced approach. He did not order Christians to withdraw from

---

[1]FC 40:144. [2]FC 23:105. [3]CSEL 81.116. [4]NTA 15:440. [5]FC 67:152. [6]NPNF 1 12:144. [7]NTA 15:259. [8]Ps 24:1. [9]NPNF 1 12:144. [10]FC 12:229. [11]FC 23:101.

associating with unbelievers, but neither did he forbid it. People who make scrupulous inquiries do so out of fear, and that is wrong. On the other hand, if someone happens to find out that the food has been sacrificed to idols and then makes a conscious decision to abstain, he does so out of contempt and aversion toward the idolatry, not out of fear, and that is acceptable in God's sight. Homilies on the Epistles of Paul to the Corinthians 25.1.[12]

10:29 Balancing Liberty and Scruples

Liberty Not Bound to Another's Scruples.
Chrysostom: What Paul means is this. God has made him free and put him beyond harm's reach, but the Gentile does not understand his rule of life. He cannot see the nature of Christian freedom and will say to himself that Christianity is a lie, because although Christians shun demons, they are prepared to eat things which have been offered to them, so great is their gluttony. Such a judgment may be unfair, but it is better not to give the Gentile any room for judging at all. Homilies on the Epistles of Paul to the Corinthians 25.2.[13]

---

[12]NPNF 1 12:144. [13]NPNF 1 12:145.

10:30-33 THE RIGHT APPROACH

[30]*If I partake with thankfulness, why am I denounced because of that for which I give thanks?*
[31]*So, whether you eat or drink, or whatever you do, do all to the glory of God.* [32]*Give no offense to Jews or to Greeks or to the church of God,* [33]*just as I try to please all men in everything I do, not seeking my own advantage, but that of many, that they may be saved.*

Overview: In giving thanks to the Creator (Ambrosiaster), do everything with care so that others may glorify God (Chrysostom, Jerome) through you so as not to be scandalized (Severian of Gabala). One who is light and leaven and salt ought to enlighten others and draw unbelievers to him or her and not drive them away (Chrysostom, Cassiodorus). One who is aware of Christ's companionship is ashamed to do evil (Maximus of Turin). Be content; avoid suspicion (Basil).

10:30 Why Be Denounced?

The Idolater Tries to Have It Both Ways.
Ambrosiaster: Paul is saying that an idolater can have it both ways. On the one hand, he can glory in his idols, and on the other hand he can attack the apostle for eating what has been sacrificed to them, even if the latter does so after giving thanks to God. Such a person has an excuse for remaining in his error and sets a bad example to the brethren. Commentary on Paul's Epistles.[1]

10:31 To God's Glory

Giving Thanks. Ambrosiaster: To eat and

---

[1]CSEL 81.118.

drink to God's glory is to eat and drink after giving thanks to the Creator. COMMENTARY ON PAUL'S EPISTLES.[2]

WHATEVER YOU DO. CHRYSOSTOM: Let all the things which you undertake and accomplish have this root and foundation, namely, that they tend to the glory of God. . . . When Paul said "If you do anything" ["whatever you do"], he has enclosed our whole existence in a single word, desiring that we never perform any act of virtue with an eye to human glory. BAPTISMAL INSTRUCTIONS 6.10.[3]

EMBODYING GOD'S GLORY. JEROME: Even if I merely stretch forth my hand in almsgiving, I am meditating on the law of God. If I visit the sick, my feet are meditating on the law of God. If I do what is prescribed, I am praying with my whole body what others are praying with their lips. HOMILIES ON THE PSALMS, HOMILY 1.[4]

WITH CHRIST OUR COMPANION. MAXIMUS OF TURIN: He wishes, then, for all our actions to be accomplished with Christ as companion and witness, that we may do good things for him as the author and avoid what is evil for the sake of his fellowship. One who knows that Christ is his companion is ashamed to do evil. In good things, however, Christ is our helper, and in the face of evil things he is our defender. SERMONS 73.1.[5]

THAT OTHERS MAY GLORIFY GOD. SEVERIAN OF GABALA: Do everything with care so that others may glorify God through you and not be scandalized. PAULINE COMMENTARY FROM THE GREEK CHURCH.[6]

10:32 Offending No One

GIVE NO UNNECESSARY OFFENSE. AMBROSIASTER: Offense is given to the Jews when they see that a Christian, who claims the inheritance of the law and the prophets, is not afraid of idols, which they detest. Offense is given to the

Greeks, that is, to the Gentiles, if their sin of idolatry is not only not contested but actually encouraged by people in the church who fail to reject things sacrificed to idols. COMMENTARY ON PAUL'S EPISTLES.[7]

AVOID SUSPICION. BASIL: Do all things decently and according to order for the purpose of edification. The person, the time, the need and the place all should be properly chosen and determined upon. By consideration of all these details every shadow of evil suspicion will be avoided. THE LONG RULES 33.[8]

BE CONTENT. BASIL: Do not be a stumbling block in any way to those you meet. Be cheerful, a lover of the brethren, gentle, humble. Do not demean the aim of hospitality by seeking extravagant foods. Be content with what is at hand. LETTERS 42.[9]

10:33 Seeking the Advantage of Others

TRY TO PLEASE ALL. CHRYSOSTOM: Not only should the brethren receive no hurt from us, but neither should those who are outside the church. If we are light and leaven and luminaries and salt, we ought to enlighten, not to darken, to bind, not to loose, to draw unbelievers to us and not drive them away. The Gentiles are hurt when they see us doing such things, because they do not understand that we have been set free from them. Likewise, Jews and the weaker brethren will also suffer, for the same reason. HOMILIES ON THE EPISTLES OF PAUL TO THE CORINTHIANS 25.3.[10]

BEING EDIFIED IN CHRIST. AUGUSTINE: The apostle wanted believers to please all men, and he took pleasure in pleasing them, not because he swelled up inside at their praise but because

---

[2]CSEL 81.118. [3]ACW 31:96-97*. [4]FC 48:6. [5]ACW 50:178*.
[6]NTA 15:260. [7]CSEL 81.119. [8]FC 9:297*. [9]FC 13:106*.
[10]NPNF 1 12:146.

by being pleasing all might be edified in Christ. LETTERS 231.[11]

THE PEACE TO COME. CASSIODORUS: It was not for his own temporal advantage that he has spoken of the peace of the era to come but for his fellow believers and neighbors, so that they should long for it to gain salvation and chain themselves with the bonds of unanimity. EXPLANATION OF THE PSALMS 121.9.[12]

---

[11]FC 32:161*. [12]ACW 53:277*.

11:1-3 THE IMITATION OF CHRIST

[1]*Be imitators of me, as I am of Christ.*

[2]*I commend you because you remember me in everything and maintain the traditions even as I have delivered them to you.* [3]*But I want you to understand that the head of every man is Christ, the head of a woman is her husband, and the head of Christ is God.*

OVERVIEW: Everything in the Christian life hinges on following Christ in love (CHRYSOSTOM), as Paul did (CLEMENT OF ALEXANDRIA). As the Father sent the Son as the teacher and author of life, so Christ sent the apostles to be our teachers (AMBROSIASTER, BASIL). In the natural order the man is head of the woman, but in Christ there is neither male nor female (PELAGIUS). The Father is the head of the Son because he is eternally begotten of the Father. Christ is the head of the man because he created him, and the man is the head of the woman because she was taken from him (CYRIL OF JERUSALEM, AMBROSIASTER). Christ and God are equal in substance but different in relationship, and the same applies to man and woman, equal in dignity but different in relationship (TERTULLIAN, NOVATIAN, CHRYSOSTOM, AMBROSE). The nature of man and woman is the same (SEVERIAN OF GABALA). Paul admonished those who held to the local tradition that women would prophesy with bared heads and men with long hair would pray with heads covered (CHRYSOSTOM).

11:1 *Imitating Paul and Christ*

IMITATORS OF PAUL. CLEMENT OF ALEXANDRIA: If you imitate Paul as he imitated Christ, then you will be imitating Christ as he represented God. STROMATA 2.136.5.[1]

IMITATING OUR TEACHERS. AMBROSIASTER: It is normal that we should imitate those whom God has set over us as teachers. For if they imitate God, why should we not imitate them? For just as God the Father sent Christ as the teacher and author of life, so Christ sent the apostles to be our teachers, so that we should imitate them, for we are unable to imitate him directly. COMMENTARY ON PAUL'S EPISTLES.[2]

GUIDING OTHERS IN THE HUMILITY OF THE INCARNATE LORD. BASIL: If, indeed, the goal of Christianity is the imitation of Christ according to the measure of his incarnation, insofar as is conformable with the vocation of each individual, they

---

[1]FC 85:249. [2]CSEL 81.119.

who are entrusted with the guidance of many others are obliged to animate those still weaker than themselves, by their assistance, to the imitation of Christ. THE LONG RULES 43.[3]

THE PRECISE LANDMARK. CHRYSOSTOM: This is the rule of the most perfect Christianity, a landmark exactly laid down, the point that stands highest of all. Nothing can make a person like Christ more than caring for one's neighbors. HOMILIES ON THE EPISTLES OF PAUL TO THE CORINTHIANS 25.3.[4]

11:2 Maintaining Paul's Teachings

REMOLDING LOCAL TRADITIONS. AMBROSIASTER: Having attacked their morals and behavior, Paul now goes on to correct their traditions. COMMENTARY ON PAUL'S EPISTLES.[5]

THE TRADITION OF HEAD COVERINGS. CHRYSOSTOM: The Corinthian women used to pray and to prophesy (for in those days women also prophesied) with their heads bare. Meanwhile the men, who had spent a long time in philosophy, wore their hair long and covered their heads when praying, which was a Greek custom. Paul had already admonished them about these things. It seems that some had listened to him but that others disobeyed. Here he praises the obedient before going on to correct the others. HOMILIES ON THE EPISTLES OF PAUL TO THE CORINTHIANS 26.2.[6]

11:3 Christ's Headship

CHRIST'S SUBMISSION A MODEL FOR BOTH SEXES. TERTULLIAN: To what kind of a crown, I ask, did Christ Jesus submit for the salvation of both sexes? What crown has he who is the head of man and the glory of the woman and the husband of the church? It was made from thorns and thistles. THE CHAPLET 14.[7]

HOW THE TWO BECAME ONE. NOVATIAN: Scripture states: "And the two shall be but one

flesh,"[8] so that what was once one may become one again. . . . The head matches its own limbs and the limbs their own head, a natural bond uniting both in complete harmony, lest the closeness of the divine covenant be shattered by some sort of discord arising from the division of members. . . . Husbands are to love their wives even as Christ loved the church, and wives are to love their husbands as the church loves Christ. IN PRAISE OF PURITY 5.[9]

THE CRUCIFIED HEAD BECOMES THE HEAD OF ALL POWER. CYRIL OF JERUSALEM: The Head suffered in the "place of the skull." O great and prophetic appellation! The very name all but reminds you to think not of the crucified as a mere man. He is the head of every principality and power. The Head which was crucified is the Head of all power. CATECHESIS 13.23.[10]

THE NATURAL ORDER AND CHRIST'S HEADSHIP. PELAGIUS: The man is head of the woman in the natural order but not in Christ, in whom there is neither male nor female. Nevertheless, Paul wanted women to be subject to their husbands. God is the head of Christ's humanity, because the divinity which was in the human Jesus controlled his doings. COMMENTARY ON THE FIRST EPISTLE TO THE CORINTHIANS 11.[11]

THE ORDERING OF FATHER, SON, MAN AND WOMAN. AMBROSIASTER: God is the head of Christ because he begat him; Christ is the head of the man because he created him, and the man is the head of the woman because she was taken from his side.[12] Thus one expression has different meanings, according to the difference of person and substantive relationship. COMMENTARY ON PAUL'S EPISTLES.[13]

EQUAL SUBSTANTIALLY, DIFFERENT RELATION-

---

[3]FC 9:319. [4]NPNF 1 12:146. [5]CSEL 81.120. [6]NPNF 1 12:149. [7]FC 40:265*. [8]Gen 2:22. [9]FC 67:168-69*. [10]FC 64:20. [11]Migne PL 30:749C. [12]Gen 2:21-22. [13]CSEL 81.120-21.

ally. Chrysostom: The word *head* is used in two different senses here, since otherwise absurdity would result. The distance between Christ and man is far greater than between man and woman, on the one hand, or between Christ and God on the other, and is of a different kind. Christ and God are equal in substance but different in relationship, and the same applies to man and woman. But between God and Christ the Son on the one hand and man [and woman] on the other, there is a vast difference of substance as well as of relationship. Homilies on the Epistles of Paul to the Corinthians 26.3.[14]

Protecting the Helper. Ambrose: This is a warning that no one ought to rely on oneself. She who was made as a helper needs the protection of the stronger. In this sense "the head of the woman is the man." Yet while he believed that he would have the assistance of his wife, he fell because of her. Hence no one ought to entrust himself lightly to another unless he has first put that person's virtue to the test. Neither should he claim for himself in the role of protec-

tor one whom he believes is lesser to his strength. Rather, each one should share his special grace with the other. Especially is this true of the man, who is in the position of greater strength, who plays the part of protector. Paradise 4.25.[15]

To Whom Is the Man Responsible? Augustine: For the man is the head of the woman in perfect order when Christ who is the Wisdom of God is the head of the man. Against the Manichaeans 2.12.16.[16]

The Nature of Man and Woman the Same. Severian of Gabala: Since man did not make woman, the question here does not concern the origin of woman. Rather it concerns only [the relation of] submission. The nature of God and Christ is the same. Similarly the nature of man and woman is the same. Pauline Commentary from the Greek Church.[17]

---

[14]NPNF 1 12:150. [15]FC 42:302*. [16]FC 84:113*. [17]NTA 15:260.

11:4-16 PRACTICAL APPLICATION

[4]*Any man who prays or prophesies with his head covered dishonors his head,* [5]*but any woman who prays or prophesies with her head unveiled dishonors her head—it is the same as if her head were shaven.* [6]*For if a woman will not veil herself, then she should cut off her hair; but if it is disgraceful for a woman to be shorn or shaven, let her wear a veil.* [7]*For a man ought not to cover his head, since he is the image and glory of God; but woman is the glory of man.* [8]*(For man was not made from woman, but woman from man.* [9]*Neither was man created for woman, but woman for man.)* [10]*That is why a woman ought to have a veil*ʳ *on her head, because of the angels.* [11]*(Nevertheless, in the Lord woman is not independent of man nor man of woman;* [12]*for as woman was made from man, so man is now born of woman. And all things are from God.)* [13]*Judge for yourselves; is it proper for*

a woman to pray to God with her head uncovered? [14]*Does not nature itself teach you that for a man to wear long hair is degrading to him,* [15]*but if a woman has long hair, it is her pride? For her hair is given to her for a covering.* [16]*If any one is disposed to be contentious, we recognize no other practice, nor do the churches of God.*

r *Greek authority (the veil being a symbol of this)*

Overview: The difference between man and woman lies not in their nature but in their relationship (Chrysostom, Severian of Gabala). Woman is the glory of man, but there is an enormous distance between that and the glory of God (Ambrosiaster). A man who approaches the throne of God should wear the symbols of his office, which in this case is represented by having his head uncovered (Chrysostom). Just as God has nobody over him in all creation, so man has no one over him in the natural world. But woman lives under the protection of man (Severian). The relation of man and woman to God makes all the difference in understanding their relation to each other (Ambrosiaster, Chrysostom). Being covered is a mark of voluntary subjection (Ambrosiaster), calling the woman to be humble and preserve her virtue (Tertullian, Chrysostom). Since woman is the glory of man, it is shameful for a woman to desire to be like a man (Chrysostom). In the Genesis narrative man precedes woman in the order of their creation (Epiphanius, Theodoret of Cyr). The woman was created with gifts of serving, the man with gifts of ordering (Theodoret of Cyr). Paul appears to be not confining his instruction about hair to a particular place and time (Tertullian). He appealed to church tradition (Chrysostom), to nature (Ambrosiaster, Ambrose) and to the argument from general consent of reasonable people in these matters (Chrysostom). Since hair is potentially erotic, it can play into temptation (Pelagius). Natural hair is preferred to deceptive wigs (Clement of Alexandria).

11:4 When a Man Prays or Prophesies

Dishonoring the Head. Pelagius: Paul was complaining because men were fussing about their hair and women were flaunting their locks in church. Not only was this dishonoring to them, but it was also an incitement to fornication. Commentary on the First Epistle to the Corinthians 11.[1]

Distinguishing Prophecy, Ancient and Modern. Severian of Gabala: There is a difference between ancient and recent prophets, as follows. The ancients prophesied about the redemption of Israel, the calling of the Gentiles and the incarnation of Christ, whereas recent prophets prophesy about particular things or people, as Peter prophesied about Ananias, for example.[2] Pauline Commentary from the Greek Church.[3]

11:5 When a Woman Prays or Prophesies

A General Instruction to Women. Tertullian: What is the meaning of the expression "every woman" except women of every age, every rank and every circumstance? No one is excepted. Prayer 22.4.[4]

Self-Restraint of Mary. Anonymous: Could not the holy Mary, mother of God, have written books under her own name? But she did not, that she might not bring shame on her head by exercising authority over men. Montanist Oracles and Testimonia, Debate of a Montanist and an Orthodox.[5]

11:6 Wearing a Veil

---

[1]Migne PL 30:749D. [2]Acts 5:3. [3]NTA 15:261. [4]FC 40:178. [5]MOT 14:125. The Orthodox Christian is speaking.

Her Desire to Be Like Man. Chrysostom: A woman does not acquire a man's dignity by having her head uncovered but rather loses her own. Her shame and reproach thus derive from her desire to be like a man as well as from her actions. Homilies on the Epistles of Paul to the Corinthians 25.4.[6]

11:7a Man the Image and Glory of God

Different in Social Ordering. Ambrosiaster: Although man and woman are of the same substance, the man has relational priority because he is the head of the woman. He is greater than she is by cause and order, but not by substance. Woman is the glory of man, but there is an enormous distance between that and being the glory of God. Commentary on Paul's Epistles.[7]

The Approach to God. Chrysostom: No governor should come before the king without the symbols of his office. Such a person would never dare to approach the royal throne without his military girdle and cloak, and in the same way, a man who approaches the throne of God should wear the symbols of his office, which in this case is represented by having one's head uncovered. Homilies on the Epistles of Paul to the Corinthians 26.4.[8]

Made in the Image of the Triune God. Augustine: This image made to the image of God is not equal to and coeternal with him whose image he is, and it would not be, even if it had not sinned at all. The meaning of the words of God when he said: "Let us make man to our image and likeness" must be understood. They were not spoken in the singular but in the plural. For man was not made in the image of the Father alone, or of the Son alone, or of the Holy Spirit alone, but in the image of the Trinity. Literal Interpretation of Genesis 61.[9]

11:7b The Glory of Man

Woman the Glory of Man. Augustine: It is not as though one part of humanity belongs to God as its author and another to darkness, as some claim. Rather the part that has the power of ruling and the part that is ruled are both from God.

Thus the apostle says, "A man certainly should not cover his head, since he is the image and glory of God, but a woman is the glory of man."[10] Against the Manichaeans 2.26.40.[11]

Augustine: [The Manichaeans say]: "The devil should not have been allowed to approach the woman." On the contrary, she should not have allowed the devil to approach her. She was made so that, if she were unwilling, she could have prevented his approach. Then they say: "Maybe the woman should not even have been made." This would be to admit that something good should not have been made. For there can be no doubt that the woman is good—so good that the apostle says that she is the glory of man and that all things are from God. Against the Manichaeans 2.28.42.[12]

Different in Relationship. Severian of Gabala: From this we learn that man is not the image of God because of his soul or because of his body. If that were the case, woman would be the image of God in exactly the same way as man, because she too has a soul and a body. What we are talking about here is not nature but a relationship. For just as God has nobody over him in all creation, so man has no one over him in the natural world. But a woman does—she has man over her. Pauline Commentary from the Greek Church.[13]

11:8 Woman Made from Man

Against the Montanists. Epiphanius: For

---

[6]NPNF 1 12:152. [7]CSEL 81:121. [8]NPNF 1 12:153. [9]FC 84:187*. [10]1 Cor 11:6-7. [11]FC 84:137*. [12]FC 84:139*. [13]NTA 15:261.

even if women among them [the Montanists] are appointed to the office of bishop and presbyter by appealing to Eve, they hear the Lord saying: "Your resort shall be to your husband, and he shall rule over you."[14] And the apostolic word has also escaped their notice: "I do not permit a woman to teach in such a way as to exercise authority over men. She is to preserve the virtue of quietness."[15] And again, "For man is not from woman, but woman from man." Panarion 49.3.[16]

Order of Creation. Theodoret of Cyr: Man has the first place because of the order of creation. Commentary on the First Epistle to the Corinthians 234.[17]

11:9 *Woman Created for Man*

Primacy of Man. Theodoret of Cyr: This is all that is needed to demonstrate the primacy of the man, for the woman was created to serve him, not the other way round. Commentary on the First Epistle to the Corinthians 234.[18]

11:10 *Veiled Because of the Angels*

The Angels' Revolt. Tertullian: It is on account of the angels, he says, that the woman's head is to be covered, because the angels revolted from God on account of the daughters of men. Prayer 22.5.[19]

Because of the Angels. Ambrosiaster: The veil signifies power, and the angels are bishops. Commentary on Paul's Epistles.[20]

Why a Woman Ought to Wear a Veil. Chrysostom: Being covered is a mark of subjection and authority. It induces the woman to be humble and preserve her virtue, for the virtue and honor of the governed is to dwell in obedience. Homilies on the Epistles of Paul to the Corinthians 265.[21]

11:11 *Men and Women Interdependent*

Checking the Pride of Man. Chrysostom: Having talked about the glory of the man, Paul now reestablishes the balance so as not to exalt the man beyond what is his due nor to oppress the woman. In the Lord woman is not independent of man, nor is man independent of woman. . . . Each one of the two is the cause of the other, God being the cause of all. Homilies on the Epistles of Paul to the Corinthians 26.5.[22]

11:12 *Man Born of Woman*

All Things Are from God. Ambrosiaster: Paul adds that all things are from God so that the woman will not be upset because of her dependent condition nor will the man be proud of his responsible position. Commentary on Paul's Epistles.[23]

The Relation to God. Chrysostom: Yet whatever excellencies belong to man, they belong ultimately to God. We should therefore obey him and not complain about it. Homilies on the Epistles of Paul to the Corinthians 27.5.[24]

Countering Manichaean Dualism. Augustine: Concerning the male and female sexes, what has the son of perdition[25] to say? That the two sexes are not from God but from the devil? What has the vessel of election[26] to say about this? "For as the woman is from the man, so also is the man through the woman—but all things are from God." What does the devil say through the mouths of the Manichaeans about the flesh? That it is an evil substance, a creature not of God but of the enemy. Continence 10.24.[27]

11:13 *Judging Propriety*

---

[14]Gen 3:16. [15]1 Tim 2:12. [16]Migne PG 82:311. [17]Migne PG 82:311. [18]Migne PG 82:311. [19]FC 40:178. [20]CSEL 81.122. [21]NPNF 1 12:153. [22]NPNF 1 12:153. [23]CSEL 81.123. [24]NPNF 1 12:153. [25]The Manichaean. [26]Paul. [27]FC 16:219*.

God's Just Judgment. Origen: Here then we see the just judgment of God's providence, that diversity of conduct is taken into account and that each is treated according to the deserts of his departure and defection from goodness. First Principles 1.7.[28]

Appeal to Tradition and Nature. Ambrosiaster: This was the church's tradition, but since the Corinthians were ignoring it, Paul made his appeal to nature. Commentary on Paul's Epistles.[29]

Judge for Yourselves. Chrysostom: Paul has a habit of referring to ordinary everyday things in order to shame his hearers. After all, if even barbarians know these things, what is wrong with them? Can they not see the obvious? Homilies on the Epistles of Paul to the Corinthians 26.5.[30]

11:14 Teaching from Nature

The Tablets of Natural Law. Tertullian: If you demand a divine law, you have that common one prevailing all over the world, written on the tablets of nature, to which also St. Paul is accustomed to appeal. Thus he says concerning the veiling of women: "Does not nature teach you this?" Again, in saying in his letter to the Romans that the Gentiles do by nature what the law prescribes, he hints at the existence of natural law and a nature founded on law. The Chaplet 6.1.[31]

Levitical Law on Long Hair. Ambrosiaster: This is in line with Leviticus [19:27], which prohibits a man from having long hair. Commentary on Paul's Epistles.[32]

Nature Itself Teaches. Ambrose: One act is becoming to a man, another to a woman. . . . How unsightly it is for a man to act like a woman! Letters to Laymen 78.[33]

Why Such Long Hair? Augustine: What is the reason, I wonder, why men wear their hair long contrary to the precept of the apostle? Is it to furnish greater leisure to the barbers? Or is it because they wish to imitate the birds of the gospel? Maybe they fear being plucked so that they might be unable to fly? I refrain from saying more concerning this habit, because of certain long-haired brothers whom, in almost all other respects, we hold in high esteem. But in proportion as we love them the more in Christ, to that degree do we advise them the more earnestly. The Work of Monks 31.[34]

11:15 Long Hair a Woman's Pride

A Woman's Pride. Clement of Alexandria: It is unholy and deceptive for a woman to wear a wig. If the man is the head of the woman, is it not impious for her to deceive him with all that extra hair and at the same time offend the Lord by dressing like a harlot, when her own natural hair is so beautiful? Christ the Educator 3.63.[35]

11:16 No Other Practice

The Churches. Chrysostom: To oppose this teaching is contentiousness, which is irrational. The Corinthians might object, but if they do so, they are going against the practice of the universal church. Homilies on the Epistles of Paul to the Corinthians 26.5.[36]

---

[28]OFP 54. [29]CSEL 81.124. [30]NPNF 1 12:153-54. [31]FC 40:242*. [32]CSEL 81.124; cf. Lev 10:6. [33]FC 26:436. [34]FC 16:389*. [35]FC 23:248. [36]NPNF 1 12:154.

11:17-22 THE ORDER OF SERVICE

> [17]But in the following instructions I do not commend you, because when you come together it is not for the better but for the worse. [18]For, in the first place, when you assemble as a church, I hear that there are divisions among you; and I partly believe it, [19]for there must be factions among you in order that those who are genuine among you may be recognized. [20]When you meet together, it is not the Lord's supper that you eat. [21]For in eating, each one goes ahead with his own meal, and one is hungry and another is drunk. [22]What! Do you not have houses to eat and drink in? Or do you despise the church of God and humiliate those who have nothing? What shall I say to you? Shall I commend you in this? No, I will not.

OVERVIEW: Paul was upset about what was happening when the Corinthians met for worship. Something had gone wrong with the way in which they received the Lord's Supper. Those who had nothing to offer were ashamed, and those who came late found nothing to eat (AMBROSIASTER). The Corinthians were disgracing the Lord's Supper (THEODORET OF CYR) by turning it into a private meal (CHRYSOSTOM). The gluttonous were offending against those who have nothing and displaying their own intemperance (CLEMENT OF ALEXANDRIA). Although it was unwished, such divisiveness had been foretold (AMBROSIASTER, CHRYSOSTOM). Once schismatics are outside the church they do us good, not by teaching the truth but by provoking spiritual Christians to expound it more accurately (CYPRIAN, AUGUSTINE). God does not destroy the human freedom to plunge into error (CHRYSOSTOM). The overruling justice of God permits schism temporarily in order to strengthen and vindicate faith (VINCENT OF LÉRINS).

1:17 No Commendation

A REBUKE. CHRYSOSTOM: Paul recognized that the Corinthians, instead of growing closer to God, were falling into the habits of the world, and so they needed a rebuke from him, in order that they might return to their former state.

HOMILIES ON THE EPISTLES OF PAUL TO THE CORINTHIANS 27.2.[1]

11:18 Divisions Among Them

RETURN TO A RIGHT STATE. CHRYSOSTOM: Paul tempers his criticism by saying that he only partly believes what he has been told [of their factions] because he wants to encourage them to return to the right state of affairs. HOMILIES ON THE EPISTLES OF PAUL TO THE CORINTHIANS 27.2.[2]

11:19 Factions Among Them

THAT THE GENUINE MAY BE RECOGNIZED. CYPRIAN: In this way the faithful are approved and the faithless are detected. UNITY OF THE CATHOLIC CHURCH 10.[3]

FACTIONS. AMBROSIASTER: Paul did not want heresies or choose them, but he foresaw the future and knew that they would come. COMMENTARY ON PAUL'S EPISTLES.[4]

DIVISIONS FORETOLD. CHRYSOSTOM: In speaking

---

[1]NPNF 1 12:158. [2]NPNF 1 12:158. [3]LCC 5:130. [4]CSEL 81.125.

here of factions, Paul did not have doctrinal heresies in mind, though it would apply to them as well. Christ himself said that occasions of stumbling would have to come (Mt 18:7). He did not thereby destroy man's free will or decree any necessity or compulsion over human life, but he foretold what would be the inevitable result of the evil in the human mind. Divisions did not come about because Christ foretold them; rather he foretold them because they were inevitable. Homilies on the Epistles of Paul to the Corinthians 27.3.[5]

The Good Done Inadvertently by Heretics. Augustine: People become heretics, even though they would still have held wrong opinions if they had remained within the church. Now that they are outside, they do us more good, not by teaching the truth, for they do not know it, but by provoking carnal Christians to seek the truth and spiritual Christians to expound it. In the church there are innumerable people who are approved by God, but they do not become manifest among us as long as we are content with the darkness of our ignorance and prefer to sleep rather than to behold the light of truth. Of True Religion 7.15.[6]

Moral Failure. Severian of Gabala: Paul is not talking here about doctrinal error but about moral failures. Pauline Commentary from the Greek Church.[7]

Why Schismatics Are Not Instantly Rooted Out. Vincent of Lérins: It is as if the apostle meant that the authors of heresies are not instantly rooted out by God, in order to make manifest those who are approved, that is, in order to make evident to what degree each one is a steadfast, faithful and firm lover of the orthodox faith. Commonitories 20.[8]

11:20 Not the Lord's Supper

All Participate in the Table Equally. Theodoret of Cyr: The Lord's Supper is the sacrament of the Lord. Everyone participates equally in it, whether they are poor or rich, slaves or lords, rulers or ruled. Common tables must at all costs be truly common so as to imitate the table of the Lord, which is open to all equally. Commentary on the First Epistle to the Corinthians 236-37.[9]

11:21 One Hungry, Another Drunk

Each One Goes Ahead with His Own Meal. Clement of Alexandria: If a person is wealthy and eats without restraint or is insatiable, he disgraces himself in a special way and does wrong on two accounts. First, he adds to the burden of those who do not have, and second, he lays his own intemperance bare in front of those who do have. Christ the Educator 2.13.[10]

The Disgrace of the Supper. Chrysostom: The Corinthians were disgracing themselves by turning the Lord's Supper into a private meal and thus depriving it of its greatest prerogative. The Lord's Supper ought to be common to all, because it is the Master's, whose property does not belong to one servant or to another but ought to be shared by all together. Homilies on the Epistles of Paul to the Corinthians 27.4.[11]

11:22 Despising the Church

Those Who Had Nothing Were Ashamed. Ambrosiaster: The false apostles had sown divisions among them so that they were possessive of their offerings. Although they were all blessed with one and the same prayer, those who had not offered or who had nothing to offer were covered with shame and did not take part. Furthermore, it all happened so quickly that those who came later found nothing left to eat. Commentary on Paul's Epistles.[12]

[5]NPNF 1 12:158. [6]LCC 6:233. [7]NTA 15:262. [8]FC 7:304. [9]Migne PG 82:315. [10]FC 23:104. [11]NPNF 1 12:159. [12]CSEL 81.126.

11:23-26 THE INSTITUTION OF HOLY COMMUNION

[23]*For I received from the Lord what I also delivered to you, that the Lord Jesus on the night when he was betrayed took bread,* [24]*and when he had given thanks, he broke it, and said, "This is my body which is for[s] you. Do this in remembrance of me."* [25]*In the same way also the cup, after supper, saying, "This cup is the new covenant in my blood. Do this, as often as you drink it, in remembrance of me."* [26]*For as often as you eat this bread and drink the cup, you proclaim the Lord's death until he comes.*

s *Other ancient authorities read* broken for

OVERVIEW: The Lord's Supper is not just a meal but spiritual medicine that purifies recipients who partake of it reverently (AMBROSIASTER). In blessing the bread even before his suffering, Jesus left this last commemoration (AMBROSE, CYRIL OF JERUSALEM, PELAGIUS). Paul delivered to Corinth what he had been taught about the Lord's Supper (OECUMENIUS). Now instead of the blood of beasts Christ has made a sacrificial offering of his own blood (CHRYSOSTOM, CYRIL OF JERUSALEM). Those who come for this offering must not do anything unworthy of it, and this applies especially to not withholding mercy from the needy neighbor (CHRYSOSTOM).

11:23 Received from the Lord

PAUL'S TEACHING. OECUMENIUS: By "received" Paul means that he was taught. PAULINE COMMENTARY FROM THE GREEK CHURCH.[1]

NO OTHER CUP. FULGENTIUS: The blessed Paul, recalling the most sacred mystery of that supper, makes known no other cup than the one called the new covenant by the Lord: "For I received from the Lord what I also handed on to you." TO FERRANDUS, LETTERS 14.40.[2]

11:24 The Broken Bread

THE WORDS OF CONSECRATION OF THE EUCHA- RIST. AMBROSE: Do you wish to know how it is consecrated with heavenly words? Accept what the words are. The priest speaks. He says: Perform for us this oblation written, reasonable, acceptable, which is a figure of the body and blood of our Lord Jesus Christ. . . . Before it is consecrated, it is bread; but when Christ's words have been added, it is the body of Christ. . . . And before the words of Christ, the chalice is full of wine and water. When the words of Christ have been added, then blood is effected which redeemed the people. THE SACRAMENTS 4.5.21-23.[3]

FULL ASSURANCE OF THE DIVINE MYSTERIES. CYRIL OF JERUSALEM: The teaching of the blessed Paul is of itself sufficient to give you full assurance about the divine mysteries by admission to which you have become one body and blood with Christ. . . . When the Master himself has explicitly said of the bread, "This is my body," will anyone still dare to doubt? When he is himself our warranty saying, "This is my blood," who will ever waver and say it is not his blood? . . . With perfect confidence, then, we partake as of the body and blood of Christ. ON THE MYSTERIES, FOURTH LECTURE 1.2.[4]

A SACRIFICE OF THANKSGIVING. CHRYSOSTOM:

[1]NTA 15:440. [2]FC 95:554-55. [3]FC 44:304-5. [4]FC 64:181.

112

Paul reminds us that the Master gave up everything, including himself, for us, whereas we are reluctant even to share a little food with our fellow believers. But if you come for a sacrifice of thanksgiving, do not do anything unworthy of that sacrifice. Do not dishonor your brothers or neglect them in their hunger, do not get drunk, and do not insult the church. When you come, give thanks for what you have enjoyed, and do not cut yourselves off from your neighbors. HOMILIES ON THE EPISTLES OF PAUL TO THE CORINTHIANS 27.5.[5]

IN REMEMBRANCE OF ME. PELAGIUS: In blessing the bread even before his suffering, Jesus left behind a last commemoration, or memorial. This is rather like someone who, when about to go on a journey, leaves some token of himself with his loved one, so that whenever she looks at it she will be reminded of his goodness and love toward her. COMMENTARY ON THE FIRST EPISTLE TO THE CORINTHIANS 11.[6]

11:25 The Cup of the New Covenant

THE NEW COVENANT. CHRYSOSTOM: Why does Paul mention that the cup is that of the new covenant? Because there was also a cup of the old covenant, which contained the libations and the blood of animals. For after sacrificing, the priests used to catch the blood in a chalice and bowl and then pour it out.[7] But now, instead of the blood of beasts, Christ has introduced his own blood. HOMILIES ON THE EPISTLES OF PAUL TO THE CORINTHIANS 27.5.[8]

THE OLD COVENANT YIELDS TO THE NEW. AUGUSTINE: Old things are passed away and are made new in Christ, so that altar yields to altar, sword to sword, fire to fire, bread to bread, victim to Victim, blood to Blood. LETTERS 36.[9]

THE CUP OF SUFFERING. FULGENTIUS: The word cup means nothing other than the new cove-

nant in the Lord. . . . The grace of suffering was intended by the Lord when the word cup is used. For what did he wish to be understood when he said to the sons of Zebedee, "Can you drink the cup that I am going to drink?"[10] . . . and "Shall I not drink the cup that the Father gave me?"[11] A stone's throw from his disciples he is torn away to die for the sins of humanity. This is his cup of suffering. He shows his feelings of human weakness, saying . . . "Father, if you are willing, take this cup away from me."[12] TO FERRANDUS, LETTERS 14.41.[13]

11:26 The Bread and the Cup

AS OFTEN AS WE RECEIVE, WE PROCLAIM. AMBROSE: As often as we receive, we proclaim the death of the Lord. If death, we proclaim the remission of sins. If, as often as blood is shed, it is shed for the remission of sins, I ought always to accept him, that he may always dismiss my sins. I, who always sin, should always have a remedy. THE SACRAMENTS 4.6.29.[14]

PROCLAIMING THE LORD'S DEATH. AMBROSIASTER: Paul shows that the Lord's Supper is not a meal in the normal sense but spiritual medicine, which purifies the recipient if he partakes of it reverently. It is the memorial of our redemption, so that mindful of our Redeemer we might follow him more closely. COMMENTARY ON PAUL'S EPISTLES.[15]

BECOMING PARTAKERS. CYRIL OF ALEXANDRIA: Proclaiming the death according to the flesh of the only begotten Son of God, that is, of Jesus Christ, and confessing his resurrection from the dead and his ascension into heaven, we celebrate the unbloody sacrifice in the churches, and we thus approach the spiritual blessings

[5]NPNF 1 12:161. [6]Migne PL 30:752A. [7]Lev 4:5-7, 16-18, 25, 30, 34. [8]NPNF 1 12:161. [9]FC 12:159. [10]Mt 20:22. [11]Jn 18:11. [12]Lk 22:42. [13]FC 95:555. [14]FC 44:306. [15]CSEL 81.127-28.

and are made holy, becoming partakers of the holy flesh and of the precious blood of Christ, the Savior of us all. LETTERS 17.12.[16]

[16]FC 76:86.

11:27-34 PREPARING FOR COMMUNION

[27]*Whoever, therefore, eats the bread or drinks the cup of the Lord in an unworthy manner will be guilty of profaning the body and blood of the Lord.* [28]*Let a man examine himself, and so eat of the bread and drink of the cup.* [29]*For any one who eats and drinks without discerning the body eats and drinks judgment upon himself.* [30]*That is why many of you are weak and ill, and some have died.[t]* [31]*But if we judged ourselves truly, we should not be judged.* [32]*But when we are judged by the Lord, we are chastened [u] so that we may not be condemned along with the world.*

[33]*So then, my brethren, when you come together to eat, wait for one another—* [34]*if any one is hungry, let him eat at home—lest you come together to be condemned. About the other things I will give directions when I come.*

t *Greek* have fallen asleep (*as in* 15:6, 20) u *Or* when we are judged we are being chastened by the Lord

---

OVERVIEW: Holy Communion becomes a punishment to those who partake unworthily (CHRYSOSTOM). This explains why some have died. It is unlawful to approach or touch the Lord's table with profane lusts of the body, of money, of anger or of malice (CHRYSOSTOM). We are to revere the one of whose body we have come to partake (AMBROSIASTER). We do well to avoid future judgment by judging ourselves truly (CHRYSOSTOM). Irreverent communicants are no better than unbelievers (AMBROSIASTER). One who profanes the Lord's Supper is like a priest who pours blood out so as to make the death appear to be a trivial slaughter and not a sacrifice (CHRYSOSTOM). Our chastening before Communion is more like admonition than condemnation, more like healing than vengeance and more like correction than punishment (CHRYSOSTOM, CLEMENT OF ALEXAN-DRIA). Paul promises to give further instructions when he comes (CHRYSOSTOM, AUGUSTINE). Meanwhile they are to make their offering together (AMBROSIASTER).

11:27 Eating and Drinking Unworthily

PROFANING THE BODY AND BLOOD OF THE LORD. CHRYSOSTOM: Why so? It is because someone who profanes the supper is like a priest who pours the blood out, making the death appear to be a slaughter and not a sacrifice. It is like those who pierced Jesus on the cross.[1] They did not do it in order to drink his blood but in order to shed it. The person who comes to the supper unworthily does much the same

[1]Jn 19:34.

thing and gains nothing by it. Homilies on the Epistles of Paul to the Corinthians 27.6.[2]

Receiving Unworthily. Augustine: What does it mean to receive unworthily? To receive in mockery, to receive in contempt. Sermons 227.[3]

11:28 Examining Oneself

A Reverent Mind. Ambrosiaster: Paul teaches that one should come to Communion with a reverent mind and with fear, so that the mind will understand that it must revere the one whose body it is coming to consume. Commentary on Paul's Epistles.[4]

Be Emptied of Profane Lusts. Chrysostom: It is unlawful for us to touch the table with profane lusts, which are more harmful than diseases. By profane lusts I mean those of the body, of money, of anger, of malice, and so on. It is fitting for anyone who approaches to empty himself of all these things first and then touch that pure sacrifice. Homilies on the Epistles of Paul to the Corinthians 28.1.[5]

Self-Examination Before Eucharist. Chrysostom: In your conscience, where no one is present except God who sees all, there judge yourself, examine your sins. When you reflect upon your whole life, bring your sins to the court of the mind. Correct your mistakes, and in this way, with a clean conscience, touch the sacred table and participate in the holy sacrifice. On Fasting, Homily 6.5.22.[6]

11:29 Eating and Drinking Judgment

Discerning the Body. Chrysostom: How can the table which is the cause of so many blessings, and which is teeming with life, become a cause of judgment? It is not from its own nature, says Paul, but because of the attitude of the one who comes to it. For just as the presence of Christ, which conveyed to us those great and unspeakable blessings, condemned those who did not receive them, so also the holy Communion becomes a means of greater punishment to those who partake unworthily. Homilies on the Epistles of Paul to the Corinthians 28.2.[7]

11:30 Some Have Died

Reinforcing the Lesson. Chrysostom: Here Paul does not take his example from ancient Israel, as he did earlier, but from the Corinthians themselves, so that the lesson would strike home more deeply. People were looking for an explanation for the untimely deaths in their midst, and here Paul gives it. Homilies on the Epistles of Paul to the Corinthians 28.2.[8]

11:31 Judging Oneself Truly

Avoid Future Judgment. Chrysostom: Paul did not say, "if we punished ourselves" but only if we were prepared to recognize our offense, to judge ourselves truly, to condemn our own wrongdoing, then we should be rid of the punishment both in this world and in the next. For the one who condemns himself propitiates God in two ways, first by acknowledging his sins and second by being more careful in the future. Homilies on the Epistles of Paul to the Corinthians 28.2.[9]

Assessing Urgent Need. Aphrahat: Judge in yourself what I am going to tell you: suppose you happen to go on a long journey and, parched with thirst in the heat, you chance upon one of the brothers. You say to him, "Refresh me in my exhaustion from thirst," and he replies, "It is the time for prayer; I will pray and then I will come to your aid"; and while he is praying, before coming to you, you die of thirst. What seems to you the

---

[2]NPNF 1 12:161. [3]FC 38:198. [4]CSEL 81.129. [5]NPNF 1 12:163-64. [6]FC 96:85. [7]NPNF 1 12:164. [8]NPNF 1 12:164. [9]NPNF 1 12:164.

better, that he should go and pray, or alleviate your exhaustion? DEMONSTRATION 4.15.[10]

TEMPORAL AND FUTURE JUDGMENT. AUGUSTINE: Indeed, many sins seem to be ignored and go unpunished. But their punishment is reserved for the future. It is not in vain that the day when the Judge of the living and the dead shall come is rightly called the day of judgment. Just so, on the other hand, some sins are punished here, and if they are forgiven will certainly bring no harm upon us in the future age. Hence, referring to certain temporal punishments which are visited upon sinners in this life, the apostle, speaking to those whose sins are blotted out and not reserved to the end says: "But if we judged ourselves truly we should not be judged. But when we are judged by the Lord, we are chastened so that we may not be condemned along with the world." ENCHIRIDION 17.66.[11]

11:32 Chastened by the Lord

CHASTENED FOR OUR EDUCATION. CLEMENT OF ALEXANDRIA: When we are judged by the Lord, it is for our education, so that we may not be condemned along with the world. Earlier the prophet said, "The Lord has given me a stern lesson but not handed me over to death."[12] STROMATA 1.27.171-72.[13]

JUDGED BY THE LORD. AMBROSIASTER: The person who comes to the Lord's table irreverently is no better than an unbeliever. COMMENTARY ON PAUL'S EPISTLES.[14]

CHASTENED THAT WE MAY NOT BE CONDEMNED. CHRYSOSTOM: Paul calls our punishment a chastening, because it is more like admonition than condemnation, more like healing than vengeance, and more like correction than punishment. He makes the present seem less burdensome by comparing it with a greater evil from which we shall escape, namely, the judgment of the world. HOMILIES ON THE EPISTLES

OF PAUL TO THE CORINTHIANS 28.2.[15]

REQUIRING AN ACCOUNT. CHRYSOSTOM: Instead of passing idly by what are considered slight sins, let us daily require an account of ourselves for words and glances and execute sentence upon ourselves so as to be free from punishment later. This is the reason Paul said, "If we judge ourselves, we would not be judged." Thus if we judge ourselves for our sins every day here, we shall preclude the severity of the judgment in that other place. But if we should be remiss, "we will be judged and chastised by the Lord." So let us take the initiative in passing sentence on ourselves with all good will, holding the court of conscience unbeknown to anyone. Let us examine our own thoughts and determine a proper verdict so that through fear of imminent punishment our mind may forbear to be dragged down and instead may check its impulses, and by keeping in view that unsleeping eye may ward off the devil's advances. ON GENESIS, HOMILY 60.16.[16]

11:33 Wait for One Another

SERVING ONE ANOTHER. AMBROSIASTER: Paul tells them to wait for one another so that they may make their offering together and serve one another. COMMENTARY ON PAUL'S EPISTLES.[17]

11:34 Paul to Give Further Directions

WHEN HE VISITS. CHRYSOSTOM: Paul adds that he will deal with everything else when he comes. It is likely that the Corinthians would have objected that not everything could be put right by letter. Therefore, Paul tells them to get on with these things in the meantime and that he will do the rest in due course. HOMILIES ON THE EPISTLES OF PAUL TO THE CORINTHIANS 28.3.[18]

---

[10]SFPSL 20. [11]LCC 8:378. [12]Ps 118:18. [13]FC 85:149.
[14]CSEL 81.130. [15]NPNF 1 12:164. [16]FC 87:184-85*. [17]CSEL 81.130. [18]NPNF 1 12:165.

UNIVERSAL PRACTICES. AUGUSTINE: We are given to understand by this that it was too much for him to set forth in a letter the whole manner of proceeding to be observed by the universal church and that what he set in order personally cannot be altered. LETTER 54 TO JANUARIUS.[19]

[19]FC 12:259.

12:1-3 SPIRITUAL GIFTS

[1]*Now concerning spiritual gifts,[x] brethren, I do not want you to be uninformed. [2]You know that when you were heathen, you were led astray to dumb idols, however you may have been moved.*

[3]*Therefore I want you to understand that no one speaking by the Spirit of God ever says "Jesus be cursed!" and no one can say "Jesus is Lord" except by the Holy Spirit.*

x *Or spiritual persons*

OVERVIEW: Spiritual gifts owe nothing to human effort (CHRYSOSTOM). They are visible signs that the grace of the Holy Spirit is at work in the faithful (THEODORET OF CYR). Christ cannot be proclaimed without the Holy Spirit (BASIL, AMBROSE, CHRYSOSTOM). The Holy Spirit proclaims his lordship (THEODORET OF CYR) in a way that the demons cannot, even if they say these words (ORIGEN, SEVERIAN OF GABALA). Having formerly been worshipers of idols and led about by demons, so now, as worshipers of God, the faithful walk in a way that is pleasing to God (AMBROSIASTER). Wherever any truth is spoken, it is spoken by the Holy Spirit (AMBROSIASTER). Pagan spirit possession in soothsaying is entirely different from prophecy (CHRYSOSTOM, SEVERIAN).

12:1 Concerning Spiritual Gifts

THE WORK OF THE SPIRIT ALONE. CHRYSOSTOM: Paul calls the gifts spiritual because they are the work of the Spirit alone, owing nothing to human initiative. HOMILIES ON THE EPISTLES OF PAUL TO THE CORINTHIANS 29.2.[1]

VISIBLE SIGNS OF GRACE. THEODORET OF CYR: In former times those who accepted the divine preaching and who were baptized for their salvation were given visible signs of the grace of the Holy Spirit at work in them. Some spoke in tongues which they did not know and which nobody had taught them, while others performed miracles or prophesied. The Corinthians also did these things, but they did not use the gifts as they should have done. They were more interested in showing off than in using them for the edification of the church. COMMENTARY ON THE FIRST EPISTLE TO THE CORINTHIANS 240.[2]

12:2 Led Astray to Idols

THEIR FORMER LIFE. AMBROSIASTER: Now that he is about to give them spiritual teaching, Paul recalls their former way of life. His intention is

[1]NPNF 1 12:169. [2]Migne PG 82:319.

that, just as they have been worshipers of idols in the shape of statues and used to be led about by the will of demons, so now, as worshipers of God, they may walk according to the model of the law, so as to be pleasing to God. Commentary on Paul's Epistles.[3]

Possessed by an Unclean Spirit. Chrysostom: What Paul means is that if anyone in a pagan temple was at any time possessed by an unclean spirit and began to divine, he was led away by that spirit like a man in chains and had no idea what he was saying. For it is peculiar to the soothsayer to be beside himself, to be under compulsion, to be pushed, to be dragged, to be greeted as a madman. But the prophet is not like this, because he has a sober mind and composed temper and knows exactly what he is saying. Homilies on the Epistles of Paul to the Corinthians 29.2.[4]

Christian Prophecy Versus Pagan Soothsaying. Severian of Gabala: Paul shows that there is a very big difference between Christian prophecy and pagan soothsaying. Pagans do not address the unclean spirit but are possessed by it and say things which they do not understand. The soothsayer's soul is darkened, and he does not know what he is saying, whereas the prophet's soul is enlightened and reveals what the prophet has learned and understood. Pauline Commentary from the Greek Church.[5]

12:3 Speaking by the Spirit

The Gift of Discernment. Origen: There are so many different kinds of spirit that without the gift of discernment, who can know which is which? Commentary on 1 Corinthians 4.47.2-3.[6]

Rightly Praising God. Basil: If two yardsticks are compared with each other, their straightness is in agreement. But if a distorted piece of

wood is compared with a ruler, the crooked one will be at variance with the straight. Since, therefore, the praise of God is righteous, there is need of a righteous heart, in order that the praise may be fitting and adapted to it. "No one can say 'Jesus is Lord,' except in the Holy Spirit." So how can one offer due praise if one does not have the right spirit in one's heart? Homily on Psalm 32 15.1.[7]

Except by the Holy Spirit. Ambrose: If we cannot name the Lord Jesus without the Spirit, surely we cannot proclaim him without the Spirit. The Holy Spirit 1.11.124.[8]

The Speaker of Truth. Ambrosiaster: Any truth spoken by anyone is spoken by the Holy Spirit. Commentary on Paul's Epistles.[9]

Without the Holy Spirit? Chrysostom: If no one can say that Jesus is Lord except by the Spirit, what can we say about those who do name his name but do not have the Spirit? Here we have to understand that Paul was not talking about catechumens who had not yet been baptized but about believers and unbelievers. Homilies on the Epistles of Paul to the Corinthians 29.3.[10]

Whether Legion Confessed Jesus as Lord. Severian of Gabala: When the demoniac Legion acknowledged Jesus as Lord, he did not do so in a believing sense, but he merely confessed his knowledge of the lordship and rule of Christ over all things. Pauline Commentary from the Greek Church.[11]

The Spirit Proclaims His Lordship. Theodoret of Cyr: There is no disharmony between the teaching of the only-begotten Son and that of the Holy Spirit. In the Gospels, Christ the

---

[3]CSEL 81.130-31. [4]NPNF 1 12:169. [5]NTA 15:262. [6]JTS 10:29-30. [7]FC 46:229*. [8]FC 44:80. [9]CSEL 81.132. [10]NPNF 1 12:170. [11]NTA 15:263. See Mk 5:9.

Lord taught us how great the Holy Spirit is, and the Spirit has proclaimed his lordship. No one who is truly moved by the Spirit can say that Christ is not divine. COMMENTARY ON THE

FIRST EPISTLE TO THE CORINTHIANS 242.[12]

[12]Migne PG 82:322.

12:4-11 UNITY IN DIVERSITY

⁴Now there are varieties of gifts, but the same Spirit; ⁵and there are varieties of service, but the same Lord; ⁶and there are varieties of working, but it is the same God who inspires them all in every one. ⁷To each is given the manifestation of the Spirit for the common good. ⁸To one is given through the Spirit the utterance of wisdom, and to another the utterance of knowledge according to the same Spirit, ⁹to another faith by the same Spirit, to another gifts of healing by the one Spirit, ¹⁰to another the working of miracles, to another prophecy, to another the ability to distinguish between spirits, to another various kinds of tongues, to another the interpretation of tongues. ¹¹All these are inspired by one and the same Spirit, who apportions to each one individually as he wills.

OVERVIEW: The giver of varied gifts is God the Holy Spirit (HILARY OF POITIERS, CHRYSOSTOM). Gifts, service and working are different forms of the same ministry (CYRIL OF JERUSALEM, CHRYSOSTOM) of the triune God (AMBROSIASTER) whose gifts cannot be artificially separated as to persons of the Godhead. There is only one God, whose grace is distributed by the Spirit to individuals as he wishes, according to his incomparable justice and power (AMBROSE), not according to the merits or will (JEROME) of any particular person (AMBROSIASTER). They are for the upbuilding of his church (BASIL, AMBROSIASTER, CHRYSOSTOM) . Even today (THEODORET OF CYR) each baptized person receives the Spirit's gift so that he or she may be useful both to self and others (AMBROSIASTER). The utterance of wisdom refers to the knowledge of divine things (AUGUSTINE) through the Scriptures (SEVERIAN OF GABALA). The utterance of knowledge refers to human science (AUGUSTINE) or the revelation of things forgotten (SEVERIAN). It is the Spirit who enlightens (AMBROSIASTER). The faith mentioned here is the faith that moves mountains (THEODORET OF CYR), not just a formal doctrine (CYRIL OF JERUSALEM). Even the shy can lay claim to such bold faith (AMBROSIASTER). The gift of tongues and the interpretation of tongues (AMBROSIASTER), as well as the gift of prophecy, is the gift of the triune God, given through the Holy Spirit (AMBROSE) to whomever God sees fit, both to women and men (THEODORET OF CYR). Hence it is not for boasting (CHRYSOSTOM).

12:4 Different Gifts

VARIETIES OF GIFTS. CHRYSOSTOM: Even if the gift bestowed on you is less than the gift bestowed on someone else, the Giver is the same, and therefore you have equal honor with him.

It is the same Fountain from which you draw refreshment. HOMILIES ON THE EPISTLES OF PAUL TO THE CORINTHIANS 29.4.[1]

THE SPIRIT NOT DIVIDED IN DIVERSE GIFTS. AMBROSE: This does not pertain to the fullness nor to a portion of the Spirit, because neither does the human mind grasp God's fullness, nor is God divided into any portions of himself. But he pours out the gift of the grace of the Spirit in which God is adored, as he is also adored in truth, for no one adores him except he who draws in the truth of his godhead with pious affection. THE HOLY SPIRIT 11.71.[2]

12:5 Different Kinds of Service

ADAPTING TO EACH. CYRIL OF JERUSALEM: The Holy Spirit adapts himself to each person. He sees the dispositions of each. He sees into our reasoning and our conscience, what we say, what we think, what we believe. CATECHESIS 14.22.[3]

ONE BODY, MANY MEMBERS. AMBROSE: We are all the one body of Christ, whose head is God, whose members we are. Some perhaps are the eyes, like the prophets. Others are more like teeth, as the apostles who passed the food of the gospel teaching into our hearts. . . . Some are hands who are seen carrying out good works. Those who bestow the strength of nourishment upon the poor are his belly. Some are his feet, and would that I were worthy to be his heel! He pours water on the feet of Christ who forgives the lowly their sins, and, in setting free the common man, he bathes the feet of Christ. LETTER TO HIS SISTER 62.[4]

VARIETIES OF SERVICE. CHRYSOSTOM: One who hears about gifts might be upset if someone else has a greater one. But when it comes to service, things are the other way round. In this case, labor and sweat are implied. Why do you complain if they have been given more to do so as to spare you? HOMILIES ON THE EPISTLES OF PAUL TO THE CORINTHIANS 29.4.[5]

THE FACULTIES OF BODY AND SOUL COMPARED. HILARY OF POITIERS: Just as a faculty of the human body will be idle when the causes that stir it into activity are not present, so with the soul. The eyes will not perform their functions except through the light or the brightness of day. The ears will not comprehend their task when no voice or sound is heard. The nostrils will not be aware of their office if no odor is detected. It is not that the faculty is lost because the cause is absent. Rather the employment of the faculty comes from the cause. It is the same with the soul of man. If the soul has not breathed in the gift of the Spirit through faith, even though it will continue to possess the faculty for understanding, it will not have the light of knowledge. The one gift, which is in Christ, is available to everyone in its entirety, and what is present in every place is given insofar as we desire to receive it and will remain with us insofar as we desire to become worthy of it. This gift is with us even to the consummation of the world. This is the consolation of our expectation. This, through the efficacy of the gifts, is the pledge of our future hope. This is the light of the mind, the splendor of the soul. For this reason we must pray for this Holy Spirit. TRINITY 2.35.[6]

12:6 The Work of the Same God

THE ONE WORK OF THE TRIUNE GOD. AMBROSIASTER: Paul is emphatic in asserting that the distribution of gifts is not to be attributed to human causes as if they were achievable by men. The varied gifts of the Holy Spirit and the grace of the Lord Jesus are the work of one and the same God. The grace and the gift cannot be divided according to the persons of the Father, Son and Holy Spirit but must be understood as

---

[1]NPNF 1 12:171. [2]FC 44:178-79*. [3]FC 64:89*. [4]FC 26:389*.
[5]NPNF 1 12:171. [6]FC 25:63*.

constituting the one work of the undivided unity and nature of the Three. Commentary on Paul's Epistles.[7]

The Fourfold Sequence. Hilary of Poitiers: There is a fourfold meaning in the words that lie before us: There is the same Spirit in the varieties of the gifts. There is the same Lord in the varieties of ministries. There is the same God in these varieties. And there is a manifestation of the Spirit in the bestowal of what is profitable. Trinity 8.29.[8]

The Same God Who Inspires. Chrysostom: Gifts, service and working all amount to the same thing in the end, for they are different forms of the same ministry. Homilies on the Epistles of Paul to the Corinthians 29.4.[9]

12:7 Gifts Given for the Common Good

Manifestation of the Spirit. Ambrosiaster: Each person receives a gift so that, governing his life by divine constraints, he may be useful both to himself and to others while presenting an example of good behavior. Commentary on Paul's Epistles.[10]

For Your Benefit. Chrysostom: Whatever measure of the Spirit has been given to you, it is for your benefit, so there is no reason to complain of what seems like a small gift. Homilies on the Epistles of Paul to the Corinthians 29.5.[11]

For the Common Good. Basil: Since no one has the capacity to receive all spiritual gifts, but the grace of the Spirit is given proportionately to the faith of each, when one is living in community with others, the grace privately bestowed on each individual becomes the common possession of the others. . . . One who receives any of these gifts does not possess it for his own sake but rather for the sake of others. The Long Rules 7.[12]

In Our Time Grace Given. Theodoret of Cyr: Even in our time grace is given to those who are deemed worthy of holy baptism, but it may not take the same form as it did in those days. Commentary on the First Epistle to the Corinthians 243.[13]

12:8 Utterance of Wisdom and Knowledge

Wisdom and Knowledge. Ambrosiaster: In other words, he is given knowledge not by book learning but by the enlightenment of the Holy Spirit. Commentary on Paul's Epistles.[14]

Divine Things and Human Science. Augustine: *Wisdom* refers to the knowledge of divine things, and *knowledge* to human science. Trinity 14.[15]

Revelation of Things Forgotten. Severian of Gabala: The utterance of wisdom means understanding what God has said through the prophets and evangelists and communicating this to those who are listening. The utterance of knowledge is the revelation of things which have been forgotten, which someone learns for the first time and then shares with others. Pauline Commentary from the Greek Church.[16]

12:9 Gifts of Faith and of Healing

Surpassing Human Nature. Cyril of Jerusalem: This faith which is given by the Spirit as a grace is not just doctrinal faith but a faith which empowers activities surpassing human nature, a faith which moves mountains. . . . For just as a grain of mustard seed is of little bulk but of explosive energy, taking a trifling space for its planting and then sending out great branches all around, so that when it is grown it

---

[7]CSEL 81.133. [8]FC 25:297*. [9]NPNF 1 12:171. [10]CSEL 81.134. [11]NPNF 1 12:171. [12]FC 9:250*. [13]Migne PG 82:323. [14]CSEL 81.134. [15]FC 45:413. [16]NTA 15:263.

can give shelter to the birds, so in like manner the faith present in one's soul achieves the greatest things by the most summary decision. For such a one places the thought of God before his mind and as enlightenment of faith permits it, beholds God. His mind also ranges through the world from end to end, and with the end of this age not yet come, beholds the judgment already, and the bestowal of the promised rewards. Catechetical Lecture on Faith 5.11.[17]

Lay Claim to Faith. Ambrosiaster: Paul says this to encourage the person concerned to suppress his shyness and receive the ability to profess and lay claim to faith. Commentary on Paul's Epistles.[18]

Not Many Spirits. Augustine: Without the spirit of faith no one will rightly believe. Without the spirit of prayer no one will profitably pray. It is not that there are so many spirits, "but in all things one and the same Spirit works, who apportions to each one individually as he wills." Letter to Sixtus 191.[19]

Faith That Moves Mountains. Theodoret of Cyr: The faith mentioned here is not the kind given to every believer but the kind which can move mountains. Commentary on the First Epistle to the Corinthians 244.[20]

12:10a Prophecy

The Grace Is One. Ambrose: According to Paul, prophecy is not only through the Father and the Son but also through the Holy Spirit. On this account the office is one, the grace is one. The Holy Spirit 2.13.143.[21]

Distinguishing Between Spirits. Origen: In the distribution of spiritual gifts, it is also added that "discernment of spirits" is given to some. It is a spiritual gift, therefore, by which the spirit is discerned, as the apostle says: "Test the spirits, if they are from God."[22] Homily 3 on Exodus.[23]

12:10b Tongues and Interpretation

Interpretation of Tongues. Ambrosiaster: To interpret is to interpret faithfully by God's gift the sayings of those who speak in tongues or in writing. Commentary on Paul's Epistles.[24]

Not to Boast. Chrysostom: The Corinthians boasted of their speaking in tongues, which is why Paul put it last in his list. Homilies on the Epistles of Paul to the Corinthians 29.5.[25]

Given to Women Also. Theodoret of Cyr: These gifts were given to women as well as men, as the Acts of the Apostles makes plain. Commentary on the First Epistle to the Corinthians 245.[26]

12:11a Inspired by the Same Spirit

The Written Word Inspired by the Spirit. Cyril of Jerusalem: Let us assert of the Holy Spirit only what is written. Let us not busy ourselves about what is not written. The Holy Spirit has authored the Scriptures. He has spoken of himself all that he wished, or all that we could grasp. Let us confine ourselves to what he has said, for it is reckless to do otherwise. Catechesis 16.2.[27]

The Same Spirit. Chrysostom: The universal medicine of his consolation stems from the same root, from the same treasure, the same stream. Therefore Paul occasionally dwells on this expression so as to level out apparent inequalities and console them. Homilies on the Epistles of Paul to the Corinthians 29.5.[28]

---

[17]LCC 4:123. [18]CSEL 81.134. [19]FC 30:312-13*. [20]Migne PG 82:323. [21]FC 44:147. [22]1 Jn 4:1. [23]FC 71:250. [24]CSEL 81.134-35. [25]NPNF 1 12:172. [26]Migne PG 82:326. [27]FC 64:76-77*. [28]NPNF 1 12:172.

The Spirit Not Divided. Ambrose: The Spirit spoke also in the patriarchs and the prophets, and finally the apostles then began to be more perfect after they had received the Holy Spirit. Thus there is no separation of the divine power and grace, for although "there are varieties of gifts, yet there is the same Spirit." The Holy Spirit 2.12.138.[29]

The Comfort of Supposed Lesser Gifts. Theodoret of Cyr: Here Paul is comforting those who received the lesser gifts, pointing out that they too come from the Holy Spirit. Commentary on the First Epistle to the Corinthians 246.[30]

12:11b Gifts Apportioned Individually

According to God's Justice and Power. Ambrose: It belongs to God's justice that he divides and to his power that he divides according to his will or because he wishes to give to each one what he knows will be of profit. Letter 20 to Bishops.[31]

The Three Do What the One Does. Ambrosiaster: Paul is here attributing to the Holy Spirit what he earlier attributed to all three persons.[32] Because they are of one nature and power, the Three do what the One does. There is only one God, whose grace is distributed to individuals as he wishes, not according to the merits of any particular person but for the upbuilding of his church. All those things which the world wants to imitate but cannot, because it is carnal, may be seen in the church, which is the house of God, where they are granted by the gift and instruction of the Holy Spirit. Commentary on Paul's Epistles.[33]

The Will of the Spirit. Jerome: Notice that Paul does not say "according to the will of each and every member" but "according to the will of the Spirit." Against the Pelagians 16.[34]

The One Spirit Adapts to Personal Diversity. Cyril of Jerusalem: One and the same rain comes down on all the world, yet it becomes white in the lily, red in the rose, purple in the violets and hyacinths, different and many-colored in manifold species. Thus it is one in the palm tree and another in the vine, and all in all things, though it is uniform and does not vary in itself. For the rain does not change, coming down now as one thing and now as another, but it adapts itself to the thing receiving it and becomes what is suitable to each. Similarly the Holy Spirit, being One and of one nature and indivisible, imparts to each one his grace "according as he will." The dry tree when watered brings forth shoots. So too does the soul in sin, once made worthy through repentance of the grace of the Holy Spirit, flower into justice. Though the Spirit is one in nature, yet by the will of God and in the name of the Son, he brings about many virtuous effects. For he employs the tongue of one for wisdom, illumines the soul of another by prophecy, to another he grants the power of driving out devils, to another the gift of interpreting the sacred Scriptures. He strengthens the self-control of one while teaching another the nature of almsgiving, and still another to fast and humble himself, and another to despise the things of the body. He prepares another for martyrdom. He acts differently in different persons, though he himself is not diverse. Catechesis 14.12.[35]

The Gift Himself. Augustine: For not everyone has all of them, but some have these and others those, although each has the Gift himself by whom the things proper to each one are divided, namely, the Holy Spirit. Trinity 15.[36]

---

[29]FC 44:144-45*. [30]Migne PG 82:326. [31]FC 26:108. [32]1 Cor 12:4-6. [33]CSEL 81.135. [34]FC 53:255. [35]FC 64:83*. [36]FC 45:500.

12:12-26 THE BODY

¹²*For just as the body is one and has many members, and all the members of the body, though many, are one body, so it is with Christ.* ¹³*For by one Spirit we were all baptized into one body—Jews or Greeks, slaves or free—and all were made to drink of one Spirit.*

¹⁴*For the body does not consist of one member but of many.* ¹⁵*If the foot should say, "Because I am not a hand, I do not belong to the body," that would not make it any less a part of the body.* ¹⁶*And if the ear should say, "Because I am not an eye, I do not belong to the body," that would not make it any less a part of the body.* ¹⁷*If the whole body were an eye, where would be the hearing? If the whole body were an ear, where would be the sense of smell?* ¹⁸*But as it is, God arranged the organs in the body, each one of them, as he chose.* ¹⁹*If all were a single organ, where would the body be?* ²⁰*As it is, there are many parts, yet one body.* ²¹*The eye cannot say to the hand, "I have no need of you," nor again the head to the feet, "I have no need of you."* ²²*On the contrary, the parts of the body which seem to be weaker are indispensable,* ²³*and those parts of the body which we think less honorable we invest with the greater honor, and our unpresentable parts are treated with greater modesty,* ²⁴*which our more presentable parts do not require. But God has so composed the body, giving the greater honor to the inferior part,* ²⁵*that there may be no discord in the body, but that the members may have the same care for one another.* ²⁶*If one member suffers, all suffer together; if one member is honored, all rejoice together.*

OVERVIEW: Once again Paul uses a metaphor, this time to describe the nature of the Christian church. We are one in Christ (CLEMENT OF ALEXANDRIA), baptized into one body (AMBROSE). God who formed the body is one, and the body he formed is one (CHRYSOSTOM). So treat no one with contempt (AMBROSIASTER, SEVERIAN OF GABALA), since each member is necessary (THEODORET OF CYR). The foot is no less a part of the body because it is not a hand (AMBROSIASTER, JEROME). Do not envy those slightly above you, as if the ear might envy the eye (CHRYSOSTOM). Suppose that the body possessed only its most important member—it would still be useless without the others (THEODORET OF CYR). There is no better explanation for this mystery than it pleased the Creator to arrange the members in the way he chose (CHRYSOSTOM). The diversity in the members,

without which the body would not be a body (GREGORY OF NYSSA, CHRYSOSTOM), unites to ensure that the body fulfills its potential (AMBROSIASTER). The eye will have no joy if other members are missing (ORIGEN). Iron can do what gold cannot (AMBROSIASTER). The greater gifts cannot do without the lesser ones (CHRYSOSTOM). What we may find despicable God finds beautiful (AMBROSIASTER). Though our genitals may be hidden, they are given the greater honor (CHRYSOSTOM, AUGUSTINE). So no one is to be despised as useless (AMBROSIASTER). The whole body suffers as one (CYPRIAN, BASIL, AUGUSTINE).

12:12 Many Members, One Body

MANY MEMBERS IN ONE BODY. CHRYSOSTOM: Paul talks about Christ when perhaps he might well have said the church. In doing so, he raises the level of discourse and appeals more and more to the hearers' sense of awe. Homilies on the Epistles of Paul to the Corinthians 30.1.[1]

Every Member Necessary. Theodoret of Cyr: Paul is pointing out that just as the body has many members, some of which are more important than others, so it is with the church also. But every member is necessary and useful. Commentary on the First Epistle to the Corinthians 246.[2]

12:13 Baptized into One Body

One in Christ. Clement of Alexandria: You are all one in Christ Jesus. It is not that some are enlightened gnostics and others less perfect spirituals. Everyone, putting aside all carnal desires, is equal and spiritual before the Lord. Christ the Educator 1.5.31.[3]

One Mystery. Ambrose: There is one work because there is one mystery, there is one baptism because there was one death for the world. There is a unity of outlook which cannot be separated. The Holy Spirit 1.3.45.[4]

Treat No One with Contempt. Ambrosiaster: Paul is teaching that we should not treat anyone with contempt, nor should we regard anyone as perfect. Commentary on Paul's Epistles.[5]

The Body Is One. Chrysostom: He who formed the body is one, and the body which he formed is also one. Homilies on the Epistles of Paul to the Corinthians 30.2.[6]

12:14 Not One Member but Many

The Unity of the Virtues. Gregory of Nyssa: Those who are experts in such matters say that the virtues are not separate from each other and that it is not possible to grasp one of the virtues properly without attaining to the rest of them, but where one of the virtues is present the oth-

ers will necessarily follow. On Virginity 15.[7]

Many Members Supply What Other Parts Lack. Ambrosiaster: The unity of the body consists in the fact that its many members supply the things which the other parts lack. Commentary on Paul's Epistles.[8]

Do Not Overlook Humbler Members. Severian of Gabala: Paul says this in order not to overlook the humbler members of the church. For even if someone is lesser by nature, he still belongs to the body of the church. Pauline Commentary from the Greek Church.[9]

12:15 No Less a Part

Weak and Strong. Ambrosiaster: This means that a weak brother cannot say that he is not a part of the body simply because he is not strong. Commentary on Paul's Epistles.[10]

12:16 "I Do Not Belong"

None Unneeded. Ambrosiaster: Paul is saying that the person who is slightly inferior should not for that reason think that he is unnecessary to the body. Commentary on Paul's Epistles.[11]

Absurd Envy. Chrysostom: Note that Paul couples the foot with the hand, which is mounted a little above it, and the ear with the eye likewise. This is because we are prone to envy not those who are far above us but those who are only a little bit above. Homilies on the Epistles of Paul to the Corinthians 30.3.[12]

12:17 If the Whole Body Were an Eye

Useless Alone. Theodoret of Cyr: Even if the

---

[1]NPNF 1 12:176. [2]Migne PG 82:326. [3]FC 23:31. [4]FC 44:51*. [5]CSEL 81.135. [6]NPNF 1 12:176. [7]FC 58:52. [8]CSEL 81.136. [9]NTA 15:263. [10]CSEL 81.136. [11]CSEL 81.136. [12]NPNF 1 12:177.

body had only its most important member, it would still be useless without the others. Commentary on the First Epistle to the Corinthians 247.[13]

12:18 Arranged as God Chose

It Pleased the Creator. Chrysostom: God has placed each part of the body where he has chosen, so we must not enquire any further as to why he has done it the way he has. For even if we could come up with ten thousand explanations, we would never find one better than this—that it pleased the Creator to make it the way he chose. Homilies on the Epistles of Paul to the Corinthians 30.4.[14]

12:19 If All Were a Single Organ

Different Functions. Ambrosiaster: If everyone in the church were equal, there would be no body, because a body is governed according to the difference in the functions of its members. Commentary on Paul's Epistles.[15]

12:20 Many Parts, One Body

Diversity Unites. Ambrosiaster: The diversity in the members of the body unites for the purpose of ensuring that the body fulfills its potential. Commentary on Paul's Epistles.[16]

No Body Without Diversity. Chrysostom: If there were not great diversity among you, you could not be a body. If you were not a body, you could not be unified. If you were not one, you would not be equal in honor. It is because you are not all endowed with the same gift that you are a body. Homilies on the Epistles of Paul to the Corinthians 30.5.[17]

12:21 "I Have No Need of You"

No Joy If Other Members Missing. Origen: If the eye is healthy and one can see clearly, what joy will it have if the other members of the body are missing? How would it appear to be perfect without the hands, the feet or the other parts of the body? Leviticus Homily 7.[18]

Iron Can Do What Gold Cannot. Ambrosiaster: The person who is greater in rank or dignity cannot do without those who are lower. For there are things which a humbler person can do which an exalted one cannot, just as iron can do things which gold cannot. Because of this, the feet perform an honorable function for the head. Commentary on Paul's Epistles.[19]

Greater Gifts Cannot Do Without the Lesser. Chrysostom: The greater gifts cannot do without the lesser ones, because if even the lesser ones are harmed, the body will not function properly. What is lower than the foot? Or what is more honorable or necessary than the head? But the head, however important it is, is not self-sufficient, nor can it do everything by itself. If that were so, there would be no need to have feet. Homilies on the Epistles of Paul to the Corinthians 31.1.[20]

Eyes, Hands and Feet Need Each Other. Jerome: The church has real eyes: its teachers and leaders who see in sacred Scripture the mysteries of God. . . . It also has hands, effective persons who are not eyes but hands. Do they plumb the mysteries of sacred Scripture? No, but they are powerful in works. The church has feet: those who make official journeys of all kinds. The foot runs that the hand may find the work it is to do. The eye does not scorn the hand, nor do these three scorn the belly as if it were idle and unemployed. Homily 85 on Matthew 18:7-9.[21]

12:22 Weaker Members Necessary

[13]Migne PG 82:327.   [14]NPNF 1 12:177.   [15]CSEL 81.137.   [16]CSEL 81.137.   [17]NPNF 1 12:178.   [18]FC 83:137.   [19]CSEL 81.138.   [20]NPNF 1 12:181.   [21]FC 57:197*.

The Emperor Needs an Army. Ambrosiaster: No matter how elevated a person may be, if he has no one under him, his rank is worthless. The greatest emperor still needs an army. Commentary on Paul's Epistles.[22]

12:23 Lesser Members

Less Honorable Parts. Ambrosiaster: Because our feet are lowly and lacking in dignity, we adorn them with shoes. It is clear that our private parts, which are thought to be shameful, cover themselves with respectability by avoiding public display, so as not to obtrude irreverently. Likewise, some of the brothers who are poor and unseemly in their dress are nevertheless not without grace, because they are members of our body. They go about in dirty little garments and barefoot. Though they may look contemptible, they are more to be honored because they usually lead a cleaner life. What men find despicable, God may find quite beautiful. Commentary on Paul's Epistles.[23]

Using the Unseemly Well in Procreation. Augustine: Just as it is good to use evils well, so it is honest to use the unseemly well. Not because of the beauty of the divine work, but because of the ugliness of lust, the apostle calls these members of the body unseemly. The chaste are not bound by a necessity to depravity, for they resist lust lest it compel them to commit unseemly acts. Yet not even honorable procreation can exist without lust. In this way in chaste spouses there is both the voluntary, in the procreation of offspring, and the necessary, in lust. Honesty arises from unseemliness when chaste union accepts, but does not love, lust. Against Julian 5.9.37.[24]

12:24 Honoring the Inferior Part

Greater Honor to the Inferior Part. Ambrosiaster: We do not have to add anything to those whose eagerness for expertise and respect-ability is obvious—the honor due to them is given already. But an exhortation is necessary regarding the despised and lowly, to ensure that due honor is given to them, so that they may be seen as useful. Otherwise, if these people are despised, they will become more negligent about themselves. Commentary on Paul's Epistles.[25]

Given Greater Honor. Chrysostom: Nothing in us is dishonorable, seeing that it is God's work. What is there in us which is less esteemed than our genitals? Nevertheless, they enjoy greater honor, and even the very poor, who may be completely naked otherwise, cannot allow those parts to be uncovered. Homilies on the Epistles of Paul to the Corinthians 31.2.[26]

The Analogy of the Bad Haircut. Augustine: Aren't the hairs of your head certainly of less value than your other members? What is cheaper, more despicable, more lowly in your body than the hairs of your head? Yet if the barber trims your hair unskillfully, you become angry at him because he does not cut your hair evenly. Yet you do not maintain that same concern for unity of the members in the church. The Usefulness of Fasting 6.[27]

12:25 The Same Care for One Another

Where the Bond of Peace Is Not Preserved. Basil: With those among whom harmony is not secured, however, the bond of peace is not preserved, mildness of spirit is not maintained, but there is dissension, strife and rivalry. It would be a great piece of audacity to call such persons "members of Christ" or to say that they are ruled by him. It would be the expression of an honest mind to say openly that the wisdom of the flesh is master there and wields a royal sovereignty. On the Judgment of God.[28]

---

[22]CSEL 81.138. [23]CSEL 81.138-39. [24]FC 35:281*. [25]CSEL 81.139-40. [26]NPNF 1 12:181. [27]FC 16:413*. [28]FC 9:41*.

No One Despised as Useless. Ambrosiaster: Paul is saying that the human body is so organized that all its members are necessary, and because of this, all are concerned for one another. One cannot exist without the other, and parts which are thought to be inferior are usually more necessary. No one ought to be despised as useless. Commentary on Paul's Epistles.[29]

Greater Attention to Inferior Parts. Chrysostom: Paul points out that if division in the body is to be avoided, greater attention must be given to the lesser parts, so that they will not be harmed or feel excluded. If they were badly treated they would be destroyed, and their destruction would be the ruin of the body. Homilies on the Epistles of Paul to the Corinthians 32.3.[30]

12:26 Suffering and Rejoicing

The Grief of the Church Under Persecution. Cyprian: I suffer with, I grieve with our fellow believers who, having lapsed and fallen by the impetus of persecution, drawing part of our hearts with them, have brought a like sorrow on us with their wounds. Letters 17.[31]

The Church Suffers over the Whole World. Basil: Our sufferings are such as to have reached even to the limits of our inhabited world. When one member suffers, all the members suffer along with it. Letters 242, To the Westerners.[32]

All Rejoice Together. Chrysostom: Sharing all things in common, both good and bad, is the only way to achieve complete communion. Homilies on the Epistles of Paul to the Corinthians 31.5.[33]

If One Member Suffers. Augustine: Suppose you had a disjointed finger. Would you not tremble in all your limbs? Would you not hurry to the doctor to have the finger set? Surely, then, your body is in good condition when all its members are in agreement, the one with the other. Then you are considered healthy, and really are well. The Usefulness of Fasting 6.[34]

All Suffer Together. Augustine: Far be it from us to refuse to hear what is bitter and sad to those whom we love. It is not possible for one member to suffer without the other members suffering with it. Letters 99.[35]

---

[29]CSEL 81.140. [30]NPNF 1 12:182. [31]FC 51:49. [32]FC 28:182*. [33]NPNF 1 12:184. [34]FC 16:413*. [35]FC 18:140.

12:27-31 THE SPIRITUAL HIERARCHY

[27]*Now you are the body of Christ and individually members of it.* [28]*And God has appointed in the church first apostles, second prophets, third teachers, then workers of miracles, then healers, helpers, administrators, speakers in various kinds of tongues.* [29]*Are all apostles? Are all prophets? Are all teachers? Do all work miracles?* [30]*Do all possess gifts of healing? Do all speak with tongues? Do all interpret?* [31]*But earnestly desire the higher gifts.*

And I will show you a still more excellent way.

OVERVIEW: The body does not consist of members electing to join themselves together (SEVERIAN OF GABALA). No special gift is given to everyone. None is merited (AMBROSIASTER). They are diversely distributed to enable us to see our need of each other. The church in Corinth belongs to the worldwide community of resurrection faith (MAXIMUS OF TURIN, CHRYSOSTOM). The order by which Paul lists the gifts is deliberate, because the Corinthians put speaking in tongues at the top of the list (CHRYSOSTOM).

12:27 The Body of Christ

BE AT PEACE WITH THE CHURCH EVERYWHERE. CHRYSOSTOM: The Corinthian church was not the whole body by itself but was part of a worldwide community of faith. Therefore the Corinthians ought to be at peace with the church in every other place, if it is a true member of the body. HOMILIES ON THE EPISTLES OF PAUL TO THE CORINTHIANS 32.1.[1]

NOT INDIVIDUALS VOLUNTARILY JOINED. SEVERIAN OF GABALA: We are not individual members who elect to join together to form a whole but rather organic members of a wider whole, which is the whole body. PAULINE COMMENTARY FROM THE GREEK CHURCH.[2]

RISEN WITH HIM. MAXIMUS OF TURIN: In Christ's resurrection, all his members have necessarily risen with him. For while he passes from the depths to the heights, he has made us pass from death to life. SERMONS 54.[3]

12:28 Gifts Given by God

GOD HAS APPOINTED. AMBROSIASTER: Paul has placed the apostles at the head of the church. They may be identified with bishops, as Peter said of Judas: "Let another take his bishopric."[4] There are two types of prophets, those who predict the future and those who interpret the Scriptures. The apostles are also prophets, because the top rank has all the others subordinated to it. Even a wicked man like Caiaphas uttered prophecies on the strength of his rank, not for any virtue he might have possessed.[5] Teachers are those who instructed boys in the synagogue, a practice which has come down to us as well. COMMENTARY ON PAUL'S EPISTLES.[6]

WHY TONGUES LISTED LAST. CHRYSOSTOM: The order goes from the higher to the lower, and quite deliberately, because the Corinthians were in the habit of putting speaking in tongues at the top of the list. HOMILIES ON THE EPISTLES OF PAUL TO THE CORINTHIANS 32.2.[7]

12:29 Given the Same Gift?

ONLY ONE BISHOP. AMBROSIASTER: A church has only one bishop, and prophecy is not given to everybody. COMMENTARY ON PAUL'S EPISTLES.[8]

12:30 Other Gifts

GIVEN TO MAXIMIZE HARMONY. CHRYSOSTOM: Even as God did not grant the greater gifts to everyone, so also did he give the lesser gifts to some and not to others. He did this in order to obtain the maximum of harmony and love, since each one would see his need of the others and therefore be brought closer to them. HOMILIES ON THE EPISTLES OF PAUL TO THE CORINTHIANS 32.4.[9]

12:31 A More Excellent Way

NOT BY MERIT. AMBROSIASTER: The graces of the Lord which are seen in persons do not relate to the merit of the individual but to the honoring of God. COMMENTARY ON PAUL'S EPISTLES.[10]

THE GREATEST GIFT. CHRYSOSTOM: All along he

---

[1]NPNF 1 12:186. [2]NTA 15:263. [3]ACW 50:131. [4]*Episkopen;* cf. Acts 1:20. [5]Jn 11:49-51. [6]CSEL 81.141-42. [7]NPNF 1 12:186. [8]CSEL 81.142. [9]NPNF 1 12:188. [10]CSEL 81.143.

wants to point them higher still and whets their appetite for the greatest gift of all. Homilies on the Epistles of Paul to the Corinthians 32.5.[11]

[11]NPNF 1 12:188.

13:1-3 THE LAW OF LOVE

[1]*If I speak in the tongues of men and of angels, but have not love, I am a noisy gong or a clanging cymbal. [2]And if I have prophetic powers, and understand all mysteries and all knowledge, and if I have all faith, so as to remove mountains, but have not love, I am nothing. [3]If I give away all I have, and if I deliver my body to be burned,[v] but have not love, I gain nothing.*

v *Other ancient authorities read* body that I may glory

Overview: The tongues of men are human languages (Severian of Gabala). Without love they are like a noisy gong (Ambrosiaster). The tongues of angels are perceived by the mind, not the ear (Theodoret of Cyr). One may have prophetic powers yet be filled with an evil spirit, as in the case of Saul. Even Balaam's ass prophesied in a human language to demonstrate the majesty of God (Ambrosiaster). By faith Paul does not mean common and universal faith but the spiritual gift of faith (Gennadius of Constantinople). Love, which fulfills the law (Severian), is the head of religion (Ambrosiaster). Love does not hate anyone (Caesarius of Arles). Paul discounts even the most extreme sacrifices if they are made without love (Chrysostom). Offering one's body to be burned is not permission to commit suicide but a command not to resist suffering if the alternative is being forced to do wrong (Augustine).

13:1 Speaking Without Love

A Noisy Gong. Ambrosiaster: It is a great gift to be able to speak in different languages. To speak with the tongues of angels is even greater. But in order to show that none of this can be ascribed to merit and that every tongue is subject to the glory of God, Paul adds that a man without love is like a noisy gong or a clanging cymbal.

Balaam's ass spoke a human language in order to demonstrate the majesty of God,[1] and children sang the praises of Christ in order to confound the Jews.[2] In fact the Savior went further and declared than even stones could cry out if necessary.[3] Commentary on Paul's Epistles.[4]

A Nuisance Without Love. Chrysostom: In other words, says Paul, if I have no love I am not just useless but a positive nuisance. Homilies on the Epistles of Paul to the Corinthians 32.6.[5]

Tongues of Men Are Languages. Severian of Gabala: The tongues of angels refer to the differ-

[1]Num 22:28-31. [2]Mt 21:15. [3]Lk 19:40. [4]CSEL 81.144-45. [5]NPNF 1 12:189.

ent languages spoken on earth since the destruction of the tower of Babel. As Moses says in Deuteronomy [32:8]: "God has set the boundaries of the nations according to the number of angels." It is therefore the task of each angel to defend the distinction of nations. The tongues of men on the other hand are languages which we learn; they do not come to us naturally. PAULINE COMMENTARY FROM THE GREEK CHURCH.[6]

TONGUES OF ANGELS NOT PERCEIVED BY THE EAR. THEODORET OF CYR: Paul chooses speaking in tongues as his example because the Corinthians thought that it was the greatest of the gifts. This was because it had been given to the apostles on the day of Pentecost, before any of the others. The tongues of angels are those which are perceived by the mind, not by the ear. COMMENTARY ON THE FIRST EPISTLE TO THE CORINTHIANS 251.[7]

13:2 Nothing Without Love

THE LIMITS OF PROPHETIC POWERS. AMBROSIASTER: Balaam prophesied even though he was not a prophet,[8] and Caiaphas also prophesied.[9] So did Saul when, because of his disobedience, he was filled with an evil spirit.[10] Judas accompanied the other disciples and understood all the mysteries and knowledge given to them, but as an enemy of love he betrayed the Savior.[11] Both Tertullian and Novatian were men of no small learning, but because of their pride they lost the fellowship of love and falling into schism devised heresies, to their own damnation. COMMENTARY ON PAUL'S EPISTLES.[12]

MIRACLES OF WORD AND DEED. CHRYSOSTOM: By naming prophecy and faith, Paul included every spiritual gift, since miracles are either in word or in deed. HOMILIES ON THE EPISTLES OF PAUL TO THE CORINTHIANS 32.7.[13]

THE SPIRITUAL GIFT OF FAITH. GENNADIUS OF CONSTANTINOPLE: By faith, Paul does not mean the common and universal faith of believers but the spiritual gift of faith. The two things have the same name, because when the Holy Spirit comes upon us it is our human faith which expands to make room for the divine gift. PAULINE COMMENTARY FROM THE GREEK CHURCH.[14]

13:3a Giving Away All

EXTREME SACRIFICES. CHRYSOSTOM: Paul discounts even the most extreme sacrifices, if they are made without love. HOMILIES ON THE EPISTLES OF PAUL TO THE CORINTHIANS 32.8.[15]

GIVING ONE'S BODY TO BE BURNED. AUGUSTINE: Giving one's body to be burned is not a license to commit suicide but a command not to resist suffering if the alternative is being forced to do wrong. LETTER 173 TO DONATUS.[16]

13:3b Gaining Nothing Without Love

THE HEAD OF RELIGION. AMBROSIASTER: Love is the very head of religion, and someone who has no head is dead. COMMENTARY ON PAUL'S EPISTLES.[17]

LOVE DOES NOT HATE ANYONE. CAESARIUS OF ARLES: Since true charity loves all, if someone knows that he hates even one other person he should hasten to vomit up this bitter gall, in order to be ready to receive the sweetness of charity himself. SERMONS 23.4.[18]

LOVE FULFILLS THE LAW. SEVERIAN OF GABALA: The one who loves fulfills the law. The one who fulfills the law is well respected. The one who is well respected receives a spiritual gift. PAULINE COMMENTARY FROM THE GREEK CHURCH.[19]

---

[6]NTA 15:265. [7]Migne PG 82:331. [8]Num 22:38—24:25. [9]Jn 11:49-51. [10]1 Sam 16:14-23; 19:9. [11]Mt 26:47-50; Mk 14:43-46; Lk 22:47-48; Jn 18:2-5. [12]CSEL 81.145-46. [13]NPNF 1 12:189. [14]NTA 15:418-19. [15]NPNF 1 12:189. [16]FC 30:77. [17]CSEL 81.147. [18]FC 31:122. [19]NTA 15:264.

13:4-7 THE NATURE OF LOVE

⁴Love is patient and kind; love is not jealous or boastful; ⁵it is not arrogant or rude. Love does not insist on its own way; it is not irritable or resentful; ⁶it does not rejoice at wrong, but rejoices in the right. ⁷Love bears all things, believes all things, hopes all things, endures all things.

OVERVIEW: Love seeks the good of others (CHRYSOSTOM, CASSIODORUS), hating what is unjust and rejoicing in what is good (THEODORET OF CYR), discerning its own limitations (BASIL). The greater the love of God the saints share, the more they learn to endure all things (GREGORY NAZIANZEN, AUGUSTINE).

13:4 Love Is Patient and Kind

THE ADORNMENT OF LOVE. CHRYSOSTOM: He next makes an outline of love's matchless beauty, adorning its image with all aspects of virtue, as if with many colors brought together with precision. HOMILIES ON THE EPISTLES OF PAUL TO THE CORINTHIANS 33.1.[1]

LOVE NOT ENVIOUS. AUGUSTINE: The reason why love does not envy is because it is not puffed up. For where puffing up precedes, envy follows, because pride is the mother of envy. LETTER TO HONORATUS 22.[2]

13:5 Not Arrogant or Rude

LOVE SEEKS TO DISCERN ITS OWN DEFECTS. BASIL: A person living in solitary retirement will not readily discern his own defects, since he has no one to admonish or correct him with mildness and compassion. In fact, admonition from an enemy often produces in a prudent man the desire for amendment. THE LONG RULES 7.[3]

REMOVING VICE. CHRYSOSTOM: He adorns love not only for what it has but also for what it has not. Love both elicits virtue and expels vice, not permitting it to spring up at all. HOMILIES ON THE EPISTLES OF PAUL TO THE CORINTHIANS 33.3.[4]

FREE SERVITUDE TRANSCENDING DOMINANCE. CASSIODORUS: So those who serve the Lord with gladness are they who love him above all else and show brotherly charity to each other. What free servitude is this! What service, excelling all forms of dominance! EXPLANATION OF THE PSALMS 2.[5]

13:6 Rejoicing in the Right

CAST OFF SULLENNESS. BASIL: Cast off the sullenness of an angry man which you are evincing by your silence, and regain joy in your heart, peace toward your likeminded brothers and sisters, and zeal and solicitude for the preservation of the churches of the Lord. LETTERS 65, TO ATARBIUS.[6]

WHAT IS GOOD. THEODORET OF CYR: Love hates what is unjust and rejoices in what is good and honorable. COMMENTARY ON THE FIRST EPISTLE TO THE CORINTHIANS 253.[7]

13:7 Love Bears All Things

ENDURING ALL THINGS. GREGORY NAZIANZEN: Bearing all things, enduring all things for our love and hope regarding him, let us give thanks

---

[1]CSEL 81.195. [2]FC 20:103*. [3]FC 9:248. [4]NPNF 1 12:195. [5]ACW 52:444. [6]FC 13:158. [7]Migne PG 82:335.

for all things, both favorable and unfavorable alike—I mean the pleasant and the painful— since reason often knows even these as arms of salvation. On His Brother, St. Caesarius 24.[8]

Love Casts Out Fear. Ambrose: A man with this charity fears nothing, for charity casts out fear. When fear is banished and cast out, charity endures all things, bears all things. One who bears all things through love cannot fear martyrdom. Letters to Priests 49, Ambrose to Horonatianus.[9]

Believing All Things. Augustine: For what is it to hear about oneself from you but to know oneself? Who, then, can know himself and say "It is false," unless he himself lies? But because "charity believes all things," certainly among those whom it makes one, in intimate union

with each other, I, also, O Lord, do even confess to you in such a way that men may hear, though I cannot prove to them the things I confess are true. But those whose ears charity opens to me, they believe. Confessions 10.3.[10]

Even Death. Chrysostom: Out of long suffering love bears all things, whether they are burdensome or grievous, whether insults, lashes or even death. Homily on the Epistles of Paul to the Corinthians 33.4.[11]

Love Endures All Things. Augustine: The greater the love of God that the saints possess, the more they endure all things for him. Patience 17.[12]

---

[8]FC 22:25*. [9]FC 26:254. [10]FC 21:265*. [11]NPNF 1 12:198. [12]FC 16:251.

13:8-13 THE FUTURE OF LOVE

[8]*Love never ends; as for prophecies, they will pass away; as for tongues, they will cease; as for knowledge, it will pass away.* [9]*For our knowledge is imperfect and our prophecy is imperfect;* [10]*but when the perfect comes, the imperfect will pass away.* [11]*When I was a child, I spoke like a child, I thought like a child, I reasoned like a child; when I became a man, I gave up childish ways.* [12]*For now we see in a mirror dimly, but then face to face. Now I know in part; then I shall understand fully, even as I have been fully understood.* [13]*So faith, hope, love abide, these three; but the greatest of these is love.*

Overview: In this life we are children, compared with what we shall become in the next life (Ambrosiaster, Chrysostom). Our knowledge now is imperfect (Basil), but it is proximately reliable within its limits (Augustine). If now we see as if in a mirror only dimly (Clement of Alexandria, Origen, Pelagius), after the resurrection we shall understand fully (Montanist Oracles). We shall know as we are known (Gregory Nazianzen), as if face to face (Chrysostom, Augustine). We shall know everything we know now, but much more as well (Chrysostom). Tongues cease as in this sentence (Origen), but love never fails by falling irremediably into sin (Severian of Gabala). Final judgment occurs by making the imperfect perfect (AMBROSIASTER). Faith embraces, hope envisions, love reigns (AMBROSIASTER). Love, which will never cease (CYPRIAN, MACRINA, CHRYSOSTOM), is the greatest of these (THEODORE OF MOPSUESTIA, SEVERIAN, THEODORET OF CYR).

13:8a Love Never Ends

LOVE ALONE PERSEVERES. MACRINA (THE SISTER OF GREGORY OF NYSSA): Love is first among all the activities connected with virtue and all the commandments of the law. If, therefore, the soul ever attains this love, it will need none of the others, having reached the fullness of its being. It seems that love alone preserves in itself the character of the divine blessedness. And knowledge becomes love because what is known is by nature beautiful. [THE TEACHING OF MACRINA] ON THE SOUL AND THE RESURRECTION.[1]

LOVE NEVER FAILS. SEVERIAN OF GABALA: Love never fails, which means that it never falls into sin. PAULINE COMMENTARY FROM THE GREEK CHURCH.[2]

UNCHANGING LOVE. THEODORET OF CYR: Love always remains firm and stable, unchanged and unchanging. COMMENTARY ON THE FIRST EPISTLE TO THE CORINTHIANS 254.[3]

13:8b Tongues and Knowledge Will End

TONGUES WILL CEASE. ORIGEN: "Tongues will cease" when I express what I want to say with my mind. COMMENTARY ON 1 CORINTHIANS 4.52.[4]

KNOWLEDGE WILL PASS AWAY. CHRYSOSTOM: What about our enemies and the heathen? Should we not hate them? No, we do not hate them but their teaching; not the person but the wicked conduct and the corrupt mind. It is no surprise to discover that prophecies and tongues will pass away, but what about knowl-

edge? Paul goes on to explain why he includes that as well. HOMILIES ON THE EPISTLES OF PAUL TO THE CORINTHIANS 35.2.[5]

USE KNOWLEDGE TO BUILD UP LOVE. AUGUSTINE: Use your knowledge as a sort of tool to build the edifice of charity, which remains forever, even when "knowledge passes away." For knowledge which is used to promote love is useful, but in itself and separated from love it turns out to be not only useless but even harmful. LETTERS 55.[6]

13:9 Knowledge and Prophecy Imperfect

OUR KNOWLEDGE IS IMPERFECT. AUGUSTINE: Our knowledge in this life remains imperfect, but it is reliable within its limits. Believers trust the witness of their senses, which are subservient to their intelligence. They may occasionally be deceived, but even so they are still better off than those who maintain that the senses can never be trusted. CITY OF GOD 19.18.[7]

13:10 The Imperfect Will Pass Away

THE PARTIAL AND THE COMPLETE. BASIL: Even though more knowledge is always being acquired by everyone, it will ever fall short in all things of its rightful completeness until the time when that which is perfect being comes, that which is in part will be done away. CONCERNING FAITH.[8]

WHEN THE PERFECT COMES. AMBROSIASTER: Everything which is imperfect will be destroyed. But destruction occurs by making the imperfect perfect, not by removing it altogether. COMMENTARY ON PAUL'S EPISTLES.[9]

IMPERFECTION SEEN AS LIMITED. CHRYSOSTOM: What is implied from this is not that our knowl-

---

[1]FC 58:241. [2]NTA 15:266. [3]Migne PG 82:335. [4]JTS 10:35. [5]NPNF 1 12:198, 202. [6]FC 12:293*. [7]FC 24:229. [8]FC 9:62. [9]CSEL 81.148.

edge will disappear altogether, but that its imperfections will be seen as very limited. We shall know everything we know now imperfectly, but so much more as well. For example, we know now that God is everywhere, but we do not know how this is possible. We know that he made the creation out of nothing, but we have no idea how. We know that Christ was born of a virgin, but we do not know how. And so on. Homilies on the Epistles of Paul to the Corinthians 36.2.[10]

Then We Shall Know. Ambrose: For now we know in part and understand in part. But then we shall be able to comprehend what is perfect, when not the shadow but the reality of the majesty and eternity of God shall begin to shine and to reveal itself unveiled before our eyes. On His Brother Satyrus 2.32.[11]

Faith and Sight. Augustine: But, as this faith, which works by love, begins to penetrate the soul, it tends, through the vital power of goodness, to change into sight, so that the holy and perfect in heart catch glimpses of that ineffable beauty whose full vision is our highest happiness. . . . We begin in faith, we are perfected in sight. Enchiridion 1.5.[12]

13:11a Like a Child

When I Was a Child. Clement of Alexandria: This is a figure of speech for the way Paul lived under the law, when he persecuted the Word and was still senseless and childish, blaspheming God. Christ the Educator 1.6.33.[13]

13:11b Giving Up Childish Ways

Childish Ways. Clement of Alexandria: He is not referring to the growing stature that comes with age, nor any definite period of time, nor even to any secret teaching reserved only for mature adults, when he claims that he

left and put away all childishness. Rather he means to say that those who live by the law are childish in the sense that they are subject to fear, like children afraid of ghosts, while those who are obedient to the Word and are completely free are in his opinion mature. Christ the Educator 1.6.33.[14]

From Child to Adult. Basil: "When I was a child"—that is, fresh from committing to memory the first elements of the divine Word—"I spoke as a child, I understood as a child, I thought as a child. But now that I have become a man"—that is, and am hastening to attain the measure of the age of the fullness of Christ—"I have put away the things of a child." Concerning Faith.[15]

This Life and the Next. Ambrosiaster: In this life we are children, compared with what we shall become in the next life. For everything in this life is imperfect, including knowledge. Commentary on Paul's Epistles.[16]

What We Shall Know. Chrysostom: Here Paul points out just how great the difference is between what we know now and what we shall know in the future. Homilies on the Epistles of Paul to the Corinthians 34.2.[17]

13:12a Seeing in a Mirror

Self-Knowledge by Reflection. Clement of Alexandria: We know ourselves by reflection, as in a mirror. We contemplate, as far as we may, the creative cause on the basis of the divine element in us. Stromata 1.94.[18]

In a Mirror Dimly. Origen: If the knowledge manifested to those worthy of it comes through a mirror and is an enigma in the present age and

---

[10]NPNF 1 12:202. [11]FC 22:210. [12]LCC 7:338. [13]FC 23:32. [14]FC 23:32. [15]FC 9:61. [16]CSEL 81.149 [17]NPNF 1 12:202. [18]FC 85:94.

will be fully revealed only "then," it is foolish to suppose that it will not be the same for the other virtues as well. ON PRAYER 11.2.[19]

THEN FACE TO FACE. CHRYSOSTOM: God does not have a face, of course. Paul uses this image to denote greater clarity and perspicuity. Someone sitting in the darkness at night will not run after the light of the sun as long as he cannot see it. But when the dawn comes and the sun's brightness begins to shine on him, he will eventually follow after its light. HOMILIES ON THE EPISTLES OF PAUL TO THE CORINTHIANS 34.2.[20]

AS THE ANGELS SEE GOD. AUGUSTINE: Face to face—this is how the holy angels, who are called our angels, already see. They are our angels in the sense that once we have been delivered from the power of darkness, have received the pledge of the spirit and have been translated to the kingdom of Christ, we shall have begun to belong to the angels. CITY OF GOD 22.29.[21]

AS TYPES AND SHADOWS. PELAGIUS: The dim mirror is the law of Moses, which contains everything in types and shadows. COMMENTARY ON THE FIRST EPISTLE TO THE CORINTHIANS 13.[22]

13:12b Understanding Fully

THEN I SHALL UNDERSTAND FULLY. DIDYMUS THE BLIND: This means that the things which we now hear on the authority of the Scriptures we believe to be so. After the resurrection we shall see them with our eyes and know them in reality, when partial knowledge has ceased, for the knowledge which depends on hearing is part of the knowledge of an eyewitness and of experience. MONTANIST ORACLES, ON THE TRINITY 103.2.[23]

WE SHALL KNOW AS WE ARE KNOWN. GREGORY NAZIANZEN: No one has yet discovered or shall ever discover what God is in his nature and essence. As for a discovery some time in the fu-

ture, let those who have a mind for it research and speculate. The discovery will take place, so my reason tells me, when this Godlike, divine thing, I mean our mind and reason, mingles with its kin, when the copy returns to the pattern it now longs after. This seems to me to be the meaning of the great dictum that we shall, in time to come, know even as we are known. ORATION 28.17.[24]

SEEING WITHOUT SPATIAL LIMITATIONS. AUGUSTINE: But when we begin to have a spiritual body as we are promised in the resurrection, let us see it even in the body, either by an intellectual vision or in some miraculous manner, since the grace of the spiritual body is indescribable. We shall then see it according to our capacity, without limitations of space, not larger in one part and smaller in another, since it is not a body, and it is wholly present everywhere. LETTER TO CONSENTIUS 120.[25]

13:13a Faith, Hope, Love Abide

LOVE ABIDES. CYPRIAN: There will always be love in the kingdom, it will abide forever in the unity of a harmonious brotherhood. Discord cannot enter the kingdom of heaven. One who has violated the love of Christ by faithless dissension cannot attain to the reward of Christ. UNITY OF THE CATHOLIC CHURCH 14.[26]

LOVE REIGNS. AMBROSIASTER: Love is the greatest because while faith is preached and hope pertains to the future life, love reigns. As 1 John [3:16] says: "By this we know his love, that he laid down his life for us." Love is therefore the greatest of the three, because by it the human race has been renewed. COMMENTARY ON PAUL'S EPISTLES.[27]

---

[19]CWS 102. [20]NPNF 1 12:202. [21]FC 24:497. [22]Migne PL 759A. [23]MOT 14:143. [24]FGFR 233. [25]FC 18:314. [26]LCC 5:134. [27]CSEL 81.149.

LOVE WILL NEVER CEASE. CHRYSOSTOM: Faith and hope will cease when the things believed in and hoped for appear. But love then becomes even greater and more ardent. HOMILIES ON THE EPISTLES OF PAUL TO THE CORINTHIANS 34.5.[28]

13:13b The Greatest of These Is Love

LOVE ABIDES ETERNALLY. CYPRIAN: Charity is the bond of brotherhood, the foundation of peace, the steadfastness and firmness of unity. It is greater than both hope and faith. It excels both good works and suffering of the faith. As an eternal virtue, it will abide with us forever in the kingdom of heaven. THE GOOD OF PATIENCE 15.[29]

OVERCOMING STRIFE. THEODORE OF MOPSUESTIA: Paul tells the Corinthians that love is the greatest of all because there was jealousy and strife among them, and the church was in danger of being divided. PAULINE COMMENTARY FROM THE GREEK CHURCH.[30]

FULFILLING THE LAW. SEVERIAN OF GABALA: Love is the greatest because it is the fulfilling of the law. PAULINE COMMENTARY FROM THE GREEK CHURCH.[31]

LOVE IS THE GREATEST. THEODORET OF CYR: If faith is the substance of things hoped for, as Hebrews [11:1] tells us, it will be superfluous once these things have arrived. Similarly with hope. But love is greater than these, because when our troubles are over and our bodies have been changed in the resurrection, our minds will be steadied by it, so that they will no longer desire now one thing, now another. COMMENTARY ON THE FIRST EPISTLE TO THE CORINTHIANS 255-56.[32]

---

[28]NPNF 1 12:203. [29]FC 36:277. [30]NTA 15:192. [31]NTA 15:267. [32]Migne PG 82:338.

14:1-12 PROPHECY VERSUS TONGUES

[1]*Make love your aim, and earnestly desire the spiritual gifts, especially that you may prophesy.* [2]*For one who speaks in a tongue speaks not to men but to God; for no one understands him, but he utters mysteries in the Spirit.* [3]*On the other hand, he who prophesies speaks to men for their upbuilding and encouragement and consolation.* [4]*He who speaks in a tongue edifies himself, but he who prophesies edifies the church.* [5]*Now I want you all to speak in tongues, but even more to prophesy. He who prophesies is greater than he who speaks in tongues, unless some one interprets, so that the church may be edified.*

[6]*Now, brethren, if I come to you speaking in tongues, how shall I benefit you unless I bring you some revelation or knowledge or prophecy or teaching?* [7]*If even lifeless instruments, such as the flute or the harp, do not give distinct notes, how will any one know what is played?* [8]*And if the bugle gives an indistinct sound, who will get ready for battle?* [9]*So with yourselves; if you in a tongue utter speech that is not intelligible, how will any one know what is said? For you will be speaking into the air.* [10]*There are doubtless many*

different languages in the world, and none is without meaning; [11]but if I do not know the meaning of the language, I shall be a foreigner to the speaker and the speaker a foreigner to me. [12]So with yourselves; since you are eager for manifestations of the Spirit, strive to excel in building up the church.

OVERVIEW: All languages are intended to convey meaning (SEVERIAN OF GABALA, PELAGIUS). Paul did not forbid speaking in tongues but regarded prophecy as more useful (AMBROSIASTER). Even if Paul himself spoke in tongues, this would be useless if not interpreted (CHRYSOSTOM). The apostles received the gift of tongues first as a sign that they were to go to all the world preaching the gospel (CHRYSOSTOM). Gifts are greater when given for the benefit of many, not one (CHRYSOSTOM). Prophecy is a greater gift than tongues because it is used for the benefit of the whole church (CHRYSOSTOM) to bring edification, encouragement and consolation (AMBROSIASTER). Prophecy interprets Scripture usefully (AMBROSIASTER) for the common good (CHRYSOSTOM). By prophecy the whole church learns God's plan (AMBROSIASTER). Like distinct notes in music, speech requires precision (CHRYSOSTOM). Do not let your words have an indistinct sound, lest like a bugle in combat they might confuse (ORIGEN, PELAGIUS).

14:1 Desire Spiritual Gifts

PROPHECY THE HIGHEST GIFT. AMBROSIASTER: Paul says that prophecy is the highest gift after love because it is to the benefit and advantage of the church, since by it everybody learns the principles of God's law. COMMENTARY ON PAUL'S EPISTLES.[1]

14:2 Uttering Mysteries

WHY THE CORINTHIANS VALUED TONGUES. CHRYSOSTOM: The Corinthians thought that speaking in tongues was a great gift because it was the one which the apostles received first, and with a

great display. But this was no reason to think it was the greatest gift of all. The reason the apostles got it first was because it was a sign that they were to go everywhere, preaching the gospel. HOMILIES ON THE EPISTLES OF PAUL TO THE CORINTHIANS 35.1.[2]

14:3 Prophecy Encourages and Consoles

UPBUILDING, ENCOURAGEMENT AND CONSOLATION. AMBROSIASTER: A person is built up when he finds out the answer to disputed points. Encouragement comes to him when he is enabled to endure. He is consoled when he continues in hope even when others are viewing his discipline with contempt. Knowledge of the law strengthens his soul and encourages him to hope for better things. COMMENTARY ON PAUL'S EPISTLES.[3]

TO THE BENEFIT OF EVERYONE. CHRYSOSTOM: Paul reckons this gift as a higher one because it is used for the common good. He always gives the greater honor to those gifts that will be used for the benefit of everyone. HOMILIES ON THE EPISTLES OF PAUL TO THE CORINTHIANS 35.1.[4]

14:4 Prophecy Edifies the Church

THE PROPHETS INTERPRET SCRIPTURE. AMBROSIASTER: Paul is saying that prophets are interpreters of the Scriptures. COMMENTARY ON PAUL'S EPISTLES.[5]

INDIVIDUAL AND CHURCH EDIFICATION. CHRYSOS-

---

[1]CSEL 81.149. [2]NPNF 1 12:208-9. [3]CSEL 81.150. [4]NPNF 1 12:209. [5]CSEL 81.150.

tom: The difference between tongues and prophecy is precisely the difference between benefit to the individual and benefit to the entire church. Homilies on the Epistles of Paul to the Corinthians 35.1.[6]

14:5 Prophecy Greater Than Tongues

Prophecy Is More Useful. Ambrosiaster: Paul could not forbid speaking in tongues, because this is a gift of the Holy Spirit, but the pursuit of prophecy is more acceptable because it is more useful. Commentary on Paul's Epistles.[7]

14:6 Benefiting the Church

Not Belittling Tongues. Chrysostom: Paul says this in order to show that he is interested in benefiting the church, not in belittling those who have the gift of tongues. He could have this gift himself, but it would be useless and would make no difference to the church if uninterpreted. Homilies on the Epistles of Paul to the Corinthians 35.2.[8]

14:7 Giving Distinct Notes

Speech Requires Precision. Chrysostom: If we require precision even in lifeless instruments, how much more will we require it in living beings? Homilies on the Epistles of Paul to the Corinthians 35.3.[9]

14:8 An Indistinct Sound

Make No Uncertain Sound. Pelagius: If it is uncertain whether the bugle is sounding for relaxation or for war, nobody will get ready for battle. The latter is how your own words should be understood, for they are meant to prepare soldiers for spiritual warfare. Commentary on the First Epistle to the Corinthians 14.[10]

Readiness for Battle. Origen: The trumpet is

a sign of war. Therefore, when the soul perceives itself armed with so many and such important virtues, it necessarily goes forth to the war it has against principalities and powers and against the world rulers. Numbers, Homily 27.[11]

14:9 Speaking into the Air

Interpretation Required. Chrysostom: If speaking in tongues is useless, why was it given? It was given for the benefit of the person who has it. But if it is to help others also, then there must be some interpretation. Homilies on the Epistles of Paul to the Corinthians 35.4.[12]

14:10 Language Has Meaning

No Language Meaningless. Severian of Gabala: There is no language without meaning because all languages are human. Pauline Commentary from the Greek Church.[13]

14:11 Interpretation

Meaning of a Language. Pelagius: Any language we cannot understand we look down on as barbaric. Commentary on the First Epistle to the Corinthians 14.[14]

14:12 Excel in Building Up the Church

Eager for the Spirit. Ambrosiaster: The soul is stirred and rejoices when it learns something more about the Scriptures. The more it tends in this direction, the more it abandons vices. It is for these reasons that Paul advises that one should make efforts to communicate clearly. Commentary on Paul's Epistles.[15]

Edifying the Church. Chrysostom: The building up of the church is Paul's touchstone in

---

[6]NPNF 1 12:209. [7]CSEL 81.151. [8]NPNF 1 12:209. [9]NPNF 1 12:210. [10]Migne PL 30:760A. [11]CWS 264. [12]NPNF 1 12:210. [13]NTA 15:268. [14]Migne PL 30:760B. [15]CSEL 81.152.

everything he says. HOMILIES ON THE EPISTLES
OF PAUL TO THE CORINTHIANS 35.5.[16]

[16]NPNF 1 12:211.

14:13-25 CONTROLLING THE POWER OF TONGUES

[13]*Therefore, he who speaks in a tongue should pray for the power to interpret.* [14]*For if I pray in a tongue, my spirit prays but my mind is unfruitful.* [15]*What am I to do? I will pray with the spirit and I will pray with the mind also; I will sing with the spirit and I will sing with the mind also.* [16]*Otherwise, if you bless*[w] *with the spirit, how can any one in the position of an outsider*[x] *say the "Amen" to your thanksgiving when he does not know what you are saying?* [17]*For you may give thanks well enough, but the other man is not edified.* [18]*I thank God that I speak in tongues more than you all;* [19]*nevertheless, in church I would rather speak five words with my mind, in order to instruct others, than ten thousand words in a tongue.*

[20]*Brethren, do not be children in your thinking; be babes in evil, but in thinking be mature.* [21]*In the law it is written, "By men of strange tongues and by the lips of foreigners will I speak to this people, and even then they will not listen to me, says the Lord."* [22]*Thus, tongues are a sign not for believers but for unbelievers, while prophecy is not for unbelievers but for believers.* [23]*If, therefore, the whole church assembles and all speak in tongues, and outsiders or unbelievers enter, will they not say that you are mad?* [24]*But if all prophesy, and an unbeliever or outsider enters, he is convicted by all, he is called to account by all,* [25]*the secrets of his heart are disclosed; and so, falling on his face, he will worship God and declare that God is really among you.*

w *That is*, give thanks to God   x *Or* him that is without gifts

OVERVIEW: When the church prays in the Spirit, the Spirit is offering the prayer (GREGORY NAZIANZEN). Prayer with the Spirit and in song (ORIGEN, CASSIODORUS) is more profound and inward than is any external composite sound (ABRAHAM OF NATHPAR). "Amen" is spoken by the whole laity (PELAGIUS) to confirm the truth of the prayer (AMBROSIASTER). Paul calls the Corinthians to be mature intellectually so they will grasp accurately what is needed for the upbuilding of the church (AMBROSIASTER) while at the same time being innocent with respect to evil (CHRYSOSTOM). The prophecies of God are hidden that they should not be garbled by unbelievers. Tongues are a wonderful sign (SEVERIAN OF GABALA) for unbelievers (PELAGIUS) but not for the instruction of believers (AMBROSIASTER, CHRYSOSTOM). The speaker of tongues may be moved, but if interpretation is lacking, others may not be edified (ORIGEN, BASIL, SEVERIAN, AMBROSIASTER). Paul claims for himself the gift of speaking in tongues in order to show how unimportant it is when taken alone (CHRYSOSTOM). The language of the believer should be a blessing to everyone (PELAGIUS).

14:13 The Power to Interpret

PRAY FOR THE POWER TO INTERPRET. ORIGEN: If the one who speaks in tongues does not have the power to interpret them, others will not understand, but he will know what he was moved by the Spirit to say. When this is understood by others as well, there will be fruit from it. Here as elsewhere, we are taught to seek the common good of the church. COMMENTARY ON 1 CORINTHIANS 4.61-62.[1]

14:14 My Mind Is Unfruitful

THE STERILITY OF YESTERDAY'S FLESH. ORIGEN: If you have brought a word in praise of God, not new and fresh from the learning of the spirit, from the teaching of God's grace, your mouth indeed offers "a sacrifice of praise," but your mind is accused on account of the sterility of yesterday's flesh. HOMILIES ON LEVITICUS 5.[2]

THE MIND UNFRUITFUL. AMBROSIASTER: What can a person achieve if he does not know what he is saying? COMMENTARY ON PAUL'S EPISTLES.[3]

MY SPIRIT PRAYS. AUGUSTINE: For he speaks thus, when that which is said is not understood, because it cannot even be uttered, unless the images of corporeal sounds precede the oral sounds by the thought of the spirit. THE TRINITY 14.16.[4]

14:15 Praying with the Spirit

PRAY WITH THE SPIRIT AND THE MIND. ORIGEN: For our mind would not even be able to pray unless the Spirit prayed for it as if obeying it, so that we cannot even sing and hymn the Father in Christ with proper rhythm, melody, measure and harmony unless the Spirit who searches everything, even the depths of God, first praises and hymns him whose depths he has searched out and has understood as far as he is able. ON PRAYER 4.[5]

PRAY WITH THE SPIRIT. GREGORY NAZIANZEN: Worshiping and praying in the Spirit seem to me to be simply the Spirit presenting prayer and worship to himself. ORATION 31.12.[6]

PRAYER BEYOND PSALMODY. ABRAHAM OF NATHPAR: It is in spirit and mind that one should pray and sing to God. Paul does not say anything about the tongue. The reason is that this spiritual prayer is not offered up or prayed by the tongue, for it is deeper than the lips and the tongue, more interiorized than any composite sounds, lying beyond psalmody and wisdom. ON PRAYER 2.[7]

SING WITH THE SPIRIT. CASSIODORUS: The prayer of those who sing is acceptable to God only if a pure heart carries the same message which the words of the hymn unfold. EXPLANATION OF THE PSALMS 2.[8]

14:16 Responding with Amen

CONFIRMING THE PRAYER. AMBROSIASTER: The confirmation of the prayer comes about when people say "Amen" to it. The words spoken are confirmed in the minds of the hearers by the confession of truth. COMMENTARY ON PAUL'S EPISTLES.[9]

THE WHOLE PEOPLE OF GOD. PELAGIUS: Paul is thinking here of laypeople, who do not hold office in the church. COMMENTARY ON THE FIRST EPISTLE TO THE CORINTHIANS 14.[10]

14:17 Others Not Edified

---

[1]JTS 10:37-38. [2]FC 83:105*. [3]CSEL 81.153. [4]FC 45:442. [5]CWS 85. [6]FGFR 285. [7]SFPSL 192. [8]ACW 53:3. [9]CSEL 81.153-54. [10]Migne PL 30:760C.

LANGUAGE SHOULD BLESS EVERYONE. PELAGIUS: Here Paul explains what he said above, which is that a believer should be a blessing to everyone. COMMENTARY ON THE FIRST EPISTLE TO THE CORINTHIANS 14.[11]

14:18 I Speak in Tongues

PAUL CLAIMS THE GIFT. CHRYSOSTOM: Paul claims the gift for himself in order to show how unimportant it is. He does the same thing elsewhere when he points out that he is a better-qualified Jew than his critics are.[12] HOMILIES ON THE EPISTLES OF PAUL TO THE CORINTHIANS 35.7.[13]

14:19 Speaking to Instruct

SPEAK WITH A CLEAR MIND. SEVERIAN OF GABALA: Paul wants to speak with a clear mind and in a normal language. PAULINE COMMENTARY FROM THE GREEK CHURCH.[14]

14:20 Be Mature in Thinking

MATURE INTELLECTUALLY. AMBROSIASTER: Paul wants them to be mature intellectually so they will grasp accurately what is needed for the upbuilding of the church. In this way they will leave behind malice and errors, striving instead for the things which are conducive to the good of the brotherhood. COMMENTARY ON PAUL'S EPISTLES.[15]

BE BABES IN EVIL. CHRYSOSTOM: To be a babe in evil is not even to know what evil is. HOMILIES ON THE EPISTLES OF PAUL TO THE CORINTHIANS 36.1.[16]

14:21 A Prophetic Writing

AQUILA AS PAUL'S SOURCE. ORIGEN: Note that Paul refers to the prophetic writings also as the "law." In this passage he is quoting Isaiah [28:11] according to Aquila's translation, and not according to the Septuagint. COMMENTARY ON 1 CORINTHIANS 4.65.[17]

FOREKNOWLEDGE OF UNBELIEF. AMBROSIASTER: The Lord said this about those whom he knew in advance would not believe in the Savior. For to speak in other tongues and with other lips is to preach the New Testament. COMMENTARY ON PAUL'S EPISTLES.[18]

14:22 Tongues for Unbelievers

THE VEIL OF TONGUES. AMBROSIASTER: The utterances of God are hidden beneath the veil of an unknown tongue, so that they should not be seen by unbelievers. Paul was saying that tongues are useful for hiding ideas from unbelievers. COMMENTARY ON PAUL'S EPISTLES.[19]

TONGUES NOT FOR INSTRUCTION. CHRYSOSTOM: Tongues are a sign to unbelievers not for their instruction, as prophecy is for both believers and unbelievers, but to astonish them. HOMILIES ON THE EPISTLES OF PAUL TO THE CORINTHIANS 36.2.[20]

TONGUES, PROPHECY AND MIRACLE. SEVERIAN OF GABALA: Tongues are a miracle in themselves. Prophecy, however, is a miracle in the substance of what it contains but not in the way in which it is uttered. PAULINE COMMENTARY FROM THE GREEK CHURCH.[21]

14:23 The Impression on Unbelievers

GOOD ORDER VALUED. BASIL: Even if a stranger should address his inquiries through ignorance to some other person and although he who is questioned by mistake is able to make a satisfactory reply, yet, for the sake of good order, he

---

[11]Migne PL 30:760D. [12]Phil 3:4-7. [13]NPNF 1 12:211. [14]NTA 15:268. [15]CSEL 81.155. [16]NPNF 1 12:215. [17]JTS 10:38. Paul was as familiar with rabbinic text as with the LXX. [18]CSEL 81.155. [19]CSEL 81.156. [20]NPNF 1 12:216. [21]NTA 15:269.

should keep silence and direct the stranger to him whose function it is, as the apostles did when the Lord was present. In this way, speech will be employed in a well-ordered and fitting manner. THE LONG RULES 45.[22]

TONGUES IN THE ASSEMBLY. PELAGIUS: On the day of Pentecost the Jews said that the apostles were full of new wine.[23] It is more or less the same thing here. COMMENTARY ON THE FIRST EPISTLE TO THE CORINTHIANS 14.[24]

14:24 Called to Account by Prophecy

THE UNBELIEVER CONVICTED. PELAGIUS: The unbeliever is convicted when his conscience is struck by the teaching being given. COMMENTARY ON THE FIRST EPISTLE TO THE CORINTHIANS 14.[25]

14:25 Declaring God Is Among You

THE UNBELIEVER WILL WORSHIP GOD. AMBROSIASTER: When he sees that God is being praised and that Christ is being adored and that nothing is disguised or being done in secret, as happens among pagans, he will understand clearly that this is true religion. COMMENTARY ON PAUL'S EPISTLES.[26]

THE SPIRIT IS GOD. THEODORET OF CYR: Note that here the Holy Spirit is directly called God. COMMENTARY ON THE FIRST EPISTLE TO THE CORINTHIANS 261.[27]

---

[22]FC 9:323. [23]Acts 2:13. [24]Migne PL 30:761C. [25]Migne PL 30:761C. [26]CSEL 81.157. [27]Migne PG 82:343.

14:26-32 ORDERING PUBLIC WORSHIP

[26]*What then, brethren? When you come together, each one has a hymn, a lesson, a revelation, a tongue, or an interpretation. Let all things be done for edification.* [27]*If any speak in a tongue, let there be only two or at most three, and each in turn; and let one interpret.* [28]*But if there is no one to interpret, let each of them keep silence in church and speak to himself and to God.* [29]*Let two or three prophets speak, and let the others weigh what is said.* [30]*If a revelation is made to another sitting by, let the first be silent.* [31]*For you can all prophesy one by one, so that all may learn and all be encouraged;* [32]*and the spirits of prophets are subject to prophets.*

OVERVIEW: Those possessed by unclean spirits tend to speak even when they do not want to (SEVERIAN OF GABALA). Such speech should be kept under control in public worship (CYPRIAN, CHRYSOSTOM), leaving sufficient time for the interpretation of Scripture (AMBROSIASTER, CASSIODORUS). Allow all a fair hearing by taking turns (THEODORET OF CYR). Follow the tradition of the synagogue whereby the people dispute while seated in chairs, on benches or on the floor, according to their rank (AMBROSIASTER).

14:26 Do All Things to Edify

For Edification. Ambrosiaster: Particular effort should be made to ensure that unlearned people will benefit. Nothing should be done to hide things from them because of their lack of learning. Commentary on Paul's Epistles.[1]

14:27 Speaking in Turn and Interpreting

Time for Scripture Interpretation. Ambrosiaster: Paul does not want these people to take up the whole day and leave insufficient time for expounding the Scriptures. Commentary on Paul's Epistles.[2]

If Any Speak in a Tongue. Chrysostom: Paul does not forbid speaking in tongues, however much he may belittle the gift, but he insists that it be kept under control and used for the edification of the whole church. Homilies on the Epistles of Paul to the Corinthians 36.5.[3]

14:28 Keeping Silence

If There Is No Interpreter. Severian of Gabala: The person who speaks in the Holy Spirit speaks when he chooses to do so and then can be silent, like the prophets. But those who are possessed by an unclean spirit speak even when they do not want to. They say things that they do not understand. Pauline Commentary from the Greek Church.[4]

14:29 Weighing What Is Said

Restraining Obstinate Strife. Cyprian: Each one ought not to strive obstinately for that which he learned and once held, but if anything better or more useful should exist, he should embrace it willingly. Letters 71.[5]

Asking Questions. Ambrosiaster: Paul allowed others to ask questions about ambiguous matters, so that they might be elucidated by clearer discussion. Commentary on Paul's Epistles.[6]

14:30 If a Revelation Is Made

Allow a Fair Hearing. Ambrosiaster: In particular, the higher-ranking person should give way to the lower. It is simply not the case that every privilege can be granted to a single individual. Nor can it be that anyone, however low in the hierarchy, should have nothing given to him. No one is without the grace of God. Commentary on Paul's Epistles.[7]

14:31 All May Learn and Be Encouraged

Prophesy One by One. Ambrosiaster: It is a tradition of the synagogue which Paul is asking us to follow, whereby the people dispute while seated in chairs, on benches or on the floor, according to their rank. If a revelation has been given to someone sitting on the floor, he should be allowed to speak and not be despised because of his low rank. Commentary on Paul's Epistles.[8]

Take Turns. Theodoret of Cyr: This rule is still applied in the church today, in that preachers take turns to teach the people. Commentary on the First Epistle to the Corinthians 262.[9]

That All May Learn. Cassiodorus: Clearly the prophet builds up the church when through the function of his foretelling he makes wholly clear matters exceedingly vital which were unknown. Those who have been granted the ability to understand well and to interpret the divine Scriptures are obviously not excluded from the gift of prophecy. Explanation of the Psalms, Preface 1.[10]

14:32 Spirits of Prophets Subject to Prophets

---

[1]CSEL 81.158. [2]CSEL 81.159. [3]NPNF 1 12:218-19. [4]NTA 15:270. [5]FC 51:264. [6]CSEL 81.159. [7]CSEL 81.159. [8]CSEL 81.160. [9]Migne PG 82:346. [10]ACW 51:28.

THE SPIRITS OF PROPHETS. AMBROSIASTER:
The Spirit is said to be subject so that he may
facilitate the good efforts which he prompts.
COMMENTARY ON PAUL'S EPISTLES.[11]

THE GIFT OF PROPHECY. OECUMENIUS: If the gift
is subject to the prophets, how can it not also
be subject to you, so that you may keep quiet
when you are meant to? PAULINE COMMENTARY
FROM THE GREEK CHURCH.[12]

---

[11]CSEL 81.160. [12]NTA 15:441.

14:33-40 DECENCY AND ORDER

[33]*For God is not a God of confusion but of peace.*

As in all the churches of the saints, [34]*the women should keep silence in the churches.
For they are not permitted to speak, but should be subordinate, as even the law says.* [35]*If
there is anything they desire to know, let them ask their husbands at home. For it is
shameful for a woman to speak in church.* [36]*What! Did the word of God originate with
you, or are you the only ones it has reached?*

[37]*If any one thinks that he is a prophet, or spiritual, he should acknowledge that what
I am writing to you is a command of the Lord.* [38]*If any one does not recognize this, he is
not recognized.* [39]*So, my brethren, earnestly desire to prophesy, and do not forbid speaking
in tongues;* [40]*but all things should be done decently and in order.*

OVERVIEW: The present church is like a woman
who retains only the outward signs of her former prosperity, displaying the empty boxes and
caskets in which she once kept her wealth (CHRY-
SOSTOM). By saying that he handed on nothing
of his own, Paul indicated that what he was
writing came as a command from God (AM-
BROSIASTER). After the fall, Eve's desire is destined to be toward her husband (CHRYSOS-
TOM). While her mouth is now restrained (ORI-
GEN), it is destined to sing as a harp the Creator's praise (EPHREM THE SYRIAN). When
women are insolent, their husbands receive the
blame (AMBROSIASTER). In ordering the church,
God seeks husbands who are as lovingly attentive
as the women are orderly (CYRIL OF JERUSALEM,
CHRYSOSTOM). Good order is upbuilding (ORI-
GEN, BASIL, CHRYSOSTOM, FULGENTIUS). All
should aim for patience that the laws of peace are
not broken (AMBROSIASTER, AUGUSTINE).

14:33 A God of Peace

AIM FOR PATIENCE. AMBROSIASTER: Those who
are called in peace ought to aim for patience, so
that the laws of peace are not broken. COMMEN-
TARY ON PAUL'S EPISTLES.[1]

EMPTY BOXES THAT ONCE STORED WEALTH.

---

[1]CSEL 81.161.

CHRYSOSTOM: Truly, the church was more like heaven in Paul's time, because the Spirit governed everything and moved each one of the members in turn. But now it seems we have only the symbols of those gifts. We also have only two or three speaking in the service, but these are only a pale shadow of what prevailed then. The present church is like a woman who has fallen from her former, prosperous days and who retains only the outward signs of that prosperity, displaying the boxes and caskets in which she kept her wealth, but which are now empty. This is true not only in the matter of gifts but in life and virtue as well. HOMILIES ON THE EPISTLES OF PAUL TO THE CORINTHIANS 36.7.[2]

14:34 Women Should Be Silent in Church

HOW ARE WOMEN TO KEEP SILENCE? ORIGEN: If this was the case, what are we to make of the fact that Philip had four daughters who prophesied?[3] If they could do it, why can we not let our own prophetesses speak? We may answer this question as follows. First, if our prophetesses have spoken, show us the signs of prophecy in them. Second, even if the daughters of Philip did prophesy, they did not do so inside the church. Likewise in the Old Testament, although Deborah was reputed to be a prophetess,[4] there is no indication that she ever corporately addressed the people in the way that Isaiah or Jeremiah did. The same is true of Huldah.[5] COMMENTARY ON 1 CORINTHIANS 4.74.6-16.[6]

DESIRE TOWARD HER HUSBAND. CHRYSOSTOM: Where does the law say this? In Genesis [3:16]: "Your desire shall be toward your husband, and he shall rule over you." HOMILIES ON THE EPISTLES OF PAUL TO THE CORINTHIANS 37.1.[7]

EVE'S MOUTH WILL YET SERVE. EPHREM THE SYRIAN: The serpent is crippled and bound by the curse, while Eve's mouth is sealed with a silence that is beneficial, but she will also serve again as a harp to sing the praises of the Crea-

tor. HYMNS ON PARADISE 6.8.[8]

14:35 Asking Questions at Home

WOMEN VEILED IN CHURCH TO APPEAR HUMBLE. AMBROSIASTER: It is shameful because it is contrary to discipline for them to presume to speak about the law in the house of God, who has taught that they are subject to their husbands, when they know that men have the primacy there and that for them it is more fitting to be free to pray while holding their tongues. If they dare to speak in church, it is a disgrace, because they are veiled in order to appear humble. Moreover, women like this show that they are immodest, which is a disgrace to their husbands too. For when women are insolent, their husbands receive the blame as well. COMMENTARY ON PAUL'S EPISTLES.[9]

WOMEN ORDERLY, HUSBANDS ATTENTIVE. CHRYSOSTOM: A woman is softer of mind than a man and more subject to being flooded with emotion. Thus he sets husbands as protectors for the benefit of both. Paul calls for husbands to be attentive and for women to be orderly. In this way husbands would have to communicate with their wives about exactly what they heard. HOMILIES ON THE EPISTLES OF PAUL TO THE CORINTHIANS 37.1.[10]

LET PARADISE OPEN. CYRIL OF JERUSALEM: I wish to see each man's earnestness and each woman's devotion. Burn out impiety from your mind, put your soul on the anvil and your stubborn infidelity under the hammer. . . . Then let the gate of paradise be opened to each man and each woman among you. CATECHETICAL LECTURES 15.[11]

14:36 The Recipients of God's Word

FILLED WITH VANITY. AMBROSIASTER: Paul is-

---

[2]NPNF 1 12:219-20. [3]Acts 21:8-9. [4]Judg 4:4. [5]2 Kings 22:14; 2 Chron 34:22. [6]JTS 10:41-42. [7]NPNF 1 12:222. [8]HOP 111. [9]CSEL 81.163-64. [10]NPNF 1 12:222. [11]LCC 4:74.

sued the Corinthians with this reproof because they were so elated with vanity. The suggestion was that if they did not obey the words of the faith, there would be no one who would believe. COMMENTARY ON PAUL'S EPISTLES.[12]

ARE YOU THE ONLY ONES? CHRYSOSTOM: Here Paul introduces the example of the other churches, indicating that Corinth has no right to claim exceptional status. HOMILIES ON THE EPISTLES OF PAUL TO THE CORINTHIANS 37.2.[13]

PROPHETESSES RESTRAINED IN SPEAKING TO THE PEOPLE. MONTANIST ORACLES: It is attested that Deborah was a prophetess. And Mariam, the sister of Aaron, took the timbrel and led the women. But you would not find that Deborah addressed the people as Jeremiah and Isaiah did. You would not find that Huldah spoke to the people although she was a prophetess. CATENAE ON PAUL'S EPISTLES TO THE CORINTHIANS 14.36.[14]

14:37 Acknowledging a Command

A COMMAND OF THE LORD. AMBROSIASTER: Paul is alluding to the false apostles mentioned above, by whom they had been misled. They were teaching things which people wanted to hear but which were not of God. By saying that he was handing on nothing of his own, Paul was trying to indicate that what he was saying came from God and not from men. He therefore preaches consistently, with a clear conscience because he does not desire to please men but God. COMMENTARY ON PAUL'S EPISTLES.[15]

14:39 Prophesy and Speak in Tongues

RECOGNIZE FOR WHOM THE APOSTLE SPEAKS. AMBROSIASTER: Anyone who does not recognize that what the apostle says is from God will not be recognized on the day of judgment. COMMENTARY ON PAUL'S EPISTLES.[16]

EARNESTLY DESIRE PROPHECY. AMBROSIASTER: In order to console them after all his rebukes, Paul calls them brothers and encourages them to have a desire to prophesy, so that by frequent discussion and exposition of the divine law they may become better equipped to be able to learn that what the false apostles were teaching was perverse. COMMENTARY ON PAUL'S EPISTLES.[17]

14:40 Decency and Order

NOTHING DISORDERED. ORIGEN: Therefore he wants all these to be set in order by you, nothing disordered, nothing restless, nothing indecent. . . . Therefore, now our true high priest, Christ, also wants his hands to be filled "with finely composed incense."[18] HOMILIES ON LEVITICUS 9.4-5.[19]

WHAT IS DECENT? AMBROSIASTER: Something is done decently when it is done peacefully and with discipline. COMMENTARY ON PAUL'S EPISTLES.[20]

WELL-ORDERED WAY OF LIFE. BASIL: Paul is referring to the decent and well-ordered way of life in the society of the faithful, where the relationship which obtains among the members of the body is maintained. THE LONG RULES 24.[21]

GOOD ORDER BUILDS UP. CHRYSOSTOM: Nothing builds up as much as good order, peace and love, just as nothing is more destructive than their opposites. It is not only in spiritual affairs but in everything that one may observe this. HOMILIES ON THE EPISTLES OF PAUL TO THE CORINTHIANS 37.4.[22]

RESISTING DISSENSION. AUGUSTINE: Those who

---

[12]CSEL 81.161. [13]NPNF 1 12:223. [14]PMS 14:99. [15]CSEL 81.161-62. [16]CSEL 81.162. [17]CSEL 81.162. [18]Lev 16:12. [19]FC 83:194. [20]CSEL 81.162-63. [21]FC 9:286. [22]NPNF 1 12:224.

make dissensions and disturbances in the church are the ones who seem to be what they are not. LETTER TO EUODIUS 169.[23]

THE FELLOWSHIP OF THE LAWGIVER. THEODORET OF CYR: Law and order come first. Let us also dedicate ourselves to this principle as members of the fellowship of the great Lawgiver. COMMENTARY ON THE FIRST EPISTLE TO THE CORINTHIANS 264.[24]

DISORDERING GOD'S ORDER. FULGENTIUS: If we take a closer look at the origin of sin, I think that it is nothing else than the inordinate love by a rational creature of the things set in order by God. TO MONIMUS 1.20.2.[25]

---

[23]FC 30:53. [24]Migne PG 82:347. [25]FC 95:214.

15:1-7 THE CONFESSION OF FAITH

[1]Now I would remind you, brethren, in what terms I preached to you the gospel, which you received, in which you stand, [2]by which you are saved, if you hold it fast—unless you believed in vain.

[3]For I delivered to you as of first importance what I also received, that Christ died for our sins in accordance with the scriptures, [4]that he was buried, that he was raised on the third day in accordance with the scriptures, [5]and that he appeared to Cephas, then to the twelve. [6]Then he appeared to more than five hundred brethren at one time, most of whom are still alive, though some have fallen asleep. [7]Then he appeared to James, then to all the apostles.

OVERVIEW: Christ could not have died for sinners if he had been a sinner himself (CHRYSOSTOM). That he died for our sins according to the Scriptures (AMBROSIASTER) is testimony to his sinlessness (CHRYSOSTOM). He did not die the death of sin but of the body. We become brothers and sisters through the work of Christ in his earthly life, death (CHRYSOSTOM) and resurrection (AMBROSIASTER). All our works are meaningless without the gospel (PELAGIUS). The justice Christ embodied when he died for us is greater than our sins (CYRIL OF JERUSALEM). He made his life an exchange for the life of all (CYRIL OF ALEXANDRIA). The Father does not suffer loss when he gives what is his own to the Son (AMBROSE). The Corinthians needed to be reminded of what they knew and to have their errors in understanding corrected (CHRYSOSTOM). The Fathers debated as to who was included in the resurrection appearances (ORIGEN, CHRYSOSTOM, OECUMENIUS, AMBROSIASTER) but agreed that many witnesses attested the resurrection truthfully (CHRYSOSTOM). We are to remember the events of the death and resurrection of Jesus according to the unbiased testimony of the apostles (CYRIL OF JERUSALEM, HILARY OF POITIERS, AMBROSE, BASIL).

15:1 The Gospel in Which You Stand

THE GOSPEL RECEIVED. AMBROSIASTER: Paul is showing the Corinthians that if they have been led away from his teaching, especially from belief in the resurrection of the dead on which it is based, they will lose everything they have believed. COMMENTARY ON PAUL'S EPISTLES.[1]

THE MESSAGE OF THE GOSPEL. CHRYSOSTOM: When Paul calls the Corinthian Christians his brothers, he establishes the basis for most of his subsequent assertions. For we became brothers through the work of Christ in his earthly life and death. After all, what is the gospel but the message that God became man, was crucified and rose again? This is what the angel Gabriel announced to the Virgin Mary,[2] what the prophets preached to the world and what all the apostles truthfully proclaimed. HOMILIES ON THE EPISTLES OF PAUL TO THE CORINTHIANS 38.2.[3]

15:2 The Gospel by Which You Are Saved

THE RESURRECTION. PELAGIUS: The resurrection of the body is the whole point of our gospel message. Without it, all the works of prayer and fasting which we do are meaningless. COMMENTARY ON THE FIRST EPISTLE TO THE CORINTHIANS 15.[4]

A REMINDER. CHRYSOSTOM: The Corinthians did not need to learn the doctrine, which they already knew, but they had to be reminded of it and corrected from their errors in understanding it. HOMILIES ON THE EPISTLES OF PAUL TO THE CORINTHIANS 38.2.[5]

15:3 Christ Died for Our Sins

IN ACCORDANCE WITH THE SCRIPTURES. AMBROSIASTER: The prophet Isaiah said: "He was led like a sheep to the slaughter" [Is 53:7] and so on. Revelation [13:8] adds that he was slain from before the foundation of the world. And Deuteronomy [28:66] says: "You will see your life hanging before your eyes, yet you will not believe." This is expressed in the future tense,

to prevent the wicked from claiming that it does not apply to Christ. COMMENTARY ON PAUL'S EPISTLES.[6]

THE JUSTICE WROUGHT IN HIS DEATH. CYRIL OF JERUSALEM: The iniquity of sinners was not as great as the justice of the One who died for them. The sins we committed were not as great as the justice he embodied, when he laid down his life for us. CATECHESIS 13.[7]

FOR OUR SINS. CHRYSOSTOM: How could Christ die for sinners if he were a sinner himself? If in fact he died for our sins, then it is clear that he himself must have been sinless. Therefore he did not die the death of sin but the death of the body. This is what the Scriptures everywhere proclaim. HOMILIES ON THE EPISTLES OF PAUL TO THE CORINTHIANS 38.3.[8]

NO LOSS IN GIVING. AMBROSE: The Son loses nothing when he bestows upon all, just as he also loses nothing when the Father receives the kingdom, nor does the Father suffer loss when he gives what is his own to the Son. THE HOLY SPIRIT 1.3.49.[9]

ONE DIED FOR ALL. CYRIL OF ALEXANDRIA: He made his life be an exchange for the life of all. One died for all, in order that we all might live to God sanctified and brought to life through his blood, justified as a gift by his grace. LETTERS 41.11.[10]

15:4 Buried, Raised on the Third Day

HE WAS BURIED. CHRYSOSTOM: This serves to confirm that Christ died a genuine human death and points us once more to the Scriptures for proof. Nowhere does Scripture mean the death of sin, when it makes mention of our

---

[1]CSEL 81.164. [2]Lk 1:26-38. [3]NPNF 1 12:227. [4]Migne PL 30:763A. [5]NPNF 1 12:227. [6]CSEL 81.164-65. [7]FC 64:27. [8]NPNF 1 12:228. [9]FC 44:52-53. [10]FC 76:174.

Lord's death, but only the death of the body, and a burial and resurrection of that same body. Homilies on the Epistles of Paul to the Corinthians 38.4.[11]

On the Third Day. Pelagius: Hosea [6:2] says: "He will revive us after two days; he will raise us up on the third day." Commentary on the First Epistle to the Corinthians 15.[12]

In Accordance with the Scriptures. Hilary of Poitiers: Paul reminded us that we are to confess the manner of the death and resurrection not so much by literally naming these things but strictly according to the testimony of the Scriptures, so that our understanding of his death might be in accord with the apostles. . . . He did this in order that we might not become helpless or to be tossed about by the winds of useless disputes or hampered by the absurd subtleties of unsound opinions. Trinity 10.67.[13]

15:5 He Appeared to the Twelve

Who Was the Twelfth? Origen: Evidently Matthias was chosen to replace Judas before Jesus ceased appearing to the disciples after his resurrection.[14] Commentary on 1 Corinthians 4.77.[15]

The Time Unspecified. Chrysostom: The gospel tells us that he appeared first to Mary.[16] But as far as men were concerned, he appeared first to those who most wanted to see him. But which of the apostles are meant here? For Matthias was not added to their number until after the ascension. However, it is likely that Christ appeared even after his ascension into heaven. Paul does not specify the time but merely records the experience. Homilies on the Epistles of Paul to the Corinthians 38.5.[17]

Matthias Included? Oecumenius: Note that

he does not say "to the eleven," and neither does John (Jn 20:24), who writes that Thomas was "one of the twelve." We should probably say that either he has included Matthias with the other apostles by anticipation or else that he is still thinking of Judas, even after his betrayal and hanging. Pauline Commentary from the Greek Church.[18]

15:6 Appearing to Five Hundred

To Five Hundred. Ambrosiaster: This is not recorded in the Gospels, but Paul knew it independently of them. Commentary on Paul's Epistles.[19]

The Compelling List of Unbiased Witnesses. Cyril of Jerusalem: "He appeared to Cephas; and after that to the twelve." So if you disbelieve one witness, you have twelve witnesses. "Then he was seen by more than five hundred people at once"—if they disbelieve the twelve, then listen to the five hundred. "After that he was seen by James," his own brother and the first overseer of this [Jerusalem] diocese. Since so noteworthy a bishop was privileged to see the risen Christ, along with the other disciples, do not disbelieve. But you may say that his brother was a biased witness. So then he continues: "He was seen by me." But who am I? I am Paul, his enemy! "I was formerly a persecutor" but now preach the good news of the resurrection. Catechesis 14.22.[20]

Some Have Fallen Asleep. Chrysostom: Paul does not say that some have died but that they have fallen asleep, thereby confirming the truth of the resurrection. Homilies on the Epistles of Paul to the Corinthians 38.5.[21]

---

[11]NPNF 1 12:228-29. [12]Migne PL 30:763C. [13]FC 25:452*. [14]Acts 1:15-26. [15]JTS 10:44. [16]Mk 16:9. [17]NPNF 1 12:229. [18]NTA 15:442. [19]CSEL 81.166. [20]FC 64:46*. [21]NPNF 1 12:229.

15:7 Appearing to James

He Appeared to James. Chrysostom: This must be James, the Lord's brother, whom he ordained as the first bishop of Jerusalem.[22] The apostles mentioned here would include the seventy and others besides the Twelve.[23] Homilies on the Epistles of Paul to the Corinthians 38.5.[24]

What We Confess. Basil: We believe and confess that, rising on the third day from the dead, according to the Scriptures, he was seen by his holy disciples and others, as it is written. He as-cended into heaven and sits on the right hand of the Father when he will come at the end of time to raise up all men and to render to each according to his works. Concerning Faith.[25]

Then to All the Apostles. Ambrose: By this he makes it clear that there are other apostles besides those eleven. On Numbers, Homily 27.11.[26]

---

[22]Acts 15:13-22; 21:18; Gal 1:19; 2:9. [23]Lk 10:1-17. [24]NPNF 1 12:229. [25]FC 9:64. [26]CWS 260.

15:8-11 PAUL'S CONFESSION

[8]*Last of all, as to one untimely born, he appeared also to me.* [9]*For I am the least of the apostles, unfit to be called an apostle, because I persecuted the church of God.* [10]*But by the grace of God I am what I am, and his grace toward me was not in vain. On the contrary, I worked harder than any of them, though it was not I, but the grace of God which is with me.* [11]*Whether then it was I or they, so we preach and so you believed.*

Overview: By "untimely" Paul means that he received his apostleship after Christ had ascended into heaven (Ambrosiaster). Paul thought of himself in the humblest terms as one unformed and unfit (Ambrosiaster, Theodoret of Cyr). Yet he shows that despite his great sins and unworthiness, the grace of God was not given to him for nothing (Ambrosiaster, Chrysostom). Grace did not find Paul inattentive (Chrysostom). He was an athlete for Christ (Augustine). God granted efficacy to his labors (Basil, Chrysostom). He did not labor in order to receive grace but received grace so that he might labor (Augustine). Paul understood his own fragility and humbled himself as unfit to be an apostle (Jerome, Chrysostom).

15:8 As One Untimely Born

Untimely Born. Ambrosiaster: By "untimely" Paul means that he was born again outside time, because he received his apostleship from Christ after the latter had ascended into heaven. Commentary on Paul's Epistles.[1]

The Last but More Illustrious. Chrysostom: Paul may have been the last but he was certainly not the least, since he was more illustrious than many who were before him, indeed,

---

[1]CSEL 81.167.

more illustrious than them all. Homilies on the Epistles of Paul to the Corinthians 38.5.[2]

Unformed. Theodoret of Cyr: Paul compares himself here to an aborted fetus which is not even regarded by some as fully born. Commentary on the First Epistle to the Corinthians 266.[3]

15:9 Least of the Apostles

Last in Time. Ambrosiaster: Paul is least because he was the last in time, not because he was inferior in any way to the others. Commentary on Paul's Epistles.[4]

Unfit. Chrysostom: Paul says this because he was a humble man and also because it is what he really thought about himself. He was forgiven for having persecuted the church, but it was a shame he never forgot. It taught him the greatness of God's grace toward him. Homilies on the Epistles of Paul to the Corinthians 38.6.[5]

Why So Fragile? Jerome: These words apply to those who complain: Why wasn't I created such that I would be free from sin forever? Why was I fashioned such a vessel that I could not endure hard like metal instead of being fragile and easily broken whenever touched? . . . Let us blush and say what those say who have already obtained their rewards. Let us, who are sinners on earth and encased in this fragile and mortal body, say what we know the saints are saying in heaven. Against the Pelagians 2.25.[6]

The Just Accuse Themselves. Jerome: If the apostle makes such a confession, how much more should the sinner? Scripture says: "The just man accuses himself when he begins to speak."[7] If the just man is prompt to accuse himself, how much more should the sinner be? Homily 47 on Psalm 135 (136).[8]

Paul Humbled Himself. Chrysostom: He who endured imprisonment, wounds and beatings, who netted the world with epistles, who was called by a heavenly voice, humbled himself, saying, "I am the least of the apostles, unfit to be called an apostle." On Repentance 5.27.[9]

The Greater Victory. Augustine: The Enemy is more completely vanquished in the case of a man over whom he holds fuller sway. Confessions 8.4.[10]

15:10a Grace Not Given in Vain

Grace Not in Vain. Ambrosiaster: Paul says all this in order to show that despite his great sins and unworthiness, the grace of God was not given to him for nothing. Commentary on Paul's Epistles.[11]

15:10b Working Harder Than Others

The Labors Imposed by Virtue. Basil: He who spends his time in softness and all laxity because of his luxurious living, who is clothed in purple and fine linen and feasting every day in splendid fashion[12] and who flees the labors imposed by virtue has neither labored in this life nor will live in the future, but he will see life afar off, while being racked in the fire of the furnace. Unto the End 19.5.[13]

I Worked Harder Than Any. Chrysostom: If Paul was so humble, why did he call attention to his labors? He had to do this in order to justify his right to be a trustworthy witness and a teacher. Homilies on the Epistles of Paul to the Corinthians 38.7.[14]

Grace Did Not Find Him Inactive. Chrysos-

---

[2]NPNF 1 12:230. [3]Migne PG 82:351. [4]CSEL 81.167. [5]NPNF 1 12:230. [6]FC 53:338*. [7]Cf. Prov 18:19. [8]FC 48:353. [9]FC 96:26. [10]FC 21:205. [11]CSEL 81.167-68. [12]Cf. Lk 16:19. [13]FC 46:319. [14]NPNF 1 12:231.

tom: You are familiar with Paul, who labored so much and erected so many trophies in combat with the devil. He physically marched throughout the known world. He orbited the earth, ocean, air—he circled the world as if he had wings. He was stoned, beaten and murdered. He suffered everything for the name of God, called from above by a heavenly voice. . . . We know, we understand, he said, the grace we have received, and it did not find me inattentive. Concerning Almsgiving and the Ten Virgins 3.22.[15]

THE ATHLETE OF CHRIST. Augustine: Gladly and with the eyes of faith do all in the City of God look up to this great man, Paul, this athlete of Christ, who was anointed by Christ and instructed by him. With him he was nailed to the cross, and through him made glorious. This man was made a spectacle to the world, to angels and to men. He lawfully carried on a great conflict in the theater of this world and strained forward to the prize of his heavenly calling. City of God 14.9.[16]

15:10c The Grace of God with Him

GOD GRANTS EFFICACY TO OUR LABORS. Basil: This is the perfect and consummate glory in God: not to exult in one's own righteousness, but recognizing oneself as lacking true righteousness, to be justified by faith in Christ alone. Paul gloried in despising his own righteousness. In seeking after the righteousness by faith which is of God through Christ, he sought only to know him and the power of his resurrection and the fellowship of his sufferings, being made conformable to his death, so as to attain to the resurrection from the dead. . . . It is God who grants efficacy to our labors. Of Humility 20.[17]

A LARGER MEASURE OF HELP. Chrysostom: Did you see how he reaped the benefit of God's liberality and then how abundantly he contributed his own share, by his zeal, his fervor, his faith, his courage, his patience, his lofty mind and his undaunted will? This is why he deserved a larger measure of help from above. Baptismal Instructions 4.10.[18]

GRACE AND LABOR. Augustine: Paul did not labor in order to receive grace, but he received grace so that he might labor. Proceedings of Pelagius 14.36.[19]

NOTHING ACCOMPLISHED WITHOUT GOD'S HELP. Augustine: How, then, is God's commandment accomplished, even with difficulty, without his help, since if the Lord does not build, the builder is said to have labored in vain. Letter from Alypius and Augustine to Paulinus 186.[20]

15:11 We Preach, You Believed

PAUL'S CREDENTIALS. Chrysostom: Paul does not expect the Corinthians to choose between him and the other apostles. He justifies his own credentials as a teacher but at the same time affirms the others as well. There is no difference between them, since their authority is the same. Homilies on the Epistles of Paul to the Corinthians 39.1.[21]

---

[15]FC 96:41*. [16]FC 14:368*. [17]FC 9:479*. [18]ACW 31:70. [19]FC 86:150. [20]FC 30:217. [21]NPNF 1 12:233.

15:12-19 THE RESURRECTION

[12]Now if Christ is preached as raised from the dead, how can some of you say that there is no resurrection of the dead? [13]But if there is no resurrection of the dead, then Christ has not been raised; [14]if Christ has not been raised, then our preaching is in vain and your faith is in vain. [15]We are even found to be misrepresenting God, because we testified of God that he raised Christ, whom he did not raise if it is true that the dead are not raised. [16]For if the dead are not raised, then Christ has not been raised. [17]If Christ has not been raised, your faith is futile and you are still in your sins. [18]Then those also who have fallen asleep in Christ have perished. [19]If for this life only we have hoped in Christ, we are of all men most to be pitied.

OVERVIEW: Paul grounds his argument for the general resurrection of the dead on the fact of Christ's resurrection (CHRYSOSTOM, PELAGIUS), in which we participate by faith (SEVERIAN OF GABALA). Without his resurrection our preaching is in vain (CYRIL OF JERUSALEM, THEODORE OF MOPSUESTIA, PELAGIUS). Christ has prepared another life for those who hope in him (AMBROSE) where they will dwell bodily in eternal glory (AMBROSIASTER). If the body does not rise again, the soul remains uncrowned with the blessings stored up for it in heaven (CHRYSOSTOM). We are not expecting a disembodied resurrection of the soul only (PELAGIUS). Some Corinthians rejected the resurrection (AUGUSTINE). It is folly to hope only in this life (MAXIMUS OF TURIN). It is bearing false witness to lie about the resurrection (AUGUSTINE).

15:12 Denying the Resurrection

CHRIST IS PREACHED AS RAISED FROM THE DEAD. CHRYSOSTOM: Paul grounds his argument for the resurrection of the dead on the fact of Christ's resurrection. The reality of the latter guarantees the reality of the former. HOMILIES ON THE EPISTLES OF PAUL TO THE CORINTHIANS 39.2.[1]

THE PIVOT OF CHRISTIAN TESTIMONY. AMBROSE: How grave an offense it is not to believe in the resurrection of the dead. If we do not rise again, Christ died in vain and did not rise again. For if he did not rise for us, he did not rise at all, because there is no reason why he should rise for himself. ON HIS BROTHER SATYRUS 2.103.[2]

HOW CAN YOU SAY THERE IS NO RESURRECTION? AUGUSTINE: When the apostle says to the Corinthians, "How can some of you say that there is no resurrection of the dead?" he shows plainly that not all of them were claiming this but that some were, and that it is clear they were not outside but among them. . . . If we had not read in the same letter that "the testimony of Christ is confirmed in you so that nothing is wanting to you in any grace," we might otherwise have concluded that all the Corinthians were carnal-minded and sensual, not discerning the Spirit of God, "quarrelsome, envious, walking according to man."[3] LETTER TO VINCENT 93.[4]

15:13 If There Is No Resurrection

---

[1]NPNF 1 12:234. [2]FC 22:243*. [3]1 Cor 2:14; 3:3. [4]FC 18:88-89*.

The General Resurrection and Christ's Being Raised. Pelagius: The one depends on the other. Either you believe both, or you believe neither. Commentary on the First Epistle to the Corinthians 15.[5]

We Are Raised. Severian of Gabala: Christ died and rose again for nothing if we are not to rise again as well. Pauline Commentary from the Greek Church.[6]

15:14 Preaching and Faith in Vain

Not a Resurrection of the Soul Only. Pelagius: Some heretics claim that there is a resurrection of the soul but not of the body, though this makes no sense. How can there be a resurrection of something which has not fallen into the ground and died? Commentary on the First Epistle to the Corinthians 15.[7]

Otherwise Faith Is in Vain. Chrysostom: Logically Paul would have said here that if Christ had not been raised, historical facts would have been denied, but instead he says something which is much more relevant and indeed frightening to the Corinthians. For if Christ had not risen from the dead, then Paul's preaching would have been useless and their faith would have no meaning. Homilies on the Epistles of Paul to the Corinthians 39.3.[8]

Preaching. Theodore of Mopsuestia: Forgiveness of sins comes through the resurrection. Pauline Commentary from the Greek Church.[9]

15:15 God Raised Christ

False Witness. Augustine: If a lie directed against the temporal life of another is detestable, how much more so is one prejudicial to his eternal life. Such is every lie voiced in the teaching of religion. On that account, the apostle terms it false witness if anyone lies about Christ, even in what might seem to pertain to his praise. On Lying 13.[10]

Misrepresenting God. Pelagius: Our preaching would not just be pointless, it would be downright false, if this were the case. Commentary on the First Epistle to the Corinthians 15.[11]

15:16 If the Dead Are Not Raised

We Shall Rise Also. Pelagius: In other words, if you accept that Christ rose from the dead, believe that we shall rise again also. Commentary on the First Epistle to the Corinthians 15.[12]

15:17 Futile Faith, Still in Sins

Forgiveness of Sins. Pelagius: If Christ lied about his resurrection, then he lied about his claim to forgive our sins also. Commentary on the First Epistle to the Corinthians 15.[13]

The Chain of Illusion. Cyril of Jerusalem: If the cross is an illusion, the resurrection is an illusion also, and "if Christ has not risen, we are still in our sins." If the cross is an illusion, the ascension is also an illusion, and everything, finally, becomes unsubstantial. Catechetical Lectures 13.[14]

If Christ Has Not Been Raised. Chrysostom: If Christ did not rise again, neither was he slain, and if he was not slain, our sins have not been taken away. If our sins have not been taken away, we are still in them, and our entire faith is meaningless. Homilies on the

---

[5]Migne PL 30:746C. [6]NTA 15:272. [7]Migne PL 30:764C. [8]NPNF 1 12:235. [9]NTA 15:194. [10]FC 16:82. [11]Migne PL 30:764D. [12]Migne PL 30:764D. [13]Migne PL 30:764D. [14]FC 64:29*.

Epistles of Paul to the Corinthians 39.4.[15]

15:18 Those Who Have Fallen Asleep

Their Dead Taken from Them. Ambrosiaster: Paul says this because the Corinthians will not want to listen to the false prophets once they realize that if they do so their dead, whom they love, will be taken from them. Commentary on Paul's Epistles.[16]

Not Dying in Vain. Pelagius: Paul has the martyrs in mind above all. They would have lost their lives in vain if there was no other life to look forward to. Commentary on the First Epistle to the Corinthians 15.[17]

15:19 Most to Be Pitied

If for This Life Only. Ambrose: Paul says this, not because to hope in Christ is miserable but because Christ has prepared another life for those who hope in him. For this life is liable to sin. The life above is reserved for our reward. On His Brother Satyrus 2.124.[18]

Hope in Christ. Ambrosiaster: It is clear that we hope in Christ both for this life and for the next one. Christ does not abandon his servants but gives them grace, and in the future they will dwell in eternal glory. Commentary on Paul's Epistles.[19]

If the Body Does Not Rise. Chrysostom: Even if the soul remains, being infinitely immortal, without the flesh it will not receive those hidden blessings. If the body does not rise again, the soul remains uncrowned with the blessings stored up for it in heaven. In that case, we have nothing to hope for, and our rewards are limited to this life. What could be more wretched than that? Homilies on the Epistles of Paul to the Corinthians 39.4.[20]

The Folly of Hoping Only in This Life. Maximus of Turin: Therefore Christ is not to be hoped in for this life only, in which the bad can do more than the good, in which those who are more evil are happier, and those who lead a more criminal life live more prosperously. Sermons 96.1.[21]

---

[15]NPNF 1 12:235. [16]CSEL 81.170. [17]Migne PL 30:765A. [18]FC 22:254. [19]CSEL 81.170. [20]NPNF 1 12:236. [21]ACW 50:258.

15:20-24 THE SECOND ADAM

[20]But in fact Christ has been raised from the dead, the first fruits of those who have fallen asleep. [21]For as by a man came death, by a man has come also the resurrection of the dead. [22]For as in Adam all die, so also in Christ shall all be made alive. [23]But each in his own order: Christ the first fruits, then at his coming those who belong to Christ. [24]Then comes the end, when he delivers the kingdom to God the Father after destroying every rule and every authority and power.

Overview: Adam, the type of Christ (Tertullian), died because he sinned. Christ, who was without sin, overcame the death that comes from sin (Ambrosiaster). This does not mean universally that all who die will be members of the body of Christ, since many will be punished in eternity by a second death (Augustine). The resurrection from the dead proves that Christ was a man and therefore able by his righteousness to merit the resurrection of the dead (Ambrosiaster). The human nature that was cast down must itself gain the victory (Basil, Chrysostom). Through Christ the church will rise (Pelagius). He tasted death for the sake of all (Athanasius, Cyril of Alexandria). There is no eternal life except in Christ (Augustine). Just because everyone will be raised from the dead, not all will enjoy the same rewards or punishments (Ambrose, Chrysostom). Then comes the end, the destruction of every shred of demonic power (Chrysostom). In the end, the faithful will pass into eternal peace and joy (Cassiodorus), and God shall be all in all (Origen, Basil).

15:20 Christ the First Fruits

Christ Has Been Raised. Ambrosiaster: Paul says this in order to get at the false prophets who claimed that Christ was never born and thus cannot have died. The resurrection from the dead proves that Christ was a man and therefore able to merit by his righteousness the resurrection of the dead. Commentary on Paul's Epistles.[1]

The Head, Then the Body. Pelagius: If the head has risen, then the rest of the body will follow in due course. Commentary on the First Epistle to the Corinthians 15.[2]

The Power of Death Destroyed. Cyril of Alexandria: For the sake of all he tasted death. Although by nature he was life and was himself the resurrection, he surrendered his own body

to death. By his ineffable power he trampled upon death in his own flesh that he might become the firstborn from the dead and the first fruits of those who have fallen asleep. . . . Even if the resurrection of the dead may be said to be through a man, the man we know it is through is the Word begotten of God. The power of death has been destroyed through him. Letter 17.11.[3]

God Assumed Flesh That Suffered. Cyril of Alexandria: The Word does not suffer insofar as he is viewed as God by nature. Yet the sufferings of his flesh were according to the economy of the dispensation. For in what way would he be "the firstborn of every creature, through whom have come to be principalities and powers, thrones and dominations, in whom all things hold together," and in what way would he become the "firstborn of the dead" and the "first fruits of those who have fallen asleep," unless the Word, being God, made his own the body born to suffer? Letter 50.14.[4]

15:21 Death Came by a Man

By a Man. Athanasius: For by the sacrifice of his own body he both put an end to the law which was against us and made a new beginning of life for us, by the hope of resurrection which he has given us. For since from man it was that death prevailed over men, for this cause conversely, by the Word of God being made man has come about the destruction of death and the resurrection of life. On the Incarnation 10.[5]

Suppose the Word Did Not Become Flesh. Basil: If the sojourn of the Lord in the flesh did not take place, the Redeemer did not pay to death the price for us. He did not by his own

---

[1]CSEL 81.170-71. [2]Migne PL 30:765A. [3]FC 76:86*. [4]FC 76:219*. [5]LCC 3:64-65.

power destroy the dominion of death. If that which is subject to death were one thing and that which was assumed by the Lord another, then death would not have ceased performing its own works, nor would the sufferings of the God-bearing flesh have been our gain. He would not have destroyed sin in the flesh. We who had died in Adam would not have been made alive in Christ. LETTERS 261, TO THE CITIZENS OF SOZOPOLIS.[6]

BY A MAN CAME THE RESURRECTION. AMBROSE: Man arose because man died. Man was raised up again, but it was God who raised him. Then he was man according to the flesh. Now God is all in all. Now we no longer know Christ according to the flesh, but we have the grace of his flesh. We know him as the first fruits of those who rest, the firstborn of the dead. Unquestionably the first fruits are of the same species and nature as the rest of the fruits. . . . Therefore, as the first fruits of death were in Adam, so also the first fruits of the resurrection are in Christ. ON HIS BROTHER SATYRUS 2.91.[7]

HE SUFFERED IN HIS HUMAN FLESH. CYRIL OF ALEXANDRIA: He tasted death on behalf of every man in his flesh, which was able to suffer without him ceasing to be life. Accordingly, even though it is stated that he suffered in his flesh, he did not receive the suffering in the nature of his divinity but in his flesh which was receptive to suffering. LETTER 55.34.[8]

BY A MAN CAME DEATH. CHRYSOSTOM: The very human nature which was cast down must itself also gain the victory. For it was by this means that the reproach was wiped away. HOMILIES ON THE EPISTLES OF PAUL TO THE CORINTHIANS 39.5.[9]

15:22a Dead in Adam

IN ADAM ALL DIE. TERTULLIAN: If Adam is a type of Christ then Adam's sleep is a symbol of the death of Christ, and by the wound in the side of Christ was typified the church, the true mother of all the living. ON THE SOUL 43.10.[10]

WHO IS INCLUDED? AUGUSTINE: This does not mean that all who die in Adam will be members of Christ, since the majority will be punished in eternity by a second death. The apostle uses the word *all* in both clauses because as no one dies in a natural body except in Adam, so no one is made to live again in a spiritual body, except in Christ. CITY OF GOD 13.23.[11]

MAN AND THE SON OF MAN. AUGUSTINE: Man indeed brought death to himself and to the Son of Man. But the Son of Man, by dying and rising again, brought life to man. TO HONORATUS 140.9.[12]

WHAT OF ENOCH AND ELIJAH? SEVERIAN OF GABALA: Strictly speaking, not everyone has died. Enoch and Elijah, for example, never did. Some will be found alive at the second coming of the Savior. PAULINE COMMENTARY FROM THE GREEK CHURCH.[13]

15:22b Made Alive in Christ

RAISED IN CHRIST. AMBROSIASTER: Adam died because he sinned,[14] and so Christ, who was without sin, overcame death, in that death comes from sin. Everyone, the righteous and the unrighteous alike, dies in Adam, and everyone, believers and unbelievers alike, will also be raised in Christ. But the unbelievers will be handed over for punishment, even though they appear to have been raised from the dead, because they will receive their bodies back again in order to suffer eternal punishment for their unbelief. COMMENTARY ON PAUL'S EPISTLES.[15]

NO ETERNAL LIFE EXCEPT IN CHRIST. AUGUS-

---

[6]FC 28:233*. [7]FC 22:237*. [8]FC 77:31*. [9]NPNF 1 12:236. [10]FC 10:277. [11]FC 14:338. [12]FC 20:77. [13]NTA 15:274. [14]Gen 3:17-19. [15]CSEL 81.171.

tine: No human enters into death except through Adam and no one into eternal life except through Christ. This is the meaning of that repeated phrase *all*, because as all men belong to Adam through their first or carnal birth, so all men who belong to Christ come to the second or spiritual birth. Therefore he says "all" in both places because as all who die die only in Adam, so all who will be made alive will not be made alive except in Christ. To Jerome 167.21.[16]

The Resurrection of the Wicked Not Included. Augustine: Notice how he emphasizes "one" and "one," that is Adam and Christ, the former for condemnation, the latter for justification. . . . Obviously he is speaking of the resurrection of the just where there is life eternal, not of the resurrection of the wicked where there will be eternal death. Those who "shall be made alive" are contrasted with the others who will be damned. To Hilarius 157.[17]

None Except Through That Door. Augustine: We commonly say that all enter a certain house through one door, not because all humanity enters that house but because no one enters except through that door. It is in this sense that as all die in Adam so do all those who live live in Christ. . . . Aside from the one Mediator of God and men, the man Christ Jesus, there is no other name under heaven whereby we must be saved. Against Julian 24.[18]

15:23 Each in Order

Variable Sequences of Maturation in Faith. Origen: Although all are contained within the one faith and washed in the one baptism, the process of maturing in faith is not the same for all, but rather "each one in his own order." Genesis, Homily 2.[19]

Each in Order. Ambrose: The fruit of divine mercy is common to all, but the order of merit differs. On His Brother Satyrus 2.92.[20]

Punishment and Benefit Occur in Differing Degrees. Chrysostom: Just because everyone will be raised from the dead, do not imagine that all will enjoy the same benefits. Even just thinking of punishment, there is a great difference in the degrees of suffering which will be inflicted. How much more then will there be a difference between the fate of sinners, on the one hand, and the righteous on the other. Homilies on the Epistles of Paul to the Corinthians 39.5.[21]

15:24 Destroying All Rule

The Kingdom Delivered. Origen: When Christ shall have delivered up the kingdom to God, even the Father, then those living beings, because they have before this been made part of Christ's kingdom, shall also be delivered up along with the whole of that kingdom to the rule of the Father, so that, when "God shall be all in all," they also, since they are a part of all, may have God even in themselves, as he is in all things. On First Principles 1.8.[22]

The End. Basil: For us the end for which we do all things and toward which we hasten is the blessed life in the world to come. Homily 19 on Psalm 48.[23]

Then Comes the End. Chrysostom: What rule and power will Christ destroy? That of the angels? Of course not! That of the faithful? No. What rule is it then? That of the devils, about which he says that our struggle is not against flesh and blood but against the principalities, the powers and the forces of darkness in this present age. Homilies on the Epistles of Paul to the Corinthians 39.6.[24]

---

[16]FC 30:25. [17]FC 20:330. [18]FC 35:392-93*. [19]FC 71:78*. [20]FC 22:238. [21]NPNF 1 12:236. [22]OFP 65*. [23]FC 46:311. [24]NPNF 1 12:237. See Eph 6:12.

When He Delivers the Kingdom to God the Father. Cassiodorus: The faithful deserve to be at his right hand. They will judge in company with the Lord. They will pass into eternal peace and joy, so that they are rightly said to be exalted, for through the Lord's wondrous devo-

tion they attain contemplation of the Lord himself. Explanation of the Psalms 14.[25]

---

[25]ACW 53:455*.

15:25-28 THE REIGN OF CHRIST

[25]*For he must reign until he has put all his enemies under his feet.* [26]*The last enemy to be destroyed is death.* [27]*"For God* [z] *has put all things in subjection under his feet." But when it says, "All things are put in subjection under him," it is plain that he is excepted who put all things under him.* [28]*When all things are subjected to him, then the Son himself will also be subjected to him who put all things under him, that God may be everything to every one.*

z *Greek* he

Overview: The demonic powers will be rendered powerless (Oecumenius). Christ's reign will be fulfilled, not ended (Theodoret of Cyr), as he begins eternally to reign in the fullest sense (Jerome). The last enemy, death, will be destroyed (Chrysostom). The subjection of Christ to the Father means that every creature will learn to be subject to Christ, who in turn is voluntarily subject to the Father (Ambrosiaster). Just as we subject ourselves to the glory of his reigning body, the Lord subjects himself in the glory of his body to the One who subjects all things to himself (Hilary of Poitiers). Some deprecate the term *subjection* in regard to the Son, not understanding that the subjection of Christ to the Father reveals the blessedness of our spiritual maturity (Origen).

When the Scriptures say that the Son is less than the Father, they refer to his assumption of humanity. But when they point out that he is equal, they refer to his deity (Augustine, Gregory Nazianzen). Even our adversities the

Lord makes his own, taking upon himself our sufferings (Basil). The Fathers sought to answer both pagan confusions (Oecumenius) and Arian exaggerations about this text (Theodoret of Cyr, Marius Victorinus). Paul is thinking of the divine dispensation of the incarnation when he says that the Son, who is fully God, has willingly subjected himself to the Father (Chrysostom, Oecumenius). It is necessary for him to make his reign so evident that his enemies will dare not deny that he reigns (Augustine). Christ does not cease to reign when he has put all his enemies under his feet (Gregory Nazianzen, Cyril of Jerusalem).

The resurrected body will no longer need nourishment for life (Cyril of Jerusalem). The alienated will no longer be an enemy (Origen, Jerome). We will be without adversary. The new life which begins now by faith is carried on by hope, but there will come the time when death shall be swallowed up in victory

(Augustine). When we have been rendered capable of receiving God, then God will be to us "all in all" (Origen). God will be the consummation of all our desiring (Augustine, Origen). This is the maturity toward which we speed (Gregory Nazianzen), when the whole number of the saints will be glorified in the whole choir of virtues, and God will be all things to all (Jerome, Augustine).

15:25 All His Enemies Under His Feet

He Will Reign. Jerome: Will the Lord rule only until he has put all his enemies under his feet? Will he then stop ruling? Obviously it is only then that he will really begin to rule in the full sense of the word! Against Helvidius 6.[1]

Until What? Gregory Nazianzen: "He must reign" till such and such a time . . . and "be received by heaven until the time of restitution" and have the seat at the right hand until the overthrow of his enemies. But after this? Must he cease to be king or be removed from heaven? Why, who shall make him cease, or for what cause? What a bold and very anarchical interpreter you are, and yet you have heard that of his kingdom there shall be no end. Your mistake arises from not understanding that "until" is not always exclusive of what comes after but asserts up to that time, without denying what comes after it. To take a single instance, how else would you understand "Lo, I am with you always, even unto the end of the world"? Does it mean that he will no longer be so afterward? Theological Orations 30, On the Son 4.[2]

All the More King After His Victory. Cyril of Jerusalem: Some say that when his enemies have been put under his feet, he will no longer be king, a bad and stupid thing to say. For if he is king before he has finally defeated his enemies, must he not be all the more king when he has completely mastered them? Catechetical Lectures 15.29.[3]

The Continuing Conflict. Augustine: He reigns forever. However, in respect to the war waged under him against the devil, this conflict will obviously continue "until he has put all his enemies under his feet." But afterward there will be no conflict, since we shall enjoy an everlasting peace. Questions 69.8.[4]

Until His Enemies Confess His Reign. Augustine: It is necessary for Christ's kingdom to be manifested to such a degree until all his enemies confess that he does reign. . . . That is, the apostle says, it is necessary for him to make his reign so clearly evident until his enemies dare not at all deny that Christ reigns. Questions 69.5.[5]

Beggaring Description. Cyril of Jerusalem: This body shall be raised but not in its present weakness. It shall be raised the very same body, but by putting aside corruption it shall be transformed, just as iron becomes fire when combined with fire, as the Lord who raises us knows. This body therefore shall rise, but it will not abide in its present condition, but as an eternal body. No longer will it, as now, need nourishment for life nor stairs for its ascent. It will become spiritual, a marvelous thing, beggaring description. Catechetical Lectures 18.[6]

Christ's Reign Fulfilled. Theodoret of Cyr: The final victory will be the fulfillment, not the end, of Christ's reign. Commentary on the First Epistle to the Corinthians 270.[7]

Rendered Powerless. Oecumenius: The principalities and powers will be abolished and will be left powerless. Pauline Commentary from the Greek Church.[8]

15:26 The Last Enemy, Death

[1]FC 53:18-19. [2]LCC 3:179. [3]LCC 4:166. [4]FC 70:174. [5]FC 70:171. [6]FC 64:130. [7]Migne PG 82:355. [8]NTA 15:442.

The Alienated Will. Origen: For the destruction of the last enemy must be understood in this way: not that its substance which was made by God shall perish, but that the hostile purpose and will which proceeded not from God but from itself will come to an end. It will be destroyed, therefore, not in the sense of ceasing to exist but of being no longer an enemy and no longer death. . . . We must not think, however, that it will happen all of a sudden, but gradually and by degrees, during the lapse of infinite and immeasurable ages, seeing that the improvement and correction will be realized slowly and separately in each individual person. On First Principles 3.6.5.[9]

"Be Exalted in the Borders of My Enemies." Jerome: As the psalmist[10] pleads that God be glorified in the borders of his enemies, so do we. When they have ceased to be enemies, then you, O Lord, will be exalted among them. Homily on Psalm 7 3.[11]

The Last Enemy. Chrysostom: In the beginning death entered last, after the counsel of the devil and our disobedience. Similarly, death will be the last thing to be destroyed. Homilies on the Epistles of Paul to the Corinthians 39.6.[12]

Without Adversary. Augustine: It is one thing to fight well, which is the case now when the struggle of death is resisted. It is something else not to have an adversary, which will be the case when death "our last enemy" is destroyed. Continence 3.6.[13]

The Mastery in Love by Vision. Augustine: The new life begins now by faith and is carried on by hope, but then will come the time when death shall be swallowed up in victory, when that "enemy, death, shall be destroyed last," when we shall be changed and become like the angels. . . . We have now mastered fear by faith, but then we shall have the mastery in love by vi-

sion. Letter to Janarius 55.[14]

Their Prize in Peace, Their Strength in Battle. Augustine: In this house God's people shall everlastingly dwell with their God and in their God, and God with his people and in his people, God filling his people, his people filled with God, so that "God may be all in all"—the very same God being their prize in peace who was their strength in battle. City of God 17.12.[15]

15:27 All Things in Subjection Under Christ

The Readiness to Receive God. Origen: Christ the Lord himself will instruct those who are able to receive him in his character of wisdom, after their preliminary training in his holy virtues, and will reign with them until such time as he subjects them to the Father who subjected all things to him. When they have been rendered capable of receiving God, then God will be to them "all in all." On First Principles 3.6.9.[16]

All Things in Subjection.[17] Origen: By this fact Christ teaches the rulers the techniques of government. On First Principles 3.5.6.[18]

Christ Takes Our Infirmities Upon Himself. Basil: He makes your subjection his own, and because of your struggle against virtue, he calls himself subjected. . . . He calls himself naked, if any of you are naked. . . . When one is in prison, he said that he himself was the one imprisoned. For he himself took up our infirmities and bore the burden of our ills. And one of our infirmities is insubordination, and this he also bore. Therefore, even the adversities which happen to us the Lord makes his own, taking upon himself our sufferings because of his fellowship

---

[9]OFP 250*. [10]Cf. Ps 7:7. [11]FC 48:30. [12]NPNF 1 12:237. [13]FC 16:195*. [14]FC 12:282. [15]FC 24:58-59. [16]OFP 254*. [17]Ps 8:6. [18]OFP 242.

with us. An Apology to the Caesareans, Letter 8.[19]

Conformable to His Body. Hilary of Poitiers: Hence the first step in the mystery is that all things have been made subject to him, and then he himself becomes subject to the One who subjects all things to himself. Just as we subject ourselves to the glory of his reigning body, the Lord himself in the same mystery subjects himself in the glory of his body to the One who subjects all things to himself. We are made subject to the glory of his body in order that we may possess the glory with which he reigns in the body, because we shall be conformable to his body. Trinity 11.36.[20]

Answering Arian Objections. Theodoret of Cyr: The Arians and the Eunomians love to play with this and the next verse, claiming that it proves that Christ is not God. But here they are confusing two different things. The apostle is not speaking about Christ in his divinity but about his humanity, since the whole discussion is about the resurrection of the flesh. It is in his humanity that he will be subject, because all humanity is subject to the divine. Commentary on the First Epistle to the Corinthians 271-72.[21]

Contrast with the Revolt of Zeus. Oecumenius: Paul is writing to converted Greeks, because the Greeks worshiped Zeus, who revolted against his own father in order to seize his kingdom. He was concerned lest they should imagine something similar in the case of Christ and his Father. Pauline Commentary from the Greek Church.[22]

15:28a *All Things Subjected to Him*

Subjection to the Father. Origen: As long as I am not subjected to the Father, neither is he said to be "subjected" to the Father. Not that he himself is in need of subjection before the Father, but for me, in whom he has not yet completed his work, he is said not to be subjected, for "we are the body of Christ and members in part."[23] Homilies on Leviticus 7.4.[24]

When All Things Are Subjected. Ambrosiaster: The subjection of Christ to the Father means that every creature will learn that he is subject to Christ, who in turn is subject to the Father, and will thus confess that there is only one God. But Christ's subjection to the Father is not the same thing as our subjection to the Son, because our subjection is one of dependence and not the union of equals. Commentary on Paul's Epistles.[25]

Source of the Son's Power. Oecumenius: The things of the Son belong to God as Father, and everything which the Son can do is attributed to the Father, for he who begot him outside time is the source of the Son's power. Pauline Commentary from the Greek Church.[26]

15:28b *The Son Subjected to Him*

Subjection the Crowning Glory of the Son's Work. Origen: But the heretics, not understanding (I cannot tell why) the apostle's meaning contained in these words, deprecate using the term *subjection* in regard to the Son. . . . Such men do not understand that the subjection of Christ to the Father reveals the blessedness of our perfection and announces the crowning glory of the work undertaken by him. On First Principles 3.5.7.[27]

Speaking About God as Substance. Marius Victorinus: Therefore God is also Being, both existing and substance, although he is above all that because he is the Father of all. We should not be afraid to use the word *substance* of God,

---

[19]FC 13:34. [20]FC 5:489*. [21]Migne PG 82:358. [22]NTA 15:442. [23]1 Cor 12:27. [24]FC 83:135*. [25]CSEL 81.173-74. [26]NTA 15:442. [27]OFP 243.

because when words are lacking to describe the highest realities, it is not inappropriate for us to take terms borrowed from what we do know and understand and use them in this special sense. Against Arius 2.2.2.[28]

The Subjection of the Father and the Son. Gregory Nazianzen: As the Son subjects all to the Father, so does the Father to the Son, the one by his work, the other by his good pleasure. Theological Orations, On the Son 30.5.[29]

The Son Willingly Subjected to the Father. Chrysostom: Why does Paul talk about the subjection of the Son to the Father, when he has just finished speaking about the subjection of everything to Christ? The apostle speaks in one way when he is talking about the Godhead alone and in another way when he is speaking about the divine dispensation. For example, once he has established the context of our Lord's incarnation, Paul is not afraid to talk about his many humiliations, because these are not inappropriate to the incarnate Christ, even though they obviously cannot apply to God. In the present context, which of these two is he talking about? Given that he has just mentioned Christ's death and resurrection, neither of which can apply to God, it is clear that he is thinking of the divine dispensation of the incarnation, in which the Son has willingly subjected himself to the Father. But note that he introduces a corrective by saying that the one who put all things under him is himself excepted from the general rule. This is meant to remind us that Christ the Son is also truly God. Homilies on the Epistles of Paul to the Corinthians 39.7.[30]

Whether the Father is Greater Than the Son. Augustine: If the Son is equal, how is the Father greater? For the Lord himself says: "because the Father is greater than I."[31] However, the rule of Catholic faith is this: when the Scriptures say of the Son that he is less than the Fa-

ther, the Scriptures mean in respect to the assumption of humanity. But when the Scriptures point out that he is equal, they are understood in respect to his deity. Questions 69.1.[32]

15:28c God Everything to Everyone

God Will Be All in All. Origen: God will be all things in each person in such a way that everything which the reasoning mind can feel or understand or think will be all God. When purified from all the dregs of its vices and utterly cleared from every cloud of wickedness, the mind will no longer be conscious of anything besides or other than God. That mind will think of God and see God and hold God. God will be the mode and measure of its every movement. In this way God will be all in all. On First Principles 3.6.3.[33]

Finishing the Work God Gave the Son. Origen: When "he shall have completed" his "work" and brought his whole creation to the height of perfection, then he is said to be "subjected" in these whom he subjected to the Father. In these "he finished the work that God had given him that God may be all in all." Homilies on Leviticus 7.6.[34]

The Maturity Toward Which We Speed. Gregory Nazianzen: "God will be all in all" at the time of restoration—"God," not "the Father." The Son will not revert to disappear completely in the Father, like a torch temporarily withdrawn from a great flame and then joined up again with it—Sabellians must not wrest this text. No, God will be "all in all" when we are no longer what we are now, a multiplicity of impulses and emotions, with little or nothing of God in us, but are fully like God, with room for God and God alone. This is the "maturity" to-

---

[28]FCC 69:201. [29]LCC 3:180. [30]NPNF 1 12:237-38. [31]Cf. Jn 14:28. [32]FC 70:166-67. [33]OFP 248*. [34]FC 83:136.

ward which we speed. Theological Orations, On the Son 30.7.[35]

The Whole Choir of Virtues. Jerome: God will be all things in all, so that there will not be only wisdom in Solomon, meekness of soul in David, zeal in Elias and Phineas, faith in Abraham, perfect love in Peter . . . , zeal of preaching in the chosen vessel [Paul], and two or three virtues each in others. But God will be completely in all. The whole number of the saints will be glorified in the whole choir of virtues, and God will be all things to all. Against the Pelagians 18.[36]

The Vision of His Own Form. Augustine: The vision itself is face to face, which is promised to the just as their supreme reward. This will come to pass when he shall deliver the kingdom to God the Father. There, he wants it understood, will also be the vision of his own form, when the whole creation, together with that form in which the Son of God has been made the Son of Man, has been made subject to God. According to this form, the Son himself will be made subject to him who subjected all things to him, that God may be all in all. The Trinity 1.12.28.[37]

All Will Share. Augustine: God will be the consummation of all our desiring—the object of our unending vision, of our unlessening love, of our unwearying praise. And in this gift of vision, the response of love, this paean of praise, all alike will share, as all will share in everlasting life. City of God 22.30.[38]

All Things Subjected to Him. Augustine: Even if there is no chance of manumission, slaves are now to make their slavery a kind of freedom by serving with love and loyalty, free from fear and feigning, until injustice becomes a thing of the past and every human sovereignty and power is done away with, so that God may be all in all. City of God 6.15.[39]

From Shadows to Light. Augustine: The allusion here is to the transformation of the saints when they pass from the old shadows of time into the new lights of eternity. City of God 20.22.[40]

Filled with God. Augustine: In heaven we shall not experience need, and on that account we shall be happy. We shall be filled, but it will be with God. He will be for us all those things which we here look upon as being of great value. Easter Sermons 255.8.[41]

---

[35]FGFR 266. [36]FC 53:258. [37]FC 45:43*. [38]FC 24:506. [39]FC 24:224*. [40]FC 24:312. [41]FC 38:357*.

15:29-34 THE DEAD

[29]*Otherwise, what do people mean by being baptized on behalf of the dead? If the dead are not raised at all, why are people baptized on their behalf?* [30]*Why am I in peril every hour?* [31]*I protest, brethren, by my pride in you which I have in Christ Jesus our Lord, I die every day!* [32]*What do I gain if, humanly speaking, I fought with beasts at Ephesus? If the dead are not raised, "Let us eat and drink, for tomorrow we die."* [33]*Do not be deceived:*

"Bad company ruins good morals." ³⁴*Come to your right mind, and sin no more. For some have no knowledge of God. I say this to your shame.*

OVERVIEW: There would be no point in taking risks for faith if there were no resurrection (DIDYMUS THE BLIND, CHRYSOSTOM, AMBROSIASTER). But providence is always greater than our risks and problems (CHRYSOSTOM, THEODORET OF CYR). The Corinthians are rebuked for their bad company (CHRYSOSTOM) and called to awaken to their right minds (DIDYMUS THE BLIND, CHRYSOSTOM). The Marcionite practice of baptizing the living on behalf of dead unbelievers does not adequately grasp that baptism saves only the person who receives it freely (DIDYMUS THE BLIND). Those who follow the Epicureans (AMBROSE) are dead already (CLEMENT OF ALEXANDRIA). Withdraw from all those who distort the Christian hope (CYPRIAN, ORIGEN, JEROME).

15:29 Baptized on Behalf of the Dead

REASON FOR BAPTIZING THE DEAD. AMBROSIASTER: It seems that some people were at that time being baptized for the dead because they were afraid that someone who was not baptized would either not rise at all or else rise merely in order to be condemned. COMMENTARY ON PAUL'S EPISTLES.[1]

THE MARCIONITE PRACTICE. DIDYMUS THE BLIND: The Marcionites baptize the living on behalf of dead unbelievers, not knowing that baptism saves only the person who receives it. PAULINE COMMENTARY FROM THE GREEK CHURCH.[2]

BAPTISM MEANINGLESS WITHOUT RESURRECTION. CHRYSOSTOM: Sin has brought death into the world, and we are baptized in the hope that our dead bodies will be raised again in the resurrection. If there is no resurrection, our baptism is meaningless and our bodies will remain as

dead as they are now. HOMILIES ON THE EPISTLES OF PAUL TO THE CORINTHIANS 40.2.[3]

15:30 In Peril Every Hour

THEME. AMBROSIASTER: The theme here is that unless there is such a fact as the resurrection of the dead, all this is pointless. COMMENTARY ON PAUL'S EPISTLES.[4]

TAKING RISKS FOR FAITH. DIDYMUS THE BLIND: If the soul is not immortal, if the body does not rise from the dead, there would be no point taking risks on behalf of the faith. PAULINE COMMENTARY FROM THE GREEK CHURCH.[5]

WHY IN PERIL? CHRYSOSTOM: Who would choose a life of constant danger if there was no point to it? Some people do this kind of thing in a moment of vain boasting, but that is not the same as dedicating one's whole life to it over a number of years. HOMILIES ON THE EPISTLES OF PAUL TO THE CORINTHIANS 40.3.[6]

15:31 Dying Every Day

THE FRUIT OF SUFFERINGS. CHRYSOSTOM: Paul rejoices in his sufferings because he sees what wonderful results they produce in people like the Corinthian Christians. HOMILIES ON THE EPISTLES OF PAUL TO THE CORINTHIANS 40.3.[7]

THE GREATNESS OF PROVIDENCE. THEODORET OF CYR: Here Paul outlines both the magnitude of the problems he faces and the greatness of God's providential care for him. COMMENTARY ON THE FIRST EPISTLE TO THE CORINTHIANS 275.[8]

---

[1]CSEL 81.175. [2]NTA 15:8 [3]NPNF 1 12:245. [4]CSEL 81.175. [5]NTA 15:8 [6]NPNF 1 12:246. [7]NPNF 1 12:246. [8]Migne PG 82:362.

15:32 *What Do I Gain?*

DEAD ALREADY. CLEMENT OF ALEXANDRIA: They are in fact dead, not tomorrow but already—dead to God. CHRIST THE EDUCATOR 3.11.81.[9]

A PROPHETIC QUOTATION. CHRYSOSTOM: Paul quotes Isaiah [22:13-14] in order to mock this suggestion. Isaiah after all was speaking about hard and reprobate people who were in the habit of talking like this. If they could find no forgiveness under the law, how much less will they be ready to be pardoned by the gospel of grace! HOMILIES ON THE EPISTLES OF PAUL TO THE CORINTHIANS 40.4.[10]

THE EPICUREAN ILLUSION. AMBROSE: If all hope of the resurrection is lost, let us eat and drink and lose not the enjoyment of the things present, for we have none to come. . . . The Epicureans say they are followers of pleasure because death means nothing to them, because that which is dissolved has no feeling, and that which has no feeling means nothing to us. Thus they show that they are living only carnally, not spiritually. They do not discharge the duty of the soul but only of the flesh. They think that all life's duty is ended with the separation of the soul and body. LETTERS TO PRIESTS 59.[11]

15:33 *Do Not Be Deceived*

BLIND GUIDES. CYPRIAN: The Lord teaches and admonishes that we must withdraw from such. "They are blinded guides of the blind. But if the blind man guide a blind man, both shall fall into a pit."[12] Such a one is to be turned away from, and whoever has separated himself from the church is to be shunned. Such a man is perverted and is condemned by his very self. Does he seem to himself to be with Christ, who acts contrary to the elders of Christ, who separates himself from association with his clergy and his people? That man bears his arms against the church; he fights against God's plan. THE UNITY OF THE CHURCH 17.[13]

GOOD CORRUPTED BY EVIL. ORIGEN: We see quiet and respectable men who, when they have become associated with turbulent and shameless people, have their good manners corrupted by evil conversations. They are turned into men to the same sort as those who are steeped in every kind of witness. This sometimes happens to men of mature age, who prove that they have lived more chastely in youth than when advanced years had granted them the opportunity of a freer life. ON FIRST PRINCIPLES 3.1.5.[14]

THE CHASTISEMENT OF GOD. CYPRIAN: An enemy of the altar, a rebel against Christ's sacrifice, a traitor to his faith, a blasphemous renegade, a disobedient servant, an undutiful son, a hostile brother, he scorns the bishops, turns his back on God's priests and dares to set up another altar, to offer another prayer in unlawful words, to profane the true offering of the Lord with false sacrifices. Does he not know that the presumption which strives against the ordinance of God is punished by the chastisement of God? THE UNITY OF THE CATHOLIC CHURCH 17.[15]

DISCRETION. JEROME: You despise gold; someone else loves it. You spurn wealth; he eagerly pursues it. You love silence, weakness and privacy. He takes delight in talking and effrontery in the public square, and streets, and apothecary shops. . . . Do not remain under the same roof with him. Do not rely on your past continence. You cannot be holier than David or wiser than Solomon. . . . If in the course of your clerical duty you have to visit a widow or a virgin, never enter the house alone. Let your companions be persons who will not disgrace you. . . . You must not sit alone with a woman secretly and without witnesses. If she has any-

---

[9]FC 23:260. [10]NPNF 1 12:246. [11]FC 26:327. [12]See Mt 15:14.
[13]FC 36:113. [14]OFP 163. [15]LCC 5:136.

thing confidential to disclose, she is sure to have some nurse or housekeeper, some virgin, some widow, some married woman. She cannot be so friendless as to have none except you to whom she can venture to confide her secrets. LETTERS 52.[16]

THE REBUKE OF BAD COMPANY. CHRYSOSTOM: Paul says this both in order to rebuke their past conduct and to show that he makes some allowance for them, in the hope that they will now repent and return to the right path. HOMILIES ON THE EPISTLES OF PAUL TO THE CORINTHIANS 40.4.[17]

15:34 Sin No More

AWAKING FROM IGNORANCE. DIDYMUS THE

BLIND: The wise are on the lookout for wrongdoing and have awakened from the sleep of ignorance. PAULINE COMMENTARY FROM THE GREEK CHURCH.[18]

COME TO YOUR RIGHT MIND. CHRYSOSTOM: Paul sounds here as if he were talking to drunkards and madmen, for it is people like that who are in the habit of making sudden changes of behavior. Those who have no knowledge of God are those who do not believe in the resurrection of the dead. HOMILIES ON THE EPISTLES OF PAUL TO THE CORINTHIANS 40.4.[19]

---

[16]LCC 5:320. [17]NPNF 1 12:247. [18]NTA 15:9. [19]NPNF 1 12:247.

15:35-44 THE RESURRECTION BODY

[35]But some one will ask, "How are the dead raised? With what kind of body do they come?" [36]You foolish man! What you sow does not come to life unless it dies. [37]And what you sow is not the body which is to be, but a bare kernel, perhaps of wheat or of some other grain. [38]But God gives it a body as he has chosen, and to each kind of seed its own body. [39]For not all flesh is alike, but there is one kind for men, another for animals, another for birds, and another for fish. [40]There are celestial bodies and there are terrestrial bodies; but the glory of the celestial is one, and the glory of the terrestrial is another. [41]There is one glory of the sun, and another glory of the moon, and another glory of the stars; for star differs from star in glory.

[42]So is it with the resurrection of the dead. What is sown is perishable, what is raised is imperishable. [43]It is sown in dishonor, it is raised in glory. It is sown in weakness, it is raised in power. [44]It is sown a physical body, it is raised a spiritual body. If there is a physical body, there is also a spiritual body.

Overview: All bodily deficits will be healed in the resurrection (Theodore of Mopsuestia, Pelagius). A better body is to be constructed, one that is no longer flesh and blood but immortal and indestructible (Theodore). Paul reasons with the analogy of seeds in order to talk about the resurrected body (Origen, Chrysostom). As a seed dies and comes back again with additional benefit, so it is credible that by God's power a human body should rise again in an equally improved form (Ambrosiaster). The resurrection of the human body transcends the power of nature (Gregory of Nyssa). As the rational soul is not good or bad in itself but is capable of becoming either, so is our body capable of becoming either perishable or imperishable (Didymus the Blind). Though it is sown in dishonor and eaten by worms, the body will rise again in glory (Ambrosiaster). Sown as a physical body, it will be raised as a spiritual body (Didymus the Blind). The mystery of the resurrection is presignified in the miracle of the seed (Macrina, Ambrose).

After the resurrection the Spirit will dwell permanently in the flesh of the righteous (Chrysostom). This is seen by analogy to the Spirit indwelling the flesh of the incarnate Son (Oecumenius). These better things have already begun, because their root and their source have been revealed (Chrysostom). The substance of our flesh was not from the outset condemned, but the guilt of the flesh is censured, having been caused by willful rebellion (Novatian). The body by itself is not the obstacle but rather our willful wickedness that prevents us from inheriting the kingdom of God (Chrysostom). Meanwhile believers continue to struggle against sin in this flesh (Augustine). Paul did not say that flesh and blood will not rise from the dead but that their corruption cannot inherit the kingdom of God. The earthly flesh and blood we have is perishable but will be clothed with immortality, and in that renewed state we shall enter the king-

dom (Severian of Gabala). If any corporeal creature were thought to be of one and the same nature as God, it would not exist in any place locally or in time (Fulgentius). God gives as he chooses (Augustine). Every nature is wholly created by God (Augustine).

15:35 What Kind of Body in the Resurrection?

The Mystery of the Growing Seed. Ambrose: Some may wonder how decayed bodies can become sound again, scattered members brought together, and destroyed parts restored. Yet no one seems to wonder how seeds softened and broken by the dampness and weight of the earth grow and become green again. Such seeds, of course, are rotted and dissolved by contact with the earth. But when the generative moisture of the soil imparts life to the buried and hidden seeds by a kind of life-giving heat, they receive the animating force of the growing plant. Then gradually, nature raises from stalk the tender life called the growing ear, and, like a careful mother, wraps it in a sheath as a protection against its being nipped at this immature stage by the frost or scorched by the sun when the kernels are emerging, as it were, from early infancy. On His Brother Satyrus 2.55.[1]

Argument and Reason. Chrysostom: Why does Paul argue like this, instead of simply referring his hearers to the power of God as he does elsewhere?[2] Here he is dealing with people who do not believe in what he is saying, so he gives them reasons for it. Homilies on the Epistles of Paul to the Corinthians 41.2.[3]

Healed Bodies. Pelagius: Everything wrong with our bodies in this life will be healed in the resurrection. Commentary on the First Epis-

---

[1]FC 22:219. [2]Phil 3:21. [3]NPNF 1 12:249.

TLE TO THE CORINTHIANS 15.[4]

5:36 *Life Through Death*

SEEDS AND HUMAN BODIES. CHRYSOSTOM: Notice how Paul utilizes language appropriate to seeds and plants, yet talks instead about life and death in a way more appropriate to our human bodies. HOMILIES ON THE EPISTLES OF PAUL TO THE CORINTHIANS 41.2.[5]

THE NATURALNESS OF RISING AGAIN. AMBROSE: We must not doubt what is more in accord with nature than against it. For it is as natural that all things living should rise again as it is unnatural that they should perish. ON HIS BROTHER SATYRUS 2.57.[6]

15:37 *Sowing a Bare Kernel*

THE GRAIN RESTORED FROM CORRUPTION. ORIGEN: The power which exists in a grain of wheat refashions and restores the grain, after its corruption and death, into a body with stalk and ear. ON FIRST PRINCIPLES 2.10.3.[7]

NOT THE BODY YET TO BE. AMBROSIASTER: If a seed dies and comes back again with so much additional benefit to the human race, why is it incredible that a human body should rise again, by the power of God, with an equally improved substance? COMMENTARY ON PAUL'S EPISTLES.[8]

15:38 *To Each Kind of Seed*

GOD TRANSCENDS THE STANDARDS OF NATURE. GREGORY OF NYSSA: It seems to me that here Paul is refuting those who ignore the particular standards of nature and assess the divine power in the light of their own strength. They think that God can do only as much as man can comprehend. They think that what is beyond us also exceeds the power of God. ON THE SOUL AND THE RESURRECTION.[9]

GOD GIVES AS HE HAS CHOSEN. AUGUSTINE: He did not say God "gave" or "ordered" but God "gives," that you may know how the Creator applies the effective power of his wisdom to the creation of things which come into existence daily at their appointed times. LETTERS 205.[10]

15:39 *Not All Flesh Is Alike*

DIFFERING TYPES OF RESURRECTION. CHRYSOSTOM: Here Paul distinguishes different kinds of resurrection. Do not suppose that just because grain is sown and it all comes up as ears of corn that therefore every resurrection will be the same in honor. For even in the world of seeds, some are more valuable than others. HOMILIES ON THE EPISTLES OF PAUL TO THE CORINTHIANS 41.4.[11]

GOD'S POWER DEMONSTRATED. AMBROSIASTER: Let the Sophists explain this if they can! All the philosophers of this world are unwilling to submit their minds to the law of God in order to believe in him. Instead they confound one another with diverse and mutually contradictory theories, none of which can be proved. God, on the other hand, does not argue. Instead, he demonstrates his power by raising Christ from the dead. COMMENTARY ON PAUL'S EPISTLES.[12]

EVERY NATURE IS WHOLLY CREATED BY GOD. AUGUSTINE: Whatever bodily or seminal causes may play a part in reproduction, by the intermingling of the two sexes, or in animals, or even by the influence of angels, and whatever longings or emotions of the mother may affect the features or the hue while the fetus is soft and pliable, nevertheless every nature as such, however affected by circumstances, is created wholly by the supreme God. It is the hidden and penetrating power of God's irresistible pres-

---

[4]Migne PL 30:768B. [5]NPNF 1 12:250. [6]FC 22:211. [7]OFP 141. [8]CSEL 81.178. [9]FC 58:268. [10]FC 32:20. [11]NPNF 1 12:251. [12]CSEL 81.178-79.

ence that gives being to every creature that can be said to be, whatever its genus and species may be. For without his creative act, a nature would not only not be in this or that genus. It simply could not have being at all. City of God 12.26.[13]

An Immortal Body. Theodore of Mopsuestia: In the resurrection a better body is constructed, one which is no longer flesh and blood as such but which is an immortal and indestructible living being. Pauline Commentary from the Greek Church.[14]

15:40 Celestial and Terrestrial Bodies

Differences Among Earthly Bodies. Origen: Even among earthly bodies there are no small differences. Take the human race, for example. Some are Greeks and some are barbarians, and among the barbarians, some are wilder than others. Some have higher laws. Some lower ones, and some follow savage customs which are not laws at all. On First Principles 2.9.3.[15]

Convince by Gradual Steps. Augustine: If any man does not believe that common flesh can be changed into a nature of this sort, he is to be convinced toward faith by gradual steps. If you ask them whether earth can be changed into water, that will not seem to him incredible because there is no great distance between these two elements. Again if you ask whether water can be changed into air, he will agree that that is not absurd because these two elements are close neighbors. Faith and the Creed 10.24.[16]

Whether the World Itself Is Eternal. Augustine: Porphyry says: "You praise the body to me without good reasons. No matter what kind of body it is, you must escape from it if you wish to be happy." Philosophers say this, but they are wrong. They are raving. . . . I read your books where you say that the world is ani-mated, that the heavens, the earth, the seas, all the huge bodies which exist, all the immense elements of all times, this whole universal body which consists of all these elements—all this, you say, is a vast living thing and has its own soul. But you claim that it does not have the senses of the body because outside of it there is nothing which can be perceived. Nevertheless you say it has intelligence, and that it leads to God, and that the soul of the world is called Jupiter. . . . You claim that the same world is eternal, that it will always exist, that it will not have an end. If then the world is eternal and remains without any end, if this world is a living thing and if its soul is always held in the world, then as a matter of fact, must we then flee every kind of body? Easter Season 241.7.[17]

God Can Make New Bodies. Pelagius: If God could make the sun, moon and stars, what problem will he have in making new bodies for us? Commentary on the First Epistle to the Corinthians 15.[18]

15:41 Star Differs from Star

Another Glory for Stars. Jerome: The members of the one church are different. Just as the sun has its own brilliance, and the moon also tempers the darkness of the night. And the five other stars called the wandering stars traverse the sky, differing both in their courses and in their brilliance. There are other countless stars that we see shining in the firmament. The brilliance of each of these is different, and yet each and every star is perfect, according to its own standard, to the degree that, in comparison with a greater star, it lacks perfection. . . . So the eye cannot say to the hand: "I do not need your help." Against the Pelagians 16.[19]

Differences in Honor. Chrysostom: Paul

---

[13]FC 14.293. [14]NTA 15:195. [15]OFP 131. [16]LCC 6:368. [17]FC 38:262-63. [18]Migne PL 30:768D. [19]FC 53:255.

switches metaphors in order to underline the fact that although there is only one resurrection, there will be great differences of honor from one body to another. Homilies on the Epistles of Paul to the Corinthians 41.4.[20]

The Eye Needs the Body. Augustine: In the body the eyes are held in high esteem. But they would be less esteemed if they were all alone or if there were no other members of seemingly less worth. In the heavens the sun outshines the moon but does not scorn it, and "star differs from star in glory" but is never measuring itself through pride. The Excellence of Widowhood 6.8.[21]

Creatures Exist Locally. Fulgentius: The diversity of corporeal natures demonstrates that each one of them is not what it is because of what it could always have had all by itself. Rather it is what it is because of what it has received from the plan and working of the one omnipotent, unchangeable and all-wise Creator. If any corporeal creature whatsoever were of one and the same nature as the holy Trinity, which is the one God, it would not exist in any place locally, nor would it ever undergo change because of passage of time, nor would it move from one place to another, nor would it be circumscribed by the fact of its mass. To Peter on the Faith 26-27.[22]

15:42 Raised Imperishable

What Is Raised Is Imperishable. Didymus the Blind: Just as the rational soul is not good or bad in itself but is capable of becoming either of these, so our body is neither perishable nor imperishable by nature but acquires these immanent, essential qualities in due course. Pauline Commentary from the Greek Church.[23]

Whether Believers Continue to Struggle with Sin. Augustine: In due time I yielded to better and more enlightened minds, or rather, to truth itself, as I heard in the words of the apostle the groaning of the saints in their battle against carnal concupiscence. Although the saints are spiritually minded, they are still carnal in the corruptible body which remains a weight upon the soul. They will, however, be spiritual also in body when the body sown animal will rise spiritual. They are still prisoners under the wall of sin, in as much as they are subject to stimulation by desires to which they do not consent. Thus I came to understand this matter as did Hilary, Gregory, Ambrose, and other holy and renowned teachers of the church, who saw that the apostle, by his own words, fought strenuously the same battle against carnal concupiscences he did not wish to have yet in fact did have. Against Julian 70.[24]

15:43 Raised in Glory

Raised in Power. Didymus the Blind: When the body formed by the copulation of male and female is sown, dishonor and weakness will be in it because it is the body of a perishing soul and shares its characteristics. But when it rises again by the power of God, it appears as a spiritual body, having imperishability, power and honor. Pauline Commentary from the Greek Church.[25]

Dishonor Will Vanish. Ambrosiaster: The body is sown in dishonor because it is placed in a coffin where it rots and is eaten by worms. But when it rises again, it will do so in glory, and all trace of this dishonor will vanish. Commentary on Paul's Epistles.[26]

Vivified by the Spirit. Augustine: We will still be bodies, so vivified by the spirit, however, as to retain the substance of the flesh without suffering the accidents of sluggishness and mortality. City of God 13.22.[27]

---

[20]NPNF 1 12:251. [21]FC 16:287*. [22]FC 95:76-77. [23]NTA 15:10. [24]FC 35:382. [25]NTA 15:10. [26]CSEL 81.181. [27]FC 14:333.

15:44 *Physical and Spiritual Bodies*

THE SAME BODY WILL RISE. ORIGEN: In regard to our bodily nature we must understand that there is not one body which we now use in lowliness and corruption and weakness and a different one which we are to use hereafter in incorruption and power and glory. Rather this same body, having cast off the weaknesses of its present existence, will be transformed into a thing of glory and made spiritual, with the result that what was a vessel of dishonor shall itself be purified and become a vessel of honor and a habitation of blessedness. ON FIRST PRINCIPLES 3.6.6.[28]

THE WHOLE CREATION TO BE DELIVERED. ORIGEN: The quality of a spiritual body is something such as will make a fitting habitation not only for all saints and perfected souls but also for that "whole creation" which is to be "delivered from the bondage of corruption." ON FIRST PRINCIPLES 3.6.4.[29]

RAISED A SPIRITUAL BODY. ORIGEN: It is from the natural body that the power and grace of the resurrection calls forth the spiritual body, when it changes it from dishonor to glory. ON FIRST PRINCIPLES 2.10.1.[30]

RESURRECTION SIGNIFIED IN THE MIRACLE OF THE SEED. MACRINA: The seed does not germinate unless it is dissolved in the earth, rarefied and made for us, so that it is mixed with the moisture nearby and dust changes into root and sprout, and it does not stop there but changes into a stalk with sections in between which are surrounded by chains, as it were, so as to be able to hold the grain in an upright position. . . . Thus the apostle says that the mystery of the resurrection is presignified before us in the miracles performed in the seeds. The divine power in its surpassing excellence not only gives back to see but adds many great and more wonderful features with which nature is magnificently adorned. [THE TEACHING OF MACRINA] ON THE SOUL AND THE RESURRECTION.[31]

GROWTH IN DUE SEASON. AMBROSE: You are sown as are all other things. Why, then, do you wonder whether you will rise again like the rest? You believe the seed because you see it. You do not believe the rising again because you do not see it. "Blessed are they who have not seen, and yet have believed."[32] Yet, before the proper season arrives, not even the seed is believed. For not every season is suitable for seeds to grow. Wheat is sown at one time and comes up at another time. At one time the vine is grafted. At another shoots begin to grow, foliage becomes luxuriant, and grapes take form. At one time, the olive tree is planted. At another, as though heavy with child and burdened with a progeny of berries, it is bent low in the abundance of its own fruit. But before the proper time arrives for each, production is restricted. Neither the tree nor the plant has the time of bearing within its own power. ON HIS BROTHER SATYRUS 2.60.[33]

THE SPIRIT WILL DWELL PERMANENTLY. CHRYSOSTOM: Is our present body not spiritual as well? Yes it is, but then it will be more so. For now the grace of the Holy Spirit often leaves people who commit great sins, and even if he remains, the life of the flesh depends on the soul, with the result that the Spirit plays no part. But after the resurrection this will no longer be so, because then the Spirit will dwell permanently in the flesh of the righteous and the victory will be his, even while the soul is also alive. HOMILIES ON THE EPISTLES OF PAUL TO THE CORINTHIANS 41.5.[34]

THE SPIRITUAL BODY. AUGUSTINE: As the Spirit, when it serves the flesh, is not improperly said to be carnal, so the flesh, when it serves the spirit, will rightly be called spiritual—not be-

---

[28]OFP 252. [29]OFP 249. [30]OFP 139. [31]FC 58:269. [32]Jn 20:29. [33]FC 22:223. [34]NPNF 1 12:252.

cause changed into spirit, as some suppose who misinterpret the text, "What is sown a natural body rises a spiritual body," but because it will be so subject to the spirit that, with a marvelous pliancy of perfect obedience, it will accept the infallible law of its indissoluble immortality, putting aside every feeling of fatigue, every shadow of suffering, every sign of slowing down. This "spiritual body" will not only be better than any body on earth in perfect health but will surpass even that of Adam or Eve before their sin. City of God 13.20.[35]

The Lord and the Spirit. Oecumenius: Christ had a spiritual body, because he had received the full presence of the Holy Spirit when the dove rested on him.[36] So the Lord had the power of the Paraclete in his humanity in a way distinguishable from his divinity, since he was himself the Spirit. Pauline Commentary from the Greek Church.[37]

---

[35]FC 214:329.   [36]Mt 3:16; Mk 1:10; Lk 3:22; Jn 1:32.   [37]NTA 15:443.

15:45-50 THE LAST ADAM

[45]*Thus it is written, "The first man Adam became a living being"; the last Adam became a life-giving spirit. [46]But it is not the spiritual which is first but the physical, and then the spiritual. [47]The first man was from the earth, a man of dust; the second man is from heaven. [48]As was the man of dust, so are those who are of the dust; and as is the man of heaven, so are those who are of heaven. [49]Just as we have borne the image of the man of dust, we shall [a] also bear the image of the man of heaven. [50]I tell you this, brethren: flesh and blood cannot inherit the kingdom of God, nor does the perishable inherit the imperishable.*

a *Other ancient authorities read* let us

Overview: The Lord who was heavenly became earthly that he might make heavenly those who were earthly (Cyril of Jerusalem, Augustine, Severian of Gabala). The spiritual body is understood as a body so subject to spirit that it may be suited to its celestial habitation (Augustine). The first man is formed of the mire (Maximus of Turin). The second or resurrected man lives in the elements and is a joint heir with Christ (Hilary of Poitiers, Isaac of Nineveh, Ambrose). Do not despise the body that is destined to be the heir of eternity (Novatian, Jerome).

The Hope of Better Things. Chrysostom: The apostle said these things so that we might learn that the signs and promises both of this present life and of that which is to come have now come upon us. He sets out the better things as matters for hope and indicates that they have already begun, because their root and their source have been revealed. If that is the case, there is no need to doubt that the fruits will appear in due course. Homilies on the Epistles of Paul to the Corinthians 41.6.[1]

15:45 A Living Being

---

[1]NPNF 1 12:252.

The Natural and the Spiritual Body Distin-guished. Augustine: The first man, Adam, was made into a living soul . . . but of all the animals it was said: "Let the earth and bring forth the living creatures." We understand, then, that the natural body is said to be like the other animals because of the dissolution and corruption of death. It is daily renewed by food, and when the bond of life is broken it is dissolved. But the spiritual body which is now with the Spirit is immortal. Letter to Consentius 205.[2]

15:46 Physical Death, Then Spiritual

Lesser and Better Things. Chrysostom: In God's plan, things keep getting better. This is why Paul says that the lesser things have al-ready come to pass and that the better ones are on the way. . . . For the farmer, seeing the grain dissolving, does not mourn. Homilies on the Epistles of Paul to the Corinthians 41.6.[3]

The Clay Becomes Gradually Molded. Augustine: First comes the clay that is only fit to be thrown away, with which we must be-gin but in which we need not remain. After-ward comes what is fit for us, that into which we can be gradually molded and in which, when molded, we may remain. City of God 15.1.[4]

Readiness for Celestial Habitation. Augus-tine: The spiritual body is understood as a body so subject to spirit that it may be suited to its celestial habitation, all earthly weakness and corruption and being changed and converted into celestial purity and stability. Faith and the Creed 6.13.[5]

15:47 A Man from Heaven

Present Life and the Life to Come. Chrysos-tom: The previous difference was between the present life and the life to come, but this differ-ence is between life before grace revealed and the life after grace is revealed. Homilies on the

Epistles of Paul to the Corinthians 42.1.[6]

The Heavenly Man. Ambrose: It is not the spiritual that comes first but the physical, and then the spiritual. . . . The last one is like the sum of the whole. It is he alone who, like the cause of the world for which all things were made, dwells in all the elements. The second man from heaven, the resurrected, heavenly man, lives amid beasts, swims with fish, flies above the birds, talks with angels, dwells on earth, does battle in heaven, ploughs the sea, feeds in the air, is a tiller of the soil, a traveler on the deep, a fisher in streams, a fowler in the air, an heir in heaven, a joint heir with Christ. Letter to Horontius 49.[7]

First the Natural Body, Then the Spiritual. Augustine: First comes in the natural body such as Adam was the first man to possess. Had he not sinned, he would never have died. Such a body we too possess, except that its nature as a result of sin has become so changed for the worse that it is now faced with inexorable death. Such a body Christ also deigned to assume for our sakes, not in-deed by necessity but in virtue of his power. Afterward, however, comes the spiritual body such as that which Christ, our head, was the first to have been, but which we, his mem-bers, will have at the final resurrection of the dead. City of God 13.23.[8]

The Second Man. Theodoret of Cyr: Paul is referring here to the second coming of Christ. Commentary on the First Epistle to the Corinthians 279.[9]

15:48a Those of the Dust

The Man of Dust. Origen: If you remain in what is of the earth, you will be turned away in

---

[2]FC 32:14. [3]NPNF 1 12:253. [4]FC 14:415. [5]LCC 6:361. [6]NPNF 1 12:255. [7]FC 26:263. [8]FC 14:336-37. [9]Migne PG 82:366.

the end. You must be changed yourself, you must be converted, you must be made "heavenly." GENESIS, HOMILY 9.[10]

CONCEIVED BY THE HOLY SPIRIT, BORN OF THE VIRGIN.

HILARY OF POITIERS: The first man was made from the slime of the earth. The second man came from heaven. By using the word *man*, he taught the birth of this man from the virgin, who in fulfilling her function as a mother acted in accordance with the nature of her sex in the conception and birth of the man. And when he asserted that the second man was from heaven, he testified that his origin was from the appearance of the Holy Spirit who came upon the virgin. Thus precisely while he was a man, he was also from heaven. The birth of this man was from the virgin. The conception was from the Spirit. TRINITY 10.[11]

FORMED FROM MIRE.

MAXIMUS OF TURIN: Adam is formed from mire by the hands of God. Christ is formed in the womb by the Spirit of God. SERMONS 50.2.[12]

15:48b *Those of Heaven*

THE MAN OF HEAVEN.

CHRYSOSTOM: The man of heaven indicates a lofty and severe life on the one hand, with something quite different [man of dust] on the other. HOMILIES ON THE EPISTLES OF PAUL TO THE CORINTHIANS 42.1.[13]

THE IMAGE OF THE EARTHLY AND THE HEAVENLY.

AUGUSTINE: If you do not like the Christian faith, say so. But you will not find another Christian faith. There is one man unto life; there is one unto death. The one is only man; the other is God and man. Through the one the world was made the enemy of God. Through the other those chosen from the world are reconciled to God. For "As in Adam all die, so in Christ all will be made alive." Therefore even as we have borne the image of the earthly, let us also bear the image of the heavenly. Whoever

tries to undermine these foundations of the Christian faith will himself be destroyed, but they will remain firm. AGAINST JULIAN 4.[14]

THE HEAVENLY BECAME EARTHLY TO MAKE THE EARTHLY HEAVENLY.

AUGUSTINE: The Lord who was heavenly became earthly that he might make heavenly those who were earthly. From immortal he became mortal by taking the form of a servant, not by changing the nature of the Lord, that he might make immortal those who were mortal by imparting the grace of the Lord, not by retaining the offense of the servant. LETTER TO CONSENTIUS 205.[15]

15:49 *Bearing the Same Image*

THE IMAGE OF THE HEAVENLY.

ORIGEN: You bore at that time "the image of the earthly." But now since these things have been heard, having been cleansed from the whole earthly mass and weight by the Word of God, make the "image of the heavenly" shine brightly in you. HOMILIES ON GENESIS 13.4.[16]

THE IMAGE OF THE MAN OF HEAVEN.

AMBROSIASTER: This means that just as we have borne the corruptible body of the earthly Adam, so we shall in the future bear an incorruptible body, like that of the resurrected Christ. COMMENTARY ON PAUL'S EPISTLES.[17]

GOD DWELLS IN THE HEAVENLY MAN.

CYRIL OF JERUSALEM: They are also a "heaven" "bearing the likeness of the heavenly man," since God is dwelling in them and mingling with them. MYSTAGOGICAL LECTURES 5.11.[18]

BY CHOICE, NOT NATURE.

CHRYSOSTOM: To "bear an image" is not so much a matter of our nature as such, as of our choices and behavior.

---

[10]FC 71:151. [11]FC 25:411*. [12]ACW 50:122. [13]NPNF 1 12:255. [14]FC 35:319. [15]FC 32:16. [16]FC 71:193. [17]CSEL 81.182-83. [18]FC 64:199.

Homilies on the Epistles of Paul to the Corinthians 42.2.[19]

Why Are We Made This Way? Augustine: Therefore, given that our nature sinned in paradise, we are now formed through a mortal begetting by the same divine providence, not according to heaven but according to earth—not according to the Spirit but according to the flesh. We have all become one mass of clay, a mass of sin. Since therefore we have forfeited our reward through sinning, and sense, in the absence of God's mercy, we as sinners deserve nothing other than eternal damnation, who then does the man from this mass think he is that he is able to question God and say: "Why have you made me this way?" If you want to know these things, do not be clay, but become a son of God through the mercy of him who has given to those believing in his name the power to become sons of God, although he has not so given, as you might want, to those desiring to know divine things before they believe. Questions 68.3.[20]

15:50 Inheriting the Kingdom of God

Flesh and Blood Cannot Inherit. Novatian: This does not mean that the substance of our flesh was condemned. On the contrary, only the guilt of the flesh is censured, the guilt which was caused by humanity's deliberate and rash rebellion against the claims of divine law. The Trinity 10.[21]

A Metaphor for Disobedience. Ambrosiaster: By "flesh" Paul means disobedience, and by "blood" he means an evil and wicked life. Not only will neither of these things inherit eternal life; both must be put under control in this life. Commentary on Paul's Epistles.[22]

Wickedness Cannot Inherit. Chrysostom: By "flesh" Paul here means willful evil deeds. The body by itself is not the obstacle; rather it is be-cause of our wickedness that we cannot inherit the kingdom of God. Homilies on the Epistles of Paul to the Corinthians 42.2.[23]

Do Not Despise the Body. Jerome: Let us by no means scorn the flesh, but let us reject its works. Let us not despise the body that will reign in heaven with Christ. "Flesh and blood can obtain no part in the kingdom of God." This does not refer to flesh and blood as such but to the works of the flesh. Homily 54 on Psalm 143.[24]

No Further Conflict. Augustine: There will then be such a common accord between flesh and Spirit—the Spirit quickening the servant flesh without any need of sustenance from it. There will be no further conflict within ourselves. And just as there will be no more external enemies to bear with, so neither shall we have to bear with ourselves as enemies within. Enchiridion 23.91.[25]

Clothed with Immortality. Severian of Gabala: Heretics get really mixed up about this. Paul did not say that flesh and blood would not rise from the dead but that they cannot inherit the kingdom of God. What this means is that the earthly flesh and blood which we now have is perishable, but it will be clothed with immortality, and in that state we shall enter the kingdom. Pauline Commentary from the Greek Church.[26]

Corruption and Incorruption. Isaac of Nineveh: By "incorruption" he means the knowledge of that other world, and by "corruption" and "flesh and blood" he designates the corrupting passions of both the soul and the body, the realm of whose motions is in the "mind of the flesh."[27] . . . And by the "kingdom

---

[19]NPNF 1 12:255. [20]FC 70:161. [21]FC 67:46. [22]CSEL 81.183. [23]NPNF 1 12:256. [24]FC 48:381*. [25]LCC 7:393*. [26]NTA 15:277. [27]Rom 8:6.

of God" he means the lofty, noetic theoria of the blessed intuitions of that eternal effulgence, into which the holy soul is permitted to enter only by means of the incorruptible intuitions that are exalted above corruption, flesh and blood. ASCETICAL HOMILIES 5.[28]

[28]AHSIS 395.

15:51-58 THE LAST TRUMPET

[51]*Lo! I tell you a mystery. We shall not all sleep, but we shall all be changed,* [52]*in a moment, in the twinkling of an eye, at the last trumpet. For the trumpet will sound, and the dead will be raised imperishable, and we shall be changed.* [53]*For this perishable nature must put on the imperishable, and this mortal nature must put on immortality.* [54]*When the perishable puts on the imperishable, and the mortal puts on immortality, then shall come to pass the saying that is written:*

"Death is swallowed up in victory."

[55]*"O death, where is thy victory?*

O death, where is thy sting?"

[56]*The sting of death is sin, and the power of sin is the law.* [57]*But thanks be to God, who gives us the victory through our Lord Jesus Christ.*

[58]*Therefore, my beloved brethren, be steadfast, immovable, always abounding in the work of the Lord, knowing that in the Lord your labor is not in vain.*

OVERVIEW: The resurrection is of real flesh. Otherwise words like "died," "was buried" and "rose again" would have little meaning (SEVERIAN OF GABALA). The body's mortality and corruption will disappear when immortality and incorruption come on it (CHRYSOSTOM). Human nature will grow more vigorous after death (AMBROSE). This mortal nature will become immortal when it loses its love for corruption and allows the practice of constant chastity (CLEMENT OF ALEXANDRIA). Carnal habits will disappear (AUGUSTINE). Without the law sin is weak (CHRYSOSTOM). The power of sin is the law (AUGUSTINE). Sin is overcome along with death (THEODORE OF MOPSUESTIA). The death of Christ defeats the devil, who was forced to surrender all those who had died because of sin (AMBROSIASTER). Rightly understood, this one teaching should cure all heresy (AUGUSTINE). Paul is viewing the mystery of the future as if it had already happened (CHRYSOSTOM, THEODORET OF CYR).

Anyone who is not changed in this world cannot experience change in the next (CASSIODORUS). At the sound of the last trumpet our vision will be clear and our joy will be full (GREGORY NAZIANZEN, JEROME, AUGUSTINE). God has made the end of life here the beginning of a true life for us (MACRINA). While the identical body is raised, it will be transformed by the putting on of incorruption, as iron exposed to the fire is made incandescent (CYRIL OF JERUSALEM,

Jerome). What has been mortal will be clad in immortality (Chrysostom). The One who was able to make you when you did not want to exist is able to make over what you once were (Augustine). The masculine and the feminine sexes will remain just as their bodies were created (Fulgentius). The resurrected person will be blessed and happy (Pseudo-Dionysius). One who puts on the faith of the cross despises even what is naturally fearful and for Christ's sake is not afraid of death (Athanasius). Death no longer exists in this resurrected condition where there are no enticements to sin, and we are made young by eternal incorruptibility (Augustine). The human race first wounded itself unto death in such a way that it made death pass to and through its offspring (Fulgentius). Baptism destroys the sting of death (Cyril of Jerusalem). Human infirmity added strength to evil even from a good law, since in the fulfilling of that law it trusted in its own strength (Augustine). We are no longer slaves to the law through fear but friends through love and slaves of the righteousness which was the very source of the law's promulgation (Augustine).

15:51 We Shall All Be Changed

All Mortals. Chrysostom: Even those who do not die will be changed, because they too are mortal. Homilies on the Epistles of Paul to the Corinthians 42.3.[1]

Transforming the Old Man. Augustine: The pious people will be raised as they transform the remnants of the "old man" that cling to them into the "new man." The impious people who have kept the "old man" from the beginning to the end will be raised in order to be precipitated into the second death. Those who read diligently can make out the divisions of the ages. They have no horror of tares or chaff. Of True Religion 27.50.[2]

A Mystery. Theodoret of Cyr: Paul calls this

a mystery because it is not clear to everyone but is believed only by the beloved. Commentary on the First Epistle to the Corinthians 280.[3]

The Necessity of Change. Cassiodorus: Anyone who is not changed in this world cannot experience change in the next. Explanation of the Psalms 20.[4]

The Radiance of the Saints. Cassiodorus: The radiance of the saints refers to when they will gleam at the resurrection like the angels of God. They will be so cleansed and radiant that they can gaze on the Majesty with the heart's eyes. They cannot gaze on that Light unless they are changed for the better. In Paul's words: "We shall all rise again, but we shall not all be changed." Explanation of the Psalms 3.[5]

15:52a The Twinkling of an Eye

The Speed of Light in a World of Wonders. Augustine: The glance of our eye does not reach nearer objects more quickly and distant ones more slowly. Rather it reaches both with equal speed. Similarly when, as the apostle says, the resurrection of the dead is effected in the twinkling of the eye, it is as easy for the omnipotence of God and his awe-inspiring authority to raise the recently dead as those long since fallen into decay. To some minds, these things are hard to accept because they are outside their experience, yet the whole universe is full of wonders which seem to us hardly worth noticing or examining, not because they are easily penetrated by our reason but because we are accustomed to seeing them. But I, and those who join me and are striving to understand the "invisible things of God by the things that are made," wonder neither more nor less at the fact that in one tiny seed all that we praise in the

---

[1]NPNF 1 12:256. [2]LCC 6:250. [3]Migne PG 82:367. [4]ACW 52:26. [5]ACW 53:120.

tree lies folded away. LETTER TO DEOGRATIAS 102.[6]

NO TIME TO ARGUE. AUGUSTINE: With the utterance of that cry and the resurrection of the dead, all comfort of human praise shall be taken away. There will be no doubt that the judgment is now present and at hand. Then there will be no time to argue about that one, or to judge of another, or to do a favor or offer support to another. LETTER TO HONORATUS 140.34.[7]

15:52b *The Trumpet Will Sound*

THE LAST TRUMPET. AMBROSIASTER: The last trumpet is the one which is sounded when the battle is over. After a thousand years, when the antichrist has been destroyed and the Savior has reigned, Satan will be released from his prison in order to lead astray the nations of Gog and Magog, who are demons, in order that they might attack the fortresses of the saints.[8] They will fail, and when they are defeated they will suffer the same fate as the antichrist and the false prophet. It is then that the last trumpet will sound the final victory. COMMENTARY ON PAUL'S EPISTLES.[9]

THEN I SHALL SEE MY BROTHER. GREGORY NAZIANZEN: Why am I so earthly in my thoughts? I shall await the voice of the archangel, the last trumpet, the transformation of heaven, the change of earth, the freedom of the elements, the renewal of the universe. Then I shall see my brother Caesarius himself, no longer in exile, no longer being buried, no longer mourned, no longer pitied, but splendid, glorious, sublime, such as you were often seen in a dream, dearest and most loving of brothers, whether my desire or truth itself represented you. FUNERAL SERMON: ON HIS BROTHER CAESARIUS 21.[10]

JUDGMENT DAY. JEROME: Then at the sound of the trumpet the earth and its people shall tremble, but you shall rejoice. The world shall la-

ment and groan when the Lord comes to judge it. The tribes of the earth shall smite the breast. Once mighty kings shall shiver in their nakedness. Then shall Jupiter, with all his progeny, indeed be shown aflame, and Plato with his disciples will be marked a fool. Aristotle's argument shall be of no avail. You may be a poor man and country bred, but then you shall exult and laugh and say: behold the crucified, my God! Behold my Judge! LETTERS 14.11.[11]

A CLEAR SIGNAL. AUGUSTINE: By "trumpet" he wants us to understand some very clear and prominent sign, which he elsewhere calls the voice of the archangel and the trumpet of God [1 Thess 4:16]. LETTERS 34.[12]

15:52c *We Shall Be Changed*

DISBELIEF BRINGS CONDEMNATION. AMBROSE: He who has not believed will be forsaken, and by his disbelief he will bring upon himself his own condemnation. ON HIS BROTHER SATYRUS 2.76.[13]

THE BEGINNING OF TRUE LIFE. MACRINA (AS REPORTED BY GREGORY OF NYSSA): At her death Macrina prayed: "O Lord, you have freed us from the fear of death. You have made the end of life here the beginning of a true life for us. You give rest to our bodies in sleep, and you awaken us again with the last trumpet. The dust from which you fashioned us with your hands you give back to the dust of the earth for safe keeping, and you who have relinquished it will recall it after reshaping with incorruptibility and grace our mortal and graceless substance." . . . As she said this, she made the sign of the cross upon her eyes and mouth and heart, and little by little, as the fever dried up her tongue, she was no longer able to speak

---

[6]FC 18:151. [7]FC 20:129. [8]Mt 24:31; 1 Thess 4:16; Rev 20:7-8. [9]CSEL 81.183-84. [10]FC 22:23. [11]LCC 5:300. [12]FC 20:128. [13]FC 22:231.

clearly. Her voice gave out and only from the trembling of her lips and motion of her hands did we know that she was continuing to pray. Then the evening came on and the lamp was brought in. . . . When she had completed the thanksgiving and indicated that the prayer was over by making the sign of the cross, she breathed a deep breath and with the prayer her life came to an end. THE LIFE OF ST. MACRINA.[14]

EASY FOR GOD. AUGUSTINE: It is as easy for God to raise the recently dead as those long since fallen into decay. LETTER TO DEOGRATIAS: SIX QUESTIONS ANSWERED FOR PAGANS.[15]

REAL FLESH. SEVERIAN OF GABALA: In saying this Paul is showing that the heretics who say that there is a resurrection of the soul but not of the flesh are wrong. These people blaspheme concerning the divine dispensation, thinking that Christ did not really rise again in his flesh but only appeared to do so. But if it was not real flesh, what do words like "died," "was buried" and "rose again" mean? If all this did not really happen, does it mean that we shall not really die either? PAULINE COMMENTARY FROM THE GREEK CHURCH.[16]

15:53 Putting On Immortality

DESIRE EDUCATED TO SELF-CONTROL. CLEMENT OF ALEXANDRIA: This nature will put on immortality when the intensity of desire that degenerates into sensuality is educated to self-control and, losing its love for corruption, allows us to practice constant chastity. CHRIST THE EDUCATOR 2.100.[17]

AS IRON TRANSFORMED BY FIRE. CYRIL OF JERUSALEM: While the identical body is raised up, it will be transformed by the putting on of incorruption, as iron exposed to fire is made incandescent. This occurs in a manner known only to the Lord who raises the dead. CATECHETICAL LECTURES 8.18.[18]

SOURCE OF GAIN. AMBROSE: The blossom of the resurrection is immortality and incorruption. What is richer than everlasting rest? What is a source of greater gain and satisfaction than perpetual security? Here is the manifold fruit, the harvest, whereby man's nature grows more vigorous and productive after death. ON HIS BROTHER SATYRUS 2.54.[19]

CORRUPTION VANISHES. CHRYSOSTOM: The body remains, but its mortality and corruption vanish when immortality and incorruption come upon it. HOMILIES ON THE EPISTLES OF PAUL TO THE CORINTHIANS 42.3.[20]

CLAD IN IMMORTALITY. CHRYSOSTOM: What has been mortal will be clad in immortality. After the resurrection of our bodies he promised to grant us enjoyment of the kingdom, life with the saints, enjoyment for all eternity, and those ineffable good things "which eye has not seen nor ear heard, nor have they been imagined by the human heart."[21] HOMILIES ON GENESIS 36.15.[22]

THE SAME BODY TRANSFORMED. JEROME: Just as before the Lord suffered his passion, when he was transformed and glorified on the mountain, he certainly had the same body that he had had down below, although of a different glory, so also after the resurrection, his body was of the same the nature as it had been before the passion but of a higher state of glory and in more majestic appearance. HOMILY ON PSALM 15 61.[23]

GOD IS ABLE TO REMAKE YOU. AUGUSTINE: People are amazed that God, who made all things from nothing, makes a heavenly body from human flesh. When he was in the flesh, did not the Lord make wine from water? Is it anything so much more wonderful if he makes a heavenly

---

[14]FC 58:181. [15]FC 18:151. [16]NTA 15:277. [17]FC 23:177. [18]LCC 4:183. [19]FC 22:219. [20]NPNF 1 12:256. [21]1 Cor 2:9. [22]FC 82:337. [23]FC 57:34.

body from human flesh? . . . Is he who was able to make you when you did not exist not able to make over what you once were? SERMONS FOR THE FEAST OF ASCENSION 264.6.[24]

BOTH SEXES WILL HAVE DISTINGUISHABLE GLORIFIED BODIES IN THE RESURRECTION. FULGENTIUS: The masculine and feminine sexes will remain just as their bodies were created. Their glory will vary according to the diversity of their good works. For all the bodies of both men and women, all that will exist in that kingdom will be glorious. TO PETER ON THE FAITH 237.[25]

BLESSEDLY HAPPY. PSEUDO-DIONYSIUS: Our minds shall be freed from passion and from earth. That is how we shall be. We shall receive a gift of light from him and, somehow, in a way we cannot know, we shall be united with him and, our understanding carried away, blessedly happy. We shall be struck by his blazing light. THE DIVINE NAMES 1.4.[26]

15:54 Death Is Swallowed Up

DESPISING WHAT IS NATURALLY FEARFUL. ATHANASIUS: For man is by nature afraid of death and of the dissolution of the body. But there is this most startling fact, that he who has put on the faith of the cross despises even what is naturally fearful and for Christ's sake is afraid of death. ON THE INCARNATION 28.[27]

NOTHING CORRUPT LEFT. CHRYSOSTOM: Incorruption will swallow up corruption, leaving nothing of the former life behind. HOMILIES ON THE EPISTLES OF PAUL TO THE CORINTHIANS 42.4.[28]

THE CURE FOR HERESY. AUGUSTINE: Were our heretics capable of grasping this one truth, they would surrender their pride and become reconciled and would never again worship God anywhere but in the church. THE WAY OF LIFE OF THE CATHOLIC CHURCH 30.64.[29]

DEATH EXISTS NO LONGER. AUGUSTINE: Where is death? Seek it in Christ, for it exists no longer. It did exist, and now death is dead. O Life, O Death of death! Be of good heart, death will die in us also. What has taken place in our Head will also take place in his members. Death will die in us also. But when? At the end of the world, at the resurrection of the dead in which we believe and about which we have no doubt. . . . These are words given to those who triumph, that you may have something to think about, something to sing about in your heart, something to hope for in your heart, something to seek with faith and good works. SERMONS FOR THE EASTER SEASON 233.4.[30]

THIS CORRUPTIBLE. AUGUSTINE: The apostle Paul seems to have directly pointed his finger at the flesh when he wrote: "*this* corruptible must put on incorruption." When he says *this*, he as good as points with his finger. That which is visible can be pointed at in this way. The soul cannot be pointed at, though it can be called corruptible, because it is corrupted by moral biases. FAITH AND THE CREED 10.22.[31]

IMMORTALITY REMOVES EARTHLY DESIRES. AUGUSTINE: There are many desires of the sick which health takes away. In just the same way as physical health undercuts those desires, so immortality does remove all other desires because immortality is our health. EASTER SEASON SERMON 55.8.[32]

NO ENTICEMENTS TO SIN IN HEAVEN. AUGUSTINE: Then not only shall we not obey any enticement of sin, but there will be no such enticements of the kind we are commanded not to obey. LETTER TO ASELLICUS 196.[33]

MADE YOUNG BY ETERNAL INCORRUPTIBILITY.

---

[24]FC 38:406*. [25]FC 95:83. [26]CWS 52-53. [27]LCC 3:82. [28]NPNF 1 12:256. [29]FC 56:49. [30]FC 38:221*. [31]LCC 6:367. [32]FC 38:357*. [33]FC 30:336.

Augustine: Because of the necessary activities of this life, health is not to be despised until "this mortal shall put on immortality." This is the true and perfect and unending health which is not refreshed by corruptible pleasure when it fails through earthly weakness but is maintained by heavenly strength and made young by eternal incorruptibility. Letter to Proba 130.[34]

15:55 O Death, Where Is Thy Sting?

The Devil Insulted. Ambrosiaster: "Death" here refers to the devil, who is being insulted. Commentary on Paul's Epistles.[35]

The Future as Present. Chrysostom: Like a man who is making a sacrifice in the hope of victory, Paul is inspired to see the future as something which has already happened, and he tramples upon death as if it has fallen at his feet. Death is gone, it is finished, it has vanished away. Christ has not only overcome it, he has destroyed it and eliminated it completely. Homilies on the Epistles of Paul to the Corinthians 42.4.[36]

The Victor Blessed. Augustine: Because human nature was subjected to an enemy as the just desert of sin, man must first be rescued from his power, that he might find him. Then if his life in this flesh is prolonged, he is assisted in the conflict that he may overcome the enemy. And finally the victor will be beatified, that he may reign, and at the very end he will ask: "Death, where is thy devouring?"[37] Against Julian 20.65.[38]

Death of Carnal Habits. Augustine: I think that "death" in this passage refers to a carnal habit which resists the good will through a delighting in temporal pleasures. Questions 70.[39]

15:56a Sin the Sting of Death

Baptism Destroys the Sting of Death. Cyril of Jerusalem: Baptism destroys the sting of death. For you descend into the water laden with your sins. But the invocation of grace causes your soul to receive this seal, and after that it does not lead you to be swallowed up by the dread dragon. You go down "deadly indeed in sin," and you come up "alive unto righteousness." Catechetical Lecture on Baptism 3.11-12.[40]

Law Increased Punishment. Chrysostom: Without the law sin was weak. It existed, to be sure, but it did not have the power to condemn, because although evil occurred, it was not clearly pointed out. Thus it was no small change which the law brought about. First, it caused us to know sin better, and then it increased the punishment. But if the effect of the law was to increase sin when it meant to check it, that is not the fault of the law but of the way it which it was abused. Homilies on the Epistles of Paul to the Corinthians 42.4.[41]

Wounded Unto Death. Fulgentius: By that sting, the human race first wounded itself unto death in such a way that he made death also pass to and through his offspring. To Scarila 35.[42]

15:56b The Power of Sin

The Power of Sin Is the Law. Augustine: Nothing could be truer. For a prohibition always increases an illicit desire so long as the love of and joy in holiness is too weak to conquer the inclination to sin. So without the aid of divine grace it is impossible for man to love and delight in sanctity. City of God 13.5.[43]

Adding Strength to Evil Even Through a Good Law. Augustine: The prohibition increased the concupiscence. It rendered it unconquered. So transgression was added, which

---

[34]FC 18:382. [35]CSEL 81.186. [36]NPNF 1 12:257. [37]Hos 15:14. [38]FC 35:377. [39]FC 70:178. [40]LCC 4:96. [41]NPNF 1 12:257. [42]FC 95:457. [43]FC 14:305.

did not exist without the law, although there was sin. . . . It is not to be wondered at that human infirmity has added the strength even from a good law to evil, since in the fulfilling of that very law it trusted in its own strength. On Continence 7.[44]

Free from the Law of Sin and Death. Augustine: Indeed, by sinning we slip down into death. For where the law forbids, we sin more seriously than if we were not forbidden by the law. However, when grace is added, we then fulfill without difficulty and most willingly that very thing which the law had oppressively commanded. We are no longer slaves of the law through fear but friends through love and slaves of the righteousness which was the very source of the law's promulgation. Accordingly the law of sin and death, that is, the law imposed upon sinning and dying men, merely commands that we do not covet. Nonetheless, we do covet. However, the law of the spirit of life—the law which belongs to grace and sets us free from law of sin and death—causes us not to covet. It causes us to fulfill the commands of law. Questions 66.[45]

Dead to the Law. Augustine: Why, if the law is good, is it the power of sin? Because sin wrought death by that which is good, that it might become exceedingly sinful, that is, might acquire greater powers by becoming also transgression. Why, if the law is good, are we "dead to the law by the body of Christ"? Because we are dead to the law's condemnation, being set free from the disposition which the law condemned and punishes. . . . So the same precept, which is law to those who fear it, is grace to those who love it. To Simplician—On Various Questions, the First Question 17.[46]

Sin Taken Along with Death. Theodore of Mopsuestia: By "law" here Paul simply means either what inheres in the flesh or what is added to it. His point is that sin is taken away along with death and that the law ceases to ex-

ist once we have become immortal and are governed by the grace of the Spirit. Pauline Commentary from the Greek Church.[47]

15:57 Thanks Be to God

The Victory. Ambrosiaster: Christ did not win the victory for himself but for our benefit. For when he became a man, he remained God, and by overcoming the devil, he who never sinned gained the victory for us, who were bound in death because of sin. The death of Christ defeated the devil, who was forced to surrender all those who had died because of sin. Commentary on Paul's Epistles.[48]

Grace Given When Unworthy. Augustine: The crown could not have been given to one who was worthy of it, unless grace had been given to him when still unworthy. Proceedings of Pelagius 35.[49]

15:58 Abounding in the Lord's Work

Be Steadfast. Ambrosiaster: Those who persevere in a life of faith and good works have the assurance that they will be accepted by God and receive their reward and that they will not be led astray by wicked arguments. Commentary on Paul's Epistles.[50]

Labor Abundantly in the Lord. Chrysostom: We ought not merely to labor in the Lord but to do so abundantly, to overflowing. The labor of man after his expulsion from paradise was punishment for his transgressions, but this labor[51] is the basis for the rewards which are to come. Homilies on the Epistles of Paul to the Corinthians 42.5.[52]

---

[44]FC 16:196*. [45]FC 70:141. [46]LCC 6:384. [47]NTA 15:196. [48]CSEL 81.186-87. [49]FC 86:148. [50]CSEL 81.187. [51]Enabled only by grace, as stated by Chrysostom frequently. [52]NPNF 1 12:257.

16:1-4 ALMSGIVING

¹*Now concerning the contribution for the saints: as I directed the churches of Galatia, so you also are to do. ²On the first day of every week, each of you is to put something aside and store it up, as he may prosper, so that contributions need not be made when I come. ³And when I arrive, I will send those whom you accredit by letter to carry your gift to Jerusalem. ⁴If it seems advisable that I should go also, they will accompany me.*

OVERVIEW: The church is called to put something aside for the Lord's day, the day of resurrection, on which we received all the blessings we now have (CHRYSOSTOM). The collection was to be doubly beneficial to the poor and to the saints of Jerusalem (AMBROSIASTER).

16:1 The Contribution

THE GALATIAN CONTRIBUTION. CHRYSOSTOM: Paul encourages the Corinthians by mentioning the Galatians, because they would surely be ashamed to be found inferior to such provincials. HOMILIES ON THE EPISTLES OF PAUL TO THE CORINTHIANS 43.1.[1]

16:2 Put Something Aside

FOR THE LORD'S DAY. CHRYSOSTOM: The day itself was enough to encourage them to give alms. For the Lord's day was the day on which we received all the blessings which we now have. It is the root and the beginning of our new life in Christ. This is not the only reason that it is suitable for almsgiving, however. It is also the day of rest, when our souls can relax from their toils and open themselves to show pity. Moreover, participation in holy Communion on that day

instills great zeal in us. HOMILIES ON THE EPISTLES OF PAUL TO THE CORINTHIANS 43.2.[2]

16:3 Carrying the Gift to Jerusalem

FOR JERUSALEM AND THE POOR. AMBROSIASTER: This collection was doubly beneficial, because it helped the saints mentioned above and also the poor people who were in the church. COMMENTARY ON PAUL'S EPISTLES.[3]

THOSE ACCREDITED. CHRYSOSTOM: Paul leaves it up to the Corinthians to choose the carriers of his message, so as to avoid showing any partiality. HOMILIES ON THE EPISTLES OF PAUL TO THE CORINTHIANS 43.4.[4]

16:4 Accompanying Paul

A GENEROUS COLLECTION. AMBROSIASTER: Paul is saying that if the collection is generous, he can go too. For if a bishop is going, he ought to take a large amount with him. COMMENTARY ON PAUL'S EPISTLES.[5]

---

[1]NPNF 1 12:259. [2]NPNF 1 12:259. [3]CSEL 81.188. [4]NPNF 1 12:260. [5]CSEL 81.188.

16:5-9 FUTURE PLANS

[5]I will visit you after passing through Macedonia, for I intend to pass through Macedonia, [6]and perhaps I will stay with you or even spend the winter, so that you may speed me on my journey, wherever I go. [7]For I do not want to see you now just in passing; I hope to spend some time with you, if the Lord permits. [8]But I will stay in Ephesus until Pentecost, [9]for a wide door for effective work has opened to me, and there are many adversaries.

OVERVIEW: Paul is writing from Ephesus (DIDYMUS THE BLIND, AMBROSIASTER). He makes it clear that he was staying there until Pentecost because he had found people thirsting for the grace of God (AMBROSIASTER), even though there were also many adversaries (CHRYSOSTOM). The one from whom the Corinthians first heard Christian teaching hopes to come to visit them (AMBROSIASTER).

16:5-6 *Passing Through Macedonia*

PAUL WILL VISIT. AMBROSIASTER: Paul is personally strengthening the admonitions by which he is putting them right. The one from whom they have heard Christian teaching is coming to visit. If so, they will be all the more concerned not to be ashamed when he arrives. COMMENTARY ON PAUL'S EPISTLES.[1]

16:7 *Spending Time with Them*

NOT JUST IN PASSING. AMBROSIASTER: Knowing that he has a lot to do in Corinth, Paul does not want to pass through on his way somewhere else but to spend time with them when he comes. COMMENTARY ON PAUL'S EPISTLES.[2]

16:8 *In Ephesus Until Pentecost*

IN EPHESUS. DIDYMUS THE BLIND: Paul wrote this letter from Ephesus. PAULINE COMMENTARY FROM THE GREEK CHURCH.[3]

16:9 *A Door for Effective Work Opened*

EFFECTIVE WORK. AMBROSIASTER: Paul made it clear that he was staying at Ephesus because he had found hearts there who were thirsting for the grace of God, and in them he could quickly instill the mystery of Christ. But because the devil is always restless and hostile to those who long for God, he adds that his enemies there are many. For the more they sought after the faith, the more there were adversaries who contradicted them and fought against the teaching of the Lord. COMMENTARY ON PAUL'S EPISTLES.[4]

MANY ADVERSARIES. CHRYSOSTOM: It was precisely because the opportunities were so great that Paul had so many adversaries. The devil is always active when he risks losing his booty. HOMILIES ON THE EPISTLES OF PAUL TO THE CORINTHIANS 43.5.[5]

---

[1]CSEL 81.189. [2]CSEL 81.189. [3]NTA 15:12. [4]CSEL 81.189-90. [5]NPNF 1 12:261.

16:10-18 FELLOW WORKERS

^{10}When Timothy comes, see that you put him at ease among you, for he is doing the work of the Lord, as I am. ^{11}So let no one despise him. Speed him on his way in peace, that he may return to me; for I am expecting him with the brethren.

^{12}As for our brother Apollos, I strongly urged him to visit you with the other brethren, but it was not at all his will ^{b} to come now. He will come when he has opportunity.

^{13}Be watchful, stand firm in your faith, be courageous, be strong. ^{14}Let all that you do be done in love.

^{15}Now, brethren, you know that the household of Stephanas were the first converts in Achaia, and they have devoted themselves to the service of the saints; ^{16}I urge you to be subject to such men and to every fellow worker and laborer. ^{17}I rejoice at the coming of Stephanas and Fortunatus and Achaicus, because they have made up for your absence; ^{18}for they refreshed my spirit as well as yours. Give recognition to such men.

b Or God's will for him

OVERVIEW: Paul commended Timothy to the Corinthians (AMBROSIASTER, CHRYSOSTOM). Due to continuing divisions in Corinth (DIDYMUS THE BLIND, AMBROSIASTER), the time was not yet right for Apollos to visit them (CHRYSOSTOM). Meanwhile they were encouraged to stand firm (AMBROSIASTER) and be strong (DIDYMUS THE BLIND) and to do all they do in love (AMBROSIASTER). If love had been present throughout, the Corinthians would not have been divided into factions or have thrown each other into law courts (CHRYSOSTOM). They are urged to follow the generous pattern of the household of Stephanas (AMBROSIASTER, CHRYSOSTOM, PELAGIUS).

16:10 Doing the Work of the Lord

WHEN TIMOTHY COMES. AMBROSIASTER: Although Timothy was preaching what he had learned from Paul and was a gifted evangelist, the apostle commends him since he did not have the same authority. Paul was afraid that Timothy might not be received as he deserved by dissidents in the church, that they would cre-

ate a fuss, that Timothy would be afraid and that his coming would do nothing for their salvation. COMMENTARY ON PAUL'S EPISTLES.[1]

PUT HIM AT EASE. CHRYSOSTOM: It might be thought that this is some criticism of Timothy's self-confidence, but Paul says this for the sake of the Corinthians, because if they turn against him they will only hurt themselves. HOMILIES ON THE EPISTLES OF PAUL TO THE CORINTHIANS 44.1.[2]

16:11 Send Him on His Way in Peace

TREATED WITH HONOR. AMBROSIASTER: Paul mentions Timothy's great merit in order to teach them not only that he should be treated with honor in their company but that once he had made preparations to leave he should be sent on his way with deference, because he was an apostle of the Lord. COMMENTARY ON PAUL'S EPISTLES.[3]

---

[1]CSEL 81.190. [2]NPNF 1 12:263. [3]CSEL 81.190.

16:12 *A Visit from Apollos*

Not His Will to Come Now. Didymus the Blind: Apollos was the bishop of Corinth, but he had left the church on account of its divisions and gone to be with Paul. He would not go back with the letter, because he did not want to return until the divisions were healed. Pauline Commentary from the Greek Church.[4]

Apollos Will Come Later. Ambrosiaster: Paul is hinting that Apollos did not want to go to Corinth because the church there was divided, in the hope that when they heard this they would be eager to make peace. Apollos would come when the church reached agreement. Commentary on Paul's Epistles.[5]

The Time Not Yet Right. Chrysostom: Apollos was probably older than Timothy, and some at Corinth may have wondered why Paul did not send him instead. Therefore, Paul reassures them by calling Apollos his brother and by saying that he did try to encourage him to go, but he did not want to at that particular point. Paul did not mean to criticize Apollos when he said this. He merely meant that the time was not right for him to come. Homilies on the Epistles of Paul to the Corinthians 44.1.[6]

16:13 *Stand Firm in Faith*

Stand Firm. Ambrosiaster: They were to be watchful, in case they were secretly attacked in their faith. They were to stand firm, being bold in confessing what they had been taught. They were to be strong in both word and deed, because it is the right combination of these which enables people to mature. Commentary on Paul's Epistles.[7]

Be Strong. Didymus the Blind: Paul tells them to be courageous and strong, like an athlete or soldier of Christ, doing everything with love toward God and each other. Pauline Commentary from the Greek Church.[8]

16:14 *Do Everything in Love*

Do All in Love. Ambrosiaster: Where there is strife and dissension, there is no love. Commentary on Paul's Epistles.[9]

All Troubles Avoidable by Love. Chrysostom: If love had been present, the Corinthians would not have been puffed up, they would not have divided into factions, they would not have gone to law before heathens, or indeed at all. If there had been love in the church, that notorious person would not have taken his father's wife, they would not have looked down on their weaker brethren, and they would not have boasted about their spiritual gifts. Homilies on the Epistles of Paul to the Corinthians 44.2.[10]

16:15 *Devoted to the Service of the Saints*

The First Fruits of Achaia. Didymus the Blind: Paul calls these people the "first fruits" of Achaia, either because they were the first to be converted or because their piety was greater than that of others or because they refused to be ordained on account of their great humility and instead dedicated themselves to the service of others. Pauline Commentary from the Greek Church.[11]

The Household of Stephanas. Chrysostom: Stephanas and his family were not only the first to be converted, they were also a shining example to everyone else. Those who are first ought to set an example to those who come afterward and be servants of others, as these people evidently were. Homilies on the Epistles of Paul to the Corinthians 44.3.[12]

---

[4]NTA 15:12-13. [5]CSEL 81.191. [6]NPNF 1 12:263-64. [7]CSEL 81.191. [8]NTA 15:13. [9]CSEL 81.192. [10]NPNF 1 12:264. [11]NTA 15:13. [12]NPNF 1 12:264.

16:16 Subject to Fellow Workers

SUBJECT TO SUCH MEN. PELAGIUS: Paul says this, because the people he is referring to dwell among the Corinthians, who can profit greatly from their presence. COMMENTARY ON THE FIRST EPISTLE TO THE CORINTHIANS 16.[13]

16:17 Stephanas, Fortunatus and Achaicus

PAUL'S LETTER BEARERS. THEODORET OF CYR: These are the people who took Paul's letter to Corinth, and they are also the ones who had brought the Corinthians' letter about marriage to him. Paul wrote the letter when he was at Philippi. COMMENTARY ON THE FIRST EPISTLE TO THE CORINTHIANS 284.[14]

16:18 Refreshing Paul's Spirit

THEY REFRESHED MY SPIRIT. DIDYMUS THE BLIND: The spirit of a holy person is refreshed by thinking and doing things which are pious, for the spirit strives after what is good. PAULINE COMMENTARY FROM THE GREEK CHURCH.[15]

SHOW THEM RESPECT. CHRYSOSTOM: It is obvious that these must have been the people who told Paul about the situation in Corinth, and no doubt the Corinthians would not have thanked them for it. This is why Paul praises them and urges the Corinthians to show them honor and respect. HOMILIES ON THE EPISTLES OF PAUL TO THE CORINTHIANS 44.3.[16]

---

[13]Migne PL 30:772B. [14]Migne PG 82:371. [15]NTA 15:13. [16]NPNF 1 12:264-65.

16:19-24 FAREWELL

[19]The churches of Asia send greetings. Aquila and Prisca, together with the church in their house, send you hearty greetings in the Lord. [20]All the brethren send greetings. Greet one another with a holy kiss.

[21]I, Paul, write this greeting with my own hand. [22]If any one has no love for the Lord, let him be accursed. Our Lord, come!^c [23]The grace of the Lord Jesus be with you. [24]My love be with you all in Christ Jesus. Amen.

c Greek Maranatha

OVERVIEW: Paul offers them this teaching from his own heart that they might learn to love each other with the same love with which they were loved by the apostle in Christ Jesus (AMBROSIASTER, CHRYSOSTOM). In doing so he rejects all who say that the Lord has not yet come (AMBROSIASTER) and prays earnestly for his coming (CHRYSOSTOM). The holy kiss with which they are to greet each other is a sign of peace (AMBROSIASTER, CHRYSOSTOM). They are not to despise the visible church (ANONYMOUS). Paul prays for grace (THEODORET OF CYR) as he notes that he wrote this in his own hand (DIDYMUS THE BLIND).

16:19 Hearty Greetings

HOUSE CHURCHES. AMBROSIASTER: Paul refers to two kinds of church—public and domestic. One in which everyone assembles, he calls public. The other, in which people gather together through friendship, he calls domestic. Any place where a presbyter celebrates the solemn rites is called a church. COMMENTARY ON PAUL'S EPISTLES.[1]

DO NOT DESPISE THE CHURCH. ANONYMOUS SYRIAC AUTHOR: We should not despise the visible church which brings up everyone as children. Nor should we despise this church of the heart, seeing that she strengthens all who are sick. And we should yearn for the church on high, for she makes perfect all the saints. BOOK OF STEPS 1.3.[2]

16:20 Sending Greetings

A HOLY KISS. AMBROSIASTER: The holy kiss is the sign of peace, doing away with discord. COMMENTARY ON PAUL'S EPISTLES.[3]

FREE FROM DECEIT. CHRYSOSTOM: Having bound them together by his exhortation, Paul goes on to bid them to set the seal on their union by means of the holy kiss, which unites and produces one body. The kiss is holy when it is free of deceit and hypocrisy. HOMILIES ON THE EPISTLES OF PAUL TO THE CORINTHIANS 44.4.[4]

16:21 A Greeting in Paul's Hand

I, PAUL. AMBROSIASTER: Paul makes it clear that he has written the subscript with his own hand. COMMENTARY ON PAUL'S EPISTLES.[5]

WITH HIS OWN HAND. DIDYMUS THE BLIND: To avoid any suspicion of forgery, Paul signs the letter with his own hand. PAULINE COMMENTARY FROM THE GREEK CHURCH.[6]

16:22 Our Lord, Come!

NO LOVE FOR THE LORD. DIDYMUS THE BLIND:

The person who does not keep the commandments has no love for the Lord. PAULINE COMMENTARY FROM THE GREEK CHURCH.[7]

THE LORD HAS NOT YET COME. AMBROSIASTER: Paul is referring to the Jews, who were accursed because they said that the Lord had not yet come. COMMENTARY ON PAUL'S EPISTLES.[8]

LORD, COME. CHRYSOSTOM: By this one word Paul strikes fear into them all. But not only that; he also points out the way of virtue. As our love for God's coming intensifies, there is no kind of sin which is not wiped out. HOMILIES ON THE EPISTLES OF PAUL TO THE CORINTHIANS 44.4.[9]

16:23 The Grace of the Lord Jesus

THE GRACE OF THE LORD. THEODORET OF CYR: It was Paul's usual custom to pray that the grace of Christ would be with those to whom he is writing. COMMENTARY ON THE FIRST EPISTLE TO THE CORINTHIANS 285.[10]

16:24 Love in Christ Jesus

MY LOVE BE WITH YOU. AMBROSIASTER: Because the Corinthians did not love one another, Paul gives them this teaching from himself, in order that they might learn to love each other with the same love with which they were loved by the apostle, not with carnal emotion but in Christ Jesus. COMMENTARY ON PAUL'S EPISTLES.[11]

IN CHRIST JESUS. CHRYSOSTOM: Paul's love is in no way carnal, but spiritual and genuine. This is why he sets the seal on it by adding the words "in Christ Jesus." HOMILIES ON THE EPISTLES OF PAUL TO THE CORINTHIANS 44.4.[12]

---

[1]CSEL 81.193. [2]SFPSL 49. [3]CSEL 81.193. [4]NPNF 1 12:265. [5]CSEL 81.193. [6]NTA 15:13-14. [7]NTA 15:14. [8]CSEL 81.194. [9]NPNF 1 12:265. [10]Migne PG 82:374. [11]CSEL 81.194. [12]NPNF 1 12:266.

THE SECOND EPISTLE
TO THE CORINTHIANS

OVERVIEW OF THE SECOND EPISTLE: Paul writes to them in haste so that, after having been grieved by his rebuke in the first letter, they may be consoled and the fruits of repentance may grow within them (AMBROSIASTER). It was right that, if he had rebuked them when they were at fault, he should commend them now that they had put things right (CHRYSOSTOM). He reminded them of his own labors, not in order to earn any praise from them but to counter the people who were trying to discredit him (THEODORET OF CYR).

LET THE FRUITS OF REPENTANCE GROW. AMBROSIASTER: Paul was aware of the beneficial effect of the first letter which he had sent to Corinth on account of their various errors and now writes a second letter to urge them to obey his teaching. In this letter he focuses on the stubbornness of those who remain incorrigible. But he was greatly relieved to hear that the problems concerning the organization of the church had been put right, and he was sure that the faults of the people would gradually be corrected, since most of them had become obedient to his teaching. The reason he writes to them in haste is so that after having been grieved by his rebuke, they may have consolation and the fruits of repentance may grow within them. Once the Corinthians saw that they were pleasing Paul, they would become all the more eager to do good.

For what is repentance, other than ceasing from error when grief of mind intrudes? COMMENTARY ON PAUL'S EPISTLES.[1]

THEY ARE COMMENDED FOR PUTTING THINGS RIGHT. CHRYSOSTOM: Why does Paul add a second epistle? In the first he had said that he would come to them,[2] but after a long interval he had not appeared but was still delaying, since the Spirit was keeping him busy with far greater matters elsewhere.

That was the first reason why he wrote, but not the only one. The Corinthians had been corrected by the first epistle, since the man who committed fornication and whom they had previously applauded and boasted about had been expelled from their fellowship.[3] In addition, they had collected the money which he had asked for[4] and shown great kindness to Titus when he visited them.[5] For all these reasons, Paul wrote a second epistle, for it was right that if he had rebuked them when they were at fault he should commend them now that they had put things right. Thus the epistle is not very severe, except toward the end. For there were some Jews among them who thought highly of themselves and accused Paul of being a boaster and someone they should pay no attention to.[6]

---

[1]CSEL 81.195. [2]1 Cor 4:19. [3]1 Cor 2:5-6. [4]1 Cor 9:2. [5]1 Cor 7:15. [6]1 Cor 10:10.

To enhance their own credit, these people made a pretense of receiving nothing, and because they had the gift of the gab they were very arrogant. As it was likely that some people would be deceived by them, Paul rebuked them gently, though only after commending what was right in their behavior and attacking their silly pride in Judaism. To sum up, then, this appears to me to be the argument of the epistle. HOMILIES ON THE EPISTLES OF PAUL TO THE CORINTHIANS 1.1-2.[7]

HE RESPONDS TO CRITICISMS. THEODORET OF CYR: The Corinthians reaped great blessing from the first letter, especially since they had such excellent men as Timothy and Titus to help them apply its teachings. But some formerly Jewish believers began to go back to their previous ways and went around blaming the apostle Paul, calling him a backslider and a breaker of the law. They wanted to restore obedience to the law, and even some of the Corin-thians joined them in this. Therefore the apostle wrote to them a second time, after his arrival in Macedonia, apologizing that he had not been able to come to them. He had not broken his promise, but he needed to go to the Macedonians first and would come to them later on. Then he compared the Old with the New Testament, not in order to downgrade the former but in order to reveal its true glory. Afterward he listed his own labors, not in order to earn any praise from them but in order to counter the people who were trying to discredit him. He also urged them to consider the needs of the saints and used the example of the Macedonians as an encouragement to their efforts in this direction. He also told of his own hardships, teaching the Corinthians that they themselves are evidence of true preaching. COMMENTARY ON THE SECOND EPISTLE TO THE CORINTHIANS 287-88.[8]

---

[7]NPNF 1 12:271-72. [8]Migne PG 82:375-78.

1:1-11 THE GOD OF ALL COMFORT

[1]*Paul, an apostle of Christ Jesus by the will of God, and Timothy our brother.*

To the church of God which is at Corinth, with all the saints who are in the whole of Achaia:

[2]*Grace to you and peace from God our Father and the Lord Jesus Christ.*

[3]*Blessed be the God and Father of our Lord Jesus Christ, the Father of mercies and God of all comfort,* [4]*who comforts us in all our affliction, so that we may be able to comfort those who are in any affliction, with the comfort with which we ourselves are comforted by God.* [5]*For as we share abundantly in Christ's sufferings, so through Christ we share abundantly in comfort too.*[a] [6]*If we are afflicted, it is for your comfort and salvation; and if we are comforted, it is for your comfort, which you experience when you patiently endure the same sufferings that we suffer.* [7]*Our hope for you is unshaken; for we know that as you share in our sufferings, you will also share in our comfort.*

[8]*For we do not want you to be ignorant, brethren, of the affliction we experienced in Asia; for we were so utterly, unbearably crushed that we despaired of life itself.* [9]*Why, we*

felt that we had received the sentence of death; but that was to make us rely not on ourselves but on God who raises the dead; [10]he delivered us from so deadly a peril, and he will deliver us; on him we have set our hope that he will deliver us again. [11]You also must help us by prayer, so that many will give thanks on our behalf for the blessing granted us in answer to many prayers.

a Or For as the sufferings of Christ abound for us, so also our comfort abounds through Christ

OVERVIEW: Paul writes as an apostle by the will of God (AMBROSIASTER). He adopts the custom of secular judges who put their name first when they write to those over whom they exercised rightful care (PELAGIUS). Paul addresses the Christians of the entire province of Achaia and not merely those of Corinth, since they all were involved in a common problem and in need of the same remedy (CHRYSOSTOM). He speaks of the Father of mercies (DIDYMUS THE BLIND) because of their many sins, aiming to console (THEODORE OF MOPSUESTIA) those who have repented (AMBROSIASTER). The gifts that the Father gives, the Son also gives (DIDYMUS THE BLIND, AMBROSIASTER, THEODORET OF CYR). Paul explains the cause of his absence (CHRYSOSTOM) and calls for reconciliation of penitents (SEVERIAN OF GABALA).

Our task of comforting those afflicted is best viewed in relation to God's comfort of us in Christ (AMBROSIASTER, GREGORY OF NYSSA). For Christ himself, for whose sake we now suffer, is present with us, consoling and rescuing us (AMBROSIASTER, ORIGEN, CHRYSOSTOM). Our salvation is manifested all the more clearly when we bear all things nobly (BASIL, CHRYSOSTOM, SEVERIAN). Paul recounts his own sufferings so that the Corinthians will realize that what they are going through is nothing by comparison (AMBROSIASTER, CHRYSOSTOM, PELAGIUS). With death staring them in the face (CHRYSOSTOM, PELAGIUS), the affliction of Paul and his companions was so great that they would not have withstood it if God had not been with them (AMBROSIASTER).

1:1a *An Apostle of Christ Jesus*

BY THE WILL OF GOD. AMBROSIASTER: Freed from all anxiety about the Corinthians, Paul confidently declares that he is an apostle of the Lord. In the first letter he said that he was "called an apostle," though he was not approved of by those who had been lured away from his teaching. In order to affirm that his apostleship has been ratified, he adds that he has been made an apostle by the will of God. He writes in association with Timothy, from whom he has heard the good news of the changes which have taken place at Corinth, and he associates the people there with believers in other churches, in order to confirm to them that they have made progress. COMMENTARY ON PAUL'S EPISTLES.[1]

PAUL, AN APOSTLE. PELAGIUS: People ask why it is that Paul puts his own name first, when the normal custom in letters is to put the name of the addressee at the beginning. The reason for this is that he is an apostle who is writing to those who are accountable to him. This is why he adopts the custom of secular judges, who do the same thing when they write to those over whom they exercise authority. Note too that he did not say "Paul and Timothy," because they were not both apostles. But in writing to the Philippians Paul did say that, because it was not so necessary for him to stress his authority in that case.[2] COMMENTARY ON THE SECOND EPIS-

[1]CSEL 81.195-96. [2]Phil 1:1.

TLE TO THE CORINTHIANS I.[3]

TIMOTHY. CHRYSOSTOM: In his first epistle, Paul said that he would send Timothy with the letter,[4] but now he associates Timothy with him. Why is this? Evidently Timothy had already accomplished his mission and returned to be with Paul. Having been for some time in Asia, they had crossed into Macedonia, from which he wrote this letter. By associating Timothy with himself, Paul increased respect for him and displayed his own great humility, since Timothy was far less well known than Paul. But love brings all things together. HOMILIES ON THE EPISTLES OF PAUL TO THE CORINTHIANS 1.2.[5]

TIMOTHY AND TITUS. THEODORET OF CYR: Timothy and Titus were both sent to Corinth, but Paul did not mention Titus in the letter because he was the one who actually carried it there. COMMENTARY ON THE SECOND EPISTLE TO THE CORINTHIANS 289.[6]

1:1b *With All the Saints*

THE CHURCH AT CORINTH. CHRYSOSTOM: Once more, Paul calls the Corinthians a church, in order to bind them together, and "saints," implying that if anyone is impure he is not included in this greeting. HOMILIES ON THE EPISTLES OF PAUL TO THE CORINTHIANS 1.2.[7]

ALL THE SAINTS. DIDYMUS THE BLIND: Paul does not always mention other people besides himself in his salutations. I think that he does this when one of his associates is well-known to the intended recipients. "With all the saints" is ambiguous. Either it means all the saints who were with Paul, or else it means all the saints who were at Corinth. PAULINE COMMENTARY FROM THE GREEK CHURCH.[8]

1:1c *The Whole of Achaia*

NEEDING THE SAME REMEDY. CHRYSOSTOM: Why

does Paul address the Christians of the entire province, and not merely those of the city? The reason, I think, is that they were all involved in a single, common problem and were therefore all in need of the same remedy. HOMILIES ON THE EPISTLES OF PAUL TO THE CORINTHIANS 1.2.[9]

1:2 *Grace to You and Peace*

THE GRACE OF GOD. AMBROSIASTER: Since the gift of God and of Christ is one and the same, Paul wants them to be partakers in the grace of God, that is, in the grace of Jesus Christ. COMMENTARY ON PAUL'S EPISTLES.[10]

THE LORD JESUS CHRIST. DIDYMUS THE BLIND: The works that the Father does the Son also does, and the gifts that the Father gives, the Son also gives. It is to be understood from this that although we know God as Father, we are still servants of Jesus Christ. We do not call him "brother" but Lord. For he is the only-begotten Son by nature, not by adoption, and is Lord of all those who have been made children of God. PAULINE COMMENTARY FROM THE GREEK CHURCH.[11]

1:3 *The God of All Comfort*

THE FATHER OF MERCIES. AMBROSIASTER: Paul always speaks in this way, indicating the personhood of the Father and the Son, even though they are of one substance. Now he is giving much relief to people who had been grieved by his rebuke, for when they hear that God is not just the Father of creation but the Father of mercies as well, they will have hope and be assured that they have been rebuked so that they may find the mercy of God, once they have mended their ways. Through repentance they were being born again and made anew, which was not just a pardon but a restoration of their

---

[3]Migne PL 30:771D—773A. [4]1 Cor 16:10. [5]NPNF 1 12:272. [6]Migne PG 82:378. [7]NPNF 1 12:272. [8]NTA 15:14. [9]NPNF 1 12:272. [10]CSEL 81.196. [11]NTA 15:14.

previous state of existence. He puts "mercies" in the plural because of their many sins, his aim being to console those who have been grieved on account of their faults. COMMENTARY ON PAUL'S EPISTLES.[12]

THE SOURCE OF MERCY. DIDYMUS THE BLIND: God alone is holy and good, sanctifying others and making them good. He alone is blessed, because he gives blessing and does not receive it from someone else. Likewise, he is the Father of mercies by nature, because he is the source of all mercy and not because he has acquired this from anyone else. PAULINE COMMENTARY FROM THE GREEK CHURCH.[13]

COMFORT IN SUFFERING. THEODORE OF MOPSUESTIA: Paul does not begin with suffering but with comfort, giving thanks for that before going on to explain that it came about through suffering. PAULINE COMMENTARY FROM THE GREEK CHURCH.[14]

THE FATHER OF OUR LORD. THEODORET OF CYR: Christ himself teaches us that God is his Father.[15] COMMENTARY ON THE SECOND EPISTLE TO THE CORINTHIANS 289.[16]

SHARED GLORY AND HONOR. CYRIL OF JERUSALEM: "Blessed be the God and Father of our Lord Jesus Christ." For in the thought of God, let the thought of Father be included, so that the glory which we ascribe to the Father and the Son with the Holy Spirit may be perfectly free from difference. For the Father has not one glory and the Son another, but their glory is one and the same, since the Son is the Father's sole-begotten. When the Father is glorified, the Son shares in enjoyment of his glory, because the Son draws his glory from the honoring of the Father. Again, whenever the Son is glorified, the Father of so excellent a Son is greatly honored. THE CATECHETICAL LECTURES 6.1.[17]

1:4 Comfort in All Our Affliction

TWO KINDS OF CONSOLATION. AMBROSIASTER: Paul mentions two kinds of consolation. One is the sort by which people who are suffering distress unjustly on account of the name of Christ find consolation in being set free. The other is the consolation of those who, when they are grieved because of sins, receive consolation from the fact that hope of forgiveness is promised to them when they mend their ways. This happens amid a community of those who have received consolation from God and been rescued from distress. COMMENTARY ON PAUL'S EPISTLES.[18]

THE CAUSE OF HIS ABSENCE. CHRYSOSTOM: The Corinthians were very upset that the apostle had not come to them, in spite of his promise, and that he had spent all his time in Macedonia, apparently preferring them to the Corinthians. Paul therefore prepares to meet this feeling against him by declaring the cause of his absence, though without stating it directly. HOMILIES ON THE EPISTLES OF PAUL TO THE CORINTHIANS 1.3.[19]

PENITENTS RECONCILED. SEVERIAN OF GABALA: Paul sets this down beforehand because he is about to say that the man who had been condemned because of his sin should be reconciled by God's comforting power. PAULINE COMMENTARY FROM THE GREEK CHURCH.[20]

COMFORT FROM THE SPIRIT. GREGORY OF NYSSA: But what does it mean to say that the kingdom of God is within us? What else than the gladness which comes from on high to souls through the Spirit? For this is like an image and a deposit and a pattern of everlasting grace which the souls of the saints enjoy in the time which is to come. So the Lord summons us through the activity of the Spirit to salvation through our afflictions and to a sharing in the

[12]CSEL 81.196-97. [13]NTA 15:15. [14]NTA 15:196. [15]Lk 10:21. [16]Migne PG 82:378. [17]LCC 4:126. [18]CSEL 81.197. [19]NPNF 1 12:273. [20]NTA 15:278.

goods of the Spirit and his own graces. For he says: "Who comforts us in our afflictions, that we also may be able to comfort those who are in any distress." ON THE CHRISTIAN MODE OF LIFE.[21]

1:5 Sharing in Suffering and Comfort

SUFFERING AND COMFORT. ORIGEN: If as the sufferings of Christ abound so also comfort abounds through Christ, let us welcome the great encouragement of Christ's sufferings and let them abound in us, if we indeed yearn for the abundant comfort with which all who mourn will be comforted, though perhaps it will not be alike for everyone. For if the comfort were alike for everyone, it would not be written, "As the sufferings of Christ abound for us, so also our comfort abounds through Christ." Those who share in sufferings will share also in the comfort in proportion to the suffering they share with Christ. And we learn this from the one who made such statements with unshaken conviction, for "we know that as you share in our sufferings, you will also share in our comfort." EXHORTATION TO MARTYRDOM 42.[22]

SHARING IN CHRIST'S COMFORT. AMBROSIASTER: It is clear that Christ himself, for whose sake we are suffering, is present with us, consoling us and rescuing us from trouble by his divine intervention. COMMENTARY ON PAUL'S EPISTLES.[23]

ABUNDANT CONSOLATION. CHRYSOSTOM: Paul did not want to depress the disciples with an exaggerated account of his sufferings, so instead of that he declares how great the consolation was that he received, reminding them of Christ. HOMILIES ON THE EPISTLES OF PAUL TO THE CORINTHIANS 1.4.[24]

VISION OF SOUL. ISAAC OF NINEVEH: Now by "consolation" he means *theoria*, which, being interpreted, is vision of soul. Vision gives birth to consolation. ASCETICAL HOMILIES 74.[25]

1:6 Afflicted for Their Comfort

A CONSOLATION TO BELIEVERS. AMBROSIASTER: Because they were suffering persecutions from unbelievers for the sake of believers, they would be set free by God's help. This was viewed as a consolation to believers, so that they would not desert their faith because of such a stumbling block. The injuries suffered by the apostles were a temptation to believers to abandon their faith. When they saw the preachers overcome by force, they were inclined to wonder whether the promise of Christ might be an empty one. COMMENTARY ON PAUL'S EPISTLES.[26]

BEARING ALL THINGS NOBLY. CHRYSOSTOM: What humility can compare with this, in that Paul raises to a level of equality with himself those who so obviously fell far short of him. Our salvation is demonstrated more clearly when we bear all things nobly. The work of salvation does not consist only of believing but of enduring evil when it is done to us. HOMILIES ON THE EPISTLES OF PAUL TO THE CORINTHIANS 2.1.[27]

THE SAME SUFFERINGS. SEVERIAN OF GABALA: If the apostles suffered, how much more are the others likely to suffer! PAULINE COMMENTARY FROM THE GREEK CHURCH.[28]

1:7 Hope Unshaken

PAUL'S COMFORT ALSO THEIRS. CHRYSOSTOM: See how far they had advanced since Paul wrote his first epistle. Now his hope for them was unshaken by their behavior. Paul also tells them that if he has been comforted, they will be comforted as well. If the Corinthians regarded Paul's sufferings as their own, then his comfort would also be theirs. By saying this, Paul hoped

[21]FC 58:152. [22]CWS 72. [23]CSEL 81.197. [24]NPNF 1 12:274. [25]AHSIS 364. [26]CSEL 81.197-98. [27]NPNF 1 12:277. [28]NTA 15:278.

that he would be able to encourage them and get them to accept his absence from them more easily. Homilies on the Epistles of Paul to the Corinthians 2.2.[29]

1:8a *The Affliction Experienced*

Affliction in Asia. Theodoret of Cyr: I think that Paul is referring here to the riot at Ephesus which was provoked by Demetrius the silversmith.[30] Commentary on the Second Epistle to the Corinthians 291.[31]

For Their Sake. Ambrosiaster: Paul wanted the Corinthians to know what evils he was enduring for the sake of their salvation. That way, they would not take it too badly if their own errors were admonished by people who were enduring such harsh treatment for their sake. Commentary on Paul's Epistles.[32]

1:8b *Despairing of Life*

Unbearably Crushed. Pelagius: Paul recounts his own sufferings so that the Corinthians will realize that what they are going through is nothing by comparison. The disciple who grieves over his own hurt will be comforted when he sees that his master is suffering far more. Commentary on the Second Epistle to the Corinthians 1.[33]

Countering Despair. Chrysostom: It was very comforting to know what others were doing and what was happening to them. If the news was bad, people would be encouraged to be energetic and thus would be less likely to fall. If the news was good, they could all rejoice together. Here, as we can see, things had been very bad indeed. Homilies on the Epistles of Paul to the Corinthians 2.3.[34]

1:9 *Relying on God*

Death Staring at Them. Ambrosiaster: Paul means that there was such a violent upsurge of evil against preachers of the faith that death was staring them in the face. But God does not refuse his protection to people in extreme danger, especially when they belong to him. He rescued them when they were in deep despair. Their affliction was so great that they would not have withstood it if God had not been with them. Commentary on Paul's Epistles.[35]

The Sentence of Death. Chrysostom: Paul was expecting death, but things had not come to that point. In the natural course of events, he should have died, but God did not allow that to happen in order that Paul would learn not to trust in himself but in God. Homilies on the Epistles of Paul to the Corinthians 2.3.[36]

To Rely Not on Ourselves. Pelagius: Death itself teaches us that all human help is inadequate and that our only hope is to rely on him who can raise us from the dead. Commentary on the Second Epistle to the Corinthians 1.[37]

A Call to Leave the Past Behind. Basil: Perfect renunciation, therefore, consists in not having an affection for this life and keeping before our minds the "answer of death, that we should not trust in ourselves." But a beginning is made by detaching oneself from all external goods: property, vainglory, life in society, useless desires, after the example of the Lord's holy disciples. James and John left their father Zebedee and the very boat upon which their whole livelihood depended. Matthew left his counting house and followed the Lord, not merely leaving behind the profits of his occupation but also paying no attention to the dangers which were sure to befall both himself and his family at the hands of the magistrates because he had left the tax accounts unfinished. To Paul, finally, the

---

[29]NPNF 1 12:277-78. [30]Acts 19:23-41. [31]Migne PG 82:379. [32]CSEL 81.198. [33]Migne PL 30:773D. [34]NPNF 1 12:278. [35]CSEL 81.198-99. [36]NPNF 1 12:279. [37]Migne PL 30:774A.

whole world was crucified, and he to the world. THE LONG RULES 8.[38]

1:10 Delivered from Peril

DELIVERED FROM DEATH. CHRYSOSTOM: Although the resurrection is a thing of the future, Paul shows that it happens every day. When a person is delivered from the gates of death, it is really a kind of resurrection. The same thing can be said of those who have been delivered out of serious illness or unbearable trials. HOMILIES ON THE EPISTLES OF PAUL TO THE CORINTHIANS 2.4.[39]

1:11 Answer to Many Prayers

HELP US BY PRAYER. CHRYSOSTOM: Paul said this both to stir them up to pray for others and to accustom them to give thanks to God for whatever happened to others. People who do this for others will be much more likely to do it for themselves as well. Paul also teaches them humility and deep, fervent love. For if he, who was so high above them, admitted that he was saved by their prayers, think how modest and humble they should have been as a result. HOMILIES ON THE EPISTLES OF PAUL TO THE CORINTHIANS 2.5.[40]

---

[38]FC 9:254. [39]NPNF 1 12:279. [40]NPNF 1 12:280.

1:12-14 PAUL'S RECORD

[12]For our boast is this, the testimony of our conscience that we have behaved in the world, and still more toward you, with holiness and godly sincerity, not by earthly wisdom but by the grace of God. [13]For we write you nothing but what you can read and understand; I hope you will understand fully, [14]as you have understood in part, that you can be proud of us as we can be of you, on the day of the Lord Jesus.

OVERVIEW: Paul's testimony of conscience was made with simplicity and sincerity (AUGUSTINE), qualities that belong most truly to God (AMBROSIASTER) and that come from grace (DIDYMUS THE BLIND, THEODORET OF CYR). They are now bearing behavioral fruit (CHRYSOSTOM). The facts of his suffering ministry (CHRYSOSTOM) speak for themselves (THEODORET OF CYR). His words are backed up by his actions (AMBROSIASTER). Regarding them as partners in his ministry (AMBROSIASTER, CHRYSOSTOM), Paul chides them for having understood him only in part (THEODORET OF CYR).

1:12a The Testimony of Our Conscience

SIMPLICITY AND SINCERITY. AMBROSIASTER: The boast of Paul's conscience was simplicity and sincerity, qualities which belong to God's teaching. In his first letter Paul had criticized teaching based on earthly wisdom, and he alludes to that again here.[1] He accused preachers of that kind both because they preached according to the wisdom of the world and because they were doing it in order to make money. For that reason, Paul was unwilling to receive any payment from the Corinthians. COMMENTARY ON PAUL'S EPISTLES.[2]

CONSOLATION FROM GOD. CHRYSOSTOM: The pre-

---

[1]1 Cor 1:17—2:16. [2]CSEL 81.200.

vious consolation was from God, but now it is the fruit of their own behavior. People who live uprightly will see the power of God at work in their lives and be comforted. Homilies on the Epistles of Paul to the Corinthians 3.1.[3]

TRUE GLORY. Augustine: Cato is rightly praised more than Caesar, for, as Sallust says of him: "The less he sought for glory the more it followed him." However, the only kind of glory they were greedy for was merely the reputation of a good name among men; whereas virtue rests not on others' judgments but on the witness of one's own conscience and therefore is better than a good name. Hence the apostle says: "For our glory is this, the testimony of our conscience." . . . Therefore, virtue should not pursue the glory, honor and dominion which they sought, even though their good men sought to reach these ends by good means, but these things should follow virtue. There is no true virtue save that which pursues the end which is man's true good. It follows, therefore, that Cato should not have sought the honors he sought, but his city should have given them to him because of his virtue and without his asking for them. City of God 5.12.[4]

1:12b By the Grace of God

NOT BY EARTHLY WISDOM. Didymus the Blind: Earthly wisdom means knowledge of material things. Those who have this kind of wisdom have no room for the wisdom of the Spirit, which they regard as foolishness. Pauline Commentary from the Greek Church.[5]

ADDING NOTHING. Theodoret of Cyr: Paul is saying that he teaches only what he has been taught by the grace of God, adding nothing of his own to it. Commentary on the Second Epistle to the Corinthians 292.[6]

1:13 What You Can Understand

BACKED BY ACTIONS. Ambrosiaster: What Paul says is backed up by his actions. It is through actions that we learn what a person really thinks. Commentary on Paul's Epistles.[7]

WRITING ONLY FACTS. Chrysostom: Paul is not boasting. All he is doing is writing facts which the Corinthians themselves would acknowledge to be true. Homilies on the Epistles of Paul to the Corinthians 3.1.[8]

WHAT YOU CAN READ AND UNDERSTAND. Theodoret of Cyr: Paul says that, in spite of the accusations leveled against him, he does not preach one thing and think another. The facts speak for themselves and prove that he is right. Commentary on the Second Epistle to the Corinthians 292.[9]

1:14 On the Day of the Lord Jesus

PROUD OF YOU. Ambrosiaster: Paul asserts that his boasting over his obedient children is noticed and that this will be to their advantage on the day of judgment. Commentary on Paul's Epistles.[10]

PARTNERS IN HIS MINISTRY. Chrysostom: Paul cuts at the root of the envy which his speech might occasion by making the Corinthians sharers and partners in the glory of his good works. Homilies on the Epistles of Paul to the Corinthians 3.2.[11]

THEY HAVE UNDERSTOOD ONLY IN PART. Theodoret of Cyr: Paul says that the Corinthians have understood only in part, because they have not yet rejected the false accusations which had been made against him. Commentary on the Second Epistle to the Corinthians 292.[12]

---

[3]NPNF 1 12:286. [4]FC 8:270. [5]NTA 15:17. [6]Migne PG 82:382. [7]CSEL 81.200. [8]NPNF 1 12:287. [9]Migne PG 82:382. [10]CSEL 81.200-201. [11]NPNF 1 12:287. [12]Migne PG 82:382.

1:15-24 PAUL'S EXCUSE

[15]Because I was sure of this, I wanted to come to you first, so that you might have a double pleasure;[b] [16]I wanted to visit you on my way to Macedonia, and to come back to you from Macedonia and have you send me on my way to Judea. [17]Was I vacillating when I wanted to do this? Do I make my plans like a worldly man, ready to say Yes and No at once? [18]As surely as God is faithful, our word to you has not been Yes and No. [19]For the Son of God, Jesus Christ, whom we preached among you, Silvanus and Timothy and I, was not Yes and No; but in him it is always Yes. [20]For all the promises of God find their Yes in him. That is why we utter the Amen through him, to the glory of God. [21]But it is God who establishes us with you in Christ, and has commissioned us; [22]he has put his seal upon us and given us his Spirit in our hearts as a guarantee.

[23]But I call God to witness against me—it was to spare you that I refrained from coming to Corinth. [24]Not that we lord it over your faith; we work with you for your joy, for you stand firm in your faith.

b Other ancient authorities read favor

Overview: The apostle had not paid Corinth the visit that he had promised, but he tells the Corinthians that he did not change his mind lightly (Ambrosiaster). When a spiritually minded person does not do what he had originally planned, it is because something more providential has emerged for the salvation of others' souls (Ambrosiaster, Chrysostom). In Christ the will to obey is never ambivalent or uncertain (Ambrosiaster). The Father's promises find their yes in him. They abide, unlike the outcome of Paul's earlier promise to come to them (Chrysostom, Augustine). Paul stayed away from Corinth because if he had gone he would have had to take on the role of disciplinarian, which neither he nor they wanted (Ambrosiaster, Chrysostom). The true flock is duly identified (Severian of Gabala). God has established us (Ambrosiaster, Chrysostom) with a firm faith in Christ, anointed us and made us worthy to receive the seal of the Holy Spirit (Cyril of Jerusalem, Ambrose, Theodoret of Cyr).

1:15 A Double Pleasure

They Have Mended Their Ways. Ambrosiaster: This is proof that the Corinthians have mended their ways, because earlier on Paul did not want to see them at all. Commentary on Paul's Epistles.[1]

A Double Pleasure to Visit. Chrysostom: The pleasure would be double because it would come both from his writings and from his presence. Homilies on the Epistles of Paul to the Corinthians 3.2.[2]

1:16 To and from Macedonia

On the Way to Macedonia. Theodoret of Cyr: Some people think that Paul said this aggressively, because in the first epistle he had promised the Corinthians that he would visit

---

[1]CSEL 81.201. [2]NPNF 1 12:288.

the Macedonians first and then come to Corinth. But as they were not willing to wait for him, he gives them a piece of his mind. COMMENTARY ON THE SECOND EPISTLE TO THE CORINTHIANS 293.[3]

1:17 Was I Vacillating?

GOOD REASONS FOR CHANGING HIS MIND. AMBROSIASTER: Paul dismisses the charge that he cannot be trusted by telling the Corinthians that he did not change his mind lightly. He had good reasons for not doing what he had originally planned. When a spiritually minded person does not do what he intends to, it is because he has in mind something more providential for the salvation of someone's soul. The apostle did not carry out his original plan in order that the Corinthians might become better men and women. He delayed his coming specifically because there were some among them who had not purified themselves, and he was waiting for that to happen first. This is spiritual thinking. Carnal thinking, by contrast, makes changes of plan in order to suit personal desires, not in order to do what is beneficial. COMMENTARY ON PAUL'S EPISTLES.[4]

LED BY THE SPIRIT. CHRYSOSTOM: The carnal man, who is riveted to the present world and completely caught up in it, is outside the sphere of the Spirit's influence and has the power to go everywhere, doing whatever he likes. But the servant of the Spirit is led by the Spirit. He cannot just do what he likes. He is dependent on the Spirit's authority. Paul was not able to come to Corinth because it was not the Spirit's will for him to go there. HOMILIES ON THE EPISTLES OF PAUL TO THE CORINTHIANS 3.3.[5]

1:18 A Trustworthy Word

FLATTERERS OMIT PARTS OF THE TRUTH. AMBROSIASTER: Paul is saying that God's preaching through him has been faithful. Flatterers, on

the other hand, frequently fail to mention things which are true in order not to offend people. COMMENTARY ON PAUL'S EPISTLES.[6]

RELIABLE PREACHING. CHRYSOSTOM: Paul had to explain why he could not keep his promise, so that the Corinthians would not distrust his preaching. In fact, what Paul preached was reliable. His promise to come to them had been from himself, but the message he proclaimed was from God, and God cannot lie. HOMILIES ON THE EPISTLES OF PAUL TO THE CORINTHIANS 3.3.[7]

1:19 In Christ It Is Always Yes

AN UNCHANGING WILL. AMBROSIASTER: Competent preachers ought to be unambiguous about what they say. Say nothing that is not beneficial. Given that our human will often tends in ambivalent directions, Paul is insistent that he is not acting according to his will but according to what he knows will be helpful. In Christ, of course, this problem does not exist, because he always wills what is beneficial. Furthermore, Christ's will never changes and is never uncertain. COMMENTARY ON PAUL'S EPISTLES.[8]

NOT UNSAYING WHAT I SAID. CHRYSOSTOM: I have never unsaid what I said before. My talk was not now this, now that. That would be not faith but a wandering mind. HOMILIES ON THE EPISTLES OF PAUL TO THE CORINTHIANS 3.4.[9]

SPEAKING THE FATHER'S TRUTH. AUGUSTINE: And when we confess that we have lied, we speak the truth, for we are saying what we know, and we know that we have lied. That Word, however, which is God and more powerful than ourselves, cannot do this. . . . And of himself he does not speak, but of that Father is

---

[3]Migne PG 82:382. [4]CSEL 81.201-2. [5]NPNF 1 12:288. [6]CSEL 81.202. [7]NPNF 1 12:289. [8]CSEL 81.202-3. [9]NPNF 1 12:289.

everything that he speaks, since the Father speaks it in a unique way. The great power of that Word is that he cannot lie, because in him there cannot be yes and no but yes, yes; no, no. For that is not even to be called a word if it is not true. THE TRINITY 15.15.[10]

1:20 All the Promises of God

THE PROMISES OF GOD FIND THEIR YES IN CHRIST. CHRYSOSTOM: Paul's preaching promised many things. He talked about being raised to life again and of being taken up into heaven. He talked about incorruption and those great rewards which awaited them. These promises abide unchanging, unlike Paul's own promise of coming to them. They are always true. HOMILIES ON THE EPISTLES OF PAUL TO THE CORINTHIANS 3.4.[11]

WE UTTER THE AMEN THROUGH THE SON. AMBROSIASTER: Paul means that the work of the Father and the Son is one. When the Father gives the Spirit, the Son gives him too, because the Holy Spirit comes from both of them. He is thinking of the Trinity here because he has been speaking about the perfecting of mankind. The whole sum of perfection is found in the Trinity. COMMENTARY ON PAUL'S EPISTLES.[12]

1:21 Established in Christ

GENTILES ESTABLISHED IN CHRIST. AMBROSIASTER: Paul is saying that Christ confirms the Gentiles in the faith promised to the Jews, because he has made us both one. COMMENTARY ON PAUL'S EPISTLES.[13]

THE ROOT AND FOUNT. CHRYSOSTOM: If the root and the fount are properly established, how can it be that we shall not enjoy the fruits which will spring from them? One thing leads inevitably to the other. HOMILIES ON THE EPISTLES OF PAUL TO THE CORINTHIANS 3.4.[14]

STAND FIRM AGAINST THE EVIL ONE. CHRYSOSTOM: After these words, after the renunciation of the devil and the covenant with Christ, inasmuch as you have henceforth become his very own and have nothing in common with that evil one, he straightway bids you to be marked and places on your forehead the sign of the cross. That savage beast is shameless, and when he hears those words, he grows more wild—as we might expect—and desires to assault you on sight. Hence God anoints your countenance and stamps thereon the sign of the cross. In this way God holds in check all the frenzy of the Evil One, for the devil will not dare to look on such a sight. Just as if he had beheld the rays of the sun and had leaped away, so will his eyes be blinded by the sight of your face and he will depart. For through the chrism the cross is stamped on you. . . . And that you may again know that it is not a man but God himself who anoints you by the hand of the priest, listen to St. Paul when he says: "It is God who makes both us and you stand firm in Christ, who has anointed us." BAPTISMAL INSTRUCTIONS 11.27.[15]

THE TRINITY'S COMMON WORK. AMBROSE: Therefore, you received of the sacraments. . . . Because you have been baptized in the name of the Trinity, in all that we have done the mystery of the Trinity has been preserved. Everywhere the Father, the Son and the Holy Spirit, one operation, one sanctification. . . . How? God, who anointed you, and the Lord sealed you and placed the Holy Spirit in your heart. Therefore, you have received the Holy Spirit in your heart. THE SACRAMENTS 6.2.5, 6.[16]

1:22 God's Seal on Us

THE SOURCE OF ALL GOOD. THEODORET OF CYR: God is the source of all good things. He has given us firm faith in Christ. He has anointed

---

[10]FC 45:488. [11]NPNF 1 12:289. [12]CSEL 81.203-4. [13]CSEL 81.203. [14]NPNF 1 12:290. [15]ACW 31:169. [16]FC 44:320.

us and made us worthy to receive the seal of the Holy Spirit. COMMENTARY ON THE SECOND EPISTLE TO THE CORINTHIANS 295.[17]

THE FLOCK IS RIGHTLY MARKED. SEVERIAN OF GABALA: Shepherds brand their sheep so as to distinguish the ones which belong to them from others. This is what Christ has done to us. PAULINE COMMENTARY FROM THE GREEK CHURCH.[18]

THE PLEDGE OF THE SPIRIT. AUGUSTINE: I have learned from your letter, as well as from the statement of the bearer, that you ardently desire a letter from me, in the belief that it will bring you the greatest consolation. I must not refuse or delay this letter, but you will have to see what good you can draw from it. Let the faith and hope and charity, which are diffused through the hearts of the faithful by the Holy Spirit, be your consolation. We receive a little of it in this life as a pledge to make us learn how to long for its fullness. You must not think of yourself as left alone, since in the interior life you have Christ, present in your heart by faith. LETTER TO ITALICA.[19]

THE SPIRIT'S PRESENCE. CYRIL OF JERUSALEM: To realize that Paul was filled with the Holy Spirit, and like him all the apostles, and all who after them believe in Father, Son and Holy Spirit, pay attention to the clear words of Paul himself. . . . "God who also stamped us with his seal and gave us the Spirit as a pledge." CATECHESIS 17.32.[20]

1:23 It Was to Spare You

HE WENT ELSEWHERE. AMBROSIASTER: Here Paul is addressing people who apparently wanted to reform but were not making much of an effort in that direction. It was to spare them until they pulled themselves together that he went elsewhere for the time being. Paul did not want them to think that he despised them as unworthy. Once they realized that, they would

mend their ways, and then the apostle would come to visit them. COMMENTARY ON PAUL'S EPISTLES.[21]

THE ALTERNATIVE WOULD HAVE BEEN DISAGREEABLE. CHRYSOSTOM: Paul stayed away from Corinth at least partly because if he had gone there he would have had to take on the role of disciplinarian, which neither he nor they wanted. HOMILIES ON THE EPISTLES OF PAUL TO THE CORINTHIANS 4.1.[22]

1:24a Not to Lord It Over Your Faith

FAITH NOT COMPELLED. AMBROSIASTER: Paul says this because faith is not a matter of compulsion but of free will. COMMENTARY ON PAUL'S EPISTLES.[23]

1:24b We Work with You

THEIR NEED TO REFORM. CHRYSOSTOM: Paul did not want to go to Corinth in order to plunge the Corinthians into despair. Instead, he stayed away so that they would reform themselves, fearing what might otherwise happen if he did come. HOMILIES ON THE EPISTLES OF PAUL TO THE CORINTHIANS 4.1.[24]

WE WORK WITH YOU. THEODORET OF CYR: Paul added this because his authority was evidently what the Corinthians were afraid of. COMMENTARY ON THE SECOND EPISTLE TO THE CORINTHIANS 296.[25]

NO FAULT WITH THEIR FAITH. THEODORE OF MOPSUESTIA: Paul says that he finds no fault with their faith. However, there are some other things which need to be put right, and he is concerned with those. PAULINE COMMENTARY FROM THE GREEK CHURCH.[26]

---

[17]Migne PG 82:383. [18]NTA 15:281. [19]FC 18:50. [20]FC 64:116. [21]CSEL 81.204. [22]NPNF 1 12:294. [23]CSEL 81.204. [24]NPNF 1 12:294. [25]Migne PG 82:386. [26]NTA 15:197.

2:1-4 PAUL'S PAIN

[1]For I made up my mind not to make you another painful visit. [2]For if I cause you pain, who is there to make me glad but the one whom I have pained? [3]And I wrote as I did, so that when I came I might not suffer pain from those who should have made me rejoice, for I felt sure of all of you, that my joy would be the joy of you all. [4]For I wrote you out of much affliction and anguish of heart and with many tears, not to cause you pain but to let you know the abundant love that I have for you.

OVERVIEW: The apostle was deeply disturbed when he wrote to the Corinthians (AMBROSIASTER). Candid communication would be the necessary prelude to the joy that would come from their obedience (AMBROSIASTER). Even if he were to make the Corinthians sorry he would be glad, since their sorrow would be proof of how much they esteemed him (CHRYSOSTOM). The physician of souls may cause temporary pain.

2:1 Not Another Painful Visit

ALL SUFFER. AMBROSIASTER: Paul was afraid that if he rebuked a few he would cause pain to many, because all the members of a body suffer when one of them is in pain. COMMENTARY ON PAUL'S EPISTLES.[1]

ANOTHER PAINFUL VISIT. CHRYSOSTOM: Paul had obviously had one bad experience at Corinth and wanted to avoid another one, for a second occasion would be even worse. HOMILIES ON THE EPISTLES OF PAUL TO THE CORINTHIANS 4.1.[2]

2:2 Causing Pain

A NECESSARY PRELUDE. AMBROSIASTER: Paul did not want to hurt the Corinthians, but he saw it as the necessary prelude to the joy which would come from their obedience. COMMENTARY ON PAUL'S EPISTLES.[3]

SORROW PROOF OF ESTEEM. CHRYSOSTOM: What Paul is saying is that even if he were to make the Corinthians sorry he would be glad, since their sorrow would be proof of how much they held him in esteem. HOMILIES ON THE EPISTLES OF PAUL TO THE CORINTHIANS 4.2.[4]

TRUST THE PHYSICIAN'S WISDOM. BASIL: It is shameful, indeed, that they who are sick in body place so much confidence in physicians that, even if these cut or burn or cause distress by their bitter medicines, they look upon them as benefactors, while we do not share this attitude toward the physicians of our souls when they secure our salvation for us by laborious discipline. The apostle says, however: "Who is he then who can make me glad, but the same who is made sorrowful by me." . . . It behooves one who looks to the end, therefore, to consider him a benefactor who causes us pain which is according to God. THE LONG RULES 52.[5]

2:3 Paul's Joy the Joy of All

THE APOSTLE'S JOY. AMBROSIASTER: The purification of the people is the apostle's joy. COMMENTARY ON PAUL'S EPISTLES.[6]

---

[1]CSEL 81.205. [2]NPNF 1 12:295. [3]CSEL 81.205. [4]NPNF 1 12:295. [5]FC 9:329. [6]CSEL 81.205.

Paul's Joy, Their Joy. Chrysostom: Paul had already said that he was gladdened by their sorrow. This may have seemed arrogant and harsh, so to soften the impact he adds this: He knew that if he were happy they would be happy and that if he were sad, they would be sad too. . . . It is with weighty meaning that I do not come to you, because I feel not hate or aversion but rather exceeding love. Homilies on the Epistles of Paul to the Corinthians 4.2.[7]

2:4 The Apostle's Abundant Love

An Abundant Love. Ambrosiaster: It is obvious that when someone admonishes another and in the process he himself suffers more grief over it than the person being rebuked, he is not doing this in order to cause grief but to show what deep love he has for the other. Someone who rebukes another without feeling this way merely tramples on his feelings. Commentary on Paul's Epistles.[8]

Wrongdoing Inflicted Pain. Chrysostom: Paul shows here that he was not less affected than those who had sinned, but more. He could hardly bear the pain which the Corinthians' wrongdoing was causing him. Homilies on the Epistle of Paul to the Corinthians 4.3.[9]

---

[7]NPNF 1 12:295. [8]CSEL 1.206. [9]NPNF 1 12:296.

2:5-11 THE CHURCH'S PAIN

[5]But if any one has caused pain, he has caused it not to me, but in some measure—not to put it too severely—to you all. [6]For such a one this punishment by the majority is enough; [7]so you should rather turn to forgive and comfort him, or he may be overwhelmed by excessive sorrow. [8]So I beg you to reaffirm your love for him. [9]For this is why I wrote, that I might test you and know whether you are obedient in everything. [10]Any one whom you forgive, I also forgive. What I have forgiven, if I have forgiven anything, has been for your sake in the presence of Christ, [11]to keep Satan from gaining the advantage over us; for we are not ignorant of his designs.

Overview: Paul asks the Corinthians not only to lift the censure of the fornicator but also to restore him to his former status (Basil, Theodoret of Cyr), for to punish a man without healing him means nothing (Chrysostom). He wanted to see that they were as obedient in restoring the sinner as they had been in disciplining him (Chrysostom, Ambrosiaster, Pelagius). Satan can destroy not only by leading into fornication but also by the immoderate sorrow that can follow on repentance for it (Chrysostom, Didymus the Blind, Ambrosiaster). The pain caused to Paul was shared by all the saints at Corinth (Ambrosiaster).

2:5 Causing Pain to All

Pain Caused to the Saints. Ambrosiaster: By "you all" Paul means the saints among the Corinthians. For they were divided into those who were saints and those who were not, but it is the former he is addressing here. COMMENTARY ON PAUL'S EPISTLES.[1]

PAUL'S ANGER SHARED BY ALL THE CORINTHIANS. CHRYSOSTOM: Paul's anger and indignation at the man who had committed fornication was shared by all the Corinthians. He thus softens their anger with him by declaring that they also suffered in his indignation. HOMILIES ON THE EPISTLES OF PAUL TO THE CORINTHIANS 4.4.[2]

2:6 Punishment Enough

THIS PUNISHMENT IS ENOUGH. CHRYSOSTOM: Notice that Paul nowhere mentions the crime, because the time had now come to forgive. HOMILIES ON THE EPISTLES OF PAUL TO THE CORINTHIANS 4.4.[3]

BY THE MAJORITY. THEODORET OF CYR: Paul reveals the zeal of the Corinthians, for they had all turned against this man, just as he had ordered them to. COMMENTARY ON THE SECOND EPISTLE TO THE CORINTHIANS 297.[4]

THE SAFETY OF COMMUNITY. BASIL: Community life offers more blessings than can be fully and easily enumerated. It is more advantageous than the solitary life both for preserving the goods bestowed on us by God and for warding off the external attacks of the Enemy. . . . For the sinner, moreover, the withdrawal from his sin is far easier if he fears the shame of incurring censure from many acting together—to him, indeed, might be applied the words: "To him who is such a one, this rebuke is sufficient which is given by many"—and for the righteous man, there is a great and full satisfaction in the esteem of the group and in their approval of his conduct. THE LONG RULES 7.[5]

THE COMMUNITY'S LOVE REAFFIRMED. CHRYSOSTOM: However, be mindful of this: if you become lazy and indifferent, sin will seize you at one time or another. Therefore, show concern, if not for your brother, then at least for yourself. Repel the disease, overpower the decay, and interrupt the spreading of the cancerous sore. Paul spoke of these things and of much more than these. Since he ordered the Christians in Corinth to hand the fornicator among them over to Satan, he said later that "the sinner changed" and became better. "For such a one this punishment by the majority is enough. Therefore, reaffirm your love for him." Even though Paul made him a common enemy, an adversary to all, expelled him from the fold and cut him off from the body, note how much concern he showed in order to bind him back indissolubly and rejoin him to the church. For he did not say, "simply love him" but "reaffirm your love for him." In other words, reveal your friendship as certain, unshakable, fervent, ardent and fiery; present your love with the same strength as the previous hatred. "What happened? Tell me, did you not surrender him to Satan?" "Yes," he said, "but not for him to remain in Satan's hands, but to be quickly delivered from his tyrannical dominion." Pay careful attention, however, to the very thing I was saying about how much Paul feared discouragement as a great weapon of the devil. He said, "Reaffirm your love for him," and then added the reason, "lest such a one should be swallowed up by excessive sorrow." ON REPENTANCE AND ALMSGIVING 1.3.22.[6]

2:7 Forgive and Comfort Him

OVERWHELMED BY SORROW. AMBROSIASTER: A person who is swallowed up in too much affliction will turn in desperation to committing sins. True repentance, on the other hand, is a turning away from sin. If this person repents, he will prove that he is sorry for what he has done. COMMENTARY ON PAUL'S EPISTLES.[7]

---

[1]CSEL 81.206. [2]NPNF 1 12:296. [3]NPNF 1 12:296. [4]Migne PG 82:387. [5]FC 9:250-51. [6]FC 96:9. [7]CSEL 81.207.

Restoring the Man. Chrysostom: Paul asks the Corinthians not only to lift the censure but also to restore the man to his former status, for to punish a man without healing him means nothing. Note too how Paul keeps the man himself humble, so that he will not become worse as a result of having been forgiven. For although he had both confessed and repented, Paul makes it clear that he obtained forgiveness not so much by his repentance as by God's free gift. Homilies on the Epistles of Paul to the Corinthians 4.4.[8]

2:8 Reaffirm Your Love for Him

Reaffirm Your Love. Pelagius: Through your love the offender will know that he has received forgiveness. Commentary on the Second Epistle to the Corinthians 2.[9]

Paul Takes On the Part of the Advocate. Chrysostom: Paul no longer commands but begs, not as a teacher but as an equal. He puts the Corinthians in the judgment seat and takes on the part of an advocate, asking them to reaffirm their love for him. Homilies on the Epistles of Paul to the Corinthians 4.4.[10]

Unite the Flock. Theodoret of Cyr: Paul's command now is that they should unite the member to the body, return the sheep to the flock and show him their most sincere love and affection. Commentary on the Second Epistle to the Corinthians 298.[11]

2:9 Testing Their Obedience

Obedient in Everything. Ambrosiaster: As far as anyone can tell, Paul was commending the Corinthians for their obedience in other respects. They had already put matters right in their church administration, and now he was asking them to be obedient in this matter as well. Commentary on Paul's Epistles.[12]

Testing Them. Chrysostom: Paul needs to see that the Corinthians are as obedient in restoring the sinner as they had been in punishing him. For the punishment might have proceeded in part from envy and malice, but if they now proceed to restore him in love, that will show that their obedience is pure. This is the test of true disciples: if they obey not only when ordered to do something but on their own as well. Homilies on the Epistles of Paul to the Corinthians 4.5.[13]

2:10 Forgiven for Their Sake

Paul's Forgiveness. Ambrosiaster: Paul is practicing what he preaches. He has the right to give orders, but he cannot refuse to do himself what he is asking others to do. In the first letter he condemned this man's crime, in the hope that everyone would loathe him for it,[14] but now he wants him to be received back and prays that they will no longer show any anger toward him. The Corinthians evidently did not have the apostle's wisdom and did not understand that this ought to be done immediately. Commentary on Paul's Epistles.[15]

Soften Contentiousness. Chrysostom: Paul lets the Corinthians take the lead and tells them that he will follow. This is the best way to soften an exasperated and contentious spirit. Then, lest he should make them careless and they should refuse forgiveness, he again constrains them by saying that he himself has already forgiven the man. Homilies on the Epistles of Paul to the Corinthians 4.5.[16]

2:11 Aware of Satan's Designs

Avoid Despair. Ambrosiaster: Paul did not want this brother, being filled with sorrow and

---

[8]NPNF 1 12:296-97. [9]Migne PL 30:776D. [10]NPNF 1 12:297. [11]Migne PG 82:387. [12]CSEL 81.207. [13]NPNF 1 12:297. [14]1 Cor 5:1-13. [15]CSEL 81.207-8. [16]NPNF 1 12:297-98.

being rigorously excluded from the love of the church, to despair of himself. The devil, who is always subtle in his tricks, would then see that this man's mind was an easy prey, approach him and suggest that at least he should enjoy the things of the present, given that he has been denied any hope of future reward. Thus the brother would perish, being possessed by the devil, even though an opportunity for repentance had been given him. Commentary on Paul's Epistles.[17]

To Deny Satan an Advantage. Chrysostom: Satan can destroy even under the show of piety. For he can destroy not only by leading into fornication but even by the opposite, the immoder-

ate sorrow which can follow on repentance for it. To take us by sin is his proper work, but to ensnare us in our repentance is an even more subtle disgrace, because that is our weapon, not his. Homilies on the Epistles of Paul to the Corinthians 4.5.[18]

Satan's Designs. Didymus the Blind: The problem is not merely to recognize Satan's designs but to play into them. Paul knows their dynamics, not so as to be engaged in them but so as not to be entrapped by them. Pauline Commentary from the Greek Church.[19]

---

[17]CSEL 81.208-9. [18]NPNF 1 12:298. [19]NTA 15:19.

2:12-17 PAUL'S PREACHING

[12]*When I came to Troas to preach the gospel of Christ, a door was opened for me in the Lord;* [13]*but my mind could not rest because I did not find my brother Titus there. So I took leave of them and went on to Macedonia.*

[14]*But thanks be to God, who in Christ always leads us in triumph, and through us spreads the fragrance of the knowledge of him everywhere.* [15]*For we are the aroma of Christ to God among those who are being saved and among those who are perishing,* [16]*to one a fragrance from death to death, to the other a fragrance from life to life. Who is sufficient for these things?* [17]*For we are not, like so many, peddlers of God's word; but as men of sincerity, as commissioned by God, in the sight of God we speak in Christ.*

Overview: Without Titus's presence Paul found the work in Troas almost unbearable, since there was so much opposition to him (Ambrosiaster, Chrysostom, Theodoret of Cyr), so he went on to Macedonia. Although the persecution there seemed like a disgrace, it was a great honor (Eusebius, Chrysostom, Ambrosiaster). As an aroma is sensed rather than seen (Pelagius), so is the knowledge of

God's grace (Ambrosiaster), which has a sweet savor (Chrysostom). So put an altar of incense in your innermost heart (Clement of Alexandria, Origen). To unbelievers the cross has the smell of death, but to believers it is the fragrance of life (Ambrosiaster, Chrysostom, Augustine). Paul refused to imitate false peddlers of God's word who claimed rewards instead of offering the free gift of salvation. He spoke not by his own wisdom but by the power that comes from Christ (Chrysostom).

2:12 A Door Opened for the Gospel

A Door Was Opened. Ambrosiaster: Paul means that when he got to Troas to preach the gospel of Christ, there were people who received the message. Commentary on Paul's Epistles.[1]

Not the Time to Say More. Didymus the Blind: In Acts [16:9] it says that a man of Macedonia appeared to Paul in a dream and asked him to come over and help them. Paul does not mention this incident in his letter, evidently because he realized that this was not the right time to say such things about himself. Pauline Commentary from the Greek Church.[2]

The Fragrance of Life and Death. Augustine: And again, in his second letter to the Corinthians, the same apostle says, "When I had come to Troas for the gospel of Christ, and a door was opened to me in the Lord, I had no rest in my spirit, because I did not find Titus my brother, but bidding them farewell, I went into Macedonia." To whom did he declare farewell except to those who had believed, that is to say, to those in whose hearts a door was opened for him to preach the gospel? But note well what he adds: "Now thanks be to God, who always makes us triumph in Christ and manifests the aroma of Christ to God, in those who are saved and in those who perish; to some indeed the odor of death to death but to others the fragrance of life to life." Behold why this most intrepid soldier, this most invincible defender of grace, gives thanks. Behold why he gives thanks—that the apostles are the good odor of Christ to God, both in those who are saved by his grace and in those who perish in virtue of his judgment. Predestination of the Saints 20.41.[3]

2:13 Going On to Macedonia

Work and Opposition. Ambrosiaster: Lacking the consolation of Titus's presence Paul found the work unbearable, because there was so much opposition to him. For although some people had opened their hearts and accepted the Word of God, there were many unbelievers who reacted with impudent hostility. One lone voice could not teach the new believers and fend off these attacks at the same time. Therefore Paul said goodbye to those who had received him and left for Macedonia. Commentary on Paul's Epistles.[4]

Titus's Absence. Chrysostom: Paul did not say that the absence of Titus hindered the salvation of those who were about to convert, nor that he neglected them for this reason, but that he continued to be concerned for Titus, showing thereby how serious a matter a brother's absence is. Homilies on the Epistles of Paul to the Corinthians 5.1.[5]

His Concern for Titus. Theodoret of Cyr: Paul mentions Titus here for a purpose. Since he was the one who took the letter to Corinth, Paul wanted the church there to appreciate his worth. Commentary on the Second Epistle to the Corinthians 299.[6]

2:14 Christ Leads Us in Triumph

Christ Is Always Ahead of Us. Ambrosiaster: For God to lead us in triumph in Christ is to make us victors in the faith of Christ, so that when unbelief has been trodden underfoot, faith may have its trophy. Commentary on Paul's Epistles.[7]

Thanks Be to God. Chrysostom: Paul was in constant affliction everywhere he went, but this did not draw him into despair. On the contrary, he rejoiced and gave thanks, because although

---

[1]CSEL 81.209. [2]NTA 15:19. [3]FC 86:267. [4]CSEL 81.209.
[5]NPNF 1 12:301. [6]Migne PG 82:390. [7]CSEL 81.209-10.

persecution might seem like a disgrace, in fact it was a very great honor. HOMILIES ON THE EPISTLES OF PAUL TO THE CORINTHIANS 5.1.[8]

COURAGE TESTED. EUSEBIUS: A whole band of soldiers, Ammon and Zeno and Ptolemy and Ingenuus, and with them an old man Theophilus, had taken their stand before the tribunal. When a certain man was being tried as a Christian and was inclined toward denying the faith, they, standing by, gnashed their teeth, and made signs with their faces, and stretched out their hands and gestured with their bodies. When the attention of all was directed toward them, before any could otherwise seize them, they rushed up first to the bench, saying that they were Christians, so that the governor and his assessors became fearful. Those who were being tried appeared most courageous in the face of what they were about to suffer, while their judges were afraid. And these paraded from the court and rejoiced in their testimony, as God "led them in triumph gloriously." ECCLESIASTICAL HISTORY 6.41.[9]

SWEET-SMELLING SERVICE. CLEMENT OF ALEXANDRIA: By washing the feet of his disciples with his own hands as he sent them forth to noble deeds, the Savior manifested in an excellent way their journeying to bestow graces upon the nations.[10] He purified that journeying in anticipation by his own power. The perfume left its aroma after it and suggests the sweet-smelling accomplishments that reach everyone. The suffering of the Lord, indeed, has filled us with its fragrance. . . . CHRIST THE EDUCATOR 2.7.63.[11]

2:15 The Aroma of Christ

A SWEET AROMA OF CHRIST. ORIGEN: Put an altar of incense in your innermost heart. Be a sweet aroma of Christ. HOMILIES ON EXODUS 9.[12]

TO SPEAK THE TRUTH IS AROMATIC. AMBROSIASTER: The aroma of the knowledge of God comes from Christ and through Christ. The reason why Paul said "aroma" was this: Some things are recognized by their smell, even though they are invisible. God, who is invisible, wishes to be understood through Christ. The preaching of Christ reaches our ears just as an aroma reaches our nostrils, bringing God and his only-begotten Son right into the midst of his creation. A person who speaks the truth about Christ is just such a good aroma from God, worthy of praise from the one who believes. But one who makes erroneous assertions about Christ has a bad smell to believers and unbelievers alike. COMMENTARY ON PAUL'S EPISTLES.[13]

A FRAGRANCE SENSED. PELAGIUS: Paul calls the knowledge of God an aroma. Its presence is sensed rather than seen. COMMENTARY ON THE SECOND EPISTLE TO THE CORINTHIANS 2.[14]

THE GOSPEL HAS A SWEET SAVOR. CHRYSOSTOM: Whether a person is saved or lost, the gospel continues to have its own power. The light, even when it blinds someone, is still light. Honey, though it is bitter to those who are sick, is still sweet. So also the gospel has a sweet savor to all, even if those who do not believe it are lost. HOMILIES ON THE EPISTLES OF PAUL TO THE CORINTHIANS 5.2.[15]

A MINISTRY OF DEATH. AUGUSTINE: Why, then, if the law is good, is it called a "ministry of death"? Because "sin, that it might be shown to be sin, worked death for me through that which is good." Do not marvel when it is said of the preaching of the gospel, "We are a sweet aroma of Christ to God, in them that are being saved and in them who perish, to the one an aroma of life to life, to the other an aroma of death to death." Now the law is called a "ministry of death" to the Jews, for whom it was written on

---

[8]NPNF 1 12:301. [9]FC 29:75. [10]Cf. Jn 13. [11]FC 23:148. [12]FC 71:342. [13]CSEL 81.210. [14]Migne PL 30:777D. [15]NPNF 1 12:302.

stone, to symbolize their hardness of heart. But this does not apply to those who fulfill the law in charity. For charity is the fulfillment of the law. To SIMPLICIAN—ON VARIOUS QUESTIONS 1.17.[16]

THE SAME FRAGRANCE, DIFFERENT RESPONSES. ORIGEN: For, as the apostle says, "We are a good aroma of Christ," but he adds, "To some a fragrance of life to life, but to others an odor of death to death." So also the prophetic word is "a sweet fragrance" to those who believe, but to the doubting and unbelieving and those who confess that they are Pharaoh's people, it becomes a detestable odor. HOMILIES ON EXODUS 3.[17]

2:16 Fragrance of Death or Life

THE SMELL OF DEATH TO UNBELIEVERS. AMBROSIASTER: To unbelievers the preaching of the cross is the smell of death. On hearing the Word of God they receive it as if it were a plague from which death knocks on the door. But to others it is the fragrance of life. To believers the Word of God is a messenger of eternal life. It affects them in accordance with their faith. COMMENTARY ON PAUL'S EPISTLES.[18]

TO CORRECT AND TO DESTROY. CHRYSOSTOM: If anyone is lost he has only himself to blame. Soothing ointment is said to suffocate pigs. Light is blinding to the weak. It is in the nature of good things not only to correct what is close to them but also to destroy the opposite, and in this way their power is displayed. HOMILIES ON THE EPISTLES OF PAUL TO THE CORINTHIANS 5.3.[19]

PUNISHMENT AND COMFORT. AUGUSTINE:

Through an evil man divine providence can both punish and comfort. For the impiety of the Jews was the Jews' downfall and yet provided salvation for the Gentiles. Again, divine providence through a good man can both condemn and help, as the apostle says: "To some we are the scent of life to life, but to others we are the scent of death to death." But every tribulation is either a punishment of the impious or a testing of the just. . . . Further, peace and quiet from disruptive times can both profit the good and corrupt the evil. EIGHTY-THREE DIFFERENT QUESTIONS 27.[20]

2:17 Commissioned by God

NOT PEDDLERS OF GOD'S WORD. AMBROSIASTER: Paul is alluding to various false apostles who used to corrupt the Word of God through bad interpretation. Some of them were so zealous for Jewish tradition that they did not teach properly about Christ. COMMENTARY ON PAUL'S EPISTLES.[21]

SPEAKING IN CHRIST. CHRYSOSTOM: Paul will not imitate the false apostles, who claim rewards for themselves. For corruption occurs when one sells for money what one ought to give freely. Paul speaks in Christ, not by his own wisdom but by the power which comes from him. HOMILIES ON THE EPISTLES OF PAUL TO THE CORINTHIANS 5.3.[22]

---

[16]LCC 6:384. [17]FC 71:257. [18]CSEL 81.211. [19]NPNF 1 12:302. [20]FC 70:52. [21]CSEL 81.212. [22]NPNF 1 12:302-3.

3:1-4 PAUL'S REFERENCES

[1]*Are we beginning to commend ourselves again? Or do we need, as some do, letters of recommendation to you, or from you?* [2]*You yourselves are our letter of recommendation, written on your[c] hearts, to be known and read by all men;* [3]*and you show that you are a letter from Christ delivered by us, written not with ink but with the Spirit of the living God, not on tablets of stone but on tablets of human hearts.*

[4]*Such is the confidence that we have through Christ toward God.*

c *Other ancient authorities read* our

OVERVIEW: The Corinthians themselves are all the recommendation Paul needed. They are like a personal letter from Christ (CLEMENT OF ALEXANDRIA, ORIGEN, BASIL, AMBROSE), written with the Spirit of God, unlike letters written in ink, which fade (AMBROSIASTER, PELAGIUS, CHRYSOSTOM, SEVERIAN OF GABALA, THEODORET OF CYR). This is the basis of our confidence in God (JEROME).

3:1 Needing Commendation?

COMMENDING OURSELVES? DIDYMUS THE BLIND: Paul gently expresses his surprise that the Corinthians are still unaware of the implication of his apostleship. PAULINE COMMENTARY FROM THE GREEK CHURCH.[1]

AVOID SEDUCTION. PELAGIUS: Paul is not saying this in order to boast but so that the Corinthians will not be seduced by others. COMMENTARY ON THE SECOND EPISTLE TO THE CORINTHIANS 3.[2]

NO MORE REMINDERS. THEODORET OF CYR: Paul is telling the Corinthians that they should have been commending him without any reminders of this kind. COMMENTARY ON THE SECOND EPISTLE TO THE CORINTHIANS 301.[3]

3:2 A Letter of Recommendation

EVIDENCE OF SALVATION. AMBROSIASTER: Evidence of salvation is an epistle in itself. The salvation of the Corinthians was in Paul's heart and in the hearts of those who were with him, for he was always thinking about it. COMMENTARY ON PAUL'S EPISTLES.[4]

A LIVING LETTER. CHRYSOSTOM: "If we needed to be commended to others," he says, "we would have produced you before them rather than a letter." HOMILIES ON THE EPISTLES OF PAUL TO THE CORINTHIANS 6.1.[5]

3:3 Written on Human Hearts

WRITTEN WITH THE SPIRIT. AMBROSIASTER: The things which are promised are eternal and are therefore said to be written with the Spirit of God, unlike temporal things written in ink, which fades and loses its power to record anything. COMMENTARY ON PAUL'S EPISTLES.[6]

RECEIVING THE SPIRIT. PELAGIUS: It was clear to everybody that the Corinthians owed their conversion to Paul's teaching, which the Holy Spirit had confirmed. We know that we belong to Christ if we have received the Spirit. COM-

[1]NTA 15:21. [2]Migne PL 30:778A. [3]Migne PG 82:391. [4]CSEL 81.213. [5]NPNF 1 12:306. [6]CSEL 81.213.

mentary on the Second Epistle to the Corinthians 3.[7]

Human Hearts. Chrysostom: Here Paul bears witness not only to their love but also to their good works, since by their behavior they can demonstrate to everybody the high worth of their teacher. What letters would have done to gain respect for the apostle, the Corinthians achieve by their life and behavior. The virtues of disciples commend the teacher more than any letter. They are an epistle of Christ, having the law of God written in their hearts. God wrote that law, but Paul and his companions prepared them to receive the writing. For just as Moses hewed stones and tables,[8] so Paul shaped their souls. Homilies on the Epistles of Paul to the Corinthians 6.1-2.[9]

Grace Higher Than Law. Severian of Gabala: Paul shows how much better the grace of the Spirit is than the law and how much higher the preaching of the apostles is than the dispensation of the prophets. Pauline Commentary from the Greek Church.[10]

The Two Testaments. Theodoret of Cyr: Forgetting the false teachers, Paul goes on to the heart of the matter and expounds the difference between the two Testaments. Commentary on the Second Epistle to the Corinthians 302.[11]

The Law of God on Human Hearts. Ambrose: But with the Word of God before us we are able to formulate opinions on what is good and what is evil. One of these we naturally understand we should avoid as evil, and the other we understand has been recommended to us as a good. In this respect we seem to be listening to the very voice of the Lord, whereby some things are forbidden and other things are advised. If a person does not comply with the injunctions which are believed to have been once ordained by God, he is considered to be liable to punishment. The commands of God are impressed in our hearts by the Spirit of the living God. We do not read these commands as if they were recorded in ink on a tablet of stone. Hence, in our own thought we formulate a law. . . . There is something, therefore, like the law of God which exists in the hearts of men. Paradise 8.39.[12]

The Finger of God. Ambrose: By this finger, as we read, God wrote on the stone tablets which Moses received. For not with a finger of flesh did God make the forms and elements of those letters which we read; by his Spirit he gave the law. And so the apostle said: "For the law is spiritual, which indeed is written not with ink but with the Spirit of the living God; not in tables of stone but in fleshly tables of the heart." For, if the letter of the apostle is written in the Spirit, what stands in the way of our being obliged to believe that the law of God was written not in ink but in the Spirit of God, which surely does not stain the secrets of our heart and mind but illuminates them? The Holy Spirit 3.3.13.[13]

The Spirit as Scribe. Basil: As the pen is an instrument for writing when the hand of an experienced person moves it to record what is being written, so also the tongue of the just man, when the Holy Spirit moves it, writes the words of eternal life in the hearts of the faithful, dipped "not in ink but in the Spirit of the living God." The scribe, therefore, is the Holy Spirit, because he is wise and an apt teacher of all. And the Spirit writes swiftly, because the movement of his mind is swift. The Spirit writes thoughts in us, "not on tablets of stone but on fleshly tablets of the heart." In proportion to the size of the heart, the Spirit writes in hearts more or less, either things evident to all or things more obscure, according to the heart's previous purity. Because of the speed with

---

[7]Migne PL 30:778B-C. [8]Ex 34:1-4. [9]NPNF 1 12:306. [10]NTA 15:284. [11]Migne PG 82:391. [12]FC 42:317. [13]FC 44:158-59.

which the writings have been finished, all the world now is filled with the gospel. HOMILY 17 ON PSALM 44.[14]

THE TABLETS OF THE HEART. CLEMENT OF ALEXANDRIA: These are the laws of reason, words that impart inspiration, written by the hand of the Lord, not on tablets of stone but inscribed in the hearts of men, provided only that those hearts are not attached to corruption. Therefore, the tablets of the hard of heart have been broken, that the faith of little ones might be formed in impressionable minds. Both laws served the Word as means of educating humanity, the one through Moses, the other through the apostles. But what a means of education is the one given through the apostles! CHRIST THE EDUCATOR 3.12.94.[15]

THE PENCIL OF CHRIST. ORIGEN: Now we have not received this longing from God on the condition that it should not or could not ever be satisfied. . . . So when even in this life men devote themselves with great labor to sacred and religious studies, although they obtain only some small fragments out of the immeasurable treasures of divine knowledge, yet [they gain this advantage, that] they occupy their mind and understanding with these questions and press onward in their eager desire. Moreover they derive much assistance from the fact that by turning their mind to the study and love of truth they render themselves more capable of receiving instruction in the future. For when one wishes to paint a picture, if he first sketches with the faint touch of a light pencil the outlines of the proposed figure and inserts suitable marks to indicate features afterward to be added, this preliminary drawing with its faint outline undoubtedly renders the canvas more

prepared to receive the true colors. So it will be with us, if only that faint form and outline is inscribed "on the tablets of our heart" by the pencil of our Lord Jesus Christ. . . . It is clear, then, that to those who have now in this life a kind of outline of truth and knowledge there shall be added in the future the beauty of the perfect image. ON FIRST PRINCIPLES 2.11.4.[16]

3:4 Confidence Through Christ

A PREPARING MINISTRY. AMBROSIASTER: Paul's purpose was to show that the ancient prophets did not have this position of trust in God's eyes, because theirs was a preparing ministry. COMMENTARY ON PAUL'S EPISTLES.[17]

THE DIVINE SUFFICIENCY. JEROME: The apostle Paul, after describing in a few words the benefits of God, states in conclusion: "And for such offices, who is sufficient?"[18] Whence he also says in another place: "Such is the assurance we have through Christ toward God. Not that we are sufficient of ourselves to think anything, as from ourselves, but our sufficiency is from God. He also it is who made us fit ministers of the new covenant, not of the letter but of the spirit; for the letter kills, but the spirit gives life." Do we still dare to boast about the free will and treat with insult the benefits of God the Giver, when the chosen vessel [Paul] also writes very clearly: "But we carry this treasure in vessels of clay, to show that the abundance of our power is God's and not ours"?[19] AGAINST THE PELAGIANS 3.9.[20]

---

[14]FC 46:281-82. [15]FC 23:270. [16]OFP 150. [17]CSEL 81.214. [18]2 Cor 2:16. [19]2 Cor 4:7. [20]FC 53:361.

3:5-11 THE NEW COVENANT

[5]*Not that we are competent of ourselves to claim anything as coming from us; our competence is from God,* [6]*who has made us competent to be ministers of a new covenant, not in a written code but in the Spirit; for the written code kills, but the Spirit gives life.* [7]*Now if the dispensation of death, carved in letters on stone, came with such splendor that the Israelites could not look at Moses' face because of its brightness, fading as this was,* [8]*will not the dispensation of the Spirit be attended with greater splendor?* [9]*For if there was splendor in the dispensation of condemnation, the dispensation of righteousness must far exceed it in splendor.* [10]*Indeed, in this case, what once had splendor has come to have no splendor at all, because of the splendor that surpasses it.* [11]*For if what faded away came with splendor, what is permanent must have much more splendor.*

OVERVIEW: Our human insufficiencies point to God's sufficiency (AUGUSTINE, FULGENTIUS, CASSIODORUS). The law kills sinners, but grace revives them if they repent (AMBROSIASTER, PELAGIUS). Moses had the written code but not the Spirit, whereas we have been entrusted with the gifts of the Spirit (ORIGEN, BASIL, AMBROSE, AUGUSTINE, PELAGIUS). Sin caused the dispensation of death, but the law brought in punishment and showed sin for what it was; the law did not cause sin (CHRYSOSTOM, THEODORE OF MOPSUESTIA). Although the law of Moses was intended to be beneficial, it became the law of death. Then came the law of faith, which not only forgives sinners but also makes them righteous (AMBROSIASTER, CHRYSOSTOM). The law condemns sinners; grace justifies them (ORIGEN, THEODORET OF CYR, AMBROSIASTER). The difference between the face of Moses and the glory of Christ is the difference between the picture and the person it portrays (AMBROSIASTER, JEROME, CHRYSOSTOM, THEODORET OF CYR).

3:5 Competence Is from God

NOT FROM US. SEVERIAN OF GABALA: By "from us" Paul means "from one another." PAULINE

COMMENTARY FROM THE GREEK CHURCH.[1]

HUMAN INSUFFICIENCY, GOD'S SUFFICIENCY.
AUGUSTINE: Therefore it rests not in human power but on God's, that we have the "power to be made the sons of God."[2] They receive it from him who inspires in the human heart devout thoughts, through which it possesses "faith which works though love."[3] For acquiring and retaining this good, and for progressing perseveringly in it to the end, "We are not sufficient to think anything as of ourselves, but our sufficiency is from God,"[4] in whose power are our heart and our thoughts. GIFT OF PERSEVERANCE 8.20.[5]

THE TRUE SOURCE OF GOODNESS AND GRACE.
CASSIODORUS: Since the Lord's call comes before all merit, and he does not find a thing deserving but makes it so, for that reason it is called gratuitous; otherwise it would be called just. So this is the good will which summons and draws us. We can think or perform nothing which benefits us without our obtaining it from the Author of goodness. As Paul says, "For we can-

---

[1]NTA 15:284. [2]Jn 1:12. [3]Gal 5:6. [4]2 Cor 3:5. [5]FC 86:286.

not think anything of ourselves, as of ourselves, but our sufficiency is from God." So let the Pelagians' madness fall silent, lest in seeking falsely to ascribe some goodness to itself the will is instead deprived of him who bestows it. EXPLANATION OF THE PSALMS 5.13.[6]

THE HOLY GIVING OF GOD. FULGENTIUS: In this debt which you demand from us and you repay, do not doubt that I am assisted, so that God, who works in us both to will and to bring to completion the work of the good will, himself gives that I may worthily think and worthily speak. For in good thoughts, "Not that of ourselves we are qualified to take credit for anything as coming from us; rather our qualification comes from God." And for this reason we do not fail for want because by a free gift our sufficiency is from him in whom there is no want. Just as he does not need our goods, so he always abounds in giving, nor does he become needy by giving who gives that by which he is always filled; nor is there any pleasing gift of thought, word or deed offered by us to him which he himself has not given with free kindness. Wherefore the holy giving of God is always free because no demand based on human merits has ever preceded, because even if a human being has any good merit, it comes from him from whom comes "every good and perfect gift."[7] TO PROBA 3.5.[8]

THE TRUE BEGINNING OF ALL GOOD THINGS. FULGENTIUS: Nor can any human being be fit either for thinking or for doing anything good unless he is first helped by the free gift of divine assistance. "For God is the one who, for his own good purpose, works 'in them' both to desire and to work,"[9] as the vessel of election [Paul] affirms; also by his teaching, we know that "we of ourselves are not qualified to take credit for anything as coming from us; rather our qualification comes from God."[10] Therefore, he supplies us with all the sufficiency of good, and his fullness is not lessened when he gives who kindly

shares every good with us that we may have them. . . . Everything which is created, just as before it was created it did not exist, so before it receives was unable to possess; and just as it cannot subsist without the working of him who made it, so it is unable to will or to do good unless God continuously deigns to help. For from him is the beginning of a good will, from him the ability to do good works, from him perseverance in a good way of life, from him in the present age is given true humility of heart and in the future the happiness of eternal reward, that they may be without end happy who now without falsity are humble. TO PROBA 4.6.[11]

3:6 Ministers of a New Covenant

MATERIAL AND SPIRITUAL. ORIGEN: The letter means what is material and the spirit what is intellectual, which we also call spiritual. ON FIRST PRINCIPLES 1.1.2.[12]

THE UNNECESSARY PART CUT OFF. AMBROSE: Rightly, then, does Paul say that "the letter kills, but the spirit gives life." The letter circumcised a small part of the body, but the understanding spirit keeps the circumcision of the entire soul and body so that chastity might be preserved, frugality loved and the unnecessary parts cut off (for nothing is so unnecessary as the vices of greed, the sins of lust, which did not belong to nature but which sin has caused). Bodily circumcision is the symbol, but the reality is the spiritual circumcision; the one cuts off a member, the other sin. LETTER TO CLEMENTIANUS 68.[13]

THE SPIRIT GIVES LIFE. AMBROSIASTER: The Spirit, who is the law of faith which is not written but which is contained in the rational soul, is life-giving, drawing to himself those who are guilty of mortal sin, so that they may be made

---

[6]ACW 51:88. [7] Jas 1:17. [8]FC 95:313. [9]Phil 2:13. [10]2 Cor 3:5. [11]FC 95:336. [12]OFP 8. [13]FC 26:407.

righteous and cease altogether from sinning. COMMENTARY ON PAUL'S EPISTLES.[14]

THE WRITTEN CODE KILLS. PELAGIUS: The law kills the sinner, but grace revives him if he repents. There are some people who say that the literal sense of Scripture is the thing which kills, but this is to forget that not all Scripture is meant to be taken literally, nor can allegory be pressed into service in every passage. For just as some things are said in an allegorical way, so other things, like the commandments, will lose all their meaning if they are taken allegorically and become destructive. The spiritual meaning of Scripture is not found in allegory but in letting the meaning of the text explain the essence of truth. COMMENTARY ON THE SECOND EPISTLE TO THE CORINTHIANS 3.[15]

MINISTERS OF A NEW COVENANT. CHRYSOSTOM: The law was spiritual, but it did not bestow the Spirit. Moses had letters but not the Spirit, whereas we have been entrusted with the giving of the Spirit. HOMILIES ON THE EPISTLES OF PAUL TO THE CORINTHIANS 6.2.[16]

THE LETTER FULFILLED. AUGUSTINE: How does the Spirit give life? By causing the letter to be fulfilled, so that it may not kill. EASTER SEASON 251.7.[17]

THE ENLIVENING SPIRIT. AMBROSE: Moreover, what wonder is it if the Spirit works life, who gives life as the Father does, who gives life as the Son does? Moreover, who would deny that to give life is of the eternal Majesty? . . . Therefore, let us see whether the Spirit is enlivened, or himself enlivens. But it is written: "The letter kills, but the Spirit gives life."[18] So the Spirit gives life. But that you may understand that the quickening of the Father and of the Son and of the Holy Spirit is not divided, learn that there is also a oneness of quickening, since God himself quickens through the Spirit; for Paul said: "He that raised up Jesus Christ from the dead

shall quicken also your mortal bodies, because of his Spirit dwelling in you."[19] THE HOLY SPIRIT 2.4.29, 30.[20]

FREEDOM, NOT FEAR. AUGUSTINE: Therefore, you that fear the Lord, praise him, and that you may worship him, not as slaves but as free men, learn to love him whom you fear, and you will be able to praise what you love. The men of the Old Testament, fearing God, because of the letter which terrifies and kills and not yet possessing "the spirit which quickens,"[21] ran to the temple with sacrifices and offered up bloody victims. They were ignorant of what was foreshadowed by them, although they were a figure of the Blood to come, by which we have been redeemed. LETTER TO HONORATUS 140.19.[22]

GOD GIVES WHAT GOD COMMANDS. AUGUSTINE: Therefore, God commands continence, and he gives continence; he commands by the law, he gives by the Spirit; for the law without grace makes sin abound,[23] and the letter without the spirit kills.[24] He commands so as to make us learn how to ask the help of grace when we try to obey his commandments and in our weakness fall wearied under the law, and also to make us grateful to him who helps us if we have been able to perform any good work. LETTER TO HILARIUS 157.[25]

FOOLISH ZEAL. AUGUSTINE: Could it be possible that the law is not of God? None but an irreligious man would think that. But, because the law commands by the letter and does not help by the Spirit, whoever listens to the letter of the law in such wise as to think that it is enough for him to know what it commands or forbids, whoever trusts in the strength of his own free will to accomplish it and does not take refuge in faith in order to be assisted in his ap-

---

[14]CSEL 81.214. [15]Migne PL 30:779A-B. [16]NPNF 1 12:307. [17]FC 38:322. [18]2 Cor 3:6. [19]Rom 8:11. [20]FC 44:107. [21]2 Cor 3:6. [22]FC 20:96. [23]Rom 5:20. [24]2 Cor 3:6. [25]FC 20:325.

proach to the Spirit that quickens lest the letter find him guilty and kill him,[26] that man has a zeal of God, but not according to knowledge. LETTER TO PAULINUS 186.[27]

THE COMMANDMENT ITSELF CANNOT OFFER LIFE. AUGUSTINE: For, if you take away the Spirit, how does the law avail? It makes a prevaricator. On that account the Scripture says: "The letter kills."[28] The law orders and you do not obey. . . . Something is commanded, and you do not do it; something is forbidden, and you do it. Behold, "the letter kills." EASTER SEASON 250.3.[29]

JOIN THE SPIRIT TO THE LAW. AUGUSTINE: Let the Spirit be joined to the law, because, if you have received the law and if you lack the help of the Spirit, you do not fulfill what is of the law. You do not carry out what is commanded you. . . . Let the Spirit be added, let him help: that which is commanded is accomplished. If the Spirit is absent, the letter kills you. . . . You cannot excuse yourself on the plea of ignorance since you have received the law. Now, because you have learned what you should do, ignorance does not excuse you. . . . But why does the apostle say: "The letter kills, but the Spirit gives life"?[30] How does the Spirit give life? Because he causes the letter to be fulfilled so that it may not kill. The sanctified are those who fulfill the law of God according to the gift of God. The law can command; it cannot help. The Spirit is added as a helper, and the commandment of God is fulfilled with joy and delight. Certainly many observe the law from fear, but those who keep the law from fear of punishment would prefer that what they fear did not exist. On the contrary, those who observe the law through love of justice rejoice even in that respect because they do not consider it hostile to them. EASTER SEASON 251.7.[31]

THE LORD GIVES US HIS SPIRIT IN HIS TEACHING. BASIL: The difference between the spirit and the letter the apostle explains succinctly in another place by comparing the law and the gospel, saying: "For the letter kills, but the spirit gives life."[32] By the "letter" he means the law, as is evident also from what precedes and follows. By the "spirit" he means the Lord's doctrine, for the Lord himself said: "My words are spirit and life."[33] CONCERNING BAPTISM 1.2.[34]

THE NEED FOR SPIRITUAL PERCEPTION. ORIGEN: For even in the Gospels, it is "the letter" that "kills." Not only in the Old Testament is "the letter that kills"[35] found; there is also in the New Testament "the letter that kills"—that one who does not spiritually perceive what is said. For, if you follow according to the letter that which is said, "Unless you eat my flesh and drink my blood," this "letter kills." Do you want me to bring out of the gospel for you another "letter" that "kills"? He says, "Let the one who does not have a sword sell his tunic and buy a sword." Behold, this is the letter of the gospel, but "it kills." But, if you take it spiritually, it does not kill, but there is in it "a spirit that gives life." For this reason, receive spiritually what is said either in the law or in the Gospels because "the spiritual one judges all things but that one is not judged by anyone." HOMILY ON LEVITICUS 7.5.5.[36]

3:7 Carved in Letters on Stone

THE LAW SHOWS UP SIN. CHRYSOSTOM: The law served death but was not its cause. What caused death was sin, but the law brought in punishment and showed the sin up for what it was—it did not cause it. The law did not minister to the existence of sin or death but to the suffering of retribution by the sinner, so that in this way it was even more destructive of sin. HOMILIES ON THE EPISTLES OF PAUL TO THE CORINTHIANS 7.1.[37]

---

[26]2 Cor 3:6. [27]FC 30:197. [28]2 Cor 3:6. [29]FC 38:314. [30]2 Cor 3:6. [31]FC 38:322. [32]2 Cor 3:6. [33]Jn 6:64. [34]FC 9:374. [35]2 Cor 3:6. [36]FC 83:146-47. [37]NPNF 1 12:310.

The Dispensation of Death. Theodore of Mopsuestia: Paul did not say the dispensation of the law but the dispensation of death, speaking rather of its result in order to lessen its attraction. Pauline Commentary from the Greek Church.[38]

The Sign of a Dull Heart. Origen: But as the apostle discusses these things with that noble understanding which he employs in other matters, he writes: "But we have the mind of Christ." He also says: "But if the ministry of death written with letters upon stones was glorious, so that the sons of Israel could not steadfastly behold the face of Moses for the glory of his countenance, which is passing away, will not the ministry of the spirit be rather in glory?"[39] And again a little later he says, "And not as Moses placed a veil on his face that the sons of Israel might not steadfastly look at the appearance of his countenance. For their senses were made dull, for up to this present day when Moses is read, the veil is upon their heart."[40] Who would not wonder at the magnitude of the mysteries? Who would not greatly fear the sign of a dulled heart? Moses' face was glorified, but "the sons of Israel" were not able "to look at the appearance of his countenance"; the people of the synagogue were not able "to look." But if anyone can be superior in conduct and life to the multitude, he can look at the glory of his countenance. For even now, as the apostle says, "The veil is placed on the reading of the Old Testament";[41] even now Moses speaks with glorified countenance, but we are not able to look at the glory which is in his countenance. We are not able, therefore, because we are still the populace, and we have no zeal or merit more than the common crowd. But because the holy apostle says, "but that same veil remains in the reading of the Old Testament,"[42] the expressed opinion of such a great apostle would have cut off all hope of understanding for us if he had not added: "But when anyone shall turn to the Lord, the veil shall be removed."[43] He says,

therefore, that the cause of the removal of the veil is our turning to the Lord. We should draw the conclusion from this that as long as we read the divine Scriptures without understanding, as long as what has been written is obscure to us and closed, we have not yet turned to the Lord. For if we had turned to the Lord, without doubt the veil would have been removed. Homilies on Exodus 12.[44]

The Call to Deep Conversion. Origen: The apostle briefly indicates the reason that these words that were read to us can be understood or not understood when he says that "the veil of the Old Testament"[45] can "be removed" from the eyes of the one "who has been converted to the Lord." From this, he wanted it understood that these things are less clear to us to the same degree as our conversion to the Lord is less complete. And for that reason, this must be worked at with all our strength so that, free from secular occupations and mundane deeds, and if possible leaving behind these unnecessary fables of friends, we may apply ourselves to the Word of God and "meditate on his law day and night."[46] The result will be the conversion of the entire heart. Then we can see the face of Moses,[47] opened and unveiled. Homilies on Leviticus 6.[48]

3:8 The Dispensation of the Spirit

Greater Splendor. Ambrosiaster: It is obvious that the grace of the law of faith is greater than that of the law of Moses. For although the law of Moses was intended to be beneficial, it became the law of death because it was flouted. Then, because there was no way it could make provision for sinners to be saved, there came the law of faith, which not only forgives sinners but also makes them righteous. There is there-

---

[38]NTA 15:197. [39]2 Cor 3:7-8. [40]2 Cor 3:13-15. [41]2 Cor 3:14. [42]2 Cor 3:14. [43]2 Cor 3:16. [44]FC 71:367-68. [45]Cf. 2 Cor 3:14, 16. [46]Cf. Ps 1:2. [47]Cf. 2 Cor 3:7. [48]FC 83:116.

fore a great deal of difference between one law and the other. COMMENTARY ON PAUL'S EPISTLES.[49]

TWO DISPENSATIONS. CHRYSOSTOM: Paul shows the results of both dispensations, but whereas in the former instance he concentrates on those results—death and separation from God—in the latter case he concentrates on the Spirit himself. HOMILIES ON THE EPISTLES OF PAUL TO THE CORINTHIANS 7.1.[50]

3:9 The Dispensation of Righteousness

MORE GLORY IN SALVATION THAN DEATH. AMBROSIASTER: Paul says this because there is more glory in salvation than there is in death. However justly a judge may condemn someone, he earns more honor if he shows mercy, so that the guilty party is given an opportunity to mend his ways. COMMENTARY ON PAUL'S EPISTLES.[51]

GRACE JUSTIFIES SINNERS. THEODORET OF CYR: The law condemned sinners, but grace receives them and justifies them by faith. It leads them to holy baptism and grants them forgiveness of sins. COMMENTARY ON THE SECOND EPISTLE TO THE CORINTHIANS 303.[52]

3:10 Surpassing Splendor

THE SPLENDOR ON MOSES' FACE. AMBROSIASTER: The law of Moses was not made glorious because of the splendor on his face.[53] That splendor was of no benefit to anyone and did not have the reward of glory. It was rather a hindrance, not through its own fault but through the fault of sinners. COMMENTARY ON PAUL'S EPISTLES.[54]

WHAT ONCE HAD SPLENDOR. CHRYSOSTOM: Paul

does not disparage the Old Testament but highly commends it, since comparisons are apt to be made between things which are basically similar in kind. HOMILIES ON THE EPISTLES OF PAUL TO THE CORINTHIANS 7.2.[55]

THE MIDDAY LAMP. THEODORET OF CYR: The light of a lamp shines brightly in the darkness of the night, but at midday it is barely visible and is not even thought of as light. COMMENTARY ON THE SECOND EPISTLE TO THE CORINTHIANS 304.[56]

GLORY COMPARED WITH GLORY. JEROME: And this is what the apostle writes in another place: "And yet what was glorified is without glory because of the surpassing glory";[57] for the justice of the law, to be sure, in comparison with the grace of the gospel would not appear to be justice. "For if that," he says, "which is done away with is glorious, much more will that be glorious which abides."[58] AGAINST THE PELAGIANS 1.15.[59]

3:11 Permanence and Splendor

THE FACE OF MOSES AND THE GLORY OF CHRIST. AMBROSIASTER: Paul does not deny that there was splendor in the law and on the face of Moses,[60] but it did not endure because in his case it was a symbol and not a reality. The difference between the face of Moses and the glory of Christ is the same as the difference between the picture and the person whom it portrays. COMMENTARY ON PAUL'S EPISTLES.[61]

---

[49]CSEL 81.215. [50]NPNF 1 12:310. [51]CSEL 81.216. [52]Migne PG 82:394. [53]Ex 34:29-35. [54]CSEL 81.216. [55]NPNF 1 12:310. [56]Migne PG 82:395. [57]2 Cor 3:10. [58]2 Cor 3:11. [59]FC 53:253. [60]Ex 34:29-35. [61]CSEL 81.216.

3:12-18 THE VEIL

[12]*Since we have such a hope, we are very bold,* [13]*not like Moses, who put a veil over his face so that the Israelites might not see the end of the fading splendor.* [14]*But their minds were hardened; for to this day, when they read the old covenant, that same veil remains unlifted, because only through Christ is it taken away.* [15]*Yes, to this day whenever Moses is read a veil lies over their minds;* [16]*but when a man turns to the Lord the veil is removed.* [17]*Now the Lord is the Spirit, and where the Spirit of the Lord is, there is freedom.* [18]*And we all, with unveiled face, beholding*[d] *the glory of the Lord, are being changed into his likeness from one degree of glory to another; for this comes from the Lord who is the Spirit.*

d Or reflecting

OVERVIEW: We have a hope of seeing glory, not the kind that was on the face of Moses, which comes to an end in Christ (THEODORET OF CYR), but the kind the three apostles saw on the mountain (AMBROSIASTER). By this our confidence will increase, because what we eventually see will be in proportion to what we now believe (AMBROSIASTER, SEVERIAN OF GABALA). There is no need for us to cover ourselves as Moses did, for we are able to look at the glory with which we are encircled, even though it is far brighter than any previous glory (CHRYSOSTOM). The covering that concealed useful truth until this day (CYRIL OF JERUSALEM) has now been removed (JEROME, AUGUSTINE, CYRIL OF ALEXANDRIA). The law has its proper glory, but the people were unable to behold it (ORIGEN, CHRYSOSTOM), hardened as they were by unbelief (AMBROSIASTER). The Lord, who is the Spirit, enables freedom (AMBROSE, THEODORE OF MOPSUESTIA). When we turn to the Lord, we see the glory of the law in the face of the Lawgiver (ORIGEN, CHRYSOSTOM, ISAAC OF NINEVEH, THEODORET OF CYR). We are being changed from knowledge of the law into the grace of the Spirit (SEVERIAN, GREGORY NAZIANZEN, GREGORY OF NYSSA, CHRYSOSTOM).

3:12 Having Such Hope

FERVENT IN LOVE. AMBROSIASTER: Paul is saying that we have a hope of seeing glory, not the kind that was on the face of Moses but the kind which the three apostles saw on the mountain when the Lord revealed himself.[1] Therefore we ought to repay the love of God as far as we can by being more fervent in our love for him, who by cleansing us from our sins has given us this confidence. Now our confidence ought to increase, because what we eventually see will be in proportion to what we now believe. COMMENTARY ON PAUL'S EPISTLES.[2]

WE HAVE SUCH HOPE. SEVERIAN OF GABALA: What hope do we have? The hope that the grace of the Spirit will not be abolished like the law but that it will remain, even after the resurrection. PAULINE COMMENTARY FROM THE GREEK CHURCH.[3]

3:13 The Fading Splendor

MOSES' VEILED FACE. CHRYSOSTOM: Paul is saying that there is no need for us to cover ourselves as Moses did,[4] for we are able to look at the glory with which we are encircled, even

---

[1]Mt 17:1-2; Mk 9:2-3. [2]CSEL 81.217. [3]NTA 15:285. [4]Ex 34:33.

though it is far brighter than the other one. HOMILIES ON THE EPISTLES OF PAUL TO THE CORINTHIANS 7.2.[5]

THE END OF SPLENDOR. THEODORET OF CYR: Paul says that the law was fading away, by which he means that it was coming to an end in Christ, whose coming was foretold by the law. COMMENTARY ON THE SECOND EPISTLE TO THE CORINTHIANS 305.[6]

THE WITNESS OF THE OLD TESTAMENT. AUGUSTINE: The truth is that the Old Testament of Mount Sinai, "producing children of slavery," now serves no purpose but to bear witness to the New. Otherwise, the words of St. Paul would not be true: "Yes, down to this very day when Moses is read, the veil covers their hearts"; but when any of them turn from the Old Testament to Christ, "the veil shall be taken away."[7] What happens is that the deepest aspirations of those who make the change are shifted from the Old Testament to the New, whereupon they begin to look for spiritual—rather than earthly—happiness. CITY OF GOD 17.7.[8]

THE TEARING OF THE VEIL. AUGUSTINE: Doubtless, there is a veil in the Old Testament, which will be removed as soon as one comes to Christ. At his crucifixion, "the veil of the temple was torn,"[9] to signify what the apostle said about the veil of the Old Testament, "Because in Christ it is made void."[10] LETTER TO HONORATUS 140.10.[11]

THE NEW CLARIFIES THE OLD. AUGUSTINE: It is not the Old Testament that is done away with in Christ but the concealing veil, so that it may be understood through Christ. That is, as it were, laid bare, which without Christ is hidden and obscure. The same apostle adds immediately: "When you shall turn to Christ, the veil shall be taken away."[12] He does not say: "The law or the Old Testament will be taken away."

It is not the case, therefore, that by the grace of the Lord that which was covered has been abolished as useless; rather the covering has been removed which concealed useful truth. This is what happens to those who earnestly and piously, not proudly and wickedly, seek the sense of the Scriptures. To them is carefully demonstrated the order of events, the reasons for words and deeds and the agreement of the Old Testament with the New, so that not a point remains where there is not complete harmony; and such secret truths are conveyed in figures. When they are brought to light by interpretation, they compel those who wished to condemn rather than to learn. THE USEFULNESS OF BELIEF 3.9.[13]

3:14 Their Minds Hardened

THE VEIL REMAINS UNLIFTED. CYRIL OF JERUSALEM: "Until this day" means not just until the time of Paul but until our time also, and indeed, till the end of the world. CATECHETICAL LECTURES 15.32.[14]

HARDENED THROUGH UNBELIEF. AMBROSIASTER: Their minds were hardened through unbelief, and this will not change until they convert and believe in Christ. COMMENTARY ON PAUL'S EPISTLES.[15]

THROUGH CHRIST IS THE VEIL TAKEN AWAY. CHRYSOSTOM: What happened once in the case of Moses happens continually in the case of the law. What is said is not an accusation of the law, nor does it reflect on Moses, who veiled himself, but only on the narrow Jewish legalists. For the law has its proper glory, but they were unable to see it. Why should we be surprised that the Jews do not believe in Christ, since they did not believe in the law either? HOMILIES

---

[5]NPNF 1 12:311. [6]Migne PG 82:395. [7]Cf. 2 Cor 3:13-16. [8]FC 24:46. [9]Mt 27:51. [10]2 Cor 3:14. [11]FC 20:79. [12]2 Cor 3:16. [13]LCC 6:298. [14]LCC 4:166. [15]CSEL 81.218.

on the Epistles of Paul to the Corinthians 7.2.[16]

3:15 A Veil Over Their Minds

CARNAL MINDS. CHRYSOSTOM: The veil is not there because of Moses but because of their gross and carnal minds. HOMILIES ON THE EPISTLES OF PAUL TO THE CORINTHIANS 7.3.[17]

DIM EYES. JEROME: The curtain of the temple is torn, for that which had been veiled in Judea is unveiled to all the nations; the curtain is torn and the mysteries of the law are revealed to the faithful, but to unbelievers they are hidden to this very day. When Moses, the Old Testament, is read aloud by the Jews on every Sabbath, according to the testimony of the apostle: "the veil covers their hearts."[18] They read the law, true enough, but they do not understand because their eyes have grown so dim that they cannot see. They are, indeed, like those of whom Scripture says: "They have eyes but see not; they have ears but hear not." HOMILY 66 ON PSALM 88 (89).[19]

BEHOLD THE NAKED TRUTH. CYRIL OF ALEXANDRIA: Yet the shadows bring forth the truth, even if they are not at all the truth themselves. Because of this, the divinely inspired Moses placed a veil upon his face and spoke thus to the children of Israel, all but shouting by this act that a person might behold the beauty of the utterances made through him, not in outwardly appearing figures but in meditations hidden within us.[20] Come, therefore, by taking off the veil of the law and by setting the face of Moses free of its coverings, let us behold the naked truth. LETTER 41.[21]

SPIRITUAL TRUTH REVEALED THROUGH THE SPIRIT. ORIGEN: The apostle also says, "Even until this day, whenever Moses is read, a veil lies upon their hearts; but when a man shall turn to the Lord, the veil shall be taken away; and where the Spirit of the Lord is, there is liberty."[22] For so long as a man does not attend to the spiritual meaning "a veil lies upon his heart," in consequence of which veil, in other words his duller understanding, the Scripture itself is said or thought to be veiled. This is the explanation of the veil which is said to have covered the face of Moses when he was speaking to the people, that is, when the law is read in public. But if we turn to the Lord, where also the Word of God is and where the Holy Spirit reveals spiritual knowledge, the veil will be taken away, and we shall then with unveiled face behold in the holy Scriptures the glory of the Lord. ON FIRST PRINCIPLES 1.1.2.[23]

THE LANGUAGE OF GOD. ORIGEN: Further, if any one ponders over the prophetic sayings with all the attention and reverence they deserve, it is certain that in the very act of reading and diligently studying them his mind and feelings will be touched by a divine breath. He will recognize that the words he is reading are not human utterances but the language of God; and so he will perceive from his own experience that these books have been composed not by human art or mortal eloquence but, if I may so speak, in a style that is divine. The splendor of Christ's advent has, therefore, by illuminating the law of Moses with the brightness of the truth, withdrawn the veil which had covered the letter of the law and has disclosed, for everyone who believes in him, all those "good things" which lay concealed within. ON FIRST PRINCIPLES 1.1.3.[24]

3:16 The Veil Removed

REMOVING ALL DARKNESS. ORIGEN: The Lord himself, the Holy Spirit himself, must be entreated by us to remove every cloud and all darkness which obscures the vision of our hearts,

---

[16]NPNF 1 12:311. [17]NPNF 1 12:312. [18]2 Cor 3:15. [19]FC 57:68. [20]2 Cor 3:15-16. [21]FC 76:172-73. [22]2 Cor 3:15-17. [23]OFP 8. [24]OFP 8.

hardened with the stains of sins, in order that we may be able to behold the spiritual and wonderful knowledge of his law. LEVITICUS HOMILY 1.[25]

THE VEIL'S PURPOSE. CHRYSOSTOM: The purpose of the veil was not to hide Moses but to prevent the Jews from seeing him, for they were unable to do so.[26] But when we turn to the Lord, the veil is naturally taken away. When Moses talked with the Jews, he had his face covered, but when he talked with God, the veil was removed. Likewise when we turn to the Lord, we shall see the glory of the law and the face of the Lawgiver uncovered. And not only this, we shall then be in the same frame of reference as Moses. HOMILIES ON THE EPISTLES OF PAUL TO THE CORINTHIANS 7.4.[27]

EVEN SO FOR YOU. THEODORET OF CYR: The same is true for you as well. When you believe in Christ, the veil of your unbelief will be taken away. COMMENTARY ON THE SECOND EPISTLE TO THE CORINTHIANS 305.[28]

A CALL FOR DILIGENT AND DISCIPLINED UNDERSTANDING. ORIGEN: Let us beware, therefore, lest not only "when Moses is read" but also when Paul is read "a veil" be "placed over" our "heart." And clearly, if we hear negligently, if we bring no zeal to learning and understanding, not only are the Scriptures of the Law and Prophets but also of the apostles and Gospels covered for us with a great veil. I fear, however, lest by too much negligence and dullness of heart the divine volumes be not only veiled to us but also sealed, so that "if a book should be put into the hands of a man who cannot read to be read, he would say, 'I cannot read'; if it should be put into the hands of a man who can read, he would say, 'It is sealed.' " Whence we see that we must not only employ zeal to learn the sacred literature, but also we must pray to the Lord and entreat "day and night" that the lamb "of the tribe of Judah" may come and himself taking "the sealed book" may deign to open

it. For it is he who "opening the Scriptures" kindles the hearts of the disciples so that they say, "Was not our heart burning within us when he opened to us the Scriptures?" May he, therefore, even now see fit to open to us what it is which he inspired his apostle to say, "But the Lord is a spirit, and where the spirit of the Lord is, there is freedom."[29] EXODUS HOMILY 12.[30]

A CLEAN HEART WILL PERCEIVE THE TRUTH. ORIGEN: For thus the apostle said, "If anyone turns to the Lord, the veil will be removed; for where the spirit of the Lord is, there is freedom."[31] Therefore, the Lord himself, the Holy Spirit himself must be entreated by us to remove every cloud and all darkness which obscures the vision of our hearts hardened with the stains of sins in order that we may be able to behold the spiritual and wonderful knowledge of his law, according to him who said, "Take the veil from my eyes and I shall observe the wonders of your law."[32] HOMILY ON LEVITICUS 1.4.[33]

3:17a The Lord Is the Spirit

THE SPIRIT IS GOD. CHRYSOSTOM: We did not say "The Lord is a spirit" but "The Spirit is the Lord." HOMILIES ON THE EPISTLES OF PAUL TO THE CORINTHIANS 7.5.[34]

THE SPIRIT. THEODORE OF MOPSUESTIA: If Paul had wanted to say that the Lord is a spirit, he would have left the article *the* out. Compare John [4:24], where in speaking to the Samaritan woman, Jesus says that God is a spirit, meaning that he does not have a body. But in this case Paul puts the article in, which proves that he is not saying that the Lord is a spirit but rather that the Spirit is Lord. PAULINE COMMENTARY FROM THE GREEK CHURCH.[35]

---

[25]FC 83:30. [26]Ex 34:30. [27]NPNF 1 12:313. [28]Migne PG 82:398. [29]2 Cor 3:17. [30]FC 71:372. [31]2 Cor 3:16-17. [32]Ps 118:18. [33]FC 83:30. [34]NPNF 1 12:313. [35]NTA 15:198.

THE SPIRIT NOT A CREATURE. THEODORET OF CYR: Paul shows here that the Spirit and God are equal. Moses turned his eyes toward God;[36] we turn ours toward the Holy Spirit. Paul would hardly have said that what the Spirit reveals is greater than what Moses saw if the Spirit were merely a creature and not God himself. COMMENTARY ON THE SECOND EPISTLE TO THE CORINTHIANS 305-6.[37]

3:17b *There Is Freedom*

THE LIBERTY OF FAITH. AMBROSIASTER: Because God is Spirit, he has given through Christ the law of the Spirit, which persuades us to believe in invisible things which our reasoning understands spiritually. This law gives liberty because it demands only faith, and because it believes what it does not see, we are able to be rescued from our condition. COMMENTARY ON PAUL'S EPISTLES.[38]

SET FREE FROM CONDEMNATION. SEVERIAN OF GABALA: The person who has been blessed with the Spirit of the Lord has been set free from the condemnation of the law, for the spiritual gifts are given their power through the Spirit. Moreover, the gift is given freely to those who are ready to receive it. PAULINE COMMENTARY FROM THE GREEK CHURCH.[39]

SHARED SUBSTANCE. AMBROSE: The same, then, is the Lord, who is the Spirit of the Lord; that is, he called the Spirit of the Lord, Lord, just as also the apostle says: "Now the Lord is a spirit, and where the Spirit of the Lord is, there is liberty."[40] You have then, the Lord called also the Holy Spirit; for the Holy Spirit and the Son are not one person but one substance. THE HOLY SPIRIT 2.1.18.[41]

FAITH LEADS TO FREEDOM. AMBROSE: Just like children, so are the Jews also under a tutor. The law is our tutor; a tutor brings us to the master; Christ is our only master. . . . A tutor is feared,

the master points out the way to salvation. Fear brings us to liberty, liberty to faith, faith to love, love obtains adoption, adoption an inheritance. Therefore, where there is faith, there is freedom, for a slave acts in fear, a free man through faith. The one is under the letter, the other under grace; the one in slavery, the other in the spirit; for "Where the Spirit of the Lord is, there is freedom."[42] LETTERS TO LAYMEN 69.[43]

3:18 *Changed into His Likeness*

WE BEHOLD THE GLORY OF THE LORD. CHRYSOSTOM: This does not refer to those things which are brought to an end but to those which remain. The Spirit is God, and we are raised to the level of the apostles, because we shall all behold him together with uncovered faces. As soon as we are baptized, the soul beams even more brightly than the sun because it is cleansed by the Spirit, and we not only behold God's glory, we receive from it a kind of splendor. HOMILIES ON THE EPISTLES OF PAUL TO THE CORINTHIANS 7.5.[44]

THE GLORY OF OUR INHERITANCE. SEVERIAN OF GABALA: We are being changed from knowledge of the law into the grace of the Spirit. And it must be remembered that from the glory of the Spirit working in us we come to the glory of our inheritance as sons. This is the work of the Spirit, for it must be held that here the word *Lord* refers to the Spirit and not to the Son of God. PAULINE COMMENTARY FROM THE GREEK CHURCH.[45]

ACQUIRING A LIKENESS. ISAAC OF NINEVEH: Although "as in a mirror" indicates "not substantially," it does show clearly, in any case, the acquisition of a likeness. ASCETICAL HOMILIES 2.[46]

---

[36]Ex 34:34. [37]Migne PG 82:398. [38]CSEL 81.219. [39]NTA 15:286. [40]2 Cor 3:17. [41]FC 44:103. [42]2 Cor 3:17. [43]FC 26:411. [44]NPNF 1 12:313-14. [45]NTA 15:286-87. [46]AHSIS 11.

GRADUAL AND DEEPER REVELATION THROUGH THE SPIRIT. GREGORY NAZIANZEN: For the matter stands thus: The Old Testament proclaimed the Father openly and the Son more obscurely. The New manifested the Son and suggested the deity of the Spirit. Now the Spirit himself dwells among us and supplies us with a clearer demonstration of himself. For it was not safe, when the Godhead of the Father was not yet acknowledged, plainly to proclaim the Son; nor when that of the Son was not yet received, to burden us further (if I may use so bold an expression) with the Holy Ghost. . . . For this reason it was, I think, that he gradually came to dwell in the disciples, measuring himself out to them according to their capacity to receive him, at the beginning of the gospel, after the passion, after the ascension, making perfect their powers, being breathed upon them and appearing in fiery tongues. And indeed it is by little and little that he is declared by Jesus, as you will learn for yourself if you will read more carefully. THE THEOLOGICAL ORATIONS 5.26.[47]

ANOTHER MOSES. CHRYSOSTOM: Do you wish to know of another way in which you were judged worthy of greater wonders? In their day the Jews were unable to see the face of Moses transfigured, although he was their fellow slave and kinsman. But you have seen the face of Christ in his glory. St. Paul cried aloud, saying: "But we all, with faces unveiled, reflect the glory of the Lord."[48] At that time the Jews had Christ following them, but all the more does he follow us now. Then Christ followed along with them thanks to Moses; he goes along with us not only thanks to [the new] Moses but thanks to your own ready obedience. For the Jews, after Egypt came the desert; for you, after your exodus will come heaven. They had Moses as their leader and excellent general; we have another Moses, God, to lead and command us. THE THIRD INSTRUCTION 3.25.[49]

CHANGE FOR THE BETTER. GREGORY OF NYSSA: Therefore, I do not think it is a fearful thing (I mean that our nature is changeable). The Logos shows that it would be a disadvantage for us not to be able to make a change for the better, as a kind of wing of flight to greater things. Therefore, let no one be grieved if he sees in his nature a penchant for change. Changing in everything for the better, let him exchange "glory for glory,"[50] becoming greater through daily increase, ever perfecting himself and never arriving too quickly at the limit of perfection. For this is truly perfection: never to stop growing toward what is better and never placing any limit on perfection. ON PERFECTION.[51]

---

[47]LCC 3:209-10. [48]2 Cor 3:18. [49]ACW 31:64. [50]2 Cor 3:18. [51]FC 58:122.

4:1-6 UNDERSTANDING THE TRUTH

[1]*Therefore, having this ministry by the mercy of God,[e] we do not lose heart. [2]We have renounced disgraceful, underhanded ways; we refuse to practice cunning or to tamper with God's word, but by the open statement of the truth we would commend ourselves to every man's conscience in the sight of God. [3]And even if our gospel is veiled, it is veiled only to*

those who are perishing. ⁴In their case the god of this world has blinded the minds of the unbelievers, to keep them from seeing the light of the gospel of the glory of Christ, who is the likeness of God. ⁵For what we preach is not ourselves, but Jesus Christ as Lord, with ourselves as your servants[f] for Jesus' sake. ⁶For it is the God who said, "Let light shine out of darkness," who has shone in our hearts to give the light of the knowledge of the glory of God in the face of Christ.

e *Greek* as we have received mercy   f *Or* slaves

OVERVIEW: Paul attributes perseverance to the mercy of God (CHRYSOSTOM), which first cleanses people, then makes them righteous, adopts them and endows them with a glory like that of God's own Son (AMBROSIASTER). The "god of this world" may be read either as the devil (PELAGIUS) or as the God of the universe who has blinded the minds of the unbelievers of this world (AMBROSIASTER, DIDYMUS THE BLIND). They cannot see the glory of Christ, who is the likeness of God (ORIGEN, GREGORY NAZIANZEN, JEROME). In the world to come there will be no unbelievers (CHRYSOSTOM, THEODORET OF CYR). Paul was not preaching the gospel for his own advantage but for the glory of the Lord (DIDYMUS THE BLIND, AMBROSIASTER, CHRYSOSTOM), whose light shines out of darkness (GREGORY OF NYSSA, THEODORET OF CYR, ISAAC OF NINEVEH, SAHDONA [MARTYRIUS]).

4:1 We Do Not Lose Heart

MINISTRY BY THE MERCY OF GOD. AMBROSIASTER: Paul attributes his perseverance not to human merit but to the mercy of God, which first cleanses a person, then makes him righteous, adopts him as a son of God and endows him with a glory like the glory of God's own Son. COMMENTARY ON PAUL'S EPISTLES.[1]

NOT LOSING HEART. CHRYSOSTOM: This perseverance is to be attributed to God's loving kindness, for not only do we not sink down under the weight of all our trials, but we even rejoice

and speak boldly. HOMILIES ON THE EPISTLES OF PAUL TO THE CORINTHIANS 8.1.[2]

4:2 Commended to Everyone's Conscience

WE RENOUNCE UNDERHANDED WAYS. AMBROSIASTER: This is really an invitation. Just while he had been speaking about himself and his associates, Paul is now exhorting the Corinthians to lead a better life. COMMENTARY ON PAUL'S EPISTLES.[3]

NO CUNNING. CHRYSOSTOM: Some were "walking in craftiness." They had a reputation for taking nothing, but in fact they took it and kept it secret. They had the seeming character of saints and apostles but were full of innumerable secret wickednesses. Paul takes nothing and calls the Corinthians as his witnesses. Likewise he does nothing wicked and asks them to testify to the truth of what he is saying. HOMILIES ON THE EPISTLES OF PAUL TO THE CORINTHIANS 8.1.[4]

OPEN STATEMENT OF TRUTH. THEODORET OF CYR: Paul is talking here about circumcision, which the false apostles were covertly forcing on newly converted Gentiles. COMMENTARY ON THE SECOND EPISTLE TO THE CORINTHIANS 307.[5]

LIVES FILLED WITH LIGHT. GREGORY OF NYSSA: Knowing Christ as the "true light,"[6] "inaccessi-

---

[1]CSEL 81.220. [2]NPNF 1 12:317. [3]CSEL 81.220. [4]NPNF 1 12:317-18. [5]Migne PG 82:399. [6]Jn 1:9.

ble"[7] to falsehood, we learn this, namely, that it is necessary for our lives also to be illuminated by the rays of the true light. But virtues are the rays of "the Sun of Justice,"[8] streaming forth for our illumination, through which we "lay aside the works of darkness,"[9] so that we "walk becomingly as in the day,"[10] and "we renounce those things which shame conceals."[11] By doing all things in the light, we become the light itself, so that it "shines" before others,[12] which is the peculiar quality of light. And if we recognize Christ as "sanctification,"[13] in whom every action is steadfast and pure, let us prove by our life that we ourselves stand apart, being ourselves true sharers of his name, coinciding in deed and not in word with the power of his sanctification. On Perfection.[14]

4:3 Veiled to the Perishing

Unbelief Darkens the Splendor of Truth. Ambrosiaster: Unbelief casts darkness over the splendor of the power of God. This is especially true in the case of the Jews. Commentary on Paul's Epistles.[15]

Those Who Are Perishing. Severian of Gabala: It is veiled only to those who are unbelievers. It is not hidden from everyone, as the face of Moses was hidden from all Israel in the Old Testament.[16] Pauline Commentary from the Greek Church.[17]

4:4 Blinded Minds

To Keep Them from Seeing. Ambrosiaster: Paul is saying that God dims the sight of worldly people because they are hostile to the faith of Christ. He is giving them what they want, since it is because they are hostile and tell lies that they move further toward not being able to believe what they do not want to believe. Commentary on Paul's Epistles.[18]

Being Enlightened. Didymus the Blind: Every

unbeliever is of this world. No one who has overcome it and been deemed worthy of the world to come is blinded in his understanding, for his eyes have been enlightened. Pauline Commentary from the Greek Church.[19]

The God of This World. Pelagius: The god of this world may be understood to be the devil, on the ground that he has claimed to rule over unbelievers. Or, on account of the attacks of the heretics it may be understood to mean that God has blinded the minds of unbelievers precisely because of their unbelief. Commentary on the Second Epistle to the Corinthians 4.[20]

The Minds of Unbelievers Blinded. Chrysostom: The "god of this world" may refer neither to the devil nor to another creator, as the Manichaeans say, but to the God of the universe, who has blinded the minds of the unbelievers of this world. In the world to come there are no unbelievers, only in this one. Homilies on the Epistles of Paul to the Corinthians 8.2.[21]

The Truth Will Be Plain. Theodoret of Cyr: Paul is saying that unbelief is limited to this world, because in the next life the truth will be plain to everyone. Commentary on the Second Epistle to the Corinthians 308.[22]

The Call to Resemble Christ. Clement of Alexandria: Our Educator, O children, resembles his Father, God, whose Son he is. He is without sin, without blame. . . . God immaculate in human form, accomplishing his Father's will. He is God the Word, who is in the bosom of the Father and also at the right hand of the Father, with even the nature of God. He it is

---

[7]1 Tim 6:16. [8]Mal 3:20. [9]Rom 13:12. [10]Rom 13:13. [11]2 Cor 4:2. [12]Cf. Mt 5:15-16. [13]1 Cor 1:30. [14]FC 58:103. [15]CSEL 81.221. [16]Ex 34:35. [17]NTA 15:287. [18]CSEL 81.221. [19]NTA 15:24. [20]Migne PL 30:781A-B. [21]NPNF 1 12:318. [22]Migne PG 82:399.

who is the spotless image.[23] We must try, then, to resemble Him in spirit as far as we are able. . . . Yet we must strive to the best of our ability to be as sinless as we can. There is nothing more important for us than first to be rid of sin and weakness and then to uproot any habitual sinful inclination. The highest perfection, of course, is never to sin in any least way, but this can be said of God alone. The next highest is never deliberately to commit wrong; this is the state proper to the man who possesses wisdom. In the third place comes not sinning except on rare occasions; this marks a man who is well educated. Finally, in the lowest degree we must place delaying in sin for a brief moment, but even this, for those who are called to recover their loss and repent, is a step on the path to salvation. CHRIST THE EDUCATOR 2.4.[24]

A LIVING IMAGE. GREGORY NAZIANZEN: And the Image,[25] as of one substance with him, and because he is of the Father, and not the Father of him. For this is of the nature of an image, to be the reproduction of its archetype and of that whose name it bears; only that there is more here. For in ordinary language an image is a motionless representation of that which has motion, but in this case it is the living reproduction of the living one and is more exactly like than was Seth to Adam[26] or any son to his father. THE THEOLOGICAL ORATIONS 4.20.[27]

THE IMAGE AND LIGHT OF THE FATHER. JEROME: What is the face of God like? As his image, certainly, for as the apostle says, the image of the Father is the Son.[28] With his image, therefore, may he shine upon us, that is, may he shine his image, the Son, upon us in order that he himself may shine upon us, for the light of the Father is the light of the Son. He who sees the Father sees also the Son, and he who sees the Son sees also the Father. Where there is no diversity between glory and glory, there glory is one and the same. HOMILY 6 ON PSALM 66 (67).[29]

BREAK FREE FROM THIS EVIL AGE. ORIGEN: For the Son of God is Word and Righteousness. But every sinner is under the tyranny of the prince of this age,[30] since every sinner is made a friend of the present evil age. For he does not hand himself over to the One who gave "himself for our sins to deliver us from the present evil age" and to deliver us "according to the will of our God and Father," according to the verse in the letter to the Galatians.[31] And the one who by voluntary sin is under the tyranny of the prince of this age is also ruled by sin. That is why we are commanded by Paul no longer to be subjected to sin that wishes to rule over us. We are so ordered through the following words, "Let not sin therefore reign in your mortal bodies, to make you obey their passions."[32] ON PRAYER 25.1.[33]

TRACES OF THE IMAGE OF GOD. ORIGEN: But if anyone dares to attribute corruption of substance to what was made according to the image and likeness of God, in my opinion he extends the charge of impiety also to the Son of God himself, since he is also called in Scripture "the image of God."[34] At least the one who holds the opinion will certainly find fault with the authority of Scripture, which says that humanity was made after the image of God. And the traces of the divine image are clearly recognized not through the likeness of the body, which undergoes corruption, but through the intelligence of the soul, its righteousness, temperance, courage, wisdom, discipline, and through the entire chorus of virtues that are present in God by substance and can be in humankind through effort and the imitation of God. The Lord points this out in the Gospel when He says, "Be merciful, even as your Father is merciful"[35] and "Be perfect, as your Fa-

---

[23]Cf. 2 Cor 4:4. [24]FC 23:5-6*. [25]2 Cor 4:4. [26]Gen 5:3. [27]LCC 3:191. [28]2 Cor 4:4; Col 1:15. [29]FC 48:43. [30]2 Cor 4:4. [31]Gal 1:4. [32]Rom 6:12. [33]CWS 132. [34]Cf. 2 Cor 4:4; Col 1:15. [35]Lk 6:36.

ther is perfect."[36] Consequently, it is quite clear that in God all these virtues can never enter or leave, but they are acquired by us little by little and one by one. On First Principles 4.10.[37]

4:5 Preaching Christ as Lord

Accepted by Our Faith. Didymus the Blind: It is not we but he who enables our faith, accepting us and judging us by it. Pauline Commentary from the Greek Church.[38]

We Preach Christ. Ambrosiaster: In expressing himself humbly, Paul spoke in a way which was designed to show that he was not preaching the gospel for his own advantage but for the glory of the Lord Christ, to whom he is obedient. Commentary on Paul's Epistles.[39]

The Lord's Mouthpiece. Chrysostom: I am a servant. I am but a minister of those who receive the gospel, transacting everything for Another, and for his glory doing what I do. In warring against me you throw down what is God's. Homilies on the Epistles of Paul to the Corinthians 8.3.[40]

Respond to the Invitation. Gregory of Nyssa: And the apostle: "For we preach not ourselves but Jesus Christ as Lord, and ourselves merely as your servants in Jesus."[41] Knowing, then, the fruits of humility and the penalty of conceit, imitate the Master by loving one another and do not shrink from death or any other punishment for the good of each other. But the way which God entered upon for you, do you enter upon for him, proceeding with one body and one soul to the invitation from above, loving God and each other. For love and fear of the Lord are the first fulfillment of the law. On the Christian Mode of Life.[42]

4:6 Light Out of Darkness

This Creation Is Greater. Chrysostom: Do you see how Paul shows the glory of Moses flashing with added luster to those who want to see it? It shines in our hearts, he says, just as it shone on the face of Moses.[43] First he reminds them of what was made at the beginning of creation,[44] and then he shows that this renewed creation is greater. Homilies on the Epistles of Paul to the Corinthians 8.3.[45]

Shining with Divine Light. Theodoret of Cyr: Since the divine nature is invisible and always remains so, it is seen for what it is in the humanity of Jesus Christ which shines with divine light and sends out its rays. Commentary on the Second Epistle to the Corinthians 309.[46]

Our Hearts Dark. Sahduna: Our hearts had been submerged in darkness. Book of Perfection 64.[47]

Dawning of Divine Wisdom. Isaac of Nineveh: When the apostle said, "God, who commanded the light to shine out of the darkness, has shined in our hearts," he referred to the resurrection. He showed this resurrection to be the exodus from the old state which in the likeness of Sheol incarcerates a person where the light of the gospel will not shine mystically upon him. This breath of life shines through hope in the resurrection. By it the dawning of divine wisdom shines in the heart, so that a person should become new, having nothing of the old. Ascetical Homilies 37.[48]

The Shining of the Spirit. Ambrose: But does anyone deny that the Godhead of the eternal Trinity is to be adored, when the Scriptures also set forth the inexplicable majesty of the divine Trinity, as the apostle says elsewhere: "For

---

[36]Mt 5:48. [37]CWS 215-16. [38]NTA 15:24. [39]CSEL 81.222. [40]NPNF 1 12:319. [41]2 Cor 4:5. [42]FC 58:147. [43]Ex 34:29-35. [44]Gen 1:3. [45]NPNF 1 12:319. [46]Migne PG 82:402. [47]SFPSL 228. [48]AHSIS 175.

the God who commanded the light to shine out of darkness has shined in our hearts, to give the light of the knowledge of the glory of God, in the face of Christ Jesus?"[49] . . . Who is it, then, who shined that we might know God in the face of Christ Jesus? For he said: "God shined," that the glory of God might be known in the face of Jesus Christ. Who else do we think but the Spirit who was made manifest? Or who else is it but the Holy Spirit, to whom the power of the Godhead is referred? For those who exclude the Spirit must introduce another to receive with the Father and the Son the glory of the Godhead. THE HOLY SPIRIT 3.12.86, 88.[50]

THE SPIRIT'S FIRE. SAHDONA: We should accordingly worship and glorify him who raised our dust to such state, recounting ceaselessly the holiness of him who mingled our spirit with his Spirit and mixed into our bodies the gift of his grace, causing the fire of his Holy Spirit to burst into flame in us. For "he has shone out in our hearts" which had been submerged in darkness. BOOK OF PERFECTION.[51]

---

[49]2 Cor 4:6. [50]FC 44:184-85. [51]SFPSL 228.

4:7-12 EARTHEN VESSELS

[7]*But we have this treasure in earthen vessels, to show that the transcendent power belongs to God and not to us.* [8]*We are afflicted in every way, but not crushed; perplexed, but not driven to despair;* [9]*persecuted, but not forsaken; struck down, but not destroyed;* [10]*always carrying in the body the death of Jesus, so that the life of Jesus may also be manifested in our bodies.* [11]*For while we live we are always being given up to death for Jesus' sake, so that the life of Jesus may be manifested in our mortal flesh.* [12]*So death is at work in us, but life in you.*

Overview: The power of God is most conspicuous when it performs mighty works by using lowly things (CHRYSOSTOM). The reference to earthen vessels is an allusion to the weakness of human nature, which can do nothing unless it receives power from God (ORIGEN, AMBROSIASTER, JEROME). Afflictions are permitted by God, not for our defeat but for our discipline (CHRYSOSTOM, AUGUSTINE, THEODORET OF CYR). In the suffering of martyrs Christ himself suffers (AMBROSIASTER). We carry in the body the death of Jesus daily (CHRYSOSTOM, PELAGIUS).

4:7a Treasure in Earthen Vessels

THIS TREASURE. AMBROSIASTER: By treasure, Paul meant the sacrament of God in Christ, which is made manifest to believers but which has been concealed from unbelievers with a veil. Just as a treasure is put in a hidden place, the sacrament of God is hidden within a person, in his heart. The reference to earthen vessels is an allusion to the weakness of human nature, which can do nothing unless empowered by God. COMMENTARY ON PAUL'S EPISTLES.[1]

---

[1]CSEL 81.223.

THE SCRIPTURE'S HUMILITY. JEROME: We have a treasure in such vessels of clay.[2] There are many who construe this last expression in reference to the body and to the Holy Spirit, meaning, of course, that we possess a treasure in earthen vessels. There is certainly that interpretation, but I think the better treasury-concept is that we have a most precious treasure in vessels of clay symbolizing the homely words of the Scripture. HOMILY 11 ON PSALM 77 (78).[3]

THE SCRIPTURE'S DEPTH. JEROME: Every word of Scripture is a symbol all its own. These rustic words that persons of every age ponder over are packed full of mystical meaning. "But we carry this treasure in vessels of clay"; we have a divine treasury of meaning in the most ordinary words. HOMILY 20 ON PSALM 90 (91).[4]

4:7b Transcendent Power

THE TRANSCENDENT POWER BELONGS TO GOD. CHRYSOSTOM: Both the greatness of the things given and the weakness of them that receive show the power of God, who not only gave great things but also gave them to those who are little. He used the term *earthen* in allusion to the frailty of our mortal nature and to declare the weakness of our flesh. For it is no better than earthenware, which is soon damaged and destroyed by death, disease and even variations of temperature. The power of God is most conspicuous when it performs mighty works by using vile and lowly things. HOMILIES ON THE EPISTLES OF PAUL TO THE CORINTHIANS 8.3.[5]

THE DEPTHS OF DIVINE INSPIRATION. ORIGEN: But just as divine providence is not proved to be a fiction, particularly for those who are convinced of its existence, because its workings and arrangements are beyond the comprehension of human minds, so neither will the divine inspiration of holy Scripture, which extends through its entire body, be supposed to be nonexistent because the weakness of our understanding cannot discover the deep and hidden thoughts in every sentence. For the treasure of divine wisdom is concealed in vessels of poor and humble words, as the apostle points out when he says: "We have this treasure in earthen vessels, that the greatness of the divine power may shine forth the more," when no taint of human eloquence is mingled with the truth of the doctrines. ON FIRST PRINCIPLES 4.1.[6]

4:8 Not Crushed or Despairing

AFFLICTED BUT NOT CRUSHED. CHRYSOSTOM: The afflictions come not only from enemies but even from our own households and friends. These things are permitted by God, not for our defeat but for our discipline. HOMILIES ON THE EPISTLES OF PAUL TO THE CORINTHIANS 9.1.[7]

GOD'S POWER REVEALED. THEODORET OF CYR: If none of these things ever happened, the greatness of God's power would never be revealed. COMMENTARY ON THE SECOND EPISTLE TO THE CORINTHIANS 310.[8]

FREEDOM IN AFFLICTION. ORIGEN: For God delivers us from afflictions not when we are no longer in affliction (. . . Paul says "we are afflicted in every way," as though there were never a time when we were not afflicted), but when in our affliction we are not crushed because of God's help. "To be afflicted," according to a colloquial usage of the Hebrews, has the meaning of a critical circumstance that happens to us without our free choice, while "to be crushed" implies our free choice and that it has been conquered by affliction and given into its power. And so Paul is right when he says, "We are afflicted in every way but not crushed." ON PRAYER 30.1.[9]

THE MYSTERY OF UNANSWERED PRAYER. ORIGEN:

---

[2]2 Cor 4:7. [3]FC 48:84. [4]FC 48:160. [5]NPNF 1 12:320. [6]OFP 267. [7]NPNF 1 12:321. [8]Migne PG 82:402. [9]CWS 162.

And unless we understand something that has escaped the notice of the many concerning praying not to enter into temptation, it is time to say that the apostles sometimes prayed and were not heard. How many thousand sufferings did they experience throughout their lifetimes with far greater labors, with far more beatings, with countless imprisonments, and often near death? Paul on his own received at the hands of the Jews the forty lashes less one, was beaten with rods three times, was stoned once, was shipwrecked three times, was adrift at sea a night and a day. He was in every way afflicted, perplexed, persecuted and struck down. ON PRAYER 29.4.[10]

4:9 Not Forsaken or Destroyed

PERSECUTED BUT NOT FORSAKEN. AMBROSIASTER: God was with them, like a shepherd, when they were in need. He looked after their interests, so that their enemies would not get the better of them. COMMENTARY ON PAUL'S EPISTLES.[11]

4:10 Manifesting Jesus' Life

JESUS' LIFE MANIFESTED IN THE BODIES OF MARTYRS. AMBROSIASTER: Christ himself shares in the death of martyrs. Their sufferings are his sufferings. His life is made manifest in their bodies. Their sufferings are evidence of the fact that they are prepared to receive the life to come which Christ promised. COMMENTARY ON PAUL'S EPISTLES.[12]

CARRYING THE DEATH OF JESUS. CHRYSOSTOM: What is the death of Jesus which they carried about with them? It is the daily deaths which they died, by which the resurrection also was shown. This is another reason for the trials, that Christ's life might be manifested in human bodies. What looks like weakness and destitution in fact proclaims his resurrection. HOMILIES ON THE EPISTLES OF PAUL TO THE CORINTHIANS 9.1.[13]

4:11 Given Up to Death

CHRISTIANS NOT AFRAID TO DIE. AMBROSIASTER: Paul is saying that Christians are not afraid to die because they have the promise of resurrection. COMMENTARY ON PAUL'S EPISTLES.[14]

FOR JESUS' SAKE. PELAGIUS: We do not suffer because of doing wrong but for the sake of the body of Christ, which is the church. He suffered for us so that his life, which is eternal, might be made manifest in our mortal bodies, so that they too might become immortal. COMMENTARY ON THE SECOND EPISTLE TO THE CORINTHIANS 4.[15]

4:12 Death at Work in Us

RISKING DEATH. AMBROSIASTER: Paul is saying this because he and Timothy were being threatened with death for their sakes. By preaching to the Gentiles they had stirred up hatred from both Jews and Gentiles, risking even death. COMMENTARY ON PAUL'S EPISTLES.[16]

ENDURING DANGERS. CHRYSOSTOM: We bear about his dying that the power of his life may be manifest. HOMILIES ON THE EPISTLES OF PAUL TO THE CORINTHIANS 9.1.[17]

---

[10]CWS:153. [11]CSEL 81.224. [12]CSEL 81.224. [13]NPNF 1 12:321. [14]CSEL 81.225. [15]Migne PL 30:782B. [16]CSEL 81.225. [17]NPNF 1 12:322.

4:13-18 THE IMPORTANCE OF FAITH

[13]*Since we have the same spirit of faith as he had who wrote, "I believed, and so I spoke," we too believe, and so we speak,* [14]*knowing that he who raised the Lord Jesus will raise us also with Jesus and bring us with you into his presence.* [15]*For it is all for your sake, so that as grace extends to more and more people it may increase thanksgiving, to the glory of God.* [16]*So we do not lose heart. Though our outer nature is wasting away, our inner nature is being renewed every day.* [17]*For this slight momentary affliction is preparing for us an eternal weight of glory beyond all comparison,* [18]*because we look not to the things that are seen but to the things that are unseen; for the things that are seen are transient, but the things that are unseen are eternal.*

OVERVIEW: Paul recalled the words of the psalmist when he was in great danger, from which there was no possibility of escape except through the power of God (CHRYSOSTOM). We have the same spirit of faith (NOVATIAN, AUGUSTINE, PELAGIUS, FULGENTIUS). All believers are made greater than death (THEODORET OF CYR) through the resurrection (POLYCARP). The body decays by being scourged and persecuted, but the inward person is renewed by faith, hope and a forward-looking will that braves those extremities (BASIL, AMBROSIASTER, CHRYSOSTOM). Our present afflictions are light because they are happening within time and space (ORIGEN, AMBROSIASTER, AUGUSTINE, CAESARIUS OF ARLES).

4:13 The Spirit of Faith

THE SAME SPIRIT OF FAITH. NOVATIAN: It is one and the same Spirit who is in the prophets and in the apostles. However, the Spirit dwelt in the prophets sporadically, whereas he abides in believers forever. THE TRINITY 29.6.[1]

ATTACKING CHEAP GRACE. PELAGIUS: Here Paul is attacking those who have believed in false apostles, who claimed that Paul was suffering because he had little faith. According to them,

faith ought to guarantee that there will be no suffering at all. But Paul shows that, on the contrary, he has endured all things precisely because of his faith. COMMENTARY ON THE SECOND EPISTLE TO THE CORINTHIANS 4.[2]

HEAVENLY WISDOM. CHRYSOSTOM: Paul reminds us of a psalm[3] which abounds in heavenly wisdom and is especially fitted to encourage us in dangers. The psalmist uttered these words when he was in great danger, from which there was no possibility of escape except in the power of God.[4] In similar circumstances, Paul says that we who have the same Spirit will be comforted likewise. Thus he shows that there is a great harmony between the Old and the New Testaments; it is the same Spirit at work in both. The men of old were in danger, just as we are. Like them, we must find a solution through faith and hope. HOMILIES ON THE EPISTLES OF PAUL TO THE CORINTHIANS 9.2.[5]

SAVED BY THE SAME FAITH. AUGUSTINE: Moreover, our Mediator, when revealed to us, wished the sacrament of our regeneration to be

---

[1]FC 67:100. [2]Migne PL 30:782B-C. [3]Ps 116:10. [4]Ps 116:10. [5]NPNF 1 12:322.

manifest. But for the just men of old it was something hidden, although they also were to be saved by the same faith which was to be revealed in its own time. For we do not dare to prefer the faithful of our own time to the friends of God by whom those prophecies were to be made, since God so announced himself as the God of Abraham, the God of Isaac, the God of Jacob, as to give himself that name forever. If the belief is correct that circumcision served instead of baptism in the saints of old, what shall be said of those who pleased God before this was commanded, except that they pleased him by faith, because, as it is written in Hebrews: "Without faith it is impossible to please God"?[6] "But having the same spirit of faith," says the apostle, "as it is written: I believed, for which cause I have spoken, we also believe, for which reason we also speak." He would not have said "the same" unless this very spirit of faith was also theirs. For, just as they, when this same mystery was hidden, believed in the incarnation of Christ which was to come, so we also believe that it has come. LETTERS TO DARDANUS 187.34.[7]

DIVERSE TIMES, A UNITED FAITH. AUGUSTINE: Those just men also were saved by their salutary faith in him as man and God. They, before he came in the flesh, believed that he was to come in the flesh. Our faith is the same as theirs, since they believed that this would be, while we believe that it has come to pass. Hence, the apostle Paul says: "But having the same spirit of faith, as it is written: I believed for which reason I have spoken: we also believe for which reason we also speak." If, then, those who foretold that Christ would come in the flesh had the same faith as those who have recorded his coming, these religious mysteries could vary according to the diversity of times yet all refer most harmoniously to the unity of the same faith. LETTERS TO OPTATUS 190.[8]

THE SAME SPIRIT OF FAITH. FULGENTIUS: Paul the apostle says that he has the same spirit of faith which the blessed David had, which the holy Moses received, just as he himself testifies, saying, "Since then we have the same spirit of faith, according to what is written: 'I believed, therefore, I spoke.' We too believe and therefore speak." How did they have the one spirit of faith, if they believed differently concerning the faithful God? For the difference in belief is great if what Paul says, "There is no injustice with God,"[9] differs from what Moses and David say, "There is no iniquity in God."[10] And if, as Paul says, he has the same spirit of faith which the prophets also had and yet his belief is different from their faith, let the apostle be declared a liar (God forbid), he who testifies that Christ speaks in him. "You are looking for proof of Christ speaking in me?" But since Christ has truly spoken in Paul, Paul is not a liar. And when he says that he has the same spirit of faith, he does not lie; the belief of each is in agreement so that what Moses and David have said. . . . This is also what Paul says. To MONIMUS 3.5.7.[11]

THE EXPANSION OF THE SPIRIT'S BLESSING. NOVATIAN: Accordingly the apostle Paul says: "Since we have the same spirit, as shown in that which is written: 'I believed, and so I spoke,' we also believe and so we speak." Therefore, it is one and the same Spirit who is in the prophets and in the apostles. He was, however, in the former only for a while; whereas he abides in the latter forever. In other words, he is in the prophets but not to remain always in them; in the apostles, that he might abide in them forever. He has been apportioned to the former in moderation; to the latter, he has been wholly poured out. He was sparingly given to the one; upon the other, lavishly bestowed. THE TRINITY 29.5-6.[12]

4:14 Brought into God's Presence

[6]Heb 11:6. [7]FC 30:248-49*. [8]FC 30:274*. [9]Rom 9:14. [10]Dt 32:4; Ps 9:16 LXX; Ps 10:16. [11]FC 95:269. [12]FC 67:100.

GOD RAISED JESUS. POLYCARP: He who raised Jesus from the dead will raise us also if we do his will and walk in his commandments and love the things which he loved, abstaining from all unrighteousness, covetousness, love of money, evil speaking and false witness. EPISTLE TO THE PHILIPPIANS 2.[13]

GOD WILL RAISE US. CHRYSOSTOM: Once again, Paul fills the Corinthians with lofty thoughts, so that they may not feel indebted to the false apostles. HOMILIES ON THE EPISTLES OF PAUL TO THE CORINTHIANS 9.2.[14]

INTO HIS PRESENCE. THEODORET OF CYR: Paul believed that through the work of Christ he and all believers were made greater than death and that they would all be brought before the terrible seat of judgment. COMMENTARY ON THE SECOND EPISTLE TO THE CORINTHIANS 311.[15]

4:15 To the Glory of God

AS GRACE EXTENDS TO MORE AND MORE. AMBROSIASTER: God does not want anyone to be excluded from his gift. But because not everyone had received the word of faith, God's apostle, who knew God's will, was not afraid to suffer persecutions and perils as long as he could preach to everyone faithfully, so that more people might believe. COMMENTARY ON PAUL'S EPISTLES.[16]

FOR THE BENEFIT OF ALL. CHRYSOSTOM: God did not raise Christ from the dead for the sake of one person only but for the benefit of us all. HOMILIES ON THE EPISTLES OF PAUL TO THE CORINTHIANS 9.2.[17]

4:16 Our Inner Nature Renewed

PERSECUTION ADVANCES THE SOUL'S MERIT. AMBROSIASTER: In times of persecution the soul advances. Every day it adds something more to its experience of faith. Even the damage done to

the body becomes conducive to immortality through the merit of the soul. COMMENTARY ON PAUL'S EPISTLES.[18]

THE HOPE OF THE SOUL. CHRYSOSTOM: The body decays by being scourged and persecuted, but the inward man is renewed by faith, hope and a forward-looking will which braves those extremities. For the hope of the soul is in direct proportion to the suffering of the body. HOMILIES ON THE EPISTLES OF PAUL TO THE CORINTHIANS 9.2.[19]

EACH GROWS AT THE PROPER SPEED. AUGUSTINE: The renewal of humankind, begun in the sacred bath of baptism, proceeds gradually and is accomplished more quickly in some individuals and more slowly in others. But many are in progress toward the new life if we consider the matter carefully and without prejudice. As the apostle says: "Even though our outer man is decaying, yet our inner man is being renewed day by day." He says that the inner man is renewed day by day in order that he may become perfect, but you would have him begin with perfection. Would that you really did desire this! But you seek to lead the unwary astray rather than to uplift the weak. THE WAY OF LIFE OF THE CATHOLIC CHURCH 1.35.80.[20]

CARING FOR THE SOUL. BASIL: A man who has his own best interest at heart will therefore be especially concerned for his soul and will spare no pains to keep it stainless and true to itself. If his body is wasted by hunger or by its struggles with heat and cold, if it is afflicted by illness or suffers violence from anyone, he will pay little attention to it, and, echoing the words of Paul, he will say in each of his adversities: "but though our outward man is corrupted, yet the inward man is renewed day by day." . . . But, if a

---

[13]AF 95. [14]NPNF 1 12:322. [15]Migne PG 82:403. [16]CSEL 81.226. [17]NPNF 1 12:322. [18]CSEL 81.227. [19]NPNF 1 12:322. [20]FC 56:61*.

man would also have mercy upon his body as being a possession necessary to the soul and its co-operator in carrying on the life on earth, he will occupy himself with its needs only so far as is required to preserve it and keep it vigorous by moderate care in the service of the soul. HOMILY 21 ON DETACHMENT.[21]

4:17 An Eternal Weight of Glory

MOMENTARY AFFLICTION. ORIGEN: It was not a light, momentary affliction to everyone, but it was to Paul and to people like him, because they had the perfect loving affection of God in Christ Jesus through the Holy Spirit poured into their hearts. COMMENTARY ON THE SONG OF SONGS.[22]

PREPARING US. AMBROSIASTER: Paul is saying that our present afflictions are light because they are happening within time and space. In return for this light tribulation, we shall gain a degree of glory beyond measure. COMMENTARY ON PAUL'S EPISTLES.[23]

PRACTICE PATIENCE IN AFFLICTION. AUGUSTINE: The human patience which is good, praiseworthy and deserving the name of virtue is said to be that by which we endure evils with equanimity so as not to abandon, through a lack of equanimity, the good through which we arrive at the better. By their unwillingness to suffer evil, the impatient do not effect their deliverance from it; instead, they bring upon themselves the suffering of more grievous ills. But the patient, who prefer to bear wrongs without committing them rather than to commit them by not enduring them, both lessen what they suffer in patience and escape worse things by which, through impatience, they would be submerged. In yielding to evils that are brief and passing, they do not destroy the good which is great and eternal, for "the sufferings of the present time are not worthy to be compared," the apostle says, "with the glory to come that will be re-

vealed in us."[24] And he also says: "Our present light affliction, which is for the moment, prepares for us an eternal weight of glory that is beyond all measure." PATIENCE 2.[25]

THE LOVE OF GOD RELIEVES OUR SUFFERING. CHRYSOSTOM: Such, after all, is the way with good people: when they endure something for his sake, far from attending to the appearance of what occurs, they understand the reason behind it and thus bear everything with equanimity. Likewise Paul, the teacher of the Gentiles, identified imprisonment, arraignment, daily peril, all those many unbearable hardships as light burdens, not because they really were so by nature but because the reason behind their happening produced such an attitude in him that he would not turn back in the face of these oncoming threats. Listen, after all, to what he says: "For the light weight of our passing distress produces in us an eternal weight of glory beyond all comparison"; expectation of the glory we are destined to attain, he is saying, and of that unceasing enjoyment makes us bear without difficulty these hardships one after another and consider them of no consequence. Do you see how love of God reduces the intensity of troubles and prevents our having any sense of them as they befall us? On this account, of course, this blessed man, too, bore everything with equanimity, sustained by faith and hope in God. HOMILY ON GENESIS 25.17.[26]

4:18 Things That Are Unseen

EARTHLY THINGS NOTHING. AMBROSIASTER: Paul is saying that people who long for heavenly things despise the things of this world, because in comparison with what they want, these things are nothing. COMMENTARY ON PAUL'S EPISTLES.[27]

---

[21]FC 9:495*. [22]CWS 230. [23]CSEL 81.227-28. [24]Rom 8:18. [25]FC 16:238*. [26]FC 82:137*. [27]CSEL 81.228.

UNSEEN THINGS ARE ETERNAL. CHRYSOSTOM: Our present afflictions will be light and our future will be glorious if we turn away from visible things and concentrate on spiritual ones instead. What excuse have we got if we choose the temporal instead of the eternal? Even if the present is enjoyable, it does not last, though the sorrow it engenders does last and cannot be alleviated. What excuse will they have if those who have been accounted worthy of receiving the Spirit and have enjoyed so great a gift grovel and fall down before the things of this earth? HOMILIES ON THE EPISTLES OF PAUL TO THE CORINTHIANS 9.3.[28]

THINGS NOT SEEN. CAESARIUS OF ARLES: If you seek temporal things, you pray publicly and with your door open. If you ask for eternal things, your prayer is secret because you long to receive not the things which are seen but those which are not seen. SERMON 146.3.[29]

ENDURE THE PRESENT IN LIGHT OF THE FUTURE. CHRYSOSTOM: Consider, dearly beloved, that life's troubles, even if distressing, are still of short duration, whereas the good things that will come to us in the next life are eternal and everlasting. "What we see is passing," Scripture says, "but what is not seen is everlasting." Accordingly, let us endure what is passing without complaint and not desist from virtue's struggle so that we may enjoy the good things that are eternal and last forever. HOMILY ON GENESIS 25.24.[30]

A SPIRITUAL TRANSACTION. CHRYSOSTOM: Far from being surprised or troubled, let us endure developments with complete fortitude and endurance, having regard not to the distress but to the gain accruing to us from it. This transaction, you see, is spiritual. People intent on making money and being involved in a transaction of this life would succeed in increasing their wealth in no other way than by being exposed to great danger on land and at sea (they must, after all, put up with the onset of brigands and wiles of pirates), and yet they are ready to accept everything with great enthusiasm, having no sense of hardship through the expectation of gain. In just the same way must we keep our mind on the wealth and spiritual riches accruing to us from this. We must rejoice and be glad, considering not what can be seen but what cannot be seen, as Paul's exhortation goes, "not considering what can be seen." HOMILY ON GENESIS 63.20.[31]

---

[28]NPNF 1 12:323. [29]FC 47:310-11. [30]FC 82:143. [31]FC 87:222*.

5:1-5 THE EARTHLY TENT

[1]*For we know that if the earthly tent we live in is destroyed, we have a building from God, a house not made with hands, eternal in the heavens.* [2]*Here indeed we groan, and long to put on our heavenly dwelling,* [3]*so that by putting it on we may not be found naked.* [4]*For while we are still in this tent, we sigh with anxiety; not that we would be unclothed, but that we would be further clothed, so that what is mortal may be swallowed up by life.*

[5]He who has prepared us for this very thing is God, who has given us the Spirit as a guarantee.

OVERVIEW: Once this body, our earthly home (AMBROSIASTER), is left behind, the soul will enter the heavenly realm (CHRYSOSTOM). It will receive its body back, transformed into a heavenly body (DIDYMUS THE BLIND). We do not look toward being delivered from a body but only from the corruption that is in it (CHRYSOSTOM). Some will rise to honor and others to dishonor (CHRYSOSTOM, DIDYMUS THE BLIND, SEVERIAN OF GABALA). Our groanings are like those of a woman in labor, awaiting a new birth (PELAGIUS). Since God the Creator foresaw the sin of Adam, he prepared a remedy for it (CHRYSOSTOM, THEODORET OF CYR). God has given us the Spirit as a guarantee so that we might know that he will not allow the temple of his Spirit to perish (AMBROSIASTER, PELAGIUS).

5:1 A Building from God

OUR PRESENT BODY. AMBROSIASTER: Our present body is our earthly home. Our resurrection body is our heavenly one. COMMENTARY ON PAUL'S EPISTLES.[1]

TWO DIFFERENT WORLDS. DIDYMUS THE BLIND: Paul is talking here about two different worlds. One is the earthly, made with hands and visible. The other is invisible, made without hands and heavenly. On earth, our soul is clothed in flesh and blood, which is the visible and organic body. But once this body is left behind, the soul will move to the heavenly realm, where it will receive its body back, but one that has been transformed into a heavenly body. PAULINE COMMENTARY FROM THE GREEK CHURCH.[2]

NOT MADE WITH HANDS. CHRYSOSTOM: Once again, Paul is alluding to the resurrection, which many of the Corinthians did not understand or accept. The earthly tent is our body.

Admittedly, it was not made with hands, but Paul is simply comparing it with the houses we live in. He was not trying to make an exact contrast between the earthly and the heavenly but rather to exalt the latter in every possible way. HOMILIES ON THE EPISTLES OF PAUL TO THE CORINTHIANS 10.1.[3]

THE TRANSFORMATION OF THE BODY. ORIGEN: In regard to our bodily nature we must understand that there is not one body which we now use in lowliness and corruption and weakness and a different one which we are to use hereafter in incorruption and power and glory, but that this same body, having cast off the weaknesses of its present existence, will be transformed into a thing of glory and made spiritual. The result is that what was a vessel of dishonor shall itself be purified and become a vessel of honor and a habitation of blessedness. And we must believe that our body remains in this condition for ever unchangeably by the will of the Creator. We are made certain of this fact by the statement of the apostle Paul in which he says, "We have a house not made with hands, eternal in the heavens." ON FIRST PRINCIPLES 3.6.6.[4]

THE PROMISE OF AN IMMORTAL BODY. AUGUSTINE: Should anyone say that the cause of vices and evil habits lies in the flesh because when the soul is influenced by the flesh it lives in such a manner, he cannot have sufficiently considered human nature as a whole. . . . But notice that the apostle who, in discussing the corruptible body, had used the words "even though our outer man is decaying," goes on, a little further, to declare: "For we know that if the earthly house in which we dwell be destroyed, we have

---

[1]CSEL 81.228-29. [2]NTA 15:26. [3]NPNF 1 12:326. [4]OFP 252.

a building from God, a house not made by human hands, eternal in the heavens." . . . On the one hand, our corruptible body may be a burden on our soul; on the other hand, the cause of this encumbrance is not in the nature and substance of the body. Therefore, aware as we are of its corruption, we do not desire to be divested of the body but rather to be clothed with its immortality. In immortal life we shall have a body, but it will no longer be a burden since it will no longer be corruptible. City of God 14.3.[5]

5:2 Our Heavenly Dwelling

We Groan Now. Chrysostom: The heavenly dwelling is the incorruptible body which we shall put on in the resurrection. We are groaning now because what is to come is far better than what we now have. Homilies on the Epistles of Paul to the Corinthians 10.2.[6]

As in Labor. Pelagius: Our groanings are like those of a woman in labor, awaiting a new birth. Commentary on the Second Epistle to the Corinthians 5.[7]

A Transformed Body. Theodoret of Cyr: The heavenly body is not some different one but the one we have now, which will be transformed. Commentary on the Second Epistle to the Corinthians 313.[8]

5:3 Putting On the New Body

Not Found Naked. Ambrosiaster: People are earnest in their prayers that they should not be excluded from the glory which is promised. This is what being found naked means. For when the soul is clothed in a body, it must also be clothed with the glory by which it is transformed into brightness. Commentary on Paul's Epistles.[9]

Clothing the Inner Person. Didymus the Blind: The unbeliever and the evil man, even if

by chance he puts on a heavenly body, will still be found naked, because he has done nothing to acquire the clothing of the inner man. Pauline Commentary from the Greek Church.[10]

Incorruptible. Chrysostom: When we discard our present body, we shall receive in heaven the same body in an incorruptible form. It is however possible to be clothed in this body and yet still be found naked, that is, without glory or security. The resurrection is common to all, but the glory is not. Some will rise to honor and others to dishonor, some to a kingdom and others to punishment. Homilies on the Epistles of Paul to the Corinthians 10.2.[11]

Immortal. Severian of Gabala: Everyone, righteous and unrighteous alike, will put on immortality. But if the latter are consigned to hell, that is the same thing as being found naked. Pauline Commentary from the Greek Church.[12]

5:4 Mortality Swallowed by Life

We Sigh with Anxiety. Ambrosiaster: Paul is saying here that we are oppressed by bodily sufferings and death. Commentary on Paul's Epistles.[13]

Taking Away Corruption. Chrysostom: We do not want to be delivered from the body but only from the corruption which is in it. Our body is a burden to us, not because it is a body but because it is corruptible and liable to suffering. But when the new life comes, it will take away this corruption—the corruption, I say, not the body itself. Homilies on the Epistles of Paul to the Corinthians 10.3.[14]

5:5 The Spirit as a Guarantee

---

[5]FC 14:351*. [6]NPNF 1 12:326-27. [7]Migne PL 30:783C. [8]Migne PG 82:406. [9]CSEL 81.229. [10]NTA 15:27. [11]NPNF 1 12:327. [12]NTA 15:290. [13]CSEL 81.230. [14]NPNF 1 12:327.

The Agent of Our Adoption. Ambrosiaster: The Spirit is our guarantee because he is the agent of our adoption. Commentary on Paul's Epistles.[15]

A Guarantee. Pelagius: God has given us the Spirit as a guarantee so that we might know that he will not allow the temple of his Spirit to perish. Commentary on the Second Epistle to the Corinthians 5.[16]

Prepared from Creation. Chrysostom: Here Paul shows that these things were prepared from the beginning. It is not now that they have been decreed but from the moment of creation, when he fashioned Adam. God did not create the first man in order that he should die but in order to make him immortal. To prove this, Paul adds that we have been given the Spirit as a guarantee. God is presented as having made a commitment to us to fulfill his promises. Paul does this in order to make what he says more credible to those less attentive. Homilies on the Epistles of Paul to the Corinthians 10.3.[17]

A Remedy Foreseen. Theodoret of Cyr: Since God the Creator foresaw the sin of Adam, he prepared a remedy for it. For he himself has given us the first fruits of the Spirit, so that by the miracles which the Spirit does in our midst we may be reassured that the promises of fu-

ture glory are true. Commentary on the Second Epistle to the Corinthians 314.[18]

Clarity from the Spirit. Augustine: However, now we see obscurely but then face to face; now we see partially but then completely.[19] But the present ability to see in the Scriptures obscurely and partially something which, nonetheless, is in accord with Catholic faith is the work of the pledge which was received by the virgin church at her bridegroom's lowly coming. She will be wed at his final coming when he will come in glory and when she will then behold face to face, for he has given to us a pledge which is the Holy Spirit, as the apostle says. Question 59.4.[20]

The Purpose of the Present Time. Augustine: For this period in God's plan, in which the Lord has deigned to appear in time and visibly as a man and has given to us as a pledge the Holy Spirit, by whose sevenfold working we are given life (apostolic authority having been added like the seasoning of a few fish), what else therefore does this period in God's plan effect but the possibility of attaining the prize of the heavenly calling without [our] powers failing us? "For we walk by faith and not by sight." Question 61.7.[21]

---

[15]CSEL 81.230. [16]Migne PL 30:783D. [17]NPNF 1 12:327. [18]Migne PG 82:407. [19]1 Cor 13:12. [20]FC 70:114*. [21]FC 70:123.

5:6-10 PAUL'S ATTITUDE

[6]So we are always of good courage; we know that while we are at home in the body we are away from the Lord, [7]for we walk by faith, not by sight. [8]We are of good courage, and we would rather be away from the body and at home with the Lord. [9]So whether we are at home or away, we make it our aim to please him. [10]For we must all appear before the

judgment seat of Christ, so that each one may receive good or evil, according to what he has done in the body.

OVERVIEW: While we are in this body, we are pressured by events in the world. Once we have left the body we know that we will be with God (PELAGIUS, AMBROSIASTER). We cannot now see what we shall be like, but we discern it by faith alone (THEODORET OF CYR, AUGUSTINE, SEVERIAN OF GABALA). If we are going to rise with a body, it is clear that we shall not be judged without a body (CLEMENT OF ALEXANDRIA, AMBROSIASTER, CHRYSOSTOM, AUGUSTINE, CYRIL OF ALEXANDRIA). All shall render a final account (ORIGEN, FULGENTIUS). Meanwhile, in this world we are wayfarers (ORIGEN, JEROME, CASSIODORUS).

5:6 Always of Good Courage

ABSENT FROM THE LORD. AMBROSIASTER: God is still present, but because we cannot see him we are said to be absent from him as long as we are in the body. COMMENTARY ON PAUL'S EPISTLES.[1]

PILGRIMS AND WANDERERS. PELAGIUS: As long as we are in this present body, we are tossed about by events in this world and do not know how it will all end. But once we have left the body, we know that we are going to be with God, since we are freed from the uncertain and hostile cares of this world. Here we are pilgrims, and as wanderers we should not worry too much about the things of this world. Let us be content with what is necessary and concentrate all our desire and longing on getting to our Father's home. COMMENTARY ON THE SECOND EPISTLE TO THE CORINTHIANS 5.[2]

FOREIGNERS FOR A BRIEF TIME. CASSIODORUS: We have been expelled in the person of Adam from our abode in paradise, and we have our lodging in this land because we do not possess the blessedness of that native land; so we are seen to be foreigners in this world. As Paul likewise says, "While we are in this body, we are absent from the Lord." EXPLANATION OF THE PSALMS 118.54.[3]

HASTENING HOME. JEROME: We who in this world "are exiled from the Lord" walk about on earth, it is true, but we are hastening on our way to heaven. For here we do not have a lasting place, but we are wayfarers and pilgrims, like all our fathers. HOMILY 63 ON PSALMS.[4]

THE HOPE OF THE FUTURE. AUGUSTINE: Man indeed brought death to himself and to the Son of Man, but the Son of Man, by dying and rising again, brought life to man. . . . He wished to suffer this in the sight of his enemies, that they might think him, as it were, forsaken, and that the grace of the New Testament might be entrusted to us, to make us learn to seek another happiness, which we now possess by faith, but then we shall behold it. "For while we are in the body," says the apostle, "we are absent from the Lord, for we walk by faith and not by sight." Therefore, we now live in hope, but then we shall enjoy reality. LETTER TO HONORATUS 140.9.[5]

5:7 Walking by Faith

WE WALK BY FAITH. SEVERIAN OF GABALA: By faith we hope in God, for his form is not visible to us. But we believe that we shall dwell with him and that we shall see him as far as it is possible for a human being to see him. For Moses saw him when he was still in the body,[6] and the angels see him in the way that is possible for them. PAULINE COMMENTARY FROM THE GREEK CHURCH.[7]

---

[1]CSEL 81.231. [2]Migne PL 30:783D—784A. [3]ACW 53:198-99. [4]FC 57:46. [5]FC 20:77. [6]Ex 24:9-11; 33:11. [7]NTA 15:291.

NOT BY SIGHT. THEODORET OF CYR: We cannot now see what we shall be like, but we discern it by faith alone. That is why after the death of the body we want to stand in the presence of God. COMMENTARY ON THE SECOND EPISTLE TO THE CORINTHIANS 314.[8]

THE EYE OF FAITH. AUGUSTINE: Therefore, amid the shadows of this life in which "we are absent from the Lord" as long as "we walk by faith and not by sight," the Christian soul should consider itself desolate and should not cease from praying and from attending with the eye of faith to the word of the divine and sacred Scriptures. TO PROBA 130.[9]

JUSTIFICATION BY FAITH, GLORIFICATION BY SIGHT. FULGENTIUS: Nevertheless, when we hear at the same time of the justified and the glorified, let us not assign both the work of justification and glorification to the same moment in the present time. For the grace of justification is given in the present time, but the grace of glorification is saved as a future grace. The one is of faith, the other of sight. Paul says that now "we walk by faith, not by sight." What the saints believe now, then they will see. TO MONIMUS 1 11.5.[10]

5:8 At Home with the Lord

EAGER TO DEPART. CHRYSOSTOM: Paul has put the greatest thing of all last, for to be with Christ is greater than having an incorruptible body. By avoiding direct mention of painful things like death and the end, Paul has dealt with them in such a way as to make his hearers long for them by calling them "presence with God." Similarly, he has passed over the sweet things of this life and expressed them in painful terms, calling them "absence from the Lord." He did this in order that we should not fondly linger among what we now have but be prepared to depart for something much better. HOMILIES ON THE EPISTLES OF PAUL TO THE CORINTHIANS 10.4.[11]

THE COURAGE OF THE PILGRIM. ORIGEN: I pray that our souls may never be disquieted, and even more that in the presence of the tribunals and of the naked swords drawn against our necks they may be guarded by the peace of God, which passes all understanding, and may be quieted when they consider that those who are foreigners from the body are at home with the Lord of all. AN EXHORTATION TO MARTYRDOM 4.[12]

5:9 Our Aim Is to Please God

OUR AIM. AMBROSIASTER: We have to put our energy into good works in order to please God. COMMENTARY ON PAUL'S EPISTLES.[13]

DEPARTING OR STAYING. CHRYSOSTOM: Departing is not good in itself, but only if it is in God's grace. Likewise, staying here is not the worst of evils, unless we are offending him. HOMILIES ON THE EPISTLES OF PAUL TO THE CORINTHIANS 10.4.[14]

5:10 The Judgment Seat of Christ

WHAT ONE HAS DONE IN THE BODY. AMBROSIASTER: If we are going to receive what we have done in the body, it is clear that we shall not be judged without a body, good or bad. Paul does not say "in the flesh," because the deeds of the flesh always deserve punishment, but "in the body," because sometimes the body acts spiritually and sometimes it acts carnally. COMMENTARY ON PAUL'S EPISTLES.[15]

THE JUDGMENT SEAT. CHRYSOSTOM: Having alarmed and shaken his hearers by mentioning the judgment seat, Paul softens what he says by mentioning the possibility of receiving good rewards, as well as bad. HOMILIES ON THE EPISTLES OF PAUL TO THE CORINTHIANS 10.5.[16]

---

[8]Migne PG 82:407. [9]FC 18:379. [10]FC 95:202. [11]NPNF 1 12:328. [12]CWS:43. [13]CSEL 81.231. [14]NPNF 1 12:328. [15]CSEL 81.232. [16]NPNF 1 12:328-29.

We Must All Appear. Augustine: Christ judges all things because when he is with God he is above all. Of True Religion 58.[17]

The Soul Did Not Exist Before the Body. Cyril of Alexandria: From this we learn that the soul was not punished for sins committed before it acquired a body. In fact, the soul did not exist before the body. Letter 81.4.[18]

All Must Appear Before Christ. Clement of Alexandria: Those who drag in a doctrine of moral indifference do violence to some few passages of Scripture, thinking that they support their own love of pleasure; in particular, the passage "Sin shall have no authority over you; for you are not subject to sin but to grace."[19] But there are other such passages, which there is no good reason to record for these purposes, as I am not equipping a pirate ship! Let me quickly cut through their attempt. The admirable apostle in person will refute their charge in the words with which he continues the previous quotation: "Well then! Shall we sin because we are no longer under law but under grace? God forbid!" With these inspired prophetic words, at a single stroke he undoes the sophistical skill at the service of pleasure. So they have not understood, it seems, that "we must all appear before Christ's tribunal, where each must receive what is due to him for his physical conduct, good or bad," that is, where a person may receive recompense for what he has done by means of his body. Stromata 3.8.61.[20]

We Must Give Account. Fulgentius: Human beings . . . because they have been made rational will render an account to God for themselves and for all the things which they have received for use in this present life and, according to the nature of their works, will receive either punishment or glory. "For we must all appear before the judgment seat of Christ, so that each one may receive recompense, according to what he did in the body, whether good or bad." . . . Therefore, eternal life will be given in the future only to the one to whom forgiveness of sins has been given in this world. Only he will receive forgiveness of sins here who renounces his sins and hastens to the highest and true God with true conversion of heart. For that [judgment] will not be a time of forgiveness but of retribution. There mercy will not justify the sinner, but justice will distinguish the just and the sinner. On the Forgiveness of Sins 2.6.1.[21]

The Mark of a Lazy Soul. Origen: Why do we ourselves not believe that we all will stand "before the judgment seat of Christ so that each one may obtain the things proper to the body according to what he has done, whether good or evil"? If we would believe these things entirely, there would be applied to us what was written, "Redemption of a man's soul is his wealth."[22] But how can we either know or believe or understand these things when we indeed do not come together to hear them? For who of you, when the Scriptures are read, really pays attention? God through the prophet threatens indeed in great anger, "I will send famine upon the earth; not a famine of bread or the thirst of water but a famine of hearing the word of God."[23] But now God has not sent "a famine" upon his church nor "a thirst to hear the word of God." For we have "living bread which came down from heaven."[24] We have "living water springing up into eternal life."[25] Why in this time of fruitfulness do we destroy ourselves by famine and thirst? It is the mark of a lazy and lingering soul to suffer want in all this abundance. Homily 9.5 on Leviticus.[26]

---

[17]LCC 6:254. [18]FC 77:106 . [19]Rom 6:14. [20]FC 85:294. [21]FC 95:154. [22]Prov 13:8. [23]Amos 8:11. [24]Cf. Jn 6:41, 33. [25]Cf. Jn 4:10, 14. [26]FC 83:191.

5:11-15 SEEING THINGS FROM GOD'S POINT OF VIEW

[11]Therefore, knowing the fear of the Lord, we persuade men; but what we are is known to God, and I hope it is known also to your conscience. [12]We are not commending ourselves to you again but giving you cause to be proud of us, so that you may be able to answer those who pride themselves on a man's position and not on his heart. [13]For if we are beside ourselves, it is for God; if we are in our right mind, it is for you. [14]For the love of Christ controls us, because we are convinced that one has died for all; therefore all have died. [15]And he died for all, that those who live might live no longer for themselves but for him who for their sake died and was raised.

OVERVIEW: We shall live because Christ died for us (AUGUSTINE, CYRIL OF ALEXANDRIA). For our sake he rose again (CHRYSOSTOM). The apostles were not obliged to be silent about the gifts they received from Christ (AMBROSIASTER), which they keep in perpetual remembrance (BASIL). Even if Paul seems to be beside himself, the love of God is in control (DIDYMUS THE BLIND). Even if people think he is mad, everything he does is for the glory of God (CHRYSOSTOM).

5:11 Known to God

KNOWN ALSO TO THE CORINTHIANS' CONSCIENCE. CHRYSOSTOM: It is because he knows the judgment which is to come that Paul does everything he can to avoid giving offense in his ministry to the Corinthians. HOMILIES ON THE EPISTLES OF PAUL TO THE CORINTHIANS 11.1.[1]

5:12 Cause for Pride

PERSONAL PRIDE. AMBROSIASTER: Paul is saying this because of some people who used to take a personal pride in making it known that they had been taught by men who had always been with the Lord. COMMENTARY ON PAUL'S EPISTLES.[2]

NOT PRAISING HIMSELF. CHRYSOSTOM: Paul is concerned to avoid giving the impression that he is praising himself. Nothing would be more offensive to his hearers than that. Since he was forced to defend himself, he insists that he is doing it for their sakes, not for his own glory. His main purpose was to stop those who were abusing their position and thereby harming the church. HOMILIES ON THE EPISTLES OF PAUL TO THE CORINTHIANS 11.1.[3]

5:13 For God and for Others

IF WE ARE BESIDE OURSELVES. AMBROSIASTER: What Paul has said is sane from his hearers' point of view, as long as it is understood in the sense in which it was uttered, but if it is thought to have been spoken out of boastfulness, it is insane. For all pride is a kind of insanity. COMMENTARY ON PAUL'S EPISTLES.[4]

FOR THE GLORY OF GOD. CHRYSOSTOM: What Paul means is that even if people think he is mad, everything he does is for the glory of God. HOMILIES ON THE EPISTLES OF PAUL TO THE CORINTHIANS 11.2.[5]

---

[1]NPNF 1 12:331. [2]CSEL 81.233. [3]NPNF 1 12:331. [4]CSEL 81.233-34. [5]NPNF 1 12:331.

5:14 *Christ's Love Controls Us*

No Need to Be Silent About Gifts from Christ. Ambrosiaster: Because of the love of Christ the apostles were not silent about the gifts they received from him. Those who love him are surrounded by such gifts. They were not boasting about them but inviting their hearers to become Christ's disciples. Commentary on Paul's Epistles.[6]

The Love of Christ. Didymus the Blind: Paul explains that although he is beside himself, the love of God controls him. Pauline Commentary from the Greek Church.[7]

One Death Worth the Life of All. Cyril of Alexandria: But how is it that "one died for all," one who is worth all others, if the suffering is considered simply that of some man? If he suffered according to his human nature, since he made the sufferings of his body his own. . . . The death of him alone according to the flesh is known to be worth the life of all, not the death of one who is as we are, even though he became like to us, but we say that he, being God by nature, became flesh and was made man according to the confession of the Fathers. Letter 50.[8]

Freedom from Death to Serve for Life. Augustine: Paul said: "Therefore all died; and Christ died for all, in order that they who are alive may live no longer for themselves, but for him who died for them and rose again." All people, consequently, without a single exception, were dead through sin, original sin or original with personal sin superadded, either by ignorance of or conscious refusal to do what is right. And for all these dead souls one living man died—a man utterly free from sin—with the intention that those who come alive by forgiveness of their sins live no longer for themselves but for him who died for all on account of our sins and rose again for our justification. City of God 20.6.[9]

Death to Sin. Augustine: As the apostle says, and as we have often repeated: "Since one died for all, therefore all died, and he died for all in order that they who are alive may live no longer for themselves but for him who died for them and rose again." The living are those for whom he who was living died in order that they might live; more plainly, they are freed from the chains of death, they for whom the one free among the dead died. Or, still more plainly: they have been freed from sin, for whom he who was never in sin died. Although he died once, he dies for each at that time when each, whatever his age, is baptized in his death; that is, the death of him who was without sin benefits each man at the time when, having been baptized in his death, he who was dead in sin shall also die to sin. Against Julian 6.15.48.[10]

The Love of the Apostle's Heart. Chrysostom: All this, in fact, blessed Paul had in mind, that fervent lover of Christ, who like a winged bird traversed the whole world. . . . See his uprightness, see the extraordinary degree of his virtue, see his fervent love. "The love of Christ," he says, "constrains us," that is, urges, impels, coerces us. Then, wishing to explain what had been said by him, he says, "convinced of this, that if one person [died] indeed for all, then all have died, he did die for all so that the living might live no longer for themselves but for the one who died and rose for them." Do you see how appropriate it was for him to say, "The love of Christ constrains us"? He is saying, you see, if he died for the sake of us all, he died for the purpose that we the living might live no longer for ourselves but for him who died and rose for us. Accordingly, let us heed the apostolic exhortation, not living for ourselves but for him who died and rose for us. Homily 34.15 on Genesis.[11]

---

[6]CSEL 81.234. [7]NTA 15:28. [8]FC 76:218. [9]FC 24:262. [10]FC 35:356-57. [11]FC 82:299-300*.

5:15 *Living for Christ*

CHRIST DIED FOR ALL. CHRYSOSTOM: What Paul says here appears to be one thing, but if you look carefully you will see that it is two. First, we live because of Christ. Second, Christ died for us. Either of these would be enough by itself to put us in his debt, but taken together, our liability is overwhelming. Indeed, we could even say that there are three things here, because it was for our sake that he rose again and took the first fruits of the resurrection up to heaven with him.[12] HOMILIES ON THE EPISTLES OF PAUL TO THE CORINTHIANS 11.2.[13]

THE MARK OF THE CHRISTIAN. BASIL: What is the mark of those who eat the bread and drink the cup of Christ? That they keep in perpetual remembrance him who died for us and rose again. What is the mark of those who keep such remembrance? That they live not for themselves but for him who died for them and rose again. What is the mark of a Christian? That his justice abound in all things more than that of the scribes and Pharisees, according to the rule of the doctrine which has been handed down in the Lord's gospel. What is the mark of the Christian? That they love one another as Christ has loved us. What is the mark of the Christian? To set the Lord always in his sight. What is the mark of the Christian? To watch daily and hourly and stand prepared in that state of perfection which is pleasing to God, knowing that at what hour he thinks not, the Lord will come. THE MORALS 22.[14]

---

[12]Mk 16:19; Lk 24:51. [13]NPNF 1 12:332. [14]FC 9:205.

5:16-21 A NEW CREATION

[16]*From now on, therefore, we regard no one from a human point of view; even though we once regarded Christ from a human point of view, we regard him thus no longer.* [17]*Therefore, if any one is in Christ, he is a new creation;* [g] *the old has passed away, behold, the new has come.* [18]*All this is from God, who through Christ reconciled us to himself and gave us the ministry of reconciliation;* [19]*that is, in Christ God was reconciling* [h] *the world to himself, not counting their trespasses against them, and entrusting to us the message of reconciliation.* [20]*So we are ambassadors for Christ, God making his appeal through us. We beseech you on behalf of Christ, be reconciled to God.* [21]*For our sake he made him to be sin who knew no sin, so that in him we might become the righteousness of God.*

g Or creature   h Or God was in Christ reconciling

OVERVIEW: Until the cross there was a suspicion that Christ was weak, but once he rose from the dead all that vanished (AMBROSIASTER). There was a time when we knew Christ in his earthly life, but now we know him from his resurrection (JEROME, CHRYSOSTOM). Those who have been baptized must put to death the ways of the world (SEVERIAN OF GABALA). It is not only God who has been reconciled to us, but we who have been reconciled to him (Hilary of Poitiers, Theodoret of Cyr, Chrysostom), making us new creatures (Basil, Gregory of Nyssa, Augustine). The old things that have passed away refer to our sins and wickedness, as well as all the ceremonial rites of Judaism (Chrysostom, Caesarius of Arles). God was in Christ reconciling the world to himself, not counting their sins against them (Ambrosiaster, Theodoret of Cyr, Chrysostom). We do not say that Christ became a sinner, but being righteous, the Father made him a victim for the sins of the world (Eusebius, Gregory Nazianzen, Cyril of Alexandria). God allowed his Son to suffer as if he was a condemned sinner, so that we might be delivered from the penalty of our sins (Chrysostom). Christ was called what we are in order to call us to be what he is (Theodoret of Cyr). He fully shared our humanity with us (Ambrose, Pelagius).

5:16a Not from a Human Point of View

We Suspected Christ Was Weak. Ambrosiaster: Now that Christ has risen from the dead, birth according to the flesh loses its importance, bodily weakness ceases to count and the sufferings of death no longer matter either. Right up until the cross there was a suspicion that Christ was weak, but once he rose from the dead all that vanished and what was previously doubted came to be believed. Commentary on Paul's Epistles.[1]

A Human Point of View. Chrysostom: Even if believers are still in their earthly bodies, we do not relate to them in that way, because the life according to the flesh has been transcended. We have been born again by the Spirit and have learned a different kind of behavior, which is that of heaven. It is Christ who has brought about this change. There was a time when we knew him in his earthly life, but now we know

him in the perfection of his resurrection. Homilies on the Epistles of Paul to the Corinthians 11.3.[2]

5:16b Regarding Christ from a Different Viewpoint

Imitating the Behavior of Heaven. Severian of Gabala: When Christ was a man, he lived in a human way, fulfilling the law. But when he died and rose again, immortal, he abolished the things of the law and took on the ways of heaven. Therefore those who have been baptized must also put the ways of the world to death and imitate the pure behavior of heaven. Pauline Commentary from the Greek Church.[3]

Regarding Him Thus No Longer. Theodoret of Cyr: There was a time when Christ had a body which was capable of suffering, but after his suffering and death it became incorruptible and immortal. Commentary on the Second Epistle to the Corinthians 317.[4]

The Body of Life. Cyril of Alexandria: After the resurrection it was the same body which had suffered except it no longer had the human infirmities in it. For we assert that it was no longer receptive of hunger, or of weariness or of anything else of such a kind but was thereafter incorruptible, and not only this but also life-giving. For it is the body of life, that is, the body of the Only Begotten, for it has been made resplendent with the glory most proper to his divinity and is known to be the body of God. Therefore, even if some might say that it is divine, just as, of course, it is the human body of a man, he would not err from proper reasoning. Whence I think that the very wise Paul said, "And even though we have known Christ according to the flesh, yet now we know him so no longer." For

---

[1]CSEL 81.235. [2]NPNF 1 12:332. [3]NTA 15:293. [4]Migne PG 82:410.

being God's own body, as I said, it transcends all human bodies. LETTER 45.12.[5]

THE GREAT ADVOCATE. GREGORY NAZIANZEN: Even at this moment he is, as man, interceding for my salvation, until he makes me divine by the power of his incarnate humanity. "As man," I say, because he still has with him the body he assumed, though he is no longer "regarded as flesh"—meaning the bodily experiences, which, sin aside, are ours and his. This is the "Advocate"[6] we have in Jesus—not a slave who falls prostrate before the Father on our behalf. Get rid of what is really a slavish suspicion, unworthy of the Spirit. It is not in God to make that demand nor in the Son to submit to it; the thought is unjust to God. No, it is by what he suffered as man that he persuades us, as Word and Encourager, to endure. That, for me, is the beginning of his "advocacy." ORATION 30: ON THE SON.[7]

CONTINUITY AND GLORIOUS DIFFERENCE. JEROME: Just as before the Lord suffered his passion, when he was transformed and glorified on the mountain, he certainly had the same body that he had had down below, although of a different glory. So also after the resurrection, his body was of the same nature as it had been before the passion but of a higher state of glory and in more majestic appearance, in fulfillment of the words of Paul: "So that henceforth we know no one according to the flesh. And even though we have known Christ according to the flesh, yet now we know him so no longer." HOMILY 61 ON PSALMS.[8]

5:17 A New Creation

WE HAVE A NEW LIFE. CHRYSOSTOM: We ought to live for Christ not just because we belong to him, not just because he died for us and not just because he rose again on our behalf. We ought to live for him because we have been made into something different. We now have a new life.

The old things which have passed away refer to our sins and impiety, as well as all the observances of Judaism. HOMILIES ON THE EPISTLES OF PAUL TO THE CORINTHIANS 11.4.[9]

BORN AGAIN IN BAPTISM. THEODORET OF CYR: Those who believe in Christ have entered a new life. They must be born again in baptism and renounce their former sins. COMMENTARY ON THE SECOND EPISTLE TO THE CORINTHIANS 317.[10]

THE ODOR OF LIFE. CAESARIUS OF ARLES: The Old Testament was good, but without spiritual understanding it dies with the letter. The New Testament, through grace, restores the odor of life. SERMONS 168.4.[11]

ORDERED FREEDOM. AUGUSTINE: We are then truly free when God orders our lives, that is, forms and creates us not as human beings—this he has already done—but as good people, which he is now doing by his grace, that we may indeed be new creatures in Christ Jesus. Accordingly the prayer: "Create in me a clean heart, O God."[12] ENCHIRIDION 9.31.[13]

THREE CREATIONS. BASIL: But, if we must go on with our discussion and make a deeper study, let us from this point contemplate especially the divine power of the Holy Spirit. We find three creations mentioned in the Scripture; the first, the education from nonexistence into existence; the second, the change from worse to better; and the third, the resurrection of the dead. In these you will find the Holy Spirit co-operating with the Father and the Son. . . . Now, humanity is created a second time through baptism, "for if any man is in Christ, he is a new creature." LETTERS 8.[14]

A NEW AND SHINING CLOAK. CHRYSOSTOM: You

---

[5]FC 76:195-96. [6]1 Jn 2:1. [7]FGFR 272. [8]FC 57:34*. [9]NPNF 1 12:332. [10]Migne PG 82:410-11. [11]FC 47:411. [12]Ps 51:10. [13]LCC 7:357. [14]FC 13:36.

heard today that the blessed Paul . . . told us in his letter to the Corinthians: "If any man is in Christ, he is a new creature." To prevent us from interpreting the text as applying to a visible creation, he stated: "If any man is in Christ," teaching us that if any man has gone over to the side of those who believe in Christ, he is an example of a new creature. Tell me, if we see new heavens and other portions of his creation, is there a profit in this which can match the benefit we gain from seeing a man converted from evil to virtue and changing from the side of error to that of truth? This is what the blessed Paul called a new creature, and so immediately he went on to say: "The former things have passed away; behold, they are all made new!" By this he briefly showed that those who, by their faith in Christ, had put off like an old cloak the burden of their sins, those who had been set free from their error and been illumined by the light of justification, had put on this new and shining cloak, this royal robe. This is why he said: "If any man is in Christ, he is a new creature: the former things have passed away; behold, they are all made new." THE FOURTH INSTRUCTION 12.[15]

CITIZENS OF A NEW WORLD. CHRYSOSTOM: Do you see why faith in Christ and the return to virtue are called a new creation? I exhort you, therefore, both you who have previously been initiated and you who have just now enjoyed the Master's generosity, let us all listen to the exhortation of the apostle, who tells us: "The former things have passed away; behold, they are all made new." Let us forget the whole past and, like citizens in a new world, let us reform our lives, and let us consider in our every word and deed the dignity of him who dwells within us. THE FOURTH INSTRUCTION 16.[16]

THE APOSTOLIC RULE. GREGORY OF NYSSA: "If any man is in Christ, he is a new creature, the former things have passed away." The "new creation" is the apostolic rule. And what this is

Paul makes abundantly clear in another section, saying: "In order that I might present to myself the church in all her glory, not having spot or wrinkle or any such thing, but that she might be holy and without blemish."[17] A new creature he called the indwelling of the Holy Spirit in a pure and blameless soul removed from evil and wickedness and shamefulness. For, when the soul hates sin, it closely unites itself with God, as far as it can, in the regimen of virtue; having been transformed in life, it receives the grace of the Spirit to itself, becomes entirely new again and is recreated. ON THE CHRISTIAN MODE OF LIFE.[18]

5:18 The Ministry of Reconciliation

ALL THINGS COME FROM GOD. AMBROSIASTER: Although Christ has redeemed us all things come from God, because all fatherhood comes from him. Therefore [in triune reasoning] precedence must be given to the person of the Father. COMMENTARY ON PAUL'S EPISTLES.[19]

GOD GAVE US THE MINISTRY. CHRYSOSTOM: When I say that Christ is the cause of our reconciliation, I say that the Father is also. When I say that the Father gave, I mean that the Son gave also. HOMILIES ON THE EPISTLES OF PAUL TO THE CORINTHIANS 11.4.[20]

GOD HAS RECONCILED US TO HIMSELF. THEODORET OF CYR: It is not just that God has been reconciled to us; we also have been reconciled to him. COMMENTARY ON THE SECOND EPISTLE TO THE CORINTHIANS 317.[21]

THE RECONCILIATION OF THE WORLD. HILARY OF POITIERS: Since all things are reconciled in him, recognize . . . that he reconciles all things to the Father in himself, which he will reconcile through himself. The same apostle says: "But all things are from God, who has reconciled us

---

[15]ACW 31:71. [16]ACW 31:72. [17]Eph 5:27. [18]FC 58:141-42*. [19]CSEL 81.236. [20]NPNF 1 12:333. [21]Migne PG 82:411.

to himself through Christ and has given to us the ministry of reconciliation. For God was truly in Christ, reconciling the world to himself." Compare the entire mystery of the evangelical faith with these words! He who is seen in him who is seen, he who works in him who works, he who speaks in him who speaks is the same one who will reconcile in him who reconciles. Accordingly, there is the reconciliation in him and through him, because the Father himself, who remains in him through the identical nature, restored the world to himself through him and in him by this reconciliation. THE TRINITY 8.51.[22]

5:19 Reconciling the World to Himself

NOT COUNTING OUR TRESPASSES. AMBROSIASTER: God was in Christ, that is to say, the Father was in the Son, reconciling the world to himself, not counting their sins against them. Creation sinned against God and did not repent, so God, who did not want his work to perish, sent his Son in order to preach through him the forgiveness of sins and thus reconcile them to himself. COMMENTARY ON PAUL'S EPISTLES.[23]

IN CHRIST. CHRYSOSTOM: Can you see how great God's love is for us? Who was the offended party? He was. Who took the first steps toward reconciliation? He did. Some will say that he sent the Son in his place, but this is a misunderstanding. Christ did not come apart from the Father who sent him. They were both involved together in the work of reconciliation. HOMILIES ON THE EPISTLES OF PAUL TO THE CORINTHIANS 11.5.[24]

5:20 God Makes His Appeal Through Us

DEVOTION AND BELIEF. AMBROSIASTER: Paul wants to show both his devotion to God's providence and his belief that it is his duty to love the whole human race. COMMENTARY ON PAUL'S EPISTLES.[25]

BE RECONCILED. PELAGIUS: We are reconciled to God if we believe in Christ. COMMENTARY ON THE SECOND EPISTLE TO THE CORINTHIANS 5.[26]

AMBASSADORS FOR CHRIST. CHRYSOSTOM: The apostles are ambassadors for Christ because they have succeeded to his ministry. And not only his, for they represent the Father as well. HOMILIES ON THE EPISTLES OF PAUL TO THE CORINTHIANS 11.5.[27]

THE SIGN OF THE NEW LIFE. AUGUSTINE: He says, "He [Christ] who knew no sin, he [God] made to be sin for us." The God to whom we are to be reconciled has thus made him the sacrifice for sin by which we may be reconciled. He himself is therefore sin as we ourselves are righteousness—not our own but God's, not in ourselves but in him. Just as he was sin—not his own but ours, rooted not in himself but in us—so he showed forth through the likeness of sinful flesh, in which he was crucified, that since sin was not in him he could then, so to say, die to sin by dying in the flesh, which was "the likeness of sin." And since he had never lived in the old manner of sinning, he might, in his resurrection, signify the new life which is ours, which is springing to life anew from the old death in which we had been dead to sin. ENCHIRIDION 13.41.[28]

5:21 Becoming the Righteousness of God

THE SAME SUBSTANCE. AMBROSE: This proves that his body and soul are of the same substance as ours. THE SACRAMENT OF THE INCARNATION OF OUR LORD 7.76.[29]

AN OFFERING FOR OUR SINS. AMBROSIASTER: Christ did not have to be born as a man, but he

---

[22]FC 25:316. [23]CSEL 81.237. [24]NPNF 1 12:333. [25]CSEL 81.239. [26]Migne PL 30:786B. [27]NPNF 1 12:334. [28]LCC 7:365. [29]FC 44:248.

became man because of sin. It was only because all flesh was subject to sin that he was made sin for us. In view of the fact that he was made an offering for sins, it is not wrong for him to be said to have been made "sin," because in the law the sacrifice which was offered for sins used to be called a "sin." After his death on the cross Christ descended to hell, because it was death, working through sin, which gave hell its power. Christ defeated death by his death and brought such benefit to sinners that now death cannot hold those who are marked with the sign of the cross. COMMENTARY ON PAUL'S EPISTLES.[30]

He Suffered as if a Condemned Sinner. CHRYSOSTOM: God allowed his Son to suffer as if a condemned sinner, so that we might be delivered from the penalty of our sins. This is God's righteousness, that we are not justified by works (for then they would have to be perfect, which is impossible), but by grace, in which case all our sin is removed. HOMILIES ON THE EPISTLES OF PAUL TO THE CORINTHIANS 11.5.[31]

A Victim for Sinners. CYRIL OF ALEXANDRIA: We do not say that Christ became a sinner, far from it, but being righteous (or rather, righteousness, because he did not know sin at all), the Father made him a victim for the sins of the world. LETTER 41.10.[32]

To Deliver Us from the Law. SEVERIAN OF GABALA: Paul shows here how much he grieved for those who obstinately kept the law. For by keeping the law, he says, we become sinners. Christ became sin in order to deliver us from the law. God says to us that we should accept this freedom by no longer remaining in bondage to the commands of the law. PAULINE COMMENTARY ON THE GREEK CHURCH.[33]

Called to Be What We Are. THEODORET OF CYR: Christ was called what we are in order to call us to be what he is. COMMENTARY ON THE

Second Epistle to the Corinthians 318.[34]

The Blessed Curse. AMBROSE: But if you hold to the letter, so as to think from what is written, namely, the Word was made flesh, that the Word of God was turned into flesh, do you not deny that it is written of the Lord that he did not make sin but was made sin?[35] So, was the Lord turned into sin? Not so, but, since he assumed our sins, he is called sin. For the Lord is also called an accursed thing, not because the Lord was turned into an accursed thing but because he himself took on our curse. He says: "For he is accursed that hangs on a tree."[36] . . . It is written that he was made sin, that is, not by the nature and operation of sin . . . ; but that he might crucify our sin in his flesh, he assumed for us the burden of the infirmities of a body already guilty of carnal sin. THE SACRAMENT OF THE INCARNATION OF OUR LORD 6.60.[37]

The Call to Discipleship. BASIL: In yet another passage, contemplating the still more wonderful benevolence of God in Christ, he says: "Him who knew no sin, he has made sin for us, that we might be made the justice of God in him." In view of these utterances and other similar ones, we are under the strictest obligation, unless we have received in vain the grace of God, first, to free ourselves from the dominion of the devil who leads a slave of sin into evils even against his will. Secondly, each of us, after denying himself present satisfactions and breaking off his attachment to this life, must become a disciple of the Lord, as he himself said: "If any man will come after me, let him deny himself and take up his cross and follow me."[38] CONCERNING BAPTISM 1.1.[39]

The Righteous Victim. CYRIL OF ALEXANDRIA: For this reason, we say that he was named sin;

---

[30]CSEL 81.238. [31]NPNF 1 12:334. [32]FC 76:174. [33]NTA 15:293. [34]Migne PG 82:411. [35]Cf. 2 Cor 5:21. [36]Cf. Gal 3:13. [37]FC 44:242. [38]Mt 16:24. [39]FC 9:343*.

wherefore, the all-wise Paul writes, "For our sakes he made him to be sin who knew nothing of sin," that is to say, God the Father. For we do not say that Christ became a sinner. Far from it, but being just, or rather in actuality justice, for he did not know sin, the Father made him a victim for the sins of the world. LETTER 41.[40]

THE WILLING SACRIFICE. EUSEBIUS: And he, since he understood at once his Father's divine counsel, and because he discerned better than any other why he was forsaken by the Father, humbled himself even more. He embraced death for us with all willingness and "became a curse for us," holy and all-blessed though he was. . . . "He that knew no sin, became sin, that we might become the righteousness of God in him." Yet more—to wash away our sins he was crucified, suffering what we who were sinful should have suffered, as our sacrifice and ransom, so that we may well say with the prophet, he bears our sins and is pained for us, and he was wounded for our sins and bruised for our iniquities, so that by his stripes we might be healed, for the Lord has given him for our sins.[41] So, as delivered up by the Father, as bruised, as bearing our sins, he was led as a sheep to the slaughter. THE PROOF OF THE GOSPEL 4.17.[42]

THE CURSE THAT DESTROYS THE CURSE. GRE-GORY NAZIANZEN: But look at it in this manner: that as for my sake he was called a curse who destroyed my curse, and sin who takes away the sin of the world, and became a new Adam to take the place of the old, just so he makes my disobedience his own as head of the whole body. As long, then, as I am disobedient and re-bellious, both by denial of God and by my passions, so long Christ is also called disobedient on my account. But when all things shall be sub-dued to him on the one hand by acknowledg-ment of him and on the other by a reformation, then he himself also will have fulfilled his sub-mission, bringing me whom he has saved to God. THE THEOLOGICAL ORATIONS 5.[43]

A WICKED BURDEN BORNE BY RIGHTEOUSNESS. GREGORY NAZIANZEN: And so the passage "The Word was made flesh" seems to me to be equiva-lent to that in which it is said that he was made sin or a curse for us; not that the Lord was trans-formed into either of these—how could he be? But because by taking them upon him he took away our sins and bore our iniquities. LETTERS ON THE APOLLINARIAN CONTROVERSY 101.[44]

---

[40]FC 76:174*. [41]Cf. Isa 53:4. [42]POG 219. [43]LCC 3:179-80. [44]LCC 3:222.

6:1-10 THE DAY OF SALVATION

[1]*Working together with him, then, we entreat you not to accept the grace of God in vain.* [2]*For he says,*
"At the acceptable time I have listened to you,
and helped you on the day of salvation."
Behold, now is the acceptable time; behold, now is the day of salvation. [3]*We put no obstacle*

in any one's way, so that no fault may be found with our ministry, ⁴but as servants of God we commend ourselves in every way: through great endurance, in afflictions, hardships, calamities, ⁵beatings, imprisonments, tumults, labors, watching, hunger; ⁶by purity, knowledge, forbearance, kindness, the Holy Spirit, genuine love, ⁷truthful speech, and the power of God; with the weapons of righteousness for the right hand and for the left; ⁸in honor and dishonor, in ill repute and good repute. We are treated as impostors, and yet are true; ⁹as unknown, and yet well known; as dying, and behold we live; as punished, and yet not killed; ¹⁰as sorrowful, yet always rejoicing; as poor, yet making many rich; as having nothing, and yet possessing everything.

OVERVIEW: The grace of the Holy Spirit possesses the soul, filling it with gladness and power, making sweet our sufferings in the Lord and taking away the perception of present pain because of the hope of the things to come (GREGORY OF NYSSA, JEROME, SAHDONA). The Christian life is the opposite of what it appears to be (ORIGEN, CHRYSOSTOM, PELAGIUS). The acceptable time is the time of the gift, the time of grace, when it is decreed that not only will no account of our sins be demanded from us but also we shall also enjoy abundant blessings, righteousness and sanctification (CHRYSOSTOM). This is the time for repentance; the next life will be the time for reward (BASIL) or judgment (FULGENTIUS). Paul like a heavenly physician (MAXIMUS OF TURIN) cuts away everything that might cause the negligent to stumble (AMBROSIASTER). The weapons of righteousness on the right hand are those which are pleasing to the mind; those on the left hand are those which are not (THEODORET OF CYR, CHRYSOSTOM, DIDYMUS THE BLIND).

6:1 Working Together with God

HASTENING TO PLEASE GOD. CHRYSOSTOM: Paul is telling his hearers that they must not relax just because God has sought them out and sent them as ambassadors. On the contrary, for that very reason we should hasten to please him and reap our spiritual blessings. HOMILIES ON THE EPISTLES OF PAUL TO THE CORINTHIANS 12.1.[1]

DO NOT ACCEPT GOD'S GRACE IN VAIN. CAESARIUS OF ARLES: What does it mean to receive the grace of God in vain except to be unwilling to perform good works with the help of his grace? SERMON 126.5.[2]

VARIED DANGERS. BASIL: That man, indeed, is in danger who does not throughout his whole life place before himself the will of God as his goal, so that in health he shows forth the labor of love by his zeal for the works of the Lord and in sickness displays endurance and cheerful patience. The first and greatest peril is that by not doing the will of God, he separates himself from the Lord and cuts himself off from fellowship with his own brothers; secondly, that he ventures, although undeserving, to claim a share in the blessings prepared for those who are worthy. Here also we must remember the words of the apostle: "And we helping do exhort you that you receive not the grace of God in vain."[3] And they who are called to be brothers of the Lord should not receive in a wanton spirit so great a divine grace nor fall from so high a dignity through negligence in doing the will of God but rather obey the same apostle, saying: "I, a prisoner in the Lord, beseech you that you walk worthy of the vocation in which you are called."[4] THE LONG RULES 34.[5]

---

[1]NPNF 1 12:336. [2]FC 47:219. [3]2 Cor 6:1. [4]Eph 4:1. [5]FC 9:300-301.

6:2 The Day of Salvation

God Decreed Grace. Ambrosiaster: Paul is teaching that God's grace in Christ was predestined. God decreed that his mercy would be poured out in this way, that help would be lavished on those who called for it in the name of Christ. Commentary on Paul's Epistles.[6]

The Present Acceptable Time. Basil: "Now is the acceptable time," says the apostle, "now is the day of salvation." This is the time for repentance; the next life, for reward. Now is the time to endure; then will be the day of consolation. Now God is the helper of such as turn aside from the evil way; then he will be the dread and unerring inquisitor of the thoughts and words and deeds of humankind. Now we enjoy his longanimity; then we shall know his just judgment, when we have risen, some to never-ending punishment, others to life everlasting, and everyone shall receive according to his works. The Long Rules.[7]

The Acceptable Time. Chrysostom: Let us not let the opportunity slip, but rather let us display a zeal worthy of his grace. We press on because we know that the time is both short and opportune. The acceptable time is the time of the gift, the time of grace, when it is decreed that not only will no account of our sins be demanded from us, but that we shall also enjoy abundant blessings, righteousness, sanctification and all the rest. Homilies on the Epistles of Paul to the Corinthians 12.1.[8]

Prophetic Testimony. Theodoret of Cyr: Paul backs his exhortation up with this prophetic testimony. Commentary on the Second Epistle to the Corinthians 318.[9]

Present Welcome—Future Judgment. Fulgentius: For the blessed Paul also knew the distance between the present world and the world to come. He knew that only in the present

world could the blessing of salvation be acquired but that only in the world to come could a just reward be given to individuals according to the quality of their works, good or wicked. So, when he had repeated the prophetic testimony which God speaks: "In an acceptable time, I heard you, and on the day of salvation, I helped you," he immediately followed it up by adding, "Behold now is a very acceptable time, now is the day of salvation." But concerning the future he says, "For we must all appear before the judgment seat of Christ, so that each one may receive recompense according to what he did in the body, whether good or evil."[10] Therefore, eternal life will be given in the future only to the one to whom forgiveness of sins has been given in this world. Only he will receive the forgiveness of sins here who renounces his sins and hastens to the highest and true God with true conversion of heart. For the future will not be a time of forgiveness but of retribution. There mercy will not justify the sinner, but justice will distinguish the just and the sinner. On the Forgiveness of Sins 5.3.[11]

Judgment Awaits Those Who Scorn the Gospel. Fulgentius: There they will be tortured endlessly, not only with the hellish punishment of soul together with body but also by the very darkness of the will set in evil. Here for such people there will be the evil will itself for a heaping up of punishment, because of which there remains for them torment without end. They now scorn the opportunity offered by the acceptable time and on the day of salvation; they do not seek to be helped by God. God has conveyed this time to us in the words of the prophet, saying, "In an acceptable time, I heard you and on the day of salvation, I helped you." When the blessed apostle inserted this testimony in his letter, he immediately added, "Behold, now is the very acceptable time; behold

---

[6]CSEL 81.239. [7]FC 9:224*. [8]NPNF 1 12:336-37. [9]Migne PG 82:411. [10]2 Cor 5:10. [11]FC 95:153-54*.

now is the day of salvation." On the Forgiveness of Sins 7.3.[12]

Heavenly Medicine for Dreadful Wounds.
Maximus of Turin: The holy apostle presents
testimony from the prophets when he says: "At
an acceptable time I heard you, and on the day
of salvation I helped you." And this follows:
"Behold, now is the acceptable time; behold,
now is the day of salvation." Hence I also testify
to you that these are the days of redemption,
that this is the time, as it were, of heavenly
medicine, when we shall be able to heal every
stain of our vices and all the wounds of our sins.
We shall do so if we faithfully implore the physician of our souls and do not, as people scarcely
worthy of the undertaking, despise his precepts.
For a person wearied of his illness has found
healing when he very carefully observes his doctor's orders; but if he does one thing when another is ordered, then the transgressor and not
the physician is guilty if the sickness is aggra-
vated. The Sermons of St. Maximus of Turin,
Sermon 35.[13]

Persistence in Prayer. Sahdona: If we go
on crying out and do not receive any answer,
this is for our advantage: instead of losing
heart and growing weary, we should go on
brazenly asking God, for it is certain that "at
an acceptable time" and at the appropriate
hour he will answer us and deliver us. Book
of Perfection.[14]

6:3 No Fault with Paul's Ministry

No Obstacle. Ambrosiaster: By his faith and
vigilance, Paul is cutting away everything which
might cause the negligent to stumble, out of
fear that their sluggishness might present his
disciples with a cause for stumbling. Fault
would have been found with their ministry if
they did not exemplify in their deeds the things
they were teaching. Commentary on Paul's
Epistles.[15]

6:4 Commended as Servants of God

Not as Flatterers. Ambrosiaster: Servants of
God teach without flattery, so that they might
please him whose servants they are, unlike the
false apostles, who sought only to please their
hearers. Commentary on Paul's Epistles.[16]

The Graceful Perception of Present Pain.
Gregory of Nyssa: This is the grace of the
Holy Spirit, possessing the entire soul and filling the dwelling place with gladness and power,
making sweet for the soul the sufferings of the
Lord, and taking away the perception of the present pain because of the hope of the things to
come. On the Christian Mode of Life.[17]

As Servants of God. Chrysostom: It is one thing
to be free from accusation, but it is a far greater
thing to appear as servants of God. To be acquitted of all accusation is not nearly as grand as to be
covered with praise. Homilies on the Epistles of
Paul to the Corinthians 12.2.[18]

A Warning Against Indifference. Gregory
of Nyssa: For this is the grace of the Holy
Spirit, possessing the entire soul and filling the
dwelling place with gladness and power, making
sweet for the soul the sufferings of the Lord
and taking away the perception of the present
pain because of the hope of the things to come.
So, govern yourselves thus as you are about to
ascend to the highest power and glory through
your co-operation with the Spirit; endure every
suffering and trial with joy with a view toward
appearing to be worthy of the dwelling of the
Spirit within you and worthy of the inheritance
of Christ. Never be puffed up or enfeebled by indifference to the point of falling yourselves or
being the cause of another's sin. On the Christian Mode of Life.[19]

---

[12]FC 95:156-57. [13]ACW 50:83-84. [14]SFPSL 232. [15]CSEL
81.239. [16]CSEL 81.240. [17]FC 58:157. [18]NPNF 1 12:337.
[19]FC 58:157.

6:5 Present Sufferings

Through Great Endurance. Chrysostom: Any one of these things is intolerable, but taken together, think what kind of soul is needed to endure them! Homilies on the Epistles of Paul to the Corinthians 12.2.[20]

6:6 Means of Endurance

By the Holy Spirit. Chrysostom: By "purity" Paul means either chastity, or general purity, or lack of corruption or even his free preaching of the gospel. By "knowledge" he means the wisdom given by God, which is the only true knowledge. When he unexpectedly mentions the Holy Spirit in this list, Paul means more than just that he does everything in the power of the Spirit. He is saying here that the Spirit himself has been given to him and that it is because of this indwelling presence that he has received the spiritual gifts. "Genuine love" was the motivating power of all these good things. It is that which made Paul what he was. It was also love which caused the Spirit to abide with him, with whose help he did everything in the right way. Homilies on the Epistles of Paul to the Corinthians 12.2.[21]

6:7 The Weapons of Righteousness

Truthful Speech. Ambrosiaster: The word of truth was in Paul's teaching, because he conveyed no message other than the one which he had received from the Lord. Commentary on Paul's Epistles.[22]

For Both Hands. Didymus the Blind: The man who rightly seeks righteousness according to human understandings is equipped with the arms of righteousness for the left hand. The man who does the same according to the teachings of the truth and who has been sought out for this task by the Son of righteousness bears the weapons of the right hand. Pauline Commentary from the Greek Church.[23]

Painful Things of the Left Hand. Chrysostom: The things on the left refer to those things which seem to be painful, because it is these which bring the reward. Homilies on the Epistles of Paul to the Corinthians 12.3.[24]

Pleasing Things of the Right Hand. Theodoret of Cyr: The weapons of righteousness on the right hand are those which are pleasing to the mind; those on the left hand are those which are not. Commentary on the Second Epistle to the Corinthians 320.[25]

Keep the Goal in View. Gregory of Nyssa: But to one who is elevated in thought, all things appear to be of equal honor, and none is preferred to another, because the course of life is run equally by opposites, and there is present in the destiny of each person the power to live well or badly, "with the armor on the right hand and on the left," as the apostle says, "in honor and dishonor." Accordingly, the one who has purified his mind and rightly examined the truth of reality will go on his way in the time assigned to him from birth to death, not spoiled by pleasures or cast down by austerity, but, in accordance with the custom of travelers, he will be little affected by what he encounters. For it is customary for travelers to hasten on to the end of their journey whether they go through meadows and fertile fields or through deserts and rough terrain; pleasure does not delay them, nor does the unpleasant impede them. So he himself will also hurry on without distraction to the goal before him, turning off into none of the byways. He will pass through life looking only to heaven, just like some good captain who guides his ship to its lofty destination. On Virginity 4.[26]

---

[20]NPNF 1 12:337. [21]NPNF 1 12:337-38. [22]CSEL 81.241-42. [23]NTA 15:31. [24]NPNF 1 12:338. [25]Migne PG 82:414. [26]FC 58:24*.

6:8 *In Honor and Dishonor*

A Faithful Preacher. Ambrosiaster: Paul is saying that he was recognized as a sincere and faithful preacher by those who believed that the gospel was the glory of God. Even to those who thought that the gospel was vile, he presented himself as a faithful servant of God and was not afraid to say things which they would have been scandalized to hear. Commentary on Paul's Epistles.[27]

In Honor and Dishonor. Chrysostom: It may seem that it is easier to bear honor than dishonor, but honor too has its perils, because the one who enjoys it may be thrown back and break his neck. Paul therefore glories in both circumstances, because he showed brightly in each of them. Homilies on the Epistles of Paul to the Corinthians 12.3.[28]

Only One Person's Opinion Matters. Jerome: Do not angle for compliments, lest while you win the popular applause, you dishonor God. "If I yet pleased men," says the apostle, "I should not be the servant of Christ."[29] He ceased to please men when he became Christ's servant. Christ's soldier marches on through good report and evil report, the one on the right hand and the other on the left. No praise elates him, no reproaches crush him. He is not puffed up by riches nor depressed by poverty. Joy and sorrow he alike despises. The sun will not burn him by day nor the moon by night.[30] Letter 52.[31]

Well-Known and Recognized. Origen: If we have lived a life deserving "good repute" and have been spoken well of, now let us also bear up under "ill repute" from the ungodly. Still more, if we have been admired as "true" by those who love truth, now let us laugh at being called "imposters." During the many dangers from which we have been delivered many said that we were "well known" by God; now let the one who wishes call us "unknown," when we are probably better known. Thus, in bearing what has happened to us we are "punished" and yet "not killed," and though "rejoicing," we resemble those who are "sorrowful." An Exhortation to Martyrdom 43.[32]

6:9 *Dying, Yet We Live*

Rescued from Death. Ambrosiaster: Those who hated the apostles thought that they were dying every day of their lives as the price for their wickedness. But because the apostles were preaching with God's approval, they kept being rescued from death by the help of Christ. Commentary on Paul's Epistles.[33]

Unknown, Yet Known. Pelagius: Paul and his companions were unknown to the wicked and reprobate but well known to the faithful and just. Commentary on the Second Epistle to the Corinthians 6.[34]

6:10 *Having Nothing Yet Everything*

Sorrowful, Yet Rejoicing. Chrysostom: People outside the church may think we are sorrowful, but in fact we are always rejoicing. We may look poor, but in fact we have enormous riches, both spiritual and physical. As usual, the Christian life is the exact opposite of what it appears to be on the surface. Homilies on the Epistles of Paul to the Corinthians 12.4.[35]

Possessing Everything. Pelagius: The person who has only the bare necessities lacks nothing. Commentary on the Second Epistle to the Corinthians 6.[36]

Keep What Matters. Augustine: It could happen that some public official would say to a

---

[27]CSEL 81.242. [28]NPNF 1 12:338. [29]Gal 1:10. [30]Ps 121 (120):6. [31]LCC 5:327. [32]CWS:73-74. [33]CSEL 81.242-43. [34]Migne PL 30:788A. [35]NPNF 1 12:339. [36]Migne PL 30:788B.

Christian: "Either you will stop being a Christian, or, if you persist in being one, you shall have no house or property." That will be the time when those rich men, who had decided to keep their riches in order to win merit with God by using them for good works, will choose to give them up for Christ's sake rather than Christ for their sake. . . . Thus they become as men "having nothing, yet possessing all things"—and everlasting life in the world to come, lest by giving up Christ for the sake of riches they be cast into everlasting death. LETTER 157 TO HILARIUS.[37]

---

[37]FC 346-47.

6:11-18 THE CHALLENGE TO THE CORINTHIANS

[11]*Our mouth is open to you, Corinthians; our heart is wide.* [12]*You are not restricted by us, but you are restricted in your own affections.* [13]*In return—I speak as to children— widen your hearts also.*

[14]*Do not be mismated with unbelievers. For what partnership have righteousness and iniquity? Or what fellowship has light with darkness?* [15]*What accord has Christ with Belial?*[i] *Or what has a believer in common with an unbeliever?* [16]*What agreement has the temple of God with idols? For we are the temple of the living God; as God said,*

"I will live in them and move among them,
and I will be their God,
and they shall be my people.
[17]*Therefore come out from them,*
and be separate from them, says the Lord,
and touch nothing unclean;
then I will welcome you,
[18]*and I will be a father to you,*
and you shall be my sons and daughters,
says the Lord Almighty."

i *Greek* Beliar

OVERVIEW: Nothing is wider than Paul's heart. He loved all the believers as one might love the object of one's dearest affection (CHRYSOSTOM, AMBROSIASTER). We are temples of the living God. There is nothing more damaging to us than idols, because they tempt us to depart from our faith (AMBROSIASTER). Nothing can deprive us of our baptism apart from the denial of God and consorting with demons (PHILOXENUS OF MABBUG). Light has no fellowship with darkness (CYPRIAN, GREGORY OF NYSSA, BASIL, JEROME, AUGUSTINE, PRUDENTIUS).

6:11 Our Heart Is Wide

A PURE CONSCIENCE. AMBROSIASTER: Paul is saying this because of the freedom he enjoyed in a pure conscience. A mind with a bad conscience is afraid to speak, loses its train of thought and makes verbal slips. People whose heart is enlarged are happy with themselves because they are confident that they have behaved well. COMMENTARY ON PAUL'S EPISTLES.[1]

SPEAKING FREELY. CHRYSOSTOM: Paul means by this that he talks to the Corinthians freely, as he would to people whom he loves. He holds nothing back and suppresses nothing. Nothing is wider than Paul's heart, which loved all the believers with all the passion which one might have toward the object of one's affection. HOMILIES ON THE EPISTLES OF PAUL TO THE CORINTHIANS 13.1.[2]

6:12 Restricted Affections

LACKING LOVE, RESTRICTIONS APPEAR. CHRYSOSTOM: The heart of one who loves is wide open. He walks with great freedom. It is when love is lacking that restrictions appear. Paul did not want to accuse them openly of lack of love. He merely points to the behavioral result and encourages them to perceive the cause for themselves. HOMILIES ON THE EPISTLES OF PAUL TO THE CORINTHIANS 13.1.[3]

6:13 Widen Your Hearts

RESPOND TO LOVE. CHRYSOSTOM: The return is not equal, because to respond to love is not as great as to offer it in the first place. Even if the amount is the same, it still comes in second place. HOMILIES ON THE EPISTLES OF PAUL TO THE CORINTHIANS 13.13.[4]

AS TO CHILDREN. THEODORET OF CYR: Paul blunts the force of his accusations by calling the Corinthians his children. COMMENTARY ON THE SECOND EPISTLE TO THE CORINTHIANS 321.[5]

6:14 Do Not Be Mismated

APPEALING TO THEIR SELF-RESPECT. CHRYSOSTOM: Paul sounds here like the father who asks a son who despises his parents and prefers wicked companions: "What are you doing? Do you not realize that you are much nobler and better than they are?" He will detach his son more easily from such people by appealing to his self-respect rather than by demeaning him. In the same way, Paul appeals to the Corinthians, not mentioning himself or God but appealing directly to their sense of who they are in themselves. HOMILIES ON THE EPISTLES OF PAUL TO THE CORINTHIANS 13.14.[6]

THE SPIRIT OF ANTICHRIST. CYPRIAN: But if we consider what the apostles thought about heretics, we shall find that in all of their epistles they execrate and abominate the sacrilegious depravity of the heretics. . . . And since they say that there is nothing in common between justice and iniquity, no communion between light and darkness, how can the darkness illuminate or iniquity justify? And since they are not from God but from the spirit of antichrist, how do they who are enemies of God and whose breasts the spirit of antichrist fills carry on both spiritual and divine affairs? LETTER 73.15 TO JUBAIAN.[7]

LIGHT AND DARKNESS. GREGORY OF NYSSA: For, says the apostle: "What fellowship has light with darkness?" Since there is a distinct and irreconcilable contradiction between light and darkness, the person partaking of both has a share in neither, because of the opposition of the parts drawn up against each other at the

---

[1]CSEL 81.243-44. [2]NPNF 1 12:342. [3]NPNF 1 12:342-43. [4]NPNF 1 12:343. [5]Migne PG 82:415. [6]NPNF 1 12:343-44. [7]FC 51:277.

same time in his mixed life. His faith provides the lighted part, but his dark habits put out the lamp of reason. Since it is impossible and inconsistent for light and darkness to exist in fellowship, the person containing each of the opposites becomes an enemy to himself, being divided in two ways between virtue and evil. He sets up an antagonistic battle line within himself. And just as it is not possible, when there are two enemies, for both to be victors over each other (for the victory of the one causes the death of his adversary), so also in this civil war brought about by the confusion in his life, it is not possible for the stronger element to win without the other becoming completely destroyed. For how will the army of reverence be stronger than evil, when the wicked phalanx of the opponents attacks it? If the stronger is going to win, the enemy must be completely slaughtered. And thus virtue will have the victory over evil only when the entire enemy gives way to it through an alliance of the reasonable elements against the unsound ones. . . . For it is not possible for the good to exist in me, unless it is made to live through the death of my enemy. As long as we keep grasping opposites with each of our hands, it is impossible for there to be participation in both elements in the same being. For, if we are holding evil, we lose the power to take hold of virtue. On Perfection.[8]

The True Baptism. Philoxenus of Mabbug: It is the same now with us who are baptized: neither the wetness of the water in which we are baptized nor the oiliness of the oil with which we are anointed remain with us after our death. But the Holy Spirit, who is mingled in our souls and bodies through the oil and the water, does remain with us, both in this life and after our death. For he is our true baptism, and for this reason we remain always baptized, for the Holy Spirit is within us always, and no sin can strip us of our baptism—neither adultery, nor theft, nor fornication, nor false testimony nor

any action of this sort: only the denial of God and consorting with demons can do this, for in such cases the Holy Spirit really does depart, for he does not consent to remain in a place where Satan dwells. "For what fellowship does Christ have with Satan or the believer with the unbeliever, or God's temple with that of demons?" On the Indwelling of the Holy Spirit.[9]

A Sinful Mingling. Prudentius: Shall we stoop to say of mammon who have been reborn in Christ? Formed to God's eternal image, shall we serve the fleeting world? God forbid that celestial flame should be mingled with earth's mire. Hymns 1.58-60.[10]

Contradictory Loves. Jerome: There cannot be two contradictory loves in one man. Just as there is no harmony between Christ and Belial, between justice and iniquity, so it is impossible for one soul to love both good and evil. You who love the Lord, hate evil, the devil; in every deed, there is love of one and hatred of the other. "He who has my commandments and keeps them, he it is who loves me."[11] . . . You who love the things that are good, hate the things that are bad. You cannot love good unless you hate evil. Homily 73 on Psalms.[12]

A Distinctive Faith with Distinctive Actions. Augustine: Now, I speak to the true Christians. If you believe, hope and love otherwise [than the pagans do], then live otherwise and gain approval for your distinctive faith, hope and charity by distinctive actions. Pay attention to the apostle when, in earnest admonition, he says: "Do not bear the yoke with unbelievers. For what has justice in common with iniquity? Or what fellowship has light with darkness?. . . Or what part has the believer with the unbeliever? And what agreement

---

[8]FC 58:100*. [9]SFPSL 112-13. [10]FC 43:100. [11]Jn 14:21. [12]FC 57:115.

has the temple of God with idols?" New Year's Day 198.3.[13]

Forbidden Acts. Basil: These words clearly indicate an act which is absolutely forbidden and is displeasing to God and perilous for the one who would venture to commit it. Concerning Baptism 2.7.[14]

6:15 What Is in Common?

What Accord Has Christ with Belial? Philoxenus of Mabbug: The Holy Spirit is our true baptism, and for this reason we remain always baptized, for he is in us always, and nothing can deprive us of our baptism apart from the denial of God and consorting with demons. In such cases the Holy Spirit really does depart, because he cannot agree to remain in a place where Satan dwells. On the Indwelling of the Holy Spirit.[15]

6:16 The Temple of the Living God

The Temple of God. Ambrosiaster: It is obvious that the things Paul lists are opposites and that we are to flee from the ones and cling to the others. No one can serve two masters. Christ has proclaimed that we should go away from the devil, who wants to represent himself falsely as God. He has promised us eternal life, so we should be strangers to the treachery and wrong-headedness of unbelievers. He has forbidden the worship of idols because they are incompatible with the temple of God. We are temples of the living God. There is nothing more damaging to us than idols, because they tempt us to depart from our faith in the one true God. Commentary on Paul's Epistles.[16]

6:17 Be Separate from Them

Touch Nothing Unclean. Chrysostom: Unclean things refer to adultery and fornication in the flesh and to evil thoughts in the soul. We must be delivered from both. Homilies on the Epistles of Paul to the Corinthians 13.17.[17]

6:18 A Father to You

Putting Up Barriers. Clement of Alexandria: Paul is prophetic in telling us to put up a barrier, not between ourselves and the married but between ourselves and the Gentiles who are still living immorally, and also from those heresies which believe neither in chastity nor in God. Stromata 3.73.4.[18]

Received as Children. Ambrosiaster: God wants us to be set apart from all contamination so that he can receive us as his children. By this testimony Paul exhorts us to a pure life. He shows that Jesus Christ was already our Lord in ancient times and was predestined to receive us in the fondness of his love. Commentary on Paul's Epistles.[19]

---

[13]FC 38:57. [14]FC 9:406. [15]SFPSL 112-13. [16]CSEL 81.245. [17]NPNF 1 12:344. [18]FC 85:301. [19]CSEL 81.246-47.

7:1-12 PAUL'S AGONY FOR THE CORINTHIANS

¹Since we have these promises, beloved, let us cleanse ourselves from every defilement of body and spirit, and make holiness perfect in the fear of God.

²Open your hearts to us; we have wronged no one, we have corrupted no one, we have taken advantage of no one. ³I do not say this to condemn you, for I said before that you are in our hearts, to die together and to live together. ⁴I have great confidence in you; I have great pride in you; I am filled with comfort. With all our affliction, I am overjoyed.

⁵For even when we came into Macedonia, our bodies had no rest but we were afflicted at every turn—fighting without and fear within. ⁶But God, who comforts the downcast, comforted us by the coming of Titus, ⁷and not only by his coming but also by the comfort with which he was comforted in you, as he told us of your longing, your mourning, your zeal for me, so that I rejoiced still more. ⁸For even if I made you sorry with my letter, I do not regret it (though I did regret it), for I see that that letter grieved you, though only for a while. ⁹As it is, I rejoice, not because you were grieved, but because you were grieved into repenting; for you felt a godly grief, so that you suffered no loss through us. ¹⁰For godly grief produces a repentance that leads to salvation and brings no regret, but worldly grief produces death. ¹¹For see what earnestness this godly grief has produced in you, what eagerness to clear yourselves, what indignation, what alarm, what longing, what zeal, what punishment! At every point you have proved yourselves guiltless in the matter. ¹²So although I wrote to you, it was not on account of the one who did the wrong, nor on account of the one who suffered the wrong, but in order that your zeal for us might be revealed to you in the sight of God.

OVERVIEW: Paul paid no attention to the pain of the lashes or the rope with which his feet were bound. Forgetting his sufferings, Paul thanked God for the godly sorrow of the church at Corinth (CHRYSOSTOM, BASIL), viewing it as a kind of reward for his troubles (AMBROSIASTER). Worldly sorrow, on the other hand, which regrets the loss of money, reputation and friends, merely leads to greater harm (AMBROSE, BASIL, CHRYSOSTOM, AUGUSTINE). Paul had to do battle not only with external foes but also with enemies within the church and fears within and fatigue (THEODORET OF CYR), but he was not afflicted in the spirit (AMBROSIASTER). It is al-ways a great comfort, when we are suffering, to have someone near us who can share it with us (AMBROSIASTER, CHRYSOSTOM), as happened with the coming of Titus (AMBROSIASTER). He was consoled by the Corinthians to such an extent that in spite of all his affliction he was overflowing with joy (AMBROSIASTER). He reminded them that not touching unclean things is not enough to make them clean (CHRYSOSTOM). Believers are called to cleanse themselves of every defilement (AMBROSIASTER) of the flesh and the spirit (BASIL, THEODORET OF CYR).

7:1 Cleansing from Defilement

Every Defilement. Ambrosiaster: What Paul is saying is clear, but "defilement of the flesh" is to be interpreted in a complex way. Notice that he did not say "from defilement of the flesh" but "from *every* defilement of the flesh" in order to encourage us to flee from all carnal vices—everything which the law prohibits—so that we might perfect holiness of the Spirit in the fear of God. We do this by pursuing the things which are right in the fear of God and which are therefore holy, abstaining from sins in the name of Christ. People who restrain themselves from vices without professing Christ may seem to be set apart according to the world but not according to the Spirit of God. Only those who believe are made clean. Others, whatever they may be like, remain unclean. Commentary on Paul's Epistles.[1]

Cleansing Ourselves. Basil: Here we are instructed to marvel at the unspeakable benevolence of God in Christ Jesus and with the greater fear to cleanse ourselves of every defilement of the flesh and the spirit. Concerning Baptism 1.2.[2]

Make Holiness Perfect. Chrysostom: Not touching unclean things is not enough to make us clean. Something else is needed for us to become holy—earnestness in faith, heedfulness and piety. Homilies on the Epistles of Paul to the Corinthians 13.[3]

Body and Spirit. Theodoret of Cyr: Paul uses the word *spirit* in this verse to mean "soul." Commentary on the Second Epistle to the Corinthians 322.[4]

7:2 Open Your Hearts to Us

Giving Thought to Paul's Comments. Ambrosiaster: Paul wants the Corinthians to give thought to what he is saying, so that when they have taken it to heart they may conclude that what he is saying is true. Commentary on Paul's Epistles.[5]

Wronging No One. Chrysostom: Paul expresses himself in this negative way in order to make his point more sharply. He does not mention all the good he has done but merely challenges the Corinthians to come up with any way he has wronged them, which of course they could not do. Homilies on the Epistles of Paul to the Corinthians 14.1.[6]

7:3 Not to Condemn

Exhorting, Not Rejecting. Ambrosiaster: Paul wants them to realize in what frame of mind he is speaking to them. He is certainly not rejecting people whom he wants to have as sharers with him, but he is exhorting them to make themselves worthy of this sharing. Commentary on Paul's Epistles.[7]

To Die Together and Live Together. Chrysostom: Paul mentions both dying and living, in order to preserve the right balance. For there are a lot of people who will sympathize with others in their misfortunes, but when things turn out well for them they become jealous and do not rejoice on their behalf. Not so the faithful, who are not wounded by envy. Homilies on the Epistles of Paul to the Corinthians 14.1.[8]

7:4 Filled with Comfort

In Spite of Afflictions. Ambrosiaster: Paul is confident because of the way the Corinthians responded to his reproof in the first letter. The fact that they did not take it badly has given him the confidence to admonish them again. He also says that he has been consoled by this to such an extent that in spite of all his affliction he is overflowing with joy. Seeing that

---

[1]CSEL 81.247. [2]FC 9:374. [3]NPNF 1 12:345. [4]Migne PG 82:415-18. [5]CSEL 81.247. [6]NPNF 1 12:347. [7]CSEL 81.248. [8]NPNF 1 12:347.

there is hope for the people on whose behalf he is enduring hardships, he is rejoicing in spite of his tribulations, being certain that he will please God for the fact that they have received salvation. COMMENTARY ON PAUL'S EPISTLES.[9]

GREAT LOVE. CHRYSOSTOM: Some might think that these expressions of praise contradict the admonitions which have gone before. But this is not so, for they help the rebukes to be more acceptable by putting them in the wider context of Paul's great love for the Corinthians. HOMILIES ON THE EPISTLES OF PAUL TO THE CORINTHIANS 14.2.[10]

7:5 Afflicted at Every Turn

FEAR WITHIN. AMBROSIASTER: It is because the flesh is irrational that Paul says that it has no rest from its suffering. But the soul, although it was suffering in the body, did have rest. This is because of the hope that God would reward them for the tribulations inflicted on them by unbelievers. Fightings were inflicted on the body, and fears attacked the soul, but Paul was not at all afflicted in the Spirit, who was given to him so that he might endure such things. COMMENTARY ON PAUL'S EPISTLES.[11]

FIGHTING WITHOUT. CHRYSOSTOM: Paul had to contend with the opposition of unbelievers without and of weak-kneed believers within. HOMILIES ON THE EPISTLES OF PAUL TO THE CORINTHIANS 14.2.[12]

ENEMIES WITHIN. THEODORET OF CYR: Paul had to do battle not only with external foes but also with enemies within the fellowship of the church. He was afraid that believers would be turned away to harmful things. COMMENTARY ON THE SECOND EPISTLE TO THE CORINTHIANS 323.[13]

7:6 God Comforts the Downcast

SHARING IN SUFFERING. AMBROSIASTER: It is always a great comfort, when we are suffering, to have someone near us who can share it with us. COMMENTARY ON PAUL'S EPISTLES.[14]

BY THE COMING OF TITUS. CHRYSOSTOM: Paul always makes a great thing of the coming of Titus, because he wants the Corinthians to hold him in honor and respect. There is nothing more guaranteed to cement a friendship than to help someone know how they have been helpful. HOMILIES ON THE EPISTLES OF PAUL TO THE CORINTHIANS 14.2.[15]

7:7 Rejoicing Still More

REWARD FOR TROUBLES. AMBROSIASTER: Paul showed what great affection he had for them. He paid no mind to the stench of the dungeon, nor of the pain of the lashes, nor of the rope with which his feet were bound. But when he heard that the Corinthians had amended their ways he rejoiced, and forgetting his sufferings, thanked God for their salvation, viewing it as a kind of reward for his troubles. COMMENTARY ON PAUL'S EPISTLES.[16]

CONSOLATION. CHRYSOSTOM: Paul was consoled by the good news from Corinth, which shows how much he loved the people there. HOMILIES ON THE EPISTLES OF PAUL TO THE CORINTHIANS 14.2.[17]

7:8 Grieved for a While

SOOTHING THEM. CHRYSOSTOM: Paul behaves toward the Corinthians as a parent does toward little children, soothing them after they have been through a painful experience. HOMILIES ON THE EPISTLES OF PAUL TO THE CORINTHIANS 15.1.[18]

---

[9]CSEL 81.248. [10]NPNF 1 12:347-48. [11]CSEL 81.249. [12]NPNF 1 12:348. [13]Migne PG 82:418. [14]CSEL 81.251. [15]NPNF 1 12:348. [16]CSEL 81.251. [17]NPNF 1 12:348. [18]NPNF 1 12:350.

A PROPER SORROW. AUGUSTINE: Moreover, even sorrow, the emotion for which, the Stoics claim, there can be found in the soul of a wise man no corresponding "attitude," is a word used in a good sense, especially in Christian writings. The apostle, for example, praises the Corinthians because they were sorrowful according to God. Of course, someone may object that the apostle congratulated the Corinthians because their sorrow led them to repentance and that such sorrow can be experienced only by those who have sinned. What he says is this: "Seeing that the same letter did for a while make you sorry, now I am glad; not because you were made sorry but because your sorrow led you to repentance. For you were made sorry according to God, that you might suffer no loss at our hands. For the sorrow that is according to God produces repentance that surely tends to salvation, whereas the sorrow that is according to the world produces death. For behold this very fact that you were made sorry according to God, what earnestness it has wrought in you." CITY OF GOD 14.8.[19]

7:9 A Godly Grief

THE ULTIMATE RESULT. CHRYSOSTOM: Like a father who watches his son being operated on, Paul rejoices not for the pain being inflicted but for the cure which is the ultimate result. He had no desire to cause harm for its own sake. HOMILIES ON THE EPISTLES OF PAUL TO THE CORINTHIANS 15.1.[20]

THE SORROW THAT PRODUCES REPENTANCE. AMBROSE: Hence Paul teaches us that that kind of sorrow is of value which has not this world but God as its end. It is right, he says, that you become sorrowful, so as to feel repentance in the face of God. . . . Take note of those who in the Old Testament were sorrowful in the midst of their bodily labors and who attained grace, while those who found delight in such pleasures continued to be punished. Hence the Hebrews,

who groaned in the works of Egypt,[21] attained the grace of the just and those "who ate bread with mourning and fear" were supplied with spiritual good.[22] PARADISE 15.77.[23]

7:10 Repentance Leading to Salvation

GODLY SORROW. AMBROSIASTER: Godly grief brings about the death of worldliness. When the sinner is found out he is grieved because he is bound to be punished, not having anyone from whom he may expect mercy. Perhaps for the moment there may be nobody who can exact retribution from him, but he knows he will not be able to escape the judgment of God. COMMENTARY ON PAUL'S EPISTLES.[24]

WORLDLY SORROW. CHRYSOSTOM: Paul was regretful before he saw the fruit of repentance, but afterward he rejoiced. This is the nature of godly sorrow. Worldly sorrow, in contrast to this, is regret for the loss of money, reputation and friends. That kind of sorrow merely leads to greater harm, because the regret is often a prelude to a thirst for revenge. Only sorrow for sin is really profitable. HOMILIES ON THE EPISTLES OF PAUL TO THE CORINTHIANS 15.2.[25]

DUNG AND WHEAT. AUGUSTINE: And, in another passage, he says: "The sorrow that is according to God produces repentance that tends to salvation of which one does not repent." He who is sad according to God is sad in repentance for his sins; sorrow because of one's own iniquity produces justice. First, let what you are displease you so that you may be able to be what you are not. "The sadness that is according to God produces repentance that tends to salvation of which one does not repent." He says: "repentance that tends to salvation." What sort of salvation? That of which one does not repent.

---

[19]FC 14:365. [20]NPNF 1 12:350. [21]Cf. Ex 2:23. [22]Cf. 1 Cor 10:3. [23]FC 42:354-558*. [24]CSEL 81.253. [25]NPNF 1 12:350-51.

What does that mean? One of which you do not repent at any time. For we have had a life of which we ought to have repented; we have had a life calculated to inspire repentance. But we cannot come to that life of which one does not repent except through repentance for an evil life. Will you, my brothers, as I had begun to say, ever find dung in a sifted mass of wheat? Nevertheless, the wheat arrives at that luster, at that fine and beautiful appearance, by means of dung; the foulness was the path to a beautiful result. EASTER SEASON 254.2.[26]

SORROW PRODUCES A FRUITFUL FIELD. AUGUSTINE: Therefore, my brothers, as I have said before, a suitable place for dung helps to produce fruit, but an unsuitable place leads to uncleanness. Someone or other has said, I have come upon this sad person; I see the dung; I examine the place. Tell me, my friend, why are you sad? He says: I have lost my money. The place is unclean; there is no fruit. Let him hear the apostle: "The sorrow that is according to the world produces death." I have looked at still another person groaning, weeping and praying; I recognize the dung and I examine the place. Moreover, I have directed my ear to this man's prayer, and I have heard him say: "O Lord, be thou merciful to me: heal my soul, for I have sinned against you."[27] He laments his sin; I recognize the field; I look for fruit. Thanks be to God! The dung is in a good place; it is not useless there; it produces fruit. This is truly the time of fruitful sorrow, so that we may lament the state of our mortality, the abundance of temptations, the stealthy attacks of sinners, the clash of desires, the conflicts of passions ever rebelling against good thoughts. On this account let us grieve; let us be sad because of this state of affairs. EASTER SEASON 254.4.[28]

REPENT WHILE TIME REMAINS. CHRYSOSTOM: However, I marvel how God, who from the beginning gave humanity pain, which came from sin, abolishes his decision with one resolution and expels the judgment with the sentence. And hear how. Sin produced pain, and through pain sin is annihilated. Pay attention carefully. God threatens the woman. He brings upon her the punishment for her disobedience, and he tells her: "You shall bring forth children in pain."[29] And he showed pain as the harvest of sin. However, oh, how munificent he is! That which he gave for punishment he changed to salvation. Sin gave birth to pain; pain destroys sin. Just as a worm that is born by a tree consumes the very same tree, likewise pain, which is born by sin, kills sin when it is supplied by repentance. For this reason Paul says: "Godly pain produces a repentance that leads to salvation and brings no regret." Pain is good for those who repent sincerely; the sorrow, matching the sin, suits those who sin. . . . Mourn for the sin so you may not lament for the punishment. Apologize to the judge before you come to the court. Or do you not know that all who want to sin flatter the judge, not when the case is being tried but before they enter the court, or through friends, or through guardians, or through another way they coax the judge? The same with God: you cannot persuade the Judge during the time of the tribunal. It is possible for you to plead with the Judge before the time of judgment. HOMILY ON REPENTANCE AND COMPUNCTION 7.6.19.[30]

7:11 Proved Guiltless

ZEAL TO BRING GOOD WORKS TO COMPLETION. AMBROSIASTER: Someone who repents is troubled by the fear that he might sin again. But a person who knows that he has been deformed by sin longs to reform himself. One who knows that he is being rebuked for his own good begins to experience a zeal for bringing good works to completion. COMMENTARY ON PAUL'S EPISTLES.[31]

[26]FC 38:343. [27]Ps 108:7. [28]FC 38:344-45. [29]Gen 3:16. [30]FC 96:102-3*. [31]CSEL 81.253.

The Benefit of Godly Grief. Basil: One who provokes godly grief in us is our benefactor. The Long Rules 52.[32]

7:12 Revealed in God's Sight

Forgiveness Granted. Ambrosiaster: Paul is making it clear that forgiveness ought to be granted to those who did wrong not only for their sake but for the sake of the church, because when one does wrong many suffer. Commentary on Paul's Epistles.[33]

---

[32]FC 9:329. [33]CSEL 81.254.

7:13-16 TITUS

[13]*Therefore we are comforted.*

And besides our own comfort we rejoiced still more at the joy of Titus, because his mind has been set at rest by you all. [14]*For if I have expressed to him some pride in you, I was not put to shame; but just as everything we said to you was true, so our boasting before Titus has proved true.* [15]*And his heart goes out all the more to you, as he remembers the obedience of you all, and the fear and trembling with which you received him.* [16]*I rejoice, because I have perfect confidence in you.*

Overview: Paul is comforted that the Corinthians wanted to reform their ways. He is pleased not only because of their good resolve but also because of the good actions by which they were correcting their former practices (Ambrosiaster). He even adds that after he had boasted about the Corinthians to Titus they had not let him down (Chrysostom).

7:13 The Joy of Titus

Consoled and Rejoicing. Ambrosiaster: Paul has been comforted by the fact that those whom he rebuked wished to mend their ways. But on learning from Titus that they were experiencing pain on account of their error, he was consoled even more and filled with joy, because their resolve had been confirmed by their behavior. Commentary on Paul's Epistles.[1]

7:14 Boasting Proved True

Not Put to Shame. Chrysostom: It is high praise when a teacher boasts that his pupils have not put him to shame. Paul even adds that after he had boasted about the Corinthians to Titus they had not let him down. Homilies on the Epistles of Paul to the Corinthians 16.1.[2]

7:15 The Corinthians' Obedience

Titus Saw Their Progress. Ambrosiaster: Paul is saying that Titus's mind and affection are concerned with them, because he has seen their progress, for the mind of a saint is con-

---

[1]CSEL 81.255. [2]NPNF 1 12:355-56.

cerned with everything that is good. COMMEN-
TARY ON PAUL'S EPISTLES.[3]

TITUS'S GRATITUDE. CHRYSOSTOM: This shows
that Titus was grateful to his benefactors and
also gives the Corinthians even greater honor in
that they were able to make such a deep impression on him. HOMILIES ON THE EPISTLES OF PAUL
TO THE CORINTHIANS 16.1.[4]

7:16 Perfect Confidence

GOOD ACTIONS. AMBROSIASTER: Paul is glad not
only because of their good resolve but because
of the good actions by which they were correcting their former sinful practices. This is why he
has perfect confidence in them. COMMENTARY
ON PAUL'S EPISTLES.[5]

---

[3]CSEL 81.256. [4]NPNF 1 12:356. [5]CSEL 81.256.

8:1-7 GENEROSITY

[1]We want you to know, brethren, about the grace of God which has been shown in the
churches of Macedonia, [2]for in a severe test of affliction, their abundance of joy and their
extreme poverty have overflowed in a wealth of liberality on their part. [3]For they gave
according to their means, as I can testify, and beyond their means, of their own free will,
[4]begging us earnestly for the favor of taking part in the relief of the saints— [5]and this, not
as we expected, but first they gave themselves to the Lord and to us by the will of God.
[6]Accordingly we have urged Titus that as he had already made a beginning, he should also
complete among you this gracious work. [7]Now as you excel in everything—in faith, in
utterance, in knowledge, in all earnestness, and in your love for us—see that you excel in
this gracious work also.

OVERVIEW: Paul offered the Macedonians the
highest praise, for even in their poverty they
gave generously of what they had (THEO-
DORET OF CYR, PELAGIUS). They wanted to offer even more than their strength allowed
(AMBROSIASTER). By giving themselves
wholly to God first (CHRYSOSTOM) and then
to their fellow believers with exceptional generosity (THEODORET OF CYR) of their own free
will (CHRYSOSTOM), the Macedonians demonstrated their sincere desire to receive spiritual
gifts (AMBROSIASTER). Paul sent Titus to
Corinth to encourage them to imitate the Macedonians (CHRYSOSTOM).

**8:1 Grace Shown in the Churches of Mace-
donia**

ACCEPTING THE WORD OF FAITH. AMBROSIASTER:
Paul says that they had received the grace of
God because they accepted the word of faith de-
voutly. COMMENTARY ON PAUL'S EPISTLES.[1]

EXHORTATION TO GENEROSITY. CHRYSOSTOM:
Having encouraged the Corinthians with these
praises, Paul now turns to exhortation once

---

[1]CSEL 81.256.

more. He wants to encourage them to give alms, but instead of saying so directly, he prepares the ground by talking about the highest things first. HOMILIES ON THE EPISTLES OF PAUL TO THE CORINTHIANS 16.2.[2]

THE GRACE OF GOD DECLARED. THEODORET OF CYR: By "the grace of God" Paul means the possession of every good thing. He is not excluding the role of free will by saying this but teaching that every good work is made possible by the help of God. COMMENTARY ON THE SECOND EPISTLE TO THE CORINTHIANS 327.[3]

8:2 A Wealth of Liberality

THEIR SOULS WERE RICH. AMBROSIASTER: Although the Macedonians were short of material resources, their souls were rich, because they ministered to the saints with a pure conscience, trying to please God rather than men. COMMENTARY ON PAUL'S EPISTLES.[4]

RICH IN THEIR SIMPLICITY. PELAGIUS: Some are poor in material terms but rich in their simplicity. They would rather give than receive. COMMENTARY ON THE SECOND EPISTLE TO THE CORINTHIANS 8.[5]

FINDING JOY. CHRYSOSTOM: The affliction of the Macedonians did not lead only to sorrow but also to great rejoicing and generosity. Paul said this in order to prepare the Corinthians to be noble and firm in their sufferings. For they were not merely to be afflicted, they were to use their afflictions as a means of growing in joy. HOMILIES ON THE EPISTLES OF PAUL TO THE CORINTHIANS 16.2.[6]

EXTREME POVERTY. THEODORET OF CYR: This is the height of praise, for in affliction they remained calm and in the depths of poverty they gave generously of what they had. COMMENTARY ON THE SECOND EPISTLE TO THE CORINTHIANS 327.[7]

8:3 Giving Freely

BEYOND THEIR MEANS. AMBROSIASTER: Because they gave themselves to God wholeheartedly, they wanted to offer even more than their strength allowed. COMMENTARY ON PAUL'S EPISTLES.[8]

IN SPITE OF POVERTY. CHRYSOSTOM: The greatness of the Macedonians can be seen from the fact that they gave voluntarily, in spite of their poverty. HOMILIES ON THE EPISTLES OF PAUL TO THE CORINTHIANS 16.3.[9]

8:4 The Relief of the Saints

TAKING PART IN RELIEF. AMBROSIASTER: Because the Macedonians were offering more than they could afford, Paul was inclined to refuse their contribution, fearing that hardship would later cause them to reconsider their good deed. But because they showed themselves to be of such character that they stood firm, with a pure mind in the confidence of faith, attaching more importance to the promises for the future than to immediate rewards in the present, in the end it seemed right for him to accept their contribution. COMMENTARY ON PAUL'S EPISTLES.[10]

DESIRING SPIRITUAL GIFTS. CHRYSOSTOM: Not only did the Macedonians give voluntarily, they insisted that Paul take what they had to offer. Their actions prove just how much they desired spiritual gifts. HOMILIES ON THE EPISTLES OF PAUL TO THE CORINTHIANS 16.3.[11]

8:5 Giving Oneself to the Lord

THEY GAVE THEMSELVES TO THE LORD. AMBROSIASTER: By giving themselves to God first and

---

[2]NPNF 1 12:356. [3]Migne PG 82:422. [4]CSEL 81.256-57. [5]Migne PL 30:792A. [6]NPNF 1 12:357. [7]Migne PG 82:422-23. [8]CSEL 81.257. [9]NPNF 1 12:357. [10]CSEL 81.257. [11]NPNF 1 12:357.

then to their fellow believers, the Macedonians demonstrated their sincere desire to be made perfect. Paul quoted their example in the hope of persuading the Corinthians to do likewise. COMMENTARY ON PAUL'S EPISTLES.[12]

HUMILITY AND WISDOM. CHRYSOSTOM: The secret of the Macedonians' zeal was that first, they gave themselves to the Lord. Everything else flowed from that. As a result, when they showed mercy they were not filled with pride but rather displayed great humility and heavenly wisdom. HOMILIES ON THE EPISTLES OF PAUL TO THE CORINTHIANS 16.3.[13]

GREAT GENEROSITY. THEODORET OF CYR: The words "not as we expected" refer not to the Macedonians' willingness to give but to the amount which they gave. COMMENTARY ON THE SECOND EPISTLE TO THE CORINTHIANS 328.[14]

8:6 Completing a Gracious Work

TITUS SHOULD COMPLETE THIS WORK. CHRYSOSTOM: Paul was sending Titus to Corinth to encourage them to imitate the Macedonians. The presence of Paul's esteemed disciple would doubtless have been a great encouragement to them to give. HOMILIES ON THE EPISTLES OF PAUL TO THE CORINTHIANS 16.4.[15]

8:7 Excel in This Work Also

SEE THAT YOU EXCEL. AMBROSIASTER: Paul is exhorting the Corinthians to take pride in these things in the sight of the other churches, for if they are keen to minister to the saints it is proof that they have mended their ways. COMMENTARY ON PAUL'S EPISTLES.[16]

---

[12]CSEL 81.258. [13]NPNF 1 12:358. [14]Migne PG 82:423.
[15]NPNF 1 12:358. [16]CSEL 81.258.

8:8-15 CHRIST'S LOVE FOR US

[8]I say this not as a command, but to prove by the earnestness of others that your love also is genuine. [9]For you know the grace of our Lord Jesus Christ, that though he was rich, yet for your sake he became poor, so that by his poverty you might become rich. [10]And in this matter I give my advice: it is best for you now to complete what a year ago you began not only to do but to desire, [11]so that your readiness in desiring it may be matched by your completing it out of what you have. [12]For if the readiness is there, it is acceptable according to what a man has, not according to what he has not. [13]I do not mean that others should be eased and you burdened, [14]but that as a matter of equality your abundance at the present time should supply their want, so that their abundance may supply your want, that there may be equality. [15]As it is written, "He who gathered much had nothing over, and he who gathered little had no lack."

OVERVIEW: Christ was made poor because God voluntarily humbled himself to be born as man (ORIGEN, BASIL, AUGUSTINE, FULGENTIUS). By this he obtained for humanity the riches of his holy love (Chrysostom) that we might share in his divine nature (Ambrosiaster). In the case of the manna, those who gathered more and those who gathered less were found to have the same quantity. Never desire more than you already have or be anxious because they have less (Chrysostom). Paul respects the Corinthians' willingness to help, but the time had come for that willingness to be translated into action (Theodoret of Cyr).

8:8 Proving Their Genuine Love

The Opportunity to Prove That Love Is Genuine. Ambrosiaster: Paul is not ordering the Corinthians to send money to those who are suffering want but encouraging them to do so, demonstrating that they have the right attitude toward God and others. In return for their generosity they will undoubtedly receive a reward. Commentary on Paul's Epistles.[1]

Not a Command. Chrysostom: Notice how Paul humors them and avoids all offensiveness. He is not violent or compulsory in his tone, even though it is quite clear what he expects. Homilies on the Epistles of Paul to the Corinthians 17.1.[2]

8:9 Becoming Rich by Christ's Poverty

Christ Was Made Poor. Ambrosiaster: Paul is saying that Christ was made poor because God deigned to be born as man, humbling the power of his might so that he might obtain for men the riches of divinity and thus share in the divine nature, as Peter says. He was made man in order to take humanity right into the Godhead. Therefore Christ was made poor, not for his sake but for ours, but we are made poor for our own benefit. Commentary on Paul's Epistles.[3]

You Become Rich. Chrysostom: If you do not believe that poverty is productive of great wealth, think of the case of Jesus and you will be persuaded otherwise. For if he had not become poor, you would not have become rich. By riches, Paul means the knowledge of godliness, the cleansing away of sins, justification, sanctification, the countless good things which God bestowed upon us and which he intends to bestow. Homilies on the Epistles of Paul to the Corinthians 17.1.[4]

Poverty or Riches? Augustine: Listen, now, to something about riches in answer to the next inquiry in your letter. In it you wrote that some are saying a rich man who continues to live rich cannot enter the kingdom of heaven unless he sells all he has and that it cannot do him any good to keep the commandments while he keeps his riches. Their arguments have overlooked our fathers, Abraham, Isaac and Jacob, who departed long ago from this life. It is a fact that all these had extensive riches, as the Scripture faithfully bears witness, yet he who became poor for our sakes, although he was truly rich,[5] foretold in a truthful promise that many would come from the east and the west and would sit down not above them nor without them but with them in the kingdom of heaven.[6] Yes, the haughty rich man, who was clothed in purple and fine linen and feasted sumptuously every day, died and was tormented in hell. Nevertheless, if he had shown mercy to the poor man covered with sores who lay at his door and was treated with scorn, he himself would have deserved mercy. And if the poor man's merit had been his poverty, not his goodness, he surely would not have been carried by angels into the bosom of Abraham who had been rich in this life. This is intended to show us that on the one hand it was not poverty in itself that was divinely honored nor that riches were condemned but that the godliness of the one and the ungodliness of the other had their own consequences.

[1]CSEL 81.259. [2]NPNF 1 12:359. [3]CSEL 81.259. [4]NPNF 1 12:360. [5]2 Cor 8:9. [6]Mt 8:11.

LETTER 157 TO HILARIUS.[7]

HIDDEN RICHES. AUGUSTINE: What human being could know all the treasures of wisdom and knowledge hidden in Christ and concealed under the poverty of his humanity? For, "being rich, he became poor for our sake that by his poverty we might become rich." When he assumed our mortality and overcame death, he manifested himself in poverty, but he promised riches though they might be deferred; he did not lose them as if they were taken from him. How great is the multitude of his sweetness which he hides from those who fear him but which he reveals to those that hope in him! For we understand only in part until that which is perfect comes to us. To make us worthy of this perfect gift, he, equal to the Father in the form of God, became like to us in the form of a servant and refashions us into the likeness of God. FEAST OF THE NATIVITY 194.3.[8]

THE LIKENESS OF CHRIST'S POVERTY. BASIL: If, then, we keep in reserve any earthly possessions or perishable wealth, the mind sinks down as into mire and the soul inevitably becomes blind to God and insensible to the desire for the beauties of heaven and the good things laid up for us by promise. These we cannot gain possession of unless a strong and single-minded desire leads us to ask for them and lightens the labor of their attainment. This, then, is renunciation, as our discourse defines it: the severance of the bonds of this material and transient life and freedom from human concerns whereby we render ourselves more fit to set out upon the road leading to God. It is the unhindered impulse toward the possession and enjoyment of inestimable goods. . . . In short, it is the transference of the human heart to a heavenly mode of life. . . . Also—and this is the chief point—it is the first step toward the likeness to Christ, who, being rich, became poor for our sake. Unless we attain to this likeness, it is impossible for us to achieve a way of life in accord with the gospel of Christ. How, indeed, can we gain either contrition of heart or humility of mind or deliverance from anger, pain, anxieties—in a word, from all destructive movements of the soul—if we are entangled in the riches and cares of a worldly life and cling to others by affection and association? THE LONG RULES 8.[9]

GENUINE POVERTY. BASIL: And why does the appellation "poor man" disturb you? Remember your nature—that you came into the world naked and naked will leave it again. What is more destitute than a naked man? You have been called nothing that is derogatory, unless you make the terms used really applicable to yourself. Who was ever haled to prison because he was poor? It is not being poor that is reprehensible but failing to bear poverty with nobility. Recall that the Lord, "being rich, became poor for our sakes." AGAINST ANGER 10.[10]

HUMAN AND DIVINE. FULGENTIUS: Therefore, it is proper to the Son alone mercifully to have received the form of a servant. That taking up of the form of a servant pertained to the person of God the Word. It did not with resulting confusion pass into the divine nature. Therefore, that taking up of the form of a servant, according to which the Son of God, who is the Lord of all things and in whom dwells all the fullness of divinity, became a true and complete human being, took away from him nothing of his divine fullness. It took away nothing of the power, because in that one person remained without confusion a divine nature and a human nature. Hence it is that in one and the same Christ both the truth of the human nature shone forth and the eternal immutability of the divine nature remained. Neither was anything diminished in him at all or changed which he had by nature from eternity, through that which he re-

---

[7]FC 20:340-41*. [8]FC 38:39. [9]FC 9:256-57. [10]FC 9:454.

ceived from time. In his exterior aspect, he became a servant, but he did not cease to be by nature the Lord of all things. According to the flesh, he became poor; nonetheless, according to his divinity, he remained rich. Hence it is that the blessed apostle asserts that Christians have been enriched by his poverty, saying, "For you know the gracious act of our Lord Jesus Christ, that for your sake he became poor although he was rich, so that by his poverty you might become rich." He would in no way have made us rich by his poverty if, having become poor, he did not have in himself the riches of his divine nature. He became poor according to the form of a servant; he remained rich according to the form of God. FULGENTIUS TO VICTOR 13.1-2.[11]

THE CRADLE OF CHRIST'S POVERTY. ORIGEN: But in this the truth is also shown to be what was written, that Jesus Christ, "although he was rich, became a poor man." Therefore, for this reason, he chose both a poor mother, from whom he was born, and a poor homeland, about which it is said, "And you, Bethlehem, you are the least among the tribes of Judah"[12] and the rest. HOMILY 8.4.3 ON LEVITICUS.[13]

8:10 Complete What You Began

TRANSLATE WILLINGNESS INTO ACTION. THEODORET OF CYR: Paul knows and respects their willingness to help, but the time has now come for that willingness to be translated into action. COMMENTARY ON THE SECOND EPISTLE TO THE CORINTHIANS 329.[14]

8:11 Readiness and Completion

GIVING AS THEY ARE ABLE. AMBROSIASTER: Paul is saying that the Corinthians should give as much as they are willing and able to give. That way their conscience would become clear and not be clouded by pretense, pleasing man but not God. COMMENTARY ON PAUL'S EPISTLES.[15]

8:12 According to What One Has

NOT UNDER COMPULSION. AMBROSIASTER: Paul is exhorting the Corinthians to give what they are able but not to overdo it, because he did not want them to feel that they were acting under compulsion and thus come to be resentful. COMMENTARY ON PAUL'S EPISTLES.[16]

EXAMPLE, NOT EXHORTATION. CHRYSOSTOM: Look at how unbelievably wise Paul is. After pointing out the need and showing them an example, Paul leaves the Corinthians to do as much as they can, letting the example of the Macedonians do its own work of persuasion. He knew that imitation was a more powerful incentive than exhortation. HOMILIES ON THE EPISTLES OF PAUL TO THE CORINTHIANS 17.2.[17]

QUALITY OF READINESS. THEODORET OF CYR: Quality, not quantity, is what counts. COMMENTARY ON THE SECOND EPISTLE TO THE CORINTHIANS 329.[18]

8:13 Not Being Burdened

FAIRNESS IN DISTRIBUTING THE LOAD. AMBROSIASTER: It is true that giving should not cause hardship to the givers. But at the same time, a person ought not to keep more than he needs for himself. COMMENTARY ON PAUL'S EPISTLES.[19]

8:14 A Matter of Equality

MINISTERING TO THE SAINTS. AMBROSIASTER: The equality Paul is speaking of consists in the fact that because they are ministering to the saints this time they will be repaid by them in the future, for they are making the saints their debtors. COMMENTARY ON PAUL'S EPISTLES.[20]

---

[11]FC 95:409. [12]Mic 5:2. [13]FC 83:160. [14]Migne PG 82:426. [15]CSEL 81.259. [16]CSEL 81.260. [17]NPNF 1 12:360. [18]Migne PG 82:426. [19]CSEL 81.260. [20]CSEL 81.261.

SPIRITUAL REWARDS. CHRYSOSTOM: Paul points out that sharing is mutual. Indeed, the Corinthians would be reaping spiritual rewards in abundance. How can they be compared with what is merely carnal? HOMILIES ON THE EPISTLES OF PAUL TO THE CORINTHIANS 17.2.[21]

8:15 As It Is Written

ALL MADE EQUAL. AMBROSIASTER: The saints, with their hope in the world to come, have more than those who appear to be rich in this world. But both will be made equal, because those who give of their wealth to help the saints now will be helped by them at some future time, when they are in need. COMMEN-TARY ON PAUL'S EPISTLES.[22]

THE CASE OF THE MANNA. CHRYSOSTOM: This happened in the case of the manna, when those who gathered more and those who gathered less were found to have the same quantity.[23] God did this in order to punish greed, and Paul recalls it both to alarm them by what happened then and to persuade them never to desire more than they already have or to be anxious because they have less. HOMILIES ON THE EPISTLES OF PAUL TO THE CORINTHIANS 17.2.[24]

---

[21]NPNF 1 12:361. [22]CSEL 81.261. [23]Ex 16:18. [24]NPNF 1 12:361.

8:16-24 TEAMWORK

[16]But thanks be to God who puts the same earnest care for you into the heart of Titus. [17]For he not only accepted our appeal, but being himself very earnest he is going to you of his own accord. [18]With him we are sending the brother who is famous among all the churches for his preaching of the gospel; [19]and not only that, but he has been appointed by the churches to travel with us in this gracious work which we are carrying on, for the glory of the Lord and to show our good will. [20]We intend that no one should blame us about this liberal gift which we are administering, [21]for we aim at what is honorable not only in the Lord's sight but also in the sight of men. [22]And with them we are sending our brother whom we have often tested and found earnest in many matters, but who is now more earnest than ever because of his great confidence in you. [23]As for Titus, he is my partner and fellow worker in your service; and as for our brethren, they are messengers[j] of the churches, the glory of Christ. [24]So give proof, before the churches, of your love and of our boasting about you to these men.

j Greek apostles

OVERVIEW: Paul urged the Corinthians to demonstrate their love by the way they would treat those he is sending to them (AMBROSIASTER).

Since the Corinthians were making progress, Titus had become particularly concerned about them and even volunteered to visit them. The identity of the "famous brother" was debated by the Fathers (CHRYSOSTOM) as to whether it might be Barnabas (THEODORET OF CYR), Luke (PELAGIUS, OECUMENIUS) or someone else. The presbyters are always to provide for the poor whatever is honorable in the sight of God and of men (POLYCARP).

8:16 Care for You

TRUSTWORTHINESS. CHRYSOSTOM: Again Paul praises Titus. After talking about almsgiving, Paul goes on to speak about those who are entrusted with collecting and administering the gifts. This is important, because if we trust them, we shall be inclined to give more. HOMILIES ON THE EPISTLES OF PAUL TO THE CORINTHIANS 18.1.[1]

8:17 Titus's Earnestness

TITUS VOLUNTEERED TO VISIT. AMBROSIASTER: Seeing that the Corinthians are making progress in good works, Titus has become particularly concerned about their attitude and has even volunteered to go to visit them. COMMENTARY ON PAUL'S EPISTLES.[2]

8:18 A Famous Brother

ONE WHO PREACHES. CHRYSOSTOM: Who is this famous brother? Some say it is Luke because of the history which he wrote, but others say it was Barnabas because Paul also calls unwritten preaching the gospel. Why does he not mention him by name? Perhaps it was because the Corinthians did not know him personally, and Paul was content to say only enough to allay any possible suspicion of him at Corinth. Notice that the man was praised for his preaching. HOMILIES ON THE EPISTLES OF PAUL TO THE CORINTHIANS 18.1.[3]

WHETHER LUKE. PELAGIUS: This is to be understood of Luke, who was highly honored because he had written a Gospel, not to mention the Acts of the Apostles as well. COMMENTARY ON THE SECOND EPISTLE TO THE CORINTHIANS 8.[4]

OECUMENIUS: This may refer to Luke. PAULINE COMMENTARY FROM THE GREEK CHURCH.[5]

OR BARNABAS. THEODORET OF CYR: These words refer to Barnabas. COMMENTARY ON THE SECOND EPISTLE TO THE CORINTHIANS 331.[6]

8:19 Appointed by the Churches

HE WILL TRAVEL WITH US. CHRYSOSTOM: This verse seems to point toward Barnabas, who was commissioned along with Paul. HOMILIES ON THE EPISTLES OF PAUL TO THE CORINTHIANS 18.1.[7]

8:20 Administering the Gift

REMEMBERING THE POOR. AMBROSIASTER: Since the matter had to do with administering aid, Paul makes this additional remark in order not to be thought negligent concerning the care of the poor or of the saints. For the apostles had agreed to keep the poor in mind. COMMENTARY ON PAUL'S EPISTLES.[8]

8:21 Honorable in the Lord's Sight

AIM AT WHAT IS HONORABLE. POLYCARP: The presbyters must always be compassionate and merciful toward everyone, turning back the sheep which have gone astray, visiting the sick, not neglecting a widow or an orphan or a poor man but providing always for that which is honorable in the sight of God and of men. EPISTLE TO THE PHILIPPIANS 6.[9]

---

[1]NPNF 1 12:363. [2]CSEL 81.262. [3]NPNF 1 12:363-64. [4]Migne PL 30:793D. [5]NTA 15:445. [6]Migne PG 82:427. [7]NPNF 1 12:364. [8]CSEL 81.262-63. [9]AF 97.

INCURRING NO REPROACH. AMBROSIASTER: Paul is providing goods in the sight of God when he teaches that what God commands concerning the administering of aid to the saints or to the poor ought to be put into practice. But he also provides goods in the sight of others, because he is sending people to urge them to take part in this undertaking. Paul does not want his teaching to incur reproach because of improvident assistants. COMMENTARY ON PAUL'S EPISTLES.[10]

NO APPEARANCE OF WRONGDOING. CHRYSOSTOM: Who is there who can be compared with Paul? For he did whatever he thought was right without ignoring those who might doubt his intentions. On the contrary, he was concerned not to appear to be doing wrong even in the eyes of the weak. HOMILIES ON THE EPISTLES OF PAUL TO THE CORINTHIANS 18.1.[11]

8:22 An Earnest Brother

SENDING A BROTHER. THEODORET OF CYR: Some people think this refers to Apollos, whom Paul promised in his first epistle that he would send.[12] COMMENTARY ON THE SECOND EPISTLE TO THE CORINTHIANS 332.[13]

8:23 Messengers of the Churches

TITUS KNOWN TO THEM. CHRYSOSTOM: It is clear from this that Titus had a special task relating to the church at Corinth, whereas the others were unknown there. HOMILIES ON THE EPISTLES OF PAUL TO THE CORINTHIANS 18.2.[14]

TITUS AND OUR BROTHERS. THEODORE OF MOPSUESTIA: The two "as for" phrases do not denote a contrast between them but rather emphasize the similarity. PAULINE COMMENTARY FROM THE GREEK CHURCH.[15]

8:24 Proof of Your Love

DEMONSTRATING LOVE. AMBROSIASTER: Paul is urging the Corinthians to demonstrate their love by the way they treat those he is sending to them. If they received them with honor, they would be demonstrating to all the other churches how far they had progressed and that the good things which were said about them were true. He is therefore encouraging their resolve, for someone who is well thought of usually shows improvement. COMMENTARY ON PAUL'S EPISTLES.[16]

---

[10]CSEL 81.263. [11]NPNF 1 12:364-65. [12]1 Cor 16:12. [13]Migne PG 82:427. [14]NPNF 1 12:365. [15]NTA 15:199. [16]CSEL 81.264.

9:1-15 ALMSGIVING

[1]Now it is superfluous for me to write to you about the offering for the saints, [2]for I know your readiness, of which I boast about you to the people of Macedonia, saying that Achaia has been ready since last year; and your zeal has stirred up most of them. [3]But I am sending the brethren so that our boasting about you may not prove vain in this case, so that you may be ready, as I said you would be; [4]lest if some Macedonians come with me

and find that you are not ready, we be humiliated—to say nothing of you—for being so confident. [5]*So I thought it necessary to urge the brethren to go on to you before me, and arrange in advance for this gift you have promised, so that it may be ready not as an exaction but as a willing gift.*

[6]*The point is this: he who sows sparingly will also reap sparingly, and he who sows bountifully will also reap bountifully.* [7]*Each one must do as he has made up his mind, not reluctantly or under compulsion, for God loves a cheerful giver.* [8]*And God is able to provide you with every blessing in abundance, so that you may always have enough of everything and may provide in abundance for every good work.* [9]*As it is written,*

"He scatters abroad, he gives to the poor;
his righteousness[k] *endures for ever."*

[10]*He who supplies seed to the sower and bread for food will supply and multiply your resources*[l] *and increase the harvest of your righteousness.*[k] [11]*You will be enriched in every way for great generosity, which through us will produce thanksgiving to God;* [12]*for the rendering of this service not only supplies the wants of the saints but also overflows in many thanksgivings to God.* [13]*Under the test of this service, you*[m] *will glorify God by your obedience in acknowledging the gospel of Christ, and by the generosity of your contribution for them and for all others;* [14]*while they long for you and pray for you, because of the surpassing grace of God in you.* [15]*Thanks be to God for his inexpressible gift!*

k *Or benevolence* l *Greek sowing* m *Or they*

OVERVIEW: Those who give reluctantly or under compulsion present a blemished sacrifice that will not be accepted (BASIL). Those who give with a cheerful heart (TERTULLIAN, MAXIMUS OF TURIN, SAHDONA) store up treasures in heaven (AMBROSIASTER). What is given to a few redounds in praises given by the many to God (AMBROSIASTER, THEODORET OF CYR). Paul does not pray for riches or abundance but only for enough to live on. He praises the poorer saints because they gave thanks even for things that were given to others, in spite of their own poverty (CHRYSOSTOM). Paul holds up the Macedonians to the Corinthians and the Corinthians to the Macedonians as examples to imitate (THEODORET OF CYR, AMBROSIASTER). The time to sow is now (AUGUSTINE). God's providence has allowed us to dispose of great things (as willed toward virtue enabled by grace) and reserved smaller things for himself, such as bodily nourishment, since only God can provide the rain and the seasons (CHRYSOSTOM).

9:1 Superfluous to Write

SUPERFLUOUS BUT NECESSARY. AMBROSIASTER: It is superfluous, but in order to demonstrate his diligence, it was necessary for Paul to write like this, so that they would be all the more willing to do what they were asked and to embody the truth they were being taught. For superfluities tend to show greater concern. Our Lord did not doubt Peter's love for him, but even so he asked the apostle three times: "Simon Bar-Jona, do you love me?"[1] This repetition may seem to be superfluous, but it contributed to the perfecting of the admonition. At length Peter would learn

[1]Jn 21:15-17.

from it that he must act with great diligence. COMMENTARY ON PAUL'S EPISTLES.[2]

ASHAMED TO APPEAR INFERIOR. CHRYSOSTOM: Paul says this in order to win the Corinthians over to his side. Some were of such reputation that they thought they did not need advice. They would be ashamed to appear inferior to others. They would not want to fall short of others' opinions about them. HOMILIES ON THE EPISTLES OF PAUL TO THE CORINTHIANS 19.1.[3]

9:2 Readiness and Zeal

A PATTERN FOR CORRECTIVE ACTION. AMBROSIASTER: The other churches followed after Corinth. When they heard that a church which had previously been involved in many errors had put them right, they were moved to good works. After accepting the faith and then behaving badly, they began to have this desire to improve. How much more then ought others, in whom such vices were not present, do so as well? COMMENTARY ON PAUL'S EPISTLES.[4]

BOASTING ABOUT THE CORINTHIANS. THEODORET OF CYR: Paul holds up the Macedonians to the Corinthians and the Corinthians to the Macedonians as examples to imitate. COMMENTARY ON THE SECOND EPISTLE TO THE CORINTHIANS 333.[5]

9:3 Boasting Not in Vain

THE APOSTLE'S CARE. AMBROSIASTER: Paul often reminds the Corinthians of his care for them by saying this kind of thing, so that they will not feel frustrated. COMMENTARY ON PAUL'S EPISTLES.[6]

9:4 Lest We Be Humiliated

BEING OVERCONFIDENT. AMBROSIASTER: It is obvious that if Paul arrives and finds that the Corinthians are not what they have been ex-

pected to be, he will be chagrined and they will feel even more frustrated. COMMENTARY ON PAUL'S EPISTLES.[7]

9:5 Arranging for This Gift

A WILLING GIFT. AMBROSIASTER: Paul was not asking Titus and his colleagues to go to Corinth as if they were not willing to do so, but in order to prove his love for them. Titus and his friends wanted to go, and Paul is urging them to do so without delay. COMMENTARY ON PAUL'S EPISTLES.[8]

9:6 Sparing or Bountiful

THOSE WHO SOW SPARINGLY. AMBROSIASTER: Paul is referring to misers when he talks about people who sow sparingly. He says this here because the Corinthians had promised to send something and had subsequently backtracked. COMMENTARY ON PAUL'S EPISTLES.[9]

THE TIME FOR SOWING SEED IS NOW. AUGUSTINE: And since the apostle himself says: "Now this I say: he who sows sparingly shall also reap sparingly," you should understand that now is the time, while we are still in this life, to be swift and eager to purchase the gift of eternal life, for when the end of the world comes it will be given only to those who have bought it for themselves by faith before they were able to see it. LETTER 268.[10]

A GOOD SEASON FOR GOOD SEEDS. CHRYSOSTOM: Accordingly, let us not simply have the recipient in view in showing generosity in almsgiving, but consider who it is who takes as his the kindnesses shown to the poor person and who promises recompense for favors done; and thus let us direct our attention to him while showing

---

[2]CSEL 81.264-65. [3]NPNF 1 12:367. [4]CSEL 81.265. [5]Migne PG 82:430. [6]CSEL 81.266. [7]CSEL 81.266. [8]CSEL 81.266. [9]CSEL 81.267. [10]FC 32:288.

all zeal in making offerings with complete enthusiasm, and let us sow generously in season so that we may also reap generously. Scripture says, remember, "he who sows sparingly shall also reap sparingly." Let us consequently sow these good seeds generously so that in due season we may reap generously. Now, after all, is the time for sowing, which I beseech you not to ignore, so that on the day of harvesting we may gather the returns of what was sown here and be regaled with loving kindness from the Lord. HOMILY 34.8 ON GENESIS.[11]

9:7 God Loves a Cheerful Giver

A CHEERFUL HEART. AMBROSIASTER: Paul is teaching them that if they give with a cheerful heart they will be storing up treasure for future use in heaven. COMMENTARY ON PAUL'S EPISTLES.[12]

NOT A BLEMISHED SACRIFICE. BASIL: People who give reluctantly or under compulsion present a blemished sacrifice which should not be accepted. THE LONG RULES 29.[13]

GENEROUS GIVING. CHRYSOSTOM: I think that Scripture means a generous giver, but Paul has taken it in the sense of willingness to give. HOMILIES ON THE EPISTLES OF PAUL TO THE CORINTHIANS 19.2.[14]

CHEERFULNESS IN GIVING. CHRYSOSTOM: Paul's purpose was not only for money to be contributed to the poor but for it to be contributed with great eagerness. Likewise, God appointed almsgiving not only for the nourishment of the needy but also for the benefit of the providers, and much more so for the latter than for the former. For if he considered only the interest of the poor, he would have commanded solely that the money be given, and he would not have asked for the eagerness of the providers. But now you see the apostle in every way ordering by will first and above all for the givers to be joy-ful: the suppliers to furnish in a cheerful manner. And at one time he says, "Everyone must do as he has chosen in his heart, neither out of grief nor necessity, for God loves a cheerful giver," not simply a giver but the one who does this with pleasure. HOMILY 10.4.16: A SERMON ON ALMSGIVING.[15]

THE JOY OF CHRIST'S DEBTOR. MAXIMUS OF TURIN: Blessed, then, is almsgiving, which both renews the recipient and rejoices the giver, "for God loves a cheerful giver," and for this reason it is better to give to him first. Joyful, therefore, and cheerful is the one who attends to the poor. Quite clearly he is joyful, because for a few small coins he acquires heavenly treasures for himself; on the contrary, the person who pays taxes is always sad and dejected. Rightly is he sad who is not drawn to payment by love but forced by fear. Christ's debtor, then, is joyful, and Caesar's sad, because love urges the one to payment, and punishment constrains the other; the one is invited by rewards, the other compelled by penalties. SERMON 71 ON FASTING AND ALMSGIVING.[16]

DEPOSITS OF PIETY. TERTULLIAN: Even if there is some kind of treasury, it is not accumulated from a high initiation fee as if the religion were something bought and paid for. Each man deposits a small amount on a certain day of the month or whenever he wishes, and only on condition that he is willing and able to do so. No one is forced; each makes his contribution voluntarily. These are, so to speak, the deposits of piety. The money therefrom is spent not for banquets or drinking parties or good-for-nothing eating houses but for the support and burial of the poor, for children who are without their parents and means of subsistence, for aged men who are confined to the house; likewise, for shipwrecked sailors, and for any in the mines, on islands or in prisons. APOLOGY 39.[17]

---

[11]FC 82:294*. [12]CSEL 81.267. [13]FC 9:292. [14]NPNF 1 12:369. [15]FC 96:141*. [16]ACW 50:175. [17]FC 10:98-99.

9:8 *Every Blessing in Abundance*

God Is Able to Provide. Ambrosiaster: Paul points out that the grace of God is present in them. Just as it has led their hearts to amend their faults and accept the truth of Christian teaching, so it will assist them, once they have begun, to abound in every good work. Commentary on Paul's Epistles.[18]

Spiritual Blessings. Chrysostom: Note how Paul does not pray for riches or abundance but only for enough to live on. Nor is this the only thing he should be admired for. He asks the same thing of the Corinthians. . . . He wants them to have enough of this world's goods but moreso an overflowing abundance of spiritual blessings. Homilies on the Epistles of Paul to the Corinthians 19.2.[19]

9:9 *He Gives to the Poor*

Giving to the Saints. Ambrosiaster: If the righteousness of a man who gives to the poor[20] endures forever, how much more will this be true of a man who gives to the saints. For the poor are obvious to all, but the saints are known only to those who can discern them, for they are servants of God who are constant in prayer and fasting and who lead a pure life. Commentary on Paul's Epistles.[21]

Righteousness Endures. Chrysostom: The things themselves do not remain, but their effects do. Therefore we should not be mean and calculating with what we have but give with a generous hand. Look at how much people give to players and dancers—why not give just half as much to Christ? Homilies on the Epistles of Paul to the Corinthians 19.23.[22]

The Beginning of Eternal Life. Theodoret of Cyr: Paul adds the prophetic testimony which shows that indifference to money is the beginning of eternal life. Commentary on the Second Epistle to the Corinthians 335.[23]

9:10 *The Harvest of Righteousness*

He Who Supplies Will Multiply. Chrysostom: If God rewards those who till the earth with abundance, how much more will he reward those who till the soil of heaven in caring for the soul? Homilies on the Epistles of Paul to the Corinthians 20.1.[24]

9:11 *Enriched in Every Way*

Providence Great and Small. Chrysostom: God allowed us to dispose of great things and reserved smaller things for himself. Bodily nourishment belongs exclusively to him, because only he can control the rain and the seasons. But spiritual nourishment he has entrusted to us, since by our own will we can decide whether our fruit will be abundant or not. Homilies on the Epistles of Paul to the Corinthians 20.1.[25]

9:12 *Thanksgivings to God*

This Service Overflows. Ambrosiaster: It is not only those who have been delivered from beggary to the service of God who rejoice but all those who see the want being supplied. Thus it is that what is given to a few redounds in praises given by the many to God. Commentary on Paul's Epistles.[26]

Blessings of Different Kinds. Theodoret of Cyr: Paul is pointing out that giving to the saints is not just a matter of supplying their immediate wants. It has many other ramifications as well and leads to blessings of different kinds. Commentary on the Second Epistle to the Corinthians 336.[27]

---

[18]CSEL 81.267. [19]NPNF 1 12:369. [20]Ps 112:9. [21]CSEL 81.268-69. [22]NPNF 1 12:369. [23]Migne PG 82:431. [24]NPNF 1 12:372. [25]NPNF 1 12:372. [26]CSEL 81.270-71. [27]Migne PG 82:431.

9:13 *Glorifying God*

TESTING ATTITUDES. AMBROSIASTER: By this service Paul and his companions are testing the Corinthians' attitude and magnifying the Lord. COMMENTARY ON PAUL'S EPISTLES.[28]

9:14 *God's Surpassing Grace*

ABLE TO REJOICE. CHRYSOSTOM: Paul praises them because they gave thanks even for things which were given to others, in spite of their own poverty. No one is more envious than the poor, but these people were free of that passion, so much so that they were able to rejoice in the blessings given to others. HOMILIES ON THE EPISTLES OF PAUL TO THE CORINTHIANS 20.2.[29]

PRAYERS OF THE RECIPIENTS. THEODORET OF CYR: The Corinthians will reap the benefit of the prayers of the poor. Those prayers come out of great love. COMMENTARY ON THE SECOND EPISTLE TO THE CORINTHIANS 336.[30]

9:15 *Thanks Be to God!*

GOD'S INEXPRESSIBLE GIFT. CHRYSOSTOM: The word *gift* refers to all the blessings which come from almsgiving, both to those who receive and to those who give. Or it refers to the inexpressible gift which Christ bestowed liberally on the whole world by his incarnation. The second interpretation seems to be the more likely meaning. HOMILIES ON THE EPISTLES OF PAUL TO THE CORINTHIANS 20.2.[31]

PRAISING GOD. THEODORET OF CYR: It is Paul's custom to praise God every time he expounds some divine dispensation or other. COMMENTARY ON THE SECOND EPISTLE TO THE CORINTHIANS 336.[32]

SPIRITUAL SERVICE. SAHDONA: We should be discerning and aware of the grace that has been effected in us, giving thanks for it to the Maker, praising God for this great and "ineffable gift" to us. We should put aside from ourselves any hateful habits of slackness and neglect which only destroy our lives; instead, we should persevere from the beginning to the end of the times of our offices. And we should behave with all the greater awe and love during the great and perfect mysteries of our salvation, standing firmly before God continually with wakefulness of heart in spiritual service, resembling servants who are eagerly at the ready to serve their master. BOOK OF PERFECTION.[33]

---

[28]CSEL 81.271. [29]NPNF 1 12:373. [30]Migne PG 82:434. [31]NPNF 1 12:373. [32]Migne PG 82:434. [33]SFPSL 218.

10:1-12 PAUL'S REPUTATION

[1]I, Paul, myself entreat you, by the meekness and gentleness of Christ—I who am humble when face to face with you, but bold to you when I am away!— [2]I beg of you that when I am present I may not have to show boldness with such confidence as I count on showing against some who suspect us of acting in worldly fashion. [3]For though we live in the world we are not carrying on a worldly war, [4]for the weapons of our warfare are not worldly but have divine power to destroy strongholds. [5]We destroy arguments and every

proud obstacle to the knowledge of God, and take every thought captive to obey Christ, [6]being ready to punish every disobedience, when your obedience is complete.

[7]Look at what is before your eyes. If any one is confident that he is Christ's, let him remind himself that as he is Christ's, so are we. [8]For even if I boast a little too much of our authority, which the Lord gave for building you up and not for destroying you, I shall not be put to shame. [9]I would not seem to be frightening you with letters. [10]For they say, "His letters are weighty and strong, but his bodily presence is weak, and his speech of no account." [11]Let such people understand that what we say by letter when absent, we do when present. [12]Not that we venture to class or compare ourselves with some of those who commend themselves. But when they measure themselves by one another, and compare themselves with one another, they are without understanding.

Overview: A person who is sent on a mission lays claim to power, not on his own behalf but on behalf of the one who sent him (Ambrosiaster). Paul warns that he can be severe with the Corinthians if he has to be. If they do not put things right in his absence, they may get an unpleasant surprise when he comes (Ambrosiaster). Paul's work of answering arguments, deflating pride (Ambrosiaster, Pelagius), detecting what is unsound and laying the proper foundation is all intended for the upbuilding of the community (Chrysostom). The apostles take every thought captive to Christ by conquering it in its contradictions and by leading it, humbled and tame, to the Christian faith (Ambrosiaster, Chrysostom). Paul criticizes not only the deceivers but the deceived as well, for they are also accountable for their actions (Chrysostom, Gennadius of Constantinople). Paul avenges disobedience when he condemns it through obedience, so that unbelief may be condemned by those who used to defend it (Ambrosiaster). Although we are surrounded by the world, we do not give in to it (Theodoret of Cyr), nor do we make misleading comparisons (Augustine, Fulgentius) when every thought is taken captive to Christ (Basil).

By Letter and in Person. Ambrosiaster: Paul is saying that he is the same person whether present or absent. He refers here to the meekness and gentleness of Christ because he does not want to appear to be harsher in person than in a letter. At the same time, he warns them that he can be severe with them if he has to be and that if they do not put things right in his absence, they may get an unpleasant surprise when he comes. Commentary on Paul's Epistles.[1]

Humble but Bold. Chrysostom: Here Paul is speaking ironically, using the words of his critics to good effect. Homilies on the Epistles of Paul to the Corinthians 21.1.[2]

Deflecting the Judaizers. Theodoret of Cyr: Some Jewish believers were ordering Gentile converts to follow the law of Moses. They condemned Paul, calling him base and stupid, and claiming that although he kept the law in secret himself, he was prepared to dispense the Gentiles from it publicly, because he thought they were too ignorant to be able to keep it. Paul refutes this charge by reminding the Corinthians of the miracles which he had done among them

10:1 Paul's Entreaty

[1]CSEL 81.271-72. [2]NPNF 1 12:375.

and of the gifts which they had received because of him. COMMENTARY ON THE SECOND EPISTLE TO THE CORINTHIANS 337.[3]

10:2 *Showing Boldness*

THOSE WHO SUSPECTED US. AMBROSIASTER: Paul is referring here to those who did not accept that his teaching was spiritual. COMMENTARY ON PAUL'S EPISTLES.[4]

BOLDNESS AGAINST FALSE APOSTLES. CHRYSOSTOM: Having completed his discourse on almsgiving, Paul now turns to less pleasant matters, concluding his epistle with denunciations of the false apostles. He offers explanations of himself and his ministry. Indeed, it would not be wrong to say that the whole epistle is an apology for Paul, because he makes so much mention of the grace and patience given to him. HOMILIES ON THE EPISTLES OF PAUL TO THE CORINTHIANS 21.1.[5]

10:3 *Living in the World*

ACTING SPIRITUALLY. AMBROSIASTER: This means that although we are living in the body we act in a spiritual way. Anyone who does what is pleasing to God is acting spiritually. COMMENTARY ON PAUL'S EPISTLES.[6]

NOT A WORLDLY WAR. THEODORET OF CYR: Although we are surrounded by the world, we do not give in to it. COMMENTARY ON THE SECOND EPISTLE TO THE CORINTHIANS 337.[7]

10:4 *Weapons with Divine Power*

UNCORRUPTED WEAPONS. AMBROSIASTER: All worldly things are corrupt, but Paul is strong because he is fighting with uncorrupted weapons. COMMENTARY ON PAUL'S EPISTLES.[8]

SPIRITUAL WEAPONS. CHRYSOSTOM: By "worldly weapons" he means wealth, glory, power, loquaciousness, cleverness, half-truths, flatteries,

hypocrisies and so on. The apostle does not use such weapons but only those which are spiritual. HOMILIES ON THE EPISTLES OF PAUL TO THE CORINTHIANS 21.2.[9]

NOT MOSES' LAW. THEODORE OF MOPSUESTIA: By "worldly weapons" Paul means the law of Moses. PAULINE COMMENTARY FROM THE GREEK CHURCH.[10]

EVERY SIN IS SERIOUS. BASIL: Here, also, one who examines each word minutely can gain a very accurate knowledge of the meaning of the Holy Scripture, so that there is no excuse for any of us being led astray into the snare of sin by an erroneous belief that some sins are punished while others may be committed with impunity. For, what says the apostle?—"destroying counsels and every height that exalts itself against the knowledge of God"; so that every sin, because it is an expression of contempt for the divine law, is called a "height that exalts itself against the knowledge of God." ON THE JUDGMENT OF GOD.[11]

10:5 *Taking Every Thought Captive*

TAMING THE INTELLECT. AMBROSIASTER: Paul takes an intellect captive when he conquers it just as it is contradicting him by its reasonings, and he leads it, humbled and tame, to the Christian faith. COMMENTARY ON PAUL'S EPISTLES.[12]

DESTROYING ARGUMENTS. CHRYSOSTOM: The arguments referred to here are those of Greek philosophy, of which they were so proud. The word *captive* sounds bad, because it might be thought to suppress freedom, but here Paul gives it its own special meaning. It might also indicate something which has been so violently overpowered that it will never rise again. This is

[3]Migne PG 82:434. [4]CSEL 81.272. [5]NPNF 1 12:375. [6]CSEL 81.273. [7]Migne PG 82:434. [8]CSEL 81.273. [9]NPNF 1 12:376. [10]NTA 15:199. [11]FC 9:48. [12]CSEL 81.274.

the sense in which Paul uses it here. Moreover, the captivity in question is one of obedience to Christ, which means the passage from slavery to liberty, from death to life and from destruction to salvation. Homilies on the Epistles of Paul to the Corinthians 2.5.[13]

A Wicked Convention. Basil: A very wicked convention, however, leads us astray, and a perverted human tradition is the source of great evil for us; I mean that tradition according to which some sins are denounced and others are viewed indifferently. Crimes like homicide and adultery are the object of a violent but feigned indignation, while others, such as anger or reviling or drunkenness or avarice, are not considered deserving of even a simple rebuke. . . . And certainly, where every height that exalts itself against the knowledge of God is brought into captivity to the obedience of Christ and every disobedience receives just punishment, there nothing is left undestroyed. On the Judgment of God.[14]

10:6 When Obedience Is Complete

Avenging Disobedience. Ambrosiaster: Paul avenges disobedience when he condemns it through obedience, destroying it at the same time as he leads those who resist to the faith, in order that unbelief may be condemned by those who used to defend it. Commentary on Paul's Epistles.[15]

Paul's Pastoral Skill. Chrysostom: Paul says that he will punish those who deserve it in due course, but first he wants to make sure that the Corinthians have been properly counseled. He sees that his people are mixed up with strangers. He wants them to withdraw from them first, before admonishing the latter. This is yet another sign of his great pastoral skill. Homilies on the Epistles of Paul to the Corinthians 21.3.[16]

Patience Leads to Repentance. Theodoret of

Cyr: Paul explains why he is being patient. He wants to try to persuade as many as possible to amend their ways. He will punish only those who continue to resist his exhortations. Commentary on the Second Epistle to the Corinthians 338.[17]

10:7 Examining Oneself

Inflated Pride. Ambrosiaster: Paul is criticizing those who in the inflated pride of their own presumption have a lower opinion of him than he deserved and who imagined that they had no need of his teaching. Commentary on Paul's Epistles.[18]

Belonging to Christ. Pelagius: No one is more foolish than the person who thinks that he alone belongs to Christ. Commentary on the Second Epistle to the Corinthians 10.[19]

Deceivers and Deceived. Chrysostom: Paul criticizes not only the deceivers but the deceived as well, for they are also accountable for their actions. Furthermore, he rebukes each one in the way which is most appropriate to their case. Those who imagine they belong to Christ must consider who Paul belongs to. If the answer is also Christ, then they must listen to what he has to say to them. Homilies on the Epistles of Paul to the Corinthians 22.1.[20]

Appearances Only. Gennadius of Constantinople: This is to be read as a censorious remark, for the people were not judging the truth from works but from superficial appearances only. Pauline Commentary from the Greek Church.[21]

10:8 For Building Them Up

---

[13]NPNF 1 12:376-77. [14]FC 9:49. [15]CSEL 81.274. [16]NPNF 1 12:377. [17]Migne PG 82:435. [18]CSEL 81.274. [19]Migne PL 30:797C. [20]NPNF 1 12:379. [21]NTA 15:419.

AUTHORITY FOR THE COMMON GOOD. CHRYSOSTOM: Paul ascribes his gift to God and points out that it was given for the common good. His work of answering arguments, detecting what is unsound and laying the proper foundation is all intended for the upbuilding of the community. But if anybody is hostile and wants to do battle with him, he also has the power to answer arguments and will use it as and when it is appropriate to do so. HOMILIES ON THE EPISTLES OF PAUL TO THE CORINTHIANS 22.1.[22]

10:9 Not Frightening Them

A SLANDER. THEODORET OF CYR: This is what Paul's enemies were saying he was trying to do. COMMENTARY ON THE SECOND EPISTLE TO THE CORINTHIANS 339.[23]

10:10 Strong Letters, Weak Presence

ANTICIPATING DISMISSIVE CRITICISM. PELAGIUS: Paul is saying all this precisely in order to avoid charges of this kind. COMMENTARY ON THE SECOND EPISTLE TO THE CORINTHIANS 10.[24]

10:11 Consistent Behavior

BOLD WHEN ABSENT. AMBROSIASTER: Someone to whom power has not been given is capable of being bold when absent but when present he is put to shame. The apostle will not be put to shame when issuing his rebuke. He is doing this in bold reliance on his spiritual power. COMMENTARY ON PAUL'S EPISTLES.[25]

10:12 Without Understanding

THOSE WHO COMMEND THEMSELVES. AMBROSIASTER: People who commend themselves are those who wish to dominate, claiming authority for their own name. A person who is sent on a mission lays claim to power, not on his own behalf but on behalf of the one who sent him. Here Paul is saying that he has been chosen as a steward of the Lord. By not presuming to anything beyond what has been granted to him, he is not associating himself with those who preach without a commission. COMMENTARY ON PAUL'S EPISTLES.[26]

A FAULTY MEASURE. AUGUSTINE: The fundamental fallacy of these men, who prefer to walk in roundabout error than keep to the straight path of truth, is that they have nothing but their own tiny, changing, human minds to measure the divine mind, infinitely capacious and utterly immutable, a mind that can count uncountable things without passing from one to the next. Such men, to use the words of the apostle, "comparing themselves with themselves," end by understanding nothing. Of course, every time such philosophers decide to do something, they have to form a new mental resolution because their minds are mutable, and they imagine it is the same with God. Without having a notion of God, they mistake themselves for him, and instead of measuring God by God, they compare themselves to themselves. CITY OF GOD 12.17.[27]

THE FOLLY OF FALSE COMPARISONS. FULGENTIUS: As often as you think of the perfection of the virtues, do not consider what others have less than you have but what you have less than you ought to have. You should not think that you are perfect in virtue if you see other women given over to sins; nor consequently should you credit yourself with any greater speed if you see some women either backsliding or walking feebly. Nor, therefore, must one with watery eyes be proclaimed to have healthy eyes because a blind man seems thoroughly closed off from the light, nor must someone be declared healthy who lies half-dead with a serious wound, if another is found dead because of a more serious wound. Nor must anyone lay claim to glory as a

[22]NPNF 1 12:379-80. [23]Migne PG 82:435. [24]Migne PL 30:797D—798A. [25]CSEL 81.276. [26]CSEL 81.276. [27]FC 14:278.

victor who, although not killed by the enemy, still is being held captive by the enemy. Therefore, do not compare yourself to others but to yourself. Hear the apostle doing this and salutarily warning us to do the same. For, writing to the Corinthians, he says, "Not that we dare to class or compare ourselves with some of those who recommend themselves. But when they measure themselves by one another and compare themselves with one another, they are without understanding." To PROBA.[28]

[28]FC 95:329.

10:13-18 PAUL'S MODESTY

[13]*But we will not boast beyond limit, but will keep to the limits God has apportioned us, to reach even to you.* [14]*For we are not overextending ourselves, as though we did not reach you; we were the first to come all the way to you with the gospel of Christ.* [15]*We do not boast beyond limit, in other men's labors; but our hope is that as your faith increases, our field among you may be greatly enlarged,* [16]*so that we may preach the gospel in lands beyond you, without boasting of work already done in another's field.* [17]*"Let him who boasts, boast of the Lord."* [18]*For it is not the man who commends himself that is accepted, but the man whom the Lord commends.*

OVERVIEW: Paul is modest, but not to the point where he neglects to tell the truth about himself. There was a real danger that the disciples might be persuaded to have a low opinion of Paul precisely because of his modesty. Paul did not seek human praise, but when he was accused of being a braggart he defended himself (CHRYSOSTOM). One who has confidence in the power of the gospel has confidence in the God who enables it (AMBROSIASTER). Paul accuses the false apostles not merely of boasting too much but also of claiming the credit for other people's labors (CHRYSOSTOM).

10:13 Keeping to God's Limits

POWER CONDUCIVE TO SALVATION. AMBROSIASTER: Paul takes advantage of his authority only to the extent that he glories in the progress of believers, so that his power may be conducive to salvation and not self-aggrandizement. He did not boast beyond the power that was given to him, nor did he claim any authority in places where his preaching had not been heard. COMMENTARY ON PAUL'S EPISTLES.[1]

EXCESSIVE BOASTING. CHRYSOSTOM: Excessive boasting was evidently a characteristic of the false apostles. HOMILIES ON THE EPISTLES OF PAUL TO THE CORINTHIANS 22.2.[2]

10:14 Reaching Them with the Gospel

NOT OVEREXTENDED. AMBROSIASTER: Paul did not go too far in what he was doing but stayed

[1]CSEL 81.277. [2]NPNF 1 12:380.

within the limits set for his task by God. He makes this explicit here so that the Corinthians will know that God has sent him to them and so they ought to obey his warnings. Otherwise they might appear to be resisting God, by whom Paul was sent. COMMENTARY ON PAUL'S EPISTLES.[3]

10:15 As Faith Increases

NO EXCESSIVE PRIDE. AMBROSIASTER: Someone who takes pride in his own work is not being excessively proud of himself. A prudent man does not rely on the labors of others. This is why Paul does not claim any credit for those who have come to faith by the preaching of other evangelists. COMMENTARY ON PAUL'S EPISTLES.[4]

OTHERS' LABOR. CHRYSOSTOM: Paul accuses the false apostles not merely of boasting too much but also of claiming the credit for other people's labors. HOMILIES ON THE EPISTLES OF PAUL TO THE CORINTHIANS 22.3.[5]

10:16 Preaching in Other Lands

GLORY FROM HIS LABOR. AMBROSIASTER: What Paul wants is to preach the gospel to those to whom the message has not yet been given, so that God will be glorified by his labor. COMMENTARY ON PAUL'S EPISTLES.[6]

10:17 Boasting of the Lord

BY THE LORD'S FAVOR. AMBROSIASTER: By saying this Paul intimates that even his assurance and pride are to be given to the Lord, because it is by his favor that he has them. Someone who has confidence in the power of the gospel has confidence in the God who enables it. Thus God is glorified by all godly work. A person who has not received power from God cannot glory in the Lord, because he is seeking his own glory. COMMENTARY ON PAUL'S EPISTLES.[7]

10:18 One the Lord Commends

SENT AND COMMENDED. AMBROSIASTER: God does not commend someone whom he does not send. COMMENTARY ON PAUL'S EPISTLES.[8]

PROPER MODESTY. CHRYSOSTOM: Paul did not claim this for himself but left it to the Lord. Paul is modest, but not to the point where he neglects to tell the truth about himself. It is possible to do harm by ill-timed modesty or to do good by saying something admirable of oneself at the right time. There was a real danger that the disciples might be persuaded to have a low opinion of Paul, precisely because of his modesty. Paul did not seek human praise, but when he was accused of being a braggart he defended himself. HOMILIES ON THE EPISTLES OF PAUL TO THE CORINTHIANS 23.3.[9]

---

[3]CSEL 81.277-78. [4]CSEL 81.278. [5]NPNF 1 12:381. [6]CSEL 81.279. [7]CSEL 81.279. [8]CSEL 81.279. [9]NPNF 1 12:381.

11:1-6 PAUL'S APPARENT FOOLISHNESS

[1]*I wish you would bear with me in a little foolishness. Do bear with me!* [2]*I feel a divine jealousy for you, for I betrothed you to Christ to present you as a pure bride to her one husband.* [3]*But I am afraid that as the serpent deceived Eve by his cunning, your thoughts*

will be led astray from a sincere and pure devotion to Christ. [4]For if some one comes and preaches another Jesus than the one we preached, or if you receive a different spirit from the one you received, or if you accept a different gospel from the one you accepted, you submit to it readily enough. [5]I think that I am not in the least inferior to these superlative apostles. [6]Even if I am unskilled in speaking, I am not in knowledge; in every way we have made this plain to you in all things.

OVERVIEW: Paul uses heavy irony to make his point. What he is about to say he says out of love for the Corinthians (AMBROSIASTER), even to the point of jealousy (CHRYSOSTOM). For God is said to be jealous, not in a human way but that everyone may know that he claims sovereign rights over those whom he loves and does what he does for their exclusive benefit (CHRYSOSTOM). They are to be regarded as spouses of Christ in their faith, hope and love (AUGUSTINE), provided they are willing to preserve both bodily chastity and virginity of heart (ORIGEN, NOVATIAN, AUGUSTINE, CAESARIUS OF ARLES). He is afraid that they will be led astray like the serpent who deceived Eve by lying to her about God, saying that God merely threatened humanity with death but would never kill anyone (PELAGIUS, AMBROSIASTER). What probably happened was that false teachers appeared from elsewhere and added to what the apostles had already taught. Their claim would have been that the apostles had not said all that there was to say, which Paul is at pains to deny (CHRYSOSTOM). In reference to "unskilled speech," he did not mean that he did not know how to speak but that commendation did not depend on mere eloquence (AMBROSIASTER, JEROME, CHRYSOSTOM).

11:1 *Bearing with Foolishness*

BEING FOOLISH. AMBROSIASTER: Paul says that he is being foolish when he starts to talk about himself but that he is forced to do so because these people were harboring unworthy thoughts, when they of all people ought to be thinking well of him. COMMENTARY ON PAUL'S EPISTLES.[1]

THE FOOLISH ONES. PELAGIUS: Paul calls himself foolish in order to demonstrate that it is those who boast about themselves who really are the foolish ones. COMMENTARY ON THE SECOND EPISTLE TO THE CORINTHIANS 11.[2]

FORCED TO BOAST. THEODORET OF CYR: Paul realizes that wise people do not boast of themselves, but he has been forced to do so. COMMENTARY ON THE SECOND EPISTLE TO THE CORINTHIANS 340.[3]

11:2 *A Divine Jealousy*

OUT OF LOVE. AMBROSIASTER: Paul is making it clear that what he is about to say he will say out of love for them, so that it may be conducive to their progress as much as to his praise and that they may learn from it how to do a favor to their father in the gospel. For to speak ill of a father harms the sons, and the praise of sons is a father's glory. COMMENTARY ON PAUL'S EPISTLES.[4]

JEALOUSY. CHRYSOSTOM: Paul uses a word here which is far stronger than mere love. Jealous souls burn ardently for those whom they love, and jealousy presupposes a strong affection. Then, in order that they should not think that Paul is after power, wealth or honor, he adds

---

[1]CSEL 81.279-80. [2]Migne PL 30:798D. [3]Migne PG 82:438. [4]CSEL 81.280.

that his jealousy is "divine." For God is said to be jealous, not in a human way but so that everyone may know that he claims sovereign rights over those whom he loves and does what he does for their exclusive benefit. Human jealousy is basically selfish, but divine jealousy is both intense and pure.

Note the difference between human brides and the church. In the world, a woman is a virgin before her marriage, when she loses her virginity. But in the church, those who were anything but virgins before they turned to Christ acquire virginity in him. As a result, the whole church is a virgin. Homilies on the Epistles of Paul to the Corinthians 23.1.[5]

A Pure Bride. Augustine: Why does Paul address all these different people as a "chaste virgin," unless he is referring to their faith, hope and love? Feast of the Nativity 188.[6]

The Spouse of Souls. Caesarius of Arles: The souls of all men and women know that they are spouses of Christ if they are willing to preserve both bodily chastity and virginity of heart. For Christ is to be understood as the spouse of their souls, not of their bodies. Sermon 155.4 on the Ten Virgins.[7]

A Chaste Virgin. Augustine: To the same church the apostle says: "For I have promised you to one spouse, that I might present you as a chaste virgin to Christ." . . . The church, then, like Mary, has inviolate integrity and incorrupt fecundity. What Mary merited physically, the church has guarded spiritually, with the exception that Mary brought forth one Child, while the church has many children destined to be gathered into one body by One. Feast of the Nativity 195.2.[8]

The Church Is a Virgin. Augustine: Do you wish to know how the church is a virgin? Hear the apostle Paul; hear the friend of the Bridegroom who is zealous not for himself but for

the Bridegroom: "I betrothed you to one spouse." He spoke to the church. To which church? To all that his letter could reach. "I betrothed you to one spouse, that I might present you a chaste virgin to Christ. But I fear lest," he said, "as the serpent seduced Eve by his guile . . ." That serpent never physically defiled Eve, did he? Yet he did destroy her virginity of heart. On that account Paul said: "I fear lest . . . your minds may be corrupted from that chastity which is in Christ." Therefore, the church is a virgin; she is a virgin, may she be a virgin. Let her beware of the deceiver, lest he turn out to be a corrupter. The church is a virgin. Are you, perhaps, going to say to me: "If the church is a virgin, how does she bring forth children? Or, if she does not bring forth children, how did we give our names so that we might be born of her?" I answer: "She is a virgin and she also brings forth children." She imitates Mary, who gave birth to the Lord. Did not the holy Mary bring forth her Child and remain a virgin? So, too, the church both brings forth children and is a virgin. And if you would give some consideration to the matter, she brings forth Christ, because they who are baptized are his members. Converts and the Creed 213.7.[9]

The Pure Virgin Bride. Novatian: May purity, then—that purity which goes above and beyond the will and which we should will always to possess—be also given to us for the sake of redemption, so that what has been consecrated by Christ cannot be corrupted. If the apostle states that the church is the bride of Christ, I ask you now to reflect just what purity is required of you, when the church herself is given in marriage as a virgin bride. In Praise of Purity 1.[10]

The Chastity of the Soul. Origen: The apostle Paul says, "But I want you all to present

---

[5]NPNF 1 12:383. [6]FC 38:20. [7]FC 47:347. [8]FC 38:42. [9]FC 38:127. [10]FC 67:166.

yourselves as a pure virgin to one man, Christ. For I fear lest, as the serpent seduced Eve by his cunning, your minds may be corrupted from the simplicity which is in Christ." Therefore, Paul wants "all the Corinthians" to present themselves as a pure "virgin to Christ"; certainly he would never want that unless it would seem possible. Whence also it would appear wonderful how these, who although corrupted by diverse sins, came to the faith of Christ, all at once are called "a pure virgin"; a virgin which is so holy and so pure that she is worthy also to be joined in marriage to Christ. However, since we cannot refer these things to the chastity of the flesh, it is sure that they refer to the chastity of the soul, whose "simplicity of the faith which is in Christ," according to the understanding of Paul himself, was called his virginity. HOMILY 12.5 ON LEVITICUS.[11]

11:3 Led Astray from Devotion to Christ

BEING SEDUCED. AMBROSIASTER: Paul is saying that glory has been given to him not so that he might praise himself but so that he might cast blame on those who, in the name of Christ, were preaching against Christ and by whom the Corinthians were being seduced. COMMENTARY ON PAUL'S EPISTLES.[12]

AS THE SERPENT DECEIVED EVE. PELAGIUS: The serpent deceived Eve by lying to her about God, saying that God merely threatened men with death, but would never actually kill anyone.[13] Likewise, the false apostles in Paul's day were saying that the gospel was merely added to the Old Testament and that it was therefore necessary to go on keeping the law of Moses as before. In our own time, there are those who claim that hell is merely a threat, either because it does not exist at all or because it is not an eternal punishment—notions which are contrary to the teaching of Scripture. COMMENTARY ON THE SECOND EPISTLE TO THE CORINTHIANS 11.[14]

CAUGHT BETWEEN TRUST AND DOUBT. CHRYSOSTOM: Paul does not say that this will happen, but he is afraid that it might. He stands midway between trust and doubt, hoping that they will do the right thing but not being entirely certain of it. HOMILIES ON THE EPISTLES OF PAUL TO THE CORINTHIANS 23.1.[15]

11:4 A Different Gospel

ADDING TO THE GOSPEL. CHRYSOSTOM: What probably happened was that false teachers appeared from elsewhere and added to what the apostles had already taught. Their claim would have been that the apostles had not said all that there was to say, which Paul is at pains to deny. HOMILIES ON THE EPISTLES OF PAUL TO THE CORINTHIANS 23.2.[16]

11:5 Superlative Apostles

NOT INFERIOR. AMBROSIASTER: Paul does not think that he is inferior to the other apostles because he has taught the same things and done the same miracles. COMMENTARY ON PAUL'S EPISTLES.[17]

WHO HE IS. CHRYSOSTOM: Paul does not appeal to what he taught but to who he is. His status is at least equal (indeed, it is far superior) to that of those who had led the Corinthians astray. HOMILIES ON THE EPISTLES OF PAUL TO THE CORINTHIANS 23.3.[18]

11:6 Knowledge Made Plain

RHETORICAL SKILL. AMBROSIASTER: This does not refer to the apostles, who were unlettered men of no eloquence, but to the false teachers whose rhetorical skill the Corinthians preferred. Paul did not mean by this that he did

---

[11]FC 83:226-27. [12]CSEL 81.281. [13]Gen 3:4. [14]Migne PL 30:799A. [15]NPNF 1 12:384. [16]NPNF 1 12:384-85. [17]CSEL 81.282. [18]NPNF 1 12:385.

not know how to speak but that commendation did not depend on mere eloquence. A person of little eloquence is not guilty before God, but someone who does not know God is liable to be charged with ignorance, because it was a sin to be ignorant of what is conducive to salvation. It was not eloquence which would commend Paul's message but the power to save which accompanied it. COMMENTARY ON PAUL'S EPISTLES.[19]

LEARNED IN HEBREW. JEROME: Paul was learned in Hebrew letters and sat at the feet of Gamaliel, whom he was not ashamed to acknowledge,[20] but he showed a contempt for Greek eloquence, or at least he kept quiet about it because of his humility, so that his preaching lay not in the persuasiveness of his words but in the power of his signs. AGAINST RUFINUS 1.17.[21]

UNSKILLED IN SPEAKING. CHRYSOSTOM: The false apostles obviously had the gift of eloquence which Paul lacked. But that means nothing as far as the substance of the preaching is concerned and may even cast a shadow over the glory of the cross, which is anything but superficially attractive. HOMILIES ON THE EPISTLES OF PAUL TO THE CORINTHIANS 23.3.[22]

---

[19]CSEL 81.283. [20]Acts 22:3. [21]FC 53:81. [22]NPNF 1 12:385.

11:7-11 PAUL'S FINANCIAL INDEPENDENCE

[7]*Did I commit a sin in abasing myself so that you might be exalted, because I preached God's gospel without cost to you?* [8]*I robbed other churches by accepting support from them in order to serve you.* [9]*And when I was with you and was in want, I did not burden any one, for my needs were supplied by the brethren who came from Macedonia. So I refrained and will refrain from burdening you in any way.* [10]*As the truth of Christ is in me, this boast of mine shall not be silenced in the regions of Achaia.* [11]*And why? Because I do not love you? God knows I do!*

OVERVIEW: Paul accepted contributions from the Macedonians because they corrected their faults, but he refused anything from the Corinthians because they were less ready to correct theirs (AMBROSIASTER, THEODORET OF CYR). One who accepts payment from sinners loses authority to admonish them (AMBROSIASTER). By indicating love as the motive for his behavior, Paul makes his admonition even more serious (CHRYSOSTOM). Beware of Satan's disguises (CYPRIAN, CYRIL OF JERUSALEM, AUGUSTINE).

11:7 Preaching Without Cost

REFUSING PAYMENT. AMBROSIASTER: Paul refused payment for two reasons. He would not resemble the false apostles who were preaching for their own advantage and not for the glory of God, nor would he allow the vigor of his message to become sluggish. For the person who accepts payment from sinners loses the authority to censor them. COMMENTARY ON PAUL'S EPISTLES.[1]

---

[1]CSEL 81.284.

11:8 *Accepting Support from Other Churches*

Robbing Other Churches. Ambrosiaster: Paul makes it clear that not only did other churches encourage him in his ministry to the Corinthians but also that they gave him significant financial support. Commentary on Paul's Epistles.[2]

Exaggerated Foolishness. Chrysostom: Paul is clearly exaggerating for effect, but we must remember that he warned the Corinthians at the beginning of the chapter to bear with a little foolishness as he made his point. Homilies on the Epistles of Paul to the Corinthians 23.4.[3]

11:9 *Not a Burden to Them*

Those Who Corrected Their Faults. Ambrosiaster: Paul accepted contributions from the Macedonians because they corrected their faults. But he refused anything from the Corinthians because they were less ready to correct theirs. Commentary on Paul's Epistles.[4]

Funded by Others. Theodoret of Cyr: This is the greatest condemnation of the Corinthians imaginable. For while he was benefiting them,

Paul was being funded by others elsewhere. Commentary on the Second Epistle to the Corinthians 343.[5]

11:10 *His Boast Not Silenced*

Refusing to Take Any Aid. Ambrosiaster: Paul urges the whole of Achaia to give aid to the saints, but at the same time he refuses to take anything for himself from any of them. Commentary on Paul's Epistles.[6]

11:11 *The Apostle's Love for Them*

A Beneficial Love. Ambrosiaster: Paul wanted the Corinthians to understand that his love for them was beneficial, not harmful. Commentary on Paul's Epistles.[7]

Love Makes Admonition Serious. Chrysostom: By giving love as the motive for his behavior, Paul makes his admonition even more serious. Homilies on the Epistles of Paul to the Corinthians 23.6.[8]

---

[2]CSEL 81.285. [3]NPNF 1 12:386. [4]CSEL 81.285-86. [5]Migne PG 82:442. [6]CSEL 81.286. [7]CSEL 81.286. [8]NPNF 1 12:387.

11:12-15 THE FALSE TEACHERS

[12]*And what I do I will continue to do, in order to undermine the claim of those who would like to claim that in their boasted mission they work on the same terms as we do.* [13]*For such men are false apostles, deceitful workmen, disguising themselves as apostles of Christ.* [14]*And no wonder, for even Satan disguises himself as an angel of light.* [15]*So it is not strange if his servants also disguise themselves as servants of righteousness. Their end will correspond to their deeds.*

Overview: An angel of light is one who is free to speak because he stands close to God. This is what the devil pretends to be (Chrysostom, Cyril of Jerusalem, Augustine). It is the devil's custom to imitate the things of God (THEODORET OF CYR). The boast of the false apostles was that they received money. Paul's reason for rejecting this practice was that he would not appear to be in any way like them (AMBROSIASTER). Nothing but the great mercy of God can save one from mistaking bad demons for good angels and false friends for true ones and from suffering the full damages of diabolical deception (AUGUSTINE).

11:12 Undermining False Claims

HIS VULNERABILITY. CHRYSOSTOM: This was the point on which the false apostles evidently felt they could attack Paul, and so he had to refute them at such great length. HOMILIES ON THE EPISTLES OF PAUL TO THE CORINTHIANS 23.6.[1]

11:13 False Apostles

ROBBING THE SOUL. CHRYSOSTOM: The false apostles looked good on the surface, but underneath they robbed the soul. Indeed, they took money as well, though they were careful to conceal that as much as possible. HOMILIES ON THE EPISTLES OF PAUL TO THE CORINTHIANS 24.1.[2]

11:14 Even Satan Disguises Himself

AN ANGEL OF LIGHT. CHRYSOSTOM: An angel of light is one who is free to speak because he stands close to God. This is what the devil pretends to be. HOMILIES ON THE EPISTLES OF PAUL TO THE CORINTHIANS 24.1.[3]

ENSNARING SOULS. AUGUSTINE: These illusions are apparitions of that spirit who seeks to ensnare unhappy souls in the deceptive rites of a multitude of false gods and to turn them aside from the true worship of the true God, by whom alone they can be purified and healed. CITY OF GOD 10.10.[4]

DIABOLICAL DECEPTION. AUGUSTINE: Satan

sometimes transforms himself into an angel of light in order to test those who need testing or to deceive those who deserve deception. Nothing but the great mercy of God can save a man from mistaking bad demons for good angels and false friends for true ones and from suffering the full damages of this diabolical deception which is all the more deadly in that it is wily beyond words. CITY OF GOD 19.9.[5]

DECENCY DEFORMED. AUGUSTINE: So powerful is the attraction of the virtue of purity that practically every human being is pleased to hear it praised, and no one is so sunk in depravity as to have lost all sense of decency. Hence, unless the malignity of the demons somewhere "transforms itself into an angel of light," as we read in our Scripture, it cannot carry out its business of deception. CITY OF GOD 2.26.[6]

ANGELS OF LIGHT, ANGELS OF DARKNESS. AUGUSTINE: As for the power of darkness, what is it but the power of the devil and his angels, who, after being angels of light, did not use their free will to stand in the truth but by falling from it became darkness? I am not teaching you this; I am advising you to call to mind what you know. So, the human race became subject to this power of darkness by the fall of the first man who was induced by that power to commit sin, and in him we have all fallen. LETTER 217 TO VITALIS.[7]

THE GREAT MIMICS. CYRIL OF JERUSALEM: Evil apes respectability, and tares do their best to look like wheat, but however close a similarity to wheat they have in appearance their taste completely undeceives the discerning. Even the devil "transforms himself into an angel of light," not meaning to ascend again to his former place (for he possesses a heart as hard as an anvil and has no intention of repenting ever) but to snare

---

[1]NPNF 1 12:387-88. [2]NPNF 1 12:390. [3]NPNF 1 12:390. [4]FC 14:135. [5]FC 24:209. [6]FC 8:121. [7]FC 32:81.

those who are living the angelic life in blinding darkness and infest them with a condition of faithlessness. There are many wolves going about "in sheep's clothing,"[8] but though they wear the coats of sheep, they possess nonetheless both talons and teeth. They wrap themselves in the gentle creature's hide and with this disguise deceive the innocent only to inject with their teeth the deadly poison of their irreligion. We therefore need the grace of God, a sober mind and watchful eyes, so as not to eat tares for wheat and come to harm for not knowing better; so as not to mistake the wolf for a sheep and be ravaged; and so as not to take the death-dealing devil for a good angel and be devoured. THE CATECHETICAL LECTURES 4.1.[9]

DESERTING THE DOCTRINE OF HEAVEN. CYPRIAN: He invented heresies and schisms to undermine faith, pervert truth and break unity. Unable to keep us in the dark ways of former error, he draws us into a new maze of deceit. He snatches men away from the church itself and, just when they think they have drawn near to the light and escaped the night of the world, he plunges them unawares into a new darkness. Though they do not stand by the gospel and discipline and law of Christ, they call themselves Christians. Though they are walking in darkness, they think they are in the light, through the deceitful flattery of the adversary who, as the apostle said, transforms himself into an angel of light and adorns his ministers as ministers of righteousness. They call night day, death salvation, despair hope, perfidy faith, antichrist Christ, cunningly to frustrate truth by their lying show of truth. That is what happens, my brothers, when we do not return to the fount of truth, when we are not looking to the head and keeping the doctrine taught from heaven. THE UNITY OF THE CATHOLIC CHURCH 3.[10]

11:15 The End Corresponds to Deeds

TO DECEIVE. AMBROSIASTER: The servants of righteousness are the apostles, whose associates these people falsely pretended to be, so as to deceive their hearers. COMMENTARY ON PAUL'S EPISTLES.[11]

IMITATING THE THINGS OF GOD. THEODORET OF CYR: It is the devil's custom to imitate the things of God. He sets up false prophets to oppose the true ones and assumes the form of an angel in order to deceive men. COMMENTARY ON THE SECOND EPISTLE TO THE CORINTHIANS 344.[12]

---

[8]Mt 7:15. [9]LCC 4:98. [10]LCC 5:125-26. [11]CSEL 81.287. [12]Migne PG 82:442.

11:16-29 PAUL'S BOASTING

[16]I repeat, let no one think me foolish; but even if you do, accept me as a fool, so that I too may boast a little. [17](What I am saying I say not with the Lord's authority but as a fool, in this boastful confidence; [18]since many boast of worldly things, I too will boast.) [19]For you gladly bear with fools, being wise yourselves! [20]For you bear it if a man makes slaves of you, or preys upon you, or takes advantage of you, or puts on airs, or strikes you in the face. [21]To my shame, I must say, we were too weak for that!

But whatever any one dares to boast of—I am speaking as a fool—I also dare to boast of that. [22]Are they Hebrews? So am I. Are they Israelites? So am I. Are they descendants of Abraham? So am I. [23]Are they servants of Christ? I am a better one—I am talking like a madman—with far greater labors, far more imprisonments, with countless beatings, and often near death. [24]Five times I have received at the hands of the Jews the forty lashes less one. [25]Three times I have been beaten with rods; once I was stoned. Three times I have been shipwrecked; a night and a day I have been adrift at sea; [26]on frequent journeys, in danger from rivers, danger from robbers, danger from my own people, danger from Gentiles, danger in the city, danger in the wilderness, danger at sea, danger from false brethren; [27]in toil and hardship, through many a sleepless night, in hunger and thirst, often without food, in cold and exposure. [28]And, apart from other things, there is the daily pressure upon me of my anxiety for all the churches. [29]Who is weak, and I am not weak? Who is made to fall, and I am not indignant?

Overview: In the pretended posture of foolishness (Theodoret of Cyr), Paul boasts of worldly things: his birth, wealth, wisdom, circumcision and popular reputation. He knows that none of these things matter before God, which is why he called this way of speaking foolish (Chrysostom). He earned his living with his own hands, from early morning until about eleven o'clock, and from then until four in the afternoon he would engage in public disputation with enormous energy (Ambrosiaster). He had been beaten, stoned and shipwrecked, in danger from rivers in winter, in danger at sea from soldiers who in a shipwreck would have killed him rather than risk his escape by letting him swim to safety (Ambrosiaster). Paul shared the suffering of all the saints (Cyprian, Ephrem the Syrian, Augustine). Such discipline is beneficial not only for bringing the body into subjection but also for showing charity to neighbors (Basil). Meanwhile, the false apostles rob the Corinthians privately while they exalt them publicly (Chrysostom).

11:16 Accept Me as a Fool

Appearing Foolish. Ambrosiaster: Paul returns here to what he said at the beginning of the chapter. What he is about to say is true, though it may make him appear to be foolish, because these truths redound to his praise. Paul is not really boasting but merely wants to show that others who boast have nothing more to show for themselves than he has, so that if they are worthy of praise so is he. Commentary on Paul's Epistles.[1]

11:17 Boastful Confidence

Without the Lord's Authority. Ambrosiaster: God does not approve of boasting, so this mode of speaking does not come from him. But the content of what he is saying is still true. Commentary on Paul's Epistles.[2]

Unprofitable Servants. Theodoret of Cyr: Jesus said that when we have done all, we should confess that we are no more than unprofitable servants.[3] This is why Paul says here that he is not speaking with the Lord's authority. Commentary on the Second Epistle to the Corinthians 344.[4]

---

[1]CSEL 81.288. [2]CSEL 81.288-89. [3]Lk 17:10. [4]Migne PG 82:443.

11:18 Boasting of Worldly Things

CLAIMING SUPERIORITY. AMBROSIASTER: Paul is saying this because some Jewish believers were claiming superiority as children of Israel. To glorify oneself according to the flesh is to claim nobility of the flesh. The Jews claimed this because they are the children of Abraham, who believed in God. COMMENTARY ON PAUL'S EPISTLES.[5]

WORLDLY THINGS. CHRYSOSTOM: What are these worldly things Paul will boast of? His birth, his wealth, his wisdom, his being circumcised, his Hebrew ancestry and his popular reputation. Of course he knew that none of these things mattered in the slightest, which is why he called this way of speaking foolish. HOMILIES ON THE EPISTLES OF PAUL TO THE CORINTHIANS 24.2.[6]

11:19 Gladly Bearing with Fools

PRIDE IN CIRCUMCISION. AMBROSIASTER: Paul gives the name of fools to those who prided themselves in the circumcision of the flesh. It was because these people were accepted by the Corinthians that Paul wants them to recognize that he too can boast of this. But he does not glorify himself as a result. On the contrary, he points out that such boasting is foolish and worldly. COMMENTARY ON PAUL'S EPISTLES.[7]

RIDICULING FOLLY. CHRYSOSTOM: To boast about such things was a sign of foolishness, and Paul ridicules them accordingly. HOMILIES ON THE EPISTLES OF PAUL TO THE CORINTHIANS 24.2.[8]

11:20 Taking Advantage

BEARING HUMILIATION. AMBROSIASTER: Paul is referring to certain Jews who were maltreating them because they were uncircumcised. They were claiming high rank for themselves and hu-miliating everyone else. COMMENTARY ON PAUL'S EPISTLES.[9]

11:21 Speaking as a Fool

EXALTED PUBLICLY, ROBBED PRIVATELY. CHRYSOSTOM: Paul means by this that he can do all the things mentioned here, but he does not do so. Meanwhile, the false apostles exalt the Corinthians publicly and then rob them privately. But the people seem not to notice, having been deceived by them. HOMILIES ON THE EPISTLES OF PAUL TO THE CORINTHIANS 24.2.[10]

11:22 Descendants of Abraham

THEIR EQUAL. AMBROSIASTER: Paul is making it clear that he is the equal of the men to whom he referred above. His purpose was to show that the disparaging opinions by which they were judging him were false. COMMENTARY ON PAUL'S EPISTLES.[11]

ISRAELITES. CHRYSOSTOM: Not all Hebrews were Israelites, for the Ammonites and the Moabites were Hebrews as well. HOMILIES ON THE EPISTLES OF PAUL TO THE CORINTHIANS 25.1.[12]

11:23 A Servant of Christ

PAUL'S LABORS. AMBROSIASTER: The other apostles labored, but not as much as Paul. He used to earn his living with his own hands, from early morning until about eleven o'clock, and from then until four in the afternoon he would engage in public disputation with such energy that he would usually persuade those who spoke in opposition to him. COMMENTARY ON PAUL'S EPISTLES.[13]

---

[5]CSEL 81.289. [6]NPNF 1 12:391. [7]CSEL 81.289. [8]NPNF 1 12:391-92. [9]CSEL 81.290-91. [10]NPNF 1 12:392. [11]CSEL 81.292. [12]NPNF 1 12:394. [13]CSEL 81.292-93.

The Apostle of Love. Chrysostom: No one else has been granted such a love of the Lord as this blessed spirit. I mean, as though freed from the body and raised on high, so to say, and not considering himself to tread the earth, he delivers himself of all these remarks. You see, desire for God and burning love elevated his thinking from material things to spiritual, from present to future, from visible to unseen. This is what faith is like, after all, and love of God. For proof of his sound attitude, see this man, with his great love for the Lord and his burning desire for him hunted, persecuted, chastised, suffering countless abuses and exclaiming, "In toils more frequently, in scourgings beyond counting, at death's door often; at the Jews' hands I five times received forty lashes bar one; I was thrice beaten with rods; once I was stoned; a day and night I spent adrift at sea, always traveling, at peril from rivers, at peril from false brothers, in toil and hardship"—and while suffering such things he rejoiced and was glad. You see, he was quite convinced that the labors of the present life proved an occasion of great reward for him, and dangers were the source of a crown. After all, if out of love for Rachel Jacob regarded as a few days the period of seven years, much more did this blessed man count it all of no consequence, on fire as he was with love of God and prepared to endure everything for the Christ he loved. Let us too, therefore, I beseech you, be concerned to love Christ. Christ looks for nothing else from you, in fact, Scripture says, than loving him with all your heart and carrying out his commands. Homily 55 on Genesis.[14]

11:24 Receiving Lashes

Forty Lashes Less One. Chrysostom: There was an ancient law that anyone who received more than forty lashes would be permanently disgraced among the Jews. So in order to prevent this from happening as a result of the impetuosity of the executioner, the law decreed that the forty lashes should be inflicted excepting one, so that even if the executioner overdid it he would not go past forty. Homilies on the Epistles of Paul to the Corinthians 25.1.[15]

11:25 Beaten, Stoned, Adrift

Beaten, Stoned and Shipwrecked. Ambrosiaster: Paul suffered the beating with rods at the hands of Gentiles.[16] He was stoned by the Jews in a city of Lycaonia.[17] Someone who sailed as much as he did would easily have been shipwrecked three times. He was adrift at sea on his journey to Rome, when he had appealed to Caesar.[18] Commentary on Paul's Epistles.[19]

Going Down to the Sea. Ephrem the Syrian: The East has grown luminous with the saints, with them the West has become brilliant, the North is raised up by them, from them the South has learned. They have ascended to the firmament and opened it,[20] they have gone down to the sea and explored it. Hymns on Paradise 6.22.[21]

11:26 Frequent Journeys and Dangers

In Danger. Ambrosiaster: Paul was in danger from rivers in winter, when there was constant rain and rivers often overflowed their banks. The danger at sea which he is alluding to here was the danger that in a shipwreck the soldiers guarding prisoners on board would kill them all rather than risk letting them swim to safety.[22] Commentary on Paul's Epistles.[23]

Set Apart. Augustine: What great complaints the apostle Paul makes of false brothers. Yet he was not defiled by their physical companionship, because he was set apart from them by

---

[14]FC 87:112-13. [15]NPNF 1 12:394-95. [16]Acts 16:16-23. [17]Acts 14:19. [18]Acts 27:1-44. [19]CSEL 81.293. [20]Cf. 2 Cor 12:3. [21]HOP 117. [22]Acts 27:42-44. [23]CSEL 81.294-95.

this distinction: purity of heart. LETTER 108 TO MACROBIUS.[24]

TWO KINDS OF PASTORS. AUGUSTINE: Therefore, there are some who occupy the pastoral chair in order to care for the flock of Christ, but there are others who sit in it to gratify themselves by temporal honors and worldly advantages. These are the two kinds of pastors, some dying, some being born, who must needs continue in the Catholic church itself until the end of the world and the judgment of the Lord. If there were such men in the times of the apostles, whom the apostle lamented as false brothers when he said: "Perils from false brothers," yet whom he did not proudly dismiss but bore with them and tolerated them, how much more likely is it that there should be such men in our times. LETTER 208 TO FELICIA.[25]

11:27 Toil and Hardship

COLD AND EXPOSED. AMBROSIASTER: Some of Paul's sleepless nights were voluntary, but others were forced on him. When he was in dire straits, he had to stay awake and seek God's help. Furthermore he taught not only in the daytime but at night as well. He was cold and exposed when he was shipwrecked on the island of Malta, where the local people came to his rescue.[26] COMMENTARY ON PAUL'S EPISTLES.[27]

THE BENEFIT OF RIGOROUS EXERTION. BASIL: Such exertion is beneficial not only for bringing the body into subjection but also for showing charity to our neighbor, so that through us God might grant sufficiency to the weak among us. THE LONG RULES 37.[28]

11:28 Anxiety for the Churches

THE DAILY PRESSURE. AMBROSIASTER: This happened because Paul adopted the habit of teaching the people entrusted to him on a daily basis. He worked during the day and taught at night,

for he did not hesitate to put himself out for their sakes.[29] COMMENTARY ON PAUL'S EPISTLES.[30]

11:29 Who Is Weak?

THEIR CAPTIVITY IS MINE. CYPRIAN: The captivity of our brothers must be thought of as our captivity. The sorrow of those in danger is our sorrow. You may be sure that there is one body of our unity. Not only love but also religion ought to incite us and to encourage us to redeem the members of our family. LETTERS 62.1.[31]

SUFFERING IN SYMPATHY. AMBROSIASTER: Paul is saying that he suffers in sympathy with everybody and that he shares their pain in order to provide medicine for the wound. He presses the point in order to show how carefully he is guarding and ruling the church entrusted to him. In this way he shows that he should not be considered inferior to the other apostles, seeing that he labored more than all of them. COMMENTARY ON PAUL'S EPISTLES.[32]

AM I NOT WEAK? THEODORE OF MOPSUESTIA: By "weak" in this case Paul means "sinful." PAULINE COMMENTARY FROM THE GREEK CHURCH.[33]

SYMPATHIZING WITH WEAKNESS. AUGUSTINE: Paul does not mean that he was counterfeiting their weakness but that he was sympathizing with it. LETTER 40 TO JEROME.[34]

THE RESPONSIBLE PASTOR. CHRYSOSTOM: What wonderful affection in a pastor! Others' falls, he is saying, accentuate my grief, others' obstacles inflame the fire of my suffering. Let all those entrusted with the leadership of rational sheep imitate this and not prove inferior to the shepherd who for many years cares for irrational sheep. In that case no harm ensues even if some

---

[24]FC 18:222. [25]FC 32:24-25. [26]Acts 28:1-10. [27]CSEL 81.295-96. [28]FC 9:306. [29]Acts 18:1-4; 19:9. [30]CSEL 81.296. [31]FC 51:200. [32]CSEL 81.296-97. [33]NTA 15:199. [34]FC 12:177.

negligence occurs, but in our case if only one rational sheep is lost or falls to predators, the loss is extreme; the harm, terrible; the punishment, unspeakable. After all, if our Lord did not forbear to pour out his own blood for him, what excuse would such a person deserve for allowing himself

to neglect the one so esteemed by the Lord and not making every effort on his part to care for the sheep? HOMILY 57, HOMILIES ON GENESIS.[35]

---

[35]FC 87:149.

11:30-33 PAUL'S ESCAPE

[30]*If I must boast, I will boast of the things that show my weakness.* [31]*The God and Father of the Lord Jesus, he who is blessed for ever, knows that I do not lie.* [32]*At Damascus, the governor under King Aretas guarded the city of Damascus in order to seize me,* [33]*but I was let down in a basket through a window in the wall, and escaped his hands.*

OVERVIEW: The governor of Damascus intended to capture Paul in order to keep the Jews happy, but this plan was foiled (AMBROSIASTER). Paul did not refrain from accepting human help when necessary. At times when evils are inevitable, grace alone suffices, but where timely choices are to be made, one does not hesitate to seize available opportunities (CHRYSOSTOM, AUGUSTINE). The time when God's help is necessary is when all human help fails (AMBROSIASTER).

11:30 Boasting of Weakness

BOASTING IN HUMILITY. AMBROSIASTER: Paul is saying this because if a Christian must boast, he should boast in humility, from which comes growth in God's sight. COMMENTARY ON PAUL'S EPISTLES.[1]

THINGS THAT SHOW WEAKNESS. CHRYSOSTOM: Paul boasted of his trials—the very things that showed his weakness. HOMILIES ON THE EPISTLES OF PAUL TO THE CORINTHIANS 25.2.[2]

11:31 I Do Not Lie

GOD AS WITNESS. AMBROSIASTER: Paul calls God as his witness in order that what he says may be readily believed. COMMENTARY ON PAUL'S EPISTLES.[3]

11:32 A Trap at Damascus

A WICKED SCHEME. AMBROSIASTER: The governor of Damascus, seeing that the Jews had set a trap for the apostle, wanted to bring this wicked scheme to pass by a wrongful use of his power. He intended to capture Paul both in order to keep the Jews happy and to demonstrate that he was doing his job properly. This occurred at the very beginning of Paul's ministry.[4] COMMENTARY ON PAUL'S EPISTLES.[5]

11:33 An Escape

---

[1]CSEL 81.297-98. [2]NPNF 1 12:396. [3]CSEL 81.298. [4]Acts 9:19-25. [5]CSEL 81.298.

HUMAN HELP. AMBROSIASTER: Some people say that this action was not worthy of Paul, because he was not set free by the help of God. But what need was there for that when he could be delivered by the help of men?[6] The time when God's help is necessary is when human help fails. COMMENTARY ON PAUL'S EPISTLES.[7]

IN A BASKET. CHRYSOSTOM: Paul did not refrain from resorting to this kind of thing when necessary, because he wanted to keep himself free for preaching the gospel. At times when evils were inevitable, grace alone sufficed, but where there were choices to be made, he did not hesitate to seize the opportunity. HOMILIES ON THE EPISTLES OF PAUL TO THE CORINTHIANS 25.2.[8]

A TIME TO FLEE, A TIME TO REMAIN. AUGUSTINE: And the apostle Paul, when he was let down from the window in a basket so that his enemy might not capture him and so escaped from his hands, did he deprive the church, which was there, of a necessary ministry, and was that duty not discharged by other brothers appointed for that purpose? The apostle so acted in deference to their wishes that he might save himself for the church, since he was the only one whom the persecutor was seeking. Therefore, let the servants of Christ, the ministers of his word and of his sacrament, do what he has commanded or permitted. Let them by all means flee from city to city when any one of them is personally sought out by persecutors, so long as the church is not abandoned by others who are not thus pursued and who may furnish nourishment to their fellow servants, knowing that otherwise these could not live. But when the danger is common to all, that is, to bishops, clerics and laity, those who depend upon others are not to be forsaken by those on whom they depend. Therefore, either all should move to places of refuge, or those who have to stay should not be abandoned by those who minister to their spiritual needs; thus all may equally live and suffer whatever the Master of the household wishes them to endure. LETTER 228 TO HONORATUS.[9]

---

[6]Acts 9:25. [7]CSEL 81.299. [8]NPNF 1 12:396. [9]FC 32:142-43.

12:1-6 THE MYSTICAL VISION

[1]*I must boast; there is nothing to be gained by it, but I will go on to visions and revelations of the Lord.* [2]*I know a man in Christ who fourteen years ago was caught up to the third heaven—whether in the body or out of the body I do not know, God knows.* [3]*And I know that this man was caught up into Paradise—whether in the body or out of the body I do not know, God knows—* [4]*and he heard things that cannot be told, which man may not utter.* [5]*On behalf of this man I will boast, but on my own behalf I will not boast, except of my weaknesses.* [6]*Though if I wish to boast, I shall not be a fool, for I shall be speaking the truth. But I refrain from it, so that no one may think more of me than he sees in me or hears from me.*

OVERVIEW: To be caught up in the third heaven means that Paul was caught up beyond all the stars of the universe into the heaven that is third in the hierarchy of spiritual heavens

(CYRIL OF JERUSALEM, AMBROSIASTER, GRE-
GORY NAZIANZEN, PELAGIUS). It is obvious that
Paul was talking about himself, but he speaks in
this way to show that he would prefer not to
talk about things unutterable (ORIGEN, CHRY-
SOSTOM, THEODORET OF CYR, THEODORE OF
MOPSUESTIA, OECUMENIUS, ISAAC OF NINE-
VEH, AUGUSTINE). If anyone talks about the
things that have been revealed to him, that in itself is not foolish. But if he keeps quiet about
them, he may be more wise (AMBROSIASTER). It
is not so much the deeds themselves that tempt
us to pride as our telling them to others
(CHRYSOSTOM).

12:1 Visions and Revelations

RAISED UP. AMBROSIASTER: Paul is now going to
describe how he has been raised up in order
that the Corinthians might understand how
great and how wonderful the things said to him
were and that they might realize that he is not
inferior in any way to the other apostles. COM-
MENTARY ON PAUL'S EPISTLES.[1]

BOASTING CAUSES PRIDE. CHRYSOSTOM: It is not
so much the deeds themselves which are the
cause of pride, as our telling them to others.
Good deeds will not puff anybody up unless
they are witnessed to and remarked upon by
others. HOMILIES ON THE EPISTLES OF PAUL TO
THE CORINTHIANS 26.1.[2]

12:2 Caught Up to the Third Heaven

THE THIRD HEAVEN. AMBROSIASTER: Paul mentions both things because either is possible. It
may seem to someone that it is nothing much
to be caught up into the third heaven, since
that is where the moon is, but that is not
right. What this means is that he was caught
up beyond all the stars of the universe into
the heaven which is third in the hierarchy of
spiritual heavens. COMMENTARY ON PAUL'S
EPISTLES.[3]

IN OR OUT OF THE BODY. CHRYSOSTOM: Paul
specifies that it was fourteen years before in order to show that he would not normally have
spoken about it at all had he not been provoked.
And even then, notice that there are some
things he is still ignorant about. He knows that
he was in paradise, but whether he was in the
body or not he cannot tell. Why did this happen to him? I think it was probably so that he
would not feel inferior to the other apostles,
who had all been with Christ while he was on
earth. HOMILIES ON THE EPISTLES OF PAUL TO
THE CORINTHIANS 26.1-2.[4]

FOURTEEN YEARS BEFORE. PELAGIUS: You see
how pressed Paul was to make his point, if he
had to recall something which had happened as
long as fourteen years before. COMMENTARY ON
THE SECOND EPISTLE TO THE CORINTHIANS 12.[5]

INEFFABLE WONDERS. GREGORY NAZIANZEN:
Had Paul been able to express the experiences
gained from the third heaven and his progress,
ascent or assumption to it, we should perhaps
have known more about God—if this really was
the secret meaning of his rapture. But since
they were ineffable, let them have the tribute of
our silence. Let us give this much attention to
Paul when he says: "We know in part and we
prophesy in part."[6] This and the like is the confession of one who is no mere layman in knowledge, of one who threatens to give proof of
Christ speaking in him,[7] of a great champion
and teacher of truth. ORATION 28: ON THE DOC-
TRINE OF GOD.[8]

12:3 Into Paradise

CAUGHT UP TWICE. AMBROSIASTER: Paul says that
he was caught up twice—first into the third
heaven and then into paradise, which is where

---

[1]CSEL 81.299. [2]NPNF 1 12:398. [3]CSEL 81.299-300. [4]NPNF
1 12:398-99. [5]Migne PL 30:802C. [6]1 Cor 13:9. [7]2 Cor 13:2-3.
[8]FGFR 235.

the Lord said that the thief on the cross would be with him.[9] COMMENTARY ON PAUL'S EPISTLES.[10]

12:4 Things That Cannot Be Told

NO ONE CAN UTTER. ORIGEN: This means that they cannot be expressed in a human language. ON FIRST PRINCIPLES 2.7.4.[11]

THE APPEARANCE OF PARADISE. THEODORE OF MOPSUESTIA: He saw the beautiful appearance of paradise, the dances of the saints in it and the harmonious sound of its hymnody. PAULINE COMMENTARY FROM THE GREEK CHURCH.[12]

THINGS HE SAW. THEODORET OF CYR: Some argue that here Paul is referring to things which he actually saw, like the beauty of paradise and the choirs of the saints which are to be found there. COMMENTARY ON THE SECOND EPISTLE TO THE CORINTHIANS 348.[13]

A FIRSTHAND REVELATION. OECUMENIUS: So much for those who write false revelations! PAULINE COMMENTARY FROM THE GREEK CHURCH.[14]

NOT AUDIBLE SOUNDS. ISAAC OF NINEVEH: All that is heard by the ears can be spoken. He did not hear audible sounds, nor did he see a vision composed of the corporeal images of sense perception, but it was by the intuitions of the understanding, being in rapture, while his will had no fellowship with the body. ASCETICAL HOMILIES 4.[15]

THE WONDER OF THE RESURRECTION BODY. AUGUSTINE: But, even if the angels, whose nature is simple and spiritual, are said to have tongues with which they sing praises to their Lord and Creator and give him unceasing thanks, much more must the spiritualized bodies of men do so after the resurrection. For all the members of their glorified flesh will have tongues in their mouths, and they will give voice to their speaking tongues, and thus they will utter divine praises, the outpouring in words of their love and of the joys that fill even their senses. Doubtless the Lord will add this to the grace and glory of his saints in the time of his kingdom, that the more perfectly they attain to this blessed condition of body by a happy transformation, the more fully will they sing with tongue and voice. Being established in their spiritual bodies, they may speak, perchance, not with the tongues of men but with those of angels, such as the apostle heard in paradise. LETTERS 94.[16]

PAUL AND ELIJAH. CYRIL OF JERUSALEM: Elijah was taken up to heaven only, but Paul into heaven and paradise (for it was but fitting that the disciples of Jesus should receive more manifold grace) and "heard secret words that man may not repeat." But Paul came down again from heaven, not because he was unworthy to abide in the third heaven but after enjoying gifts beyond man's lot. CATECHESIS 14.16.[17]

12:5 Not on My Own Behalf

IT DOES NOT MATTER. CHRYSOSTOM: It is obvious that Paul was talking about himself, but he says this in order to show that it does not matter to him in the slightest. He would prefer not to talk about it at all. HOMILIES ON THE EPISTLES OF PAUL TO THE CORINTHIANS 26.2.[18]

12:6 Paul Refrains from Boasting

SPEAKING THE TRUTH. AMBROSIASTER: Paul says this because if someone proclaims his own worth in God's sight he is not unwise, for what he says is true. So if anyone talks about the things which have been revealed to him, he is not foolish, though if he keeps quiet about them he is wise. COMMENTARY ON PAUL'S EPISTLES.[19]

---

[9]Lk 23:39-43. [10]CSEL 81.300. [11]OFP 118. [12]NTA 15:200. [13]Migne PG 82:447. [14]NTA 15:445. [15]AHSIS 34. [16]FC 18:112-13*. [17]FC 64:49. [18]NPNF 1 12:399. [19]CSEL 81.301.

12:7-10 THE THORN IN PAUL'S FLESH

[7]*And to keep me from being too elated by the abundance of revelations, a thorn was given me in the flesh, a messenger of Satan, to harass me, to keep me from being too elated.* [8]*Three times I besought the Lord about this, that it should leave me;* [9]*but he said to me, "My grace is sufficient for you, for my power is made perfect in weakness." I will all the more gladly boast of my weaknesses, that the power of Christ may rest upon me.* [10]*For the sake of Christ, then, I am content with weaknesses, insults, hardships, persecutions, and calamities; for when I am weak, then I am strong.*

OVERVIEW: By the thorn in his flesh, Paul was referring to the persecutions he had so often suffered (SEVERIAN OF GABALA, THEODORET OF CYR) from vexing adversaries like Alexander the coppersmith and the party of Hymenaeus and Philetus (CHRYSOSTOM). Paul could hardly bear the plots that were going on behind his back, and he sought three times (meaning often) to be delivered from them (CHRYSOSTOM). But Paul's affliction was intended for a higher purpose (THEODORET OF CYR). By grace his humility overcame his frailty (AMBROSE). By this it became clear that God's power is made perfect in persecutions and sufferings (CYPRIAN, BASIL, SEVERIAN). When some infirmity or desolation attacks us, then our power is made mature if faith stands firm (NOVATIAN). The more trials we face, the more grace we are capable of receiving (CHRYSOSTOM). Does this imply that the devil is good because he is useful? On the contrary, he is evil because he is the devil, but God who is good and almighty draws many good things out of the devil's malice (TERTULLIAN, AUGUSTINE). This incident shows that even a wrong prayer may receive a right answer (PELAGIUS, CASSIODORUS).

12:7 A Thorn in the Flesh

THE DEVIL'S BORROWED POWER. TERTULLIAN: The right to tempt a man is granted to the devil ... whether God or the devil initiates the plan or for the purpose of the judgment of a sinner, who is handed over to the devil as to an executioner. This was the case with Saul. "The spirit of the Lord departed from Saul, and an evil spirit from the Lord troubled and stifled him."[1] Again, it may happen in order to humble a man, as St. Paul tells us that there was given to him a thorn, a messenger of Satan, to buffet him, and even this sort of thing is not permitted for the humiliation of holy men through torment of the flesh, unless it be done so that their power to resist may be perfected in weakness. The apostle himself handed Phigellus and Hermogenes over to Satan so that by being chastised they might not blaspheme. And so you see that, far from possessing power in his own right, the devil can more easily be granted it by the servants of God. FLIGHT IN TIME OF PERSECUTION 2.7.[2]

ENRICHED BY TRIALS. AMBROSIASTER: Paul is testifying that God makes provision for those who have done well, while at the same time he allows them to be cast down by various trials. This is both so that they shall not be deprived of the fruits of their labors and that they may be enriched by their trials so that they may have even greater eternal rewards. COMMENTARY ON PAUL'S EPISTLES.[3]

---

[1]1 Kings 16:14. [2]FC 40:280-81*. [3]CSEL 81.301.

His Adversaries. Chrysostom: There are some who have said that Paul is referring to a pain in the head caused by the devil, but God forbid! The body of Paul could never have been given over to the devil, especially when we remember that the devil submitted to Paul when he was bidden to. In Hebrew, any adversary can be called Satan. What Paul means is that God would not allow the preaching of the gospel to go forward, so that his proud thoughts might be checked. Instead, Paul was attacked by adversaries like Alexander the coppersmith, the party of Hymenaeus and Philetus and all the opponents of the Word.[4] These were the messengers of Satan. Homilies on the Epistles of Paul to the Corinthians 26.2.[5]

Is the Devil Good Because He Is Useful? Augustine: "And so," they ask, "is the devil good because he is useful?" On the contrary, he is evil insofar as he is the devil, but God who is good and almighty draws many just and good things out of the devil's malice. For the devil has to his credit only his will by which he tries to do evil, not the providence of God that draws good out of him. Against the Manichaeans 2.28.42.[6]

His Persecution. Severian of Gabala: Many people think this was some kind of headache, but in reality Paul is referring to the persecutions which he suffered, because they came from diabolical powers. Pauline Commentary from the Greek Church.[7]

Messenger of Satan. Theodoret of Cyr: By "messenger of Satan" Paul means the insults, attacks and riots which he had to face. Commentary on the Second Epistle to the Corinthians 349.[8]

Prayer in Our Suffering. Augustine: Therefore, in these trials which can be both our blessing and our bane, "we don't know how we should pray," yet, because they are hard, because they are painful, because they go against the feeling of our human weakness, by a universal human will we pray that our troubles may depart from us. But this need of devotion we owe to the Lord our God, that, if he does not remove them, we are not to think that he has deserted us but rather, by lovingly bearing evil, we are to hope for greater good. This is how power is made perfect in infirmity. To some, indeed, who lack patience, the Lord God, in his wrath, grants them what they ask, just as, on the other hand, he in his mercy refused the apostle's requests.[9] To Proba 130.[10]

The Advantage of Unanswered Prayer. Cassiodorus: Paul begged that the flesh's thorn be removed from him, but he was not heard by the Lord. The devil prayed that he might strike Job with the harshest of disasters, and we know that this was subsequently granted him. But Paul was denied the fulfillment of his prayer for his glory, whereas the devil was granted his for the devil's pain. Thus it is often an advantage not to be heard even though postponement of our desires depresses us. Explanation of the Psalms 21.3.[11]

Faith Perfected in Weakness. Cyprian: Thus also the apostle Paul, after shipwrecks, after scourgings, after many grievous tortures of the flesh and body, says that he was not harassed but was corrected by adversity, in order that while he was the more heavily afflicted he might the more truly be tried. There was given to me, he says, a thorn in my flesh, an angel of Satan, to buffet me lest I be exalted. Concerning this thorn I asked the Lord three times that it might depart from me. And he said to me: "My grace is sufficient for you: for power is made perfect in weakness." When, therefore, some infirmity and weakness and desolation at-

---

[4]1 Tim 1:18-20; 2 Tim 2:16-18; 4:14-15. [5]NPNF 1 12:400. [6]FC 84:140. [7]NTA 15:297. [8]Migne PG 82:450. [9]Num 11:1-34. [10]FC 18:396**. [11]ACW 51:218.

tacks us, then is our power made perfect, then our faith is crowned, if though tempted it has stood firm. . . . This finally is the difference between us and the others who do not know God, that they complain and murmur in adversity, while adversity does not turn us from the truth of virtue and faith but proves us in suffering. Mortality 13.[12]

The Severity of a Friend. Augustine: Not everyone who spares is a friend, nor is everyone who strikes an enemy. . . . Love mingled with severity is better than deceit with indulgence. It is more profitable for bread to be taken away from the hungry, if he neglects right living because he is sure of his food, than for bread to be broken to the hungry, to lead him astray into compliance with wrongdoing. The one who confines the madman, as well as the one who rouses the lethargic, is troublesome to both but loves both. Who could love us more than God does? Yet he continually teaches us sweetly as well as frightens us for our good. Often adding the most stinging medicine of trouble to the gentle remedies with which he comforts us, he tries the patriarchs, even good and devout ones, by famine;[13] he chastises a stubborn people with heavier punishments; he does not take away from the apostle the sting of the flesh, though asked three times, so as to perfect strength in weakness. Letter 93 to Vincent.[14]

12:8 I Besought the Lord

A Plea Not Granted. Ambrosiaster: Although he asked three times, his request was not granted. It is not that he was disregarded but that he was making a plea which was against his own best interests. Commentary on Paul's Epistles.[15]

Three Times. Chrysostom: Three times means repeatedly. Paul could not bear the plots which were going on behind his back, and he sought to be delivered from them. Homilies on the

Epistles of Paul to the Corinthians 26.3.[16]

Answers to Our Advantage. Chrysostom: Accordingly, whether we have our requests granted or not, let us persist in asking and render thanks not only when we gain what we ask but also when we fail to. Failure to gain, you see, when that is what God wants, is not worse than succeeding; we do not know what is to our advantage in this regard in the way he does understand. The result is, then, that succeeding or failing we ought to give thanks. Why are you surprised that we don't know what is to our advantage? Paul, a man of such quality and stature, judged worthy of ineffable blessings, did not know what was advantageous in his requests: when he saw himself beset with trouble and diverse tribulations, he prayed to be rid of them, not once or twice but many times. "Three times I asked the Lord," he says. . . . "Three" means he asked frequently without success. So let us see how he was affected by it: surely he didn't take it badly? He didn't turn fainthearted, did he? He didn't become dispirited, did he? Not at all. On the contrary, what? God said, "My grace is sufficient for you; my power has its full effect in weakness." Not only did he not free him of the troubles afflicting him, but he even allowed him to persevere in them. True enough; but how does it emerge that he did not take it badly? Listen to Paul's own words when he learned what the Lord had decided: "I will gladly boast of my weaknesses." Not only, he says, do I no longer seek to be rid of them, but I even boast of them with greater satisfaction. Do you see his grateful spirit? Do you see his love for God? . . . So we ought to yield to the Creator of our nature, and with joy and great relish accept those things that he has decided on and have an eye not to the appearance of events but to the decisions of the Lord. After all, he who knows better than we what is

[12]FC 36:209*. [13]Gen 12:10; 26:1; 41:54; 42:1; 43:1. [14]FC 18:60. [15]CSEL 81.302. [16]NPNF 1 12:400.

for our benefit also knows what steps must be taken for our salvation. HOMILY 30.16 ON GENESIS.[17]

12:9 The Power of Christ

FAITH CROWNED. CYPRIAN: When some infirmity and weakness and desolation attacks us, then our power is made perfect, and our faith is crowned if it has stood firm through temptation. MORTALITY 12.[18]

UNJUST INJURIES. AMBROSIASTER: Paul is clearly teaching that the time for boasting is when one is being humiliated by unjust injuries. Christ gives us the power to endure these so that what previously appeared to be painful and loathsome may be accepted with gladness. COMMENTARY ON PAUL'S EPISTLES.[19]

THE IRONY OF WRONG PRAYER. PELAGIUS: We learn from this that even a wrong prayer will receive an answer, even if it does not get what it wants. COMMENTARY ON THE SECOND EPISTLE TO THE CORINTHIANS 12.[20]

MORE TRIALS, MORE GRACE. CHRYSOSTOM: God told Paul that it was enough that he could raise the dead, cure the blind, cleanse lepers and do other miracles. He did not need exemption from danger and fear as well, or complete freedom to preach without any form of hindrance. Indeed, when these troubles come, God's power of deliverance is shown, and the gospel triumphs in spite of persecution. The more the trials increased, the more grace increased as well. HOMILIES ON THE EPISTLES OF PAUL TO THE CORINTHIANS 26.3.[21]

MATURITY THROUGH PERSECUTION. SEVERIAN OF GABALA: God's power is made perfect in persecutions and sufferings. PAULINE COMMENTARY FROM THE GREEK CHURCH.[22]

FOR A HIGHER PURPOSE. THEODORET OF CYR:

Paul wanted to make it clear that his affliction was not a natural property of the body but something which was intended by God for a higher purpose. COMMENTARY ON THE SECOND EPISTLE TO THE CORINTHIANS 350.[23]

THE SOURCE OF OUR STRUGGLE. AUGUSTINE: The more one easily conquers, the less one needs combat. But who would fight within himself if there were no opposition from self? And why is there opposition from self if nothing remains in us to be healed and cured? Therefore, the sole cause of our fighting is weakness in ourselves. Again, weakness cautions against pride. Truly, that strength and virtue by which one is not proud in this life where he could be proud is made perfect in weakness. AGAINST JULIAN 4.2.11.[24]

EVIL'S TESTIMONY TO GOODNESS. TERTULLIAN: Still, we must realize that as you cannot have a persecution without evil on the part of the devil or a trial of faith without a persecution, the evil that seems required for the trial of faith is not the cause of persecution but only its instrument. The real cause of the persecution is the act of God's will, choosing that there be a trial of faith; then there follows evil on the part of the devil as the chosen instrument of persecution which is the proximate cause of the trial of faith. For in other respects too, insofar as evil is the rival of justice, to that extent it provides material to give testimony of that of which it is a rival, and so justice may be said to be perfected in injustice, as strength is perfected in weakness. For the weak things of the world are chosen by God that the strong may be put to shame, and the foolish things of this world to put to shame its wisdom.[25] Thus even evil may be used that justice may be glorified when evil is put to shame. FLIGHT IN TIME OF PERSECUTION 2.1.[26]

---

[17]FC 82:232-33*. [18]FC 36:208. [19]CSEL 81.302. [20]Migne PL 30:803B. [21]NPNF 1 12:400-401. [22]NTA 15:298. [23]Migne PG 82:450. [24]FC 35:175. [25]1 Cor 1:27. [26]FC 40:278.

12:10 *Content for Christ's Sake*

STRONG IN WEAKNESS. AMBROSE: Humility like this does away with frailty. LETTERS TO EMPERORS 1.[27]

CONSOLATION IN AFFLICTION. CHRYSOSTOM: Paul wanted to be delivered from these things, but when God told him otherwise he accepted it and was even glad about it. There is consolation in affliction and grace in consolation. HOMILIES ON THE EPISTLES OF PAUL TO THE CORINTHIANS 26.3-4.[28]

PAUL COPED. THEODORET OF CYR: Paul does not say that he enjoyed these things but that he had learned to cope with them. COMMENTARY ON THE SECOND EPISTLE TO THE CORINTHIANS 350.[29]

TRUE GLORY'S LOCATION. BASIL: Not in the amount of money, not in the pride of power, not in the height of glory is victory gained, but the Lord freely gives his help to those who seek him through excessive affliction. Such was Paul, who made his afflictions his boast. Therefore he was able to say, "When I am weak, then I am strong." . . . Do you see where affliction leads you? To hope that does not disappoint.[30] HOMILY 20 ON PSALM 59.[31]

---

[27]FC 26:5. [28]NPNF 1 12:401. [29]Migne PG 82:450. [30]Cf. Rom 5:3. [31]FC 46:340.

12:11-13 PAUL'S CREDENTIALS

[11]*I have been a fool! You forced me to it, for I ought to have been commended by you. For I was not at all inferior to these superlative apostles, even though I am nothing.* [12]*The signs of a true apostle were performed among you in all patience, with signs and wonders and mighty works.* [13]*For in what were you less favored than the rest of the churches, except that I myself did not burden you? Forgive me this wrong!*

OVERVIEW: Paul has been forced to disclose the truth. He makes it clear that he is not putting his own merits on display voluntarily (AMBROSIASTER). He rightly puts patience before signs and wonders, because attitudes matter more than abilities (THEODORET OF CYR). To bear all things nobly is the sign of an apostle (CHRYSOSTOM).

12:11 *Not Inferior*

FORCED TO SPEAK. AMBROSIASTER: Paul is saying that he has been forced to disclose the truth of the matter. He is certainly not foolish, having spoken the truth about himself, but is abasing himself in this way in order to make it clear that he is not putting his own merits on display voluntarily. COMMENTARY ON PAUL'S EPISTLES.[1]

12:12 *Signs of a True Apostle*

---

[1]CSEL 81.303.

HIS PATIENCE. AMBROSIASTER: Paul humbles himself only to rise to his true height. He talks about his patience because for a long time he put up with them as if they were sick people. His intention was to cure them of their errors by using the medicine of signs and wonders. COMMENTARY ON PAUL'S EPISTLES.[2]

SIGNS OF AN APOSTLE. CHRYSOSTOM: Notice that Paul says that all these things were done in great patience, for to bear all things nobly is the sign of an apostle. HOMILIES ON THE EPISTLES OF PAUL TO THE CORINTHIANS 27.1.[3]

ATTITUDES MATTER MORE THAN ABILITIES. THEODORET OF CYR: Paul rightly puts patience before signs and wonders, because attitudes matter more than abilities. COMMENTARY ON THE SECOND EPISTLE TO THE CORINTHIANS 350.[4]

12:13 Not Less Favored

CORINTH NOT LESS FAVORED. AMBROSIASTER: Paul is telling the Corinthians that they were better off than other churches. Corinth was the only place where he preached the gospel without being paid for it. COMMENTARY ON PAUL'S EPISTLES.[5]

HIS IRONY. CHRYSOSTOM: Paul says that the Corinthians insult the apostles by regarding him as inferior to these false teachers. His irony merely makes his rebuke more severe. HOMILIES ON THE EPISTLES OF PAUL TO THE CORINTHIANS 27.2.[6]

---

[2]CSEL 81.303. [3]NPNF 1 12:404. [4]Migne PG 82:451. [5]CSEL 81.304. [6]NPNF 1 12:404.

12:14-21 PAUL'S IMPENDING ARRIVAL

[14]Here for the third time I am ready to come to you. And I will not be a burden, for I seek not what is yours but you; for children ought not to lay up for their parents, but parents for their children. [15]I will most gladly spend and be spent for your souls. If I love you the more, am I to be loved the less? [16]But granting that I myself did not burden you, I was crafty, you say, and got the better of you by guile. [17]Did I take advantage of you through any of those whom I sent to you? [18]I urged Titus to go, and sent the brother with him. Did Titus take advantage of you? Did we not act in the same spirit? Did we not take the same steps?

[19]Have you been thinking all along that we have been defending ourselves before you? It is in the sight of God that we have been speaking in Christ, and all for your upbuilding, beloved. [20]For I fear that perhaps I may come and find you not what I wish, and that you may find me not what you wish; that perhaps there may be quarreling, jealousy, anger, selfishness, slander, gossip, conceit, and disorder. [21]I fear that when I come again my God may humble me before you, and I may have to mourn over many of those who sinned before and have not repented of the impurity, immorality, and licentiousness which they have practiced.

OVERVIEW: Paul is prepared even to die for the salvation of the Corinthians' souls (AMBROSIASTER). He did not say that he was afraid of finding them in sin but rather that they might not be all he would wish (CHRYSOSTOM). Paul makes explicit all the charges an opponent might make against him in order to clear himself on all counts. He wanted to make spiritual provision for them in the sight of God yet did not want their material wealth (AMBROSIASTER). If he had more to give them, he would be bound to do so, as a loving parent (PELAGIUS). Forgiveness is effective only among converted hearts (FULGENTIUS).

12:14 Seeking Them, Not Their Goods

TO GAIN THEM. AMBROSIASTER: Paul's desire was to gain the Corinthians themselves and not their money. Once they understood that, they would have more affection for him. COMMENTARY ON PAUL'S EPISTLES.[1]

AS A LOVING PARENT. PELAGIUS: Paul is telling the Corinthians that if he had more to give them, he would be bound to do so, as a loving parent. COMMENTARY ON THE SECOND EPISTLE TO THE CORINTHIANS 12.[2]

NOT A BURDEN. CHRYSOSTOM: Paul adds this in order to dispel any lingering suspicion about his motives and intentions. He will not be a burden to them when he comes. On the contrary, he will give them far more than he will take from them. HOMILIES ON THE EPISTLES OF PAUL TO THE CORINTHIANS 27.2.[3]

12:15 Spending and Being Spent

SPENDING LAVISHLY. AMBROSIASTER: Now Paul is openly expressing the love and affection which he had for them, since he is prepared not only to spend lavishly on their behalf but even to die for the salvation of their souls. COMMENTARY ON PAUL'S EPISTLES.[4]

RECEIVING LOVE. CHRYSOSTOM: Paul had a right to receive, but he would not do so. We too should imitate his behavior! HOMILIES ON THE EPISTLES OF PAUL TO THE CORINTHIANS 27.2-3.[5]

12:16 Craft and Guile?

WAS PAUL CRAFTY? AMBROSIASTER: Paul makes explicit all the charges which an opponent might make against him in order to clear himself on all counts. For he did not deal deviously with the Corinthians but straightforwardly. On the one hand he wanted to make provision for them in the sight of God and on the other he did not want their wealth in this life. He might have been suspected of despising them because the sums which they offered him were too small, but this was not the case. COMMENTARY ON PAUL'S EPISTLES.[6]

12:17 Taking Advantage?

HIS EMISSARIES. AMBROSIASTER: Paul is saying that the people whom he sent to them did not suggest that if they wanted the apostle to be well-disposed toward them they should offer him more money. COMMENTARY ON PAUL'S EPISTLES.[7]

12:18 Titus and the Brother

OF GOOD CHARACTER. AMBROSIASTER: It is obvious that since nothing like this was done by any of Paul's colleagues, the unanimous verdict on him was that he was of good character, with no trace of avarice in him. COMMENTARY ON PAUL'S EPISTLES.[8]

12:19 For Their Upbuilding

LOVE AND RESPECT. AMBROSIASTER: Paul wants

---

[1]CSEL 81.305. [2]Migne PL 30:803D. [3]NPNF 1 12:405. [4]CSEL 81.306. [5]NPNF 1 12:405. [6]CSEL 81.306. [7]CSEL 81.307. [8]CSEL 81.307.

the Corinthians to love and respect him, without becoming a burden on their finances. COMMENTARY ON PAUL'S EPISTLES.[9]

CAREFUL SPEECH. CHRYSOSTOM: Paul is constantly afraid of giving the wrong impression, which is why he is always careful to talk like this. HOMILIES ON THE EPISTLES OF PAUL TO THE CORINTHIANS 28.2.[10]

12:20 Fear of Discord

NOT WHAT I WISH. CHRYSOSTOM: Paul did not say that he was afraid of finding them in sin but rather that they might not be all he would wish. Furthermore, he balances this by saying that their expectations of him might be disappointed as well. HOMILIES ON THE EPISTLES OF PAUL TO THE CORINTHIANS 28.2.[11]

12:21 Lack of Repentance?

THOSE WHO HAVE NOT REPENTED. AMBROSIASTER: Paul is saying that some have repented but others have not. This contradicts Novatian, who claims that fornicators cannot repent or be received back into communion. Paul is affirming that they have indeed repented, and because of this they have been received back into the peace of the church. COMMENTARY ON PAUL'S EPISTLES.[12]

HUMBLING FROM GOD. CHRYSOSTOM: Paul would come as their accuser and judge, and yet he regards this as a humbling from God, not as a cause of exaltation. He had no desire to assume such an unpleasant role. HOMILIES ON THE EPISTLES OF PAUL TO THE CORINTHIANS 28.2.[13]

THE CALL TO CONVERSION. FULGENTIUS: Concerning those who though within the church persisted in their evil deeds, he spoke thus to the Corinthians with these words of comfort: "I fear that when I come again, my God may humiliate me before you, and I may have to mourn over many of those who sinned earlier and have not repented of the impurity, immorality and licentiousness they practiced." The apostle would not be saddened or humiliated in mourning over them if he believed that the forgiveness of sins would be granted to sinners and the wicked who continue to exasperate the divine justice without conversion of heart. The forgiveness of sins has no effect except in the conversion of the heart. We refer to those who have been converted by divine aid through the exercise of their own freedom of choice and whose lives are genuinely changed for the better. These converts will still occasionally sin, either through ignorance or through the stubbornness of a will that is knowingly lured by evil. They do not, however, stop asking for the forgiveness of their sins. ON THE FORGIVENESS OF SINS 1.13.2.[14]

---

[9]CSEL 81.307. [10]NPNF 1 12:408. [11]NPNF 1 12:408. [12]CSEL 81.309. [13]NPNF 1 12:409. [14]FC 95:126.

13:1-4 PAUL'S STRENGTH

[1]This is the third time I am coming to you. Any charge must be sustained by the evidence of two or three witnesses. [2]I warned those who sinned before and all the others, and I warn them now while absent, as I did when present on my second visit, that if I come again I

---

will not spare them — ³since you desire proof that Christ is speaking in me. He is not weak in dealing with you, but is powerful in you. ⁴For he was crucified in weakness, but lives by the power of God. For we are weak in him, but in dealing with you we shall live with him by the power of God.

OVERVIEW: Paul takes great pains to write in advance of his coming, because he hopes that the church will put things right before he gets there (CHRYSOSTOM). The Corinthians wanted to test him to see whether he would dare to exact retribution (AMBROSIASTER). Paul had rebuked them so often and so many people had heard his threats that if he comes and nothing has changed, he will be forced to carry them out (CHRYSOSTOM). Christ was crucified in weakness, even though this weakness was not his own but rather something which he assumed on our behalf (SEVERIAN OF GABALA).

13:1 Evidence of Witnesses

WITNESSES REQUIRED. AMBROSIASTER: Paul is here appealing to the law, saying that it applies to the Corinthians as well. COMMENTARY ON PAUL'S EPISTLES.[1]

ADVANCE NOTICE. CHRYSOSTOM: Paul takes great pains to write in advance of his coming, because he hopes that the church will put things right before he gets there, so that what he threatens to do will prove to be unnecessary. HOMILIES ON THE EPISTLES OF PAUL TO THE CORINTHIANS 29.1.[2]

13:2 Two Warnings

A DEFEAT. CHRYSOSTOM: Paul is saying that he has stuck his neck out so often and so many people have heard his threats that if he comes and nothing has changed he will have to carry them out. Even so, he will see it more as a humbling and as a defeat than as anything else. HOMILIES ON THE EPISTLES OF PAUL TO THE CORINTHIANS 29.1.[3]

13:3 Christ Speaking in Me

SEEKING PROOF. AMBROSIASTER: The Corinthians are seeking proof that Christ is speaking in the apostles. When they do not obey Paul's teachings, they want to test him to see whether he will dare to exact retribution. COMMENTARY ON PAUL'S EPISTLES.[4]

LONG-SUFFERING. CHRYSOSTOM: Paul will not punish the Corinthians just to prove that he has the power to do so. His patience with them does not stem from weakness but from love and long-suffering. HOMILIES ON THE EPISTLES OF PAUL TO THE CORINTHIANS 29.2.[5]

13:4 Living by the Power of God

BELIEVERS MADE STRONG BY BEING WEAK. AMBROSIASTER: Paul is referring here to the personal experience of the apostles, who were made weak by being treated badly, imprisoned and beaten. . . . Believers are made strong by being weak. Death inflicted by unbelievers is life as far as believers are concerned, for they will rise again to reign with Christ. COMMENTARY ON PAUL'S EPISTLES.[6]

CRUCIFIED IN WEAKNESS. CHRYSOSTOM: This is a difficult passage which causes problems for many people. What is meant here by "weakness"? In Scripture *weakness* can refer to bodily illness, and it can also mean not being securely grounded in faith. But there is a third possibility, and that is what we find here. *Weakness*

[1]CSEL 81.309. [2]NPNF 1 12:411-12. [3]NPNF 1 12:412. [4]CSEL 81.310. [5]NPNF 1 12:412. [6]CSEL 81.310-11.

can mean persecutions, trials, plottings and the like. Christ was not weak in body or in spirit, but he was persecuted and put to death. It was not because of any inherent weakness that he went to the cross; on the contrary, he chose to die in that way in order to give us life in the power of God. HOMILIES ON THE EPISTLES OF PAUL TO THE CORINTHIANS 29.2-3.[7]

WEAKNESS HE ASSUMED. SEVERIAN OF GABALA:

Earlier Paul said that Christ became sin and a curse for us, even though he knew no sin and was not a curse in himself.[8] Likewise here he says that Christ was crucified in weakness, even though this weakness was not his own but rather something which he assumed on our behalf. PAULINE COMMENTARY FROM THE GREEK CHURCH.[9]

---

[7]NPNF 1 12:412-13. [8]2 Cor 5:21. [9]NTA 15:298.

13:5-14 SELF-EXAMINATION

[5]*Examine yourselves, to see whether you are holding to your faith. Test yourselves. Do you not realize that Jesus Christ is in you?—unless indeed you fail to meet the test!* [6]*I hope you will find out that we have not failed.* [7]*But we pray God that you may not do wrong—not that we may appear to have met the test, but that you may do what is right, though we may seem to have failed.* [8]*For we cannot do anything against the truth, but only for the truth.* [9]*For we are glad when we are weak and you are strong. What we pray for is your improvement.* [10]*I write this while I am away from you, in order that when I come I may not have to be severe in my use of the authority which the Lord has given me for building up and not for tearing down.*

[11]*Finally, brethren, farewell. Mend your ways, heed my appeal, agree with one another, live in peace, and the God of love and peace will be with you.* [12]*Greet one another with a holy kiss.* [13]*All the saints greet you.*

[14]*The grace of the Lord Jesus Christ and the love of God and the fellowship of* [n] *the Holy Spirit be with you all.*

n *Or and participation in*

OVERVIEW: If we do not know how to put one another to the test, we do not know whether Christ is in us or not (AMBROSIASTER). There is one grace, one love and one fellowship on the part of the Father and of the Son and of the Holy Spirit in the one operation of one God whose power cannot be divided (AMBROSE).

Chastisement is a form of edification for the whole church (THEODORET OF CYR). The Son is not less than the Father (PELAGIUS). Grace saves apart from works (DIDYMUS THE BLIND). The holy kiss is given in order to stimulate love and instill the right attitude in us toward each other. When we return after an absence we kiss

---

each other, for our souls hasten to bond together (CHRYSOSTOM).

13:5 Test Yourselves

CHRIST WITHIN US. AMBROSIASTER: Paul is saying this because if we do not know how to put one another to the test, we do not know whether Christ is in us or not. To fail to meet the test is not to know the faith inherent in our religious profession. A person who has a sense of faith in his heart knows that Jesus Christ is within him. COMMENTARY ON PAUL'S EPISTLES.[1]

CHRIST IN THEIR TEACHER. CHRYSOSTOM: Look into yourselves and you will find that you have Christ in you. But if Christ is in you, how much more is he in your teacher! HOMILIES ON THE EPISTLES OF PAUL TO THE CORINTHIANS 29.4.[2]

13:6 We Have Not Failed

KNOWLEDGE OF FAITH. AMBROSIASTER: Paul is calling them to a knowledge of the faith and an upright life. Once they have recognized the authority of the apostle and his worth in God's sight, they will start to be concerned about themselves. COMMENTARY ON PAUL'S EPISTLES.[3]

13:7 Do What Is Right

PAUL'S PRAYER. AMBROSIASTER: Paul is praying that he and his colleagues will be humbled, as it were, by seeing the Corinthians so well behaved that he will not dare rebuke them. If they are humbled in this way, they will appear to be false. It is when they judge sinners with the authority granted to them that they are seen to be approved as genuine by God. If then there are no people for them to judge, it looks as if they have been proved false through the lessening of their authority. COMMENTARY ON PAUL'S EPISTLES.[4]

13:8 Only for the Truth

NO POWER AGAINST THE TRUTH. AMBROSIASTER: Paul is saying this because there is no power against the truth. They cannot reprove someone who is living a good life, but only someone who is an enemy of the law. This power will come to nothing if people have done what is good. COMMENTARY ON PAUL'S EPISTLES.[5]

13:9 Praying for Their Improvement

WE ARE WEAK, YOU ARE STRONG. CHRYSOSTOM: Who is there who can equal Paul? He was despised, spat upon, ridiculed, mocked as mean and contemptible, accused of being a braggart. But although he sees the need for making a show of his power, he puts it off and prays that it will not be necessary. He does not want his claims to be proved. On the contrary, he would rather that the situation be cleared up in advance so that such proof will be unnecessary. HOMILIES ON THE EPISTLES OF PAUL TO THE CORINTHIANS 29.5.[6]

13:10 Building Up, Not Tearing Down

THE PURPOSE OF AUTHORITY. CHRYSOSTOM: Paul would rather that his authority be shown in his words and not have to be demonstrated in deeds. But he left the Corinthians to draw the conclusion that if they did not put things right, he would have to come and do it for them. HOMILIES ON THE EPISTLES OF PAUL TO THE CORINTHIANS 30.1.[7]

CORRECTION AS EDIFICATION. THEODORET OF CYR: Paul shows that chastisement is a form of edification. If one or two are punished, the entire fellowship learns the lesson. COMMENTARY ON THE SECOND EPISTLE TO THE CORINTHIANS 356.[8]

---

[1]CSEL 81.311. [2]NPNF 1 12:414. [3]CSEL 81.311. [4]CSEL 81.312. [5]CSEL 81.312. [6]NPNF 1 12:415. [7]NPNF 1 12:417. [8]Migne PG 82:458.

13:11 *Live in Peace*

MENDING THEIR WAYS. AMBROSIASTER: The joy referred to here will come when the Corinthians mend their ways, after which it will be possible for them to mature in faith. But before that there will be consolation, enabling them to abandon the pleasure of the present in favor of hope for things to come. The peace of God is one thing, but the peace of the world is another. People in the world have peace, but it works to their damnation. The peace of Christ is free from sins, and therefore it is pleasing to God. A person who has peace will also have love, and the God of both will protect him forever. COMMENTARY ON PAUL'S EPISTLES.[9]

FOLLOWING PAUL'S COMMANDS. CHRYSOSTOM: How can Paul expect them to rejoice after he has said this kind of thing to them? It is for this very reason that he says it. For if they follow what he commands, there will be nothing to prevent them from rejoicing. Nothing is more comforting than a pure conscience. HOMILIES ON THE EPISTLES OF PAUL TO THE CORINTHIANS 30.1.[10]

13:12 *Greet One Another*

A HOLY KISS. CHRYSOSTOM: What is a holy kiss? It is one that is not hypocritical, like the kiss of Judas. The kiss is given in order to stimulate love and instill the right attitude in us toward each other. When we return after an absence, we kiss each other, for our souls hasten to bond together. But there is something else which might be said about this. We are the temple of Christ, and when we kiss each other we are kissing the porch and entrance of the temple. HOMILIES ON THE EPISTLES OF PAUL TO THE CORINTHIANS 30.2.[11]

13:13 *The Saints Greet You*

RETURN THE GREETING. AMBROSIASTER: Paul is calling the Corinthians to holiness, so that they may be bold enough to return the greeting of the saints. For they are greeted by the saints with the intention that they should imitate them. COMMENTARY ON PAUL'S EPISTLES.[12]

ALL THE SAINTS. PELAGIUS: All the saints sent their greetings, not just the leaders. COMMENTARY ON THE SECOND EPISTLE TO THE CORINTHIANS 13.[13]

13:14 *Grace, Love and Fellowship*

ONE UNDIVIDED OPERATION. AMBROSE: If there is one grace, one peace, one love and one fellowship on the part of the Father and of the Son and of the Holy Spirit, surely there is one operation, and where there is one operation, certainly the power cannot be divided or the substance separated. THE HOLY SPIRIT 1.12.13.[14]

THE UNITY OF TRIUNE POWER. AMBROSIASTER: Here is the intertwining of the Trinity and the unity of power which brings all salvation to fulfillment. The love of God has sent us Jesus the Savior, by whose grace we have been saved. The fellowship of the Holy Spirit makes it possible for us to possess the grace of salvation, for he guards those who are loved by God and saved by the grace of Christ, so that the completeness of the Three may be the saving fulfillment of mankind. COMMENTARY ON PAUL'S EPISTLES.[15]

GRACE SAVES APART FROM WORKS. DIDYMUS THE BLIND: The grace of our Lord Jesus Christ saves us apart from works and fills us with grace. PAULINE COMMENTARY FROM THE GREEK CHURCH.[16]

THE SON NOT LESS THAN THE FATHER. PELAGIUS: This is written against the Arians, who

---

[9]CSEL 81.313-14. [10]NPNF 1 12:417-18. [11]NPNF 1 12:418. [12]CSEL 81.314. [13]Migne PL 30:806B. [14]FC 44:82-83. [15]CSEL 81.314. [16]NTA 15:44.

maintain that the Father is greater than the Son on the ground that he is usually mentioned first. COMMENTARY ON THE SECOND EPISTLE TO THE CORINTHIANS 13.[17]

THE DISTINCTIVENESS OF THE PERSONS UNCONFUSED. CHRYSOSTOM: Paul closes his letter with prayer, taking great care to unite them all with God. Those who claim that the Holy Spirit is not God because he is not inserted with the Father and the Son at the beginning of Paul's letters are sufficiently refuted by this verse. All that belongs to the Trinity is undivided. Where the fellowship is of the Spirit, it is also of the Son, and where the grace is of the Son, it is also of the Father and the Spirit. I say these things without confusing the distinctiveness of the Persons but recognizing both their individuality and the unity of their common substance. HOMILIES ON THE EPISTLES OF PAUL TO THE CORINTHIANS 30.3.[18]

---

[17]Migne PL 30:806C. [18]NPNF 1 12:418-19.

APPENDIX

The following table lists where various early documents may be found in Cetedoc and TLG digital CD-Rom databases.

Ambrose

"Cain and Abel" (De Cain et Abel)	Cetedoc 0125
"The Holy Spirit" (De Spiritu Sancto)	Cetedoc 0151
"Letter to His Sister" (Epistulae)	Cetedoc 0160
"Letters to Bishops" (Epistulae)	Cetedoc 0160
"Letters to Emperors" (Epistulae)	Cetedoc 0160
"Letters to Laymen" (Epistulae)	Cetedoc 0160
"Letters to Priests" (Epistulae)	Cetedoc 0160
"The Mysteries" (De Mysterii)	Cetedoc 0155
"On His Brother Satyrus" (De Excessu Fratis Satyri)	Cetedoc 0157
"On Theodosius" (De Obitu Theodosii)	Cetedoc 0159
"Paradise" (De Paradiso)	Cetedoc 0124
"Six Days of Creation" (Exameron)	Cetedoc 0123
"Synagogue at Callinicum" (Epistulae)	Cetedoc 0160
"Synodal Letters" (Epistulae)	Cetedoc 0160

Athanasius

"On the Incarnation of the Word" (De Incarnatione Verbi)	TLG 2035.002

Augustine

"Adulterous Marriages" (De Adulterinis Coniugiis)	Cetedoc 0302
"Against Julian" (Contra Julianum)	Cetedoc 0351
"Against the Manichaeans" (De Genesi Contra Manichaeos)	Cetedoc 0265
"The Ascension" (Sermones)	Cetedoc 0284
"City of God" (De Civitate Dei)	Cetedoc 0313
"Confessions" (Confessionum Libri Tredecium)	Cetedoc 0251
"Converts and the Creed" (Sermones)	Cetedoc 0298
"Easter Season" (Sermones)	Cetedoc 0298
"Eight Questions of Dulcitius" (De Octo Dulcitii Quaestionibus)	Cetedoc 0291
"Enchiridion" (Enchiridion de Fide, Spe et Caritate)	Cetedoc 0295
"The Excellence of Widowhood" (De Bono Uiduitatis)	Cetedoc 0301
"Feast of the Nativity" (Sermones)	Cetedoc 0284
"Gift of Perseverance" (De Dono Perseverantiae)	Cetedoc 0355

"Letters" (Epistulae)	Cetedoc 0262
"Literal Interpretation of Genesis" (De Genesi ad Litteram Imperfectus Liber)	Cetedoc 0268
"New Year's Day" (Sermones)	Cetedoc 0284
"Of True Religion" (De Vera Religione)	Cetedoc 0264
"On Continence" (De Continentia)	Cetedoc 0298
"On Diverse Questions/To Simplician" (De Diversus Quesionibus ad Simplicianum)	Cetedoc 0290
"On Faith and the Creed" (De Fide et Symbolo)	Cetedoc 0293
"On Lying" (De Mendacio)	Cetedoc 0303
"On Patience" (De Patientia)	Cetedoc 0308
"On the Trinity" (De Trinitate)	Cetedoc 0329
"Predestination of the Saints" (De Praedestinatione Sanctorum)	Cetedoc 0354
"Proceedings of Pelagius" (De Gestis Pelagii)	Cetedoc 0348
"Questions" (De Diuersis Quaestionibus Octoginta Tribus)	Cetedoc 0289
"The Usefulness of Belief" (De Utilitate Credendi)	Cetedoc 0316
"The Usefulness of Fasting" (De Utilitate Ieiunii)	Cetedoc 0311
"The Way of Life of the Catholic Church" (De Moribus Ecclesia Catholicae et de Moribus)	Cetedoc 0261
"The Work of Monks" (De Opera Monachorum)	Cetedoc 0305

Basil of Caesarea

"Against Anger" (Homilia Adversus Eos Qui Irascuntur)	TLG 2040.026
"Concerning Baptism" (De Baptismo Libri Duo)	TLG 2040.052
"Concerning Faith" (De Fide)	TLG 2040.031
"Give Heed to Thyself" (Attende Tibi Ipsi)	TLG 2040.006
"Homilies on Psalms" (Homiliae Super Psalmos)	TLG 2040.018
"Letters" (Epistulae)	TLG 2040.004
"The Long Rules" (Regulae Fusius Tractae)	TLG 2040.048
"The Morals" (Regulae Morales)	TLG 2040.051
"Of Humility" (De Humilitate)	TLG 2040.036
"On the Judgment of God" (De Judicio Dei)	TLG 2040.043

Caesarius of Arles

"Sermons" (Sermones Caesarii Uel Ex Aliis Fontibus Hausti)	Cetedoc 1008

Clement of Alexandria

"Christ the Educator" (Paedagogus)	TLG 0555.002
"Stromateis" (Stromata)	TLG 0555.004

Clement of Rome
"Epistle to the Corinthians" (Epistula I ad Corinthios)   TLG 1271.001

Cyprian
"The Good of Patience" (De Bono Patientiae)   Cetedoc 0048
"On Mortality" (De Mortalitate)   Cetedoc 0044
"Unity of the Catholic Church" (De Ecclesiae Catholicae
    Unitate)   Cetedoc 0041

Cyril of Jerusalem
"Catechetical Lectures" (Procatechesis)   TLG 2110.001
"Mystagogical Lectures/On the Mysteries" (Mystagogiae)   TLG 2110.002
"Sermon on the Paralytic" (Homilia in Paralyticum Juxta Piscinam
    Jacentem)   TLG 2110.006

Epiphanius
"Panarion" (Panarion)   TLG 2021.002

Eusebius
"Ecclesiastical History" (Historia Ecclesiastica)   TLG 2018.002
"The Proof of the Gospel" (Demonstratio Evangelica)   TLG 2018.005

Fulgentius
"Letters" (Epistulae XVIII)   Cetedoc 0817
"On the Forgiveness of Sins" (Ad Euthymium de Remissione
    Peccatorum Libri II)   Cetedoc 0821
"To Monimus" (Ad Monimum Libri III)   Cetedoc 0814
"To Peter on the Faith" (De Fide ad Petrum Seu de Regula
    Fidei)   Cetedoc 0826
"To Proba" (Epistulae XVIII)   Cetedoc 0817
"To Victor" (Epistulae XVIII)   Cetedoc 0817

Gennadius of Constantinople
"Pauline Commentary from the Greek Church" (Fragmenta in
    Epistulam ad Romanos)   TLG 2762.004

Gregory Nazianzen
"On His Brother Caesarius" (Funeribus in Laudem Caesarii Fratris
    Oratio)   TLG 2002.005
"Theological Orations" (In Dictum Evangelii cum Consummasset
    Jesus hos Sermones)   TLG 2002.045

Gregory of Nyssa
"On Perfection" (De Perfectione Christiana ad Olympium Monachum)   TLG 2017.026
"On the Christian Mode of Life" (De Instituto Christiano)   TLG 2017.024
"On the Soul and the Resurrection" (Dialogus de Anima et Reurrectione)   TLG 2017.056
"On Virginity" (De Virginitate)   TLG 2017.043

Gregory the Great
"Dialogue" (Dialogorum Libri IV)   Cetedoc 1713

Hermas
"Shepherd" (Pastor)   TLG 1419.001

Hilary of Poitiers
"On the Trinity" (De Trinitate)   Cetedoc 0433

Ignatius of Antioch
"Epistle to the Ephesians" (Epistulae Interpolatae et Epistulae
    Suppositiciae)   TLG 1443.002
"Epistle to the Romans" (Ad Romanos)   TLG 1443.001

Jerome
"Against Helvidius" (Adversus Helvidium de Mariae Virginitate Perpetua)   Cetedoc 0609
"Against Rufinus" (Apologia Adversus Libros Rufini)   Cetedoc 0613
"Against the Pelagians" (Dialogi contra Pelagianos Libri III)   Cetedoc 0615
"Homilies" (Tractatus LIX in Psalmos)   Cetedoc 0592
"Homilies on Matthew" (Homilia in Euangelium Secundum Matthaeum)   Cetedoc 0595
"Homilies on the Psalms" (Tractatus LIV in Psalmos)   Cetedoc 0592

John Chrysostom
"Baptismal Instructions" (Catechesis ad Illuminandos)   TLG 2062.382
"Concerning Almsgiving and the Ten Virgins" (In Decem Virgines)   TLG 2062.234
"Fourth Catechetical Instruction" (Catechesis ad Illuminados)   TLG 2062.382
"Homilies on Genesis" (Homilae 67 in Genesim)   TLG 2062.112
"Homilies on the First Epistle of Paul to the Corinthians"
    (In Epistulam I ad Corinthos)   TLG 2062.156
"Homilies on the Second Epistle of Paul to the Corinthians"
    (In Epistulam II ad Corinthos)   TLG 2062.157
"On Repentance and Almsgiving" (De Paenitentia)   TLG 2062.027

Marius Victorinus
"Against Arius" (Adversus Arium)   Cetedoc 0095

Maximus of Turin
"Sermons" (Collectio Sermonum Antiqua)   Cetedoc 0219

Novatian
"In Praise of Purity" (De Bono Pudicitiae)   Cetedoc 0069
"Jewish Foods" (De Cibis Judaicis)   Cetedoc 0068
"On the Trinity" (De Trinitate)   Cetedoc 0071

Oecumenius
"Pauline Commentary from the Greek Church" (Fragmenta in Epistulam
    ad Romanos)   TLG 2866.002

Origen
"Commentary on First Corinthians" (Fragmenta ex Commentariis in
    Epistulam I ad Corinthios)   TLG 2042.034
"Commentary on the Song of Songs" (Commentarium in Canticum
    Canticorum)   Cetedoc 0198
"Exhortation to Martyrdom" (Exhortatio ad Martyrium)   TLG 2042.007
"Homilies on Exodus" (Homiliae in Exodum)   TLG 2042.023
"Homilies on Genesis" (Homiliae in Genesim)   TLG 2042.022
"Homilies on Leviticus" (Homiliae in Leviticum)   TLG 2042.024
"Homilies on Numbers" (Homiliae in Numeros)   Cetedoc 0198
"On First Principles" (De Principiis)   TLG 2042.002
"On Prayer" (De Oratione)   TLG 2042.008

Polycarp
"Epistle to the Philippians" (Epistula ad Philippenses)   TLG 1622.001

Prudentius
"Hymns" (Liber Peristefanon)   Cetedoc 1443

Pseudo-Dionysius
"The Divine Names" (De Divinis Nominibus)   TLG 2798.004
"The Ecclesiastical Hierarchy" (De Ecclesiastica Hierarchia)   TLG 1798.002

The So-Called Second Letter of Clement
"The So-Called Second Letter of Clement" (Epistula II ad Corinthios)   TLG 1271.002

Severian of Gabala
"Pauline Commentary from the Greek Church" (Fragmenta in Epistulam
    ad Romanos)   TLG 4139.039

Tertullian
"Apology" (Apologeticum)   Cetedoc 0003
"The Apparel of Women" (Ad Uxorem)   Cetedoc 0012
"The Chaplet" (De Corona)   Cetedoc 0021
"Flight in Time of Persecution" (De Fuga in Persecutione)   Cetedoc 0025
"On Prayer" (De Oratione)   Cetedoc 0007
"On the Soul" (De Anima)   Cetedoc 0017
"To the Martyrs" (Ad Martyrs)   Cetedoc 0001

Theodore of Mopsuestia
"Pauline Commentary from the Greek Church" (Fragmenta in Epistulam
    ad Romanos)   TLG 4135.015

Theodoret of Cyrus
"Commentary on the First Epistle to the Corinthians" (Interpretatio
    in XIV Epistulas Sancti Pauli)   TLG 4089.030
"Commentary on the Second Epistle to the Corinthians" (Interpretatio
    in XIV Epistulas Sancti Pauli)   TLG 4089.030

Vincent of Lérins
"Commonitories" (Commonitorium)   Cetedoc 0510

CHRONOLOGICAL LIST OF PERSONS & WRITINGS

The following chronology will assist readers in locating patristic writers, writings and recipients of letters referred to in this patristic commentary. Persons are arranged chronologically according to the terminal date of the years during which they flourished (fl.) or, where that cannot be determined, the date of death or approximate date of writing or influence. Writings are arranged according to the approximate date of composition.

Clement of Rome (pope), regn. 92-101?

Ignatius of Antioch, d. c. 110-112

Didache, c. 140

Shepherd of Hermas, c. 140/155

Marcion of Sinope, fl. 144, d. c. 154

Second Letter of Clement (so-called), c. 150

Polycarp of Smyrna, c. 69-155

Justin Martyr (of Flavia Neapolis in Palestine), c. 100/110-165, fl. c. 148-161

Montanist Oracles, c. latter half-2nd cent.

Theophilus of Antioch, late second century

Tatian the Syrian, c. 170

Athenagoras of Athens, c. 177

Irenaeus of Lyons, b. c. 135, fl. 180-199; d. c. 202

Clement of Alexandria, b. c. 150, fl. 190-215

Tertullian of Carthage, c. 155/160-225/250; fl. c. 197-222

Callistus of Rome (pope), regn. 217-222

Hippolytus of Rome, d. 235

Minucius Felix of Rome, fl. 218/235

Origen of Alexandria, b. 185, fl. c. 200-254

Novatian of Rome, fl. 235-258

Cyprian of Carthage, fl. 248-258

Dionysius the Great of Alexandria, fl. c. 247-265

Gregory Thaumaturgus (the Wonder-worker), c. 213-270/275

Euthalius the Deacon, fourth century?

Victorinus of Petovium (Pettau), d. c. 304

Methodius of Olympus, d. c. 311

Lactantius (Africa), c. 250-325; fl. c. 304-321

Eusebius of Caesarea, b. c. 260/263; fl. c. 315-340

Aphrahat (Aphraates), c. 270-c. 345

Hegemonius (Pseudo-Archelaus), fl. c. 325-350

Cyril of Jerusalem, c. 315-386; fl. c. 348

Marius Victorinus, c. 280/285-c. 363; fl. 355-363

Acacius of Caesarea, d. 366

Macedonius of Constantinople, d. c. 362

Hilary of Poitiers, c. 315-367; fl. 350-367

Athanasius of Alexandria, c. 295-373; fl. 325-373

Ephrem the Syrian, b. c. 306; fl. 363-373

Macrina the Younger, c. 327-380

Basil the Great of Caesarea, b. c. 330; fl. 357-379

Gregory Nazianzen, b. 329/330, fl. 372-389

Gregory of Nyssa, c. 335-394

Amphilochius of Iconium, c. 340/345-post 394

Paulinus of Nola, 355-431; fl. 389-396

Ambrose of Milan, c. 333-397; fl. 374-397

Didymus the Blind, c. 313-398

Evagrius of Pontus, 345-399; fl. 382-399
Syriac *Book of Steps (Liber Graduum)*, c. 400
Apostolic Constitutions, c. 400
Severian of Gabala, fl. c. 400
Prudentius, c. 348-after 405
John Chrysostom, 344/354-407; fl. 386-407
Jerome, c. 347-420
Maximus of Turin, d. 408/423
Pelagius, c. 350/354-c. 420/425
Palladius, c. 365-425; fl. 399-420
Theodore of Mopsuestia, c. 350-428
Honoratus of Arles, fl. 425, d. 429/430
Augustine of Hippo, 354-430; fl. 387-430
John Cassian, c. 360-432
Sixtus III of Rome (pope), regn. 432-440
Cyril of Alexandria, 375-444; fl. 412-444
Pseudo-Victor of Antioch, fifth century
Peter Chrysologus, c. 405-450
Leo the Great of Rome (pope), regn. 440-461
Theodoret of Cyr, 393-466; fl. 447-466
Basil of Selucia, fl. 440-468

Salvian the Presbyter of Marseilles, c. 400-c. 480
Euthymius (Palestine), 377-473
Gennadius of Constantinople, d. 471; fl. 458-471
Pseudo-Dionysius the Areopagite, c. 482-c. 532; fl c. 500
Symmachus of Rome (pope), regn. 498-514
Jacob of Sarug, 451-521
Philoxenus of Mabbug, c. 440-523
Fulgentius of Ruspe, c. 467-532
Caesarius of Arles, 470-542
Cyril of Scythopolis, b. 525; fl. c. 550
Oecumenius, sixth century
Gregory the Great (pope), 540-604; regn. 590-604
Isidore of Seville, c. 560-636
Sahdona (Martyrius), fl. 635-640
Isaac of Nineveh, d. c. 700
Bede the Venerable, 673-735
John of Damascus, c. 645-c. 749

Biographical Sketches & Short Descriptions of Select Anonymous Works

Ambrose of Milan (c. 333-397; fl. 374-397). Bishop of Milan and teacher of Augustine who defended the divinity of the Holy Spirit and the perpetual virginity of Mary.

Ambrosiaster (fl. c. 366-384). Name given by Erasmus to the author of a work once thought to have been composed by Ambrose.

Aphrahat (c. 270-350 fl. 337-345). "The Persian Sage" and first major Syriac writer whose work survives. He is also known by his Greek name Aphraates.

Apollinarius of Laodicea (310-c. 392). Bishop of Laodicea who was attacked by Gregory of Nazianzus, Gregory of Nyssa and Theodore for denying that Christ had a human mind.

Arius (fl. c. 320). Heretic condemned at the Council of Nicaea (325) for refusing to accept that the Son was not a creature but was God by nature like the Father.

Athanasius of Alexandria (c. 295-373; fl. 325-373). Bishop of Alexandria from 328, though often in exile. He wrote his classic polemics against the Arians while most of the eastern bishops were against him.

Augustine of Hippo (354-430). Bishop of Hippo and a voluminous writer on philosophical, exegetical, theological and ecclesiological topics. He formulated the Western doctrines of predestination and original sin in his writings against the Pelagians.

Basil the Great (b. c. 330; fl. 357-379). One of the Cappadocian fathers, bishop of Caesarea and champion of the teaching on the Trinity propounded at Nicaea in 325. He was a great administrator and founded a monastic rule.

Basilides (fl. second century). Alexandrian heretic of the early second century who is said to have believed that souls migrate from body to body and that we do not sin if we lie to protect the body from martyrdom.

Book of Steps (c. 400). Written by an anonymous Syriac author, this work consists of thirty homilies or discourses and which specifically deal with the more advanced stages of growth in the spiritual life.

Caesarius of Arles (c. 470-542). Bishop of Arles from 503 known primarily for his pastoral preaching.

Cassian, John (360-432). Author of a compilation of ascetic sayings highly influential in the development of Western monasticism.

Cassiodorus (c. 485-c. 540). Founder of Western monasticism whose writings include valuable histories and less valuable commentaries.

Chromatius (fl. 400). Friend of Rufinus and Jerome and author of tracts and sermons.

Clement of Alexandria (c. 150-215). A highly educated Christian convert from paganism, head of the catechetical school in Alexandria and pioneer of Christian scholarship. His major works, *Protrepticus, Paedagogus* and the *Stromata*, bring Christian doctrine face to face with the ideas and achievements of his time.

Clement of Rome (fl. c. 92-101). Pope whose *Epistle to the Corinthians* is one of the most important documents of subapostolic times.

Cyprian of Carthage (fl. 248-258). Martyred bishop of Carthage who maintained that those baptized by schismatics and heretics had no share in the blessings of the church.

Cyril of Alexandria (375-444; fl. 412-444). Patriarch of Alexandria whose strong espousal of the unity of Christ led to the condemnation of Nestorius in 431.

Cyril of Jerusalem (c. 315-386; fl. c. 348). Bishop of Jerusalem after 350 and author of *Catechetical Homilies*.

Didymus the Blind (c. 313-398). Alexandrian exegete who was much influenced by Origen and admired by Jerome.

Dionysius the Areopagite. The name of Dionysius the Areopagite was long given to the author of four mystical writings, probably from the late fifth century, which were the foundation of the apophatic school of mysticism in their denial that anything can be truly predicated of God.

Epiphanius of Salamis (c. 315-403). Bishop of Salamis in Cyprus, author of a refutation of eighty heresies (the *Panarion*) and instrumental in the condemnation of Origen.

Ephrem the Syrian (b. c. 306; fl. 363-373). Syrian writer of commentaries and devotional hymns which are sometimes regarded as the greatest specimens of Christian poetry prior to Dante.

Eunomius (d. 393). Bishop of Cyzicus who was attacked by Basil and Gregory of Nyssa for maintaining that the Father and the Son were of different natures, one ingenerate, one generate.

Eusebius of Caesarea (c. 260/263-340). Bishop of Caesarea, partisan of the Emperor Constantine and first historian of the Christian church. He argued that the truth of the gospel had been foreshadowed in pagan writings but had to defend his own doctrine against suspicion of Arian sympathies.

Eusebius of Vercelli (fl. c. 360). Bishop of Vercelli who supported the trinitarian teaching of Nicaea (325) when it was being undermined by compromise in the West.

Faustinus (fl. 380). A priest in Rome and supporter of Lucifer and author of a treatise on the Trinity.

Filastrius (fl. 380). Bishop of Brescia and author of a compilation against all heresies.

Fulgentius of Ruspe (c. 467-532). Bishop of Ruspe and author of many orthodox sermons and tracts under the influence of Augustine.

Gaudentius of Brescia (fl. 395). Successor of Filastrius as bishop of Brescia and author of numerous tracts.

Gennadius of Constantinople (d. 471). Patriarch of Constantinople, author of numerous commentaries and an opponent of the Christology of Cyril of Alexandria.

Gnostics. Name now given generally to followers of Basilides, Marcion, Valentinus, Mani and others. The characteristic belief is that matter is a prison made for the spirit by an evil or ignorant creator, and that redemption depends on fate, not on free will.

Gregory of Elvira (fl. 359-385). Bishop of Elvira who wrote allegorical treatises in the style of Origen and defended the Nicene faith against the Arians.

Gregory Nazianzen (b. 329/330; fl. 372-389). Bishop of Nazianzus and friend of Basil and Gregory of Nyssa. He is famous for maintaining the humanity of Christ as well as the orthodox doctrine of the Trinity.

Gregory of Nyssa (c. 335-394). Bishop of Nyssa and brother of Basil, he is famous for maintaining the equality in unity of the Father, Son and Holy Spirit.

Gregory the Great (c. 540-604). Pope from 590, the fourth and last of the Latin "Doctors of the Church." He was a prolific author and a powerful unifying force within the Latin Church, initiating the liturgical reform that brought about the Gregorian Sacramentary and Gregorian chant.

Hilary of Poitiers (c. 315-367). Bishop of Poitiers and called the "Athanasius of the West" because of his defense (against the Arians) of the common nature of Father and Son.

Ignatius of Antioch (c. 35-107/112). Bishop of Antioch who wrote several letters to local churches while being taken from Antioch to Rome to be martyred. In the letters, which warn against heresy, he stresses orthodox Christology, the centrality of the Eucharist and unique role of the bishop in preserving the unity of the church.

Irenaeus of Lyon (c. 135-c. 202). Bishop of Lyons who published the most famous and influential refutation of Gnostic thought.

Isaac of Nineveh (d. c. 700). Also known as Isaac the Syrian or Isaac Syrus, this monastic writer served for a short while as bishop of Nineveh before retiring to live a secluded monastic life. His writings on ascetic subjects survive in the form of numerous homilies.

Jerome (c. 347-420). Gifted exegete and exponent of a classical Latin style, now best known as the translator of the Latin Vulgate. He defended the perpetual virginity of Mary, attacked Origen and Pelagius and supported extreme ascetic practices.

John Chrysostom (344/354-407; fl. 386-407). Bishop of Antioch and of Constantinople who was famous for his orthodoxy, his eloquence and his attacks on Christian laxity in high places.

Leo the Great (regn. 440-461). Bishop of Rome whose *Tome to Flavian* helped to strike a balance between Nestorian and Cyrilline positions at the Council of Chalcedon in 451.

Lucifer (fl. 370). Bishop of Cagliari and fanatical partisan of Athanasius. He and his followers entered into schism after refusing to acknowledge less orthodox bishops appointed by the Emperor Constantius.

Macrina the Younger (c. 327-380). The elder sister of Basil the Great and Gregory of Nyssa, she is known as 'the Younger" to distinguish her from her paternal grandmother. She had a powerful influence on her younger brothers, especially on Gregory, who called her his teacher and relates her teaching in *On the Soul and the Resurrection*.

Manichaeans. A religious movement that originated circa 241 in Persia under the leadership of Mani but was apparently of complex Christian origin. It is said to have denied free will and the universal sovereignty of God, teaching that kingdoms of light and darkness are coeternal and that the redeemed are particles of a spiritual man of light held captive in the darkness of matter (*see* Gnostics).

Marcion (fl. 144). Heretic of the mid-second century who rejected the Old Testament and much of the New Testament, claiming that the Father of Jesus Christ was other than the Creator God (*see* Gnostics).

Marius Victorinus (b. c. 280/285; fl. c. 355-363). Grammarian who translated works of Platonists and, after his late conversion (c. 355), used them against the Arians.

Maximus of Turin (d. 408/423). Bishop of Turin who died during the reigns of Honorius and Theodosius the Younger (408-423). Over one hundred of his sermons survive.

Methodius of Olympus (fl. 290). Bishop of Olympus who celebrated virginity in a *Symposium* partly modeled on Plato's dialogue of that name.

Montanist Oracles. Montanism was an apocalyptic and strictly ascetic movement begun in the latter half of the second century by a certain Montanus in Phrygia, who, along with certain of his followers, uttered oracles they claimed were inspired by the Holy Spirit. Little of the authentic oracles remains and most of what is known of Montanism comes from the authors who wrote against the movement. Montanism was formally condemned as a heresy before A.D. 200 by Asiatic synods.

Nestorius (b. 381; fl. 430). Patriarch of Constantinople 428-431 and credited with the foundation of the heresy which says that the divine and human natures were associated, rather than truly united, in the incarnation of Christ.

Novatian of Rome (fl. 235-258). Roman theologian, otherwise orthodox, who formed a schismatic church after failing to become pope. His treatise on the Trinity states the classic western doctrine.

Oecumenius (sixth century). Called the Rhetor or the Philosopher, Oecumenius wrote the earliest extant Greek commentary on Revelation. Scholia by Oecumenius on some of John Chrysostom's commentaries on the Pauline Epistles are still extant.

Origen of Alexandria (b. 185; fl. c. 200-254). Influential exegete and systematic theologian. He was condemned (perhaps unfairly) for maintaining the preexistence of souls while denying the resurrection of the body, the literal truth of Scripture and the equality of the Father and the Son in the Trinity.

Pelagius (c. 354-c. 420). Christian teacher whose followers were condemned in 418 and 431 for maintaining that a Christian could be perfect and that salvation depended on free will.

Philoxenus of Mabbug (c. 440-523). Bishop of Mabbug (Hierapolis) and a leading thinker in the early Syrian Orthodox Church. His extensive writings in Syriac include a set of thirteen *Discourses on the Christian Life*, several works on the incarnation and a number of exegetical works.

Polycarp of Smyrna (c. 69-155). Bishop of Smyrna who vigorously fought heretics such as the Marcionites and Valentinians. He was the leading Christian figure in Roman Asia in the middle of the second century.

Prudentius (c. 348-c. 410). Aurelius Prudentius Clemens was a Latin poet and hymn-writer who devoted his later life to Christian writing. He wrote didactic poems on the theology of the incarnation, against the heretic Marcion and against the resurgence of paganism.

Quodvultdeus (fl. 430). Carthaginian deacon and friend of Augustine who endeavored to show at length how the New Testament fulfilled the Old Testament.

Rufinus of Aquileia (c. 345-411). Orthodox Christian thinker and historian who nonetheless translated Origen and defended him against the strictures of Jerome and Epiphanius.

Sabellius (fl. 200). Allegedly the author of the heresy which maintains that the Father and Son are a single person. The patripassian variant of this heresy states that the Father suffered on the cross.

Sahdona (fl. 635-640). Known in Greek as Martyrius, this Syriac author was bishop of Beth Garmai for a short time. His most important work is the deeply scriptural *Book of Perfection* which ranks as one of the masterpieces of Syriac monastic literature.

Second Letter of Clement (c. 150). The so-called *Second Letter of Clement* is the earliest surviving Christian sermon probably written by a Corinthian author, though some scholars have assigned it to a Roman or Alexandrian author.

Severian of Gabala (fl. c. 400). A contemporary of John Chrysostom, he was highly regarded preacher in Constantinople, particularly at the imperial court, and ultimately sided with Chrysostom's accusers. His sermons are dominated by antiheretical concerns.

Shepherd of Hermas (second century). Divided into five *Visions*, twelve *Mandates* and ten *Similitudes*, this Christian apocalypse was written by a former slave and named for the form of the second angel said to have granted him his visions. This work was highly esteemed for its moral value and was used as a textbook for catechumens in the early church.

Tertullian of Carthage (c. 155/160-225/250; fl. c. 197-222). Brilliant Carthaginian apologist and polemicist who laid the foundations of Christology and trinitarian orthodoxy in the West, though he himself was estranged from the main church by its laxity.

Theodore of Mopsuestia (c. 350-428). Bishop of Mopsuestia, founder of the Antiochene, or literalistic, school of exegesis. A great man in his day, he was later condemned as a precursor of Nestorius.

Theodoret of Cyr (c. 393-466). Bishop of Cyr (Cyrrhus), he was an opponent of Cyril, whose doctrine of Christ's person was finally vindicated in 451 at the Council of Chalcedon.

Valentinus (fl. c. 140). Alexandrian heretic of the mid-second century who taught that the material world was created by the transgression of God's Wisdom, or Sophia (*see* Gnostics).

Subject Index

Aaron, 147

Abel, 57

Abraham, 140, 141, 165, 235, 272, 296, 297

Achaicus, 2, 3, 187, 189

Adam, 156-59, 174-76, 239, 241, 242, 253

adoption, 8, 53, 54, 91, 194, 225, 241, 299

adultery, 53, 59-61, 79, 261, 262, 285. *See also* sin, and marriage

adversary, 52, 160, 162, 206, 261, 295, 305

affliction
    endurance of, 237, 254, 269, 270
    overwhelmed by, 206
    of Paul, 193, 204, 209, 304, 308
    present, 234, 237, 238
    salvation through, 41, 192, 195-97, 231, 232, 264, 270, 304, 307, 308. *See also* suffering

age
    future, 162, 179
    present, 13, 20-22, 27, 35, 93, 95, 122, 135, 159, 167, 179, 216, 229, 232, 246, 280

allegory, 91, 217

almsgiving, 102, 123, 153, 185, 206, 270, 276, 277, 279, 280, 282, 284

altar
    Eucharistic, 99, 113, 167
    as heart, 58, 208
    of temple, 85, 96, 98, 113

angels
    becoming like, 130, 131, 303, 162, 175, 179, 295, 303
    evil, 293-95, 305. *See also* Satan
    good, 39-41, 49, 51, 85, 105, 108, 130, 131,

136, 149, 153, 159, 170, 180, 272

anger, 1, 40, 41, 43, 46, 57, 59, 61, 86, 114, 115, 127, 132, 206, 207, 244, 273, 285, 309

anointed, 88, 89, 153, 200, 202, 261

antichrist, 180, 260, 295

anxiety, 71, 272, 275

Apollinarians, 21, 22

Apollos, 1, 3, 9, 10, 27, 29, 30, 35, 38-40, 187, 188, 277

apostasy, 64

apostle/apostles
    alms to, 82-84, 234, 256, 284, 287, 292, 296
    authority of, 3, 4, 6, 7, 12, 39, 56, 79, 80, 82, 86, 103, 120, 123, 128, 129, 143, 151, 182, 193, 203, 212-14, 224, 227, 234, 241, 246, 250, 299, 302
    and Christ, 13, 15, 148, 150, 151, 209, 221, 222, 225
    false, 2, 4, 5, 10, 12, 38, 43, 59, 83, 95, 11, 289, 291, 292, 308
    and hardship, 40, 41, 95, 196, 258, 312
    and partisanship, 10, 37, 38
    power of, 12, 14, 23, 30, 41, 50, 51, 81, 82, 87, 89, 131, 138, 143, 236, 283, 291, 292
    preaching of, 14, 16, 28, 149, 258, 312
    service of, 37, 85, 267, 279, 297

Aquila, 142, 189

archetype, 229

Aretas, 300

Arian, 21, 22, 160, 163, 315

Arius, 19, 22, 164

aroma, 208-11

ascension
    of Christ, 23, 113, 150, 151, 155, 226
    of saints, 256, 298

ashamed, 41, 49, 54, 72,

101, 102, 110, 111, 185, 186, 279, 292

Asia, 189, 192, 194, 197

asleep, 73, 114, 148, 150, 154, 156, 157. *See also* death

assembly, 5, 143

atonement, 17, 18, 45. *See also* Jesus Christ, atoning death of

Babel, 131

baptism
    as adoption, 91
    as becoming Christ, 290
    benefits of, 54, 90, 119
    as cleansing, 29, 54, 90, 225, 236
    and death, 91, 165, 166, 179, 183, 246-48
    efficacy of, 9, 11, 12, 29-30, 93, 98, 121, 166, 202, 259, 261
    as forgiveness of sins, 30, 220
    and Holy Communion, 94
    and the Holy Spirit, 118, 262
    as new life, 27, 53, 249
    prefigured, 91, 235

Barnabas, 32, 79, 81, 276

beating, 2, 19, 95, 152, 153, 233, 296, 298, 312. *See also* affliction; suffering

beauty
    carnal, 18, 109
    spiritual, 23, 25, 127, 132, 134, 135, 214, 223, 267, 273, 303

Belial, 259, 261, 262

belief
    and action, 6, 87-89, 102, 113, 128
    apostolic, 3, 12, 13, 14, 17, 29, 40, 147-49
    and demons, 118
    and hardship, 43, 196, 209, 265, 312. *See also* affliction; suffering
    and the Holy Spirit, 27, 35, 122
    and Jesus Christ, 3, 13-15, 19, 22, 66, 208-9,

211

    and judgment, 7, 44, 49, 50, 51, 70

    and knowledge, 15, 20, 22, 26, 50, 134, 170, 223

    and marriage, 59, 61, 63-65

    and nonbelievers, 15, 80, 99-101, 283, 297

    personal, 2, 3, 15, 20, 72

    and resurrection, 2, 5, 12, 19, 48, 56, 136, 149, 151, 153, 155, 158, 166, 168, 171, 173, 183, 221, 239, 248

    and sacrament, 53, 54, 90, 116, 249

    and spiritual gifts, 36, 132, 133, 137, 140-43, 151, 153

    and unity, 10, 97, 103, 131

beloved, 27, 41-43, 96, 178, 179, 238, 263, 309

benefactor, 5, 204, 268

Bethlehem, 98, 274

betrayed, 71, 288, 290

bird, 109, 122, 168, 175, 246

bishop, 12, 49, 96, 108, 123, 129, 150, 151, 167, 185, 188, 301

blameless, 37, 39, 88, 89, 250

blasphemy, 67, 167, 181, 304

blessings
    of Christ, 252, 253, 300
    of creation, 100, 173
    of ecclesiastical life, 54, 192, 206
    and Eucharist, 96, 97, 112, 113, 115
    of God, 192, 195, 278, 281
    of the gospel, 85, 87
    of the kingdom of heaven, 154, 156, 159, 179, 182, 242, 254, 255, 303
    spiritual, 70, 71, 73, 111, 134, 140-42, 173, 185, 225, 235, 254, 280-82

blindness, 25, 26, 136, 166-69, 172, 186-90, 193-95, 198, 199, 205, 208, 209,

333